An Introduction to Politics

Peter Joyce

Hodder & Stoughton

A MEMBER OF THE HODDER HEADLINE GROUP

Dedication

To my wife, Julie, and my daughter, Emmeline

Orders: please contact Bookpoint Ltd, 39 Milton Park, Abingdon, Oxon OX14 4TD, UK. Telephone: (44) 01235 400414, Fax: (44) 01235 400454. Lines are open from 9.00–6.00, Monday to Saturday, with a 24-hour message answering service. Email address: orders@bookpoint.co.uk

A catalogue record for this title is available from The British Library

ISBN 0 340 704802

First published 1999
Impression number   10   9   8   7   6   5   4   3   2   1
Year   2004   2003   2002   2001   2000   1999

Copyright © 1999, Peter Joyce

Cover illustration by Gary Thompson Studio

Typeset by Wearset, Boldon, Tyne and Wear.
Printed in Great Britain for Hodder & Stoughton Educational, a division of Hodder Headline Plc, 338 Euston Road, London NW1 3BH by Scotprint, Musselburgh, Scotland.

Contents

Acknowledgements

The publishers would like to thank copyright holders for permission to reproduce materials in this book. Every effort has been made to trace and acknowledge all copyright holders, but if any have been overlooked, the publishers will be pleased to make the necessary arrangements.

For permission to reproduce copyright photographs:

Associated Press pp 31, 36, 192, 269, 546; Corbis/Hulton Deutsch Collection pp 14 and 478; David Simson p 460; Don Smith p 114; PA News pp 79, 142, 173, 226, 260, 290, 301, 365, 534, 544, 567, 576, 587; Peter Crystal p 69; UPPA p 400.

Introduction

This book is written for those students embarking on the study of politics who have little, or no, knowledge of the subject area. Its main focus is British politics, and in particular the changes which have occurred since the election of a Labour government in 1997. This is supplemented by material which is concerned with the government and politics of other states, especially those in the European Union and United States of America.

The structure and content of this book reflect the guidelines laid down by the Qualifications and Curriculum Authority (QCA) for the development of AS/A level core syllabuses in Government and Politics. These guidelines insist that such courses must 'include some comparative study of aspects of other political systems' in conjunction with an examination of the government and politics of the UK. This requirement is, for example, reflected in the Northern Examination Board syllabuses which seek to promote an understanding of the British system of government by comparing British practice with that in other systems. Other examining bodies (such as the Associated Examining Board) have prepared syllabuses which reflect the 1988 resolutions of the Council of the European Union, requiring students to 'acquire knowledge and understanding of government and politics in a selection of European countries' (especially France, the Irish Republic and Germany) and also the USA. The material presented in this book caters for these requirements. Much material of a comparative nature is included in the various chapters. It is deliberately not presented in a complex theoretical framework, but instead, consists of examples and case studies which provide contrasting or complementary material designed to aid the overall understanding of British government and politics.

The subject matter reflects the issues most commonly found in the compulsory components of A level syllabuses. Additionally, it includes a wide range of material found in option papers which focus on British government and politics. These include EdExcel's paper 2, Issues in British Politics, the contents of which are given very wide coverage in this book, and option paper 1 of the AEB (Power in the United Kingdom). A large number of issues specified for study in the NEAB's 1999 and 2000 option papers are also covered in this book. These include the development of Liberalism, Conservatism and Socialism in British politics, Northern Ireland, Governing Northern Ireland,

Scotland and Wales, feminist politics and the politics of race. Additionally, there is much material which is relevant to the AEB's option paper 2, Government and Politics in the USA, particularly those sections of the syllabus which seek to compare British and American politics.

The organisation of each chapter is similar. Questions are regularly posed, seeking to assess understanding of the subject matter which has been covered, but also encouraging readers to extend their knowledge by undertaking additional study. The nature of the questions also reflects SCAA's concerns about the need to analyse and evaluate political events and controversies, and to be able to put forward coherent, critical arguments.

Although the content of this book reflects developments in the study of A level politics, it will be of relevance both to general readers seeking to broaden their knowledge of politics, and also to undergraduate students embarking on courses (such as Social Science) which require them to study politics without having previously done so. To aid this, each chapter has suggestions for additional reading, and illustrative case studies are included in boxes.

Key Concepts and Issues | PART ONE

Chapter One | Key Concepts in Politics

The aims of this chapter are:

> 1 To provide an understanding of the scope and nature of the study of politics.
>
> 2 To differentiate between various forms of political systems and to analyse the key features of political structures.
>
> 3 To analyse a number of key concepts concerned with the study of politics.
>
> 4 To evaluate a number of key concepts linked to the relationship between the state and the citizen.

The Discipline of Politics

Politics is all around us. It is encountered in the workplace, perhaps in the form of 'office politics'. Reference is frequently made to the 'political environment' which fashions the content of public policy. This section seeks to briefly assess what the *study of politics* is concerned with.

Human relationships are crucial to the study of politics. Human beings do not live in isolation but in communities. These may be small (such as a family), or large (such as a country). The study of politics involves two crucial dimensions:

○ *Analysing the behaviour of individuals within a group context:* the focus of political study is broad and includes issues such as the formation and management of groups, inter-group relationships, the operations of their collective decision-making processes, and the implementation and enforcement of decisions.

○ *Examining the nature of conflict and the manner in which it is resolved:* this is a particular focus of political analysis and is especially concerned with competition for resources. This may be analysed from a number of perspectives which include the study of organisations, policy-making processes affecting sub-national, national and supranational bodies, and international relations.

THE POLITICAL SPECTRUM

Conflict within society is underpinned by competing ideas concerning the nature of the social system it is desired to create. These competing ideas provide the basis for political ideology, the study of which is an important area of politics. The terms 'left', 'right' and 'centre' are frequently used to classify political parties and ideologies. Such terminology derived from the French Revolution in the late eighteenth century: the Left was associated with revolution while the Right was identified with reaction.

The terms left, right and centre lack precise definition but broadly indicate stances adopted towards political, economic and social change: historically, the Right opposed it, preferring the established order of the past. The Left advocated change while the Centre was associated with the desire to introduce gradual reform. Conservatism is identified with the right of the spectrum, socialism with the left, while liberalism and social democracy is commonly depicted as occupying the centre ground.

The Classification of Political Systems and Structures

A political system embraces a wide range of formal and informal processes which exert influence on a state's decision-making machinery. These include both the formal institutions of the state (such as the executive, legislative and judicial branches of government which are discussed in Chapters 10–15) but also embrace the influences exerted by individuals and organisations which are not formally incorporated into it. The latter include public opinion, the media and pressure groups. A political system has no physical dimension or formal existence but embraces a wide range of organisations, bodies and activities whose operations influence decision-making.

Types of political systems

Political systems can be distinguished from each other in a number of ways. This process of differentiation is termed *classification*. Alan Ball (*Modern Politics and Government*) identifies three broad types of political systems:

1 liberal democratic
2 socialist democratic
3 oligarchic or authoritarian.

Liberal Democratic

This term is discussed more fully in Chapter 2: a key feature of these political systems is that the actions of government reflect the will of the people (or at least the majority of them). Open competition for power between political parties, the existence of a wide range of personal and civil liberties, and an acceptance of the legitimacy of pressure groups seeking to influence public policy characterise such political systems. To avoid tyranny, the branches of government are to some extent separated rather than being held in one set of hands, and the scope of government is limited.

THE SEPARATION OF POWERS

The separation of powers was advocated by Montesquieu in his work *De l'Esprit des Lois*, written in 1748. He believed that tyranny was most effectively avoided if the three branches of government (the legislature, executive and judiciary) were separate. This implied that each branch would possess a degree of autonomy and that its personnel should be different.

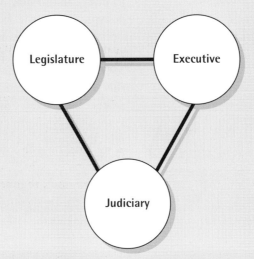

The separation of powers.

An important consequence of this is the existence of an independent judiciary, which is usually regarded as a crucial aspect of a liberal-democratic political system which guarantees that civil and political liberties are adequately protected.

Socialist Democratic

This system was formerly associated with the Soviet Union and its East European satellite neighbours but, following the collapse of communism, is confined to a smaller number of countries which include the People's Republic of China, Vietnam and Cuba. The main feature of this system of government is the paramount position of an official socialist ideology and the domination or total monopolisation of political affairs by the official Communist Party. The role of the state is to fulfil an ideology and build a society characterised by equality and classlessness. State control of the economy is viewed as essential in order to achieve this ideal. As the massacre of opponents to the communist regime in China at Tiananmen Square in 1989 evidenced, dissent is not encouraged in such political systems. The control which the Communist Party exerts over government means that the judiciary is less able to defend civil and political liberties than in liberal-democratic political systems.

Oligarchic or Authoritarian

A wide variety of political structures exist under this heading which include regimes controlled directly or indirectly by the military, traditional monarchies and dictatorships. Government is typically in the hands of one person or a small group of people. In common with socialist democracies, oligarchic political structures permit few political freedoms, and are frequently characterised by brutality and coercion meted out by the police or military, who perform a prominent part in civil affairs. The key difference which separates oligarchic or authoritarian regimes from socialist democracy is ideology which, in turn, gives rise to a number of different forms of this regime. These are:

○ self-interest regimes

○ fascist dictatorships

○ theocracies.

Self-Interest Regimes

These regimes operate in the interests of those who hold power. Here there is no ideology governing the actions of the government, which is motivated by defending and advancing the interests of its rulers. Military dictatorships often constitute this form of oligarchic government.

Fascist Dictatorships

These are oligarchic regimes whose operations are guided by the ideology of fascism. This ideology is difficult to define precisely, and varies widely within countries which have practised it. Its characteristics include the distrust of liberal democratic political structures (especially independent legislatures). Government is exercised by powerful dictators (which in twentieth-century Europe have included Hitler in Germany, Mussolini in Italy, Franco in Spain and Salazar in Portugal) who head the political party which dominates all state institutions. Fascist regimes are typically nationalistic and this may lead to genocide being practiced against those who are not members of the dominant race which lives in that country. Free enterprise usually exists within fascist countries, but its operations may be subject to regulation by the state.

Theocracies

These are regimes based upon a religious ideology. Examples exist in Iran and in those areas of Afghanistan governed by the Taliban. A main feature of theocratic government is the dominance of viewpoints and opinions held by the dominant religious sect.

Question

Undertake your own study of political systems. To do this select ONE example of a country with a liberal democratic system of government and ONE with any of the alternatives described above. Compare and contrast the operations of these two political systems using the following headings:

○ **The Formal Structure of Government:** examine this in each of the two countries you have selected (particularly the composition of the executive and legislature in each case).

○ **People Power:** look at the extent to which the general public has the ability to control or influence the selection of members of the government and the policies it pursues (and in particular the relevance of elections to these processes).

○ **Liberty**: assess the civil and political liberties which exist in these two countries (this includes factors such as the independence of the media).

Political Structures

The study of political structures is concerned with the operations or workings of a political system. There are a number of key features which can be used to distinguish between different forms of political structures. Such structures are not peculiar to any particular political system. These are discussed more fully in Chapters 11 and 16, but are briefly referred to here.

Federal and Unitary

These two contrasting political structures are primarily concerned with the division of power between the national government and sub-national bodies (such as state, regional or local government):

○ *Federal government:* in a federal political structure, power is divided between the national government and sub-national units, each of which have their own respective responsibilities which the other should not intrude upon. This division of power is typically provided for in a codified constitution. The United States of America, Australia and Canada are countries with federal political structures.

○ *Unitary government:* in a unitary political structure power is centralised in the hands of the national government. Other units of government may exist but they are subordinate to the national government which may create or abolish them, and allocate or remove functions from them as it wishes. France is an example of a country with a unitary political structure.

Presidential and Parliamentary Forms of Government

These two contrasting political structures are concerned with the nature of the executive branch of government, particularly its relationship to the legislative branch.

○ *Parliamentary:* in countries with a parliamentary form of government the executive branch of government is drawn from and is accountable to the legislature. Its tenure in office is dependent on the legislature's support. The United Kingdom has this structure: the prime minister, who is the chief executive, and cabinet are members of Parliament, and are accountable to this body (primarily the House of Commons) which possesses the sanction of dismissal.

○ *Presidential:* in countries with a presidential form of government the chief executive is not part of the legislature and is elected separately from that body. This structure exists in the USA where the President is elected every four years by the vote of the entire nation. The President is not allowed to be a member of Congress and has no formal relationship with this body, other than through their ability to remove him by impeachment, which is discussed in Chapters 2 and 11.

Question

○ How would you classify the UK's political structure?

○ To what extent will the operations of the Welsh Assembly and Scottish Parliament affect these basic characteristics?

Key Political Concepts

This section discusses a number of key issues which relate to the study of politics. These are usually referred to as 'concepts', and provide an underpinning on which a more detailed examination of the political process in liberal democracies can be built.

Political Culture

This is concerned with the conduct of a country's political affairs. In particular it seeks to explain why political conduct differs within similar political systems.

It has been suggested above that liberal-democratic political systems embrace a wide range of similar features. These include:

❍ *Institutions of government:* government in liberal-democratic political systems consists of the executive (which is headed by a chief executive), the legislature, and the judiciary (or courts).

❍ *Political organisations:* bodies such as political parties and pressure groups are important components of a liberal-democratic political system. It is through these organisations that members of the general public can exert influence over the conduct of political affairs.

❍ *Political processes:* these are concerned with matters such as the composition of government and the determination of public policy. Procedures such as elections and referendums are used in liberal democratic political systems to decide these matters.

❍ *Personal freedoms:* liberal-democratic political systems guarantee individual citizens a range of freedoms. These secure political freedom and safeguard them in their dealings with the state.

However, the composition, conduct, powers, relationships, and operations of these common features differ from one country to another. Within a common framework, the conduct of political affairs in each liberal democracy is subject to wide variation. In France, for example (as is discussed in Chapter 8), there is tolerance of conflict as a means of settling political disputes. In Sweden, however, the spirit of compromise tends to guide the actions of key participants in the political process. In the UK there is a tradition of evolutionary rather than revolutionary change.

Political culture refers to an underlying set of political values held by most people living in a particular country. These attitudes influence the conduct of political activity by both politicians and the general public. When reference is made to a country's political culture, emphasis is being placed on the similarity of views held within any particular country. This implies that within any one country there is a tendency for the majority of persons to think, feel and act in the same way concerning the manner in which political affairs should be

CONVENTIONAL AND EXTRA-PARLIAMENTARY POLITICAL ACTION

Political activity may be conducted in a number of different ways. A key distinction, however, is between conventional and extra-parliamentary political action.

Conventional political activity views a country's legislative assembly as the main arena in which political decisions are made. Citizens indirectly participate in a state's decision-making process by their involvement in elections contested by political parties with alternative ideologies.

Extra-parliamentary political activity entails action undertaken by groups of citizens who directly involve themselves in attempts to influence a state's decision-making process. This may include direct action which is discussed in Chapter 8.

Political culture determines the relative importance of these two methods of political activity in any particular country.

conducted. But these people may hold different core values to those citizens in another liberal democracy.

The extent of a common political culture can, however, be overstated. Within any country, differences are likely to exist concerning fundamental values related to political behaviour. Factors such as *deindustrialisation* (which has resulted in the emergence of an 'underclass' in many liberal democracies) or *immigration* (which has led to the development of multi-ethnic societies) have fundamental significance for the existence of universally-agreed sentiments underpinning political conduct. These factors may give rise to a society in which dominant attitudes coexist alongside sub-cultural values, or result in a looser attachment to mainstream values by some sections of society.

Contrasting Views of Political Culture

Liberal theorists suggest that a country's political culture is fashioned by its unique historical development and that its underlying values are transmitted across the generations by a process termed *political socialisation*. Agencies such as the family, schools, the media and political parties are responsible for instructing citizens in such beliefs and attitudes. The traditional reluctance of citizens in the UK to carry identity cards is derived from an historic dislike of the State being able to intrude into the lives of its individual citizens. Continued support for such a view is derived from history, law and political studies, and contemporary political debate.

Marxists, however, tend to view political culture as an artificial creation rather than the product of history. They view political culture as an ideological weapon through which society is indoctrinated to accept views which are in the interests of its dominant classes (whose control is based on economic power). Thus from this perspective, public support for elections as the main way to change the composition of government and the content of policy is an attitude which has been deliberately manufactured by those fearful of alternative methods to achieve these ends (such as riots or revolution). Riot and revolution may produce radical change not to the liking of society's ruling class.

States and Government

Although the terms 'state' and 'government' are sometimes used interchangeably, important distinctions exist between them.

State

A state consists of a wide range of permanent official institutions involved in formulating and enforcing collective decisions for a society. These usually include the institutions of government, the bureaucracy, courts and police. Decisions made by these bodies are binding on all members of that society and may, if necessary, be enforced by the deployment of sanctions or force in the name of the state. The geographic boundaries of a state are referred to as a 'nation' or a 'country'.

Government

The term 'government' refers to the institutions which are concerned with making, implementing, and enforcing laws. In a narrower sense, however, government is often associated with those who wield executive power within a state. It refers to a specific group of people who give direction to the activities of the state and function as its political arm.

Power and Authority

The terms 'power' and 'authority' have crucial bearing on an issue which is fundamental to the study of politics – the manner in which conflict is resolved. Both are concerned with explaining how one group of persons has the ability to influence the behaviour of another, and in particular the terms explain how a government is able to secure the obedience of citizens to its decisions. These terms may be defined as follows:

○ *Power:* this is the ability to compel obedience by utilising sanctions against disobedience. The fear of the sanction thus ensures that citizens obey the government.

○ *Authority:* an individual or institution which possesses authority secures compliance because there is general agreement that those who put forward ideas have the right to propose and implement them. Thus governments which possess authority are able to influence the actions of their citizens because there is a general consensus that it has the right to take decisions, even if the content of them is not generally popular.

In liberal democracies governments possess both power and authority. They are obeyed partly because there is general consent that they have the right to govern, but also because the courts may be used as a sanction to force compliance with their laws. Power which is divorced from authority is likely to produce an unstable political structure in which violence, disorder and revolution threaten the existence of the government.

The Distribution of Power

The resolution of conflict is determined by the way in which power is distributed within society. This influences the consent (or legitimacy) given to the decisions which are arrived at. There is, however, considerable disagreement concerning how power is distributed within a society.

○ *Pluralism:* pluralists argue that power is widely distributed throughout society and that the role of the state is to adjudicate in the constant competition which exists between different groups and interests. Decisions thus reflect the process of bargaining between such diverse bodies.

○ *Elitism:* elitist theories contend that power is concentrated in the hands of a relatively small, organised group of people and that this minority is able to enforce its will on the majority of citizens.

○ *Marxism:* Marxists identify the ruling elite as those who possess economic power and are able to use the political system to further their own interests. Popular consent to decisions is especially reliant on the ideological control exerted over the population by this economically powerful elite.

Sources of Authority

The sociologist Max Weber suggested that authority could be derived from one or other of three sources. These were:

❍ *Traditional authority:* here acceptance of the right to rule is based on custom. Popular consent is accorded to decisions made by those from a background which traditionally exercises the functions of government within a state. Hereditary monarchs (who rule by virtue of birth) enjoy this form of authority.

❍ *Charismatic authority:* this is derived from characteristics which are personal to a political leader. The main criteria for obedience is that the public stand in awe of the person taking decisions. Charisma is particularly associated with dictators, who include Adolf Hitler in Germany and Juan Peron, President of Argentina 1946–55 and 1973–4.

❍ *Legal-bureaucratic or legal-rational authority:* here compliance to decisions made by rulers is based upon the office which an individual holds within a state, and not his or her personal characteristics. It is thus the prestige accorded by the public to an office which influences the ability of an official to secure acceptance to his or her wishes.

In liberal democratic political systems the political office occupied by those who give orders forms the main basis of their authority. It is accepted that presidents or prime ministers have the right to give orders by virtue of the positions which they occupy. However, political leaders frequently derive their authority from more than one source: in the UK the association of the prime minister with government *carried out in the name of the monarch* gives this office holder authority derived from both traditional and legal-bureaucratic sources.

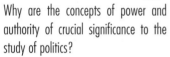

Question

Why are the concepts of power and authority of crucial significance to the study of politics?

The Citizen and the State

The relationship between the state and its citizens is a key issue in liberal democratic political systems. This relationship is affected by key concepts which are discussed below.

Citizenship

A major issue in assessing the relationship between a state and those who live in it concerns the definition of citizenship, which gives people a sense of common identity. Citizenship can be based on factors such as pride in one's nation, but usually involves giving inhabitants a stake in the society in which they live. This may be provided by the allocation of political rights, and social and economic entitlements. The receipt of such privileges is usually balanced by responsibilities being placed upon the beneficiaries. In the UK, for example, those in receipt of political and socio-economic rights are expected to accept the status quo in society and not engage in revolutionary activities designed to bring about its downfall.

Political Inclusion

In many liberal democracies citizenship was initially based on the ability to vote in local and national elections. This was usually determined by property ownership. Thus the extension of the right to vote meant extending citizenship to ever increasing numbers of people.

ENFRANCHISEMENT

Initially in the nineteenth century the right to vote, or franchise, was limited to men who owned property. Slowly the right to vote was extended through legislation passed in 1832, 1867 and 1884. However, by the end of the nineteenth century many men (mainly, but not solely, members of the working classes) and all women still were denied a vote.

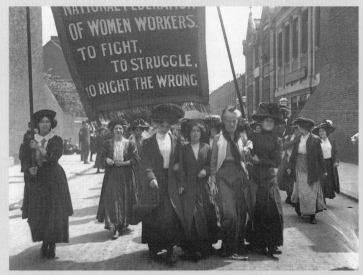

Suffragettes fought for women's right to vote.

In the early twentieth century campaigners (who were termed 'suffragettes') sought to give women the right to vote. This right was ultimately conceded when the Representation of the People Act 1918 gave all men over 21 years of age and all women over 30 the right to vote. In 1928 the age qualification for women was lowered to 21.

The current legislation, which gives all men and women the right to vote when they reach 18, was passed in 1969.

Social Inclusion

The increase in the ability to vote did not, however, guarantee a common identity since this was eroded by the presence of economic and social divisions within a society. There was no common identity between the 'haves' and 'have nots'. Increasingly, therefore, citizenship entailed social and economic reforms directed at the poorer and least fortunate members of society. These reforms were designed to create a sense of national cohesion. The welfare reforms initiated by the Liberal governments of 1905–14, and subsequently embraced within the welfare state created and advanced by Labour and Conservative governments after 1945, contained ideals (such as the right to a job, access to a comprehensive national health service, and entitlement to a range of social welfare benefits) which extended the social and economic aspects of citizenship to large numbers of people. Those who were excluded from any or all of these arrangements were not regarded as 'full' citizens. In the early postwar period this included members of ethnic minority communities whose prospects in areas such as employment and housing were adversely affected by racial prejudice and discrimination.

Conservative governments between 1979 and 1997 shifted the focus of citizenship away from the state provision of services, which were designed to create a unified society, to the exercise of individual initiative and consumer choice. Those able to take advantage of the opportunities offered by the free market economy constituted the new basis of citizenship. Those who were unable to play any part in the operations of this economic system became viewed as the 'underclass'. They were thus excluded from full membership of the newly constituted society. As Chapter 3 argues, the Labour government elected in 1997 sought to end this situation by pursuing policies to secure social inclusion.

The Rule of Law

The rule of law is regarded as a fundamental constitutional principle in liberal democracies. It asserts the supremacy of the law as an instrument which both governs the actions of individual citizens in their relationships with each other and also controls the conduct of the state towards them. This principle may be incorporated into a codified constitution (as is the case in the USA), or it may be grounded in common law (which is the situation in the UK).

The paramount position accorded to the law as the means of regulating actions undertaken by citizens and the state has a number of important implications. It suggests:

❍ *Open justice:* citizens can only be punished by the state using formalised procedures when they have transgressed the law.

❍ *Equality before the law:* this means that all citizens will be treated in the same way when they commit wrongdoings. Nobody is 'above the law', and the punishments meted out for similar crimes should be the same regardless of who committed them.

Many of the requirements embodied in the principle of the rule of law constitute practices which are widely adhered to in liberal democracies. Citizens are given legal protection against arbitrary actions committed by the state and its officials, and the law is applied to all citizens. However, most liberal democratic states deviate from the strict application of the rule of law. For example, equality before the law does not constitute equality of access to it. Factors which include social background, financial means, class, race or gender may play an influential part in determining whether a citizen who transgresses the law is proceeded against by the state, and may also have a major bearing on the outcome of any trial.

The Rule of Law in the USA

In the USA the freedom of citizens from arbitrary actions undertaken by government is incorporated into the Constitution. The procedure and practices which must be followed when citizens are accused of criminal actions are laid down in this document, most notably in the fifth and fourteenth amendments. The requirement that no citizen shall be deprived of 'life, liberty or property' without 'due process of law' is imposed as a condition affecting the operations of both federal and state governments. The fifth amendment also provides the citizen with further protection in their dealings with government. No person can be tried twice for the same offence nor be compelled to give self-incriminatory evidence in a criminal trial.

Further Reading

Maurice Duverger, *The Study of Politics* (London: Nelson, 1972).

Although written some time ago, this work remains a classic text concerning the study of politics. It covers a wide ground, discussing issues which include political and social structures, the roots of political struggles, and the way in which these antagonisms are reconciled.

Discussions of key political concepts are found in a number of general books on politics:

Alan Ball, *Modern Politics and Government* (Basingstoke: Macmillan, 1988, 4th edition).

Rod Hague, **Martin Harrop** and **Shaun Breslin**, *Comparative Government and Politics, An Introduction* (Basingstoke: Macmillan, 1992, 3rd edition).

Chapter Two | The Operations of Liberal Democracy

The aims of this chapter are:

> 1 To differentiate between 'democracy' and 'liberal democracy'.
>
> 2 To identify key political freedoms which are essential to liberal democracy.
>
> 3 To analyse key factors which relate to the representative nature of liberal-democratic political systems.
>
> 4 To evaluate mechanisms enabling members of the general public to play a role in policy making.
>
> 5 To assess the implications which corruption and abuse of power pose for the vitality of liberal democracy and to evaluate the measures taken in Britain during the 1990s to respond to this problem.

The Characteristics of Liberal Democracy

Direct and Liberal Democracy

A democratic society is one in which political power resides with the people who live there: it is they who are sovereign.

Democratic government was initiated in the Greek city of Athens in the fifth century BC. The word 'democracy' is derived from two Greek words, *demos* (meaning people) and *kratos* (meaning rule). The term thus literally means 'government by the people'. Initially major decisions were taken by meetings at which all free males attended. This system is referred to as *direct democracy*. It was possible for government to function in this way when the population was small and the activity of the State limited. Today, however, ancient city states have been replaced by bigger units of government with a greater range of responsibilities to larger numbers of people. It became necessary, therefore, to find ways whereby the notion of popular sovereignty could be made compatible with a workable decision-making process. This gave rise to a political system known as 'liberal democracy'.

The key principle underlying liberal democracy is that of *representation*: liberal (or, as it is sometimes referred to, representative) democracy is a system in which a small group of people take political decisions on behalf of all the citizens who live in a particular country. Those who exercise this responsibility do so with the consent of the citizens and govern in their name. However, their right to take decisions depends on popular approval and may be withdrawn should they lose the support of the population to whom they are accountable for their actions. In such cases citizens reclaim the political power they have ceded and reallocate the responsibility of government to an alternative group of people who subsequently govern in the name of the people.

Chapter 1 provided a brief discussion of the characteristics of liberal-democratic political systems and observed that there are wide variations between their political structures. A major distinction is between those (such as the United States of America) which have presidential systems of government and those (such as the United Kingdom) which have parliamentary systems. In some the executive branch of government tends to be derived from one political party but in others it is drawn from a coalition of parties, perhaps making for a more consensual style of government.

Question ?

Compare and contrast the terms 'direct democracy' and 'liberal (or representative) democracy'.

Politics examination questions frequently ask students to compare and contrast issues. This question can be tackled using the following steps:

◯ Define in your own words what you understand by the term 'direct democracy'.

◯ State in your own words what the term 'representative democracy' means to you.

◯ Consider whether there are any similarities in the underlying principles or operations of these systems.

◯ List TWO main differences between these terms.

Political Freedom and Liberal Democracy

It is an essential feature of liberal-democratic political systems that citizens have the ability to directly influence the policy-making process, including the right to join pressure groups and engage in their activities. This is discussed in Chapter 8. Here the discussion will be confined to considering the representative nature of such political systems and will focus on elections.

Elections in a Liberal Democracy

Representative institutions in liberal democracies are based on the principle of majority rule. This requires mechanisms to enable the general public to exercise choice over who will represent them, and also to dismiss these representatives if they feel that policies lacking popular support are being pursued. This suggests that elections are essential to the operations of liberal-democratic political systems. They enable the public to exert influence over the composition of government (especially the legislative and executive branches) and to hold it accountable for its subsequent actions. They also serve as the means whereby a country's citizens can make a retrospective judgement (that is, an assessment based on actions which have been previously carried out) on the record of those who have exercised the functions of government.

However, elections are not confined to liberal democracies. Countries with alternative political systems may also utilise them. In October 1995 over 99 per cent of the Iraqi people voted for Saddam Hussein to be that country's president. He was the only candidate in that election. An essential characteristic, therefore, of elections in liberal democracies is that such contests should provide a *genuine opportunity* to exert popular choice over the personnel and policies of government. To ensure this, it is necessary for elections to be accompanied by a range of political freedoms. The key ones are as follows:

○ the timing of elections is not totally determined by existing public-office holders

○ freedom of political expression

○ a wide electorate

○ fair electoral practices

○ a willingness to accept the verdict of elections.

Control over the Timing of Elections

Elections provide for popular control over the activities of government only if they are held regularly and their timing is not exclusively determined by those who occupy public office. There are various methods whereby these objectives are attained in liberal democracies:

○ *Fixed term elections:* in some countries, legislators or executives hold office for a fixed period of time at the end of which fresh elections must be held. In the USA, for example, the President is elected for a four-year term while members of the House of Representatives and the Senate serve for two and six years respectively.

❍ *Variable elections:* in some countries elections are not held at predetermined intervals. In the UK, for example, the Prime Minister has the ability to determine when general elections are held. However, this choice is subject to the legal requirement that fresh elections to the House of Commons must take place at least every five years, and to the theoretical possibility that the Monarch may deny the Prime Minister's request for an election.

Question ❓

❍ Consider the strengths and weaknesses of fixed term elections.

❍ Do you believe that the British system (whereby the timing of a general election is determined by the Prime Minister) is a preferable system?

Freedom of Political Expression

Elections will only provide the public with genuine political choice if a wide range of opinions can be voiced. This entails political parties being able to openly compete for power, and the existence of a range of political freedoms. The freedoms of speech, thought and assembly are essential features of liberal democracies, distinguishing them from more totalitarian systems in which dissent is not permitted. This implies that censorship on the media or restrictions on the activities of political parties, trade unions or other forms of political activity are incompatible with the operations of liberal democracy. An impartial judicial system and freedom from arbitrary arrest are also necessary aspects of such political systems which ensure that the leading opponents to a government are free to put their arguments before the nation's voters.

Nonetheless, a line needs to be drawn within liberal democracies concerning what members of political parties can say and the methods which they are permitted to use to present their case to the electorate. This issue is discussed below.

THE FREEDOM OF POLITICAL EXPRESSION

Restrictions on the total freedom of political expression exist in a number of countries. They may be justified for reasons which are discussed below.

Failure to Endorse Liberal-Democratic Principles

One reason for curtailing political freedom arises if parties fail to support the basic principles underlying liberal democracy: thus a party might achieve power through the ballot box but once installed into power will radically alter a country's political system. On grounds such as these the 1947 Italian constitution banned the reformation of the Fascist Party. The French constitution stipulates that political parties must respect the principles of national sovereignty and democracy. A similar provision applies in Germany where the Federal Constitutional Court may ban parties perceived to be undemocratic.

Threat Posed to the State

The doctrines espoused by a political party may, further, be viewed as threatening not merely to a country's political system but to the very existence of the state itself. Fear of the Soviet Union and communism (which was believed to be on a quest for world domination) was prominent in the USA during the 1950s. The American Communist Party was theoretically banned by the 1954 Communist Control Act, but its enforcement was lax. However perceived sympathy for communism led to discriminatory actions against individuals, such as dismissal from employment.

Methods Used to Advance a Cause

The tactics used by political organisations may also justify restrictions being imposed by the state. Organisations which provoke violence because their statements or actions are viewed as offensive by other groups of citizens may be subject to restrictions in order to maintain public order. Groups which actually carry out acts of violence to further their political objectives are also likely to be the subject of state regulation. In the UK, for example, groups which utilised violence to further their political ends were banned (or 'proscribed') by the Prevention of Terrorism legislation which was initially enacted in 1974. One difficulty with this course of action is that parties which are outlawed may continue their activities as secret organisations. This may make it more difficult for the police and other agencies of the state to monitor their activities, and may also encourage more extreme forms of violent activity by the members of the banned organisation.

Question

Assess the strengths and weaknesses of THREE reasons which might be presented for placing limits on political expression and activity in a liberal democracy.

A Wide Electorate

Popular control over government requires a large electorate in which the vast majority of the population possess the right to vote (or franchise). In the nineteenth century this right was based on property ownership in many countries: those who owned little or no property were not regarded as citizens and thus were unable to play any part in conventional political activities. The enfranchisement of adults, regardless of wealth, gender or race is necessary for systems of government to accurately reflect the wishes of their populations. However, the enfranchisement of every individual is rarely accomplished since most liberal democracies deny the vote to some groups of people. In Britain current exclusions include convicted prisoners whilst detained in a penal institution.

Fair Electoral Practices

Elections permit public involvement in key political activities
only when they are conducted fairly. Factors which include the
secret ballot, freedom from intimidation and the absence of
corruption are required to ensure that the outcome of an
election reflects genuine public sentiments. The geographic
areas used as the basis for elections should also be fairly
constructed to avoid *gerrymandering*. This entails a governing
party seeking to maintain its power by drawing up ward or
constituency boundaries which will disadvantage its opponents.
This term derived from early nineteenth century America (being
named after the activities of Governor Elbridge Gerry of
Massachussetts) but was used in more recent times by the
Unionist party in Northern Ireland as a means to minimise the
impact of the Catholic vote.

In Britain the secret ballot was introduced in 1872 so that a
voter could not be subjected to pressure (for example, from an
employer or landlord) when casting a vote. The amount which
candidates may spend is also subject to regulation, and corrupt
practices such as candidates seeking to bribe voters or voters
seeking to vote more than once in the same election are subject
to legal penalties if discovered.

The composition of Parliamentary constituencies is determined
by independent bodies, the Boundary Commissions. There are
four of these (one each for England, Wales, Scotland and
Northern Ireland) and they report at periodic intervals
concerning the need for changes in the existing arrangements. A
government may, however, use their majority in the House of
Commons to delay the implementation of proposals made by
these Commissions, a course of action which Harold Wilson's
Labour government adopted in 1969. It is, however, impossible
to attain the theoretically ideal situation whereby every
constituency contains the same number of electors. Since 1944
Scotland and Wales have been over-represented due to an
arrangement whereby each country is guaranteed a minimum
number of MPs: this was set at 71 for Scotland and 36 for Wales
although these figures may be exceeded. In the 1997 General
Election Scotland returned 72 MPs and Wales 40. It is
additionally necessary to make special arrangements for remote
areas (especially the Scottish Highlands and Islands) so that MPs
can physically consult, and be consulted by, their constituents.

Question

List TWO arguments to support the argument that 'the UK is a democratic country' and TWO which oppose it.

Willingness to Accept the Verdict of Elections

Liberal democracy requires that those who govern a country accept the verdict delivered by the electorate. Rulers in non-democratic political systems may often challenge the outcome of an election when this has demonstrated popular support for fundamental change. There are a number of ways whereby they may do this which include setting election results aside by declaring them null and void, or supporting a military take over to preserve the political status quo.

The Representative Nature of Liberal Democracy

It has been argued that liberal democracy involves a small group of people taking political decisions on behalf of the entire population. It is thus necessary to consider whether those entrusted with this responsibility represent public opinion. There are a number of factors which need to be considered in relationship to this objective.

The Party System

Parties constitute one mechanism through which the views of the general public can be acted upon by elected officials. However, these may distort the relationship between an elected official and his or her electorate. Voters may support candidates for public office on the basis of their party label rather than their perceived ability to articulate the needs of local electors. While in office, party discipline may require an official to sacrifice locality to party if these interests do not coincide. The extent to which this happens depends on the strength of party discipline, which is stronger in some liberal democracies (such as the UK, Australia and New Zealand) than in others (such as the USA). In America *parochialism* (that is, the advancement of local interests) remains a potent force in politics, forcing elected officials to place local considerations at the forefront of their actions.

Majority Rule and Minority Interests

It is clearly impossible for those elected to public office to represent the views of all citizens. It is rare for residents of any country to display total unity on the conduct of civil affairs. The system of representative democracy, therefore, ensures that government caters for the opinions of the *majority* of its citizens. This poses the problem concerning how representative democracy should treat minorities whose views or needs may be irrelevant to (and even opposed to) majority opinion.

There is no easy answer to this problem. The division of sovereignty within a state between national and sub-national governments may help to ensure that minorities located in particular areas enjoy a degree of self-government and can thus secure attention to their particular needs or problems.

The electoral system may also have a crucial bearing on the extent to which minorities can influence the agenda of politics. In the UK, for example, the first-past-the-post electoral system has been charged with distorting the wishes of the electorate and producing a legislative body which does not accord with popular opinion as expressed at a general election. The paramount need to ensure that minorities are formally represented explains the use of proportional representation in elections to the Northern Ireland Forum in 1996 (which used the party list system with a 'top-up' for the most successful parties) and to the Northern Ireland Assembly in 1998 (which utilised the Single Transferable Vote). Electoral systems are discussed in detail in Chapter 4, and Northern Irish politics in Chapter 20. However, no electoral system can ensure effective representation for all minorities. In the 1998 Northern Ireland Assembly elections, the six-member constituency of West Belfast returned 4 Sein Fein and 2 Social Democratic and Labour Party members. This result meant that no Loyalist politician was elected to represent the Protestant minority living on the Shankhill Road.

If minorities are unrepresented they may seek to further their political ends through pressure groups or through the use of protest and dissent. In extreme cases, perceptions by minorities of neglect or unfair treatment may result in their withdrawing from mainstream society and seeking to conduct their own lifestyle. This tactic may result in minority groups undertaking activities which are illegal. Disorder may occur if the state refuses to accept such cultural diversity and intervenes to put down these practices.

The Status of Elected Officials

Those who are elected to public office may fulfil the role of either a delegate or a representative:

○ *Delegate:* this is an elected official who follows the instructions of the electorate as and when these are given. He or she has little freedom of action and is effectively mandated by voters to act in a particular manner.

○ *Representative:* such a person claims the right to exercise his or her judgement on matters which arise. Once elected to office, a representative's actions are determined by that person's conscience and not by instructions delivered by voters. A representative is, however, subsequently held accountable by the public for actions undertaken whilst occupying public office.

THE STATUS OF A BRITISH MEMBER OF PARLIAMENT

The eighteenth century statesman, Edmund Burke, argued that an MP should apply his judgement to serve the interests of the nation as a whole rather than having to obey the wishes of the local electorate. His assertion that an MP was a representative and not a delegate has been subsequently followed in practice.

A British Member of Parliament is thus subject to no formal restraints on his or her actions once elected. The system of recall which is practised in some American States (whereby those who elect a public official can end that person's tenure in office before he or she has served a full term) has never operated in the UK. A Member of Parliament cannot be forced to resign by local electors: their only power is their ultimate ability to select an alternative representative when the next election occurs. There are informal pressures which may influence the behaviour of a Member of Parliament, for example the discipline exerted by the party system. But this may prove an ineffective restraint on an MP's behaviour.

In 1998, the Conservative Member for Leominster, Peter Temple-Morris, 'crossed the floor' of the House of Commons and joined the Labour Party. Neither the Conservative Party nor his local electorate possessed any power to respond to this situation and make him resign. In South Africa, however, members of the National Assembly who cease to be members of the Party which nominated them are required to vacate their seats.

The Social Composition of Legislatures

In many liberal democracies the institutions of representative government do not mirror the make up of the population and fail to reflect key social divisions, such as a country's occupational make up, or its class, ethnic, gender or religious divisions. This is a particular problem for legislative assemblies. White, male, middle class persons of above-average education frequently dominate the composition of such bodies which are thus socially unrepresentative, although they may reflect the characteristics required to occupy influential positions elsewhere in society. This may mean that the opinions or needs of groups which are inadequately represented in the composition of such assemblies (such as women, and racial minorities) receive insufficient attention. In the UK, for example, only six out of the 651 MPs elected in 1992 came from ethnic minority communities. In 1997 the figure was nine (out of an increased total of 659). The issue of women MPs is discussed in Chapter 23.

> ## YOUNG PEOPLE AND CONVENTIONAL POLITICAL ACTIVITY
>
> The problem posed by the disaffection of young people with conventional political activity is especially acute. A 1995 report from the think tank Demos (entitled *Freedom's Children*) stated that people under 25 in the UK were four times less likely to be registered to vote than any other group, were less likely to vote for or join a political party, and only 6 per cent of the 15–34-year-olds described themselves as 'very interested in politics'. This distrust of conventional political activity has given rise to involvement by younger people in direct action (particularly in connection with the conservation of the environment) and in the activities of the voluntary sector. A survey of 16–24-year-olds by the British Youth Council in 1998 revealed that 1 in 10 could not name the new Labour prime minister, and only 2 in 100 knew the name of the Health Secretary. Only 50 per cent of those aged 18–24 had voted in the 1997 General Election.

A key danger which arises when legislatures are not socially representative is that government becomes out of tune with public opinion, and may be viewed as anachronistic (that is, out-of-date) when the national mood demands reform and innovation. The seriousness of this problem may be aggravated by the procedures adopted by legislative bodies: the seniority system used by the American Congress (whereby the chairs of influential Congressional committees were allocated to the longest serving committee member whose party was in control of Congress) tended to entrench the conservative influence over postwar American domestic affairs and persisted until changes to these procedures were introduced during the 1960s and 1970s.

Question

List and evaluate TWO arguments to suggest that the requirements of a liberal-democratic political system are not fully met in contemporary Britain.

Policy-Making and the General Public

It has been argued that elections play a major role in liberal-democratic political systems. They enable the population to select a small group of people who perform the tasks of government. However, the ability to elect representatives and (at a subsequent election) to deliver a verdict on their performance in public office does not give the general public a prominent role in political affairs. In many liberal democracies, therefore, there are mechanisms which seek to provide citizens with a more constant role in policy formulation. Some of these (such as membership of political parties and pressure groups, and the ability to engage in protest and dissent) are discussed throughout this work. This section considers some additional methods through which public involvement in public policy-making can be achieved.

Referendums

Referendums give the general public the opportunity to vote on specific policy issues. They are utilised widely in some liberal democracies such as Switzerland and the Scandinavian countries, but more sparingly in others such as the UK.

Advantages of Referendums

Referendums bring a number of benefits to the operations of a liberal-democratic political system:

○ they facilitate direct democracy

○ they allow the public to determine constitutional issues.

Facilitate Direct Democracy

Referendums permit mass public involvement in the formulation of public policy. A proposal requires the approval of the majority of citizens in order for it to be implemented. The danger that those elected to govern do not accurately reflect public opinion is avoided through the operation of a system of direct democracy which enables the citizens themselves to express their approval or disapproval of issues which affect their everyday lives.

It is important, however, that the initiative to hold a referendum should not solely rest with those in government. It is desirable that the public themselves should have the right both to call a referendum and to exercise some control over its content in order for it to provide a mechanism to secure public involvement in policy making. In New Zealand, for example, the 1993 Citizens Initiated Referenda Act gave 10 per cent of the country's registered electors the opportunity to initiate a non-binding referenda on any subject. This must be held within one year of the initial call for a referendum unless 75 per cent of Members of Parliament vote to defer it.

Determine Constitutional Issues

It is not feasible to suggest that referendums should be held to judge the mood of the public on every single item of public policy. However, they do provide a means whereby major issues (perhaps of considerable constitutional importance) can be resolved. In many European countries referendums were held on membership of the European Union or treaties (such as Maastricht) which were associated with it, due to their implications for fundamental matters such as national sovereignty. In the UK, a Referendum Party was established in 1994 calling for a referendum on the Maastricht Treaty and its subsequent revisions. British membership of the single European currency (the Euro) will be determined by a referendum likely to be held in the early years of the twenty-first century.

Disadvantages

There are, however, a number of problems associated with referendums:

○ they devalue the role of the legislature and the executive

○ they may provide for an unequal competition

○ the issues may be too complex for a fair vote

○ the motive for calling a referendum may not be a progressive one

○ they may promote 'mob rule'.

Devalue the Role of the Legislature and Executive

Referendums may devalue the role performed by legislatures by undermining their role as law-making bodies. They were deliberately introduced in some countries (such as France) to weaken the power of parliament. They may be reconciled with the concept of Parliamentary sovereignty by viewing them as *consultative* rather than *binding* on the actions of the legislature, (that is, if a referendum is consultative, the legislature is not forced to act according to the outcome, thus retaining its ultimate power to determine public policy). However, it is difficult to ignore the outcome of a popular vote even when it does not theoretically tie the hands of public policy makers. Thus the Norwegian Parliament announced in advance of the 1972 consultative referendum on entry into the European Economic Community that its outcome would determine the country's stance on this issue.

The power of the executive branch of government may be limited by the use of referendums. Governments may be forced to follow public opinion at the expense of their ability to lead it.

Unequal Competition

Competing groups in a referendum do not necessarily possess equality in the resources they have at their disposal, which may give one side an unfair advantage over another in putting its case across to the electorate. This problem becomes more acute if the government contributes to the financing of one side's campaign, as occurred in the early stages of the 1995 Irish referendum on divorce. In 1998, Lord Neill's reforms to party funding (which are discussed more fully in Chapter 6) proposed new laws for referendums in the UK, to include equal State funding for 'yes' and 'no' campaigns.

Complexity of Issues

The general public may be unable to understand the complexities of the issues which are the subject of a referendum. This may result in the level of public participation being low, or cause the outcome to be swayed by factors other than the issue placed before the voters. For example, a referendum may become a mechanism for voters to express an opinion on their government, especially if it has become unpopular and is closely associated with the proposal for which popular sanction is sought. Thus the outcome of the French referendum in 1969 to re-establish the region as a unit of government was heavily influenced by the unpopularity of President de Gaulle with whom the proposal was closely identified.

Motive May not be Progressive

A referendum is not always associated with the progressive political intention of bringing government closer to the people. Dictators may use them instead of representative institutions such as parliament, asserting that such bodies are unnecessary since the people are directly consulted on government policy. The extent of public involvement may, however, be minimal, especially when referendums are used to seek public endorsement of an action which has already taken place.

Referendums may also be proposed by executives as a means to preserve party unity on an issue which is extremely divisive. The British referendum in 1975 on the Labour government's renegotiated terms for membership of the European Economic Community was primarily put forward for such partisan reasons. This avoided the government having to take a decision which might have split the Party.

'Mob Rule'

A referendum may facilitate the tyranny of the majority whereby minority interests become sacrificed at the behest of mob rule. One danger associated with this objection is that political issues may be resolved by orchestrated hysteria rather than through a calm reflection of the issues which are involved. There is thus a danger that a referendum on the UK joining the single European currency will become dominated by the tabloid press appealing to sentiments such as 'defence of the British Pound', rather than promoting a calm analysis of the benefits and disadvantages associated with such a course of action.

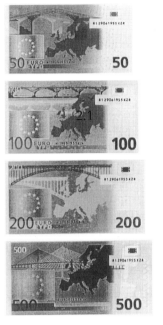

Look: no Queen's head! Prototypes of the euro.

THE CASE OF THE MISSING QUEEN'S HEAD

The danger that a referendum on the UK joining the single European currency would be dominated by emotion rather than an assessment of the economic advantages and disadvantages arising from this course of action was evidenced towards the end of 1998. The European Central Bank determined that Euro bank notes should contain images to symbolise cooperation. This meant that if the UK ultimately decided to join, the Queen's head would not appear on the currency.

Although the Queen's head has appeared on British bank notes only since the early 1960s, the leader of the Conservative Party declared this decision was a 'warning signal to British people', and a senior Conservative MP asserted that it constituted 'an insult to Britain and the Royal Family'. The *Sun* newspaper attacked the unelected bankers who had 'goose-stepped over the people of Europe', and a leading constitutional historian posed the question, 'What next? Will we have to remove the Queen's head from postage stamps?'

Examples of the Use of Referendums

Referendums are widely used by liberal democracies. Switzerland makes the greatest use of them (279 being held between 1941 and 1993), but they are also a feature of the government of other countries, as the following examples demonstrate.

○ *The UK:* since 1945 referendums have been used on a limited number of occasions. Recent examples include the Labour government's devolution proposals for Scotland and Wales in 1997 and the 1998 vote to judge popular approval in Northern Ireland for the 'Good Friday' peace accord (which is discussed in Chapter 21).

○ *Ireland:* proposals to amend the constitution, following enactment by the Oireachtas (parliament), must be submitted to a referendum. In 1995, a proposal to amend the constitution

Question

On the basis of the arguments presented above, do you believe that the extended use of referendums is a desirable or undesirable development in British politics?

and legalise divorce was narrowly approved, having been decisively rejected in 1986. In 1998, Irish people overwhelmingly expressed approval for amending the Constitution in line with the 'Good Friday' peace agreement.

○ *France:* referendums have been initiated by some Presidents to appeal directly to the public over the heads of either the National Assembly or the government. De Gaulle's 1962 referendum secured popular approval for the direct election of the president and demonstrated how a referendum can be used to enhance presidential power.

○ *Italy:* a number of referendums were held in the 1990s on the issue of electoral reform. They may be initiated by 500,000 of the country's electors.

'Teledemocracy'

Referendums are one mechanism of direct democracy. But there are others. 'Teledemocracy' could also be used to achieve the objective of enhanced popular involvement in public policy-making. This involves a television audience being supplied with the technology to make an instant response to matters which appear on their screens. Experiments have taken place in countries which include the USA and New Zealand. Although these experiments have been concerned mainly with marketing commercial products and entertainment, the technique could be developed further to involve members of the general public in the formulation of policy, perhaps through their participation in spontaneous polls concerning options which are debated before them.

Participatory Democracy

The perception that legislative bodies were controlled by capital and bureaucracies, and thus could never inaugurate radical reform, was the key underpinning of demands for 'participatory democracy' or 'people power'. Such sentiments emerged during the 1960s, as a reaction to the emergence of the Corporate State. The British Liberal Party's endorsement of community politics was initially based upon the desire for popular empowerment at local level, enabling citizens to regain control over a range of activities affecting the conduct of their everyday lives.

Corruption and Abuse of Power

A major issue considered in connection with the vitality of liberal democracy is concerned with the conduct of those who are elected to public office. The system of representative democracy involves citizens electing officials to serve them. However, it is sometimes alleged that the main concern of elected public office holders is to use their positions to further their own interests or those of people who are close to them.

Allegations against public officials are not always substantiated. Indeed, they may be made maliciously for political reasons. But it is important that those elected to public office should act honestly and that mechanisms should exist to investigate (and if necessary punish) those whose integrity is found to be lacking. For, if the general public feel that the main aim of seeking election to public office is to pursue self-interest rather than advance the needs of constituents or the interests of the nation, the prestige of elected officials will suffer and their authority will be undermined. Ultimately the legitimacy of the system of liberal democracy may be discredited.

The Behaviour of Elected Officials

Accusations of conflict of interest, abuse of power or corruption have often been levelled against elected officials in many countries. Many liberal democracies were rocked by such allegations in the 1990s, some examples of which are discussed below.

Italy

In 1995, the Italian elder statesman and seven-times prime minister, Giulio Andreotti, was placed on trial for 'mafia conspiracy' (that is, using his political power to shield members of this organisation). The same year, Francesco Musotto, one of the senior aides of a former prime minister, Silvio Berlusconi, was charged with mafia conspiracy, and a former foreign minister, Gianni de Michelis, was jailed for four years for corruption. Also in 1995, Silvio Berlusconi, was committed for trial for corruption. It was alleged that he had bribed the tax inspectors who audited his publishing and television companies' books. He was found guilty of this offence in 1998, and sentenced to a two year and nine month prison sentence. The following week he received a further two year and four month prison sentence for illegal party funding. He was also convicted in December 1997 of false accounting, for which he received a 16 month prison sentence.

Ireland

A number of scandals emerged towards the end of the 1990s. In 1997, the former Taioseach, Charles Haughey, admitted that he had accepted a secret £1 million payment from supermarket chief Ben Dunne. He had previously misled a judicial tribunal (the McCracken Inquiry) investigating payments to politicians on this matter. He was subsequently summoned to appear in court to answer allegations that he had obstructed and hindered this body.

The minister for Foreign Affairs, Ray Burke, resigned in 1998 over allegations of financial impropriety which included taking IR30,000 (that is, 30,000 Irish Pounds) from a builder, allegedly in order to secure planning permission. Burke admitted receiving this payment, but vehemently denied it was designed to procure favours. The Taoiseach, Bertie Ahern, ordered a judicial inquiry into this matter. Burke, it was also alleged, accepted a political donation in 1989 from a company whose chairman then secured television transmission licences from Burke (who was at that time Minister of Communications). Although there was no suggestion or evidence that this payment was improper, it led to questions in the Irish Parliament as to whether it had influenced official decisions.

Concern has also been expressed about the 'Ansbacher accounts'. These consisted of around IR38 million in off-shore funds operated by Des Trainor, Mr Haughey's late accountant. It is not known precisely whose money the accounts contained and who benefited from the funds, although it has been alleged that several politicians were among the beneficiaries.

Belgium

The Belgian Parliament's decision to lift the immunity of a former defence minister, Guy Coeme, and a former minister for economic affairs, Willy Claes, in a case involving corruption, led to the latter's resignation as General Secretary of NATO in 1995. It was alleged that companies seeking government defence contracts had paid bribes to the Flemish socialist party. The Belgium foreign minister, Frank Vandenbroucke, also resigned over this issue in 1995. In December 1998 Claes was found guilty of military contract corruption by a Belgian court.

The United States of America

In the USA, the Iran-Contra affair (which concerned the secret and illegal transfer of profits, made from the sale of arms to Iraq, to guerrilla groups fighting the Sandinista government in Nicaragua in the mid-1980s) had an adverse effect on the credibility of the Reagan presidency and resulted in the new incumbent, President Clinton, promising to provide an 'ethical administration'. However this aim was adversely affected by a number of scandals involving leading members of his cabinet. President Clinton and his wife were, themselves, involved in a real estate venture in Arkansas ('Whitewater') which became the subject of a Congressional probe in 1995. Later that year, a Grand Jury charged Clinton's Whitewater associates, James McDougal, Susan McDougal and Jim Guy Tucker (Governor of Arkansas), with fraud and they were subsequently convicted in May 1996.

The Whitewater episode resulted in the appointment in 1994 of a special counsel to investigate President Clinton's past activities. This post was briefly held by Robert Fiske, and latterly by Kenneth Starr. A new area of investigation focused on alleged sexual misbehaviour by the President. In May 1994, Paula Jones initiated a sexual harassment claim against Clinton, for an event which allegedly occurred in 1991 when he was Governor of Arkansas. This case eventually collapsed in 1998, following an unsuccessful attempt to undermine the President's character by accusing him of having a sexual relationship with Monica Lewinsky. Both Clinton and Lewinsky swore on oath that they had not had an affair, and Clinton also denied this charge on television.

However, doubt was subsequently cast on the truthfulness of these denials. Additional evidence appeared in the form of records of telephone conversations with Monica Lewinsky, taped by Linda Tripp. The focus of attention shifted to determining whether Clinton and Lewinsky had lied on oath concerning a sexual relationship, and whether there was a subsequent attempt, initiated by the President, to cover up this affair. Such allegations, if proved, involved criminal charges of obstructing justice and incitement to perjury. In July 1998, Lewinsky accepted immunity from future prosecution in return for agreeing to testify before a grand jury appointed to examine these matters. A subpoena was then issued for Clinton to appear, although this was withdrawn when he voluntarily agreed to testify to Starr's investigatory team in August 1998.

In this testimony, Clinton admitted to having had an 'inappropriate' physical relationship with Lewinsky. But no admission was obtained that the President had initially induced Lewinsky to lie about this matter. That same evening he made a television broadcast to the American people in which he publicly confessed to a relationship with Lewinsky. Lurid details of this relationship were subsequently contained in Starr's report to the House of Representative's Judiciary Committee. The report was also released onto the Internet. It made a number of serious allegations against the President, which are discussed below.

THE STARR REPORT

The report of the special counsel, Kenneth Starr, accused President Clinton of the following offences.

◆ *Perjury:* he was accused of having lied under oath in his deposition in the Paula Jones lawsuit in January 1998 and also in his grand jury testimony in August of that year.

◆ *Abuse of power:* he was accused of trying to persuade Lewinsky to deny any relationship with him and of seeking the aid of a White House secretary, Betty Currie, to help cover his tracks.

◆ *Obstruction of justice and witness tampering:* the report alleged a pattern of lying by the President and attempts to sustain these lies by the use of government employees and resources to prevent key witnesses from giving testimonies which could damage him.

President Clinton, shortly before making a personal statement to the nation about his relationship with former intern, Monica Lewinsky.

The allegations contained in the Starr Report were potentially very serious. A sitting president cannot be prosecuted for criminal actions but may be impeached if such wrongdoings constitute 'high crimes and misdemeanours'. For this to succeed, however, there would need to be a wide level of agreement – shared by Democrats as well as Republicans – that Clinton merited such treatment. The likelihood of such bipartisan agreement would, however, be eroded if it was thought that the entire affair was designed to advance the political fortunes of the Republican Party.

Those who supported the president believe that sinister political motives underlaid the Starr investigation. Starr was not a neutral figure, having served as Solicitor General in President Bush's Republican administration (1989–93). It was argued (most notably by the president's wife, Hillary Clinton in January 1998) that a vast plot had been initiated by the right. This allegedly sought to use the courts and media to undo the verdict delivered by the vote which elected Clinton in 1992, and again in 1996. This argument was repeated in the *Observer* on 2 August 1998 when it was alleged that 'the men promoting the scandal which has brought the Clinton presidency to crisis include racists, religious fanatics, far-right billionaires, a convicted embezzler and Moonies'.

The initiation of the impeachment process was also influenced by political considerations. If they succeeded and the President was removed from office, the Vice President (Al Gore) would have replaced him. This would have given Gore time to aid his own election prospects in the subsequent Presidential Election in the year 2000. On the other hand, the prospects of the Republican Party in that election may have been advanced by tarnishing Clinton's reputation.

In December 1998 the House of Representatives' judicial committee approved four articles of impeachment. Two of these (one concerned with perjury and the other with obstruction of justice) were subsequently passed by the House of Representatives. The decision to impeach the President meant that he had to undergo a trial before the Senate. However, the partisan nature of the impeachment vote coupled with Clinton's sustained popularity resulted in his acquittal in February 1999.

Spain

In Spain, the Supreme Court launched an investigation into accusations that the Prime Minister, Felipe González, was involved in the death squads which operated against Basque separatists in the mid-1980s. Between 1983 and 1987, 28 people were killed by the Anti-Terrorist Liberation Group. Many of these people had no connection with the separatist group, ETA. One of González's close associates, Jose Barrionuevo (who was Interior Minister at the time), was stripped of his parliamentary immunity so that he could be tried for involvement in such activities. Allegations of an involvement in this 'dirty war' played a significant role in González's election defeat in 1996. In 1997, the Supreme Court ruled that he should be called as a witness in the trial of Barrionuevo and 11 former senior officials and police officers charged in connection with the bungled kidnapping of Segundo Marey in 1983. The Court ruled that was insufficient evidence to prosecute González personally for involvement in this matter. This trial took place in 1998, and resulted in the supreme court sentencing Barrionuevo and his deputy, Rafael Vera, to 10 years imprisonment for kidnapping and the misappropriation of public funds.

Britain

Accusations of corruption and 'sleaze' exerted a major influence on British politics in the 1990s. The following section examines the main issues and the attempts which have been made to respond to these problems.

'Sleaze' in British Politics

In 1994, two Conservative Members of Parliament were accused of accepting money to table parliamentary questions to ministers in the House of Commons. It was subsequently alleged that two additional Members had been paid by a lobbyist to ask parliamentary questions. These episodes suggested that some Members of Parliament had used their positions for personal gain. The Prime Minister, John Major, responded by appointing a Committee on Standards in Public Life, initially chaired by Lord Nolan (and latterly by Lord Neill). A major report was published in 1995.

The Nolan Report

Nolan's report was broadly supportive of the standards which existed in British public life but it indicated that there was some public concern over the conduct of people involved in public affairs, and that this had increased in recent years. The report thus urged action to ensure that corruption and malpractice did not become an accepted aspect of public affairs in the UK. To achieve this goal, the Nolan Committee put forward seven principles of public life. These were:

○ selflessness

○ integrity

○ objectivity

○ accountability

○ openness

○ honesty

○ leadership.

The report then made a number of specific recommendations to govern the subsequent behaviour of elected officials.

With specific reference to the legislature, it was proposed that Members of Parliament should be prohibited from acting as consultants to lobbying companies. Consultancies to other bodies, such as commercial organisations, would be permitted but would be subject to enhanced scrutiny. Nolan recommended that MPs would be required to make a full entry in the Register of Members' Interests of all contracts which they secured as a result of being a Member of Parliament. They would also indicate the amount they were paid for the services they provided.

The report also suggested that parliament's self-regulation (by the Select Committee on Members' Interests and the Privileges Committee) should cease and that an independent Parliamentary Commissioner should be appointed. One difficulty with the Select Committee was the ability of party whips to seek to influence its proceedings: it was alleged that Conservative whips had meddled in its operations in connection with the cases of Jonathan Aitken and Neil Hamilton. The proposed Commissioner would maintain the Register of Members' Interests, give advice to Members on matters of conduct and would investigate and report on allegations of misconduct. The House of Commons' Privileges Committee (which was retitled the Standards and Privilege Committee) would be the recipient of the Commissioner's reports. It may, if it wished, conduct further examination into the subject of a report and also act as a court of appeal for an MP whose actions have been criticised by the Commissioner. The operation of this system is referred to in connection with the Hamilton case which is discussed below. If the Committee agreed with the Commissioner that an MP had acted improperly, it would possess the power to punish the offender. This could entail suspension from the House of Commons or, in serious cases, expulsion from it.

The Prime Minister referred the implementation of the report to a special Select Committee of the House of Commons. Many of Nolan's recommendations were endorsed but the majority of the Committee was unwilling to sanction disclosure of income derived from consultancy work. However, the report and the Select Committee's responses were subsequently put to the full House of Commons. In November 1995, the House decided to support Nolan and voted that Members would have to declare income which arose from their position as Members of Parliament. Some saw this as the prelude to an era of full-time, professional politicians.

The House of Commons subsequently voted to introduce new rules governing the behaviour of MPs.

IMPLEMENTATION OF THE NOLAN REPORT

The response of the House of Commons to allegations of sleaze were:

◆ *Outside earnings:* MPs were required to disclose earnings from all consultancies which arose from their position as an MP. They were to provide details in the Register of MPs' Interests

◆ *'Paid advocacy':* MPs were to be restricted from performing Parliamentary activity on behalf of outside interests, including tabling amendments, motions or questions. In order to do so, they were required to deposit an 'employment agreement' in the Register of Members' Interests.

◆ *Appointment of a Parliamentary Commissioner for Standards:* the first holder of this post was Sir George Downey. MPs would register all details of contracts with this official, whose authority to conduct detailed investigations of alleged wrongdoing by MPs surpassed the capacity of an enquiry conducted by a Parliamentary committee.

◆ *Code of practice:* a code to regulate the general conduct of Members in connection with outside interests was approved in principle.

The House of Lords also voted to set up a register of Peers' financial interests.

The New System in Operation

The Hamilton Case

A number of MPs were investigated by the Commissioner in 1997 in relation to the 'cash for questions affair' but avoided punishment by the Select Committee when they lost their seats in that year's General Election. One of these was the former

Trade Minister, Neil Hamilton. Sir Gordon Downey alleged there was 'compelling evidence' that he took money (which could have amounted to as much as £25,000) from the owner of Harrods, Mohamed Al Fayed. Also, that he had misled the then President of the Board of Trade, Michael Heseltine. At the 1997 General Election the Labour and Liberal Democrats withdrew their candidates in Hamilton's constituency of Tatton. This was to allow the BBC war correspondent, Martin Bell, a free run against Hamilton who had been renominated to stand as a Parliamentary candidate by the local Conservative association. Bell campaigned on an 'anti-sleaze' ticket and succeeded in winning one of the safest Conservative seats in the UK by a majority in excess of 11,000 votes.

Following the election, Hamilton sought to reopen the issue by requesting that the Committee reinterview a number of witnesses who had been questioned by Sir Gordon Downey. There was speculation at Westminster that the Commissioner would have resigned if the Committee agreed to such a course of action. The Committee permitted Hamilton to address them on this matter but resolved by majority vote in October 1997 not to agree to his request. The Committee subsequently accepted Sir Gordon's findings, stating that Hamilton had 'persistently and seriously' fallen below the standards expected of MPs. In August 1998, Hamilton sought to secure the reinvestigation of this issue when he launched a libel action against claims by Al Fayed that he had received from him free shopping, gift vouchers, a holiday at the Paris Ritz, and cash.

The Robinson Case

In 1997, the Labour Paymaster General, Geoffrey Robinson, was accused of breaking House of Commons rules for not declaring his family interest in a multi-million-pound tax-free offshore trust. Robinson's argument for not doing so was that he personally received no financial advantage from the Trust. In 1998, following the investigation of the matter by the Commissioner for Standards, he was cleared by the Privileges Committee of the accusation that he had broken the rules of the House of Commons. However, the Commissioner rebuked the minister for not consulting with him on this matter and indicated that he would have recommended the registering of the interest under a discretionary clause in the House of Commons rule book. Robinson was subsequently accused of failing to declare a paid directorship but was exonerated of the main charge following a lengthy investigation by the Commissioner.

Further Reforms to Tackle 'Sleaze'

Further measures were contemplated to tackle sleaze following the 1997 General Election. These included a proposal to *extend* the requirement concerning disclosure of consultancies. It was proposed that MPs should disclose *all* paid outside employment, unless they could prove that they were performing the same work before they were first elected. This reform, which was suggested to the House of Commons Standards and Privileges Committee by Sir Gordon Downey, was directed against directorships which were awarded to a number of MPs.

Reform was also contemplated concerning the conduct of ministers whose conduct is governed by a ministerial code. This requires ministers to consult with their permanent secretaries on a wide range of issues, and the system is policed by the Cabinet Secretary and the Prime Minister. A particular objection to this arrangement is that the executive branch of government investigates its own ministers. This has led to suggestions that this role could be performed by an 'ethic commissioner' who would perform a similar role to that of the Parliamentary Commissioner for Standards in relation to the conduct of MPs.

Lobbying

A particular concern arose in connection with lobbying companies following the election of a Labour government in 1997. This activity is not extensive in the UK, compared to the USA. There lobbying is big business: the *Observer* estimating on 19 July 1998 that business and commercial interests in the USA spend approximately £700 million a year to field 14,000 official registered lobbyists in Washington DC. This amounts to 27 lobbyists for each member of Congress. By comparison the British lobbying industry has earnings of around £70 million a year.

The main role of lobbying companies is to promote a cause for which they are paid. One particular aspect of the work of these organisations in the UK involves the Parliamentary lobbyists, or parliamentary consultants. Their key purpose is to provide political advice and analysis. This service may be sought by commercial companies or by other governmental organisations who then become the clients of the lobbying companies. Most of this work is uncontroversial: indeed, much of the information is already within the public domain and could easily be secured at no cost. However, it is perceived that lobbying companies may sometimes extend their role beyond these activities and seek to provide their clients with access to politicians or sensitive information secured from them. One major company, Lawson Lucas Mendelsohn, was established soon after the 1997

Election, a key advantage being that its three founders had close ties with the new government. Neal Lawson had formerly been an adviser to the new Chancellor, Gordon Brown, and Ben Lucas and Jon Mendelsohn had acted as advisers to Tony Blair. This raised the issue of the access and influence which firms such as this possessed in the machinery of government and gave rise to the accusation of 'cronyism'.

In July 1998, the *Observer* newspaper made an allegation of 'cash for secrets' which asserted that a number of former aides to senior Labour ministers had obtained classified government information. They allegedly sold this information to lobbying firms who passed it on to their commercial clients. The most serious accusation was levelled at Roger Liddle, who was a senior member of the Downing Street Policy Unit. He was accused of conspiring with a lobbyist to offer access to ministers and of offering sensitive information to a representative of an American energy firm. Unlike earlier accusations of 'sleaze' during John Major's government, no politician was involved: Liddle was the only person inside the governmental machine to be linked with allegedly seeking to trade access for cash.

There were two important aspects to the *Observer's* allegations:

❍ *The style of government:* the importance attached to securing access to a relatively small group of ministers implies that power is highly centralised in the Labour administration. Access to them is thus likely to result in influence over government policy.

❍ *The need for reform:* the *Observer's* allegations raised the need for reforms to the operations of lobbying companies. One possible response to charges of 'cronyism' would be to introduce a period of 'quarantine' whereby a time limit would be imposed on former aides to MPs taking up jobs in lobbying firms. In the USA a one year period was introduced in 1995.

In the wake of these accusations, the government produced a new code to regulate lobbying in 1998. This forbade civil servants and minister's political aides from leaking confidential information to lobbyists, and ordered these officials not to aid lobbyists by arranging for their clients to have privileged access to ministers or undue influence over policy. The breaching of such procedures would be regarded as a serious disciplinary offence which could lead to dismissal. Other sections of the new code warned about accepting gifts or hospitality from lobbyists. Some ministers, including the Home Secretary, Jack Straw, also expressed support for ending the Parliamentary immunity of MPs found guilty of dishonesty or corrupt practices. This would mean that issues of this nature would cease to be internal to the

House of Commons and would instead be treated as criminal offences.

Further Reading

In addition to the general works cited in Chapter 1, an informative account of democratic politics in contemporary Europe is to be found in:

Michael Gallagher et al, *Representative Government in Western Europe* (London: McGraw Hill, 1992).

An up-to-date account of the use of referendums is to be found in:

Jurg Steiner, *European Democracies* (Harlow: Longman, 1998). This work also contains useful material on a wide variety of other topics related to the study of politics.

Chapter Three | Political Ideology

The aims of this chapter are:

> 1 To discuss the key principles underlying the ideology of the United Kingdom's major political parties.
>
> 2 To analyse changes to the ideology and policies of the Labour Party since 1979.
>
> 3 To assess the factors which led to the formation of the Social Democratic Party in 1981.
>
> 4 To discuss events which led to the formation of the Liberal Democrats (initially called Social and Liberal Democrats) in 1988.

The UK's Major Political Parties

Ideology and Historical Development

This section will analyse briefly the development of the Conservative, Liberal and Labour Parties in the nineteenth and early years of the twentieth centuries. It will seek to provide an understanding of the ideology which underpins these political Parties.

Conservatism and the Conservative Party

The essence of Conservative ideology is a resistance to change. This desire to 'retain things as they are' is especially concerned with the key institutions on which society is based. These include the *constitution*, vested interests such as the *Church of England*, and *private property ownership*. The early Tories (who were the forerunners of the contemporary Conservative Party) in the seventeenth century supported the powers of the Monarchy as a defence against the interests then represented within Parliament. Although the governments of William Pitt the Younger (1783–1801 and 1804–6) were associated with some reform of trade and finance, the impact on British politics of the French Revolution after 1792 identified Tories with the defence of the status quo.

In the late eighteenth and early nineteenth centuries, conservatism was defined in connection with political reform. The initial attitude of the Tories was that the existing constitution was perfect and required no improvement through

INFLUENCE OF THE FRENCH REVOLUTION

British conservatism was considerably influenced by *Reflexions on the Revolution in France*, written by Edmund Burke in 1792. Although he had initially been sympathetic to the French Revolution, he turned against it. Events which included the execution of the King, Louis XVI, in 1793 further justified this change of heart. He explained this alteration in the direction of his thought by providing a summary of the 'British way' which constituted a classic statement of conservatism. He argued that an Englishman's freedom was a national inheritance, which was most effectively secured by government which balanced democracy, aristocracy and Monarchy. Although he accepted that changes would sometimes be necessary, he advocated that these should be minimal, seeking to preserve as much of the old as was possible.

political reform. Thus Tory leaders (termed 'Ultras') sought to preserve the existing structure of society through legislation such as the 'Two Acts' of 1795 or the 'Six Acts' of 1819 which limited the ability of political reformers to put their case forward.

However, the endorsement of reform by the rival Whig Party, presented the Conservatives with a challenge. As discussed below, the Whigs became identified with the interests of the middle class, which had emerged as a new social grouping during the Industrial Revolution. The Conservative Party, in order to survive politically, was thus required to move with the times and endorse policies which would enable it to rival the Whig appeal to the middle class electorate. This task was initially undertaken by Sir Robert Peel.

Peel's Contribution to Conservatism

Peel became leader of the Tory Party in 1833. He realised that if the Party confined itself to being the political vehicle of the landed aristocracy and gentry, it would be swept aside by the middle classes. Accordingly, Peel adopted a policy of 'reform in order to preserve': this entailed making concessions to middle class opinion in order to neuter its more extreme demands, which included the disestablishment of the Church of England and the replacement of local control of local affairs by centralised control. (This centralisation was a key feature of the reforms advocated by Jeremy Bentham and his followers.)

However, the ability of the Conservative Party to court support from two electorates with different needs and values was tested in connection with the issue of protection of the agricultural industry. Middle class manufacturers believed their interests required the removal of tariffs, so that the goods they exported would benefit from world-wide free trade. Their concerns were directed at the Corn Laws (initially enacted in 1804). These laws were designed to keep cheap foreign grain out of Britain so that British farmers would face no competition in the home market. The middle class were opposed to such laws, not simply because they breached the principle of free trade, but also because they symbolised the power of the landed classes to dominate the British political system and secure the enactment of laws which were designed solely to benefit them.

The middle class case for repeal was mounted by a pressure group, the Anti-Corn Law League. This was first founded in London in 1836, although the association formed in Manchester in 1838 was of greater political significance. Peel determined that the laws should be abandoned in order to secure middle class support for his Party. He used the pretext of the Irish Famine (1845–46) to repeal the Corn Laws in 1846. In the short term his actions split the Party between those who endorsed reform (termed 'Peelites'), and those representing the landed interest who were unwilling to agree to such a radical measure.

Peel's attempt to embrace the interests of different social groupings in the one Party (which increasingly used the name of 'Conservative' rather than 'Tory' after 1846) was developed by Benjamin Disraeli. He became leader of the Conservative Party in 1849, and served as Prime Minister in 1868 and 1874–80. Under his leadership the Party made considerable inroads into the middle class support of the Liberal Party during the latter decades of the nineteenth century.

'Tory Democracy'

Although based upon actions initially undertaken by Sir Robert Peel, Benjamin Disraeli developed what is termed the 'one nation' philosophy of the Conservative Party. The key characteristic of this approach was a willingness to endorse pragmatic reform (that is, reform guided by a desire to solve a pressing problem, rather than being underpinned by a political ideology). Disraeli endorsed this approach in response to the existence of the two nations (rich and poor) which he wished to unify through policies pursued by the Conservative Party.

The term 'Tory democracy' is used to describe the actions undertaken by Disraeli's Conservative government between 1874 and 1880. During this period a number of reforms were introduced to aid the circumstances of the working class.

DISRAELI AND 'TORY DEMOCRACY'

Disraeli wished to counter the problems arising from unregulated free enterprise, especially exploitation of the working class. His approach was based on the old Tory tradition of paternalism (which insisted that those in a position of social authority had obligation towards the poorer and weaker members of society).

The key reforms associated with Disraeli's 'Tory democracy' were:

◆ *The 1874 Factory Act:* this regulated the hours which women and children could work.

◆ *The 1878 Factory Act:* this was designed to improve safety at work.

◆ *the 1875 Artisans Dwellings Act:* this enabled local authorities to acquire slum property and rebuild more modern housing.

◆ *The 1875 Public Health Act:* this gave all municipal authorities general powers in this field.

◆ *The 1875 Conspiracy and Protection of Property Act:* this gave trade unions the rights of peaceful picketing and legalised collective bargaining.

◆ *The 1876 Education Act:* this hesitantly introduced the principle of compulsory school attendance.

However, the scope and significance of the reforms which were introduced by late nineteenth century Conservative governments were restricted. Many of the new State functions were allocated to local authorities in the form of discretionary powers: that is, local government could choose whether or not to perform them and, if it did so, had to raise the necessary funds from its own resources. Additionally, the Conservative interest in domestic policies was surpassed by the dominant position accorded to foreign policy, which included the government's purchase of the Khedive (King) of Egypt's shares in the Suez Canal in 1875, the award to Queen Victoria of the title 'Empress of India' in 1876, and the successful resistance to Russian territorial claims on the Turkish Empire, endorsed at the 1878 Congress of European Powers at Berlin.

The Second World War and Its Aftermath

This period witnessed a further development of the 'one nation' approach through the support given by Conservatives to social reform. The extent of social difficulty was revealed by (and in many cases made worse as a result of) the Second World War. A key advocate of this approach was Richard 'Rab' Butler, whose 1944 Education Act was a crucial aspect of the welfare state, subsequently developed by the postwar Labour governments (1945–51). Although the new educational system tended to entrench existing social divisions in society, it paved the way for a limited amount of postwar social mobility. The sons and daughters of working class Britons could take advantage of the facilities provided (initially by grammar schools, and latterly through an expansion of higher education in the 1960s) to 'climb' the social ladder.

Butler's influence succeeded in moving the Conservative Party to accept the welfare state and the goal of full employment. Both were key aspects of the postwar consensus (which is discussed in Chapter 19). This included the further development of the welfare state, and an acceptance that it was the duty of governments to maintain full employment.

Thatcherism

In the 1970s, conservatism was influenced by a new, radical tradition which was termed the 'New Right'. It involved a rejection of 'one nation' pragmatism which was replaced with an ideological commitment to the free market. This approach was inspired by Friedrich Hayek and Milton Friedman and exercised a significant influence on the governments of Ronald Reagan in the United States of America (1981–89) and Margaret Thatcher in the United Kingdom (1979–90). The approach, which in the UK was termed 'Thatcherism', embraced two broad themes: 'neoliberalism' and 'neoconservatism'.

❍ *Neo-liberalism:* this involved economic liberalism or 'rolling back the frontiers of the state'. It endorsed private enterprise, the free market and individual responsibility. This, and the policies associated with it, are discussed in Chapter 19.

❍ *Neo-conservatism:* this entailed social authoritarianism, which argued that social malaise (evidenced by crime, disorder, hooliganism, indiscipline among young people, and moral decay) was caused by the decline of 'traditional' values. These were being replaced by liberal and permissive attitudes and multi-cultural values. It demanded a return to traditional forms of authority (such as the family), and in this sense was compatible with the Conservative tradition discussed above.

Liberalism and the Liberal Party

Modern liberalism emerged from the fight for religious freedom waged in late sixteenth and early seventeenth century Western Europe. The close link which existed between Church and

THE FREE MARKET

A market is a forum in which those who wish to sell goods or services are brought into contact with those wishing to buy them. The price paid for them is determined by the 'natural' market forces of *supply* and *demand*.

The principle of the free market had been undermined by the constant growth of State activity since 1945, especially in economic affairs. Those who opposed this development believed that government intervention in the economy had led to inefficiency. They argued that growth, employment, productivity and widespread prosperity would be secured if the government ceased its attempts to regulate wages and prices. The free market was thus associated with policies which included limited public ownership and minimal welfare provision (since wealthier people would be better placed to look after their own social requirements).

State ensured that the objective of religious freedom became associated with political dissent. The advocacy of religious and civil freedom led liberalism to oppose absolutism, which at that time was associated with the authoritarian rule exercised by monarchs. Absolutism was identified with tyranny and led Liberals to argue that social order was a contract voluntarily entered into by those who were party to it, rather than being a structure handed down by God. The belief that government emerged as the result of rational choice, made by those who subsequently accorded their consent to its operations, ensured that the rights of the individual became prominent concerns of Liberal philosophers. The people were viewed as the ultimate source of political power and government was legitimate only while it operated with their consent.

The philosophy of liberalism existed independently of the developing party system which operated in the late seventeenth and early eighteenth centuries, although it exerted some influence on the Whigs who traditionally supported civil and religious liberty, and opposed arbitrary government. The issue of political reform separated the Whigs from the Tories in the early nineteenth century. Although the Whigs were not democrats (as their belief in 'government by the people' applied only to those who owned property) they saw the logic of political reform, which would benefit those whose property was derived from new forms of wealth associated with the Industrial Revolution rather than from the ownership of land. Whigs feared that an alliance of unenfranchised middle and working classes could result in revolution and sought to prevent this by a limited measure of political reform. These proposals were ultimately embodied in the 1832 Reform Act.

Subsequently liberalism passed through *four* main phases during the nineteenth and twentieth centuries.

Early Nineteenth-Century Liberalism

The major influences on the development of early nineteenth-century liberalism are discussed below.

○ *Adam Smith, David Ricardo and the political economists:* these emphasised the importance of free trade and laisser faire (a doctrine which advocated that the state should not interfere in social or economic affairs). Such views exerted influence over the Tories as well as the Whigs.

○ *Jeremy Bentham and the philosophical radicals:* these rejected the doctrine of natural rights in favour of the principle of *utility*. This suggested that when government was forced to intervene in the lives of its citizens, its actions should be designed to promote the greatest good of the greatest number and that all rights should be subordinate to this rule.

The emphasis which utilitarianism placed on the individual as the focus of social action ensured that the first phase of nineteenth century liberalism was essentially a political creed operating in the interests of the newly emerging middle classes. Ideally, government would not intervene in the lives of its citizens unless such involvement was required to enable one individual to exercise individual initiative which another sought to prevent.

Mid-Victorian Liberalism

The second phase of nineteenth-century British liberalism commenced around 1850 and witnessed the formation of the Liberal Party as the key vehicle of Liberal political philosophy. The Liberal Party was formed through the coalescence (that is, coming together) of a number of Parliamentary groupings, most notably the Whigs, radicals and Peelites (these being Tories who had supported Peel's decision to repeal the Corn Laws in 1846). This political coalition initially emerged as a government under the premiership of Lord Aberdeen in 1852 and was formalised in 1859 in response to the issue of Italian independence, indicating a sympathy for national struggles, especially those waged by small nations. The Party subsequently drew popular support from the Celtic Fringe (which embraces south-west England, Scotland and Wales), the middle and enfranchised members of the working classes, and sectional groupings (referred to as 'fads') who attached themselves to the Liberal 'umbrella'. The Party's strength was much aided by the development of the cheap press.

The key thinkers associated with this stage of liberalism were:

❍ *Richard Cobden, John Bright and the Manchester School:* these emphasised laisser faire principles in economic affairs and led the Liberal Party to view free trade as its most important policy.

❍ *John Stuart Mill:* he asserted individual freedom to be an underlying value on which Liberal policies should be based. Mill argued that liberty was desirable not merely because it contributed to the greatest good to the greatest number, but also because it was a desirable end in itself. In his essay, *On Liberty* (1859), he viewed liberty and the institutions of representative government as essential to the full development of human individuality.

The political effectiveness of the Party relied heavily on the leadership provided by William Ewart Gladstone.

WILLIAM GLADSTONE

Affectionately known as the 'grand old man' in the latter part of his career, Gladstone served as Prime Minister on four occasions between 1868 and 1894. In government he was identified with policies which sought to promote free trade and *retrenchment* (that is, efficiency in administration and economy in expenditure). His concern with political and administrative reform identified the Party with progressive measures. Gladstone's mission to 'pacify' Ireland also revealed a commitment to reform, as did limited moves which his governments undertook against the Church of England (such as the abolition of religious tests for University and College teaching posts at Oxford and Cambridge Universities in 1871). In foreign policy, Gladstone demonstrated his ability to raise liberalism away from being a selfish middle class creed and to identify it with higher moral ideals. His ability to identify liberalism with moral crusades was an important factor which won the Party nonconformist support in this period.

New Liberalism

The enfranchisement of some working class males in the 1867 and 1884 Reform Acts made it important for political parties to develop policies attractive to this new electorate. The Liberal Party's belief in laisser faire was mirrored by a view that the State should not play a large role in social affairs. This attitude was underlaid with a belief that problems such as poverty derived from personal failings and weaknesses. It was thus argued that the solution of social problems was the responsibility of the individual and not the concern of the State. Self-help reinforced by voluntary effort and charity were seen as the main mechanisms for improving the conditions of the socially disadvantaged. This essentially moral stance possessed some credibility in times of general affluence, but became far less acceptable when poverty became more widespread in the latter decades of the nineteenth century.

The Liberal Party responded to these changed circumstances, and began to develop ideals which appealed to the working class. The 1870 Education Act accepted the need for government action where voluntary effort could be shown to be inadequate. Joseph Chamberlain, in particular, advocated activity by both central and local government to improve social conditions. Such measures were not, however, viewed as completely adequate by those who believed in wider-reaching social justice. A more forthright appeal to the working classes was provided by 'new' liberalism (sometimes referred to as 'social liberalism') which sought a compromise between *individualism* and *collectivism* and formed the third phase of nineteenth–century liberalism.

INDIVIDUALISM AND COLLECTIVISM

The extent to which the State should intervene in the lives of its citizens is a subject which traditionally separated the main political Parties. There were fundamental differences between those who endorsed individualism and those who were collectivists.

♦ *Individualism:* individualists place individual needs at the forefront of their concerns. The aim of politics is viewed as the creation of conditions in which human beings are able to pursue their own interests and thereby achieve self-fulfilment. This is associated with a reduced role for the State.

♦ *Collectivism:* collectivists believe in the sacrifice of self-interest to commonly-agreed goals. Group needs thus supersede individual interests. This often results in the State taking an active role, directing resources to achieve group objectives.

New liberalism emerged between 1880 and 1914 and sought to direct the Party's reforming energies to the economic, political and social circumstances of late nineteenth and early twentieth century Britain, particularly the problems caused by industrialisation and urbanisation. The advocacy of State intervention to secure social justice was made compatible with more traditional Liberal beliefs through the argument that individuals could only enjoy freedom when social and economic impediments to it had first been removed. This resulted in legislation underlaid by collectivist principles being implemented by the Liberal governments of 1905–14.

Radical Liberalism

This movement emerged during the Second World War and was particularly influential in shaping the contents of the Liberal Party's election manifesto at the 1945 General Election. It was inspired by John Maynard Keynes and Sir William Beveridge and entailed a further move away from individualism, towards collectivism. This approach supported wide-ranging State activity in economic policy and in the provision of welfare services. These views underpinned the postwar social democratic consensus which is discussed in Chapter 19.

Socialism and the Labour Party

The Reform Acts of 1867 and 1884 extended the franchise to large numbers of urban and rural working class males. Initially the Liberal Party secured much of the working class vote. The belief that the interests of employer and employee were essentially similar appealed to the skilled (or 'respectable') workers who constituted the urban working class electorate. This spirit of cooperation across the social classes resulted in 'Lib–Labism': the craft unions which dominated the Trades Union Congress cooperated with the Liberal Party. In return they secured legislation favourable to their interests (such as the Trade Union Act, 1871) and the adoption of some working class candidates by Liberal constituency associations. These candidates, if elected, championed working class views in Parliament and took the Liberal whip.

The extent of poverty in the latter decades of the nineteenth century had a profound effect on working class politics. Poverty was especially felt in urban areas by unskilled or semi-skilled workers, and it additionally emerged as a major problem in rural areas. The Liberal belief that poverty could always be attributed to the failings of the individual was challenged by social scientific investigations. The results of these studies gave support to the belief that urban working class interests would be served best by the formation of an independent political party.

There were two developments which were crucial to the development of an independent working class political party during the later decades of the nineteenth century. These were:

○ the emergence of socialist societies

○ the altering attitude of the unions towards cooperation with the Liberal Party.

Both of these issues are discussed below.

The Emergence of the Socialist Societies

British socialism rejected the existing society in which inequalities in the distribution of wealth and political power resulted in social injustice. The development of socialism was influenced by a number of sources.

○ *The economic theories of David Ricardo:* he suggested that the interests of capital and labour were opposed.

○ *The reforming activities of Robert Owen:* he advocated the ownership of the means of production by small groups of producers organised into societies based upon the spirit of cooperation.

○ *The Christian impulse:* Christianity was relevant to socialism through its concern for the poor and the early experiences of Christians living in a society in which property was held in common. Christian attitudes were voiced by Christian socialists such as Charles Kingsley and by organisations such as the Guild of St. Matthew.

○ *Marx and Engels:* their works affected the development of British socialism towards the end of the century. Marx stressed that the exploitive nature of capitalism made a proletarian (that is, working class) revolution inevitable. Exploitation would result in increased class consciousness. This would develop into class conflict, resulting in a revolution to overthrow the ruling class and the emergence of a new society based on the dictatorship of the proletariat.

Divisions Within Socialism

Socialists did not agree on the manner in which reform should be attempted nor on the nature of the just society they wished to create. These divisions constituted the basis for the constant dispute within British socialism between *fundamentalism* and *social democracy*.

○ *Fundamentalism:* this emphasised that ownership of the means of production had to be removed from private hands in order for a just society to be established: this objective was latterly incorporated into Clause IV of the constitution of the Labour Party, thus theoretically committing the Party to the policy of *nationalisation*.

❍ *Social democracy:* this implied that social and economic inequalities could be redressed through reforms directed at the poor and underprivileged within the existing economic system. This approach identified social democracy with *reformism*.

The existence of disputes within British socialism is an explanation for the formation of a number of socialist political organisations in the late nineteenth century. Such divisions did not, however, prevent an attempt being made to form a single working class political organisation. The Independent Labour Party (ILP) was established in 1893. This sought a compromise between fundamentalism and social democracy by advocating collective ownership of the means of production, distribution and exchange, but giving prominence to a programme of reforms designed to benefit the working class from within the existing framework of capitalism.

Trade Unions and the Working Class

An independent working class political party required trade union backing to provide it with widespread working class support. But, as is argued above, unions traditionally represented skilled workers and endorsed 'Lib–Labism'. However, in the 1880s semi-skilled and unskilled workers began to organise and the resultant 'new' unions were involved in a number of major industrial disputes. Their leaders included Will Thorne (of the Gasworkers' and General Labourers' Union) and Ben Tillett (of the Dockers' Union). These men were socialists who preached political as well as industrial action. The entry of new unions into the TUC adversely affected the 'Lib–Lab' stance of that organisation.

'Lib–Labism' was also undermined by the changing views of the older unions. The introduction of mechanisation, and the adoption of increasingly hostile attitudes by employers towards unions made members of craft unions more willing to cooperate with other sections of the working class in industrial action. Such new-found class consciousness resulted in the formation of the Labour Representation Committee (LRC) in 1900. This was an umbrella group representing the ILP, Fabians, some trade unions and – briefly – the Marxist Socialist Democratic Federation. In 1900, it secured the election of two Members of Parliament and fared much better in 1906.

The philosophy of the LRC (which assumed the name of 'Labour Party' following the 1906 General Election) was *labourism*: this emphasised the importance of the trade unions to an independent working class political party and viewed the role of the Party to be that of representing the needs of organised labour. It emphasised working class self-reliance and independence from employers, and provided the Labour Party with a broad framework within which a range of political ideologies could be accommodated.

Revisionism

It has been argued above that the Labour Party straddled two different socialist impulses – fundamentalism and social democracy. Although the latter (which was supported by the Right wing of the Party) was the dominant force in Labour politics, many on the Labour's Left identified with fundamentalism. Disputes between these two wings of the Party were toned down both by labourism (which made debates of ideology largely unnecessary), and also by placating the Left through occasional acts of nationalisation pursued by Labour governments. However, Labour's defeat at the 1951 General Election led to the emergence of factionalism, which intensified following the Conservative victory in 1955 and the subsequent change in Labour's leadership. The new leader, Hugh Gaitskell, was identified with the social democratic wing of the Party which soon became locked in a dispute with the fundamentalists, who had emerged as an organised body under the leadership of Aneurin Bevan.

THE CASE FOR REVISIONISM

As stated above, the argument between the Left and Right wings of the Labour Party in the late 1950s and early 1960s were based on the differences between fundamentalism and social democracy.

Fundamentalists believed that public ownership was indispensable to socialism. Their goal was working class supremacy, which depended for its success on basic changes to the country's economic structure.

Social democrats, however, were coming to the conclusion that the changed structure of postwar capitalism (especially the separation of ownership and capital) and the decline in class antagonisms (resulting from a number of social and economic policies pursued after 1945) meant that the class struggle should no longer be a central feature of Labour's political approach.

Thus social democrats sought to move the Party away from fundamentalism by updating social democratic philosophy and policies. This approach was referred to as 'revisionism' and was associated with Labour politicians who included Roy Jenkins and Tony Crosland. Crosland's *The Future of Socialism*, published in 1956, provided a full account of the revisionist case.

Revisionists did not seek to transform society's economic and social structures but instead wished to pursue reformist aims within the context of a mixed economy. Their brand of socialism was defined in *distributive* terms (that is, emphasis was placed on equality and social justice). The goals of redistribution might be achieved in a number of ways: through taxation policies, the consolidation and improvement of social welfare provision to aid the least well-off members of society, and the introduction of comprehensive education to provide equality of educational opportunity. Sustained economic growth was the crucial underpinning of revisionism, with the State performing a positive role in the quest for social justice and the eradication of inequality. Ownership of the means of production was not seen in strategic terms, but was viewed tactically: it was merely one option which could be employed to achieve equality. Labour's third election defeat in a row in 1959 intensified the debate within the Party between revisionism and fundamentalism.

○ *Fundamentalists:* they wished to prevent the movement towards revisionism, and believed that the correct way forward for Labour was to 'sell' the case for fundamentalism to the electorate more vigorously.

○ *Revisionists:* they wished to broaden the electoral support of the Party beyond the working class. They felt the Party should abandon policies perceived to be unpopular (such as nationalisation), cease promoting the interests of sectional groupings (particularly the trade unions), and leave behind out of date attitudes (such as the class struggle). Such associations were felt to be particularly damaging to the level of Labour support among younger voters.

Gaitskell set about providing the Party with an image which would more easily accommodate revisionist policies and political outlooks. However, his attempt to do this foundered. At the 1959 Party conference he suggested that Clause IV of the constitution needed re-examination. This possessed symbolic importance for both fundamentalists and revisionists, but the support given to the fundamentalists by the unions ensured that no such change would occur. Gaitskell's authority as Party leader was at stake, which led to bitter disputes at the 1960 and 1961 conferences (ostensibly on the topic of defence policy). His failure to rewrite Labour's constitution meant that the Party continued to embrace both fundamentalism and social democracy.

Question

Conduct your own study of a political party in the UK. To do this, organise your material under the following headings:

○ **Origins** – that is, when the party was established and who were the key people associated with its development.

○ **Ideology** – that is, the ideas which guided the party and the values it sought to promote.

○ **Policies** – a brief summary of the key issues which were at the forefront of the party's development and an assessment of how these related to its ideology.

Developments in Labour Party Ideology after 1970

The failure of successive governments after 1964 to rejuvenate the economy was a dominant feature of British political debate. Factors which included increased levels of unemployment, sluggish economic growth and high inflation were constant problems. The inability of policies based on the postwar political consensus to solve these problems prompted attempts by both major parties to put forward alternative ideological solutions. The Conservative Party in 1970, led by Ted Heath, briefly flirted with 'Selsdon Man' policies (which included placing enhanced faith in the free market). However, they readily abandoned these policies in favour of intervention in industry, including selective acts of nationalisation.

In 1975, the new Conservative leader, Margaret Thatcher, adopted *monetarism* in place of Keynesian economics. This change justified attempts to transform the Labour Party into a vehicle which endorsed fundamentalist policies (such as nationalisation).

The Left and Labour Policy After 1970

The campaign of the Left to dominate the affairs of the Labour Party began in the late 1960s and was intensified following Labour's defeat in 1970. The Party conference of that year commenced a review of Labour policy which resulted in a challenge to revisionist socialism through what ultimately became known as the 'Alternative Economic Strategy'. This new approach was first expressed in the Home Policy Committee's document *Labour's Programme for Britain* (1973, revised in 1976 and 1982). It was designed to secure a shift in the balance of power and wealth in favour of working people and their families. This was to be achieved through policies which included the nationalisation of the UK's top 25 companies through a state holding company (when implemented by the Labour government in the 1975 Industry Act, this took the name of the National Enterprise Board) and by other large companies entering into planning agreements with the government.

THE ALTERNATIVE ECONOMIC STRATEGY

The aims of the Alternative Economic Strategy went much further than the revisionist goal of enhanced equality and sought not merely to reform society, but to transform it. The approach adopted, however, also went beyond the historic commitment of the fundamentalists to common ownership of the means of production, and in this sense it was an original economic strategy endorsed by the Labour Left. Public ownership was coupled with new mechanisms to secure State economic planning. Accountability and industrial democracy were at the forefront of this new approach. The use of public corporations to run the nationalised industries (which dominated the industrial policy of the postwar Labour governments under the influence of Herbert Morrison) was thus abandoned. The move to the Left which was apparent in economic policy was also mirrored elsewhere, especially in defence.

The Left and the Labour Party After 1979

The General Election defeat in 1979 intensified the attempts by the Left to dominate the affairs of the Labour Party. The Left believed that the actions undertaken by Labour governments between 1964–70 and 1974–79 had not made the UK a more socialist country. Particular criticism was directed at the actions of the Wilson/Callaghan governments in the 1970s for abandoning some of the Party's election manifesto promises. Very little of the Alternative Economic Strategy had been implemented, and the government had also persisted with an incomes policy (governing wages) to which many of the Left were opposed.

Although economic problems (which forced the government to seek a loan from the International Monetary Fund in 1976) and its precarious Parliamentary situation (which led the Prime Minister, James Callaghan, to conclude an agreement with the Liberal Party in 1977–78) helped to explain the government's inability to satisfy leftwing opinion, widespread acceptance that the Party had failed served to radicalise opinion within it. These sentiments underpinned a campaign by the Left to transform the Party in their own image. This involved a series of constitutional reforms directed at Labour's leadership, organisation and policy-making processes. These reforms sought to ensure that the Labour movement would exert a far greater degree of control over the actions of a future Labour government than had been the case under Wilson and Callaghan.

The Left and Constitutional Reform After 1979

The aim of constitutional reform was to establish leftwing control of the Party, under the guise of enhancing internal democracy. The success with which this transformation was achieved after the 1979 General Election defeat was primarily dependent on changing attitudes held by the trade unions and constituency activists, rather than infiltration by extreme leftwing groups. The views of the trade unions (which had traditionally supported the party's leadership) were fuelled by a sense of betrayal by the Wilson and Callaghan governments, and their dissatisfaction with the manner in which the election date had been determined. Such sentiments resulted in the Right of the Party being placed in a minority position.

The pressure for constitutional reform was aided by organisational developments affecting the Left of the Party. In 1980, the Rank and File Mobilising Committee was established as an umbrella group which brought the Campaign for Labour Party Democracy and the Labour Coordinating Committee into contact with Militant Tendency and the Socialist Campaign for Labour Victory.

The 1979 Labour conference accordingly accepted the mandatory (that is, compulsory) reselection of Labour MPs, and endorsed the principle of ending the dominance exerted over the election manifesto by the Party leader. Concrete proposals for achieving this objective would be debated in 1980 (although they were finally rejected in 1981).

Perhaps the most significant innovation was the removal of the exclusive power of Labour MPs to choose the leader and deputy leader. The introduction of an *electoral college* was debated at the Party conferences in 1979 (when it was rejected) and 1980 (when it was approved in principle). A special conference was subsequently held at Wembley in January 1981 to determine the mechanics of the new system. Initially (until the system was revised in 1993), the Labour leader would be elected by a process in which unions were allocated 40 per cent of the vote, while the MPs and constituency Labour Parties each received 30 per cent. This result went against the advice of Michael Foot and the National Executive Committee (NEC) who wished to give the Parliamentary Labour Party (PLP) half of the vote in such a mechanism. Callaghan's resignation in 1980 (before the Wembley conference) meant that the new leader, Michael Foot, was elected under the old system involving MPs alone. The new college was first used in the election for Labour's deputy leader in 1981, when Denis Healey narrowly defeated Tony Benn.

Developments Affecting Policy

The apparent strength of the Left was demonstrated at the 1979 conference by a policy resolution which pledged that the Party would reconsider the UK's membership of the European Community. Another resolution promised to take over, without compensation, all State assets subjected to the government's privatisation policies. The 1980 Party conference voted to withdraw the UK from the EEC, to embark upon a policy of unilateral nuclear disarmament, to extend the programme of public ownership, and to abolish the House of Lords. In 1981, party resolutions expressed support for unilateral nuclear disarmament, unconditional and immediate withdrawal from the EEC, a 35-hour week with no loss of earnings, total rejection of an incomes policy, and measures to extend nationalisation to create 'a fully socialised economy'. In 1982, the Party conference endorsed unilateralism by a two-thirds majority.

The Right and the Labour Party

Social democrats were concerned with many of the developments which took place within the Labour Party after 1970. They were, however, suffering from ideological weakness. The Sterling crisis (which resulted in the UK seeking aid from the International Monetary Fund in 1976) provided conclusive evidence that the economic growth, on which social welfare programmes depended, could not be sustained. The shortcomings of revisionism resulted in a vacuum into which the Left moved. Increasingly after 1970, the Right perceived itself to be a besieged minority in a party where it had traditionally exercised a dominant position. The main concerns of the right were as follows.

○ *Economic policy:* they were critical of many aspects of the Alternative Economic Strategy, especially its hostility towards private enterprise.

○ *The European Economic Community:* to revisionists, Europe became the means through which Britain would be modernised economically, institutionally, culturally and socially. In 1971, 69

Labour MPs supported the terms of entry negotiated by the Conservative leader, Ted Heath. They were in defiance of a 3-line whip to vote against, and the following year a number of prominent MPs associated with the right resigned from the Shadow Cabinet on this issue.

❍ *Trade union power:* the success of the unions in bringing down Heath's Conservative government in February 1974 ensured a dominant position for the unions in the subsequent actions of a Labour government. This alarmed social democrats who did not wish Labour to be seen exclusively as a working class political party.

The Defection of the Social Democrats

Following the 1979 election defeat, the Parliamentary Labour Party and Shadow Cabinet were dominated by the Left. Social democrats initially pinned their hopes on Callaghan serving as a figurehead to resist the Left's demands. However, his agreement to an electoral college for choosing the Labour leader (to which the social democrats were opposed) disqualified him from such a role in the eyes of many on the Right. The unwillingness of either Callaghan or Healey to take the lead in combating the Left, and the resistance of the Parliamentary Party to lead a challenge to them, were major factors in the eventual formation of the Social Democratic Party (the SDP).

THE FORMATION OF THE SOCIAL DEMOCRATIC PARTY

In addition to the issues referred to above, there were other factors which caused the social democrats to abandon the Labour Party in the early 1980s. These were:

◆ *The absence of principles to guide political actions:* social democrats were concerned about the absence of a philosophy to underpin the actions of Labour government after 1964. Particularly under Harold Wilson government reacted pragmatically to a constant series of crises.

◆ *Experience of cross-party cooperation:* the referendum in 1975 on Britain's membership of the European Economic Community was preceded by a campaign of a cross-party nature. Leading members of Labour's Right worked with Liberals and Conservatives to secure a 'yes' vote in opposition to the hostile stance adopted by Labour's Left.

◆ *A belief that a new party would have political 'space' in which to thrive:* this view was based on the swing of the Conservatives to the Right of the political spectrum and

Labour's move to the Left during the course of the 1970s and early 1980s. This created space on the Centre-Left which a new political party might exploit.

◆ *The weakened hold of the two major parties on the electorate:* between 1951 and 1979, Labour's share of the vote declined at each successive General Election. While this was also the case with the Conservative Party (until it succeeded in reversing this trend in 1979), Labour also fared badly in by-elections. It was conceivable, therefore, that a newly-formed SDP would secure a considerable degree of political support, rather than being consigned to political oblivion.

◆ *Foot's election as Labour Leader in 1980:* Michael Foot actively supported many of the policies which social democrats could not tolerate. Had Healey become leader, it is likely that most social democrats would have felt duty bound to give him support.

◆ *Roy Jenkins and British politics:* Jenkins became the UK's first President of the European Commission in 1977. Before he left this office in 1979, he gave the Dimbleby Lecture on BBC television. His support for the Atlantic Alliance, the UK's position in Europe and for Keynesian economic policies were at odds with contemporary developments in the Labour Party and his stance provided potential leadership for those who agreed with him.

◆ *The role of the media:* the treatment given by the media to the divisions within the Labour Party after its 1979 election defeat (and especially to the rise of the Left) both enhanced the intensity of these divisions and encouraged leading social democrats to desert their Party. A more balanced treatment may have put these divisions into perspective and persuaded the Right to stay within the Party and fight the Left.

The Social Democratic Party and the Liberal Party

The Social Democratic Party was launched in March 1981. It was conceived, not as a Centre party, but one on the Left of the political spectrum, founded on the principle of one member, one vote. By the end of 1981 it had the support of 26 Labour MPs (and 1 Conservative), 18 Peers, and 31 former Labour MPs. Its membership totalled 65,000. Two more Labour MPs subsequently joined in 1982. In the period between the launch of the Party and the ratification of its Constitution in June 1982,

Party affairs were conducted by a Steering Committee, whose role included the handling of relations with the Liberal Party.

SDP Policies and Ideology

The policies and principles of the SDP were put forward in the *Limehouse Declaration* (a statement of Social Democratic aims and objectives which was published before the Party was officially formed). These ideas were expanded upon in the writings of leading SDP members, especially in David Owen's *Face the Future* and Shirley Williams's *Politics is For People* (both published in 1981). The ideology of the Social Democrats differed from that of the earlier revisionists in a number of key ways. Although they also rejected the view that class warfare was necessary to secure a socialist society, they failed to support the active role of the State which was an essential aspect of revisionism. Social Democrats were aware of the need to tailor their objectives, since the economic growth which underpinned the revisionist pursuit of equality could no longer be assumed. Social Democratic thought was especially influenced by Richard Tawney, who condemned the acquisitive society based upon the pursuit of individual gain and placed community at the heart of his thinking. The ultimate vision was of a society based upon the principles of fraternity, fellowship, community and participation.

Social Democrats coupled their support for the system of parliamentary democracy with proposals to diffuse power and develop a strong sense of community. The emphasis which the revisionists placed on egalitarianism was replaced by the endorsement of political change underpinned by decentralisation. Mechanisms designed to secure popular involvement across a wide range of policy areas and to promote participation through voluntary action were prominent.

The SDP was also an *internationalist* party. It endorsed the UK's membership of the EEC and NATO, desired multilateral nuclear disarmament and sought to give support to the Third World. The ideology and policies put forward by the SDP emphasised the importance of *consensus*. It was argued that adversarial politics harmed the economy and that a return to the postwar consensus was required to restore the UK's economic fortunes.

Many of the SDP attitudes and policies found support within the Liberal Party. The relationship between the two Parties had a major impact on the course of politics in the 1980s. In particular, the theme of *participation* was a traditional Liberal concern.

Core Support for the New Party

The SDP depicted itself as a classless party, in the sense that it did not seek to closely identify itself with the traditional classes associated with the Labour and Conservative Parties. However, it has been observed that the membership of the SDP, and the support which it obtained, was overwhelmingly middle class. A key element of this support was derived from a particular social grouping, namely the well-educated, public service 'salariat' (that is, salaried rather than weekly wage earners). The features of this segment of the electorate were that they were upwardly mobile (being of the 1937–56 generation which had reaped the benefits of educational reform, the postwar establishment of social services and the National Health Service), their success was due to education and professional training, and they were concentrated in the public service sector of the economy. Their guiding philosophy was public service as opposed to profit-making. The political attitudes of such electors thus favoured key aspects of the postwar consensus.

Problems Encountered by the SDP

The development of the SDP was impeded by a number of factors which are discussed below.

Lack of Clarity

There was a great deal of debate about what sort of party the SDP should be. This led to lack of clarity regarding ideology and political positioning. Some saw it as a 'Mark 2 Labour Party', which was designed to replace the existing leftwing Labour Party. They wished to direct its appeal at the working class and sought to erode Labour's traditional electoral support. Bill Rodgers (and latterly David Owen) became associated with this objective.

This view was challenged by an alternative belief that the SDP should be a *radical, idealist movement*, rejecting the Labour Party because of the leftwing dominance which had occurred since 1979 and the conservatism which stemmed from the influence exerted by the unions. The intention was to appeal to a broader section of the electorate than the working class and to put forward policies (such as devolution and participation) not traditionally associated with Labour. David Owen was initially associated with such a course of action.

The final model for the new party was that of a *Centre party*, which was designed to repudiate extremism and promote social harmony. Its policies were based on consensus and it was a course of action initially put forward by Roy Jenkins. This could be justified on the basis that the swing to the Right in the Conservative Party and to the Left in Labour created a political vacuum in the Centre which such a party would fill. The unpopularity of both major Parties when the SDP was formed implied that the electorate was sympathetic to a party which could promote an image of moderation. This also aided cooperation with the Liberal Party whose politics had traditionally been based on a rejection of extremist politics.

The diverse views concerning the nature of the SDP which have been outlined above had significant consequences for the image, ideology and policies of the Party and for its relationship with the Liberal Party.

Failure to Attract all Social Democrats

The SDP proved unable to unite all Social Democratic opinion. Decisions by Labour MPs not to defect to the SDP were governed by a variety of factors which included the strength of their emotional ties to the Labour movement, and their individual relationships with their Constituency Labour Parties: moderate MPs whose constituency parties had not been taken over by the Left were more likely to remain in the party.

Failure to Secure Support from Tory 'Wets'

The dismissal of Ian Gilmour, Christopher Soames and Mark Carlisle from the Conservative cabinet in 1981 suggested the possibility of disaffected Conservative 'wets' defecting to the SDP. (The term 'wets' was used to describe those on the Left of the Party whose views derive from the earlier 'one nation' tradition of conservatism.) However, with the exception of Christopher Brocklebank-Fowler, no Conservative MP joined the SDP. This failure to attract leading Conservative supporters arose for a number of reasons. No concerted attempt was mounted to secure the defection of Conservative MPs as had been directed at members of the Parliamentary Labour Party. No leading Conservative 'wet' gave support to such a course of action. One explanation for this is that the Conservatives' disenchantment with Thatcher's leadership was not as significant as the disillusionment felt by Social Democrats towards the rise of the Left in the Labour Party.

Any incentive which may have existed for the Conservative Left to desert the Party increasingly declined in late 1981 and early 1982. Factors, such as the improvement of the economy and the suggestion in opinion polls that the Liberal–SDP Alliance (which is referred to below) was losing support, exerted pressure on disaffected Conservative MPs to remain in the Party. These

> **Question**
>
> To what extent can it be argued that divisions in the Labour Party were solely responsible for the formation of the SDP in 1981?

sentiments were enhanced by the Falklands War which rendered desertion almost unthinkable. So, the SDP assumed the image of a breakaway Labour Party which was less likely to attract wavering Conservative voters, other than as a consequence of protest voting.

Relationship with the Liberal Party

The Liberal Party's then leader, David Steel, rejected the possibility that his Party would be able to achieve power independently. Instead he sought to create a new party which would serve as the vehicle of progressive politics on the Centre-Left of the political spectrum. This would be based upon a fusion of the Liberal Party and Labour's Social Democrats. It was crucial to the attainment of such a strategy, however, that rank and file Social Democrats, rather than a relatively small number of leading figures, should participate in a process of realignment. It was in this context that Roy Jenkins was especially crucial to developments in the early 1980s. Steel believed that if a Social Democratic party was established it would be possible for the Liberals to closely cooperate with it, and from that situation the process of realignment could be advanced.

Liberal–SDP Cooperation After 1981

Steel actively sought to secure the cooperation of Liberals and Social Democrats following the formation of the SDP in 1981. He believed that this would be necessary for a number of reasons. These reasons included political expediency – it made no sense for two parties seeking to occupy the Centre-Left of the British political spectrum to fight against each other. A working arrangement between the two parties could further be justified by the political benefits which it was assumed would arise. It was believed that a party which had emerged from Labour would be able to attract working class support and succeed in urban and industrial areas where the Liberal Party's appeal had been generally weak after 1945. Two Parties polling different electorates but working together would produce a strong challenge to the two major Parties. There was a belief that a single candidate representing both Parties would succeed to a greater extent than a candidate representing one Party alone – an alliance of the two Parties would approach parts of the electorate which the two Parties singly could not reach, referred to as the 'Heineken Effect' (a term which took its name from a popular television commercial advertising lager).

Similarity of ideology and policy could also be used as a justification for the cooperation of the Liberal and Social

Democratic Parties. Agreement between the two Parties was given practical substance in the 1981 'Königswinter Compact', which stemmed from a meeting of leading Liberals and members of the SDP at the Anglo-German Society's annual Königswinter conference. This compact committed both parties to broad agreement on principles, cooperation in election contests, and Joint Policy Commissions on major issues. The term applied to these various forms of cooperation was the 'Liberal–SDP Alliance'. Specifically this involved joint planning and activity in a number of areas. There followed coordination at Parliamentary level and publication of a joint policy document in 1981 (*A Fresh Start for Britain – A Statement of Principles*). The key feature of the Alliance was an agreement on the allocation of Parliamentary constituencies between the two parties for the 1983 General Election. The procedures which were adopted ultimately resulted in a single Alliance candidate in all but three constituencies.

Breaking the mould of British politics? The Liberal leader, David Steel, and a leading member of the SDP, Shirley Williams, advertise the benefits of two-party cooperation in the May 1981 local elections.

The 1983 General Election

The Alliance experienced chequered fortunes between 1981 and the 1983 General Election. Momentum was provided by by-election victories at Croydon North West, Crosby, Glasgow-Hillhead and Bermondsey, but other factors suggested the Party was failing to live up to its early lofty expectations. Events which included the improvement of the economy (evidenced by the slowing down of the rise in unemployment and inflation), the reduced intensity of Labour's internal wrangling after Healey's victory in the election for deputy leader in 1981, and the euphoria surrounding the successful liberation of the Falkland Islands by a British Task Force served to reduce the impact of the Alliance on the electorate.

The Alliance polled 25.4 per cent of the vote in 1983, the strongest showing obtained for a third party for 60 years, yet they secured only 23 seats. Under a system of proportional representation it would have secured around 161 seats. The Alliance suffered from a problem that had bedevilled the Liberal Party for many years – its ability to secure support more or less evenly across the social strata failed to provide it with sufficient votes to emerge as the victor in individual constituencies. Those who voted for the Alliance were virtually a microcosm of the electorate as a whole, in terms of sex, age and social class. Although the Alliance harmed the Labour Party more than it did the Conservatives, the Labour Party's support was heavily concentrated within mainly working class constituencies. This resulted in Labour winning 209 seats with a very similar percentage vote to that polled by the Alliance (27.6 per cent).

The balance between the two Alliance Parties at Parliamentary level changed to the Liberal Party's advantage. They managed to retain 12 of the 13 seats they held before the election (losing only Croydon North West) and gaining a further five seats. Of the 28 MPs who had defected to the SDP and stood in 1983, only five retained their seats. One further gain was made.

Failure to Merge Following the 1983 General Election

David Owen's election as Party leader in place of Jenkins in June 1983 led the SDP to officially consider the merits of the Alliance. Unlike Jenkins, who sought the eventual merger of the Liberal and Social Democratic Parties, Owen viewed the Alliance as no more than an electoral pact which would operate until the SDP had developed sufficiently as a political force, able to make its own independent contribution to British political affairs. Thus, while he wished to retain working arrangements with the Liberal Party he opposed any consideration of merger with them.

Development of a Distinct SDP Ideology

A key dilemma faced by David Owen when he became leader of the SDP was to demonstrate political space between his Party and both the revisionist socialists (who remained in the Labour Party) and the Liberal Party. The former was required in order to secure support from Labour voters while the latter was necessary to resist pressures for merger by emphasising ideas and policies which associated the SDP with Western European social democratic parties rather than the British Liberal Party. Owen's response to these issues was to advance the concept of the *social market*.

The Social Market

The social market was originally pioneered by postwar West German economic liberals in reaction to the 'overmighty state and cartelised economy'. The term was used briefly by the Conservative New Right in the 1970s, principally by Sir Keith Joseph. Owen's use of this concept after 1983 included abandoning the term 'mixed economy', and was based upon an acceptance of a new consensus. This consensus was based on the market economy, but sought to instil social objectives into its operations. These objectives offered a solution to the problems of social exclusion whose potential to create social disharmony had been manifested in the riots of 1981. The social market was officially adopted as SDP policy at its 1984 conference in Buxton, and was articulated in works written by Owen, especially *A Future That Will Work* (1984).

One problem with the social market was the lack of a precise definition. A particular difficulty was whether it entailed a market economy accompanied by a State that intervened on a highly selective basis, or by an active enabling State which sought to correct market failures and promote social welfare and justice. One definition suggested that it was an approach whereby wealth was created by market forces but would be redistributed according to social principles. This would result in the creation of a classless, more equal and more humane society, especially through the relief of deprivation and poverty. However, other uses of the term placed reduced emphasis on social objectives and devoted rather more attention to the role of the State in promoting the market. This was contrasted with the perception held by many on the Left of the political spectrum that it was the operations of the market which were a prime cause of social problems justifying intervention by government.

The 1987 General Election

The Alliance continued to secure some good results after 1983. By-election gains were secured at Portsmouth South (1984), Brecon and Radnor (1985), Ryedale (1986) and Greenwich (1987), and the Liberal Party held its seat in Truro in 1987 following the death of the sitting MP, David Penhaligon. In the 16 by-elections which occurred during the Parliament elected in 1983, the Alliance polled 39 per cent of the vote, compared to the Conservative's 30 per cent and Labour's 28 per cent. Successes were also achieved in local government contests. The Alliance gained 260 seats in the 1985 County Council elections and 450 in the May 1987 Council elections. Thus by 1987 the Alliance either controlled or held the balance in 100 local authorities.

In 1986, an Alliance Planning Group was formed to prepare the Alliance campaign for the forthcoming General Election. A joint manifesto, *Britain United – The Time Has Come*, was produced for the election. Owen did not believe that it was possible for the Alliance to win power singlehandedly and that the most realisable objective was participation in a coalition government in which power was shared with a major party. This stance was similar to that adopted by Steel towards Callaghan's Labour government in the 1970s and thus the Alliance moved towards endorsing the balance of power (termed a 'balanced Parliament') as its electoral objective.

The Alliance polled 7.3 million votes (23.1 per cent of the national vote) but secured the return of only 22 MPs (17 Liberal and 5 SDP). An arithmetical share of the seats would have given them 143 MPs. This result failed to live up to the high expectations which the Alliance had for the election – they had assumed that the figure of 50–100 seats was a realisable objective. The election was a total disaster for the SDP. This Party was reduced from eight MPs to five, and had failed to gain a single seat. Fourteen of the Alliance MPs represented rural constituencies. The Party had thus become the political vehicle of the Celtic Fringe. The reduced level of support obtained by the Alliance was slightly to the benefit of the Labour Party although additional Alliance support was picked up from both major Parties. A perceived defect in the Alliance campaign was its dual leadership. This was the prime reason for Steel's subsequent attempts to secure the merger of the Parties.

The Merger of the Two Parties

Steel called for a merger of the two Parties following the 1987 General Election. There were several factors which prompted him to act as he did. The SDP largely failed to attract Labour working class voters to the Alliance. The Alliance had become a strong force in London and the South, but at the 1987 election it lost support in Labour's Northern heartlands, emerging from the election heavily dependent on sources of electoral support which the Liberal Party was largely capable of attracting for itself. There were also practical considerations in favour of a merger, especially the demoralisation felt by many SDP activists concerning their Party's performance in 1987. They were thus likely to be receptive to this course of action.

The SDP's members voted (in a 77 per cent turnout) for a merger to be negotiated with the Liberal Party. The result was 25,987 votes in favour (57.4 per cent) to 19,228 against (42.6 per cent). Owen immediately resigned as leader and was replaced by Robert Maclennan, SDP MP for Caithness and Sutherland. The desire to merge was affirmed at the SDP conference at the end of August, and in September the Liberal Assembly also voted to proceed with discussions of this nature. The Alliance was formally ended on 26 August 1987 and Owen and Steel agreed to go their separate political ways. Both parties then entered into negotiations (a key concern of which was to draw up a constitution) which lasted from September 1987 until January 1988.

On 23 January 1988 a special Liberal Assembly approved the merger, and the SDP Council for Social Democracy subsequently approved it by 273:28. It was subsequently endorsed by a postal ballot of Party members. On 3 March 1988, the Social and Liberal Democrats were officially launched, under the interim leadership of Steel and Maclennan. A leadership contest was held later in 1988 which resulted in victory for **Paddy Ashdown** over Alan Beith. The Party subsequently changed its name to the Liberal Democrats in 1989.

The Labour Party, 1983–92

The scale of Labour's defeat in the 1983 General Election intensified feelings against the Left, while the size of Neil Kinnock's victory in the subsequent Labour leadership contest indicated he had a clear mandate to initiate reforms in the party and lead it in a new direction. The actions of the Conservative government against the trade unions made their leaders receptive to Kinnock and to a policy which was sufficiently credible to win an election. Accordingly, moves were initiated against the influence which the Trotskyite Militant Tendency possessed in some constituency parties. Perhaps more importantly, attempts were made to broaden Labour's electoral appeal by making its policy and underlying ideology more 'electable'. These key changes are discussed below.

Reforms to the Labour Party, 1983–87

Ideology

Kinnock delivered a Fabian lecture on the *Future of Socialism* in 1985 which differentiated between what he referred to as 'democratic socialism' and both 'democratic centralism' and 'social democracy'. The values of democratic socialism were stated to be the interdependent ones of *liberty, equality and democracy*.

○ *Liberty* required action to reduce disadvantage and give individuals greater control over their own destiny.

○ *Equality* entailed both the elimination of those institutions which protected, rewarded and perpetuated inequalities and the promotion of the principle of equality of opportunity in all policy areas.

○ *Democracy* rejected the centralisation of power in the hands of unaccountable bureaucrats in favour of participation in areas as diverse as the workplace, the housing estate or within the community, thus enhancing the goal of popular involvement in activities which affect the day-to-day life of the individual.

Policy

Kinnock's re-examination of Labour ideology was accompanied by changes in the direction of Labour policy. The unpopularity of nationalisation and the level of deindustrialisation by the mid-1980s justified changes to the Alternative Economic Strategy. Thus in 1986, the policy of 'social ownership' indicated a movement away from old style nationalisation, towards endorsement of the market economy. Although Labour continued to propose that industries such as British Telecom and British Gas (which had been privatised) would be renationalised, support was also expressed for alternative mechanisms to secure public and democratic control over the economy. These wider forms of social ownership included developments such as cooperative ventures and enterprise boards.

Organisation

The aim of organisational reform was to create a more centralised and disciplined Party, with power located in its leadership, at the expense of the National Executive Committee and the constituency Labour Parties. Such reforms were underlaid with the belief that Labour could only win elections when it was viewed as a respectable, orderly and united Party, able to tame the Left and reduce the influence of those who advocated extra-parliamentary activity, including the trade unions.

Presentation and Packaging

Considerable emphasis was also placed on the packaging and presentation of the Party. There was modernisation of organisation, programme and strategy. A key step taken after the 1983 election was the setting up of the Campaign Strategy Committee, chaired by Kinnock. In 1985, Peter Mandelson was appointed as Director of Campaigns and Communications.

The 1987 General Election

Presentation dominated the Party's 1987 election campaign at the expense of policy, much of which remained vague or non-committal, borne out of the need to reconcile divergent views within the Party and indicating the relatively slow progress of reforms to ideology and policy. Labour fared relatively badly in 1987, increasing its poll to 30.8 per cent, and gaining a small number of seats. Kinnock's response to this perceived deficiency was the Policy Review which is discussed below.

Modernisation

The process described as 'modernisation' involved two main elements. The first was a restatement of Labour ideology, contained in the publication *Democratic Socialist Aims and Values* (published in 1988). This document was designed to provide the framework for a detailed review of policy. This was undertaken in seven Policy Reviews initiated by Kinnock in 1987 and which were due to report to the Party conference in 1989. An interim document, *Social Justice, Economic Efficiency* was presented to Party conference in 1988. Further proposals were embodied in the statement *Meet the Challenge, Make the Change* (published in 1989 and containing many similarities to the policies latterly associated with Tony Blair) and *Looking to the Future: A Dynamic Economy, a Decent Society, Strong in Europe* (published in 1990). The review resulted in public ownership being abandoned as a major item of Labour policy, and the Party's anti-EEC stance being replaced by a pro-European one. Labour's commitment to unilateral nuclear disarmament was also dropped. The Party adopted a more flexible attitude towards taxation policies and moderated its response to Conservative trade union reforms.

Labour and the Market Economy

The Policy Review reflected the need for Labour to adjust to the beliefs, values and aspirations advocated by conservatism, a key aspect of which was that personal betterment would not be secured through the operations of the State, but rested in the hands of individuals. The developments which took place after 1983 and particularly between 1987 and 1989 transformed Labour into a Party which openly accepted the market orientated mixed economy. Nonetheless, the case for intervention by the State to provide services (such as health care and education) and to intervene selectively in the operations of the market to prevent abuse or unfair exploitation (for example, in connection with monopolies) was accepted. Terms such as 'new realism' or 'market socialism' were applied to the outlook and policies adopted by the Labour Party during the 1980s.

Thus Labour's new approach was to endorse the market economy but seek to intervene selectively in its operations in pursuit of collective purposes serving social needs. This was latterly endorsed in part two of the new Clause IV of the Party constitution adopted in 1995. The Party endorsed the goal of 'a dynamic economy . . . in which the enterprise of the market and the rigour of competition are joined with the forces of partnership and cooperation'.

Organisational Reforms

A number of organisational reforms were implemented after 1987. Limited moves were made towards the implementation of the 'one member, one vote' principle. This was viewed as necessary in order to mobilise moderate Party members and to reduce the grip of the 'hard Left' on the Party, as well as to reduce the hold of the trade unions on Labour affairs. Reforms which were implemented in 1987 concerned the introduction of localised electoral colleges for the selection and deselection of parliamentary candidates. In 1988, new voting procedures for the constituency sections of the leadership electoral college and the NEC were introduced. The loss of the Left's influence was demonstrated by Tony Benn's unsuccessful challenge for the leadership of the Party in 1988. Kinnock secured almost 90 per cent of the vote. It was left to Kinnock's successor, John Smith, to conclude this process of organisational reform with the implementation of a form of 'one member, one vote' in 1993.

The Labour Party After 1992

Labour's narrow failure to oust the Conservative Party in the 1992 General Election led to Kinnock's resignation. The new leader of the Labour Party was John Smith, who advanced the process of modernisation through the organisational reform (which has been referred to above) and by his appointment of the Commission on Social Justice which is discussed below.

The Commission on Social Justice

The role of the Commission on Social Justice was to consider the relationship between social justice and the goals of economic competitiveness and prosperity. The final report, *Social Justice: Strategies for National Renewal* (published in 1994), gave considerable prominence to five broad policy areas – education, employment, welfare, social policy and taxation. There were ideas to improve nursery education, cut long term unemployment and tackle pension provision. Economic success was perceived as the crucial underpinning of social justice. Priority was also given to political and civil rights. The Commission spoke of the need to construct a new relationship between those who govern and those who are governed. This theme formed the basis of the proposals for constitutional reform subsequently agreed to in 1997 by the Joint Consultative Committee composed of senior figures from the Labour Party and Liberal Democrats.

Blair and Renewal

Attempts by Labour leaders to bring Labour ideology up to date were accompanied by suggestions of the need to abandon or rewrite Clause IV of the Party's constitution. John Smith commenced work on preparing a statement of values which would have been debated at the Party conference in 1995, but his initiatives were halted by his premature death in 1994. The new Labour leader was Tony Blair. Like Kinnock, Blair initially described his ideology as 'democratic socialism' which he defined in terms of social justice, the equal worth of each citizen, equality of opportunity, and community. Initially his leadership diverted attention back to ideology at the expense of policy, which had been the pre-eminent consideration of Smith's leadership.

Reforms to Labour's ideology and organisation speeded up under Blair's leadership. At the 1994 Labour conference he proposed to rewrite Clause IV. A number of changes affecting the postwar world could be cited to justify a move away from old-style, Clause IV socialism. These included the collapse of communism, and globalisation (which made economic isolation neither desirable nor feasible and which additionally made it problematic to seek egalitarianism through the use of taxation and social welfare policies, since capital would go elsewhere).

Other relevant issues included the massive growth in service industries coupled with the development of a consumer culture, and changes to the composition of the workforce (particularly the number of women who were employed, many on a part-time basis). Additionally, the revision of Clause IV would prevent the Party being misunderstood or misrepresented in future elections (especially in being associated with high taxation and state socialism), and would further provide a symbol of the Party's modernisation.

In December 1994, the NEC voted to hold a special conference the following April to vote on the proposed constitutional change which differentiated between the purposes or objectives of the Party and the policies designed to achieve them. The new Clause IV was approved by the NEC on 13 March 1995. It emphasised the value of community, social justice and democracy, and part two redefined the Party's economic aims. These included accepting the competitive market economy operating in the public interest, and espousing a partnership between private and public ownership. These changes meant that profit was no longer decried as a dirty word and that centralised planning and State control were not deemed to be indispensable to socialism. The special conference approved this new statement on 29 April 1995. These changes amounted to Labour's acquiescence to a capitalist society, which they would seek to improve and reform.

The Party was christened 'New Labour' to indicate its social-democratic transformation.

NEW LABOUR

The policy and ideological changes associated with Kinnock, Smith and Blair were also reflected in the composition of the Party, especially at Parliamentary level. At the 1997 General Election, only 13 per cent of Labour MPs were drawn from manual backgrounds, whereas 45 per cent came from the professions (especially law and education), 9 per cent from business, and 33 per cent came from a range of non-manual jobs which included journalism.

These changes prompted the Amalgamated Engineering and Electrical Union (AEEU) in 1997 to withhold a £250,000 donation in protest at the changing profile of the Party. It subsequently announced that £1 million would be switched from its political fund (used to make donations to political parties) to its general fund. It would be used to groom working class AEEU members as candidates for future elections.

The Labour Party and the Liberal Democrats

The changes, which have been discussed earlier in this chapter, increased the possibility of enhanced cooperation between the Liberal Democrats and the Labour Party.

Individualism and Collectivism

Cooperation between the Labour and Liberal Parties had formerly been hindered by Labour's theoretical commitment to State socialism. This included a powerful role for the State which was contrary to the emphasis which Liberals placed on individual liberty. However, the concept of individual freedom received prominent attention in the ideological changes which took place in the Labour Party during the 1980s. Labour politicians denied there was any inherent contradiction between collective provision and individual freedom. Democratic socialism was thus seen as an ideology whose key objective was to protect and extend individual liberty.

Community

Liberals in the postwar UK had sought to reconcile the traditional importance which was attached to individualism with a collectivist age. The problem faced by Labour in the 1980s was the reverse – the need to make their traditional emphasis on collectivism acceptable in an era which had been dominated by Thatcherite individualism. Both Parties, therefore, came to

Tony Blair addressing the National Assembly in Paris on the 'third way'.

support the notion of *community* as the mechanism through which individual interests could be reconciled with collective action. Labour's new approach was based upon ethical socialism which emphasised the importance of fellowship, fraternity and participation, and emphasised the fact that individuals are socially interdependent human beings who can not be divorced from the society they live in. The key exponent of these views, Richard Tawney, was a common intellectual influence on both New Labour and the Liberal Democrats. Strong communities were presented as one of the main principles underpinning what was described as Labour's 'third way' between statism and unrestricted individualism.

THE THIRD WAY

The term 'third way' was increasingly used after 1997 to describe the ideology underpinning the actions of the Labour government.

The first way was the neo-liberal approach identified with Mrs Thatcher. Labour criticised this approach because it resulted in a society divided between the 'haves' and 'have nots'.

The second way consisted of the form of socialism associated with the 1945–51 Labour governments, in which nationalisation figured prominently.

The third way embraced the goals of opportunity and social inclusion based on support for capitalism. Emphasis was placed on the obligations of citizens (for example, to bring up their children to act responsibly) as well as their rights.

Apart from the French socialist government, most social democratic parties in Europe shifted towards the 'third way' during the late 1990s. It is compatible with coalition government (or realignment) involving the parties of the Centre and Centre-Left.

New Labour and the Market Economy

Labour's endorsement of a market economy provided a further basis of agreement between themselves and the Liberal Democrats. Liberal Democrats supported the free market, although they were also aware of its potential weaknesses and, like New Labour, they supported the view that there was a need for some level of government provision of services.

A key problem with a market economy, however, was that it tended to promote selfish individualism which was in opposition with the emphasis placed upon community. There was a need, therefore, to reconcile the tendency of a market economy to create social divisions between the 'haves' and 'have nots' with objectives which sought a more unified society and thereby secured social harmony. This was provided through *stakeholding*. This concept was the key to what has been termed 'one nation socialism', and was intimately linked to community.

Stakeholding

The adoption of the market economy by Conservative governments after 1979 intensified social divisions. Much of the wealth which had been created had not been invested, but had been stored up as profits and paid out as dividends to shareholders and as large salaries to 'fat cat' chief executives. This meant that wealth had failed to filter throughout society and an 'underclass' had been created who felt permanently excluded from society, deprived of work, power and prospects. There was a need, therefore, to ensure that society as a whole benefited from the operations of a market economy. Labour thus sought to move away from the emphasis on shareholding to that of stakeholding. This sought to combine a company's responsibilities to its shareholders with responsibility to a broader community, embracing customers, workers and localities in which firms were located.

THE STAKEHOLDER ECONOMY

Stakeholding was directed towards the pursuit of social justice and the provision of wider opportunities for all within a market economy. It was also depicted as a reform which was essential for the smooth operation of a market economy. The stakeholder economy was thus a reform which would provide economic efficiency, at the same time as providing a measure of social justice. Stakeholding could be governed by individual or collective principles. Both provided a framework within which Liberal Democrats and Labour were able to cooperate. Individualism is focused on equipping individuals with the skills they require in the highly flexible and constantly changing labour market of modern capitalism. Collectivism emphasised the collective obligations and rights conferred by membership of communities and organisations. This model of stakeholding embraced issues which included the ownership and control of companies and constitutional change. These were compatible with long-standing Liberal/Liberal Democrat policies which sought to promote popular involvement in political and economic structures.

Further Reading

There is a wide range of literature on the UK's major political parties. A brief selection of these is as follows:

Tudor Jones, *Remaking the Labour Party from Gaitskell to Blair* (London: Routledge, 1996).

Eric Shaw, *The Labour Party since 1979: Crisis and Transformation* (London: Routledge, 1994). Both these provide excellent accounts of the developments affecting the ideology, policy and organisation of the Labour Party.

A briefer, but highly readable account of the development of the Labour Party from its origins to the present time, is provided by **Steven Fielding**, *Labour: Decline and Renewal* (Manchester: Baseline Books, 1995).

Chris Cook, *A Short History of the Liberal Party, 1900–1997* (Basingstoke: Macmillan, 1998, 5th edition) provides the best summary of developments affecting the Liberal Party/Liberal Democrats. This work also offers a very useful introductory chapter, dealing with the Liberal tradition in the nineteenth century.

Ivor Crewe and **Anthony King**, *The Birth, Life and Death of the Social Democratic Party* (Oxford: Oxford University Press, 1995) gives a very detailed evaluation of the history of the SDP.

Andrew Heywood, *Political Ideas and Concepts: An Introduction* (Basingstoke: Macmillan, 1994). This provides a lucid and easy-to-follow account of key political ideas and concepts.

Also useful is **Ian Adams**, *Political Ideology Today* (Manchester: Manchester University Press, 1993) which discusses the evolution and subsequent development of a wide range of political ideologies.

Robert Blake, *The Conservative Party from Peel to Major* (London: Heinemann, 1997). This offers a detailed study of the contribution of key Conservative leaders to the development of the Party's ideology and policies.

The specific contribution of Margaret Thatcher (who led the Party between 1975 and 1990) is contained in a number of works which include, **Andrew Gamble**, *The Free Economy and the Strong State: The Politics of Thatcherism* (Basingstoke: Macmillan, 1994, 2nd edition).

Political Systems
and Policy-Making

PART TWO

Chapter Four | Elections and Electoral Systems

The aims of this chapter are:

> 1 To assess the purpose served by elections in liberal-democratic political systems.
>
> 2 To evaluate the significance of, and reasons for, citizens' decisions not to vote in elections.
>
> 3 To analyse the concept of the electoral mandate and to evaluate its strengths and weaknesses.
>
> 4 To discuss the main features of first-past-the-post and proportional representation and of variants to these two electoral systems.
>
> 5 To evaluate the strengths and weaknesses of first-past-the-post and proportional representation.
>
> 6 To assess the factors which influenced the emergence of electoral reform on the British political agenda and discuss the progress of reform after 1997.

Elections and Liberal-Democratic Political Systems

The Purpose of Elections

People who live in liberal democracies will be invited to vote periodically. They may be asked to choose representatives for local, State or national office. Elections, therefore, are a key mechanism to enable citizens in a liberal-democratic political system to play some part in the political affairs of their country. They serve a number of key roles which include:

○ *Facilitating popular sovereignty:* elections provide citizens with ultimate political power. They enable citizens to participate in key political activities which include selecting the personnel of government and determining the content of public policy.

○ *Securing accountability:* it is an essential feature of liberal democracy that sovereignty rests with the people. Governments must be accountable to the people for their actions. If they lose the backing of public opinion they can be replaced at the next round of elections.

○ *Providing an essential link between the government and the governed:* they serve as a barometer of public opinion and ensure that the holders of public office, and the policies which they pursue, are broadly in accord with the wishes of the general public.

Non-Voting

In some liberal democracies voting is compulsory: this is the case in Australia and Belgium, for example. In others, however, it is optional. Where voting is optional, the level of voter participation varies. In 1996, the turnout for the American Presidential Election was a mere 49 per cent. The following year, 71.4 per cent of the British public voted in the General Election.

It is sometimes argued that the extent to which citizens exercise their right to vote (where it is optional) is an indicator of the 'health' of that system of government. A high level of voter participation (which is referred to as 'turnout') suggests enthusiasm by members of the public to become involved in the affairs of government. In more general terms it implies support for the political system.

There are two contrasting views concerning low turnout. This may result in public policy failing to represent the national interest. If public opinion is imperfectly represented, governments may be swayed to act at the behest of organised voting minorities. Lack of popular involvement in the affairs of government may pave the way for authoritarianism, in which the public are effectively frozen out of participation in government. This is the case in Nigeria where the public hold political parties in low esteem. In 1998, only 1 per cent of the population voted in the elections for the national assembly. An alternative interpretation, however, suggests that low voting levels are not of great importance. Non-voting may indicate a general level of popular satisfaction with the way in which public affairs are conducted.

Various reasons may explain non-voting. Factors such as social class, education and income may be influential forces in determining whether a person votes or abstains. Generally, low voting rates are found among persons from low socio-economic backgrounds. Voting laws and registration procedures may also influence turnout. The following procedures apply in the United Kingdom.

○ *Registration of voters:* in order to vote, a person must be included on the Register of Electors. This is compiled annually by local authorities, many of whom actively seek to ensure that all eligible persons are registered. This process fails to take account of population mobility, and the Labour Party estimated that four million people were effectively disenfranchised at the 1997 General Election because of this factor.

○ *Registration of parties:* any British citizen over the age of 21 (subject to disqualifications laid down in legislation enacted in 1975) may seek election to Parliament. A candidate merely requires endorsement from 10 registered voters in the constituency he or she wishes to contest and a deposit of £500 (which is returned if the candidate secures over 5 per cent of the votes cast in the election).

A wide variety of procedures are used in liberal-democratic political systems. Candidates may be required to be nominees of political parties which in turn may be subject to controls governing their right to contest elections. Candidates often require a party to demonstrate a stipulated level of support in order to be entered on the ballot paper. In the 1995 elections to the Russian Parliament, for example, each party had to submit 200,000 signatures gathered in at least 15 of the regions in order to enter the contest. The situation in the United States of America is considered in more detail below.

REGISTRATION PROCEDURES IN THE USA

Registration procedures apply to both voters and political parties. Citizens are required to register in advance of election contests in order to vote. The effort to be registered falls squarely on the shoulders of the individual. The criteria governing registration are controlled by the States and are subject to wide variation across the country. In some States' regulations they are extremely complex and may deter voting.

Additionally political parties are required to display a stipulated level of registered supporters by a determined date before they can be entered on ballot papers. This process may make it difficult for new national parties to enter the political arena and thus works in favour of the two established national parties. This is illustrated by the example of the Ross Perot's Reform Party in the State of California. In order to be entered for the March 1996 presidential primaries and the November 1996 Presidential Election it was necessary for the Party to lodge 89,007 signed forms with the State's county registrars by 25 October 1995.

The Mandate

Candidates for public office in liberal-democratic political systems are usually selected by political parties. To contest

> ## Question
>
> Use the headings below to compare and contrast the mechanics of the electoral system in any TWO liberal democracies.
> - **Registration of voters**
> - **Nomination of candidates**
> - **Turnout in national elections.**

elections, parties generally put forward a statement of the principles or policies which will guide their future actions if they succeed in taking control of public affairs. In the UK such a statement is called an *election manifesto*. A party which succeeds in gaining control of a public body through the election of its nominees claims to have a mandate to administer it in line with the statements contained in its manifesto. Its right to do this has been legitimised by the process of popular election.

The Influence of the Mandate

The concept of the electoral mandate is influential in some liberal democracies such as the UK. The reasons for this are described below.

- *Electors are provided with information:* a political party is forced to declare the policies which will determine its subsequent actions if it gains control of a public authority. Parties, therefore, are not unknown quantities: electors vote in an informed manner, their choice being determined by policy statements issued during an election contest.

- *Victors possess authority for their subsequent actions:* those who win an election can claim the right to carry out their policies on the grounds that the public has endorsed them. This provides their actions with authority based on popular support.

- *There is a check on unauthorised actions:* the mandate implies that candidates, parties or governments which embark on a course of action not placed before the electorate previously, should seek popular approval in a new election rather than acting without it.

In other countries, this concept may be of less importance. In the USA, for example, voters are heavily influenced by the previous record of incumbent candidates (that is, those who are seeking re-election to the office they currently occupy). There is a tendency to look back and cast votes in accordance with a candidates' past record rather than seeking to evaluate the merits of proposed future actions. Nonetheless, those seeking public office usually put forward a statement of future intentions: candidates for the Presidency, for example, announce their platform at the nominating convention.

Weaknesses of the Mandate

There are, however, several weaknesses associated with the concept of the mandate. The main problems associated with it are amplified below:

❍ Issues may emerge after an election.

❍ Voters may endorse parties not policies.

❍ Voting may be influenced by negative factors.

The Emergence of Issues Following an Election

It would be unrealistic to expect that a party could include every item of policy which it intended to carry out over a period of several years in a single document prepared for a specific election. Previously unforeseen issues emerge. Governments have to respond even though the public have not had the opportunity to express their views. British people, for example, were not invited to vote on the despatch of a task force to recapture the Falkland Islands in 1982, nor whether they wanted to commit British troops to the Gulf in 1990 or join the Americans in bombing Iraq in 1998. This suggests that, while it is useful in a liberal democracy that parties should declare their policies to the voters at election time, it is unrealistic to expect that election manifestos can give a total guide to what a party will do.

Instead, it must be accepted that, once installed into office, governments need to exercise a certain amount of discretion, responding to pressing problems when they arise. This capacity to act without consulting the general public is referred to as *trusteeship*.

Voters Endorse Parties not Policies

A party cannot claim the right to carry out all of its promises on the grounds that the public expressed support for them. Electors are unable to pick and choose between policies contained in a manifesto. It is a question of supporting the whole manifesto, or none of it. As Chapter 5 will argue, voters may also support a party for reasons other than the policies which it advances. Factors such as social class may determine a voter's political allegiance. In extreme circumstances this may mean that parties

Question

Evaluate the strengths and weaknesses of the concept of the electoral mandate as it applies to the operations of British politics.

secure support in spite of, rather than because of, the policies they put forward.

Voting may be Influenced by Negative Factors

A party or its candidates may secure support for negative rather than positive reasons. For example, it was argued that the 1992 American Presidential Election was primarily a referendum on the Presidency of George Bush, especially his handling of the economy. Many voters supported Bill Clinton and the independent candidate, Ross Perot, because they were dissatisfied with Bush. In Britain, public dissatisfaction with the record of the Conservative Party in the 1990s was a significant factor in the scale of Labour's victory at the 1997 General Election. Such negative support makes it difficult for parties and their candidates to claim they have a mandate to carry out their policies.

Electoral Systems

The First-Past-the-Post System

The first-past-the-post system is used in countries which include the UK, the USA, Canada and India.

Under this system, it is necessary for a winning candidate to secure more votes than the person who comes second. But there is *no* requirement that the winning candidate should secure an *overall majority* of the votes cast in an election. It is thus possible for a candidate to be victorious under this system despite having secured a minority of the votes cast.

Party	Votes	Percentage
Conservative	20,313	39.1
Liberal Democrat	13,981	26.9
Labour	12,939	24.9
Referendum Party	4,188	8.0
Others	629	1.1

DIFFICULTIES OF THE FIRST-PAST-THE-POST SYSTEM

The difficulties of the first-past-the-post electoral system were illustrated by the following example. In the Parliamentary constituency of Folkestone and Hythe at the 1997 General Election the result in the table opposite was obtained.

The Conservative candidate was returned as MP although he obtained only 39.1 per cent of the vote cast in that constituency.

A further difficulty with the first-past-the-post system concerns the extent to which constituencies contain equal numbers of electors. The ideal of equal constituencies was provided for in the 1885 Redistribution Act, but has not been achieved in practice. Labour's good performance in small-sized constituencies in the 1997 General Election had a major effect on the size of its majority.

Variants of the First-Past-the-Post Electoral System

In some countries, systems of election have been devised which seek to adjust the deficiencies associated with the first-past-the-post system. Two of these (the second ballot and the Alternative Vote) are discussed below.

The Second Ballot

The second ballot is a two-stage process. It is necessary for a candidate to obtain an *overall majority* of votes cast in the first round election in order to be elected to public office. Thus if 50,000 people voted in a constituency, it would be necessary for a candidate to secure 25,001 votes to be elected. If no candidate obtains a majority, a second-round election is held. Candidates with least votes in the first round stand down. In the second ballot (which is ideally between the candidates who secured first and second place in the first round) the candidate with most votes is elected. This system seeks to ensure that the winning candidate gets the endorsement of the majority of the electors who cast their vote in the second round.

This system is used in France for elections to the Presidency and National Assembly (although proportional representation was used for the 1986 elections to the latter body). The key features of elections in France have been:

○ *Presidential elections:* for Presidential contests the second ballot is between the top two candidates from the first round. In 1995, the second-round contest was between Lionel Jospin and Jacques Chirac with the seven other first-round candidates eliminated.

○ *National Assembly:* for elections to the National Assembly, any candidate who obtains 12.5 per cent of the vote in the first round may enter the second ballot. In practice, however, parties of the Left and Right have often agreed in advance to rally behind one candidate for the second ballot.

The Alternative Vote

The Aternative Vote is used in Ireland for Presidential elections, and for by-elections to the lower house, the Dail. It is also used to select members for the Australian House of Representatives. As with the second ballot, a candidate cannot be elected without obtaining majority support from the electorate (namely

50 per cent + 1 of the votes cast). Unlike the second ballot, however, there is no second election.

Voters number candidates in order of preference. If, when the votes are counted, no candidate possesses an overall majority, the candidate with the fewest first-preference votes is eliminated. These votes are redistributed to the candidate placed second on each ballot paper. This process is repeated until a candidate has an overall majority composed of first-preference votes coupled with the redistributed votes of candidates who have been eliminated.

Proportional Representation

Proportional representation indicates an objective rather than a specific method of election. It seeks to guarantee that the wishes of the electorate are arithmetically reflected in the composition of public authorities. This is achieved by ensuring that parties are represented on public bodies according to the level of popular support they enjoy at an election contest. Various forms of proportional representation are used in the countries which comprise the European Union. This section will consider two of these forms – the single transferable vote, and the party list system.

The Single Transferable Vote

The Single Transferable Vote applies to elections to legislative bodies. It requires an area to be divided into a number of multi-member constituencies (that is, constituencies which return more than one member to the legislative body). When electors cast their votes, they are required to number candidates in order of preference. They may indicate a preference for as many, or as few, candidates as they wish. To be elected, a candidate has to secure a quota of votes which determines the subsequent process of redistribution. The redistribution (or transfer) of votes from one candidate to another is the key distinguishing feature of this form of proportional representation.

The aim of the Single Transferable Vote system is to ensure that each successful candidate is elected by the same number of votes. It is used in Ireland for elections to the Dail (the lower House of Parliament) and for 49 out of 60 seats in the upper chamber (the Seanad). This system is employed in Malta, and since 1979 in Northern Ireland for the election of Members of the European Parliament. Elections to the Northern Ireland Assembly in 1998 also used this electoral system.

THE SINGLE TRANSFERABLE VOTE AND THE QUOTA

Under the Single Transferable Vote, a candidate is required to obtain a set number (or quota) of votes to secure election. This quota (which is termed the 'droop quota', after its nineteenth century inventor, Henry Droop) is calculated by the following formula:

$$\left(\frac{\text{Total Number of Votes Cast in the Constituency}}{\text{Total Number of Seats to be Filled} + 1} \right) + 1$$

Thus in a constituency in which 100,000 electors voted and in which there were four seats to be filled, the quota would be 20,001. Any candidate who obtains the necessary number of first preference votes is declared elected. Additional first-preference votes cast for such candidates are then redistributed to the candidates listed second on each ballot paper.

If, when the count is complete, no candidate has obtained the necessary number of first-preference votes, the candidate with fewest is eliminated and these are redistributed to the candidates listed as second choice on the eliminated candidate's ballot papers. The process of eliminating candidates with fewest first-preference votes and redistributing their votes is continued until the required number of seats are filled.

The Party List System

The other main system of proportional representation is the party list system. A main objective of this system is to ensure that parties are represented in legislative bodies in proportion to the votes which were cast for them. Political parties are responsible for drawing up lists of candidates which may be compiled on a national or on a regional basis. Elections to the Northern Ireland Forum in 1996 were conducted on the basis of the regional party list. In South Africa two hundred members of the National Assembly were elected from regional party lists and the other two hundred from national party lists.

Unlike the Single Transferable Vote, proportionality does not involve any transfer of votes from one candidate to another. Instead, each party prepares a list of candidates which it draws up in order of preference. When the votes are counted a party's representation in the legislative body arithmetically reflects the proportion of votes which it obtained. In a very simplistic form (in what is termed a 'closed party list'), a party which obtained 20 per cent of the total national poll would be entitled to 20 per cent of the seats in the legislative chamber. If this chamber contained 300 members, this party would be entitled to fill 60 places. The actual nominees would be those numbered 1 to 60 on that party's list.

This system affects the *status* of those elected who become *delegates* rather than *representatives*. They are not elected in their own right but as nominees of a political party. One logical consequence of this is for a party leader to have the power to dismiss representatives and replace them with alternatives drawn from the original list. Members elected to the Northern Ireland Forum in 1996 were subject to such party discipline.

Varieties of the Party List System

There are several varieties of party list systems. A popular one in Europe is the *D'Hondt system* which is used for national elections in Belgium, the Netherlands, Portugal, and Spain. Under this system it is possible for electors to vote for specific candidates selected from the lists drawn up by the parties. This enables the voters to indicate their views on the standing of candidates put forward by a political party. In this case what is termed the 'highest average' formula seeks to ensure that approximately the same number of votes are required to elect candidates drawn from the same political party.

Other variations include the *Hagenbach-Bischoff system* which is used in elections to the Greek Parliament, and the *Panochage system* which is used for elections to the Luxembourg Parliament. A particular feature of the latter system is the 'mix-in' whereby voters are not confined to selecting candidates from one party's list but may support candidates nominated by different parties. This is termed a 'free party list'.

Hybrid Electoral Systems

Hybrid electoral systems also exist which seek to blend the first-past-the-post system with proportional representation. In Germany, for example, both systems are used concurrently in order that minority parties who fare badly under the former system can be compensated under the latter. Under Germany's Additional Member System, electors have two votes in Parliamentary elections. The first (*erststimme*) is for a constituency candidate, elected under the first-past-the-post system. Approximately half of the Bundestag's 672 members are directly elected in this manner. The second (*zweitstimme*) is for a party list drawn up in each state (or *Länder*). The *Niemeyer system* is used to allocate additional members according to the following formula:

$$\frac{\text{Total Votes Obtained by a Party} \times \text{Number of Seats Available}}{\text{Total Number of Votes of All Parties Getting above 5\%}}$$

Question

What are the key features of electoral systems based upon proportional representation? How do these differ from the first-past-the-post system?

This system serves as a 'top up' seeking to ensure that there is a degree of proportionality between the parties. The remaining members of the Bundestag are elected in this fashion. This hybrid system gives electors the opportunity of 'split ticket' voting: that is they can support a constituency candidate of one party and the party list of another. This is a growing feature in German elections.

Elections to the lower house of the Russian Parliament, the Duma, in 1995 utilised a mixed system of first-past-the-post and proportional representation by the party list system. In 1993 a referendum in New Zealand narrowly supported changing the electoral system from first-past-the-post to a mixed member system, whose main features were similar to the electoral system used in Germany. It was subsequently used in the 1996 General Election.

The Strengths and Weaknesses of the First-Past-the-Post System

Strengths

The main strengths of the first-past-the-post electoral system are as follows.

❍ *Simplicity:* the system is relatively easy to understand. Voting is a simple process and it is easy to see how the result is arrived at. The winner takes all.

❍ *Executive strength:* the winner-take-all aspect of the first-past-the-post system is greatly to the benefit of the executive branch of government. This is regardless of whether this branch is drawn from the legislature (as it is in the UK) or is separately elected (as in the USA).

FIRST-PAST-THE-POST ELECTIONS

◆ *Britain, 1992:* the Conservative Party obtained only 41.9 per cent of the votes cast, but the workings of the first-past-the-post system gave it an overall majority of 21 in the House of Commons (51.6 per cent of the seats). This majority, although a reduced figure from that obtained in the previous election, was sufficient to enable the government to pursue its policies and govern for a reasonable period of time.

◆ *Britain, 1997:* the Labour Party's share of the vote (43.2 per cent) in this election gave it 418 seats in the House of Commons (63.4 per cent of the total number). This guaranteed it the ability to govern for a full five year term.

♦ *America, 1992:* Bill Clinton defeated the incumbent President Bush but obtained only 43 per cent of the popular votes cast. However, the electoral college vote for each state was allocated on the winner-take-all principle of the first-past-the-post system. Accordingly, Clinton obtained 370 votes to Bush's 168. This gave the former an aura of political strength.

♦ *America, 1996:* President Clinton obtained 49 per cent of the popular vote compared to 41 per cent secured by his Republican Party rival, Robert Dole. However, his margin of victory in electoral college votes was 379:159 which implied his record in office secured overwhelming backing from the American public.

○ *Aids party unity:* the manner in which this system treats minorities may serve as an inducement for parties either to remain united or to form electoral alliances in order to secure political power. This may be an advantage in those countries where the executive is drawn from the legislative body. Support for the government within the legislature is likely to be durable.

○ *Enhances the link between the citizens and legislators:* the first-past-the-post system may strengthen the relationship between members of the legislative branch of government and their constituents. In the UK, the House of Commons is composed of Members elected from 659 single-member constituencies. This facilitates a close relationship between individual legislators and their constituents and may also enhance the extent to which legislators can be held accountable for their actions. Local relationships are also of great significance to the conduct of American politics.

Weaknesses

There are, however, a number of disadvantages associated with this electoral system.

○ *Distorts public opinion:* a key purpose served by elections is to ensure that public office holders and the policies they pursue reflect public opinion. A major problem with the first-past-the-post system is that it distorts public opinion – in particular it fails to ensure that the wishes of the electorate are arithmetically reflected in the composition of the legislative branch of government. This may thus result in public policy being out of line with the views or wishes of the majority of the general public.

○ *Encourages adversarial politics:* the first-past-the-post system is capable of producing extreme political changes which do not necessarily reflect the feelings of the electorate. Major political parties can be virtually wiped out by such a system. An extreme example of this occurred in the 1993 Canadian General Election when the ruling Conservative Party was reduced from 157 seats to 2 in the House of Commons. Such changes in the composition of the legislature or executive may result in the loss of experienced personnel and may also create a system of adversarial politics. Parties have less incentive to cooperate in an electoral system which may translate them overnight from a minority to majority position.

❍ *Leads to unfair treatment of minority parties:* the system traditionally discriminates against minority parties. Ross Perot's performances in the 1992 and 1996 American Presidential Elections (in which he obtained 19 per cent and 8 per cent of the total national vote respectively) failed to secure him a single vote in the electoral college in either of these contests. The British Liberal Democrats seek electoral reform in part because their Parliamentary strength does not reflect their popular appeal. The electoral system fails to translate the Party's national vote into seats within the legislature.

CONSEQUENCES OF THE BRITISH ELECTORAL SYSTEM

1992 General Election

In the 1992 General Election the Liberal Democrats secured 17.9 per cent of the total vote, yet only 3 per cent of the seats in the House of Commons. Had the electoral system reflected the views of the electorate, the Party would have gained 117 seats rather than the 20 it succeeded in winning. Expressing the figures another way:

◆ it took 41,957 votes to elect a Conservative MP

◆ it took 42,646 votes to elect a Labour MP

◆ it took 299,735 votes to elect a Liberal Democrat MP.

This contravenes the principle of 'one vote, one value'.

The Scottish National Party also suffered at this election, securing 21.5 per cent of the total vote in Scotland but returning only 3 MPs.

1997 General Election

At the 1997 British general election:

◆ it took 32,419 votes to elect a Labour MP

◆ it took 58,124 votes to elect a Conservative MP

◆ it took 113,985 votes to elect a Liberal Democrat MP.

The electoral system continued to discriminate against the Liberal Democrats, but not as significantly as in 1992. In 1997, the support which the Liberal Democrats obtained was more highly concentrated in certain areas, rather than being evenly spread. This secured the election of 46 MPs even though the Party's share of the vote was lower than that obtained in 1992. Nonetheless, the Liberal Democrats share of the total national poll (16.1 per cent) arithmetically entitled it to 106 seats.

○ *Discourages voter participation:* the first-past-the-post system may discourage voter participation. Areas may be considered 'safe' political territory for one party and this may deter opponents from voting because their vote would be effectively 'wasted'. This may have a significant effect on the turnout in British local elections.

○ *Encourages downplaying of ideology:* the first-past-the-post system tends to discourage parties from fragmenting, and thus promotes the conduct of politics within the confines of a two-party system. It may also result in ideology becoming diluted, obscured or played down in order to attract a wide range of political opinions. The absence of a distinct identity may result in voters becoming disinterested. The consequence of this is low turnouts in elections and the utilisation of alternative ways (such as pressure group activity) in order to bring about political change.

Realising the Benefits of the First-Past-the-Post System

A final consideration of the first-past-the-post electoral system is the extent to which the stated advantages of this system are realised in practice, using the UK as an example.

In the UK, the executive branch of government comes from the majority party in the House of Commons. However, strong governments (in the sense of having a large Parliamentary majority) have not been a consistent feature of postwar politics. Fifteen General Elections have been held between 1945 and 1997: in six of these (1950, 1951, 1964, February 1974, October 1974 and 1992) governments were returned with a relatively small (and in February 1974, no) overall majority. Governments in this position cannot guarantee to stay in office and carry out their policies. On one occasion (1977–78) the Labour and Liberal Parliamentary Parties concluded a pact which had the effect of sustaining what had become a minority Labour government. Thus the first-past-the-post electoral system does not always deliver all of the benefits which supporters claim this system possesses.

The Strengths and Weaknesses of Proportional Representation

This section assesses the benefits and disadvantages associated with proportional representation.

Strengths

The main advantage of proportional representation is that the system addresses many of the defects of the first-past-the-post system.

○ *Minorities are fairly treated:* legislative bodies throughout Europe contain members drawn from parties such as the Greens, and thus provide an inducement for such groups to operate within the conventional political system. This inducement is absent in the UK where the poll obtained by the Green Party in the 1989 European elections (15 per cent) failed to secure the return of any members to the European Parliament.

○ *Encourages inter-party cooperation:* proportional representation may encourage parties to cooperate (especially in cases where the executive is drawn from the legislature). This may, in turn, divert politics away from extremes and foster consensus politics.

○ *Encourages diversity in candidate selection:* a party will put forward a number of candidates in a multi-member constituency. This may encourage the selection of candidates who are more socially representative in terms of race, gender and class.

Weaknesses

In 1986, the French socialist president, Francois Mitterrand, introduced proportional representation (in the form of the party list system) for the French legislative elections in order to dilute the strength of the dominant Conservative forces in the country (the RPR and the UDF). One consequence of this was the election of a number of representatives from the National Front. This party obtained 9.7 per cent of the vote and secured 35 seats. In 1988, the second ballot system was restored, and the National Front was virtually eliminated as a legislative force, winning just 1 seat, despite securing 9.6 per cent of the total poll. In the 1993 elections the National Front's share of the vote increased to 12.5 per cent, but it failed to win any seats in the National Assembly.

These episodes illustrate two problems which are associated with proportional representation and which are discussed below.

○ *Furtherance of vested interests:* these examples suggest that the motive for introducing proportional representation may be to further political vested interests. In France, this reform was not viewed as a progressive measure designed to improve the relationship between government and the people, but was put forward for selfish, partisan reasons – the desire of the Left to reduce the power of the Right in French elections.

○ *Representation of political extremists:* these examples also suggest that proportional representation may facilitate the representation of the political extremes which, once established within a legislative body, gain respectability and may enjoy a growth in their support. Some countries which use this system seek to guard against this problem by imposing a requirement that a party needs to secure a minimum threshold of support in order to benefit from proportional representation. In Denmark this figure is 2 per cent and in Germany, 5 per cent (although a variation was introduced for the 1990 and 1994 elections). In the 1998 German General Election, the 5 per cent threshold figure required for a party to benefit from the Additional Member System ensured that the Greens, Liberals and Communists secured proportional representation in Parliament whilst denying it to the neo-nazis.

○ *Promotion of multi-party systems:* the encouragement which proportional representation provides for political extremes is symptomatic of a more general problem, which is that this system may promote the development of a multi-party system. The use of the regional party list system of proportional representation for elections to the Northern Ireland Forum in 1996 seemed to encourage the formation of political parties to the detriment of the established, larger parties. This factor is of particular significance for countries whose executives are drawn from the legislature. In these cases, multi-party systems may make it difficult either to select the personnel which constitute the executive or to determine what policies should be enacted. Executives may consist of a coalition of parties, which are often seen as being weak and unstable.

○ *Minority interests secure unfair advantages:* proportional representation may result in minor parties securing a role in a country's political affairs which is out of all proportion to their levels of support. For example, the German Free Democratic Party enjoyed participation in government between 1969 and 1998. This is due to the fact that it held a pivotal position between the Christian Democrats and the Social Democrats. It could keep either out of office by siding with the other.

In cases where the balance between the main parties is narrow, proportional representation may give considerable favour and other benefits to individual MPs. In October 1998, the Italian government, led by Romano Prodi, was forced to resign after losing a vote of no confidence in the chamber of deputies. The margin of defeat was one vote. This situation arose after one of the government's supporters, Silvio Liotta, defected to the opposition.

The influence which individual MPs may wield in Italian politics has given rise to what is termed a 'votes market'. This precedes crucial votes when, it is alleged, political affiliations are traded for personal benefits such as policy changes or ministerial office.

❍ *Complexity:* critics of proportional representation argue that the system is difficult in the sense that it may not be obvious how the eventual result has been arrived at. This is especially the case with the single transferable vote which requires a process of redistribution (either of the surplus votes of an elected candidate or of the redundant votes of one who has been eliminated). Such votes are not randomly redistributed, and electors may not fully understand the manner by which this process is carried out. A danger is that, if the process by which the result is arrived at is not fully understood, the result itself may be deprived of popular legitimacy.

❍ *Enhancement of party leadership:* proportional representation has been accused of enhancing the power of party leadership. This is especially the case with the party list system which gives regional or national party leaders the ability to place candidates in-order of preference. So, the system improves the chances of loyal party members being elected ahead of those who are regarded as dissentients. This objection can be mitigated by the nature of candidate selection. The process governing candidate selection is not necessarily controlled by the party hierarchy. The Official Unionist Party in Northern Ireland, for example, permitted delegates at regional level to select and rank candidates who stood in the 1996 Northern Ireland Forum elections. In addition, in many countries which utilise the party list method of election, electors have the ability to vote for individual candidates.

❍ *Impact on constituency relationships:* proportional representation may weaken the link between legislator and constituent, which in countries such as the UK and the USA is regarded as a crucial aspect of political affairs. But this is not necessarily the case if multi-member constituencies are used. Further, the ability of electors to express support for individual candidates under some versions of the party list system may serve to enhance the relationship between constituent and representative.

Coalition Government Assessed

A key argument made in connection with proportional representation is its tendency to promote coalition government. This section analyses the operation of such governments.

Absence of Popular Choice

It might be argued that the formation of a coalition government and the determination of its policies are not conducted in a democratic manner. Although separate political parties can enter into pacts or alliances *prior* to an election contest, coalition governments are frequently formed *after* an election has taken place. Negotiations between parties may be drawn out and the electorate is not consulted on the composition of the executive or the choice of policy.

This problem occurred in New Zealand which first used a system of proportional representation at the 1996 General Election. The result gave the New Zealand First Party the balance of power between the Labour and National Parties. In the campaign, the leader of New Zealand First intimated support for Labour. After the election, however, this Party sided with the National Party (which held only 44 seats of the total of 120), giving the country a government it did not vote for, and which opinion polls subsequently estimated to lack popular approval.

Ineffective Accountability

It is also argued that accountability is impaired by coalition governments. When several parties are involved in government, it is difficult for the electorate to know who is responsible for decisions or to make a single party answerable for its actions.

Instability

Coalition governments are accused of being unwieldy. If a minor party deserts the government, the whole structure tumbles down. Examples of this include:

○ *Italy:* the downfall of Silvio Berlusconi's government in 1994 was due to the desertion of the Northern League.

○ *Ireland:* the demise of Albert Reynolds's government in Ireland in 1994 followed its abandonment by the Irish Labour Party.

Difficulties such as these were part of the consideration which prompted Italian voters to move away from proportional representation. Italy has had in excess of 50 postwar governments. Following a referendum to end proportional representation for elections to the Senate in 1993, new rules were introduced under which 75 per cent of the seats in a General Election were subject to the first-past-the-post system of election. The remaining seats were allocated by the regional party list system of proportional representation.

However, coalition governments are not inevitably weak and unstable. A coalition of the Christian Democrats, the Christian-Social Union, and the Free Democrats provided Germany's government between 1982 and 1998. The existence of local authorities in the UK in which no single party possesses an overall majority (termed 'hung councils') has in some cases forced political parties to cooperate. This could help legitimate coalition government in a country which has previously resorted to this only in times of emergency (1931 and 1940).

Electoral Reform in the UK

Electoral Reform and the British Political Agenda

Traditionally the case for electoral reform in the UK has been underlaid by vested interests. A belief by a political party that electoral reform would benefit them and/or harm their opponents has sometimes prompted calls for reform. This is illustrated by the following examples.

Electoral Reform and the Liberals

The most consistent demands for electoral reform since 1945 have been voiced by the Liberal Party and Liberal Democrats. Only when it became apparent in the late 1920s that the Liberal Party was unlikely to secure power in its own right, did the Party actively endorse electoral reform. This has been subsequently justified on the grounds that the electoral system has consistently failed to give this Party a share of seats in the House of Commons which reflects the level of popular support obtained in General Elections.

Seeking Support Through Electoral Reform

Electoral reform has been advocated by both major parties in the postwar period in an attempt to secure support from the Liberal Party and Liberal Democrats. However, the main parties have historically abandoned support for this reform when their need for Liberal support ended. Examples include:

❍ *1950:* the substantial reduction in Labour's majority at the 1950 General Election prompted the then leader of the Conservative Party, Winston Churchill, to urge the appointment of a Select Committee to consider electoral reform. He justified this by the under-representation of the Liberal Party at this election, although a key objective was to turn the Liberal Party's vote against the government in Parliamentary divisions.

○ *1965:* the then leader of the House of Commons, Ted Short, suggested the Labour government might be prepared to consider electoral reform. The main intention of this proposal was to seek the votes of the Liberal Parliamentary Party to keep the Labour government (which had been elected in 1964 with a majority of four) in office.

○ *1978:* the use of proportional representation for elections to the European Parliament secured the support of the Labour government's leadership to further the spirit of the Lib–Lab pact which was then in operation. This measure was, however, voted down in the House of Commons.

Seeking to End the One-Party State

The emergence of what appeared to be a one-party state after 1979 was one reason why some members of the Labour Party began to display an interest in electoral reform. Four consecutive Conservative victories in General Elections held in 1979, 1983, 1987 and 1992 led to concerns that this dominance could be broken only by electoral reform. This assertion could be justified by the failure of Conservative governments to secure an overall majority of votes at any of these General Elections, and the manner in which the electoral system disadvantaged the Liberal Party, Liberal–SDP Alliance and Liberal Democrats at all of them.

A Conservative Change of Heart?

The Conservative Party adopted a negative stance towards proportional representation. In 1998 the Party's leader, William Hague, stated that his Party would fight every inch of the way to resist the use of proportional representation for Westminster elections, because it would undermine the fundamental principle of democratic accountability. He argued that it took political power away from the electorate and gave it to small political parties.

However, the results of the 1997 General Election indicated that the Conservative Party might benefit if electoral reform was introduced. Although this Party secured 17.5 per cent of the vote in Scotland and 19.6 per cent in Wales, it failed to elect a single MP in either country. Proportional representation would ensure that in future general elections and contests for the

Scottish Parliament and Welsh Assembly, the Conservatives would receive fair representation.

On the other hand, electoral reform may encourage splits in the ranks of this Party over Europe. Conservative pro-Europeans who were unhappy with the Euro-sceptic stance of the leadership might break away, encouraged by the prospect of electoral success.

Reform Proposals After 1997

In the mid-1990s, the interest in electoral reform was no longer based on political self-interest. Many on the Left of the political spectrum began to view electoral reform as a mechanism to develop a new relationship between government and the governed, with a particular objective of bringing government and the people closer together.

Thus following the 1997 General Election Labour's new Prime Minister, Tony Blair, initiated a series of measures concerned with electoral reform. These were supported by the Liberal Democrats, whose leaders were included on a Cabinet sub-committee to consider the area of constitutional reform. The main proposals were to reform elections as follows.

Parliamentary Elections

An electoral commission was appointed to examine the introduction of proportional representation for elections to the House of Commons. The proposals put forward by this body would then be put to the electorate in a referendum. This commission was appointed in 1997, and was chaired by Lord Roy Jenkins. An all-party group, (composed of members drawn from Labour, the Liberal Democrats, Charter 88, the SNP, Plaid Cymru, and the Greens) was established in June 1998, pledged to promote whatever voting system the Jenkins Commission proposed in its October 1998 report.

THE JENKINS COMMISSION

As the diagram on p. 107 illustrates, the voting system is of crucial importance to the outcome of a general election contest.

In October 1998, the commission headed by Lord Jenkins proposed to replace the first-past-the-post system in UK Parliamentary elections with a system referred to as the *Alternative Vote Top-Up*. This entails giving voters two votes at general elections.

The first vote would be to elect a local constituency MP, using the alternative vote system. The number of Parliamentary constituencies would be reduced in number (to 530–560).

The second vote would elect additional members on a city-wide or countrywide basis. These would be chosen from lists put forward by the political parties.

The top-up element of the new system (comprising around 15 to 20 per cent of the membership of the House of Commons) is designed to ensure that the vote cast for parties is more accurately reflected in the seats secured in Westminster.

Elections in Northern Ireland, Wales and Scotland

Elections to the Northern Irish Assembly were held in 1998 using the single transferable vote. The outcome of these elections is discussed in Chapter 21.

The Scottish Parliament and Welsh Assemblies were established by legislation passed in 1998 and the first elections were held in 1999. Members to both bodies were elected by the additional member system (whose characteristics are outlined above). Forty members of the Welsh Assembly and 73 members of the Scottish Parliament were elected by the first-past-the-post system. The remaining members (20 in Wales and 56 in Scotland) were elected by the party list system.

European Elections

The 1999 European Parliamentary Elections Act introduced the regional party list system for future elections to the European Parliament. Those held in 1999 were the first to use this new method of election which required the parties to select candidates in each of the regions into which the UK was divided (although voters would be able to opt for an independent candidate). The use of this 'closed list' system of proportional representation enabled individual parties to introduce initiatives to make elected bodies more socially representative. One reform to achieve this was *zipping* which sought to secure an equal number of male and female candidates at these elections.

Zipping

This system, utilised by the Liberal Democrats, entailed candidates being chosen and ranked by ballot of Party members.

System	First Past The Post (FPTP)	Alternative Vote (AV)	Supplementary Vote (SV)	Additional Member System (AMS)	Single Transferable Vote (STV)
How it works	Very simple, the Westminster way. It retains traditional single-member constituencies in which the candidate who gets the most votes wins the election	Single-member constituencies, but voters list preferences among the candidates (1, 2, 3, 4, etc). Unless one gets more than 50 per cent of the first-preference votes - and wins outright - the subsequent preferences of candidates with fewest votes are distributed until someone does pass the 50 per cent mark	Simpler variation of AV, being used to elect London's Mayor. Voters only get two votes. If no one wins in the first ballot, the second-preference votes of candidates with fewest votes are distributed between top two candidates. ('AV-Plus' or 'SV-Plus' is a mixed system in which up to half the seats are not directly elected. Instead they are distributed to candidates on a party list)	Voters have two votes. One would be used to elect up to two-thirds of MPs in traditional way under FPTP. The other would be cast for the party, and remaining MPs would be elected from party lists	Large multi-member constituencies would each have 4 or 5 MPs. Voters list candidates in order of preference and can pick between contenders in the same party as well as rival ones
1997 election result	Lab **419** Con **165** Lib Dem **46** Others **29** **Lab majority 179**	Lab **436** Con **110** Lib Dem **84** Others **29** **Lab majority 213**	Lab **436** Con **110** Lib Dem **84** Others **29** **Lab majority 213**	Lab **303** Con **203** Lib Dem **115** Others **38** **Lab majority 27 short**	Lab **342** Con **144** Lib Dem **131** Others **42** **Lab majority 25**
Pros	Clear result; tends towards stable one-party government; good link between local MP and local voter	Retains direct link between MP and constituents; ensures winner has majority support at local level; fairer to small parties	SV is straightforward. SV and AV Plus variations produce highly proportional results	Produces effective proportional results while retaining constituency link and increasing voter choice	Gives the voter what he wants, no wasted votes and due weight to minority views. Encourages turnout in areas previously 'safe' for one party
Cons	Can deliver near-absolute power via huge majorities on less than half the popular vote; unkind to small parties; limits voter choice	Can produce wildly unproportional results, thanks to tactical voting. Was recommended for Westminster in 1910 and 1916	Under landslide conditions the leading party gets too much dominance at constituency level	Makes it hard for one party to win outright majority and thus gives small parties power out of proportion to their votes or seats	Complex, hard to understand or count votes. Too parochial. Huge 200,000-plus constituencies

Source: the *Guardian*, 19 September 1998.

Separate lists of male and female candidates were drawn up in each region and members were asked to place candidates in order of preference. The two lists were then amalgamated into one which formed the party's slate of candidates for the election.

Zipping described the process used to amalgamate the separate lists of male and female candidates and rank the candidates. The candidate (male or female) with the highest number of first-preference votes would be ranked number one on the regional list. If that person were male, the candidate ranked number two would be the female with the highest number of individual first-preference votes on the 'female only' list. If the most popular candidate were female, she would be ranked first, and the male who topped the 'male only' list would be ranked number two. This process of alternating male and female candidates would continue until the Party had the same number of candidates as there were seats to be filled at the election.

Further Reading

Michael Dummett, *Principles of Electoral Reform* (Oxford: Oxford University Press, 1997). This book provides a detailed account of the operations of various electoral systems and a discussion of what an electoral system is designed to achieve.

A wide range of alternative electoral systems are also evaluated in **David Farrell**, *Comparing Electoral Systems* (Hemel Hempstead: Prentice Hall/Harvester Wheatsheaf, 1997).

Chapter Five | Voting Behaviour

The aims of this chapter are:

---

1 To distinguish between the role performed by candidates and political parties in determining why citizens vote the way they do.

2 To examine the factors which may underpin the support given to political parties.

3 To analyse the limits on social class as an explanation of voting behaviour in the postwar United Kingdom.

4 To evaluate the impact of social and economic changes on voting behaviour between 1945 and 1970.

5 To analyse the emergence of new factors influencing voting behaviour after 1970.

6 To examine the changing nature of General Election campaigns in the United Kingdom.

Factors Influencing Voting Behaviour

Chapter 2 has described the principles underlying representative democracy. Elections constitute the basis to this form of political system. This chapter seeks to provide an understanding of voting behaviour, the study of which is referred to as *psephology*.

There are various reasons which might explain why citizens vote the way they do. These include the personality or track record of candidates standing for public office: in British elections, votes are cast for individual candidates whose appeal might be enhanced by factors such as personality. In the case of *incumbents* (that is, candidates who were elected to public office at the previous election and are standing again, seeking to be re-elected), his or her track record might be important. As is discussed in Chapter 14, in the USA, incumbency has a major bearing on voting behaviour for Congressional Elections, but in the UK is of lesser importance. Here a candidate's affiliation to a political party is far more important than his or her personality.

In most liberal democracies, citizens vote for a political party as opposed to a candidate. The following factors may be important to particular political parties:

○ religion

○ local and regional influences

○ age

○ race and gender.

Religion

In the nineteenth century this was a major factor governing the support secured by political parties. The Conservative Party drew considerable support from the members of the Church of England which was popularly described as 'the Conservative Party at prayer'. Alternatively, support for the Liberal Party was underpinned by nonconformity. The adverse impact of the First World War on religious belief tended to undermine this basis of support for the political parties. In modern times this factor has limited relevance to a voter's party affiliation outside of Northern Ireland, where it remains the crucial factor in determining political allegiance. However, religion provides some influence over voting behaviour in countries such as Germany. In the State of Bavaria, for example, Roman Catholicism underpins the electoral support obtained by the Christian Social Union.

Local and Regional Influences

In many liberal democracies, local and regional influences play a major role in providing the basis of political parties. The Spanish Conservative government, elected in 1996, relied on the support of regional parties from Catalonia, the Basque country and the Canary Islands for its governing majority. In the UK such factors assumed some relevance to voting behaviour after 1960 and was manifested in the support obtained by Plaid Cymru in Wales and by the Scottish National Party. The belief that in political terms Britain comprised two nations – the North of England, Scotland, and Wales (whose voters were more inclined to vote Liberal or Labour when the latter Party replaced the former as the main force on the Left of the political spectrum) and the rest of England (where citizens favoured the Conservative Party) – has been perceived by political scientists since 1918. During the 1980s this factor became prominent when an apparent *North–South divide* emerged (which is discussed below).

Age

In postwar elections it was suggested that younger people were more prone to support the Labour Party than were elder voters, who had a marked tendency to vote Conservative. One explanation for this was the so-called 'life cycle effect': that is, younger electors were more idealistic and favoured social and political change, whereas age brought with it responsibilities and a stake in society which induced suspicion of change.

Race and Gender

In the UK, neither race nor gender underpin any significant political party, but they do exert some impact on the support obtained by the major political Parties. Studies in the 1950s and 1960s observed that men were less likely to vote Conservative and were more inclined to vote Labour. The ethnic minority vote initially assumed minimal significance in British postwar elections due to its small size, but its importance subsequently increased. It has been estimated that at the 1987 General Election, 67 per cent of Asian voters and 86 per cent of Afro-Caribbean electors supported the Labour Party, and that this high level of support was maintained at the 1997 General Election.

Question ?

General Elections are commonly viewed as occasions when the general public select representatives to defend their individual interests, and those of the area in which they live, in Parliament. This implies that electors carefully consider the character and policies advocated by individual candidates and vote for the one they most prefer. However, the above section has argued that a citizen's choice of candidate in the UK is usually governed by factors other than preference for a particular candidate and his or her Party.

Write a paragraph which assesses the importance of any TWO of these issues to voting behaviour in the UK:

○ party

○ religion

○ race

○ nationalism.

In undertaking this research it would be helpful to consider the election results from the last General Election, indicating the extent to which each of these factors influenced the outcome of results locally, regionally or nationally.

Voting Behaviour in the UK, 1945–70

Models of Voting Behaviour

Models of voting behaviour which were developed after 1945 initially drew heavily on American political science. The aim of a model is to provide an explanation for voting behaviour which holds good for a significant proportion of the electorate and, additionally, seems to apply from one generation to the next. In each generation citizens become eligible to vote for the first time, replacing former voters who have died.

The Michigan Model

The main model which seemed appropriate for British voting behaviour was the *Michigan model*, the key focus of which was

	Percentage of popular vote							Seats in House of Commons					
	Turnout	Con.	Lab.	Lib.[a]	Nat.[b]	Other	Swing[c]	Con.	Lab.	Lib.	Nat.	Other	Government majority
1945	72.7	39.8	48.3	9.1	0.2	2.5	−12.2	213	393	12	0	22	146
1950	84.0	43.5	46.1	9.1	0.1	1.2	+3.0	299	315	9	0	2	5
1951	82.5	48.0	48.8	2.5	0.1	0.6	+0.9	321	295	6	0	3	17
1955	76.7	49.7	46.4	2.7	0.2	0.9	+2.1	345	277	6	0	2	60
1959	78.8	49.4	43.8	5.9	0.4	0.6	+1.2	365	258	6	0	1	100
1964	77.1	43.4	44.1	11.2	0.5	0.8	−3.2	304	317	9	0	0	4
1966	75.8	41.9	47.9	8.5	0.7	0.9	−2.7	253	363	12	0	2	95
1970	72.0	46.4	43.0	7.5	1.3	1.8	+4.7	330	288	6	1	5	30
Feb 1974	78.7	37.8	37.1	19.3	2.6	3.2	−1.4	297	301	14	9	14	−34[d]
Oct 1974	72.8	35.8	39.2	18.3	3.5	3.2	−2.1	277	319	13	14	12	3
1979	76.0	43.9	37.0	13.8	2.0	3.3	+5.2	339	269	11	4	12	43
1983	72.7	42.4	27.6	25.4	1.5	3.1	+4.0	397	209	23	4	17	144
1987	75.3	42.3	30.8	22.6	1.7	2.6	−1.7	376	229	22	6	17	102
1992	77.7	41.9	34.4	17.8	2.3	3.5	−2.0	336	271	20	7	17	21
1997	71.4	30.7	43.2	16.8	2.6	6.7	−10.0	165	419	46	10	18	179

a. Liberal Party 1945–79; Liberal/Social Democrat Alliance 1983–87; Liberal Democrat Party 1992–97.

b. Combined vote of Scottish National Party (SNP) and Welsh National Party (Plaid Cymru).

c. 'Swing' compares the results of each election with the results of the previous election. It is calculated as the average of the winning party's percentage-point increase in its share of the vote and the losing major party's decrease in its percentage-point share of the vote. In the table, a positive sign denotes a swing to the Conservatives, a negative sign a swing to Labour.

d. Following the February 1974 election, the Labour Party was 34 seats short of having an overall majority. It formed a minority government until it obtained a majority in the October 1974 election.

The results of British General Election contests between 1945 and 1997. Source: Anthony King et al, *New Labour Triumphs: Britain at the Polls* (New Jersey: Chatham House, 1998).

party identification. This suggested that the basis of voting behaviour was an attachment formed between voters and political parties. It was perceived that an individual's association with a political party was determined by his or her social relationships. The major factor was the family which effectively *socialised* a person into identification with a political party. This explained why a son or daughter tended to vote the same way as a father or mother, effectively translating existing trends of voting behaviour across the generations. This provided an understanding of the stability in the support which the political parties obtained from one general election to the next.

Social Class

The Michigan model (as developed in research conducted by David Butler and Donald Stokes, first published in 1969), explained the phenomenon of *partisan alignment.* This term indicated the existence of a strong attachment between voters and a political party. The choice of party was underpinned by *social class* which dominated explanations of voting behaviour in this period. Labour was viewed as the Party of the working class and the Conservatives were seen as the political vehicle of the middle class and those higher up on the social ladder. This *class alignment* thus formed the basis of assumptions made about voting behaviour in postwar British elections.

The role once played by religion as the basis of party affiliation in the UK was replaced increasingly after 1918 by social class. In 1967, Pultzer asserted the dominance of social class in determining postwar voting behaviour by stating that 'class is the basis of British party politics; all else is embellishment and detail.' The main political parties were thus identified with social class and some of the factors referred to above may relate back to this factor. For example, the high level of attachment of Afro-Caribbeans to the Labour Party may be determined less by race and more by their position in the social ladder. The higher proportion of working class voters in the North of England may help to explain the increased tendency for these voters to identify with the Labour Party.

The Limitations of a Social Class Model

The view that social class was a determinant of voting behaviour was a generalisation which clearly did not apply to all electors. If it did, Labour would have won every postwar general election – the working class was the largest grouping in the electorate. It followed, therefore, that while social class was a key factor in determining why citizens gave their allegiance to political

The views and attitudes of working-class Conservatives were represented by the television character Alf Garnett whose allegiance to the Queen (and Winston Churchill) was mirrored by an intense dislike of the Labour Party and its then leader, Harold Wilson.

parties, it was not a total explanation of voting behaviour. Particular attention was devoted by political science to those whose voting behaviour was *not* underlaid by social class.

Working Class Conservatives

The Conservative Party attracted a considerable degree of working class support at each election held in the period 1945–70: Jean Blondel estimated that between one-third and two-fifths of the working class voted Conservative during this time. The existence of Conservative working class voters presented the Labour Party with a major political choice: to downplay socialism, or to advocate it more aggressively.

❍ *Downplay socialism:* this involved an acceptance that Labour would never secure the support of all members of the working class. Therefore, elections could only be won if the loss of these 'natural' voters could be offset by gaining votes from other sections of the electorate. Downplaying socialism was designed to secure support from middle class voters.

❍ *Advocate socialism more aggressively:* those who advocated this course of action believed it would secure support from those members of the working class who failed regularly to vote for the Labour Party. It was perceived that their disenchantment stemmed from Labour's being insufficiently radical.

THE WORKING CLASS CONSERVATIVE VOTE

Political scientists sought explanations for those whose voting behaviour represented a 'betrayal of class'. The main arguments put forward were:

◆ deference

◆ self-assignment of class

◆ the relationship between social values and Conservative ideology

◆ lack of tradition.

Deference

This view, which was put forward in a study by McKenzie and Silver in 1968, suggested that some members of the working class voted Conservative as they viewed this Party as the natural ruler of the UK, sensitive to the nation's traditions and uniquely qualified by birth, experience and outlook to govern. This study differentiated between deferential Conservative working class voters and those termed 'seculars'. Whereas the former embraced the Conservative

Party because of its perceived 'innate transcendent superiority', the support of the seculars was determined by a satisfactory assessment of the Party's policies and performance. The study suggested that the basis of working class Conservative voting was moving from away from deference towards secularism (especially among younger voters) and this would result in the increased volatility of working class support for this Party.

Self-Assignment of Class

This explanation of working class support for the Conservative Party was developed by Runciman in 1966. This view was especially linked to enhanced working class affluence in the postwar period, which led well paid workers to identify with a higher social grouping. Although they objectively remained members of the working class, they switched allegiance to the Conservative Party.

The Relationship between Social Values and Conservative Ideology

A further theory put forward by Parkin in 1967 was the identity between social values and Conservative ideology. This implied that it was thus 'natural' in the UK to vote Conservative since Conservatives were associated with the key values of British society (private property ownership, and support for the monarchy and for the Church of England). These values were not traditionally sanctioned by the Labour Party. This view (which was derived from a sociological as opposed to a political science approach) could be challenged for making assumptions about the core values of British society and the extent to which these influenced voting behaviour.

Lack of Tradition

The tendency of some members of the working class not to support the Labour Party could also be explained by family traditions deriving from a period when the Labour Party was not a major political force. This explanation would logically decline in significance as older generations were replaced by younger ones whose political views would be influenced by the emergence of Labour as a major political party.

The Middle Class Vote

The voting habits of middle class electors were subject to fluctuation from one election to the next and they were not constantly identified with any of the major political parties. Studies of the 1945 General Election indicate the importance of the middle class vote to the size of Labour's victory. It was subsequently argued in a study by John Bonham in 1954 that a number of middle class voters were not regular supporters of either of the two major parties. The main explanation for the

Conservative victory in 1951, therefore, was that between 1945 and 1951 the Labour Party lost the support of 600,000 middle class voters. One difficulty in assessing the political loyalty of the middle class was in providing a precise definition of such voters. Bonham utilised a very broad definition which suggested the middle class vote comprised around 12 million electors. Other studies estimated that the middle class vote consisted of far fewer electors: the *Economist* on 24 January 1948, for example, referred to a figure of 1.5 million.

Clerks

One particular group of lower middle class voters which were the subject of political analysis were clerks, whom Lockwood described as 'black coated workers' in his study. He argued that these people were poised between the middle and working classes, indulging in middle class pretensions but achieving a working class standard of living. Although clerks increasingly joined trade unions after 1945, Lockwood alleged that there were 'powerful and enduring' features of their work situation which prevented full class identification with either the working or middle classes.

Social Change and Voting Behaviour

In 1957 the then Prime Minister, Harold Macmillan, informed the working class that 'you've never had it so good'. The scale of the Conservative victory at the 1959 General Election (in which large numbers of working class people voted Conservative) led to the assertion that class was no longer of relevance to political behaviour. The operations of the welfare state defused the intensity of class hostility in comparison to the inter-war years (1919–39) and there were two other key social changes which had a potential impact on voting behaviour: *embourgeoisement* and *social mobility*.

Embourgeoisement

This referred to the increased affluence (or prosperity) of some members of the working class, especially those engaged in growth areas of economic activity such as the motor car industry. The real earnings of such members of the working class substantially increased during the 1950s and gave rise to *class hybrids* that is, those who in terms of occupation, education, speech and cultural norms were working class but whose income and material comforts identified them with the middle class. The main political significance of this development was whether such well-off workers would continue to support the Labour Party.

Question

Based on your reading of the above section, list TWO arguments which suggest that social class was not a totally accurate explanation of voting behaviour after 1945.

This issue was investigated in a study of car workers in Luton researched by Goldthorpe, Lockwood, Bechhofer and Platt in 1968. It was concluded that although such workers were affluent, they retained a high level of support for the Labour Party. However, such support was stated to be 'less solidaristic and more instrumental' than that traditionally accorded to the Labour Party by the working class. This suggested that, in the long term, affluent workers might switch their allegiance to other political parties if these seemed more likely to bring them material benefits. Thus Labour had to 'deliver the goods' to be assured of such working class support. This study further suggested that the level of trade union membership in the car industry was a factor which explained these workers' continued loyalty to the Labour Party. This implied that affluent workers in less unionised industries were less likely to retain such voting habits.

Social Mobility

A further change in postwar society was social mobility (which in this context referred to the ability of members of the working class to become members of the middle class). The ability to climb the social ladder was facilitated by the increased educational opportunities made available to a limited number of the working class through the operations of the 1944 Education Act (and latterly the establishment of the 'new' Universities), and was made possible by factors which included the increase in the number of white collar jobs in industry from the 1950s onwards. These arose as the result of the application of science and technology to productive processes which brought about a decline in the number of manual jobs but an increase in the number of clerical, administrative and technical posts. These jobs were filled by upwardly mobile children from working class homes. A study by Abrams in 1962 concluded that such upward social mobility prevented political loyalties from being totally repeated from one generation to the next. He believed that this was to the benefit of the parties of the Centre and Right of the political spectrum.

The Liberal Party 'Revival'

Factors which included social mobility and changes relating to the application of technology to industry attracted the attention of the political Parties after the 1959 General Election. In 1962, the Liberal Party succeeded in capturing the formerly safe Conservative seat of Orpington at a by-election. Although several factors accounted for this victory (particularly the unpopularity of the Conservative government at that time), the one which was seized upon by both academics and the media was that upwardly mobile, young people who lived in the commuter belts outside major cities were transferring their support from Labour to the Liberal Party. The Liberal victory was thus accredited to 'Orpington man' or the 'new' middle class. The Liberal Party deliberately pitched its appeal to such voters, making them the focus of a range of policy proposals which were designed to modernise Britain.

The 1964 General Election provided evidence of a Liberal 'revival'. The Party's total vote rose to just over 3 million (11.2 per cent of the total votes cast in the election) and the number of Liberal MPs increased from the six who had been elected in 1959 to nine.

LIBERAL PERFORMANCE AT THE 1964 GENERAL ELECTION

Analysis of the Liberal Party's performance at the 1964 General Election suggested that although the Party had sought the support from the type of voter described as 'Orpington Man', their additional votes mainly came from other sections of the electorate. These included:

◆ *Protest voters:* these were disenchanted with the record of the Conservative government and turned to the Liberal Party, not because they wished to endorse its policies, but for negative reasons. Theirs was a short term transfer of political allegiance, designed to force changes onto the Conservative Party which, when accomplished, would result in them returning to their former political home.

◆ *Rural voters:* Liberal Party support in this period also derived from rural voters, especially in the areas of the UK in which the Party had traditionally been strong. The term 'Celtic fringe' refers to such areas of traditional strength in South West England, Wales and Scotland. It seemed, therefore, that the Liberal revival of this period was fuelled by rural voters in the remoter parts of the country who were concerned that the government based at Westminster was neglecting them.

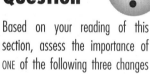

Question

Based on your reading of this section, assess the importance of ONE of the following three changes which affected patterns of voting behaviour after 1945.

○ upward social mobility

○ increased working class affluence

○ support for the Liberal Party in the 1960s.

Voting Behaviour After 1970

After 1970, two significant changes occurred governing the way in which electors in the UK voted.

Partisan Dealignment

Partisan dealignment means that a large number of electors either desert the party to which they were traditionally committed, or identify with the party which they traditionally support far more weakly. A number of factors may explain this phenomenon. These include the increased education and political awareness of many members of the electorate, making them base their vote on logical as opposed to emotional or traditional considerations. They may also perceive that the party they have traditionally supported does not reflect their own views on key issues. The loss of support for the Labour Party in the early 1980s was attributed to the 'swing to the left' which occurred after the 1979 General Election defeat. This move to the Left caused an *ideological disjuncture* between the views and values of the Party and those of its supporters.

Class Dealignment

A further factor affecting voting behaviour after 1970 was *class dealignment*. This means that the historic identity between a political party and a particular social class becomes of reduced significance. Class dealignment can be explained by the reduced intensity of class consciousness in this period, caused by a number of factors which include embourgeoisement (which has been discussed above), the decline in the number of manual workers, and the rise in the service sector of employment. Class dealignment was perceived to have had a particularly damaging effect on the electoral prospects of the Labour Party which failed to win a general election between 1979 and 1997.

Decline of Working Class Solidarity

Although (as has been noted above) the support accorded by the working class to the Labour Party has never been complete, it declined after 1970. One explanation for this has been the impact of a number of social and economic changes after 1970 (and particularly after 1979). Such changes have been explained in *sectoral* terms (which emphasise the political significance of the division between the public and private sectors in both employment and consumption). More generally, these changes have resulted in the *fragmentation* of the working class. Key divisions include:

❍ *The North–South divide:* this suggested that the South of England was more prone to support the Conservative Party and the North of England backed Labour. This division became especially marked during the 1980s and was explained by the relative affluence of the South resulting from Conservative policies introduced after the 1979 General Election. At the 1983 General Election, Labour won only three constituencies in southern England outside of London, and until 1997 made only modest gains in the South in subsequent elections.

○ *The public and private sectors:* this implied that workers in the private sector tended to support the Conservative Party whose endorsement of the market economy aided this sector of the economy. Those who worked in the public sector (which was subject to a range of cutbacks and changes after 1979) were increasingly prone to support the Labour Party.

○ *Property owners and non-property owners:* this suggests that those who owned their own homes (perhaps as the result of the 'right to buy' provisions of the 1980 Housing Act) were increasingly likely to support the Conservative Party, whose support for a property-owning democracy had benefited them. Those who relied on the public provision of housing (which was adversely affected by the policies of the Conservative Party) were more likely to support Labour.

Such divisions were not isolated factors but seem to have had a cumulative effect. This meant, for example, that a relatively well-paid local government employee in the North of England was more likely to support the Labour Party after 1979, whereas a worker who was not relatively well-off but who was employed in the private sector in the South of England was more likely to vote Conservative.

Consequences of Partisan and Class Dealignment

Partisan and class dealignment after 1970 had two main consequences for the conduct of British politics:

○ an increase in support given to third parties

○ a volatility of support for all political parties.

The Increase in Support given to Third Parties

The grip exerted over the electorate by the Conservative and Labour Parties, which were perceived to represent the class interests of capital and labour, was almost total in the 1950s. In the 1951 General Election, 97 per cent of those who voted supported either the Conservative or Labour Parties. In both of the 1974 General Elections this figure had fallen to 75 per cent.

At the February 1974 General Election, the Liberal Party's total national vote increased to over 6 million and prompted the Party's then leader, Jeremy Thorpe, to declare that 'we are all minorities now'. Although this figure was reduced in the two subsequent elections, in 1983 the Liberal Party, operating within the context of an Alliance with the newly-formed SDP, succeeded in securing 23.2 per cent of the vote, only marginally less than the 25.4 per cent obtained by the Labour Party.

As Chapter 4 has argued, the extent of popular support for minor parties has traditionally been masked by the manner in which the first-past-the-post electoral system fail to translate votes cast for a party into parliamentary seats. However, even this began to change. In 1997, the Liberal Democrats polled 16.8 per cent of the popular vote (less than their 1992 figure) yet managed to return a Parliamentary Party of 46, the best performance of a third party since 1929.

The Volatility of Support for All Political Parties

A main consequence of social class determining voting behaviour was that the core support given to the two main Parties was relatively consistent from one general election to the next. Reduced partisan and class alignment made voting behaviour more *volatile*. Electors were less likely to consistently support one political party and more likely to change allegiance between elections (especially at by-election contests), and from one election to another. This affected the main political Parties and also the minor ones. One study conducted of the support obtained by the Liberal Party at the two General Elections held in February and October 1974 suggested that the Party lost around 3 million votes it secured in the first of these elections. This was offset to a large extent by gaining the support in October of around 2 million voters who had not voted for them in February.

The Prospect of Realignment

Partisan and class dealignment might be the prelude of *realignment* in which the relationship between parties and key social groups is redefined and constitutes the new basis of party support. The formation of such new coalitions is usually ratified in what is termed a 'realigning election', which is seen as the start of new patterns of political behaviour. The 1932 American Presidential Election which witnessed the birth of the 'new deal coalition' was an example of this. There is some debate as to whether President Reagan's victories in 1980 and 1984 were based on the emergence of a new coalition. The preference of white male voters in the southern States of America for the Republican Party indicated a major shift in this group's political affiliation. However, such changes have not been sufficient to bring about an era of total Republican political dominance.

ESSEX MAN

Labour's support amongst the working class vote declined after 1979. At the 1983 General Election, the Party polled less than 50 per cent of the working class vote. It was thus concluded that Labour had become the Party of only a *segment* of the working class – those who resided on council estates, who were employed in the public sector or in the 'traditional' manufacturing industries, and who lived in Northern England and Scotland. The traditional working class was viewed as a declining group and this suggested that Labour was facing an electoral crisis. It also provided a key explanation for the Conservative Party's political dominance between 1979 and 1997.

There was a 'new' working class of private sector workers (many of whom were employed in the new service industries) and who were home owners living in southern England. These had prospered after 1979 from the policies pursued by Margaret Thatcher's Conservative government and were inclined towards the Conservative Party. In 1983, Labour's working class support trailed behind the Conservative and Alliance Parties in southern England. 'Essex Man' was a particularly significant factor in the Conservative Party's victories in 1983, 1987 and 1992, being demonstrated by the Party's ability to secure victories in parliamentary constituencies such as Basildon, Billericay, and Harlow. This suggested that the 'new' working class in the South was realigning itself with the Conservative Party, constituting as significant a political development as the transfer of white voters in the southern States of America from the Democratic to the Republican party after 1972.

New Models of Voting Behaviour

The belief of social scientists that the importance of social class to voting behaviour declined after the 1970 General Election resulted in new models to explain why electors vote the way they do. These include:

○ issue voting

○ the consumer model.

Issue Voting

Issue voting or judgemental voting suggested that specific topical events or policies exert an influence on a person's political behaviour. This meant that an elector's choice of political party was determined by the policies advanced by that party. While it would be impossible for an elector to positively identify with

Question

○ In what senses has voting in the UK since 1970 become dealigned?

○ What are the consequences of this for the UK's three main political Parties?

every item of party policy, they would support their party because of a combination of factors based on policies which they deemed to be important, performance in government or opposition, and leadership.

The Consumer Model

This model was suggested in work by Hilda Himmelweit and associates in 1981. It built upon the concept of issue-based voting, and suggested that a person's choice of political party is similar to a shopper's choice of goods in a supermarket. Although 'brand loyalty' may influence the decision to buy a particular product, the consumer will 'shop around' and may purchase a different product because of factors which include value for money or attractive packaging. Similarly a voter may pay close attention to the policies put forward by the various parties and opt for those of a party they have not supported before.

General Election Campaigns in the UK

Aims of Election Campaigns

Election campaigns may fulfil one of three roles:

○ *Reinforcement:* this is designed to reinforce a voter's existing loyalty to a political party.

○ *Activation:* this seeks to mobilise a party's existing supporters and ensure they turn out and vote on election day. The identification by a party of its supporters is an important feature of constituency campaigning.

○ *Conversion:* here the aim is to convert members of the general public and thus gain new sources of electoral support for a party.

The importance of election campaigns has been enhanced by partisan and class dealignment. These factors have resulted in an increased number of voters who are undecided as to which party to vote for or who have transferred their political allegiance to another party. People who change their choice of party are called *floating voters*, the overall number of which has increased. Factors such as perceptions of party leaders, record in government or opposition, and specific policy issues all contribute towards shaping the choice of political party for the 'don't knows' and floating voters.

Changing Styles of Election Campaigns

Canvassing

Electors are traditionally sent election literature detailing the policies of individual candidates and they may be approached by individual candidates or party workers to ask how they intend to vote. This seeks to identify potential or actual supporters of a party and this information can be followed up on election day to ensure that they actually vote.

Political Meetings

Political meetings were the traditional form of political activity, enabling members of the general public to meet those campaigning for political office. At election time, national political leaders would address audiences throughout the country and individual candidates would appear before their local electorates at events referred to as the *hustings*. Political meetings are now a less important feature of election campaigns.

The Role of the Media

Politicians seize the opportunities offered by the media to project themselves to the electorate: the photo opportunity, the walkabout, the press conference, televised debates and political broadcasts have diminished the importance of the old-style political meeting.

Television in particular has had a number of consequences for the conduct of national elections. It provides candidates with an opportunity to address large audiences and 'head to head' televised debates are common in countries with directly elected Presidents. In 1995, an estimated audience of over 30 million people watched the televised debate between Jacques Chirac and Lionel Jospin which was held before the final ballot in the French Presidential Election. In 1998, however, Helmut Kohl refused a televised debate with his challenger, Gerhard Schröder, preferring to put his case for re-election in a speech delivered to the Bundestag.

Even in countries such as the UK with a parliamentary executive, television has tended to focus attention on party leaders and thus transform General Elections into contests for the office of Prime Minister. In such countries, national elections have become 'presidentialised'. Central control over party affairs has been enhanced by this development, which has also tended to reduce the importance of activities performed by local party members. Nonetheless, the personality of a party leader is only one factor among many which can influence an elector's choice of political party: in 1979 James Callaghan was more popular than Margaret Thatcher, yet the Conservatives won the election. However, leadership may be crucial when the outcome of an election is very close. It has been speculated for example that in 1992, had John Smith rather than Neil Kinnock been leader of the Labour Party he might have secured a Labour victory.

Additionally, television has placed emphasis on presentation: major political events such as campaign rallies are carefully orchestrated so that viewers are presented with an image of a united and enthusiastic party. Leading politicians are carefully schooled in television techniques, since the ability to perform professionally on television has become an essential political skill. Advertising companies play an ever increasing role in 'selling' political parties and their leaders. The danger with such developments is that policy may be of secondary importance to what advertisers refer to as 'packaging'.

Use of Technology

Campaigns at national level now utilise technology and market research techniques. Computerised mailing lists, opinion polls and advertising are commonly utilised in an attempt to assess the views of voters and to design and deliver campaign messages. These developments, coupled with the enhanced role of the media, particularly television, are costly. In the USA (where it is possible for politicians and political parties to buy air time) it was estimated that $1 billion was spent on the national elections held in 1992.

Opinion Polls

Opinion polls are distinct from *exit polls*. Exit polls are taken as voters leave polling stations and they seek to assess how that person has just voted. They are used to predict the outcome of a contest.

Opinion polls seek to determine the views of the public in advance of voting, by putting questions to a small group of people. There are several ways in which such a group might be selected. The two main ways are through the use of a *random* or a *quota* sample. The first addresses questions to a segment of the public who are chosen by chance. In the UK, for example, a random sample might consist of every thousandth name on the Register of Electors. A quota sample, however, seeks to address questions to a group of people whose composition is determined in advance. By this method, questions are directed at a group who are perceived to be a cross-section of the public.

Quota sampling will attempt, for example, to reflect the overall balance between old and young people, men and women, black and white, and working and middle class persons.

Polls constitute a major aspect of contemporary political activity. Labour's policy review, 1987–92 (discussed in Chapter 3), made considerable use of opinion polls and sample surveys. Polls are used in election campaigns to:

○ *Assess the views of voters on particular issues:* this enables parties to adjust the emphasis of their campaigns (or the content of their policy) to match the popular mood.

○ *Evaluate the standing of the parties at various stages of the campaign:* polls provide a snapshot of voters' intentions on the days over which the poll was conducted. This may not, however, provide an accurate prediction of how voters will subsequently act.

OPINION POLLS AND VOTING BEHAVIOUR

It is believed that polls influence voting behaviour in one of two ways:

◆ *By creating a bandwagon effect:* this means that additional support is attracted for the party judged by the polls to be in the lead. This arises because voters wish to be associated with a winner, but also because supporters of the trailing party lose heart.

◆ *By providing a boomerang or underdog effect:* this means that voters are induced to support the party which appears to be performing badly in the polls. This is caused in part by sympathy, but also by the complacency of the party in the lead, which may relax and campaign less vigorously.

There is no conclusive evidence that polls exert any significant influence on the outcome of General Elections (although they may be important in by-elections). However, the perception that polls do exert some influence over electoral behaviour has prompted some countries to ban the publication of poll results close to an actual election contest. In France (where the second ballot system is used for elections to the National Assembly and the Presidency), opinion polls are banned from publication one week before the final round of voting.

The Accuracy of Opinion Polls

Although opinion polls are widely used, especially during election campaigns, they are not consistently accurate. In 1995, the polls wrongly predicted a major victory for Silvio Berlusconi in the Italian regional elections (which his party lost) and a clear victory for Jacques Chirac in the first round of the French Presidential Election (in which he was defeated by the Socialist, Lionel Jospin). In 1998, Denmark's socialist prime minister, Poul Nyrup Rasmussen, narrowly secured victory for his Left and Centre-Left coalition in the General Election which opinion polls had predicted he would lose.

There are several explanations for the shortcoming of opinion polls.

○ *Technical problems:* these include the failure by the respondent to understand the question put to him or her (perhaps because it was ambiguous) or the pollster's inability to correctly record the answers which have been given.

○ *Refusal to answer:* some people may refuse to answer the pollsters' questions. This can distort the result if such refusals are disproportionately made by one segment of electoral opinion. It was believed that, in the 1992 British General Election, Conservative supporters were reluctant to admit their preference, resulting in polls which underestimated the strength of the Conservative vote. In the subsequent 1997 General Election polls built in a figure to deal with 'ashamed' Conservatives.

○ *Honesty:* polls rely on those who are questioned to tell the truth. If they fail to do this (for whatever reason) the findings of the poll will be inaccurate.

○ *Opinions may not be translated into actions:* polls assume that those who are questioned will subsequently act in accordance with their expressed intentions. But this may not always happen. Those questioned may not be eligible to vote. Some electors will be more inclined to vote than others. The perception that the Conservative Party's organisation is more successful than that of the other parties in 'getting its vote out' (that is, in ensuring that its supporters turn out and vote) may skew the findings expressed in opinion polls.

○ *The 'last minute swing' phenomenon:* this suggests that members of the general public may alter their minds at the last moment of an election campaign (perhaps on voting day itself) and depart from a previously expressed opinion.

○ *'Too close to call':* polls may find accuracy difficult when the public is evenly divided on the matter under investigation. This was the case in the British 1992 General Election when it was estimated that the Conservative Party's parliamentary majority rested on 1,233 voters in the 11 most marginal constituencies.

Had these voted Labour rather than Conservative, the slim majority would have been wiped out.

SWING

The term 'swing' is used to assess the movement of support from one party to another. It is calculated according to a formula devised by David Butler which is as follows:

$$\frac{C2{-}C1 + L1{-}L2}{2}$$

in which C1 and L1 are the percentage shares of the vote obtained by the Conservative and Labour Parties in election one. C2 and L2 are those Parties' percentage shares of the vote in election two.

Consider the simplified results in the table below: there would have been a 16 per cent swing to the Conservative Party in election two.

In early televised election contests in the UK, swing was graphically illustrated by the use of the 'swingometer'. However, this method of assessing the movement of public opinion from one party to another is accurate only when there are two political parties. The rise in electoral support for the Liberal Democrats, the SNP and Plaid Cymru since 1970 have made it more difficult to accurately assess 'swing'.

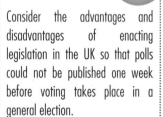

Question

Consider the advantages and disadvantages of enacting legislation in the UK so that polls could not be published one week before voting takes place in a general election.

	Election 1				Election 2	
Party	Vote	Percentage	Party	Vote	Percentage
Labour	30,000	60	Labour	22,000	44
Conservative	20,000	40	Conservative	28,000	56

References

The studies referred to in this chapter are as follows:

Peter Pultzer, *Political Representation and Elections in Great Britain* (London: Allen and Unwin, 1967)

Jean Blondel, *Voters, Parties, Leaders: The Social Fabric of British Politics* (Harmondsworth: Penguin, 1967)

Robert McKenzie and **Alan Silver**, *Angels in Marble: Working Class Conservatives in Urban England* (London: Heinemann, 1968)

Walter Runciman, *Relative Deprivation and Social Justice: A Study of Attitudes to Social Life* (London: Routledge and Kegan Paul, 1966)

Frank Parkin, 'Working Class Conservatives: A Theory of Political Deviance', in *British Journal of Sociology*, 1967

John Bonham, *The Middle Class Vote* (London: Faber and Faber, 1954)

David Lockwood, *The Black Coated Worker: A Study in Class Consciousness* (London: George Allen and Unwin, 1958)

John Goldthorpe, **David Lockwood**, **F Bechhofer** and **J. Platt**, *The Affluent Worker: Political Attitudes and Behaviour* (Cambridge: Cambridge University Press, 1968)

Mark Abrams, 'Social Trends and Electoral Behaviour', *British Journal of Sociology*, 1962

David Butler and **Donald Stokes**, *Political Change in Britain: The Evolution of Electoral Choice* (London: Macmillan, 1st edition 1969: 2nd edition, 1974)

David Butler and **Dennis Kavanagh**, *The British General Election of 1983* (Basingstoke: Macmillan, 1984)

David Denver, *Elections and Voting Behaviour in Britain* (Hertfordshire: Harvester Wheatsheaf, 2nd edition, 1994). This is a relatively brief but illuminating account of voting behaviour during 1950–92. It covers many of the issues dealt with in this chapter in greater detail.

The changing nature of electoral behaviour is also thoroughly dealt with by **Mark Franklin**, *The Decline of Class Voting in Britain: Changes in the Basis of Electoral Choice, 1964–83* (Oxford: Clarendon, 1985).

Eric Shaw, *The Labour Party Since 1979: Crisis and Transformation* (London: Routledge 1994). This book provides not merely an excellent account of the process of modernisation undertaken by the Labour Party after 1983, but it also provides a very informed account of the impact of dealignment on Labour's political campaigning in both the 1987 and 1992 General Elections.

Martin Rosenbaum, *From Soapbox to Soundbite: Party Political Campaigning in Britain since 1945* (Basingstoke: Macmillan, 1997). This work examines national and local campaigning techniques, and analyses the transformation of British electioneering since 1945.

Further Reading

Chapter Six | Parties and Party Systems

The aims of this chapter are:

1 To analyse the role performed by political parties in liberal-democratic political systems.

2 To evaluate the main factors which influence the way in which political parties are formed and function.

3 To discuss the problems faced by contemporary political parties and to evaluate the manner in which their vitality may be restored.

4 To discuss key factors affecting the operation of political parties.

5 To analyse the structure and organisation of the United Kingdom's two major political parties.

6 To evaluate major issues related to the funding of political parties.

Political Parties in Liberal-Democratic Political Systems

The spectre of political parties openly competing for power is often regarded as the hallmark of a liberal democracy. However, while parties are now viewed as indispensable to the conduct of political affairs within liberal democracies, they have not always been seen as helpful to the political process. The American Constitution contained no provisions for party government, and in his farewell address to the Nation in 1796 President Washington bemoaned the 'baneful effects of the spirit of party'. In France, the development of political parties was hindered by a view that they tended to undermine the national interest. However, in both countries parties are now an accepted feature of political life. The current constitution of France (and also of Germany) specifically acknowledges their existence.

Political parties may also exist in countries which do not possess a liberal-democratic political system. The ability to inaugurate meaningful change within society is thus an important qualification required by political parties in a liberal democracy. They should be able to carry out their policies without hindrance from other state institutions.

The Benefits of Political Parties

Political parties aid the operations of a liberal-democratic political system in a number of ways. They are important in:

○ selection of candidates and leaders

○ organisation of support for national government

○ stimulation of popular interest and involvement in political affairs

○ promotion of national harmony

○ patronage.

These points are discussed more fully below.

Selection of Candidates and Leaders

Parties recruit and select candidates for public office at all levels in the machinery of government: national, state, regional and local. In particular, a country's national leaders emerge through the structure of political parties as they provide the main method for selecting a nation's political elite. This function is an important one. In the nineteenth century, monarchs frequently exercised their powers of patronage to select ministers. But with the gradual extension of the right to vote, the composition of governments became determined by popular choice. This choice was facilitated by the development of party.

There are a variety of procedures which parties might use to select candidates:

○ *Choice by supporters of a political party:* the American system of primary elections opens the choice of candidate to a wide electorate. In these elections all registered party supporters are able to select candidates for public office.

○ *Choice by local party activists:* party activists at local level might choose candidates, possibly subject to the approval of the central organs of that party. This is a more restricted electorate, being confined to party members. Such is the practice in the UK in which a key role is played by the constituency organisations in the selection of candidates.

○ *Choice by the central party organisation:* the central party organisation might select candidates, perhaps taking local views into consideration. The party list form of proportional representation may encourage the selection of candidates to be made in this fashion.

Organisation of Support for National Governments

When a candidate has been selected through the party machinery, the party's role is to secure electoral support for its standard bearer. The reliance of candidates on the party organisation thus implies a situation of dependency in which those who are elected to public office are expected to follow the party line. This is important at national level since it provides governments with organised support, and is of particular significance in political structures in which the executive is drawn from the legislative branch of government. In the UK, the party whip system in the House of Commons ensures that governments have the necessary backing to implement their policies. The whip consists of written instructions indicating how the party leadership wishes its members to vote. Members who disobey such instructions may have the whip withdrawn. This entails expulsion from their Parliamentary party and their replacement with an alternative party candidate at the next election. Without the support of party and its accompanying system of party discipline, governments would be subject to the constant fear of defeat. Such organisation also affects the workings of the opposition parties who are thus able to step in to form a government should the incumbent party be defeated.

However, while parties do aid the operations of liberal-democratic political systems, they are not indispensable to it. This is shown by the following examples:

❍ *The United States of America:* candidates for public office often promote themselves through personal organisations, even if they latterly attach themselves to a political party. Membership of a major political party is not essential for those seeking national office. In the 1992 Presidential Election an independent candidate, Ross Perot, secured 19.7 million votes, showing widespread support for a person to be that country's leader who was not associated with either major political party.

❍ *Italy:* in 1995 the President, Oscar Luigi Scalfaro, appointed an ex-banker, Lamberto Dini, to be Prime Minister and head a non-party government whose cabinet consisted of non-elected technocrats. This illustrated that governments can be formed without the initial backing of established political parties. Dini's government possessed sufficient vitality to survive a vote of 'no confidence' in October 1995 which was designed to force an early general election. Dini resigned at the end of that year and subsequently headed a caretaker administration.

Stimulation of Popular Interest in Politics

Political parties are beneficial to liberal democracies because they stimulate popular interest and facilitate public involvement in political affairs. This function is performed through activities which include:

○ *Education:* parties need to mobilise the electorate in order to win votes and secure the election of their representatives to public office. Parties have to sell themselves to the general public. In theory, therefore, a party puts forward its policies and seeks to convince the electorate that these are preferable to those of its opponents. In assessing the arguments which all parties put forward, the electorate thus becomes better informed about political affairs.

○ *Popular participation:* parties enable persons other than a small elite group of public office holders to be involved in political activity. Members of the general public can join political parties and engage in matters such as candidate selection and policy formulation.

○ *Accountability:* although elections provide the ultimate means to secure the accountability of public office holders, parties are a mechanism whereby those who hold public office can be made accountable for their actions. Parties do this by subjecting the activities of their officials to regular, day-by-day scrutiny, and possess sanctions such as deselection or expulsion of those whose conduct is disapproved of by their party organisation.

Promotion of National Harmony

Political parties simplify the conduct of political affairs. They transform the claims put forward by individuals and groups into programmes which can be put before the electorate. This is known as the *aggregation of interests* and involves a process of arbitration in which a wide range of demands are given a degree of coherence by being incorporated into a party platform or manifesto.

Such activity enables parties to promote national harmony. Numerous divisions exist within societies. These may be based upon factors which include class, religion, race, nationality or locality. But to win elections, parties have to appeal to as many voters as possible. In doing this they may endorse policies and address appeals which rise above social divisions, thus aiding the process of national unity.

One consequence of this is to transform parties into 'broad churches' which seek to maximise their level of support by incorporating the claims of a wide cross-section of society. For example, the British Labour Party needs to secure support from a sizeable section of the middle class in order to form a government. Thus it may put forward policies to appeal to such voters. In doing so it bridges the gulf between the working class (whose interests the Party was formed to advance) and the middle class. One political party thus becomes the vehicle to further the claims of two distinct groups in society.

Patronage

Political parties serve as important sources of patronage. They are able to hand out perks and privileges to their members. The party in charge of the national government is in the best position to do this. The chief executive can make ministerial appointments and thus the party becomes the vehicle through which political ambitions can be realised. Party supporters can also be rewarded. In Britain this includes paid appointments to public bodies and the bestowal of a range of awards through the Honours system. This is an advantage in that it encourages politically-minded individuals to work within rather than outside the conventional political system to secure the personal advantages which may be on offer.

Question ?

Present ONE argument under each of the headings below to explain why it might be argued that political parties are essential to the operations of liberal democratic political systems.

- ○ **Selection of leaders**

- ○ **Organisation of support for national governments**

- ○ **Stimulating interest in political affairs**

- ○ **Promoting national harmony.**

Problems Associated with Political Parties

The above section discussed some of the functions performed by political parties within liberal-democratic political systems. This section suggests that some of these benefits are not realised in practice.

Failure to Provide Political Education

The role of parties to provide political education implies that electors vote for a party following an impartial examination of the policies which are put forward during an election contest. But this is rarely the case. The extent to which parties provide education in political affairs is affected by factors which include:

❍ *The relationship between policy and a party's electoral support:* many electors support a political party for reasons which go beyond the policies which it puts forward. These include factors such as traditional loyalty to a party or its association with social class. This suggests that many people are neither receptive to nor interested in detailed discussions of a party's policies or those of its opponents.

❍ *The tendency to resort to trivia or negativity:* election campaigns may be conducted around trivia rather than key issues. Parties may be more concerned to attack their opponents, rather than seeking to convince electors of the virtues of their own policies.

❍ *The desire to follow rather than lead public opinion:* parties may decide that political success depends on following public opinion rather than seeking to lead it. This may induce a party to abandon an ideology or policy which is viewed to be unpopular rather than making strenuous attempts to persuade the electorate of the wisdom of such a course of action.

❍ *The impact of the media:* the importance of television to election campaigns has placed considerable emphasis on presentation rather than on the actual content of a party's programme. This issue is discussed more fully in Chapter 9.

Absence of Popular Involvement

The extent to which parties genuinely foster widespread involvement in political affairs is questionable. This is impeded by factors which include:

❍ *Membership:* parties do not always have a mass membership. In the USA voters do not 'join' a party as they might, for example, in the UK. However, even in countries where individuals can join a political party they do not always do so in large numbers. French and Irish political parties, for example, lack a tradition of mass membership

❍ *Elite control:* those who do join a party are not guaranteed any meaningful role in its affairs. The Italian Christian Democrats, for example, have a mass membership but this has little say on issues such as Party policy. The formal accountability of party leaders to rank and file activists through mechanisms such as annual party conferences is often imperfectly achieved in practice, due to the domination which leaders exert over their parties.

Divisiveness

Political parties do not always seek to promote national harmony. Some may seek to make political capital by

Question

Give TWO arguments to suggest that political parties do not substantially aid the operations of liberal democracy in Britain.

highlighting existing divisions within society. The French National Front has sought to cultivate support by blaming France's economic and social problems on immigration, especially from North Africa. The scapegoating of racial or religious groups, depicting them as the main cause of a country's problems, is a common tactic of the extreme right and serves both to emphasise and intensify existing divisions within society.

Self-Interest

The role of parties as dispensers of patronage may lead to accusations of 'jobs for the boys' or 'snouts in the gravy train'. This may result in popular disenchantment with the conduct of political affairs since politics becomes associated with the furtherance of self-interest rather than national considerations.

Party	Membership
Labour	405,000
Conservative	350,000
Liberal Democrats	100,000
Scottish National Party	30,000
Plaid Cymru	8,000

Country	Party membership as a percentage of the population
Sweden	14.5
Italy	7.4
Belgium	6.3
Denmark	5.1
Holland	2.2
Britain	1.6

MEMBERSHIP OF THE UK'S POLITICAL PARTIES

In mid-1998, the number of members of each of the main parties was as shown in these tables.

These figures suggested that only 1.6 per cent of Britain's population were members of political parties. This constituted a major decrease in political activism: in 1974 the membership of the Conservative Party stood at 1,300,000. Membership of political parties is also less in the UK than in many of her European neighbours, as the following figures illustrate.

Shaping Party Systems

Considerable differences exist between liberal democracies concerning the nature of party systems. Some countries such as the UK, the USA and New Zealand have relatively few political parties. Scandinavia, however, is characterised by multi-party systems. This section considers the main factors which influence the development of political parties.

Social Divisions

The degree of homogeneity (that is, social uniformity) in a country is an important determinant of the formation and development of political parties. Cleavages within a society might provide the impetus for party formation, giving an array of parties which reflect society's main divisions. These might include class, nationalism, religion or race. The following examples illustrate this.

Social Class

In the UK, social class was a key factor which shaped the development of political parties in the nineteenth and early twentieth century. The landed aristocracy was identified with the Conservative Party, the industrial bourgeoisie with the Liberal Party, and the working class with the Labour Party.

Religion

In France, Italy and Germany, religion played an important part in providing the underpinning for political parties. In nineteenth century France the basic division was between clericals and anti-clericals. In the twentieth century, the vote for leftwing parties was weakest where the influence of the Catholic Church was strongest. By the 1960s, however, social class began to play an increasingly important role in determining party affiliation. In Italy, the Christian Democrats initially relied on the Catholic vote, while in Germany the coalition between the Christian Democrats and the Christian Social Union represented a religious alliance between Catholics and Protestants in opposition to the Social Democrats, who were viewed as representative of the secular (or non-religious) interests within society.

Regionalism and Nationalism

Either of these factors may provide the basis of party. Both regionalism and nationalism may arise from a belief that the national government pays insufficient regard to the interests of people living in peripheral areas (that is, places geographically distant from the centre of political power in a country). These feelings are often underpinned by cultural factors. Regional or national self-government is frequently demanded by such parties. Examples include the Italian Lega Nord, the Scottish National Party, Plaid Cymru in Wales, the Parti Québécois in Quebec, Canada, and the Catalan Republican Left and Basque National Parties in Spain.

Political Parties and Social Divisions

The importance of social divisions to political parties is illustrated by the manner in which fundamental changes to a country's economic or social structure might have a significant effect on its political parties. The decline in jobs in the French steel, coal and shipbuilding industries is one explanation for the reduced support for the Communist Party. Immigration has influenced the growth of racist political parties in countries which include the UK, France and Germany. However, while social divisions may provide parties with a degree of popular support, they do not consistently underpin party formation. Ireland is illustrative of the development of parties in the absence of key social divisions.

THE IRISH PARTY SYSTEM

A party system developed in early twentieth century Ireland. This country was relatively unified in terms of race, religion, language and social class. The key issue which divided the nation was a matter of policy – support for or opposition to the 1921 Anglo–Irish Treaty. This provided for the partitioning of Ireland, whereby six Irish counties remained part of the United Kingdom.

In response to this situation, two parties emerged – Fine Gael (which supported the treaty) and Fianna Fail (which opposed it). However, as the treaty issue became irrelevant to the conduct of Irish politics, the parties remained as permanent interests. In this sense it might be argued that the parties became the cause of divisions in Ireland rather than reflections of them.

Political Parties and Electoral Systems

It might appear that the electoral system has a major influence in shaping political parties. Arguments presented in Chapter 4 suggested that the first-past-the-post system encourages the development of a relatively small number of parties (since third parties are discriminated against), whereas proportional representation aids the representation of minor parties in legislative bodies and thus promotes a multi-party system. However, it is inaccurate to assert that proportional representation is the sole explanation for the development of a multi-party system. It has been argued above that parties are based on factors such as the social divisions which exist within society. Proportional representation may thus be justified by the need to ensure that existing social divisions are represented in the composition of a country's legislature.

However, an electoral system may have some influence over the nature of the party system and the conduct of political parties. The first-past-the-post system serves as an encouragement for groups to align with a dominant political party in order to achieve their objectives. Support obtained by the British Conservative and Labour Parties, and the American Republican and Democratic Parties illustrate this phenomenon. This electoral system further provides an inducement for such groups to stay attached to a major party due to the way in which it often works against the interests of minor parties.

Question

Comment on TWO factors which you feel help to explain the nature of the UK's party system.

FRENCH POLITICS AND THE ELECTORAL SYSTEM

The manner in which an electoral system can influence the conduct of political parties can be shown in connection with France.

France has generally used the second ballot for elections to the National Assembly. This electoral system involves a number of second-round contests. Electors may be required to cast votes for candidates who do not represent the party of their choice. This situation (coupled with the emergence of the directly elected Presidency as the key political prize) encouraged major parties and/or their supporters to cooperate. This was referred to as *bipolarisation*.

Bipolarisation emerged during the 1970s and involved the major parties of the Left and the Right cooperating to contest elections. A two-bloc, four-party system emerged. Electoral cooperation amongst the parties of the Left involved the formation of the Union of the Left, which in 1974 narrowly failed to secure the election of Francois Mitterrand to the Presidency. Although subsequent changes to the structure of the French party system have affected this development, in both 1986 and 1993 the main parties on the Right presented a common programme for government.

The Decline of Party?

This section evaluates the arguments suggesting that political parties are in decline, and analyses the steps which have been taken to revitalise them.

The Decline of Major Parties

The early 1990s provided widespread evidence of the loss of support of major political parties, with minor ones benefiting.

❍ *The UK:* 97 per cent of the vote cast in the 1955 General Election went to the Labour and Conservative Parties. In 1964, this figure had declined to 88 per cent. In 1992, it was further reduced to 76 per cent.

❍ *France:* in the 1981 legislative elections the four main parties (RPR, UDF, PCF and PS) secured 93 per cent of the votes cast in the first round of elections. Subsequently there has been a significant move away from the two-bloc, four-party system. In 1993, the four main parties obtained 68 per cent of the vote cast. Further, 2 million voters spoiled their ballots in the second round of the 1993 legislative elections rather than give their support to a major party candidate.

○ *Italy:* in the 1993 legislative elections the support for the Italian Christian Democrats dropped to below 30 per cent.

○ *Austria:* the traditional strength of the Christian Democrats and Social Democrats has been impaired by the increased support for the far-right Freedom Party, although the Social Democrats fared unexpectedly well in the 1995 'emergency' elections.

○ *The USA:* the dominance of the two major parties was broken in the 1992 Presidential Election in which an independent candidate, Ross Perot, secured 19 per cent of the total national vote. He did, however, perform far less impressively in 1996 when he obtained only 8 per cent of the national vote.

Explanations for the Decline of Major Parties

Dealignment

The loss of support for major parties may suggest partisan dealignment and class dealignment. This issue is explored more fully in Chapter 5.

Loss of Confidence in Political Parties

A further problem affecting conventional political activity is people's loss of confidence in the operations of political parties. Evidence of popular distrust towards political parties has been seen in many countries. Although this affects all parties, it has been particularly damaging to the major ones which have been involved in government. This may be explained by a number of factors which are discussed more fully below:

○ inefficiency

○ avoidance of key issues

○ consensus in policy

○ disunity

○ hypocrisy

○ corruption.

Inefficiency

Fears have been expressed that parties are unable to 'deliver the goods': that is they make extravagant promises during election campaigns which they are unable to fulfil if returned to office. During the 1970s the *overload thesis* was put forward as an explanation of this problem in the UK. This suggested that in order to win elections political parties were forced to outbid their opponents and make promises which they could not keep. The result was popular disillusionment with the performance of political parties based on the perception that they were either inefficient or dishonest.

Avoidance of Key Issues

Political parties sometimes seem to avoid tackling what many citizens believe to be key issues of concern. Issues such as the protection of the environment did not always figure as prominently in party manifestos as many people wished. This led to a rise in support for single-issue politics which was frequently conducted by pressure groups rather than mainstream political parties.

Consensus in Policy

Parties were accused of moving closer together in terms of both ideology and policies. Leftwing parties in particular seemed to undergo significant reforms. During the 1980s the British Labour Party embarked upon a number of changes affecting its ideology, policy and organisation which involved embracing the market economy. Similarly, the New Zealand Labour Party adopted Thatcherite monetarist economic policies after 1984. This approach was called 'Rogernomics' after the Minister of Finance, Roger Douglas. However, the perception that parties of the Left and Right were drawing closer together raised the question as to whether parties really 'mattered'.

Disunity

Party disunity might also be cited as an explanation for the loss of confidence in political parties. Parties seemed to be preoccupied with their own internal disputes, to the detriment of national political concerns. In 1995, the then British Prime Minister, John Major, highlighted divisions within his own Party by inviting his opponents to 'put up or shut up'. This triggered a leadership contest in which 89 Conservative Members of Parliament declined to support him and voted for his opponent, John Redwood.

Hypocrisy

Political parties are sometimes accused of advocating courses of action to which their own leading members do not subscribe. In the UK, John Major's 1993 'Back to Basics' campaign (in which traditional Conservative values of self-discipline and the importance of the family were emphasised) was undermined by

John Major's government faced allegations of hypocrisy following the 'Back to Basics' campaign.

accusations that these values were not personally adhered to by all members of the Conservative Parliamentary Party. Similarly, the attempt by the Education and Employment Secretary, David Blunkett, to discourage parents from taking their children on holidays during school term time was undermined by the Prime Minister's actions in taking a holiday which meant his three children missed the start of their school term in January 1999.

Question

What evidence is there to suggest that Britain's two major political parties are in decline? Provide THREE arguments to support this statement.

Corruption

The belief that politicians seek public office to further their own interests rather than those of their constituents or the nation as a whole has had a detrimental effect on the level of support given to established political parties. Accusations of 'sleaze' had a particularly damaging impact on the British Conservative Party's electoral performance in 1997. This issue is explored in Chapter 2. The problem may also be associated with the funding of political parties, which is examined more fully below.

The Reform of Political Parties

It might seem that established political parties face the prospect of losing support. However, it also seems likely that they will continue to carry out important roles within liberal democratic political systems. This is because parties are adaptable and understand the importance of reform.

Reforms to restore the vitality of parties may take a number of different forms. These include:

○ *Membership drives:* attempts have been made in a number of countries to increase the number of citizens joining political parties.

○ *Democratisation:* in countries such as the USA, where local leaderships have often controlled the parties, initiatives have been put forward to introduce democracy. This ensures that members are able to exercise a greater degree of control over key party affairs including the selection of candidates and the formulation of policy.

○ *Financial improvements:* parties are able to perform an active role in political affairs if they are adequately funded. This enables them to perform functions which include publicising their policies, providing aid to candidates, and deploying information technology in election campaigns.

There have, however, been problems associated with such developments. Attempts to increase the membership of local parties may aid extremists in gaining control of organisations, which in turn makes it difficult for parties to appeal to a wide electoral base in order to win elections. What is termed 'coalition building' in the USA becomes difficult if a party is associated with extremist issues. Problems of this nature were also evidenced in the British Labour Party in the early 1980s, resulting in its disastrous showing at the 1983 General Election. The policies contained in its manifesto emerged in the wake of other reforms designed to democratise the internal affairs of the party.

The following sections examine the initiatives which have been put forward to reform key areas associated with the operations of American and British political parties.

The Reform of American Political Parties

The decay of party has been especially pronounced in the USA. In Britain a candidate's party label is crucial in securing support. American elections have tended to be candidate-centred. Incumbent office-holders use their record as a source of electoral support, and candidates utilise personal organisations and fund-raising. Such factors have served to weaken the role performed by parties in political affairs. However, attempts have been made to remedy this situation. The workings of political parties in the USA have been subject to a number of reforming initiatives, particularly directed at the process of nominating candidates and the role of parties in election campaigns.

The Nomination of Candidates

Reform of the nominating process was particularly associated with the Democratic Party and arose following the 1968 National Convention. The McGovern-Fraser Commission, 1969 (and the subsequent reform commissions of Mikulski and Winigrad in the 1970s) succeeded in initiating a number of developments. These included broadening the nomination process at the expense of the control formerly exercised by party leaders, increasing the size and demographic representativeness of the National Convention and the National Committee and introducing a charter containing rules and procedures governing key party activities.

Such developments tended to democratise the workings of the Democratic Party, although subsequent measures undertaken in the 1980s (especially the enhanced status given to selected party members, the 'superdelegates') were not compatible with this process. The Republican Party was less influenced by this process of internal democratisation, although state and local parties sometimes pursued compatible courses of action.

The Parties and Election Campaigns

The Republican Party initially attempted revitalisation through reforms to the role played by parties in election campaigns. This objective was especially associated with Bill Brock, who chaired the Republican National Committee between 1977 and 1981, and resulted in the Committee performing a more constant and active role in electioneering. This course of action was also adopted by the Democrats. Its adoption was influenced by the fortunes of these Parties (the poor showing of the Republicans in the 1974 and 1976 elections and the Democrats' loss of the Presidency and their weak Congressional performance in 1980).

The importance of parties at election time has been enhanced but there are limits to what has been achieved. In particular, the 1974 Federal Election Campaign Act and its subsequent amendments ensured that parties would not dominate the election process, as they do in other liberal democracies, by placing curbs on their fund-raising activities. However, the role of parties has become more prominent in regard to the money they raise and the services which they are able to provide. The ability of the national party organs to give or withhold aid at election times has tended to enhance their power at the expense of state and local parties.

Key Issues Affecting the Operation of Political Parties

This section briefly considers a number of general issues affecting the way in which political parties function.

The Objectives of Political Parties

The main objective of a political party is to secure power and thereby exercise control over government. Parties operate at all levels of government, but a key aim is to determine the composition of the national government, and the policies which it carries out. To achieve this control, a party may operate independently or it can cooperate with other political parties.

Major and Minor Parties

The terms 'major' and 'minor' reflect the level of support secured by parties in a political system. Major parties generally obtain a large degree of electoral support and compete for control of the national government. Minor parties do not generally expect to win national elections: the most they can usually expect is to influence the conduct of the party (or parties) which constitute the national government. In this sense they perform a role in the political system which is similar to that carried out by pressure groups.

However, while minor parties may not be able to secure power at national level, they may achieve this objective at local, regional or state level. In the UK, for example, the Scottish National Party is a main contender for power within Scotland, while the Liberal Democrats have control of a large number of local authorities.

Dominant-Party Systems and One-Party States

It might seem logical to assume that control of the national government should alternate between political parties in a liberal democracy. However, in some countries one party frequently wins national elections. This was so for Fianna Fail (which held office in Ireland for 37 of the 43 years between 1932 and 1973), and for the British Conservative Party which won four general elections between 1979 and 1992. In Germany, Dr Helmut Kohl's Christian Socialist-dominated government was in power from 1982 until 1998.

However, in all of these countries the replacement of the party holding office is theoretically possible. It is the *potential* for change which separates a one-party state from a state in which a single political party is dominant but could be replaced through the process of free elections. For example, while it is inconceivable that the Chinese Communist Party could be voted out of office, the Labour Party was able to remove the Conservatives at the 1997 General Election.

Party Discipline

Members of political parties have obligations towards their party. This is enforced by a system of party discipline which ideally should strike a balance between allowing members to express their views on topical political issues, and the need of party leaders to ensure unity. The arrangements which operate in Britain's two main parties are discussed below in connection with their structure and organisation.

Ideology

A political party is usually guided by a political ideology. Its members are thus inspired by a vision of a society which they wish to create in the country where they operate. Ideology serves as a unifying force between party leaders and supporters: all are spiritually united in the promotion of a common cause.

Ideology is not, however, always an obvious guiding force in party politics. American political parties appear far less ideological than their western European counterparts. Even in these countries, however, ideology may not be a consistent factor affecting political conduct. This may arise for a number of reasons including the nature of political issues which occur in the modern world (these may require expert or intellectual responses, rather than reaction based upon abstract ideology) and the frequent requirement of parties (especially when in power) to respond to events rather than to fashion them. Parties have sometimes been accused of abandoning ideology in favour of *pragmatism* or of redefining their ideology to make them more electable. Developments affecting the contemporary British Labour Party and its ideology are discussed more fully in Chapter 3.

A number of dangers may arise where political ideology is not prominent as a driving force motivating a political party:

○ *'Power for power's sake'*: politicians may be perceived as seeking office for the power which it gives them as individuals rather than being motivated by a desire to reform society. The ambition of individuals to secure power may have a damaging impact on party unity.

○ *Apparent consensus:* the absence of pronounced ideology may result in a situation in which electors find it difficult to differentiate between the political parties. The term 'consensus' is used to describe a situation in which similar goals and policies are espoused by competing political parties. Chapter 19 analyses arguments relating to the emergence of consensus politics in the UK between 1945 and 1979, and again during the 1980s.

○ *Popular disillusionment with conventional political activity:* both of the above situations may result in citizens becoming disenchanted with the main political parties, whose debate becomes centred on which party can manage the existing economic, social and political system most effectively. This may pave the way for the emergence of extremist political parties or result in the growth of extra-parliamentary political activity as mechanisms to bring about meaningful political change.

Structure, Organisation and Finance of British Political Parties

The following section analyses the structure, organisation and financing of the UK's Labour and Conservative Parties.

Structure

A party possesses a formal structure which involves national leadership and local organisation. The main role of the latter is to recruit party members, nominate candidates and contest elections. This organisation is permanent, although it may be most active at election times. The relationship between a party's leaders and its membership varies quite considerably, especially the extent to which a party's leaders can be held accountable for their actions by its rank-and-file supporters. Policy-making is frequently the preserve of the party's national leadership which may also possess some degree of control over the selection of candidates for public office.

Both of the UK's major parties undertook major reforms of their structure and organisation during the 1990s. This section seeks to evaluate the nature of the changes which were made.

Reform of the Labour Party

Labour is composed of two distinct elements – the rank and file members who join local organisations, and the trade unions which affiliate to the Party.

Local Organisation

The basic unit of Labour organisation was traditionally the ward. Representatives of the various wards and also of affiliated bodies (principally trade unions) formed a General Management Committee (later termed General Committee) which managed the affairs of the Constituency Labour Party (CLP). However, the 1993 Party conference approved a reform whereby union members were required to pay a levy in order to become full members of the Labour Party and participate in activities which included the selection of Parliamentary candidates. The local organisation performs a range of key activities, including the selection of candidates for local and national elections, and campaigning to support them in such contests.

National Organisation

The key national body is the Party's National Executive Committee (NEC). With the exception of the Party treasurer (who was elected by the vote of the entire conference), membership of this 26 member body was traditionally organised into a number of sections (with members being elected by the CLPs, trade unions, women members of the Labour Party, and affiliated socialist organisations). However, the organisational reforms approved in 1997 affected the composition of the NEC. Its membership was expanded to 32, the separate women's section was abolished (although the newly-constituted NEC must contain a minimum number of 12 women), and constituency parties lost the ability to elect MPs to the constituency section of the NEC.

COMPOSITION OF THE NATIONAL EXECUTIVE COMMITTEE

From 1998 the composition of the NEC is as follows:

- 6 members elected by Constituency Labour Parties
- 12 affiliated trade union members
- 3 government ministers
- 3 members appointed by the Parliamentary Labour Party and Labour MEPs
- 2 Labour Councillor representatives

◆ 1 Young Labour representative

◆ 1 representative of the Socialist Societies

The leader of the Party, deputy leader, Party treasurer and leader of the European Parliamentary Labour Party are also members of the NEC.

The minimum number of 12 women is secured by the use of quotas in all sections with more than one representative. This means, for example, that three of the members elected by the CLP and six of the trade union representatives must be women.

The NEC has a national panel to deal with internal Party disputes. However, a separate body, the National Constitutional Committee, serves as the Party disciplinary body for individual members. It is the only body with the power to expel a member. Cases may be reported to it by the NEC or CLPs.

The Annual Conference

The annual conference was (and technically remains) the supreme policy-making body of the Labour Party. It was traditionally the mechanism through which individual members of the Party were able to influence its policy through the resolutions which were submitted for debate. The power and role of this body has, however, been influenced by a number of key developments which are outlined below.

THE BLOCK VOTE

There were traditionally two ways to identify with the Labour Party: by joining a local organisation or by paying a political levy to a trade union which was affiliated to the Labour Party. The latter far outnumbered the former, thus enabling the unions to dominate Labour affairs. The union leaders who attended the annual conferences cast the entire union vote on one side or other of an issue being discussed, rather than splitting their vote to reflect differences of opinion which their members might have. This meant that a handful of leaders of the large trade unions were able to control conference proceedings.

Changes to reduce the power wielded by the unions over conference decisions were introduced in the 1990s. In 1990, the NEC voted to reduce the weighting of the union vote so that it constituted 70 per cent of the entire conference vote. It was proposed to subsequently scale this down to the figure of 40 per cent. In 1993, the conference approved the abolition of the block vote for the selection of candidates for the post of leader and deputy leader.

○ *The policy review (1987–89):* this effectively marginalised the party conference as a policy-making body, and this function was transferred to a number of policy review groups. Leading trade unionists were involved in this process and ordinary party members were consulted through initiatives which included the 'Labour listening' campaign.

○ *The Joint Policy Committee:* this stemmed from the organisational reforms which were approved at the 1997 Party conference. The JPC consists of equal numbers from the NEC and government, who work together on policy development, campaigns and elections. It is chaired by the Prime Minister when Labour is in office, and would direct the National Policy Forum.

○ *The National Policy Forum:* this also originated from the 1997 reforms. It consists of 175 members, whose role is to review party policy through the mechanism of policy commissions. It operates on a two-year programme: year one is consultative, and year two involves the drawing up of specific proposals which are then put before the Party conference.

The Party Leadership

The Party leader was initially elected by the vote of Labour Members of Parliament. However, in 1981, an electoral college was set up to considerably increase the numbers involved in this process. Under the initial arrangements, the unions had 40 per cent of the votes in a leadership (and deputy leadership) contest, and the MPs and CLPs, 30 per cent each. Parity (in the form of each of these three bodies having one-third of the total vote in such contests) was approved at the 1993 Party conference, and was implemented for the 1994 leadership election contest at which Tony Blair secured victory.

The Organisation in Parliament

The executive authority of the Parliamentary Labour Party is the Parliamentary Committee. This is composed of members elected by backbench Labour MPs, together with nominees of the Labour leader and ex officio members.

Discipline in Parliament is in the hands of the party whips. Considerable efforts (which are discussed below) were exerted after 1997 to ensure the obedience of Labour MPs to the party line.

○ *New disciplinary procedures:* the ability of the chief whip to suspend MPs from the Parliamentary Party (which had been previously abandoned as a disciplinary measure) was reintroduced by the government's chief whip, Nick Brown. Further, MPs could be expelled from the Parliamentary Labour Party for the vaguely-worded charge of 'bringing the Party into disrepute'.

○ *Reporting MPs to their constituency parties:* a new procedure was introduced whereby those MPs whose attendance was poor, or who disobeyed the party whip, could be reported to their constituency Party. This could result in the errant MP being deselected by a local Party eager to please the national organisation.

○ *Tighter discipline over ministers' Parliamentary Private Secretaries (PPSs):* such unpaid aides to ministers were forbidden from criticising *any* aspect of government policy: previously they were only prevented from criticising the affairs of the department with which they were associated.

DISSENT IN THE LABOUR PARTY AFTER 1997

The Guardian on 3 October 1997 commented that the repression of internal opposition by the measures referred to above, presented the Party as 'a dissent free zone, now entirely under the control of a small cadre of dedicated modernisers'. However, such measures did not entirely succeed in eliminating internal opposition to government policy.

'Rebellions' in which backbench Labour MPs voted against or abstained in key divisions took place in relation to benefit cuts to lone parent families (December 1997), the abolition of student maintenance grants (June 1998), and the amendment to outlaw predatory pricing in the newspaper industry (June 1998).

The chief whip has used disciplinary powers sparingly: three MPs were suspended from membership of the Parliamentary Labour Party between May 1997 and mid-1998 (Tommy Graham, Mohammed Sawar and Bob Wareing) for matters unconnected with dissent towards government policy. One MP (Llew Smith) was, however, allegedly threatened with disciplinary action for campaigning against devolution in the 1997 referendum on the establishment of the Welsh Assembly.

Members of the European Parliament

The relative autonomy traditionally enjoyed by Labour's MEPs was demonstrated in 1994 when 32 of their number signed an advertisement in the *Guardian* which criticised Tony Blair's proposals to reform Clause IV of the Party's constitution. Accordingly, the new Labour government undertook a series of measures which were designed to curtail the freedom exercised by these party representatives.

❍ *A new Code of Practice:* this was drawn up in September 1997 and required members to support Party policy. They were also forbidden from making critical comments in the media concerning the Party's future candidate selection process for MEPs.

❍ *Candidate selection:* the use of proportional representation for the 1999 elections to the European Parliament was accompanied by proposals to ensure a degree of central control (through the NEC) over candidate nomination and ranking: the other two main parties let their members determine these issues. It was perceived that one consequence of the Labour scheme would be to 'cull the awkward squad' and replace them with Blairite loyalists.

LABOUR MEPS AND PARTY DISCIPLINE

The new procedures referred to above resulted in the application of disciplinary measures against MEPs who refused to adhere to the new standards of required behaviour. In October 1997, four Labour MEPs (Ken Coates, Alex Falconer, Michael Hindley and Hugh Kerr) were suspended from membership of the European Parliamentary Labour Party for flouting the rules which prevented them criticising Labour's policy in public. The Labour Party's European leader, Wayne David, accompanied this action with language which was reminiscent of medieval religious intolerance, stating (according to the *Guardian* on 23 October 1997) that these MEPs should 'recant' and pledge to abide by the new disciplinary code to avoid such disciplinary action.

Two of these MEPs (Coates and Kerr) were subsequently expelled in 1998 from the European Parliamentary Labour Party and from the European Socialist Group to which Labour was affiliated. Such measures could be viewed as contrary to the ability of MEPs to exercise freedom of speech and contravened the rules of natural justice, since neither of the MEPs who were expelled had the opportunity to answer the case which they were accused of or nor to appeal against it.

Elections to the Scottish Parliament and Welsh Assembly

The method used by the Labour Party to select candidates for these elections involved centralised procedures. In Scotland, one panel was given the responsibility for drawing up a shortlist for the entire country. Constituency parties had to select local candidates from this list. Although this method was introduced to provide a safeguard against possibilities of local 'sleaze', opponents regarded it as a further example of an attempt to purge the Party of its Left wing.

The Professional Organisation

This consists of the staff who work full time on a number of areas of party activity. It is headed by the general secretary. The professional organisation was for many years based at Transport House, Westminster, and more recently at John Smith House in South London. However, staff and campaigning activities for the 1997 General Election were transferred to Millbank, London, which became identified as the focal point of Labour's General Election campaign. Subsequently, Labour's entire professional organisation was moved to this location.

An Assessment of Labour's Reforms

The reforms to Labour's structure and organisation which occurred after 1997 were underlaid by three main considerations:

❍ *The desire to reduce trade union influence over Labour affairs:* this objective was compatible with a number of developments which occurred during the 1990s and which have been outlined above.

❍ *The desire to reduce the role of the party conference:* this would be more closely stage-managed, in an attempt to prevent the acrimonious debates and in-fighting which had occurred during previous periods of Labour government, especially in the 1970s.

❍ *Centralisation of power:* the Joint Policy Committee in particular seeks to increase the dominance which ministers possess over Labour policy when the Party is in power, thereby securing a dominant role for a small elite.

Reform of the Conservative Party

Major reforms to the organisation of the Conservative Party were put forward in the 'Fresh Future' proposals, drawn up by William Hague in 1997. These were submitted to a vote of Party members whose approval was announced at a Special Reform Convention in March 1998.

Local Organisation

Individual members of the Conservative Party are recruited through a constituency association. The role performed by these bodies is similar to Labour's CLPs. Constituency associations are grouped in 42 new area structures to coordinate Party activity.

National Organisation

The main central body of the Party was formerly the National Union of Conservative and Unionist Associations to which the English and Welsh constituency organisations affiliated. There was a separate Scottish Unionist Association. However, the 'Fresh Future' proposed the establishment of a Board of Management. This body would become the supreme decision-making body on all matters relating to Party organisation and management, with direct powers over Central Office, senior Party appointments, and spending. It would also be responsible for Party finance and membership, providing the central organisation with the ability to refuse membership to any individual, to replace or remove constituency officers, and to disband associations. It would also oversee campaigning and organise and administer the Party conference. It is chaired by the Party Chairman, who is appointed by the leader. The remaining 13 members are either directly elected by the National Convention or serve by virtue of the offices they hold within the Party (such as the leader in the House of Lords and the chairman of the 1922 committee). Subject to the Board's approval, the leader may nominate one further member.

Key activities of the Board (in connection with candidate recruitment, conference preparation and management, membership subscriptions and guidelines for the National Membership list) are discharged by sub-committees, which may include individuals who were not members of the Board of Management.

The Annual Conference

This body never traditionally possessed the power of its Labour counterpart, and tended to display subservience to the leadership especially when the Conservatives formed the government. The 'Fresh Future' reforms supplemented the varied functions of the annual conference and the spring assembly by:

❍ *The National Conservative Convention:* this body seeks to enhance the relationship between the leadership and membership. It is composed of key local and regional officers who meet twice each year. Its meetings are attended by the party leader, party officers and members of the Board of Management.

❍ *The Conservative Policy Forum:* this body's main role is to ensure that political discussion was encouraged throughout the party. It organises regional policy congresses to survey the views of members, and makes policy proposals to the party conference.

The Party Leader

Until 1965, the leader of the Conservative Party was chosen by a process of informal soundings in which a small elite constituting the Party's 'establishment' exercised a dominant role. The last occasion when this method was used occurred in 1963 when Lord Alec Douglas Home replaced Harold Macmillan. Subsequently a process of electing the leader was introduced, whereby Conservative MPs were responsible for initiating challenges to an existing leader, nominating candidates and determining who would lead the Party. This process (subject to amendment in 1975) was used on six occasions. These were to elect Ted Heath (1965), Margaret Thatcher (1975, and to re-elect her in 1989), John Major (1990, and to re-elect him in 1995) and William Hague (1997). In the latter case, however, Hague submitted the choice by the MPs to Party members who endorsed it (and the organisational reforms which he pledged to introduce) by the margin of 143,299 to 30,092.

There were three problems with the old method used to elect the Conservative leader:

❍ *It was a complex procedure:* in order to win on the first ballot, a candidate required an overall majority and a lead of 15 per cent over the runner up.

❍ *Annual contests:* this was introduced in 1975, prior to which there was no mechanism to remove a leader once elected. This applied regardless of whether the Party was in government or opposition, and presented the possibility that a small minority of dissentients could trigger a contest. The result of one contest, rather than proving final, could mark the commencement of a war of attrition against the Party leader.

❍ *Candidates did not have to enter the leadership contest at the outset:* this meant that it was possible to use a 'stalking horse' (that is, someone who had no realistic prospects of victory, but who 'tested the water' to see whether a challenge to an existing leader by a more established candidate was feasible).

THE NEW ELECTION PROCEDURE

The 'fresh future' reforms introduced a two-stage process to elect the Conservative leader.

◆ *Stage 1:* this involves a ballot of Conservative MPs. It is necessary for a candidate to obtain the support of 10 per cent of Conservative MPs in order to stand in such a ballot. Any candidate who secures over 25 per cent of the votes cast in this first-round ballot is eligible to enter the second round.

◆ *Stage 2:* grassroots members of the Party choose the leader from the successful participants of the first ballot. The victor is determined by a simple majority on the basis of one member, one vote.

Under these new proposals, MPs alone are able to trigger a contest. One-quarter (or 45, whichever is the fewer) of MPs could trigger a vote of no confidence. If the leader fails to get 51 per cent of the vote of the MPs, he or she is not eligible to stand as a candidate in the ensuing leadership contest.

Organisation In Parliament

Conservative MPs meet as the 1922 Committee. This took its name from the gathering of Conservative MPs who voted in 1922 to end Conservative support for the premiership of David Lloyd George, and to contest the next General Election on an independent basis.

As with Labour, Party discipline was under the control of the Party whips. Their inclination to use the ultimate disciplinary sanction of withdrawal of the whip was, however, not used. This meant that between 1992 and 1997 dissent by Conservative MPs towards the actions of their own government, and improper conduct by a minority of Conservative MPs went officially unpunished. Disunity and sleaze significantly contributed to the scale of John Major's defeat in 1997.

Accordingly, reforms were introduced designed to deal with the behaviour of Conservative MPs:

○ *Integrity:* the 'Fresh Future' proposed the establishment of an Ethics and Integrity Committee, chaired by a Queen's Counsel (a senior barrister), to investigate any case of misconduct referred to it by the Party leader or Board of Management. It possesses the power to suspend or expel those who behave improperly.

○ *Applying tighter discipline to MPs:* one immediate casualty of the new emphasis on discipline was Peter Temple-Morris, Conservative MP for Leominster. He was dissatisfied with Hague's declaration that Britain would remain outside a single European currency for the lifetime of two Parliaments, and publicly questioned his continuing commitment to the Party. The party whip was withdrawn from him in 1997, and the following year he 'crossed the floor' and joined Labour.

Professional Organisation

The Conservative central organisation is termed 'Central Office', and is headed by the Party chairman. It is staffed by full-time employees and its role is to provide guidance and coordination of the Party throughout the country, to advise and assist constituency Parties, and to provide services (such as information to the public). The 'Fresh Future' proposals gave Central Office a new function with regard to the implementation of a national membership scheme. A Membership and Marketing Department was established within Central Office to oversee this initiative.

Assessment of Conservative Reforms

The reforms embarked upon by William Hague were underlaid by the following principles:

○ *Centralisation:* the reforms reflected a desire to subordinate all elements of the Party (including the Parliamentary Party) to an enhanced degree of central direction enforced by innovations which include the Board of Management.

○ *Democratisation:* the desire to involve grassroots members to a greater extent in Party affairs was evident in the establishment of the Conservative Party Forum and the facility whereby Party members would elect the leader. Hague subsequently sought to extend this to policy by proposing in 1998 that the Party membership should be balloted to endorse his opposition to European monetary union in the next General Election.

○ *Unification:* the reforms served to create a Party structure which was more unified than had been the case previously. The Party's first written constitution was at the heart of the new arrangements which provided a framework for the unification of the elected, professional and voluntary components. These reforms established that the leaders of all other Parliamentary groups would come under the authority of the Party leader.

Question

?

Compare and contrast the structure and organisation of any TWO of Britain's political parties. Which, in your view, is the more democratic of the two you have selected for study?

FACTIONS AND TENDENCIES

Pressure groups are sometimes found within political parties. There is a basic division between a *faction* and a *tendency*.

◆ *Faction:* this is a group with organisation and a reasonably stable membership. It may be viewed as 'a party in a party'. The Italian Christian Democrats, for example, are sometimes described as a coalition of several factions.

> ◆ *Tendency:* this consists of people within a party who share common opinions and emotional ties but who do not possess formal organisation. The 'Thatcherites' constituted an example of a tendency within the British Conservative Party.

Think Tanks

Think tanks are bodies concerned with the promotion of ideas and the development of policy. They may be entirely independent bodies such as the Institute of Economic Affairs. This was founded in 1955 and seeks to promote the advancement of learning through research into economic and political issues, by the education of the public in such matters, and by the dissemination of ideas, research and the results of research. Other think tanks are identified with particular political parties which may involve formal links (such as exists between the Fabian Society and the Labour Party). Others are associated with a party even if their membership is not necessarily confined to active party members. Examples of think tanks include:

○ *Demos:* although associated with Labour, this is an independent think tank, committed to radical solutions to long-term problems. Formed in 1993, it seeks to develop ideas which will shape the politics of the twenty-first century, and to improve the breadth and depth of political debate. It brings together people from a wide range of backgrounds in business, academia, government, the voluntary sector and the media to share and cross fertilise ideas and experiences.

○ *Centre for Reform:* this is a public policy think tank, pursuing the values of Liberal Democrats, but open to all progressive-minded people who wish to debate social, economic and political reform. Formed in 1988, it seeks to develop connections with policy makers and academic and other researchers sympathetic to Liberal Democrats, and commissions working groups to investigate policies.

○ *The Adam Smith Institute:* this was established in 1977 to develop policies associated with a market economy. A particular objective was to develop approaches designed to promote personal initiative.

Financing British Political Parties

British political parties are funded from a number of sources. These include:

❍ the State

❍ subscriptions

❍ sponsors and donors.

The State

In some countries, the State makes financial contributions towards the operations of political parties. This is so in Germany (in which parties represented in the Bundestag receive financial aid based on their popular support) and in the USA (where the Federal Election Commission gives grants to candidates contesting the office of President). Although there is no state funding of political parties in the UK, they do benefit from a wide range of resources which are funded by the taxpayer. The official opposition party receives financial aid towards the operation of their Parliamentary organisation. In 1998, for example, the Conservatives received around £250,000 (which contributed towards William Hague's salary as leader of the opposition, the salaries of the whips, and Hague's car driver). This sum also included around £88,000 towards the salaries of civil servants who were attached to the Conservative whips office.

Additionally political parties are given free radio and television time each year in which to address the electorate through party political broadcasts. In 1998, the Labour government proposed to limit such broadcasts to elections. Political parties also receive a range of additional benefits at election time. These include free postage for the election addresses of their candidates and the free hire of halls for public meetings.

Subscriptions

Members of political parties pay an annual membership subscription. This contributes towards the funding of the party at all levels of its organisation.

Sponsors and Donors

The accounts of the Labour Party differentiate between *sponsors* and *donors:* the former make regular payments to the funds of the Party (for example, through standing orders or direct debiting arrangements), whereas donors make 'one-off' gifts. In 1996, this Party claimed to have 80,000 donors and 65,000 sponsors.

The parties traditionally relied on financial support from sectional groupings. The Labour Party received funding from the unions (who in 1986 contributed over 77 per cent of the

Party's annual income), and the Conservatives were funded by big business. However, in more recent years the pattern of funding has altered: the financial importance of the union contribution to the Labour Party has significantly declined (and in 1996, for the first time in the Party's history, was below 50 per cent of the Party's income), whereas aid from business has increased. In 1996, for example, business contributions to the Labour Party were received from David Sainsbury, British Gas, the Sun Life Corporation and Tate and Lyle. Labour's new reliance on corporate finance was, however, adversely affected by the decision announced by Sainsbury's in 1998 that it would no longer sponsor the Party because this involvement breached the company's ethical guidelines.

Donations were also made to a number of senior Labour politicians in the lead-up to the 1997 General Election to enable them to fund the operations of their political offices. These were paid into 'blind trusts' so that the recipient was not officially aware of the identity of the donor.

Additionally, Labour Party policy development was funded by private donations. Such included research into tax policy which was conducted by the Smith Political Economy Unit between 1996 and 1998. The Labour MP Geoffrey Robinson was a key donor to this organisation.

Problems Associated with Funding

General election campaigns place considerable financial burdens on political parties.

THE COST OF ELECTION CAMPAIGNS

Fighting a modern general election is a costly business. In 1997 it was estimated that the spending of the three main political parties was:

◆ Conservative Party: £28.3 million

◆ Labour Party: £25.7 million

◆ Liberal Democrats: £2.3 million

In August 1998, it was announced that Labour was planning to build an election fighting fund of £50 million.

The high cost of contemporary electioneering (in addition to their routine running costs) forces parties to rely on donations. However, while many who donate to political parties do so because they support the party and the ideology and policies with which it is associated, there is a danger that some who donate to the funds of political parties are motivated (or, perhaps more importantly, might be perceived by the ordinary public as being guided) by factors such as the pursuit of personal or commercial advantages.

Following the 1997 General Election campaign, a number of incidents illustrated the potential problems associated with donations:

Labour's Ecclestone Donation

In January 1997, the head of Formula 1 racing, Bernie Ecclestone, made a donation of £1 million to the Labour Party. Soon after the election the Health Secretary, Frank Dobson, announced a ban on tobacco sponsorship for sport. Ecclestone had a meeting with the Prime Minister to seek an exemption for Formula 1 racing, on the grounds that the global nature of the sport made such a ban inappropriate. This pressure succeeded. There was no evidence that the donation to the Labour Party had secured a shift in its policy (an accusation which was denied by Ecclestone), but there was a danger that the public might infer that influence over government policy could be bought. The chairman of the Standards in Public Life Committee, Sir (later Lord) Patrick Neill, advised the Labour Party to return this donation, which they did. The gap in its funds was subsequently filled by a donation of the same amount from the London restaurant, Planet Hollywood.

The Conservative Party's Hong Kong Connection

Financial donations to the Conservative Party came under scrutiny after the 1997 General Election. Around £1.5 million had been received from the Ma family in Hong Kong, one of whose members (Ma Sik-Chun) was alleged to have had connections with the drugs trade. Subsequently, the Conservative Party was asked by the family to refund around £1 million on the grounds that they had failed to keep their side of the bargain which was to lift the threat of prosecution against Ma Sik-Chun.

Cash for Access

The *Observer* on 19 July 1998 alleged that the government was using lobbying firms to secure donations to Party funds from their corporate clients. A financial contribution to the Party would be exchanged for the chance to dine with a junior minister, select committee member or MP at social events such as the Party's annual conference gala dinner. The Conservative

Party also 'sells' access to its front bench in return for donations to Party funds but makes no use of lobbying firms as middlemen.

Reforms to the Funding of Political Parties

In the late 1990s, both major Parties introduced reforms which sought to remedy some of the problems which had been identified above.

❍ *The Labour Party:* in 1996 it agreed to publish the identity of any individual or organisation which contributed over £5,000 in one calendar year to the Party's funds. It did not, however, identify the amount which had been donated. Increased reliance was also placed on 'sponsorship deals' which included the cost of Party events being subsidised by business and commercial interests.

❍ *The Conservative Party:* in 1997 William Hague stated that the Party would list its major donors and would henceforth accept no foreign donations (that is, financial aid contributed by those ineligible to vote in a UK election).

Other reforms which might be considered are set out below.

❍ *Capping the national expenditure of political parties:* in the UK spending has been limited in individual constituencies since 1883, but spending by (or on behalf of) a party nationally is unregulated. In other liberal democratic political systems (such as New Zealand or Scandinavia) national spending is limited to ensure that at election times all parties contest on an 'equal playing field'.

❍ *State funding of political parties:* this usually places limits on additional party expenditure. A principle has to be devised to determine which parties secure funding. In Germany electoral success is a main determinant of such aid, but this discriminates against new parties. The system also requires strong policing to prevent parties circumventing the limits on their spending. Such problems led to Italy abandoning the State funding of parties following a referendum in 1993.

LORD NEILL'S PROPOSALS TO REFORM PARTY FUNDING

In 1997, the chairman of the Standards in Public Life Committee, Sir Patrick (and subsequently Lord) Neill, initiated an enquiry into the funding of British political parties. His report, in 1998, included the following proposals:

◆ Foreign donations should be banned.

- ◆ All national donations over £5,000 and local donations of over £1,000 should be made public.

- ◆ Anonymous donations of £50 or more should be banned.

- ◆ Blind trusts should be abolished.

- ◆ Party campaign budgets at General Election campaigns should be capped.

- ◆ State funding of opposition parties should be increased and a fund would be established to aid policy research.

- ◆ Shareholders would be required to approve donations and sponsorship by their company to political parties.

Lord Neill proposed that the reforms to party funding which he put forward should be enforced by severe sanctions (including fines for overspending during election campaigns) and be policed by an elections commission.

Question

Make a personal study of any ONE UK political party. To do this, gather information using the following headings:

○ **Membership:** how do members of the public join this party?

○ **Power:** who makes the key decisions in this party and what facilities exist for ordinary party members to influence such decisions?

○ **Leadership:** how is the party leader chosen?

Further Reading

Alan Ware, *Political Parties and Party Systems* (Oxford: Oxford University Press, 1996). This book provides a comparative evaluation of political parties and party systems. It contains much valuable material on the UK, France, Germany, the USA and Japan.

Lynton Robins, **Hilary Blackmore** and **Robert Pyper**, *Britain's Changing Party System* (Leicester: Leicester University Press, 1994). This work discusses a number of key issues related to the structure, composition, ideology, and policy of political parties in the UK.

Chapter Seven | The Public Policy-Making Process

The aims of this chapter are:

> 1 To discuss the policy-making cycle.
>
> 2 To distinguish between the main approaches adopted towards the study of policy-making.
>
> 3 To compare and contrast rational and incremental models of policy-making.
>
> 4 To evaluate the key agents involved in the policy-making process.

The Policy-Making Process

Public policy-making is a very complex area of study. This chapter, therefore, seeks to provide an introductory examination of the subject. It confines itself to public policy-making in which key choices are made by political agents or *actors*.

The Policy-Making Cycle

Policy-making involves a number of stages. The key ones are as follows:

❍ *Policy initiation:* policy-making is selective in the sense that some needs and requirements are acted upon by policy makers whereas others are not. A key aspect of studying policy-making is concerned with explaining the forces which ensure that some ideas and suggestions for action are taken up while others are ignored. *Agenda setting* is a key aspect of this stage.

❍ *Policy formulation:* this is concerned with explaining the mechanics of the process whereby ideas or objectives are translated into a specific set of policy proposals (such as legislation) which can then be executed.

❍ *Policy implementation:* once specific proposals have been formulated, they can be put into operation. This is termed 'implementation'. The way in which decisions are implemented and the forces which influence policy need to be analysed in order to explain why a decision may not be carried out to the total satisfaction of those who made it.

❍ *Policy evaluation:* this is concerned with monitoring the extent to which policy succeeds in accomplishing the goals which were initially intended. Policies which fail may need to be revised in order to attain such objectives. This may require the policy-making process to begin again, initiating new proposals to remedy the deficient outcomes of the old. It is in this sense that policy-making is viewed as a *cycle*.

Policy Implementation

A major concern with the study of public policy-making is the extent to which policy works – that is, achieves the intentions of those who devised it. The concept of *perfect implementation* suggests that policy outcomes mirror the intentions of policy makers. However, this is not usually the case. There are a number of explanations for what is sometimes termed an *implementation deficit* (that is, the differences between the initial intentions of the policy makers and the consequences of the policy which is put into operation). These include the following:

❍ *Unclear or unrealisable goals:* the intention of those who make decisions may not always be expressed in a sufficiently precise way. Ambiguities concerning aims may result in those who carry policy out placing different interpretations on their responsibilities.

❍ *The structure of government:* the political structure of a country may exert a crucial bearing on the manner in which policy is administered. Factors such as the division between the legislative and executive branches of government, and federal or unitary political arrangements may account for the implementation deficit. This may arise from poor communication between the branches or tiers of government or may result from political differences between them.

❍ *Inadequate financing:* the impact of policies may suffer from inadequate funding. In Britain this problem is especially likely to occur when central government specifies objectives which are then left to local government to implement. If the programme is not specifically funded by central government, local authorities may be unable to achieve the desired outcomes.

❍ *Resistance to the policy maker's proposals:* the aims and proposals put forward by policy makers may meet with resistance. Reservations may be expressed by members of bureaucracies charged with implementing the proposals or by those who will be on the receiving end of them. Objectives or policies may have to be modified to overcome such resistance. This situation suggests that the stages involved in policy-making are not discrete but, rather, overlap.

○ *The organisation of the machinery of government:* this may account for differences between intentions and outcomes. The physical separation in the United Kingdom between those who make policy and those who implement it (implicit in the agency arrangements which are discussed in Chapter 12) may have an important bearing on this issue. The overall coordination of the machinery of government (discussed in Chapter 13) may also impede the attainment of objectives.

Approaches to the Study of Policy-Making

Martin Burch and Bruce Wood identify two broad approaches to the study of policy-making. These are:

○ *Behavioural analysis:* this focuses on how decisions are made. In particular, it seeks to provide an understanding of the institutional setting in which policy is made, by focusing on the issue of rationality.

○ *Structural analysis:* this area of study is concerned with an analysis of who makes decisions. It seeks to provide an understanding of the groups who contribute to decision-making in society. An assessment of the relative importance of various contributors to decision-making includes a more general appreciation of the distribution of power within society (see pages 175–7).

Behavioural Analysis

Behavioural views of policy-making concentrate on the process which policy makers use to make decisions. There are two key schools of thought concerning the manner in which policy makers take decisions. The two models derived from these schools of thought, the *rational model* and the *incremental model*, are discussed below. The behavioural approach stemmed from an earlier concern with the structure of organisations, which is first discussed.

The Structure of Organisations

A belief that organisation was the key to efficient policy-making was put forward in the writings of the American, F. W. Taylor, in the early years of the twentieth century. He sought to organise industrial management according to scientific principles. Subsequently Max Weber attempted to formulate principles for the operations of bureaucracy which were based upon the idea of formal rationality. In *The Theory of Social and Economic Organisation*, published in 1947, Weber put forward a number of characteristics which defined bureaucracy. These were designed to show the best possible way for work to be organised. The main principles were:

❍ *A continuous organisation with a specified function or functions, whose operations were bound by rules:* written records were the main means of ensuring continuity and consistency within the organisation.

❍ *Division of labour:* personnel were organised on the basis of hierarchy. The span of authority within the hierarchy should be clearly defined, and the rights and duties of officials at each level should be specified.

❍ *Staff were separated from ownership of the means of administration or production:* they were subject to authority only in connection with their impersonal official obligations.

❍ *Staff were appointed on the basis of impersonal qualifications:* promotion would be according to merit.

❍ *Staff were paid fixed salaries and had defined terms of employment:* the salary scale would be graded according to the position occupied in the hierarchy. Employment was permanent with a certain degree of security of tenure. Pensions were usually paid on retirement.

Weber's approach suggested that the manner in which work was organised underpinned efficient policy-making. Other commentators, however, believed that this depended on the nature of the decision-making process used by organisations. The remainder of this section discusses two key models of decision-making – the rational and incremental approaches.

The Rational Model

A major contribution towards the study of decision-making within organisations was provided in Herbert Simon's *Administrative Behaviour*, which was published in 1945. He extended the earlier emphasis on organisations by analysing the processes through which decisions were made. The rational approach to policy-making suggests that, once a problem has been identified, the response to it proceeds through a series of logically-ordered stages. These are shown on page 168.

The rational model of policy-making has a number of strengths. These include the suggestion that organisations should have clearly defined goals to direct their operations and that a range of options should be considered before a decision is taken. The disadvantage of this approach is that policy-making is primarily viewed as an intellectual exercise. This tends to underplay the political environment within which public policy is fashioned.

STAGES IN THE RATIONAL APPROACH

The following stages outline the goals, values or objectives which guide the actions of the decision maker.

◆ Identification of all possible ways through which the solution to the problem might be achieved.

◆ Consideration of all possible consequences (the *costs* and *benefits*) arising from the adoption of each of the responses.

◆ Comparison of each alternative and its consequences with the other alternatives.

◆ Selecting the alternative (and its attendant set of consequences) which offered the most effective solution to attaining the decision maker's goals, values or objectives.

Politics may render it unnecessary to consider every conceivable response to an identified problem. To address this criticism, a second edition of Simon's *Administrative Behaviour*, published in 1957, put forward the notion of *bounded rationality*. This accepted that a decision maker did not have to examine each and every alternative course of action which might theoretically respond to a problem. Instead, it was acceptable to conclude the analysis of choices when one had been found which was 'good enough': that is, it offered an *adequate* rather than *total* advancement of a policy maker's goals. This was referred to as 'satisficing', as opposed to optimising behaviour.

The rational approach to policy-making exerted some influence on the operations of British government after the 1960s as is shown by the following examples.

PESC

In 1961 the Public Expenditure Survey Committee (PESC) was introduced as a mechanism to enable central government to exert control over the level of public spending. The overall level of public spending was set as a percentage of the gross national product, a formula designed to ensure that spending and economic resources were related. The essence of this system of control was that expenditure proposals were subject to rigorous scrutiny, including an analysis of the aims which proposals sought to accomplish and the total level of spending they would require across a number of financial years. However, while founded on a rational model of policy-making, many of the decisions seemed to be governed by incremental considerations (see pages 170–01).

There were, however, a number of problems associated with the PESC exercise. Money was allocated to specific programmes on the understanding that, once approved, funding would be forthcoming until their conclusion. Factors such as inflation resulted in initial estimates of the resources required being wildly exceeded, while the failure of the economy to grow at the predicted rate resulted in the public spending assuming a greater proportion of the gross domestic product than had originally been planned for. In 1976, the PESC exercise was replaced by cash limits. This system was governed by resources rather than programmes. Departments had a greater freedom to spend the money which was allocated to them, but it would not be supplemented by additional funds when it became exhausted. Any overspending in one financial year was clawed back in the following.

The Corporate Approach to Local Government Affairs

A particular criticism of the operations of local government in the early 1960s was directed at *departmentalism*. A local authority was essentially the product of a large number of individual activities performed by separate departments (such as Housing, Education, Town and Country Planning, and Environmental Health). These were largely independent and it was difficult to exercise strategic control over all the operations conducted by the Council. This, however, became necessary when increased financial constraints on local government required it to prioritise its activities to ensure that those deemed to be most important to local residents would be pursued to the detriment of the more peripheral functions.

The corporate approach was seen as a response to these problems. This may be defined as taking an overall view of the work of a local authority, deciding what it should do and guiding its activities towards the achievement of those purposes, in order to match community needs with the limited resources at the local authority's disposal. It involved two key processes.

○ *Corporate management:* this concerned the development of a new administrative structure able to take strategic decisions about the *entire* work of a local authority. This new organisation frequently took the form of a policy and resources committee, composed of senior councillors and supported by a central committee of chief officers (usually termed the management team).

○ *Corporate planning:* this was concerned with the policy-making process adopted by the new management team. It proceeded in a logical series of steps, similar to those outlined above in connection with the policy-making cycle.

One advantage of the corporate approach was that the key aims and policies of the local authority were contained in one document, *the corporate plan*, which was available to members of the public, who could become more informed concerning the work of their local authority. However, as is discussed in Chapter 17, a number of criticisms were directed at this approach. These included the centralisation of power within a local authority whereby all key decisions were taken by a relatively small group of councillors and officers. This resulted in other councillors being frozen out of the decision-making process, and residents feeling that the council and the services which it provided were remote.

The perception that the decision-making structure of local government was the key to its performance and efficiency was subsequently put forward by the then Environment Secretary, Michael Heseltine, in a green paper published in 1991. A number of reforms were proposed to streamline the decision-making process which included the establishment of an executive branch such as a directly elected mayor, the adaption of the committee system (which might entail enhancing the powers of the chairs of such bodies), and the appointment of a council manager to take day-to-day decisions under the guidance of policy directions issued by the council.

EFFECTIVENESS AND EFFICIENCY

These two terms are often used in evaluations of organisations.

Effectiveness focuses on the goals and outputs. An organisation is effective if it attains its objectives.

Efficiency is concerned with the use of resources to attain goals. Criteria such as cost effectiveness and value for money determine an organisation's efficiency.

Performance indicators used in the UK by public bodies such as the police service seek to measure both the effectiveness and efficiency of individual forces.

The Incremental Model

This approach to policy-making was particularly associated with the American, Charles Lindblom, whose initial contribution was contained in an article, published in 1959, entitled *The Science of 'Muddling Through'*. He argued that when policy makers made decisions they did not engage in the lengthy process encompassed by the rational model. Instead, they merely sought to make small adjustments to existing policy. This implied that policy-making was:

○ *Spasmodic:* the actions of policy makers did not conform to a coherent science, guided by the pursuit of objectives. Instead their intervention was of a reactive nature, responding to issues (which were mainly of a short-term nature) in an ad hoc fashion.

○ *Conservative:* policy makers did not substantially depart from the status quo. This meant that the content of new policies was substantially influenced by existing ones and radical innovations were not attempted.

○ *Remedial:* policy-making was not concerned with a 'once and for all' solution to a problem which had been identified. Rather, its scope was limited to managing problems as and when they arose.

This approach to policy-making was primarily viewed as *descriptive* rather than *prescriptive*. That is, it was concerned with explaining what actually happened as opposed to how decisions should ideally be made. Its advantages were that it took the political environment within which public policy was fashioned into account. One key explanation offered by Lindblom for incrementalism was *partisan mutual adjustment*. This meant that policy makers were engaged in a perpetual game of 'give and take' which might be explained by factors including competition for scarce resources. This process of negotiation resulted in policy makers having to dilute their more radical proposals in order to secure support for more modest programmes. It further explained how coordination between a range of policy makers was achieved.

There were, however, many problems with the incremental model of policy-making. The criticism that this model did not seek to examine the consequences of possible policies resulted in Lindblom and David Braybrooke putting forward the notion of *disjointed incrementalism* in a book, *A Strategy of Decision*, published in 1963. This suggested that while policy makers did not engage in a comprehensive analysis of policies, they did conduct a more limited evaluation. They examined policies which differed from each other incrementally, and which also differed incrementally from the status quo. A further criticism of this model was that it seemed to suggest that public policy could not inaugurate radical transformations. Whether this is so, however, depends on the definition given to the term 'incremental'.

HYBRID MODELS OF DECISION-MAKING

Some theorists have sought to produce models of decision-making which combine elements of both the rational and incremental approaches. These include Yehezkel Dror's *optimum model* and Amitai Etzioni's *mixed scanning model*.

Dror was critical of incrementalism, believing that it enhanced conservatism. This approach might be justified in countries in which there was political stability and consensus, but worked less well in those where significant political, economic or social change was required. His optimum model of decision-making thus combined *rational* and *non-rational* elements. Policy emerged from rational activities which included a selective review of options and a limited statement of objectives, linked to non-rational exercises such as *brainstorming*.

Etzioni argued that policy makers sometimes departed from incrementalism and took decisions which he described as 'fundamental' in the sense that they moved the policy-making process in a new direction. The mixed scanning model of decision-making combined aspects of the rational and incremental approaches by suggesting that policy makers should undertake a broad review (rather than a comprehensive analysis) of the options available. This would enable fundamental decisions to be taken. These would then form the basis for incremental decisions, at which point a more detailed survey of options could be taken.

Question

Compare and contrast the rational and incremental models of policy-making. Which, in your view, offers the most appropriate description of the policy-making process in modern British government?

To do this you should organise your material as follows:

○ Describe the main features of the rational model of policy-making.

○ Outline the major features of the incremental model of policy-making.

○ Discuss the strengths and weaknesses of each of these two models.

○ Draw a conclusion, based on the evaluation of strengths and weaknesses.

Structural Analysis

This approach to the study of policy-making concentrates on those whose views influence the outcomes of the decision-making process. There are various participants in this process whose contributions are discussed below.

Public Opinion

This suggests that the general public exert a significant influence on the content of public policy. Citizens in a participatory democracy will themselves exert a dominant influence on policy-making, but in a liberal (or representative) democracy the views of the general public are brought to bear on those who wield power on the people's behalf. Those who take decisions are ultimately accountable to the citizenry for the actions they have taken (or have failed to take), and in this sense, the people are sovereign.

The House of Commons is composed of representatives of all citizens of the United Kingdom. It is their role to advance the needs and requirements of those who elected them. If they fail to do so they run the risk of not being elected in a future contest.

The extent to which public opinion is able to influence the policy-making process is, however, variable. The weight attached to popular views is affected by factors which include the distribution of power between the executive and legislative branches of government (which is itself influenced by the party system). Government or parliament may consider it to be their duty to lead rather than follow public opinion. In this sense, elections merely provide citizens with the opportunity to cast a retrospective judgement on the actions taken by their political leaders.

Political Parties

This view suggests that political activists exert a major influence on the policy-making process. Activists are members of the general public who join political parties and are thus able to play a part in formulating policy. If and when the party attains a position of political power or influence, these views will then form the basis of the decisions which it undertakes.

The suggestion that political activists are able to exert a significant influence on the decision-making process implies that political leaders are subservient to the views of their activists. Thus when elected to public office, their role is merely to carry out predetermined policies. In reality, however, political leaders frequently claim the right to disregard party policy when this conflicts with their perception of what is the right course of political action. They may also be required to initiate policy-making to cater for issues on which their party had expressed no prior views.

Bureaucrats

This suggests that policy-making is heavily influenced by full-time officials who are employed by public bodies. It is these bureaucrats, and not the politicians, who are nominally in control of bodies such as central government or local authorities, and who effectively determine decision-making either by promoting policy themselves or by influencing the content of ideas put forward by their political leaders. This suggests that the content of public policy mainly corresponds to the views of officials, and that politicians and the general public exert a more modest level of influence. These arguments are more fully explored in Chapter 12 which is concerned with the influence exerted by the senior civil service on policy-making.

Pressure Group Activity

This suggests that decision-making is influenced by members of the general public who join pressure groups to advance their beliefs or interests. The role of government is to establish ground rules for the manner in which pressure groups operate and to adjudicate between them when competing demands are put forward. The manner in which groups seek to influence the policy-making process, and factors which influence the success they enjoy, is considered more fully in Chapter 8 and in connection with the discussion of *pluralism*, below.

Intellectual Opinion

Some policy areas are heavily determined by the views of experts. Experts may be employed within the machinery of government in response to the technical nature of some aspects of its operations, or they may be 'outsiders'. They conduct enquiries into particular problems and produce reports of their findings, on which subsequent policies are based. The development of social policy in particular has owed much to intellectual activity. In the later nineteenth century, public awareness of urban problems was promoted by the work of those who included William Preston, Charles Booth and Seebohm Rowntree. Their pioneering work was subsequently taken up in the postwar period by Richard Titmuss, Brian Abel-Smith, Peter Townsend, David Donnison and Michael Young who made a significant contribution to the development of the discipline of social administration.

Question

The above discussion has referred to some of the key actors in the decision-making process. Select one of the headings used above and evaluate that actor's role in policy-making. To do this, organise your material in the following way:

❍ State how their views regarding policy-making are put forward.

❍ Examine what factors are likely to aid the adoption of the views by the policy makers.

❍ Discuss what factors hinder the endorsement of their proposals.

The Distribution of Power within Society

The concern of structural analysis with an evaluation of the influences which determine policy-making extends beyond the various groups whose ideas may contribute to this process. Such influences may be placed within a context which focuses on the distribution of power within a state as an explanation for the nature of decision-making.

This approach is not totally exclusive and may relate to the processes of decision-making which formed the focus of behavioural analysis. Certain processes may be more appropriate to particular forms of power relationships than to others. For example, the incremental model of policy-making might be appropriate to a *pluralist society*, whereas a rational model might be easier to apply in a *totalitarian political system*.

There are a variety of power structures to be considered, which give rise to the dominance of some groups over others in the policy-making process. The key structures are discussed below.

Pluralism

Pluralist theory emphasises the importance which pressure groups play in a liberal–democratic political system. Groups are perceived as a key mechanism through which public opinion can influence the decision-making process. Thus a pluralist society is one in which citizens are organised into a variety of interest groups, all competing with each other for attention by the policy makers. The process of bargaining and conciliation is overseen by the government. Pluralist theorists are divided as to whether the government is merely a neutral arbiter of intergroup disputes or whether it is itself a key actor in the negotiating process, acting in a manner similar to a pressure group pursuing its own interests as well as responding to demands from outside.

Elitism

An ideal pluralist state would be one in which power was evenly divided between groups who thus competed on a relatively equal footing. Elite theory, however, suggests that power is not diffused (that is, widely spread throughout society) but, rather, is concentrated in the hands of a small minority of citizens. This gives rise to a situation in which the many are governed by the few. This minority constitutes a political elite which exercises a dominant position in the policy-making process.

The nature of the political elite varies between societies. In modern industrial society the elite's power is based on a wide array of sources, which include holding formal political office (such as President, Prime Minister or senior civil servant), the possession of technical or intellectual expertise, and control of economic power derived from wealth. Elite theorists differ in their opinions about whether elitism and pluralist democracy (as defined above) are incompatible. Some suggest that competition between elites upholds this principle, whereas others emphasise the similarity between elites based on factors such as social background, attitudes and values. The latter suggest that the state is dominated by elites whose loyalty to 'the establishment' constrains the scope of policy making.

Marxism

Marxist theory, like elitism, questioned the pluralist nature of society. It held, however, that in industrialised societies the elite consisted of the economically dominant class. Their wealth was the underpinning for their political power and the state was used as an instrument of class domination. Although those who owned and controlled capital were not necessarily the same as those who exercised political power, the views and values of the former determined the actions undertaken by the latter. Policy-making thus reflected the interests of those who controlled the means of production (who were termed 'the bourgeoisie').

Corporatism

Corporatist theory blended elements of pluralism and elitism. In common with pluralism it emphasised the importance of pressure groups in the formulation of public policy. In accordance with elite theory, it emphasised the dominant position which was occupied by a relatively small number of powerful and highly organised groups which were incorporated into the state's decision-making machinery. One example of a corporatist structure was the National Economic Development Council (usually referred to as NEDDY) which was set up by Harold Macmillan's Conservative government in 1961. It brought together ministers, civil servants, trade union leaders and representatives of employers, whose key role was to plan for industrial growth. The implications of this are discussed in Chapter 8.

What is Power?

A related aspect to the concern of who wields power in society is the nature of that power. There are three differing views concerning what power is, which alternatively suggest that power entails the ability:

❍ *To ensure that the views of one group prevail over those of another:* this view is compatible with the pluralist position, which concentrates on the decisions which emerge as the product of intergroup conflict. It suggests that power relates to the ability of one group to ensure that its views prevail in situations of conflict with others.

❍ *To limit the scope of the policy-making agenda:* this view suggests that power extends to nondecision-making – that is, the ability of one group to restrict the scope of policy-making so that issues viewed as contentious or problematic by a dominant group are frozen out of the political process.

❍ *To shape people's preferences:* this focuses on latent conflict and suggests that power may be used to secure social harmony based on the false notion of consensus. Here power constitutes a form of ideological control whereby those who wield it are able to maintain their dominance by influencing the attitudes and values of those they rule. This view is associated with Steven Lukes, and is termed the 'third dimension of power'.

Further Reading

Policy-making is typically studied in detail in undergraduate courses, and much of the literature reflects the intellectual capacity of advanced students. Much useful material will, however, be found in the following:

Martin Burch and **Bruce Wood**, *Public Policy in Britain* (Oxford: Blackwell, 2nd edition, 1990). This book examines the politics surrounding the acquisition of resources necessary for policy-making, discusses how these are divided between policy programmes, and examines how these programmes are implemented. Chapter 2 in particular provides a useful account of key views concerning the operation of the policy process and the behaviour of policy makers.

Christopher Ham and **Michael Hill**, *The Policy-Making Process in the Modern Capitalist State* (London: Harvester Wheatsheaf, 2nd edition, 1993). This book provides a scholarly account of a wide range of theoretical approaches to the study of policy-making and policy implementation. A particular strength of this work is its analysis of the structure of power within society.

Simon James, *British Government: A Reader in Policy-Making* (London: Routledge, 1997). This book presents a large number of case studies concerning policy-making in Britain. It explores a number of key issues which include the role of civil servants, ministers and Parliament in developing policy, and the impact of the EU on national decision-making.

Chapter Eight | Pressure Groups

The aims of this chapter are:

---

1. To define the term 'pressure group', differentiating such organisations from political parties and social movements.

2. To analyse the role performed by pressure groups.

3. To provide an understanding of the way in which pressure groups are differentiated (or classified).

4. To analyse the various methods which pressure groups may utilise to secure their objectives.

5. To evaluate the factors which influence pressure group effectiveness.

6. To assess the benefits and disadvantages which pressure groups present for the operations of parliamentary democracy.

Definition of Pressure Groups

A pressure group is an organisation:

○ with a formal structure

○ composed of a number of individuals seeking to further a common cause or interest.

These groups operate at all levels of society. Some seek to influence the activities of local, state or central government. Others exist within the workplace in the form of trade unions. The factions or tendencies found within some political parties are further examples of such organisations. Many groups perform functions which are not political, for example by providing benefits or advisory services either to their members or to the general public. For the purposes of this discussion, however, attention will be focused on those seeking to exert influence over national government policy-making.

Pressure Groups and Political Parties

The key difference between political parties and pressure groups centres on the distinction between control and influence: while a pressure group seeks to exert influence over a relatively narrow aspect of policy-making, a political party wishes to control the overall direction of public affairs.

○ *Control:* parties normally seek control over the policy-making process. They may achieve this through their own efforts or in combination with other political parties. They contest elections in the hope of securing power so that they can then carry out the policies contained in their election manifestos. Such policies cover all aspects of public affairs and the party seeks to exercise control over a wide range of issues.

○ *Influence:* pressure groups wish to influence those who control the policy-making process. They do not normally have an interest in the overall work of government but only in those aspects of its operations which are of concern to its membership. In order to pursue their aims, groups usually possess a degree of autonomy from both government and political parties.

Tactics

One further distinction between political parties and pressure groups concerns the manner in which they seek to cultivate support. Parties concentrate their activities on the general public, hoping to convince voters to support them in election contests. Although campaigns directed at the public may form one aspect of pressure group campaigning, influence may be sought throughout the political system.

The tactics thus available to pressure groups and social movements are broad. Some have utilised protest and direct action (which are discussed in greater detail below) in association with traditional methods of pressure group activity to mobilise popular support for their objectives. Greenpeace, for example, has sought to combine a range of direct action tactics with the use of lobbying and scientific inquiry designed to alert both governments and the public to the problems facing the natural world. Such groups may seek to couple conventional political activity with various forms of protest and dissent. In 1996, the British arm of the American-based International Fund for Animal Welfare made a donation of £1 million to the Labour Party to further its opposition to fox hunting.

Social Movements

Many reforms are promoted by organisations termed 'social movements'. Examples include the Peace Movement, the Women's Movement and the Environmental Movement. It is not easy to precisely differentiate between these and pressure groups.

Social movements tend to be:

○ *Loosely organised:* unlike pressure groups, social movements generally lack a formal structure.

○ *Concerned with a broader focus than are pressure groups:* rather than concentrate on one specific policy area, their concern is to instil new moral values within society.

Social movements may embrace the activities of pressure groups whose specific aims are compatible with this overall objective. For example, the British Campaign for Nuclear Disarmament would be located within the umbrella of the Peace Movement.

Social movements typically operate outside of mainstream political institutions and their tactics are thus dominated by non-conventional forms of political activity. These are frequently carried out on an international stage rather than being confined to any particular country.

THE ENVIRONMENTAL MOVEMENT

The traditional role undertaken by pressure groups to promote political change in the United Kingdom has more recently been supplemented by organisations termed 'social movements'. These are associated with the leftwing of the political spectrum but have substituted the traditional Marxist emphasis on the overthrow of capitalism with a range of direct action tactics which seek to transform society by redefining social values.

The environmental movement is an important example of a contemporary social movement. It has succeeded in bringing together a range of groups engaged in counter-cultural protest (such as New Age Travellers), and those opposed to hunting, live animal exports, motorway construction and pollution. These seemingly disparate, single-issue bodies (whose aims, in fact, seem contrasting) are united by a social vision which rejects the culture of advanced capitalist society. All stand opposed to what they view as an alliance of developers, business, the construction industry and government. They have utilised tactics of protest and direct action to project an alternative vision to a modern industrial society which emphasises environmental considerations over the pursuit of wealth and profit. All are concerned with man's damage to the planet and are opposed to materialism and consumerism.

The Role of Pressure Groups

Pressure groups seek to influence policy makers. Their actions are thus directed at politicians, civil servants and, in some cases, the general public. The complex and lengthy nature of the policy-making process provides wide scope for group activity which may be conducted at a number of different levels:

○ *Influencing the political agenda:* a major concern of pressure groups is to persuade policy makers to consider their views and then to act upon them. This involves inducing policy makers either to adopt a course of action which they did not initially intend to embark upon, or to abandon a measure which they had originally decided to introduce.

○ *Participating in the formulation of policy:* this entails the group in devising ways to achieve the objective(s) which they have succeeded in placing on the political agenda.

○ *Implementation of policy:* groups may become involved in carrying out policy.

○ *Monitoring:* groups may participate in processes designed to ensure that the objectives sought by policy are attained. If this is not the case, they may propose changes to ensure that goals are reached.

Formal Organisations and Pressure Group Activity

Pressure group activity is not confined to organisations which are specifically established to advance an interest or a cause. It may also be performed by bodies whose existence is concerned with other functions but which may, on occasions, act in the capacity of a pressure group and seek to exert influence within the policy-making process. Examples include:

○ *The Catholic Church in Ireland:* this is an example of a body which sometimes acts as a pressure group. The Roman Catholic bishops played a prominent role in the 1995 referendum campaign opposing a change in the Irish constitution to permit divorce.

○ *Chief constables and senior members of the British judiciary:* these sometimes make public pronouncements designed to influence the approach adopted by policy makers to the operations of the criminal justice system.

○ *The Pentagon:* in the United States of America the Pentagon sometimes performs a role akin to that of a pressure group on behalf of the military establishment.

Pressure Groups and The Private Sector

The discussion of pressure groups in this chapter is primarily concerned with their influence on the policy-making processes of central government. However, pressure groups frequently direct their activities towards alternative targets. These may include the practices adopted by commercial organisations. Indeed, a number of Greenpeace activists now see business rather than politics as the best arena within which to further environmental aims.

ACTIVITY DIRECTED AT THE PRIVATE SECTOR

The following examples illustrate that pressure groups sometimes direct their activities at private sector organisations.

In 1995, the environmental organisation Greenpeace mounted a campaign against the decision by the Shell Oil company to sink a disused oil rig, Brent Spar, in the North Atlantic. Adverse publicity coupled with consumer boycotts of Shell's products organised by environmental groups resulted in the company agreeing to examine alternative ways of disposing of their unwanted property.

In early 1998, farmers organised into a 'farming army' and engaged in activities which included picketing supermarkets and big food distributors in their campaign to force companies to stock British meat products in preference to those from abroad.

Question

Select a pressure group with whose activities you are familiar. With the aid of books, journals and other material concerning this group (possibly supplied by the organisation itself), build up your own analysis of it. In particular you should seek to assess:

○ its aims and objectives

○ the methods through which it seeks to achieve its goals

○ its relationship (if any) with other pressure groups or political parties.

Further questions in this chapter are designed to aid you by providing a thorough evaluation of the work and activities of the particular body you have chosen for study.

Pressure Group Activities

This section examines the way in which pressure groups can be differentiated from each other and the methods which are available to such groups in an attempt to secure influence.

Classification of Pressure Groups

Various systems may be adopted to classify the pressure groups which are to be found within liberal–democratic political systems. One method is to differentiate them according to the relationship which exists between the objective put forward by the group and its membership. This provides two broad categories into which groups might be placed: *sectional groups* and *promotional groups*.

Sectional Groups

These are groups in which the members have a vested interest in the success of their organisation. They stand to benefit materially if its aims are adopted by policy makers. Such organisations are sometimes referred to as 'interest' or 'economic' groups. The membership of sectional groups tends to be narrow and composed of people from similar backgrounds. In the UK examples include

○ *Employers' associations:* such include the Confederation of British Industry.

○ *Professional bodies:* one example is the British Medical Association.

○ *Labour organisations:* these embrace trade unions such as the Transport and General Workers' Union.

American examples of sectional groups include the American Bar Association and the American Medical Association.

Promotional (or Cause) Groups

These are organisations in which the members are united in support of a cause which does not necessarily benefit them directly. Members view the work of the group as a moral concern. The aim of such groups is thus to change social attitudes and values. Examples include:

○ *Campaign Against Racial Discrimination:* this was active in the UK during the 1960s and was a main driving force behind this country's first piece of race relations legislation, the 1965 Race Relations Act.

○ *Common Cause:* this is an American organisation which seeks honesty and efficiency in government.

The aims of promotional groups may be designed to benefit specific groups (especially minorities whose needs are often ignored by policy makers) or be directed at an issue affecting society as a whole. Membership of promotional groups is open to all who share its objectives: members are typically drawn from a wide range of social or occupational backgrounds and are united solely by their common support for the cause advocated by the organisation. A significant feature of protests against motorway construction and the export of live animals in the 1990s has been the diverse social background of the participants.

Question

Based on the above categorisation, is the pressure group you have selected for study a cause or promotional group? Give an explanation to justify your answer.

COUNTRIES ACTING AS PRESSURE GROUPS

The division between sectional and cause groups is a very broad one. Examples of groups which do not obviously fit into either of these two categories can be found. The superpower status of the USA, for example, has encouraged some countries (especially Israel and Japan) to engage in activities associated with pressure groups. They do this by employing representatives to put forward their interests in Washington.

The Operation of Pressure Groups

Pressure groups operate throughout the system of government.

The Executive Branch of Government

In Britain this consists of both ministers and civil servants. Some pressure groups have the ability to constantly liaise with, and be consulted by, these key policy makers.

The relationship between groups and the executive branch of government may be constructed in a number of ways:

❍ *A permanent formalised relationship with government departments:* members representing a group may be appointed to Joint Advisory Committees which are key mechanisms through which the concerns of a pressure group can be made known to the relevant government department.

❍ *Regular access to civil servants.*

❍ *Involvement in discussions on appointments:* these relate to bodies such as quangos which are responsible to a government department.

❍ *The 'old boy' network:* this entails former ministers or civil servants securing jobs in pressure groups whose cause might be advanced from the contacts in government possessed by such former public officials.

Organisations with links to government are termed 'insider' groups. This denotes the close relationship which they enjoy with key members of the policy-making process. It is a desirable position to occupy in countries such as the UK and France, where political power is centralised in the executive branch of government, although it is regarded as important in some federal countries such as Australia. The relationship between the British National Farmers' Union and the Ministry of Agriculture, Fisheries and Food is an example of such an 'insider' association. Groups in this position, however, are limited in the tactics they use to 'sell' their case, since they will be expected to act in a manner deemed acceptable by those in the executive branch of government with whom they enjoy a close relationship.

Other groups may secure influence from their relationship with the political arm of the executive branch of government. This was the case in the UK between 1964 and 1970 when leading trade unionists were frequently invited to Downing Street to discuss industrial affairs over 'beer and sandwiches'. This politically-fashioned link with the ministerial component of the executive is not permanent and may alter when the government changes. Thus, the introduction of monetarist economic policies in the UK after 1979 and in New Zealand after 1984 had an adverse effect on the role which organised interests such as trade unions were able to exert over public policy-making.

The Legislature

There are a number of ways whereby pressure groups may seek to exert influence over the legislature. A major mechanism is that of *lobbying*.

Lobbying

Lobbying was originally directed exclusively at legislators. Its aim is to ensure that these law-makers are fully briefed on the merits of the case advocated by a group. They are thus in a position to advance the group's interests when issues which are relevant to it come before the legislative assembly for discussion or resolution. The importance attached to this activity is much influenced by the independence of action which legislatures possess. Pressure groups may devote relatively little attention to such bodies if they perceive them to be dominated by the executive branch of government.

In the USA many groups employ professional lobbyists. These are full-time officials who work in Washington and constantly subject members of both Houses of Congress to the views and attitudes of the organisations which employ them. Although such activities also occur in the UK, the strength of the party system may serve to reduce the effectiveness of pressure group activity directed at this branch of government, unless the issue is deemed to be non-political (in the sense that the main parties have no particular view they wish to promote and thus let their MPs have a 'free vote' on it).

Influence Achieved Through the Legislature's Committee System

Pressure groups may voice their concerns to the legislature through ways other than lobbying. In the Fourth French Republic (1946–58) some groups such as the trade union and farmers' associations enjoyed permanent membership of specialised legislative standing committees. In both the UK and the USA investigations conducted by the legislature provide a mechanism for the articulation of group interests, while in Germany the committee system utilised by the Bundestag serves to enhance pressure group influence over legislation.

Iron Triangles

In the USA some pressure groups enjoy considerable power from the relationship which they have constructed with *both* the executive and legislative branch of government.

The term 'iron triangle' has been used to describe the close links (governed by ties of interdependent self-interest) which exist between an interest group, the government department or agency concerned with the interests of that organisation, and the

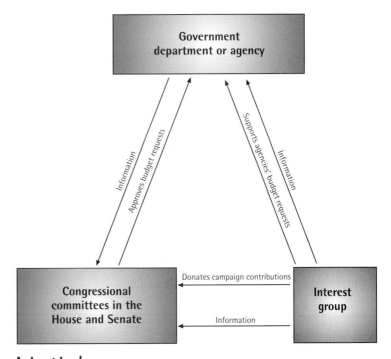

An iron triangle.

Congressional committee charged with responsibility for the policy area. One recent example of an iron triangle concerns the relationship struck between the American biotech/pharmaceutical/agri–business complex (one of whose interests is genetically modified foods) and the Foods and Drugs Administration (which regulates the American Food Industry). The former donates millions of dollars each year to political parties and members of Congress sitting on key food safety and regulatory committees. Iron triangles have been argued to be responsible for decentralising and fragmenting the policy-making process to the detriment of the exercise of central control by the executive and legislative branches of government. In more recent years, the autonomy of such 'sub governments' has been challenged by alternative centres of power (such as issue networks).

The Judiciary

Pressure groups may utilise the courts in their attempts to secure the adoption of their aims, usually by challenging the legality of legislation. This is a crucial tactic of American cause groups.

Organisations concerned with civil rights, such as the National Association for the Advancement of Colored People, used this mechanism after 1945 in their fight against the segregation practised by a number of the southern States. A landmark in education was reached in 1954 when the Supreme Court ruled (in the case of *Brown* v. *Board of Education of Topeka*) that segregation in schools was unconstitutional and thus illegal throughout the entire country. In more recent years American consumer and environmental groups have turned to the courts to advance their concerns. This procedure may also be adopted by sectional groups. President Clinton's attempt to introduce measures to reduce teenage smoking in 1995 was immediately countered by law suits filed by five cigarette manufacturing companies, asking the courts to block such initiatives.

The ability of groups to utilise the courts to advance their objectives is affected by two considerations:

❍ *Rules governing the operations of a country's judicial system:* in Australia, for example, the rules of *locus standi* have made it difficult for pressure groups to initiate legal actions, since it is necessary for plaintiffs to demonstrate a personal stake or material interest in a case. In America, however, interest groups are permitted to present arguments directly to courts, thereby enhancing their ability to influence the content of public policy.

❍ *Absence of a codified constitution:* the role of the courts is less prominent in countries such as the UK and New Zealand where judicial challenge to national legislation is precluded by the concept of parliamentary sovereignty. However, pressure groups may utilise the courts and launch test cases (when the law is in need of clarification) or challenge the legality of the way in which the law has been implemented through the process of judicial review.

Political Parties

Pressure groups may forge close links with political parties and use them to further their aims. Parties may incorporate aspects of a group's demands within their own policy statements. In the USA, the labour organisation, American Federation of Labour and Congress of Industrial Organisations (AFL-CIO), is associated with the Democratic Party while the French trade union, the Confédération Générale du Travail (CGT), has close ties with the Communist Party. The relationship which exists between pressure groups and political parties may be organisational or financial. In the UK leading trade unions are affiliated to the Labour Party, while the Conservatives have traditionally received funding and support from the business sector.

The General Public

Most pressure groups do not enjoy the status of 'insiders' and are kept at arm's length by politicians and civil servants. Civil servants often adopt a hostile attitude towards groups as they may provide politicians with information which rivals that presented to a minister by a government department. This may have an adverse effect on the role performed by civil servants in the policy-making process. The absence of 'insider' status may force pressure groups to utilise alternative tactics to advance their aims. These include attempts to secure the support of the general public for the demands of the group.

There are a number of methods which may be used by pressure groups to secure public endorsement of their aims. A basic division exists, however, between education and coercion.

Education

Education entails tactics designed to inform and thus educate the public into positively and enthusiastically supporting the objectives of a group. This may involve publicising issues, the scale or scope of which were hitherto generally unknown. This has happened with social problems such as the plight of the homeless, or humanitarian concerns such as animal welfare. The campaigns of environmentalist groups concerned with global warming and the hole in the ozone layer are examples of attempts to educate the public into endorsing the objectives of a pressure group. The protests organised by animal welfare groups such as Compassion in World Farming at British ports and airports during 1995, against the export of British calves for the Continental veal trade, also sought to alert and educate the public to the suffering experienced by animals.

Coercion

Coercion involves methods which apply a form of sanction to coerce the public into applying pressure on policy makers to give in to the group's demands. The intention of the coercive approach is to make the public inconvenienced, anxious or even frightened so that they exert pressure on the policy makers to capitulate. Alternatively, the pressure may be more directly applied to the government, seeking to persuade it to change the direction of its policy or to intervene in an essentially private dispute.

The strike weapon used by trade unionists may sometimes provide an example of the coercive approach. Indiscriminate terrorism, randomly directed against the public, is an extreme example of an attempt to alter the direction of government policy by coercive means.

Direct Action

Direct action is a key form of protest and has become a widely used tactic by pressure groups in a number of countries. In the UK the modern 'wave' of direct action commenced with anti-nuclear protests and subsequently became involved with environmental and animal welfare issues, and opposition to motorway and airport construction.

DIRECT ACTION IN BRITAIN

There are two basic forms of direct action: *positive activities* consisting of actions which give effect to the change the group wishes to promote, and *negative activities* which physically oppose those a group wishes to confront.

Specific examples of groups using positive forms of direct action include:

◆ *The workers' sit-in at the Upper Clyde shipbuilding yard:* this action undertaken in 1972 succeeded in reversing the government's decision to cease financial aid to this industry.

◆ *Squatting:* squatters' movements initially emerged in Britain in 1945–46 and reappeared in the late 1960s. Their tactic of occupying empty property to house homeless people constituted an important example of the positive use of direct action to implement a movement's cause.

◆ *Animal liberation:* the freeing of animals in research laboratories by organisations such as the British Animal Liberation Front prevents their future use in animal experiments. Similarly, the release of mink by the same organisation in 1998 prevented animals being used for commercial activities.

The negative tactics associated with direct action may involve various forms of physical obstruction. Such action has included:

◆ *The 'Stop the Seventies Tour':* this initially disrupted the South African rugby tour in 1969–70 in protest against the system of apartheid which then operated in that country. Tactics included invading playing fields and disrupting coach journeys. It was also successful in causing the abandonment of the proposed South African cricket tour in 1970.

◆ *Opposition to motorway construction:* this was initiated in 1992 to oppose the construction of the M3 extension at Twyford Down. Latterly the construction and occupation of camps and 'tree houses' have been utilised to prevent the construction of the M11 link road through East London in 1994, the M77 extension to link Glasgow with Kilmarnock and Ayr in 1995, and the A34 Newbury bypass in 1996.

◆ *Animal welfare:* groups such as Compassion in World Farming opposed the conditions under which British livestock was exported to Europe and the methods used by European farms involved in veal production. In 1995, they obstructed highways at Shoreham, Brightlingsea and Plymouth to prevent lorries reaching ports, and disrupted flights from airports such as Swansea and Coventry.

Breaking the Law

Physical obstruction may involve breaking the law. Those who do so hope that the dignity of the objective will create public sympathy for the group's aims, leading juries to refuse to convict even in the face of evidence of guilt. This occurred, for example, in 1997 when five women were acquitted of causing £1.5 million damage to a Hawk jet which was to be sold to Indonesia. The jury accepted that a 'home made' defence (the desire to prevent the aeroplane being used in a campaign of genocide by the Indonesian government) was a sufficient excuse for their actions.

DIRECT ACTION IN FRANCE

In France, where institutionalised links between groups and policy makers are not strongly developed, direct action is frequently utilised by groups seeking to alter the direction of government policy. Examples of this included the wave of industrial disputes and public demonstrations which occurred towards the end of 1995 directed at the austerity programme of the then French Prime Minister, Alain Juppé, one aspect of which was the reduction of welfare benefits. Demonstrations by the unemployed were directed against perceived inaction by France's socialist government following its election in 1997. Other forms of direct action (such as the blockade mounted by French lorry drivers across the country in 1997) were designed to force the government to intervene in a dispute with their employers over improved wages and conditions of work.

It has been observed that 'like nobody else in Europe the French still believe absolutely in the right to protest. Farmers dump Spanish tomatoes and British lamb; train drivers paralyse public transport; truckers close off motorways and blockade ports; students mount street barricades and hurl paving stones at the police. And usually, it works. The government gives in because that is also the French way of doing things' – Jon Henley, the *Guardian*, 20 January 1998.

A demonstration by homeless and unemployed people through Paris, December 1997

The French example of direct action targeted at government policy has proved to be contagious and also occurs in the UK. In June 1998, for example, lorry drivers operated a 'go slow' on the motorways to protest against the level of duty imposed on diesel fuel. They argued that, as this was lower elsewhere in Europe, foreign hauliers had an unfair advantage over them.

The International Arena

Pressure groups do not confine their activities to one country but increasingly operate on a world stage. These may be:

❍ *International organisations:* these may seek the universal adoption of standards of behaviour throughout the world. Amnesty International (which is concerned with human rights) is an example of such a body.

❍ *Groups seeking influence over policy-making in another country:* the Greek Animal Welfare Fund, for example, is a London-based organisation which seeks to alter the official and public attitudes towards the treatment accorded to animals in Greece.

❍ *Groups which operate on the supranational stage:* international institutions such as the United Nations Human Rights Committee and the European Court of Justice have been used by pressure groups seeking to question the actions undertaken by individual governments. As is discussed below, the policy makers of the EU (principally the Commission and Council of Ministers) are particularly subject to group activity.

The international arena may mean that groups whose interests or activities are prejudiced by the law of their own country may be able to call upon higher authorities for redress. In 1998, for example, the British Labour government was warned that unless it repealed legislation passed by previous Conservative governments, which allowed employers to discriminate against trade union members and deny them representation, it could have a case to answer before the European Court of Human Rights.

Pressure Groups and the European Union

European Union legislation has a considerable effect on the policies pursued by its member states. In some countries this has resulted in protest being directed against the European Commission. In 1998, Spanish miners went on strike in protest against the insistence of the EU that the Spanish government should speed up plans to cut coal production and curb subsidies to the mining industry. Pressure groups constitute an important way to influence the direction of EU policy, and some groups have reorganised themselves to use its machinery to their advantage. These reorganisations include:

○ *Coordination of groups across national boundaries:* organisations within individual countries may coordinate their activities with similar groups in other countries to secure overall influence on European Union policy. An umbrella body for farming interests (COPA) and an employers' federation (UNICE) reflects the European-wide dimension to these groups' activities.

○ *Establishment of permanent European Offices:* an example of this is the Brussels Office of the Confederation of British Industry which monitors developments in the European Union and seeks to influence the direction of European legislation to the benefit of its members.

There are advantages and disadvantages for pressure groups operating on an EU-wide stage.

Groups may use European law to their own advantage. For example, in the UK groups opposed to motorway construction have complained to the European Commission that the government failed to adequately implement the procedures of the 1988 Directive concerned with Environmental Impact Assessments. This could result in the government being taken to the European Court for contravening European law.

The EU may limit the scope of pressure group activities. In December 1997 the European Court of Justice issued a judgement against the French government for failing to prevent their farmers from disrupting the flow of vegetables and fruit from Spain. This case concerned actions undertaken by the militant farmers' organisation, Coordination Rurale, which conducted violent raids against lorries carrying Spanish strawberries and other products between 1993 and 1995. This decision made the government more vulnerable to damage suits in national courts. In the same month, British farmers blocked a number of ports in protest against the import of beef, especially from Ireland. Such actions resulted in the government being warned by the EU internal market commissioner that the UK could face legal action in the European court unless it took steps to ensure the free circulation of goods in accordance with its treaty obligations.

Question

Outline the manner in which the pressure group you have chosen for study seeks to implement its aims. Evaluate the strengths and weaknesses of the approach (or approaches) it has adopted.

Factors Determining Pressure Group Effectiveness

The previous section discussed various tactics which a pressure group might utilise to further its aims. The extent to which these tactics succeed in influencing policy makers depends on a range of factors which are now considered.

Ability to Mobilise

The ability of a group to mobilise all who adhere to a particular sectional interest or cause may be one determinant of a pressure group's effectiveness. The fragmentation of French labour organisations into a number of competing federations has tended to weaken their influence over policy makers. This stands in contrast to the organisational unity of French business interests (whose trade associations are linked by the umbrella organisation, CNPF). The strength of American labour organisations is reduced by the low affiliation rate of workers to trade unions. The cause of animal welfare in the UK may be impeded by the existence of a large number of organisations which include the Royal Society for the Prevention of Cruelty to Animals, Compassion in World Farming, the Animal Liberation Front and the International Fund For Animal Welfare.

One development which may help to overcome the fragmentation of like-minded opinion between a number of pressure groups is the banding together of bodies with similar objectives under the auspices of an umbrella organisation. Examples of such 'associations of associations' include Britain's Trade Union Congress and Confederation of British Industry and Australia's National Farmers' Federation.

Expertise Commanded by a Group

A further factor which may affect the influence groups are able to exercise over policy-making is the expertise which they command. Governments may be reliant upon such bodies for advice on the technical and complex issues which surround much contemporary public policy, and may further be reliant on a group's goodwill or support to implement policy. Such considerations had a major bearing on the influence possessed by the British Medical Association following the establishment of the National Health Service in 1946.

Resources Possessed by a Group

The resources which pressure groups are able to command may also determine the success or failure of a group. New technology (such as computer-processed direct mail) is expensive. Economically powerful groups possess the ability both to publicise their objectives and to resist sanctions which may be deployed against them. Employer organisations are often

Question

To what extent do you consider that the pressure group you have selected for your study is able to achieve its objectives?

Assess the reasons for either its relative success or its inability to influence policy makers.

influential for such reasons. By contrast, consumer groups have traditionally suffered from lack of resources which may help to explain their difficulties in securing influence over the actions of policy makers. However some governments (such as the French) and supranational bodies (such as the European Union) have contributed towards the funding of pressure groups, which offsets weaknesses which derive from lack of funds.

Sanctions Available to a Group

The sanctions which an organisation is able to deploy may be a factor in its ability to influence policy-making. Investment decisions or strikes may be used as weapons by business groups or trade unions to influence the conduct of policy makers. Groups which are involved in the implementation of public policy possess the ability to withhold their cooperation and thus prevent the progress of policies to which they object.

The Strengths and Weaknesses of Pressure Group Activity

In some liberal-democratic political systems, the ability of citizens to participate in pressure group activity is seen as a fundamental political right. The 1949 West German constitution (as extended in the 1990 unification treaty which involved the five East German states) guaranteed the right of all social groups to form alliances and coalitions. Alternatively, the attempts by the 1958 French constitution (which established the Fifth Republic) to establish a highly powerful President was influenced by a desire to limit the influence possessed by pressure groups and political parties.

This section examines the benefits which pressure groups bring to liberal-democratic political systems and then assesses the disadvantages which may arise.

Benefits of Pressure Groups

The main benefits associated with the activities of pressure groups are as follows:

○ they encourage popular involvement in policy-making

○ they contribute to political education

○ they promote reform

○ they articulate minority interests.

Popular Involvement in Policy-Making

Pressure groups enable ordinary members of the general public to play some role in policy-making. Their involvement may be institutionalised (that is, incorporated into formalised, permanent structures). In France, for example, Advisory Councils composed of representatives of interest groups, technicians and prominent personalities appointed by the government are attached to individual Ministries.

There are two main advantages associated with popular involvement in policy-making, both of which enhance the operations of liberal democratic government by enabling public policy to be fashioned according to widespread popular choice.

❍ *Permits popular participation:* pressure groups facilitate the participation of members of the general public in policy-making. Their role in political affairs is not confined merely to casting a vote in periodic elections.

❍ *Reduces the dominance exercised by elites over policy-making:* pressure groups ensure that the policy-making process is not monopolised by elites consisting of politicians or senior civil servants. Elites may be out of touch with popular sentiments.

Political Education

The need for pressure groups to 'sell' their case in order to secure influence may aid the process of public education in political affairs. Groups may need to explain what they believe in and why they endorse the views they hold. Groups who oppose government policy may engage in activities such as investigative journalism, which results in enhanced scrutiny and popular awareness of government activity.

Promote Reform

Pressure groups may raise matters which the major political parties would prefer to ignore, either because they do not consider them to be mainstream political issues (as is economy or law and order) or because they are internally divisive. The emergence of women's issues and environmental concerns onto the political agenda owed much to the activities of pressure groups.

However, pressure groups do not always perform such a progressive role. The stance taken by the National Rifle Association in the USA towards President Clinton's Crime Bill in 1994 demonstrated the reactionary role which groups sometimes adopt towards reform proposals which they view as contrary to the interests of their members.

Articulate Minority Interests

The workings of liberal-democratic political systems may also benefit from the ability of pressure groups to articulate minority opinions or concerns. Liberal democracies tend to listen to majority opinion so there is a risk that minorities get ignored. Pressure groups provide a vehicle whereby minorities can articulate their needs and encourage policy makers to pay heed to them. In the 1960s the British group Campaign Against Racial Discrimination sought to voice the opinions of ethnic minority communities. This group's activities was one factor which led to the passage of the 1965 Race Relations Act.

Disadvantages of Pressure Groups

There are a number of problems associated with the operations of pressure groups in a liberal-democratic political system. These are:

○ the unequal influence possessed by different groups

○ the lack of internal democracy

○ difficulties with the methods used to secure influence

○ the fact that groups can undermine representative democracy

○ the problem of *hyperpluralism*.

Unequal Influence

One problem associated with pressure groups is that all are not accorded the same degree of attention by policy makers. The influence they are able to command is considerably influenced by factors which include the resources at the group's disposal, and the relationships they have constructed with government departments. There are two diametrically opposed problems arising from the inequality which exists between groups.

Worthy Causes May Be Ignored

Worthy minority causes may make little impact on public policy as they are relatively ignored by the bureaucrats, ministers, political parties, the media and public opinion. Members of groups in such a position may become frustrated and resort to violence, seeking to coerce when they are denied opportunities to persuade.

Groups May Seek to Dominate the Policy-Making Process

Some groups command considerable economic resources and possess powerful sanctions which can be deployed to further their interests. These factors may result in their being in a position not merely to influence, but also to dominate, the policy-making process. The power of large American corporations has for long provided them with a wide degree of autonomy in their dealings with government.

Internal Democracy

A further difficulty encountered with the workings of pressure groups is the extent to which the opinions or actions of the leadership faithfully reflect the views of the membership. The belief by British Conservative governments that trade unions, for example, sometimes endorsed political activity which was not genuinely supported by the rank and file membership resulted in a number of pieces of legislation being enacted during the 1980s designed to ensure that such organisations were responsive to their members' opinions. These measures included requirements for compulsory secret ballots to be held before the commencement of strike action, and the periodic election of union leaders. However, most pressure groups are not subject to such internal regulation and are thus susceptible to domination by their leaders. This means they fail to extend greatly the degree of popular involvement in policy-making.

Methods Used to Secure Influence

Concern has been expressed within liberal democracies regarding the expenditure of money by pressure groups in order to achieve influence. The purposes of such spending may go beyond political education and extend into activities which are perceived to approximate to bribery or corruption. Lobbying has been a particular cause for concern and has led some countries to introduce measures to regulate such activities.

❍ *The USA:* the 1946 Federal Regulation of Lobbying Act required lobbyists both to register and state their policy goals.

❍ *Canada:* registration for lobbyists was introduced by the 1988 Lobbyists Registration Act.

American Political Action Committees

Political Action Committees were established in 1974 as a mechanism through which groups can direct funds into the individual campaign funds of candidates who supported their aims. PACs are set up by pressure groups (usually economic interest or producer groups) and registered with the Federal Election Commission. This procedure permits groups to collect money from their members which is then donated – via the PAC – to political campaigns. The number of such bodies has risen dramatically: in 1974 there were approximately 600 operating at the federal (that is, national) level. By 1988 this figure had risen to over 4,000.

The support which can be given to individual candidates has been limited by subsequent amendments to the 1974 legislation, but PACs are able to initiate independent political action. One form this may take is to campaign against the election of candidates to whom they are opposed. PACs have also been accused of buying political influence, and of weakening the role of local party organisation by reducing the importance of its fund-raising activities and thereby reducing the level of public participation in election campaigns.

Pressure Groups may Undermine Representative Democracy

Pressure groups may have a detrimental effect on the institutions of representative democracy.

The Most Effective Way to Secure Reforms

Widespread public support for conventional political activity involving political parties contesting elections may be undermined if the public believe that this form of activity is an ineffective way of bringing about political change. They may perceive that pressure group activity is a more likely way to produce reforms. In the UK, for example, the perception that business interests dominate key aspects of the policy-making process has resulted in enhanced support for groups which utilise various forms of direct action concerned with environmental and animal welfare issues. A further reason why pressure groups may secure support at the expense of political parties is that the latter put forward a wide political programme whereas pressure groups concentrate on narrower concerns and may thus attract support from those only concerned to advance a specific interest or cause.

Pressure Group Power May Eclipse that of Legislatures

In some countries a relatively small number of pressure groups enjoy a close relationship with the executive branch of government. The content of public policy may be heavily influenced by leaders of key pressure groups (especially employer and labour organisations) if they are accorded privileged access to ministers and civil servants. The term 'corporate state' is applied to such political arrangements.

○ *The UK:* the National Economic Development Council was established in 1961 to facilitate discussions between trade unions, business, civil servants and ministers.

○ *France:* the Constitution requires the government to consult with the Economic and Social Council on socio-economic legislation. This body contains civil servants, trade unions, farmers' organisations, business associations and professional groups.

The nature of the political system changes if consultations of this nature preclude the involvement of other parties, and lead to decisions being taken which cannot be discussed meaningfully in other forums. There are three main problems associated with this situation:

○ *Elections cease to enable the public to influence the content of policy:* it makes little difference which party wins a general election since all are constrained to endorse similar policies, foisted on them by corporate decision-making structures.

○ *Legislatures may be relegated to bodies which rubber-stamp decisions:* decisions are taken elsewhere and the legislature possesses little or no control over them.

○ *Lack of accountability:* meetings involving pressure groups, ministers and civil servants are conducted in secret, away from the public gaze. It is difficult to ascertain where precisely power resides and who can be held responsible for particular decisions.

Hyperpluralism

Power in a pluralist society is dispersed. Policy emerges as the result of competition, consultation, bargaining and conciliation conducted between groups who have relatively equal access to the policy-making arena. This process is overseen by the government which is viewed as a neutral arbitrator. Pressure groups thus perform a crucial role in policy-making.

A problem may arise, however, in societies in which a very wide range of groups emerge, some of which hold diametrically opposing views. Examples include the USA and Canada where a wide array of single-issue groups exist with the ability to campaign across a number of tiers of government. The processes of consultation, bargaining and conciliation may be long and drawn out. The decision-making process may stagnate and governments find it difficult, or impossible, to take any decisions. This situation (which regards all interests as being on an equal footing) is known as 'hyperpluralism'. However, the tendency for powerful groups (including the government) to dominate the policy-making process serves to reduce the likelihood of such stagnation occurring in many liberal democracies.

Question ❓

With reference to the pressure group you have selected to study, indicate whether its operations are beneficial or detrimental to the UK's system of liberal democracy.

Further Reading

Clive S. Thomas (editor), *First World Interest Groups, A Comparative Perspective* (Westport, Connecticut: Greenwood Press, 1993). This work provides a comparative examination of the operations of pressure groups in 12 Western liberal democracies. It assesses the similarities and differences in group activity in countries which include the UK, the USA, France, Italy, Sweden and Germany.

A comparative account (which includes pressure groups in the EU) is to be found in **Jeremy Richardson**, *Pressure Groups*, (Oxford: Oxford University Press, 1993).

Jeremy Richardson and **Grant Jordan**, *Governing Under Pressure: The Policy Process in a Post-Parliamentary Democracy* (Oxford: Martin Robertson, 1979). Although somewhat dated, this book provides a useful account of the role of pressure groups in policy-making.

A more up-to-date examination of pressure groups in the UK is provided in **Wyn Grant**, *Pressure Groups, Politics and Democracy in Britain* (London: Philip Allan, 1989).

Jeremy Richardson and **Sonia Mazey**, *Lobbying in the European Community* (Oxford: Oxford University Press, 1993). This work provides an important account of pressure group activity in the EU, and the changes which have occurred since the passage of the 1986 Single European Act.

Chapter Nine | The Media

The aims of this chapter are:

> 1 To examine the key media sources in the United Kingdom and to assess key contemporary developments relating to them.
>
> 2 To analyse the functions performed by the media in liberal-democratic political systems and to evaluate the problems associated with the performance of these tasks.
>
> 3 To examine media regulation in the UK, discussing the rationale for regulation and proposals for reform, including a specific law to safeguard privacy and the implications for Data Protection and Human Rights legislation on this subject.
>
> 4 To evaluate the influence exerted by the media over the conduct of political affairs.
>
> 5 To analyse reasons for the growth of cross-media ownership, to assess the problems this may pose for the conduct of political affairs and evaluate how states might seek to remedy them.
>
> 6 To examine the impact of the media on the operations of the Labour Party in opposition and in government in the 1990s.

The Media in Britain

The media is a means of communication: historically newspapers were the main means of transmitting information, but today there are far more sources. The media includes journals, radio, television and newer means of communication using computer technology. The Internet is an example. This section briefly explores some key developments affecting the scale and operations of the media in the UK.

The Newspaper Industry

The national newspaper industry has for a number of years been divided into the *tabloids* (which give prominence to entertainment over news coverage and are directed at a mass audience) and the *broadsheets* or 'serious' newspapers (which concentrate on news coverage of important national and international events and are pitched at a smaller, more educated readership).

National Newspaper Circulation, 1998

Dailies	
Sun	3, 699, 301
The Mirror	2, 312, 421
Daily Record	671, 135
Daily Star	664, 276
Daily Mail	2, 294, 124
The Express	1, 157, 207
Daily Telegraph	1, 074, 464
Guardian	399, 943
The Times	766, 358
Independent	215, 797
Financial Times	358, 742

Sundays	
News of the World	4, 273, 075
Sunday Mirror	2, 086,880
People	1, 753, 756
Mail on Sunday	2, 202, 024
Express on Sunday	1, 054, 723
Sunday Times	1, 366, 220
Sunday Telegraph	838, 359
Observer	415, 617
Independent on Sunday	259, 551

Source: ABC

The commencement of the tabloid era is usually attributed to Kelvin MacKenzie's tenure at the *Sun* which commenced in 1981. His success (measured in terms of readership) prompted other popular newspapers such as the *Daily Mirror* and *Star* to follow suit. However, the decline in sales experienced by all tabloid newspapers towards the end of the 1990s prompted a re-evaluation of their presentation. In January 1998, Kelvin MacKenzie assumed control of the Mirror Group newspapers and set about providing a more balanced approach, blending entertainment and news coverage. His success promoted other newspapers to act in a similar manner. The departure of Stuart Higgins as editor of the *Sun* later in June 1998 seemed to signal the end of the tabloid era and the introduction of a more balanced approach to journalism pitched at mass consumption.

In addition to the national press, the UK has a wide variety of national, regional and local newspapers. Towards the end of the 1980s it appeared that the regional and local press was in decline. This industry was dominated by multi-media giants such as Thompson Regional Newspapers, Reed Regional Newspapers and Northcliffe newspapers which experienced declining profits, reduced advertising revenues and increasing newsprint costs. By the late 1990s, however, the vitality of the regional and local press was re-established. Most of the former dominant organisations were replaced by companies which included Trinity International, Newsquest Media Group and United Provincial. The publication of provincial newspapers was the sole concern of many of these, some of which were controlled by people with long experience of working in the newspaper industry. The increased circulation and profits of local and regional newspapers derives from factors which include an enhanced focus on community news, economies of scale and the vigorous pursuit of advertising revenue.

The Internet

The Internet consists of networks of computers linked by the international telephone system through which information can be disseminated. It is developing into a major mechanism of international communication and is becoming widely utilised in political affairs. For example, in 1995 details of the British Chancellor of the Exchequer's Budget were circulated by this means of communication. It is a rapidly expanding area of media: by mid-1998 about 14 per cent of Britons (around 7 million) used the Internet, of whom around half had become users in the previous year. A key educational development based on the Internet is the National Grid for Learning which is designed to bring together schools, colleges, universities, libraries, the workplace and the home. It is intended that by the year 2002 all schools will be connected, and that all teachers should be able to teach using information and communications technology (ICT).

There are, however, a number of problems associated with the Internet. These include censorship, regulation and control of cyberspace. At the end of 1995, an American company, CompuServe Inc, closed worldwide access to some 280 sex discussion forums available on the Internet, following allegations that some of these were distributing child pornography (although access was later restored to almost all of these newsgroups). The Munich prosecutor subsequently initiated an action in connection with this, charging the former head of the German subsidary of CompuServe with 'knowingly' facilitating the dissemination of child and animal pornographic pictures. It was argued this could have been prevented by erecting 'firewalls' to prevent the spread of criminal material. In May 1998, the Munich court convicted the defendant, handing out a 2 year suspended sentence.

This case raised three issues − the extent to which an Internet provider could be held responsible for the contents of materials distributed by its subscribers, the adequacy of the regulation of material circulated on the Internet, and the extent to which the problem of illegal material on the Web could be tackled by national (as opposed to international) action.

The acceptance of the need to impose some form of regulation on material available on the Internet prompted the British industry to set up a watchdog body, the Internet Watch Foundation, in 1996. Its main purpose was to tackle illegal material, particularly child pornography. In its first annual report, published in March 1998, it stated it had received 781 complaints referring to 4,300 items on the Net. This resulted in 2,000 images being removed, most of which concerned children engaged in sexual activity. In 1997, Germany became the first country to seek to regulate cyberspace. Multimedia legislation enacted that year curbed what businesses could or could not do on the Internet and outlawed child pornography, Nazi propaganda and material denying the holocaust.

The Functions of the Media

A Source of Information

The media is a source of information concerning internal and international events. By reading, listening to or viewing the media, members of the general public are informed about events of which they have no first-hand knowledge and thereby become more politically aware. One advantage of this is that public participation in policy-making is facilitated. Public opinion is able to exert pressure on governments over a wide range of matters. The problems facing minorities can be made more widely known in this manner.

DIGITAL BROADCASTING

For many years radio and television were important means of communication and acted as major sources of information concerning political affairs. Both have been affected by the advent of digital broadcasting.

Digital audio broadcasting was introduced into the UK towards the end of 1998 and digital television commenced later in the same year. The main benefit of this technological development was to provide the public with a wider range of listening and viewing. Digital audio broadcasting enabled the UK public to initially receive up to 80 channels, while digital television offered a wide range of new channels, home shopping, the Internet and pay-per-view television. There are two main difficulties associated with this form of broadcasting.

The first is that of cost to the consumer. It is likely that the present television signals which are carried on analogue frequencies will be phased out before the end of the first decade of the twenty-first century, after which the only way to see any channels will be either with a set-top box which decodes digital information or by a more expensive digital television set.

The second problem raised by digital broadcasting is the extent to which the production costs will encourage cross media ownership (an issue which is discussed in more detail below), thus enabling a relatively small number of media entrepreneurs to exert disproportionate influence over this industry.

Scrutiny of Government

The media acts as a watchdog and scrutinises the activities performed by governments. The electorate has information placed at its disposal with which it can judge their records: in particular the shortcomings or errors committed by individual ministers or by the government as a whole may be exposed. Investigative journalism has especially aided this role. The impact of the media was spectacularly displayed in the downfall of the American President, Richard Nixon, in 1974 in connection with the Watergate break-in. The media performs an important function by ensuring that governments can be held effectively accountable to the electorate.

'The Fourth Estate'

The term 'fourth estate' is often used to describe the role of the media as a guardian of a country's constitution and its liberal democratic system of politics. This implies, however, that the media possesses autonomy and is independent of the State, the institutions which comprise it (including the political parties) and the economic interests which underlay it.

Problems Posed by the Media

While it is generally accepted that the media is important to the functioning of liberal democracy, its operations are frequently subject to adverse comment. The major criticisms which have been made concerning the manner in which the media operates are considered below.

Partisanship

The first problem is that of partisanship. That is, the media may project political bias in its reporting of events. A newspaper is particularly likely to support one party, which it portrays in a favourable light whilst seeking to denigrate its political opponents. Press bias is primarily effected through analysis: that is, newspapers do not simply report events, but seek to guide the public to a particular interpretation of them. One way this is done is by blurring fact and opinion. This results in a story being slanted towards a political perspective which the newspaper wishes to advance. In countries such as the UK and Ireland radio and television are subject to legislation which is designed to prevent programmes favouring one politician or political party at the expense of another. These forms of media are less regulated elsewhere, so that political partisanship may be displayed.

PRESS PARTISANSHIP

Press partisanship is not necessarily a problem. If a country possesses a press which is diverse, a relatively wide range of political opinion will be presented. Thus the biases of one newspaper can be offset by another presenting a totally different report or analysis of the same issue. However, several problems may arise from this situation.

◆ *Selectivity:* most members of the general public do not read a wide range of newspapers to secure a balanced view. People tend to be selective in their choice of newspaper and may be influenced by the interpretation which it puts forward.

◆ *Disproportionate support:* newspapers rarely reflect the wide range of political views and opinions found within a particular country. In the UK, for example, the bulk of national newspapers support the Conservative Party. In Germany they tend to articulate a moderate conservative political position.

◆ *Ownership:* the problem of bias has been compounded by recent developments in the concentration of ownership. In many liberal democracies a number of newspapers are owned by one individual, which may restrict the diversity of views expressed in that nation's press. Examples of such 'press barons' include Silvio Berlusconi in Italy, the Springer Group in Germany and Rupert Murdoch in Britain.

Selective Coverage of Events

A second criticism which is levelled against the media concerns the process by which events are selected for coverage. It is argued that stories which appear in the newspapers or on television are not chosen according to their importance but, rather, their presence is determined by the criterion of 'newsworthiness'. This may mean that stories which are sensational get media coverage at the expense of worthier events which lack such 'glamour'. Thus war coverage or an inner-city riot may get coverage at the expense of events such as famines, simply because editors believe that the spectre of a tenement block being bombed or a police car being burned is more likely to attract readers or boost listening or viewing figures than a story of quiet and resigned suffering. Such sentiments led Clare Short, the Labour government's International Development Secretary, to urge the British media in 1998 to reverse what she alleged was their 'dumbing down' in the coverage of global issues such as mass starvation.

This criticism suggests that the media does not fulfil its role of educating the public, since it is selective in the information which it provides and how this is presented. This is especially of concern if media owners or editors concentrate on trivia at the expense of key issues of national or international concern.

Editorial Freedom

A third criticism which has been directed against the media is concerned with its editorial freedom: should the media be free to publish any story which it believes is of interest to the general public? Censorship is regarded as an anathema to a liberal-democratic system of government. It is suggestive of state control and implies that the media functions as a propaganda tool of the government, as was the case, for example, in the old state of East Germany. Written constitutions in liberal democracies frequently incorporate provisions to guarantee the freedom of the press: the first amendment to the American Constitution contains such a statement and this principle is also enshrined in the German Basic Law.

Restrictions on Media Activities

Although restrictions on media activity vary in liberal-democractic systems of government (being relatively absent in America but more numerous in the UK), controls are to be found in all of such countries and are justified by the need to ensure that the media acts responsibly. It is, for example, a requirement that reports should be truthful. Those which are not might be subject to actions for slander or libel. A particularly contentious issue concerns the right of the media to publish material which may endanger the state. Legislation (such as the UK's 1989 Official Secrets Act) is designed to protect the state against subversive activities and may be used to stifle stories

Question

'A free press is essential to a liberal-democratic system of government.' Discuss this statement and assess the extent to which it applies to the UK.

In answering this question you should cover the following aspects.

○ Consider the relationship of a *free* press to liberal democracy — why is a free press so important in this system?

○ Provide examples to illustrate *how* a free press is of benefit to the operations of the British liberal-democratic political system. In doing this, use should be made of contemporary events in the press which evidence matters referred to above, such as scrutiny of government actions.

○ Put forward arguments which suggest the press is not totally free. These arguments may be derived from material above (such as ownership, political bias or restrictions on the grounds that state interests override the public's right to know).

○ Present a conclusion concerning whether the British press is able to fulfil its obligations to liberal democracy.

potentially of use to hostile governments. In Ireland, the 1939 Offences Against the State Act or the 1960 Broadcasting Act may be used to prohibit media coverage of illegal organisations.

The main problem is that state interests are difficult to define precisely. Should control of the media cover activities performed by a government which, if revealed to the general public or to world opinion, it might find politically embarrassing? This issue arose in West Germany in the 1960s in connection with the 'Speigel Affair'. The episode led to an amendment of the West German criminal code in 1968 whereby the press could be punished for revealing secrets which were clearly a threat to the State's security.

In the following section more detailed attention is devoted to the issue of media regulation in the UK.

Media Regulation in Britain

The media is subject to a number of controls in the UK. This section examines the nature and operations of these controls, and then examines the arguments for and against an enhanced form of media regulation in the UK.

The European Convention of Human Rights

Article 8 of the European Convention of Human Rights asserts that 'everyone has the right to respect for his private and family life, his home and his correspondence'. Most of the cases brought under this Article have been concerned with protecting the citizen from the state or public authorities. However, for a claim to be ruled admissible it is necessary for a number of conditions to be fulfilled. Any action must be balanced against Article 10, which guarantees the right to freedom of speech. There is also a requirement that applicants have to exhaust any legal remedies available in their home country before launching a claim at the Commission. In 1998, a claim by Earl Spencer that the government had failed to protect his family from media intrusion by publishing stories and pictures of Countess Spencer was rejected as inadmissible by the Commission. The government's lawyers argued that a claim for breach of confidence (which could have secured damages and an injunction against the publication of further similar stories) provided the Earl with a sufficient remedy had he chosen to make use of it.

The Press Complaints Commission

The issue of media invasion of individual privacy is a very contentious issue. Concerns on this matter resulted in six Private Members' Bills being introduced between 1961 and 1989, and further specific proposals to safeguard privacy were contained in a draft Bill published by the legal human rights organisation Justice in 1989 and by the Calcutt Committee in 1990. The key concern is that the media's watchdog function may involve publishing information which infringes on the personal life of a public figure. This highlights an important issue: where does the public's 'right to know' stop and a public person's 'right to privacy' begin? This is a particularly sensitive issue when information is obtained in dubious ways, including the use of telephoto lenses or bugging devices.

The boundaries between the public right to know and the privacy of an individual are often determined by the media themselves, who may operate some form of code of practice. In the UK, for example, there exists a voluntary code of practice which is policed by the Press Complaints Commission to whom those aggrieved by media intrusion may appeal. However, accusations that the British media, and especially the newspaper industry, unduly infringed on the privacy of members of the Royal Family and leading politicians led to calls for the enactment of legislation (in the form of a privacy law) to impose restrictions on the activities of the media. This would make intrusive behaviour by the newspapers a specific criminal offence.

This issue became one of public debate following the circumstances surrounding the death of Diana, Princess of Wales, in Paris in 1997. The car in which she was travelling apparently crashed while the driver tried to avoid the attention of freelance photographers (termed 'paparazzi'). Although these photographers were not employed by major media outlets, the willingness of the tabloid press to buy photographs from them effectively encouraged their work. Accordingly a revised code of practice designed to provide greater protection to members of the public against intrusion by newspapers and magazines was drawn up and came into force on 1 January 1998. This revised code was described as 'the toughest in Europe' by the chairman of the Press Complaints Commission, Lord Wakeham.

There are, however, limitations in the powers of the Press Complaints Commission. In 1998, the decision of the editor of the *Daily Mirror* and *Express* to purchase for six-figure sums the stories of the two British nurses who were found guilty in a Saudi Arabian court of murdering a colleague (but who were

REVISED CODE OF PRACTICE OF THE PCC (1998)

The key provisions of the Press Complaints Commission revised code were:

◆ *Privacy:* section 3 (i) of the new code acknowledged that 'everyone is entitled to respect for his or her private and family life, home, health and correspondence. A publication will be expected to justify intrusions into any individual's private life without consent'. A new definition of a private place as 'public or private property where there is a reasonable expectation of privacy' was provided.

◆ *Harassment:* the code specifically prohibited persistent pursuit by journalists and re-emphasised the responsibility of editors to ensure that material provided from outside sources was obtained in accordance with the provisions of the code.

◆ *Intrusion into grief:* the code called for sensitivity in the publication of such matters in addition to existing provisions related to approaches by journalists.

◆ *The treatment of children:* the code required that editors must demonstrate an exceptional public interest to override the normally paramount interests of the child.

◆ *The public interest:* intrusions into a person's privacy could be justified by demonstrating that the stories were published in the public interest. The new code offered three definitions of this – exposing crime, protecting public safety and preventing the public from being misled by some statement or action of an individual or organisation. The code also reworded the sections which related to public interest.

then subsequently pardoned by the King of that country) raised to prominence the issue of *cheque book journalism*. This concerns the payment by the press (or other media outlets) of large sums of money for publishing rights to a story. Cheque book journalism is included within the editors' code which states that 'payment or offers of payment for stories, pictures or information must not be made directly or through agents to convicted or confessed criminals or to their associates' *unless* 'the material concerned ought to be published in the public interest and payment is necessary for this to be done'. In this particular case, both newspapers justified their decision to pay for the nurses' stories on the grounds that they were victims of a miscarriage of justice and that their version of events was a public interest issue. In 1998, the Press Complaints Commission accepted this argument, stating that the nurses had a right to give their account of this episode.

One reform to this code would be to give the Press Complaints Commission the power to award damages to victims of abuses by the press, financed by fines on editors who breach the code. The broadcasting media are currently subject to more stringent regulation. The Independent Broadcasting Standards Commission has a privacy code whose rulings can be enforced by the Independent Television Commission and the Radio Authority.

Media Controls

There are a wide range of formal and informal mechanisms to regulate the British media.

Public Morality

Public morality is safeguarded by legislation which includes the 1959 Obscene Publications Act, the 1984 Video Recordings Act, the 1990 Broadcasting Act, and the 1994 Public Order and Criminal Justice Act, and through the work performed by the Broadcasting Standards Council (which was established on a statutory footing in 1990 to oversee both radio and television).

Pornography

Ireland possesses the strictest pornography legislation in Europe. Films are governed by the 1923 Censorship of Films Act, which requires that they are approved by the Official Censor. This official may refuse a certificate on the grounds of being 'unfit by reason of being indecent, obscene or blasphemous'. At the other extreme, Holland has the reputation of being the most liberal country regarding pornography. Although the open display of pornographic material is illegal, restrictions are rarely enforced. Hard-core pornography is readily available.

In the UK, moves to liberalise the censorship rules on sex videos produced a clash in 1998 between the British Board of Film Censors (which desired changes in order to undermine the black market in hard-core pornographic videos) and the Home Secretary, Jack Straw, (who opposed the Board's liberalising measures on the grounds that it permitted the distribution of obscene material). Later that year, the retiring chief film censor, James Ferman, branded Britain's Obscenity law as 'an ass' in his annual report.

State Interests

State interests are safeguarded by the 1989 Official Secrets Act (discussed in Chapter 24). However, governments have a range of other means at their disposal to influence the conduct of the media. These include the D-Notice system (which is a procedure designed to stop the reporting of security matters). A key concern here is the differentiation between State interests and government concerns. Allegations have also been made that appointments to bodies such as the British Broadcasting Corporation and the Independent Television Commission may be used in a partisan manner.

Contempt of Court

The reporting activities of the media may be controlled by contempt-of-court proceedings. In 1997, the London *Evening Standard* was fined £40,000 by the High Court for publishing a story concerning six IRA terrorists accused of escaping from Whitemoor prison in 1994. The story disclosed that some of the men on trial had previous convictions for terrorist offences and this resulted in their trial being brought to a halt.

Libel

A particularly effective way for politicians and other public figures to prevent the media from publishing detrimental stories about them is to threaten to sue for libel. This provides a defence for the victim of a published story which is false. Politicians and public figures may, however, use this device to prevent the publication of a story which, although true, would cause embarrassment. The problems posed to the media in defending themselves in such cases (especially the costs involved) may either deter the story being published, or lead to its retraction and possibly an out-of-court financial settlement. Nonetheless, the media are not totally defenceless in such situations, as the following two examples illustrate.

The Jonathan Aitken Case

The manner in which libel may serve as a mechanism to gag the media was illustrated in the episode which involved Jonathan Aitken. *The Guardian* alleged that in 1993, when serving as Minister for Defence Procurement, he had spent time with a Saudi businessman, and that the bill for his stay at the Ritz hotel in Paris had been paid for by an Arab associate. This was in contravention of ministerial rules. Mr Aitken said that his wife had paid the bill and sued the newspaper and Granada television for libel. However, in 1997 the trial collapsed when the

Guardian produced new evidence to support their allegation and to undermine the defence put forward by Mr Aitken. This further suggested he had perjured himself in the High Court. It was estimated that he faced a legal bill of around £1.8 million. In 1999, he subsequently pleaded guilty to perjury and perverting the course of justice in connection with his failed libel action.

The Albert Reynolds Case

In 1994, the Irish Republic's coalition government composed of Fianna Fail and the Labour Party collapsed. The *Sunday Times* subsequently alleged that this had arisen because the taoiseach (that is, Prime Minister) and leader of Fianna Fail had mislead the *Dail* and lied to his Labour Party colleagues. In 1996, Reynolds sued for libel in the British High Court and, although he won the case, was awarded damages of 1p and was forced to pay his own legal bills. He subsequently appealed to the Court of Appeal in 1998 and was granted a retrial. In its defence, the *Sunday Times* asserted that the article was in the public interest and should be protected by the rule of qualified privilege. This would have the effect of reinterpreting the British libel laws to protect newspapers and broadcasters who criticised politicians and other public figures, even if the allegations were inaccurate.

This reform would place British libel laws on a par with American ones. In 1964, the *Sullivan Case* provided the media with qualified privilege when reporting on public figures in order to facilitate uninhibited, robust and wide-open debate on public affairs. Additionally, American laws of defamation provide an 'absence of malice' defence which is designed to protect careful and responsible journalism even if some of the details of a story are not totally accurate.

Safeguarding Privacy in Britain

Privacy may be broadly defined as the 'right to be let alone'. There is no specific right to privacy in the UK, which has been particularly threatened by the advent of surveillance technology. There are two ways in which the intrusion of the media into an individual's privacy can be brought under control.

❍ *A privacy law:* this would be a piece of legislation specifically designed to protect an individual's privacy.

❍ *A privacy law 'through the back door':* this would defend an individual's right to privacy indirectly, through the application to the media of legislation whose ostensible purpose is not concerned with this issue.

A Privacy Law

The main alternative to media self-regulation is through privacy legislation which would enable the courts to award damages when such rights were violated. Privacy legislation exists in a number of European countries: a right to privacy is recognised in both French and German law, while in Denmark unauthorised photography on private property is forbidden. This issue is regulated by State governments in America and most have some form of privacy law. However, privacy legislation to regulate the media in Britain has been fiercely resisted on the grounds that it would interfere with the media's ability to act as a public watchdog.

The Justification for a Privacy Law

The main problem associated with the UK's current system of regulation policed by the Press Complaints Commission is that it is sometimes ineffective. The new code of practice introduced in 1998 seemed to be breached when some sections of the media ran stories concerning the private life of the Foreign Secretary, Robin Cook. Such stories seemed to confuse the concept of 'public interest' with a broader notion of 'what interests the public'. The intention of the coverage seemed less concerned with informing the public than with lowering Cook's public standing. This prompted the Lord Chancellor, Lord Irvine, to suggest that the Press Complaints Commission (PCC) should establish machinery to stop a newspaper publishing a story which infringed an individual's privacy. This involved the exercise of 'prior restraint' in which the PCC would be empowered to ban a paper from publishing a story of this nature, unless it could be demonstrated that it was in the public interest.

Opposition to a Privacy Law

The effectiveness of privacy legislation is limited in those countries which have it. In France, for example, the civil damages awarded are usually low and the sanction of the prevention of publication is rarely used. In Germany, privacy is balanced by Article 5 of the 1949 Constitution which specifically protects the freedom of speech and the press. The main objections to a specific privacy law in Britain have been that it would be very complicated to draft and would encounter key problems including the precise legal definition of 'privacy', thereby possibly preventing the reporting of issues such as corruption in government by investigative journalists.

Data-Protection and Human Rights Legislation

The debate concerning a specific law of privacy has been influenced by beliefs that other legislation concerning open government and human rights, which was put forward by the Labour government after 1997, could also safeguard privacy and would effectively secure the enactment of a privacy law 'through the back door'. This argument rested upon the ability of judges to develop a common law right of privacy derived from their interpretation of this new legislation. The new laws consisted of data protection and human rights legislation.

Data Protection Legislation

Data protection introduced in Italy in 1996 has been used to restrict media coverage. In 1998, the UK's Labour government enacted the Data Protection Act to implement a European Directive. This was designed to protect the individual's rights to privacy. It gave the public the right to inspect personal information held on them in computer files and other databases and insisted that such personal data could not be used without the subject's consent.

Human Rights Legislation

In 1997, the government proposed to introduce a Human Rights Act which would incorporate the European Convention of Human Rights into British law. This issue is discussed more fully in Chapter 24. The prospect alarmed the press, which feared that Article 8 (concerned with asserting an individual's right to privacy in connection with his or her relationship to state authority) would be applied to them and that, used in conjunction with the data protection legislation and the new offence of harassment, their ability to investigate, report and comment on matters of public interest would be curtailed.

The government's response to such fears was to deny its intention to provide for privacy legislation in this indirect manner. Accordingly, it tabled amendments which included an explicit statement that the courts should give higher priority to freedom of expression (embodied in Article 10 of the European Convention of Human Rights) when it clashed with respect for private life. Also, that the courts should be required to take into account the public interest of any disputed published item, coupled with a judgement as to whether the newspaper had acted 'fairly and reasonably' within the provisions of the Code of Practice of the Press Complaints Commission. These amendments, however, still gave judges a wide discretion which might aid them in developing a law of privacy when this legislation becomes operational.

The Attitude of the Courts

Whether privacy legislation becomes enacted 'through the back door' is dependent on the manner in which the judiciary act: they may take the view that such a law should be based on statute law passed by Parliament as opposed to common law developed by the courts. Nonetheless, the fact that the judges might create a common law right of privacy has led some press proprietors to advocate that this matter should be dealt with by legislation which would contain an adequate public interest defence for the media when intruding upon an individual's privacy, rather than leaving judges to determine what the public interest constituted. Their concerns are partly based upon the historic attitude of the courts towards these matters, which is discussed in the following section.

The Courts and the Freedom of the Media

In the USA, the determination of the boundary between freedom of speech and the right to privacy is left to the judges who deal with the matter on a case by case basis. The increased involvement of the British judiciary in matters affecting privacy was viewed sceptically by the media in the belief that judges are likely to adopt a hostile attitude towards them. This view is justified by the negative stance frequently adopted by the judiciary towards the disclosure of information, whether state or private interests are concerned. The ability of journalists to protect the sources of information is regarded by many as a key safeguard of press freedom. The judiciary, however, have frequently taken a different view of this situation and have compelled journalists to disclose the sources on which their stories are based.

DISCLOSURE OF INFORMATION

The following examples indicate that judges often require journalists to disclose the sources of their information.

◆ *1980:* Granada TV was ordered to disclose its sources in relation to a programme which was critical of the British Steel Corporation.

◆ *1983:* the *Guardian* was ordered to return documents which would enable the name of the civil servant who had leaked the date when cruise missiles would be delivered from America to Britain to be ascertained.

◆ *1985:* a journalist was fined £20,000 for refusing to disclose the sources concerning the outcome of references to the Monopolies and Mergers Commission.

Question

'Media intrusion into the private lives of public figures is never justified and thus the media should be made subject to statutory regulation.'

Consider this statement, supporting the arguments you present with examples of your own.

◆ *1997:* the Court of Appeal ruled that a journalist should return a number of documents to the organisation Camelot to enable it to ascertain who had leaked information regarding large salary increases to the directors of the National Lottery. The Court of Appeal argued that the public interest required this private company to discover a disloyal and untrustworthy employee.

These examples suggest that the judiciary have no inbuilt disposition to champion press freedom, which may be even more limited when judges implement the data protection and human rights legislation.

The Information Revolution and European Regulation

The approach of what is termed the 'information age' has a number of major implications for regulation. The birth of digital television will see the advent of hundreds of television channels, television sets used as computers to access the Internet and to transact commercial operations such as shopping and banking, and PCs used to watch moving pictures and eventually conventional broadcasting. Such developments will possess major implications for regulation which may serve one or other of the two objectives which are discussed below.

Quality

One approach views the maintenance of quality as the key task of regulation. Some of those who will be involved in the information revolution (such as broadcasters) come from a highly regulated environment. Others (such as information technology companies) come from an entrepreneurial climate in which regulation is of a limited nature.

Competition

An alternative approach towards regulation is to ensure fair and open access to the new opportunities which will become available through the enactment of new competition laws. However, the desire of multinational companies for free and open competition may clash, for example, with the protected position given to public service broadcasters in countries such as the UK. In 1994, and in 1998, the European Commissioner for Competition, Karel Van Miert, blocked attempts by three companies (Kirch, Bertelsmann and Deutsche Telekom) to establish pay-TV ventures (the latter involving digital television) on the grounds it would establish a monopoly in the German pay-TV market.

EU PROPOSALS FOR MEDIA REGULATION

Towards the end of 1997, the European Commission published a Green Paper, *Towards an Information Society Approach*. This document put forward five principles, stating that regulation should:

1   be as limited as possible to achieve goals

2   respond to the needs of users

3   operate in a clear framework

4   ensure the principle of universal service and the public service mission

5   ensure the independence of watchdogs.

It then suggested three possible ways forward for regulation:

1   retain the current regulatory structure and build upon it

2   establish a new system for the new technologies and allow systems for traditional core broadcasting and telecommunications to adapt more slowly

3   terminate the existing regulatory system and introduce a new one which would cover all existing and new services.

Most member countries of the EU have paid little regard to the implications which the information revolution possesses for regulation. Germany, however, has moved some way in this direction by introducing a graduated approach to regulation whereby controls have been lightened the further away the system becomes from straightforward broadcasting. One major difficulty of producing a policy in this area in the UK is that responsibility for the area is currently divided between the Department of Trade and Industry and the Culture and Media Department. This situation led the chairman of the Commons Culture, Media and Sport Select Committee, Gerald Kaufman, to suggest in 1997 that responsibility for the issue should be taken away from the departments and vested in the hands of a Minister for the Information Age, located in the Prime Minister's Office.

The Media and Political Affairs

The media may exert a significant degree of influence on the conduct of a nation's political affairs.

The Media and Political Campaigning

In all liberal democracies the media exerts a profound influence over the conduct of political affairs. In the nineteenth century, the only way members of the general public could see a leading politician was to physically attend meetings which they addressed. It followed, therefore, that oratory was a prized political skill in that period. But this is no longer the case. Initially the popular press made it possible for politicians to put their case to a wider audience than could attend a political meeting. Subsequently, radio and television enabled leading politicians to address the public. This has had a significant influence over the conduct of national election campaigns, which has been discussed in Chapter 5.

However, the involvement of the media in political affairs is not confined to national elections. The role performed by legislatures may also be adversely affected. Investigative journalism may provide more effective scrutiny of the actions of the executive than a legislator's speeches or questions. An appearance by a legislator in a brief televised interview will reach a wider audience than a speech delivered within the legislature. One response to this issue has been the televising of

TELEVISING THE BRITISH HOUSE OF COMMONS

Legislatures may respond to arguments that the media has taken over their traditional functions by using it to publicise their activities. In 1989, the House of Commons allowed its proceedings to be televised. The main benefit intended from this course of action was to make government more visible to members of the general public who would then understand the importance of the work performed by Parliament. Although the viewing public of live proceedings is not substantial (but is available, for example, in cable television's *Parliamentary Channel*), snippets of broadcasts are utilised in the more widely viewed news programmes.

However, there have also been disadvantages associated with this development. It has been argued that MPs 'play up' to the cameras, perhaps tailoring their speeches to include words or phrases which are likely to get reported. These references are referred to as 'sound bites'. Ministers have also been accused of 'planting' questions: this involves an MP from the government party tabling a question of which the minister has prior knowledge. This is designed to make the minister appear an effective parliamentary performer on television, thus enhancing the minister's and the government's reputation.

the proceedings of legislative bodies. The Australian parliament, for example, voted to televise the proceedings of the Senate, the House of Representatives and their committees in October 1991.

The Political Influence of the Media

Issues such as ownership and bias are regarded as important in liberal democracies, as it is assumed that the media possesses considerable ability to determine the course of political events. In this section various arguments concerning the influence of the media on political affairs are considered.

Agenda Setting

It is argued that the media has the ability to 'set the political agenda': that is, the media may publicise a particular issue in the hope of concentrating the attention of its readers, listeners or viewers on this topic. Whether this is a good or a bad development depends much on the motives behind the media's attempts to influence public perceptions. A beneficial aspect of this activity is that the media may lead public opinion in a progressive direction, perhaps securing action on a social problem which would otherwise have been ignored. In the UK, a television programme shown in 1966, *Cathy Come Home*, had a significant impact on publicising the plight of Britain's homeless and aided the growth of the organisation Shelter.

Alternatively, however, the media may be guided by partisan motives. Attention may be directed at an issue in order to secure support for a course of action favoured by the media owner or by the political interests which the owner supports. This may involve whipping up public hysteria to persuade governments to act in a manner advocated by the media or the interests which are behind it.

Reinforcement or Change?

Agenda setting is, however, only one aspect of media influence. It is sometimes argued that the media has the ability to determine, not merely the policies which governments adopt but, more fundamentally, their political complexion. This accusation implies that the media has a significant influence over voting behaviour at election times. There are two basic schools of thought concerning the ability of the media to influence how we vote. The debate centres on the extent to which the media merely reinforces existing political behaviour rather than being able to act as the agent of political change. In the UK this debate is particularly concerned with the ability of newspapers to determine the outcome of political events.

Reinforcement

Those who argue that the media reinforces existing political activity suggest that the power of the media over politics is limited, since most members of the general public have preconceived political opinions. They will either read, listen to or view material which is consistent with these existing ideas or ignore contrary ideas should they be expressed. Further, as the media knows the tastes of its clientele, it will cater for their opinions. The reinforcement theory thus suggests that issues of media bias are of no significant political importance even at election times.

Change

A contrary opinion to the reinforcement theory suggests that the media has a profound influence over political activity such as voting behaviour. It is suggested that many people are unaware of the political biases of the media and may thus be influenced by the manner in which it portrays events, especially when such exposure takes place over a long period of time.

This may be especially important when the gap between the leading parties for political office is small: the British Conservative Party's election victory in 1992 has been attributed to the influence exerted by the Conservative tabloid press on undecided voters. The front-page suggestion in the *Sun* newspaper on the day of the 1992 General Election suggesting that if Neil Kinnock won, the last person leaving Britain should turn out the lights, led to the boast the following day (when Major narrowly secured re-election) that 'it was the *Sun* wot won it!' Similarly, Silvio Berlusconi's victory in the 1994 Italian elections has been explained by the impact of his three television channels on voting behaviour. The perception that the Labour Party required to convert Conservative supporters in order to continue winning elections was one explanation for Tony Blair's decision to publicly defend his welfare reforms in an article in the *Daily Mail* in December 1997 as opposed to papers traditionally supportive of the Labour Party such as the *Daily Mirror*.

Conclusion

The extent to which the media influences political affairs is thus open to debate. It is one social agency among several others (such as the family, the workplace or the neighbourhood) which

Question

Provide a definition of the term 'soundbite', using examples of your own taken from television and newspaper reports.

may affect political conduct. Those without established political views or loyalties (who are described as 'don't knows' in opinion polls) may be most susceptible to media influence.

Promotion of Political Events

The role of the media extends beyond merely influencing the outcome of elections: it also may promote major political episodes. In the UK, it was alleged that the Social Democratic Party (formed in 1981) was a media creation. This argument suggested that the heavy emphasis of the media on ideological divisions within the Labour Party was a major factor which persuaded a number of social democrats to form a new political vehicle to advance their views.

The initial successes enjoyed by that Party were also attributed to media interest in their affairs – an interest which waned when the Falklands War commenced in 1982.

Media Ownership

The suggestion that the media can influence the political behaviour of at least some members of the general public thus implies that issues such as ownership and political bias are important in a liberal democracy. It may mean that some parties have an unfair advantage over others.

Cross-Media Ownership

Traditionally media operations were disconnected: a 'separation of media powers' existed in many liberal democracies whereby ownership of the print media was divorced from other major forms of communication such as radio and television. While it became increasingly common in the twentieth century for newspaper ownership to be concentrated in relatively few hands by a process of mergers, such processes were confined to the print media. But this is now changing. Increasingly media owners have financial interests in various forms of communication including newspapers, journals, radio and television. The largest European media organisation is the German company Bertelsmann AG, whose revenue in 1996 amounted to $14,728 million. Its interests included commercial and pay television, hardcover and paperback books, magazines and newspapers, music publishing and multimedia products. In 1998, it reportedly paid £840 million to buy the British publishing company Random House. This provides a good example of what is meant by 'cross-media ownership'. In the remainder of this section consideration is directed at why this development occurred and what problems might arise as the result of it.

Why Cross-Media Ownership Developed

The role of the private sector in television companies had a profound influence on cross-media ownership. In many European countries television was initially viewed as a form of public service. It was operated by the State (sometimes using the mechanism of public corporations) whose main duty was to ensure that news was reported in an impartial fashion: objectivity and balance were the guiding principles of public service broadcasting. This situation was different to that in the USA where broadcasting organisations were privately owned.

The monopoly enjoyed by public service broadcasting was eventually challenged by the private sector which sought to make a profit from this form of communication. This gave rise to commercial television which was exclusively funded by advertising revenue. This was unlike public service broadcasting which was mainly funded by its users' paying a licence fee (as in the UK), sometimes (as in the former state of West Germany) topped up by income derived from advertising. The costs involved in establishing a television channel made it essential that established business and commercial interests should involve themselves in commercial television. In many countries, however, the growth of commercial broadcasting was initially subject to state supervision. This was justified on the grounds that the frequencies available for transmission were limited in number and so the state had to regulate the use of this scarce commodity.

However, more recent developments concerned especially with cable and satellite television have facilitated a massive growth in the number of television channels which can be transmitted within any one particular country. Although these may also be subject to some degree of state supervision (cable and satellite channels in the UK, for example, are loosely regulated by the Independent Television Commission) these innovations have served to further increase the role of the private sector in broadcasting.

Problems Associated with Cross-Media Ownership

Cable and satellite channels are attractive to the private sector whose role in broadcasting has been further facilitated by the process of deregulation: this has especially occurred in Italy and France during the 1980s. Many of these commercial and business interests were already engaged in other aspects of media activity such as newspapers and radio. The ability of an individual or a commercial company to have interests in a wide range of media outlets may pose a number of difficulties.

The Power of Media Bosses

Media owners possess a considerable degree of power. They may seek to place ideas on the political agenda or to influence the manner in which members of the general public think or act. This may create a situation in which politicians adopt a subservient attitude towards major media owners. This allegation was made in connection with the relationship between the Blair government and Rupert Murdoch after 1997.

One explanation for Labour's success at the 1997 General Election was the support obtained from the tabloid newspapers. The perception that such support needed to be sustained in order both to sell Labour policies to the electorate and to aid future electoral success resulted in the government devoting attention to the popular press and particularly towards Rupert Murdoch. This gave rise to two accusations.

Rupert Murdoch, who owns a publishing empire on which it is said 'the sun never sets'.

1   *Murdoch influenced the content of government policy:* initial government hesitancy towards the UK entering the single European currency was possibly based on Murdoch's opposition to this venture. A front-page article in the *Sun* in 1998 queried whether Blair's support for this proposal could make him the most dangerous man in Britain. The article resulted in him advocating this course of action less eagerly.

2   *The government actively aided Murdoch's interests:* in March 1998, discussions took place between Prime Minister Blair and his Italian counterpart, Romano Prodi. Their discussion regarding the impact on Italian political opinion of Murdoch's attempt to expand his media interests in Europe was a key factor inducing him to call off his £2 billion bid for a stake in Silvio Berlusconi's television interests, Mediaset.

MURDOCH AND MANCHESTER UNITED FOOTBALL CLUB

Towards the end of 1998, BSkyB made a bid of in excess of £600 million for Manchester United Football Club. The club's board of directors voted to accept it. The forging of a link between broadcasters and football was not new in Europe. In 1986 the Italian media magnate, Silvio Berlusconi, bought the club AC Milan. The prestige associated with this may have aided his political ambitions, which briefly led to his becoming Prime Minister after the 1994 elections. Murdoch's actions were not guided by political considerations of this nature. There was a variety of other reasons to explain this decision, including a desire to prevent this club from independently operating its own television channel. If other teams followed suit, the intention of the Murdoch empire to use BSkyB's broadcasting of live football (on a pay-per-view basis) as an inducement to sell dishes for its digital satellite service would be undermined. Ownership of Manchester United would further give BSkyB a strong insider position in negotiations between UEFA and the television companies over the broadcasting of matches in a future European football league.

This arrangement was referred to the Office of Fair Trading. In April 1999, Stephen Byers, the Trade and Industry Secretary, blocked Murdoch's bid on the grounds that it would be anti-competitive, against the public interest, and would damage the quality of British football.

Lack of Diversity

Cross-ownership may erode the diversity of the media, regarded as essential in a liberal democracy. The media needs to articulate a wide range of opinions in order for members of the public to become politically educated. A similarity of views expressed in various media forms may be more compatible with a one-party state than a liberal democracy.

Censorship

Media owners may wish to suppress debate on the grounds that this may have an adverse effect on their broader commercial interests. An accusation of this nature arose in 1998 when it was alleged that Rupert Murdoch had pressurised senior managers at one of his publishing concerns, HarperCollins, to reverse a decision to publish a book written by the former Governor of Hong Kong, Chris Patten.

Patten's book contained passages which were critical of the Chinese authorities. Publication might have harmed the attempts which were being made to extend the operations of satellite and cable television owned by Murdoch into China.

Commercial Considerations May Dominate the Media

Stories or programmes may cater for the lowest common denominator in which the worst practices of the tabloid press become the standard form of activity. This problem has implications for public service broadcasting. If they lose viewers to commercial television companies their case for receiving all or any of a licence fee is undermined.

Limiting Cross-Media Ownership

Many developments connected with the application of technology to the media industry have had consequences for the conduct of politics which are desirable. Innovations which include desktop publishing, cable and satellite broadcasting theoretically facilitate a diversity of opinion which is beneficial to a healthy liberal democracy. New media ventures (such as Ted Turner's Cable News Network) have succeeded and a wide range of additional broadcasting outlets have been created, eroding the power previously enjoyed by media 'giants'. In the USA, for example, the power previously enjoyed by ABC, CBS and NBC has been broken and one feature of the 1992 Presidential Election campaign was the enhanced role of local cable television stations.

The key consideration is the extent to which companies taking advantage of these developments are able to remain independent. Developments in the mid-1990s in connection with the Information Superhighway have tended to promote takeovers and mergers, resulting in the formation of large companies with diverse media interests. If small companies are taken over or driven out of business by larger concerns with interests in a range of different forms of communication the benefits which could be derived from technological innovations will be lost. It is this concern which has prompted the enactment of national or state legislation to limit the extent of cross-media ownership.

THE REGULATION OF MEDIA OWNERSHIP IN BRITAIN

Mergers of large operations within the newspaper industry have required the consent of the Secretary of State since 1965, who may refer the matter to the Monopolies Commission. But consent to such activities is the norm. In 1981, for example, Rupert Murdoch was allowed to purchase *The Times* and the *Sunday Times*, giving him a large share of the national daily and Sunday newspaper market. But Murdoch's interests went beyond newspapers. He owned a cable television company, Sky Cable Company, which merged with British Satellite Broadcasting in 1991 to form BSkyB.

In some countries (such as Australia and America) restrictions have been imposed on cross-media ownership. In the UK, the 1981 Broadcasting Act prevented newspapers from owning Independent

Television Companies, but this provision did not extend to cable television. This matter was considered in a 1995 Green Paper. The 1996 Broadcasting Act proposed permission for national newspapers to own Independent Television Companies (with the exception of Rupert Murdoch's News International and Mirror Group Newspapers) and for such television companies to take over newspapers.

Question

What do you understand by the term 'cross-media ownership' and what problems might affect the conduct of political affairs as the result of it?

Cross-Media Subsidies

This issue is related to cross-media ownership. It concerns the ability of a media proprietor to use profits from one enterprise to subside losses on another. Although this may be a means to ensure the publication of 'quality' material with a potentially low audience, it can also be used as a mechanism to destroy competition from rival publications by undercutting them.

The policy adopted by Rupert Murdoch's News International Corporation of selling *The Times* at an artificially low price on certain days of the week supported from profits made by the tabloid *Sun* made this issue a topic of debate during the 1990s. It became an issue of political concern when the Competition Bill was debated in the House of Lords in 1998. Murdoch was accused of deliberately trying to drive competitive 'quality' newspapers (especially the *Independent* and *Daily Telegraph*) out of business by the practice of 'predatory pricing' which had far-reaching implications for the diversity and independence of the British press.

This prompted the House of Lords to support a Liberal Democrat amendment to the Bill to specifically prohibit newspaper price cuts which had the effect of 'injuring' or 'eliminating' the competition. The government rejected the need for such an amendment (which was thus voted down during the Bill's progress through the House of Commons in 1998) arguing that it would have the effect of freezing the newspaper industry in its current form and gave too much power to the regulator. However, critics of the government's stance argued that the real reason for their opposition was that the amendment was unambiguously directed at Rupert Murdoch whose goodwill the government wished to cultivate.

Politicians and Media Management

It is essential in liberal-democratic political systems for politicians to secure widespread public support. This may require enlisting the support of the media to ensure that it treats them and their policies favourably.

The Media and Official Information

Chief executives will frequently use the media to 'sell' themselves or policies with which they are associated to the general public. This may involve the regular use of the media: for example, Boris Yeltsin made regular weekly radio broadcasts to the Russian people while serving as president after 1990. Additionally, governments seek to manage the media through the release of official information at regular meetings between ministers (or their spokespersons) and journalists. In France, for example, daily information meetings for journalists take place at the foreign ministry and the Prime Minister's office. Meetings of this sort are typically public and 'on the record' (that is, the person imparting the information may be quoted). They are frequently supplemented, however, by a more restricted flow of information to selected journalists. In the UK the 'lobby system' is used in this manner.

The British Lobby System

The lobby system traditionally consisted of regular, secretive meetings between representatives of the government (usually the Prime Minister's chief press secretary) and selected journalists. This carried a possible sanction whereby a particular journalist and/or his or her employer could be excluded from such meetings and denied all forms of official information if they offended the government. Information imparted in this fashion was often 'off the record' or 'background information' from sources who could not be quoted.

Objections to the secretive nature of the lobby system came to a head in the late 1980s when three newspapers (the *Guardian*, the *Independent* and the *Scotsman*) protested against the conduct of Margaret Thatcher's press secretary, Bernard Ingham. One of their complaints was that he made disparaging remarks about Cabinet ministers which could not then be quoted. These newspapers withdrew from the lobby system until 1991 when John Major offered a compromise position whereby journalists were allowed to identify a source as one which emanated from Downing Street. The situation was further modified in 1997 when Tony Blair's government instituted an 'open' lobby system. This is discussed below.

Opposition parties will also seek to use the media for their own political advantage. The following section explores the Labour Party's management of the media between 1992 and 1997 and the consequent problems which arose.

'Spin Doctors', the Media and the Labour Party

The Labour Party's success at the 1997 General Election was heavily influenced by their ability to manage or manipulate the reporting activities of the media, particularly the newspapers, so that their policy and criticisms of the Conservative government received favourable coverage. The essence of this work was in presentation, adjusting the slant of Labour statements in order to enhance their popular appeal. Those responsible for this work were referred to as *spin doctors*. The term 'spin doctor' was first used in the USA in the 1980s, and described those whose work was essentially concerned with public relations, seeking to create a favourable media image for a political party or organisation.

Following Labour's victory at the 1997 General Election, a number of these 'spin doctors' were employed (in the status of temporary civil servants) as ministerial advisors. A key role was to secure governmental control of the media agenda so that journalists would be placed in the position of responding to government initiatives, rather than putting forward ones of their own. However, a number of problems associated with the use of techniques which had served Labour well in opposition surfaced following their election success in 1997. These are discussed below.

The Power Wielded by Spin Doctors

The ability of spin doctors to mediate between the government and the electorate provides them with considerable power. Alastair Campbell, who served as the chief press secretary to the Prime Minister, Tony Blair, has been described as 'the most powerful unelected politician at the very heart of British government' who operated as the hub of the government's publicity machine. His briefings of the Parliamentary lobby effectively made him the daily voice both of the government and the Prime Minister. One conceivable danger which might arise from this situation is that the operations of the liberal democratic political process may be undermined through the power wielded by spin doctors. This may happen in a number of ways.

❍ *Domination of elected politicians:* the pre-eminence 'spin doctors' attach to presentation may lead them to dominate (or 'rubbish') ministers and other politicians. Examples of this were Sir Bernard Ingham's dismissal of John Biffen as a 'semi-detached member' of Margaret Thatcher's cabinet and accusations in 1998 that Tony Blair's press secretary, Alastair Campbell, spoke down to ministers.

○ *Censorship:* they may seek to control the activities of the media by bullying journalists into favourably reporting the activities of the government, or denying access to government sources. In 1998, such allegations against Alastair Campbell highlighted the inconsistencies derived from status as a civil servant and his role as a Party appointee.

Presentation Dominates Policy

The emphasis placed on presentation and image could become a substitute for policy. This would devalue the liberal democratic political system since the attention of electors would be diverted from the contents of government proposals to issues such as delivery, appearance or image.

Impact on the Civil Service

The employment by leading Labour ministers of spin doctors whose status was that of temporary civil servants had an unsettling impact on the Civil Service. There were two main problems.

○ *Impact on Civil Service neutrality:* 'spin doctors' were employed to aid the interests of the Labour government. This not only cast the neutrality of the Civil Service into doubt but also raised the issue of whether it was acceptable that taxpayers' money should be used for Party political causes.

○ *Politicisation:* the relationship between 'spin doctors' and the official Government Information and Communication Service became unclear. Attempts were made to make this service seemingly more subservient to government requirements – a 'Ministry of Spin'. This included the establishment of a central media monitoring unit in 1997.

Parliament Becomes Devalued

Parliament was traditionally viewed as the forum in which government policy was released. This often took the form of ministerial statements. The pre-eminent position of Parliament in such matters was reinforced by the '12 day' rule which operated until the end of the 1950s, whereby television did not debate an issue which was to be imminently discussed within Parliament. However, the tendency of spin doctors to release statements about government policy prior to statements in Parliament effectively undermines this traditional role and was criticised by the Speaker, Mrs Betty Boothroyd, in 1998. Conservative and Liberal Democrat MPs on the Select Committee on Public Administration also levelled this charge against Alastair Campbell in 1998.

The Potential to Stir Up Internal Disunity

A spin doctor's first loyalty is to his or her minister. Thus when a minister or the policy with which he or she is associated becomes a source of conflict within the government, there is a danger that a spin doctor will rush to the minister's defence by using the media in an attempt to undermine the position of his or her opponents. The relatively large number of spin doctors employed by ministers in Tony Blair's Labour government made this problem a potentially serious one, and led to suggestions that all contacts with the press by spin doctors should be subject to the overall control of the Prime Minister's office. This development, of course, would enhance the power of the Prime Minister's 'spin doctor', the chief press secretary, Alastair Campbell.

The Determination of Government Policy

The most serious problem relates to the relationship between spin doctors and ministers in the determination of government policy. When Labour had been in opposition in the 1990s, spin doctors were viewed as authoritative sources of Party policy. In government after 1997 they continued to wield this power by methods which included giving journalists private, often unattributed, interviews in order to convey the message which they believed was best suited to advance the interests of the government or their minister. Ministers, however, were not necessarily consulted by their spin doctors before they gave a statement to the media. This resulted in the possibility of conflicting statements being publicly articulated. The most serious allegation of this nature in the early period of Blair's government concerned the UK's entry into the European single currency. It was alleged a glaring difference of opinion emerged between the statements issued by the Chancellor of the Exchequer, Gordon Brown, and his spin doctor, Charlie Whelan.

In 1997, the Chancellor suggested in an article in *The Times* that the UK would not join the single currency in the first 'wave' of memberships after 1997. But he wished to keep his options open regarding entry before the next General Election which was due, at the latest, in 2002. His spin doctor, however, sought to avoid suggestions that the Chancellor was fudging the issue and put forward a statement to the media which abandoned the Chancellor's carefully chosen words by categorically ruling out any possibility of the UK entering the single currency until after the next General Election. In doing so, Whelan had not merely provided gloss on a policy to enhance its popular appeal but he had effectively altered it. This conflict had damaging political and economic repercussions and forced the Chancellor to endorse the view of his 'spin doctor'.

Reforms of Labour–Media Relationships

Centralisation was the main theme of the reforms which took place after 1997. These entailed a number of developments which are discussed below.

The Strategic Communications Unit

This was set up within the Cabinet Office in January 1998, and is composed of senior civil servants and ministerial advisors. Its role was to coordinate ministerial announcements to avoid the possibility of giving conflicting statements to the media. Its work is discussed in more detail in Chapter 12.

The 'Enforcer'

In 1998, Jack Cunningham was appointed to a key coordinating role within the Cabinet Office which was particularly concerned with the government's relationship with the media. His work included holding daily meetings which brought together senior government and Labour Party personnel (drawn from Number 10, the Cabinet Office, Chief Whips Office, the Treasury, Foreign Office, Department of Environment, Transport and the Regions, and the Labour Party) coordinating strategy and presentation, and ensuring that immediate presentational issues were handled within a wider strategic context. Cunningham's role is also discussed in Chapter 13.

The Attribution of Sources

One problem faced by the Blair government after 1997 was the manner in which secret, 'off the record' interviews were given to journalists by numerous 'unattributable' sources (that is, where the name of the source could not be revealed). This resulted in conflicting policy statements to journalists which had an unsettling effect on the government. Accordingly, an attempt was made by the government to secure a greater degree of coordination and openness (and hence accountability) to those who briefed the media on the government's behalf.

The lobby system was accordingly made subject to greater openness, thus increasing the authority of statements made at such meetings and devaluing alternative sources of information. Pronouncements by the Prime Minister's press secretary could be officially ascribed to 'the prime minister's official spokesman'. This reform fell short of the situation in the USA where news conferences are regularly given by the President or members of the White House staff. These occasions may be broadcast and journalists can ask questions. The system of 'off the record' briefings continued, but would be described as statements made 'by a Labour source'.

However, even in countries such as the USA and Germany where such openness exists, private meetings between spin doctors and journalists continue, resulting in the publication of unattributed material.

The Media and Government in the UK After 1997

Some problems arose in the relationship between the media and the Labour government after 1997.

Media Criticisms of the Government

Those in political power tend to be critical of attacks made upon them by the media. The long period of Conservative Party political dominance between 1979 and 1997 accentuated this critical stance and led to some Conservatives voicing concern about the impartiality of bodies such as the BBC. In 1986 the then Conservative Party chairman, Norman Tebbit, accused the highly respected BBC correspondent, Kate Adie, of being a spokesperson for Colonel Gadafy of Libya, following what he perceived to be her biased reporting of the American attack on Tripoli.

Government disapproval of the media increased after 1992 and resulted in the media giving relatively favourable coverage to Labour attacks on John Major's government, particularly when these were carefully presented by the spin doctors. Newspapers which were traditionally Conservative supporters (such as the *Sun*) switched to backing Labour in this period. This may have induced the new government to believe that the media was favourably disposed towards it. The government may have 'lowered its guard' in its dealings with the media, mistakenly believing that it retained the ability to manage the media which would effectively operate as part of the government's propaganda machine.

THE BBC AND THE LABOUR GOVERNMENT

Almost as soon as the Labour government took office the media began to adopt a critical attitude towards its operations. In 1997, media criticism of issues which included the Lord Chancellor's plans to reform the legal aid system, and the donation by Bernie Ecclestone to the Labour Party embarrassed the government.

Resentment of the scrutinising role of the media climaxed in December 1997 in an interview on the BBC's Radio 4 *Today* programme between John Humphrys and the Social Security Secretary, Harriet Harman, on the subject of benefit cuts for single parents. This provoked an outburst similar to that of Tebbit's in 1986 in which the Party's chief media spokesman, David Hill, threatened to sever cooperation with the programme, thus preventing ministers being interviewed on it. This immediately led to allegations of Labour's seeking to bully the programme, of refusing to publicly discuss its policies, and of a party official trying to control the media's access to ministers.

This was followed in early 1998 with an attack on the BBC by the Prime Minister's chief press secretary, Alastair Campbell. He objected to a question put to the Prime Minister by John Sergeant, the BBC's chief political correspondent, on the eve of the Prime Minister's visit to Washington. The question concerned how Tony Blair would react if questioned in America on the sex scandal engulfing the Clinton administration. Campbell subsequently branded the BBC as a 'downmarket, dumbed-down, over-staffed, over-bureaucratic, ridiculous organisation'.

Explanations of Media Behaviour

One reason to explain the apparent enthusiasm for attacks on the Labour government in its early months was that the media saw its main role to be that of questioning the actions of those wielding political power. The need for an effective opposition to the government was intensified after the 1997 General Election when the Conservative Party was reduced to 165 MPs and the ability of the Liberal Democrats to mount opposition to the government was compromised by the close relationship it secured as the result of its policy of constructive opposition. Additionally many Conservative policies (particularly for spending limits) were adopted by the new government. The weakness of Parliamentary opposition to the government thus legitimised the media's close scrutiny.

THE RESIGNATIONS OF PETER MANDELSON (1998) AND CHARLIE WHELAN (1999)

Peter Mandelson resigned as Secretary of State at the Department of Trade and Industry in 1998 following a disclosure in the *Guardian* on 22 December that he had purchased a house in West London with the aid of a low-interest loan of £373,000 which had been made available by a fellow MP (and later a ministerial colleague), Geoffrey Robinson, in 1996. Although it was far from clear that Mandelson was guilty of any wrong-doing by failing to declare this loan either to his permanent secretary when he took charge of the DTI in 1998 or in the Register of Members' Interests, the ongoing investigation by the DTI into possible breaches of company law by Robinson may have been perceived by the public as a clash of interest. Mandelson (and also Robinson) accordingly resigned.

Key issues which emerged from this episode included who leaked the details of this loan, and what were their motives for doing so. The answers to such questions appear to date to 1994, when Mandelson lent his support to Tony Blair's campaign to become leader of the Labour Party. Such support was one factor which induced a potentially strong candidate, Gordon Brown, not to stand in the leadership contest. However, person rivalry emerged between Brown and Mandelson which continued when Labour became the governing party in 1997. It had serious implications for the authority of the Prime Minister since Mandelson was viewed as a key aide to Tony Blair. An attack on Mandelson by the Brown camp could thus be seen as a veiled attack on the Prime Minister himself.

In the 1998 government reshuffle, Blair asserted his control over the party by dismissing some ministers who were regarded as supporters of Brown. This may have prompted the Brown camp to retaliate by seeking to undermine Mandelson's position. The leak to the *Guardian* of details regarding his home loan succeeded in this objective and forced him from office. His supporters, however, wanted a corresponding sacrifice to be made which led to the resignation of Charlie Whelan, Brown's press secretary, in early 1999. Whelan had not been repsonsible for the leak to the *Guardian*, but his role as a key aide to Brown, coupled with the high profile he received from constantly having to deny any involvement in the affair which led to Mandelson's downfall, persuaded him to resign.

These resignations illustrate the manner in which the media may become the battleground in which rivalries between senior political figures are played out. Such are more likely to occur when ideology is insufficiently potent to overcome personalised rivalries.

Question

○ What do you understand by the term 'spin doctor'?

○ Using a selection of tabloid and 'serious' newspapers for one day, select a political issue and analyse how each of these newspapers treats the government's handling of this matter.

○ What do you conclude from this exercise concerning media objectivity or bias?

Further Reading

Nicholas Jones, *Soundbites and Spin Doctors: How Politicians Manipulate the Media – and Vice Versa* (London: Cassell, 1995). This book discusses the relationship between politicians and the media in contemporary British politics.

More general accounts of the role of the media in British politics is provided by **R Negrine**, *Politics and the Mass Media in Britain* (London: Routledge, 1989).

Also **J Keane**, *The Media and Democracy* (Cambridge: Polity Press, 1991).

Institutions ^{of} Government

PART THREE

Chapter Ten | Constitutions

The aims of this chapter are:

---

1 To consider the purpose of constitutions.

2 To differentiate between codified and uncodified constitutions.

3 To evaluate the manner in which codified constitutions are kept up to date through the process of amendment and judicial review.

4 To examine the nature and operations of the United Kingdom's uncodified constitution.

5 To analyse the case for constitutional reform in the UK and to assess the main proposals which have been put forward to achieve this purpose.

6 To assess progress made since 1997 in implementing constitutional reform.

The Purpose Served by Constitutions

A constitution provides a framework within which a country's system of government is conducted. It gives basic information concerning the composition and powers of government and establishes rules which those who exercise the functions of government have to obey.

The Key Features of Government

A constitution describes the essential characteristics of a country's system of government. A constitution contains a formal statement of:

❍ *The composition and powers of the key branches of government:* these 'arms' or 'branches' consist of the legislature, executive and the judiciary. A constitution will contain information concerning the process of appointment and tenure of those who carry out these functions and the role which they perform in the machinery of government.

❍ *The relationship between these branches of government:* the doctrine of the *separation of powers* (which is discussed in Chapter 1) suggests that each branch should be independent of the other.

However, such a situation is neither desirable nor possible. In practice, there is a considerable degree of overlap between the operations of each arm of government.

○ *The exercise of sovereignty:* this concerns the power to make law. In a unitary political structure this is exercised by central government but in a federal political structure it is shared between a central (or federal) government and subnational governments (such as states). A constitution will seek to provide guidance concerning the respective powers of each tier of government.

THE AMERICAN CONSTITUTION

The following example indicates how the general features discussed above are embodied in the United States of America's codified constitution. The constitution provides basic information on the organisation of government.

The Basic Framework of Government

This was to consist of three branches – a legislature (which was termed 'Congress'), consisting of two chambers (the House of Representatives and the Senate), an executive (who was termed 'the President of the United States of America') and a judiciary (consisting of a supreme court and a range of subordinate federal courts).

The Qualifications Required by Holders of Government Office

The requirements for membership of the House of Representatives and the Senate were laid down in the constitution which further stipulated conditions governing the Presidency, including eligibility to serve in that office and the length of that official's term. Issues concerned with the tenure and remuneration of federal judges were also laid down in this document.

The Functions and Powers of Each Branch of Government

For example, a key role given to Congress was that of levying and collecting taxes. One duty allocated to the President was to be commander in chief of the country's armed forces. The federal judiciary was charged with upholding federal law, including the constitution, and arbitrating disputes between two or more states.

The Relationship Between the Branches of Government

The desire of those who drafted the constitution to ensure that no one branch of government was able to act in an arbitrary manner resulted in the development of a system of *checks and balances* whereby an action undertaken by one branch of government could be reviewed, and possibly annulled, by another.

A Federal Political System

In the American system of government, sovereignty is divided between the federal (national) government and the state governments. The existence of states was guaranteed by the constitution which further sought to establish the balance of power between the federal and state governments. This objective is especially expressed in the tenth amendment which stipulated that powers not expressly delegated to the federal government in that document nor prohibited from being exercised by the states would be 'reserved to the states respectively, or to the people'. This implied that state governments would exercise a major role in law-making. The changing nature of the balance between federal and state governments in the USA will be discussed in Chapter 16.

The Conduct of Political Action

In addition to providing key information regarding the structure of government, a constitution will also lay down certain ground rules governing the conduct of political activity. These rules are subsequently enhanced by customs and practices. Deviations from these norms of political behaviour may take one of two forms which are discussed below.

Unconstitutional Acts

These are actions which contravene either the letter or the spirit of the constitution. The perpetrator usually contravenes one specific constitutional provision or convention. In the UK, a government refusing to resign following the passage of a 'no confidence' motion in the House of Commons would be accused of acting unconstitutionally.

Anti-Constitutional Actions

These are actions which display a total disregard for the entire constitutional arrangements which exist within a particular country, and may seek to overthrow them. The assassination of the Israeli Prime Minister, Yitzhak Rabin, in 1995 to alter the direction of government policy towards the Palestinians was an example of an anti-constitutional action. Military intervention to overthrow a system of liberal democracy and impose a different form of government is a further example which is sometimes referred to as a coup d'état. The forcible removal of Salvador Allende's government in Chile in 1973 and its replacement by a military regime headed by General Pinochet was an example of an anti-constitutional action.

Citizens' Rights

In liberal democratic political systems, constitutions usually contain statements concerning the relationship between the government and its citizens. Such documents typically contain safeguards against arbitrary (that is, dictatorial) conduct by a government which are designed to safeguard individual freedom.

The omission of provisions relating to the rights of citizens was regarded as a major weakness of the American constitution. Accordingly ten amendments (collectively known as the Bill of Rights) were incorporated into this document in 1791. These list a range of personal freedoms. These include the freedom of religion, speech and assembly and the right to petition for the redress of grievances. The constitution safeguards the ability of all citizens to possess arms. Provisions concerning the manner in which citizens or their property can be searched are incorporated into this document, which also establishes the right of an accused person to a speedy and public trial. Further examples of civil rights enshrined in constitutions include the following.

○ *Ireland:* personal rights such as the equality of all citizens before the law, the right of habeas corpus (that is, an obligation not to imprison a person unless this detention is authorised by the courts), and the freedom of expression (including the right to criticise government policy) are embodied into the constitution.

○ *Italy:* the right to join a political party or a trade union is enshrined in the constitution.

○ *Germany:* the German constitution contains a prominent statement of basic rights which guarantee its citizens a range of personal and political freedoms.

The Embodiment of Political Values

A constitution provides information concerning the political views and values of those who wrote it.

○ *The Italian constitution:* this was drafted in 1947 and revealed a desire on the part of its authors to organise that country's system of government in order to prevent the return of fascism. This was reflected in the widespread dispersal of political power and the absence of a provision for the direct election of the President.

○ *The French constitution:* the constitution of the fifth Republic was drawn up in 1958 and displayed a commitment by its

SOCIAL RIGHTS

Traditionally the freedoms provided for in constitutions concerned the conduct of political affairs and the operations of the criminal justice system. They were designed to prevent governments acting in an overbearing fashion towards their citizens. In the late twentieth century, however, other forms of rights have entered political debates. These include social rights such as the right to a job, the right to be housed, the right to enjoy a minimum standard of living or the right for a woman to have an abortion. The denial of the right of Irish women to abortion was included in that country's constitution until a referendum held in 1995 narrowly supported the removal of this provision. Although legislation may sometimes remove impediments to prevent specific groups of citizens from exercising defined social functions, constitutions rarely contain any fundamental, all-embracing statement of social rights.

authors that strong, effective government was an essential guarantee of national security. They sought to secure this objective by strengthening the executive branch at the expense of the legislature. This development considerably enhanced the power of the President.

❍ *The South African constitution:* the transitional arrangements in the South African constitution which provided for power sharing at all levels of government until majority rule was established in 1999 indicated a desire to protect the interests of the white minority in the formative years of the new Republic.

An examination of a constitution thus enables us to discover how theory is translated into practice and how the climate of political opinion at the time of that document's drafting subsequently influenced the conduct of a country's governing institutions. It thus embodies a statement of political theory and political history. This situation will be discussed more fully in relationship to the drafting of the American constitution.

The Principles of the American Constitution

The 55 delegates who assembled at Philadelphia in 1787 to draft the American constitution were influenced by a variety of political ideas and priorities. These included John Locke's social contract theory and Montesquieu's concept of the separation of powers (which is discussed in Chapter 1). This latter idea appealed to those who drafted the American constitution. It was widely believed that George III's unreasonable treatment of the American colonists had triggered the War of Independence in

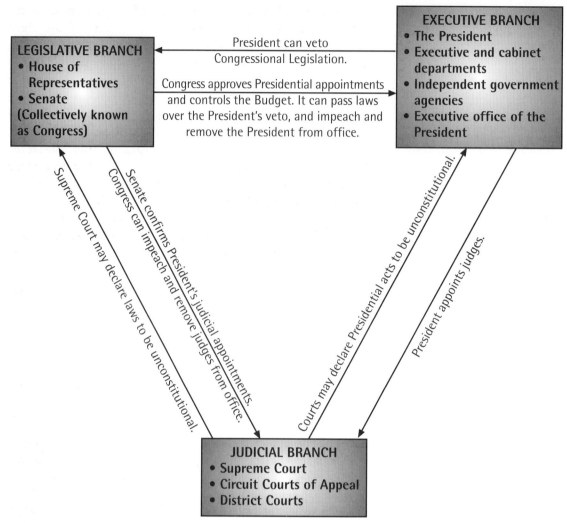

The system of checks and balances in American government. Adapted from Robert Lineberry, *Government in America: People, Politics and Policy* (Boston: Little Brown and Company, 1986, 3rd edition).

1775. The Monarch embodied all three functions of government and was thus able to act tyrannically.

Accordingly the constitution placed the legislative, executive and judicial functions of government into the hands of different bodies. The legislature consisted of the House of Representatives and the Senate, the executive was placed in the hands of the President, and the judicial function of national government was placed in the hands of justices of the supreme court and judges of subordinate federal courts. Many subsequent constitutions have adopted this principle to a greater or lesser extent.

However, it was also accepted that total autonomy exercised by the three branches of government could be prejudicial to the rights and liberties of the people. In an extreme form, three tyrannies might be substituted for one. Accordingly the American constitution deliberately instituted procedures in which the workings of one branch of government could be affected or influenced by the operations of another. This is known as checks and balances. An example of this concerns the relationship between Congress and the President in the area of law-making. According to the constitution, laws passed by Congress have to be subsequently agreed by the President. If the President is not satisfied with the content of a Bill, it may be vetoed. However, Congress may override this veto provided that two-thirds of the members of both Houses support this action. It was anticipated that these procedures would avoid unreasonable action being undertaken by the legislative or executive branches of government.

The main problem with a system of checks and balances is that it can result in inertia – that is, the involvement of numerous people in decision-making may result in nothing being done, as one group effectively cancels out the work of another. The situation of a stalemate in the relationships between the President and Congress is termed 'gridlock' and is later discussed in Chapter 11.

Question

With reference to a European country with a codified constitution (such as Germany, Italy, Belgium or France), outline the composition and structure of its government and identify the extent to which the three branches of government operate independently of each other. To do this, construct a diagram similar to that shown on page 246. This should include:

○ A brief description of the composition of the three branches of government.

○ Examples of how one branch of government can exercise a check on the operations of another.

Codified and Uncodified Constitutions

There is usually one document which contains information concerning the manner in which a country's system of government operates. Examples of such codified documents include the American Constitution which was drawn up in 1787, the Irish Constitution of 1937, and the French Constitution of 1958. The provisions of codified constitutions have a superior status to ordinary legislation and provide a key point of reference whereby the activities performed by the executive and legislative branches of government can be judged. Actions which contravene it may be set aside by the process of judicial review. It is in this sense in particular that constitutions are referred to as a country's fundamental law.

The UK and New Zealand, however, are examples of countries which do not have codified constitutions. These are thus said to be *unwritten* in the sense that there is no one single, specific document which provides information of the type referred to above. Instead such information is scattered across a number of different sources. The issue is considered below in relationship to the UK's uncodified constitution.

The Operations of Codified and Uncodified Constitutions

Codified constitutions are traditionally drawn up following some major political event or crisis which necessitates the reconstruction of the apparatus of government. There is a widely felt need to 'start afresh'. Such situations have included the following.

❍ *Securing independence:* new arrangements for government were required when America secured her independence from Britain in the late eighteenth century. A similar situation required a constitution to be written for what was then termed 'the Irish Free State' following the end of the War of Independence in 1921 which had been conducted against British rule.

❍ *Military defeat:* in Italy and the old state of West Germany, defeat in war and the collapse of fascism necessitated the construction of new governing arrangements which were embodied in the 1948 and 1949 constitutions respectively. In France, the Algerian war provided the occasion for the drafting of a new constitution in 1958, thus bringing the fifth Republic into being.

However, it is impossible to include all the material relevant to the government of a country in one single document. Codified constitutions are thus supplemented by several additional sources to provide detailed information concerning the operations of a country's system of government. A constitution sometimes establishes broad principles of action whose detailed implementation is left to legislation. Such statutes constitute a further source of information concerning the manner in which government functions. Other sources include declarations made by judges whose work may involve interpreting the constitution. These declarations are usually termed conventions.

Conventions

The manner in which a country's system of government operates is often determined by customs or practices rather than by specific constitutional enactment. Such constitutional conventions may fundamentally alter arrangements contained or implied in a country's constitution.

❍ *France:* the 1958 constitution gave the National Assembly the power to dismiss Prime Ministers. However, their willingness to accept that they could be dismissed by the President even when enjoying the support of the legislature resulted in the extension of the President's power.

❍ *The USA:* the American constitution anticipated that Congress would be the main source of legislation. In practice, however, the President subsequently assumed a major role in initiating legislation.

❍ *The UK:* in practice the monarch may veto any legislation passed by Parliament. This power was last used by Queen Anne when she rejected the Scottish Militia Bill in 1708. By convention the Royal Assent is given to all measures which have been passed by Parliament.

Judicial Review

The fact that codified constitutions are supplemented by a wide range of additional sources, including conventions, might suggest that there is little difference between these and uncodified constitutions. There is, however, one basic difference.

Codified constitutions form the basic law of those countries which have them. As such, a codified constitution has greater authority than other forms of law (including that passed by the legislature). In countries with this type of constitution the process of judicial review enables judges to determine whether or not the actions of the legislature are in accord with the constitution. If the judges decide they are not, the constitution prevails and the measures passed by the legislature are declared null and void. In the USA this process is performed by the Supreme Court.

Countries which have uncodified constitutions cannot have a similar process of judicial review. This is because the law passed by the legislature is itself a source of the constitution. It thus follows that legislatures in such countries may enact law without outside intervention. This is the case in the UK: while Parliament has ceded sovereignty to the European Union over a wide range of issues with which domestic law is required to be

Question

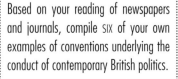

Based on your reading of newspapers and journals, compile SIX of your own examples of conventions underlying the conduct of contemporary British politics.

compatible, it retains the theoretical ability to reclaim such sovereignty merely by passing a new Act of Parliament.

Codified Constitutions as Living Documents

Codified constitutions are designed to be enduring documents. The process of drafting and ratifying a constitution is a lengthy one. No country can afford the luxury of frequently rewriting its constitution. This, however, raises the question as to how a document written at one specific point in time can endure for many subsequent years. In particular, it is necessary to consider how a constitution can adjust to subsequent social, economic and political changes and how it might it respond to circumstances which were not perceived when the document was originally drawn up.

The Process of Amendment

Amendments provide one obvious way for a constitution to be kept up to date. Constitutions generally contain provisions whereby additions or deletions can be made to the original document. The mechanics of the amending process, however, are subject to great variation. There are two main models concerning the amending process.

Flexible Constitutions

These can be amended by the normal law-making process. The uncodified British constitution (which is discussed below) is a good example of a flexible constitution, but the German constitution can also be altered by the normal law-making process.

Germany

Changes to the German constitution are constrained by two factors. One is that any changes must secure the support of at least two-thirds of the members of both houses of Parliament, the Bundestag and the Bundesrat. The other is that certain elements of the constitution cannot be amended. These concern the key principles governing the operations of the State, including its 'democratic and social' nature, the ability of the people to exercise political power through the process of voting in elections, and the functioning of government through legislative, executive and judicial organs. The role performed by the states (Länder) in the process of government may also not be altered.

Rigid Constitutions

These can be amended only by a process which is separate from the normal law-making process utilised in a particular country. Examples of these include Ireland, Belgium and the USA.

Ireland

Amendment of the Irish constitution requires that a referendum must be held to determine popular support or rejection for any constitutional change put forward by Parliament (the Oireachtas). Examples of amendments which were made using such a procedure included two in connection with Ireland's membership of the European Union (in 1972 and 1987).

Belgium

The desire to retain the allegiance of Belgium's Flemish and French-speaking populations to the State is reflected in provisions to amend the constitution. The support of two-thirds of each community is required to endorse such changes.

The USA

Changes which have been made to the American constitution include civil rights issues such as the abolition of slavery, the right of women to vote, and the universal introduction of votes at the age of eighteen. The power of federal government was enhanced by the amendment which authorised Congress to levy income tax. As discussed in Chapter 14, the American constitution can be amended in two ways.

Generally amendments are most easily secured to flexible constitutions. When the amending process is lengthy and drawn out changes become more difficult. There have only been 26 amendments made to the American constitution since 1789. One potential danger with rigid constitutions is that they fail to keep abreast of social changes.

Judicial Review

A second way whereby constitutions can be adapted to suit changed circumstances is through the process of judicial review which has been referred to above. Codified constitutions give this function to the judiciary. The American supreme court's decision (in 'Roe' v. Wade, 1973) that under certain circumstances a woman had a right to an abortion was an example of judicial interpretation of the American constitution. Judicial review enables the courts to inject contemporary views and values into a country's constitution when they deliver judgement on a specific issue which comes before them. In performing this task, judges may draw solely on their legal expertise or they may, as in the case in Germany, consider submissions from interested parties before reaching a judgement.

THE GERMAN CONSTITUTION AND COMMERCIAL BROADCASTING

One consequence of the use of judicial review to keep a constitution up to date is that the courts may adjust their interpretation of the constitution and endorse actions which they had previously sought to prevent. This is illustrated by the following example.

In 1961, the Constitutional Court restrained the actions of the Adenauer government by rejecting its attempt to set up a national commercial television channel. Ten years later, the Court upheld the independence of public service broadcasting by preventing the federal government from subjecting the licence fee to VAT. However, in 1981 the Court permitted broadcasting to expand as the result of cable and satellite technologies, and in 1986 gave its blessing to a private commercial sector existing alongside the public service sector. In 1987, the balance between these two sectors was detailed in five separate rulings of the Court.

The Limits of Judicial Review

Judicial review is most easily facilitated when the constitution lacks precision. Constitutions frequently contain statements of principle which embody the spirit of the constitution. Such declarations institute values to be observed henceforth. Generalised principles may set the tone for subsequent judicial interpretations when specific activities come before the courts for adjudication. In this manner the constitution may validly be applied to situations and events which were not envisaged when the original document was written. All that is required is to apply its principles to new and changed conditions.

There are, however, two main limitations associated with the process of judicial interpretation: the core values may lose their appeal and the actions of government may be insufficiently restrained.

The Core Values Lose Their Appeal

This may arise because broader social changes make these underlying values unfashionable. In such circumstances the constitution may lose its authority and may have to be replaced when it becomes impossible to inject new values through the process of judicial review.

The Actions of Government are Insufficiently Restrained

An important role served by constitutions is to provide a yardstick against which the actions of government can be judged. It is able to do this by being an independent source of power and, therefore, an impartial arbitrator. However, the process of judicial review may result in sanction being given to any action which the government wishes to undertake, especially when the government has some ability to appoint judges, thereby determining the personnel of the courts. This may mean that it fails to meaningfully limit the operations of government or to force such to subscribe to any basic standard of behaviour.

The UK's Uncodified Constitution

The UK possesses an uncodified constitution. With the exception of the Commonwealth period, 1649–60, there has been no political revolution or fundamental political crisis to justify the codification of one. The processes of government have been subject to evolutionary adjustments, enabling them to accommodate major changes including the agricultural and industrial revolutions in the eighteenth and nineteenth centuries and the expanded role of the State after 1945. There is thus no one document which provides a basic store of knowledge concerning the operations of the branches of government or the rights and liberties of the UK citizen. Instead information of the type normally contained in a constitution is dispersed. There are a wide range of written and unwritten sources for the British constitution.

The Sources of the UK's Constitution

The main sources of Britain's uncodified constitution are:

○ Statute law

○ European law

○ Common law

○ Conventions.

Statute Law

There are numerous examples of Acts of Parliament which govern the way in which Britain's system of government operates. Examples include the following.

Question ?

○ Discuss the operations of the process of judicial review as a mechanism to keep codified constitutions up to date.

○ What problems do you think may arise from this process?

❍ *The 1911 and 1949 Parliament Acts:* these concerned the relationship between the House of Commons and the House of Lords and specified the powers of the latter chamber.

❍ *The 1971 Courts Act:* this established the system of Crown Courts which are utilised to try the more serious criminal cases.

European Law

Britain's membership of the European Community in 1972 involved the incorporation of the European Convention, the Treaties of Rome, and 43 volumes of existing European legislation into British law. These provisions and subsequent European legislation perform an important role in determining the operation of Britain's system of government. Traditionally the British courts lacked the power to declare Parliament's statutes null and void on the grounds that their contents contravened provisions of the constitution. However, Britain's membership of the European Union enabled the courts to determine whether Parliament's legislation is compatible with European law which has precedence.

Common Law

Unlike statute law (which is made by legislatures), common law is law determined by judges. It becomes part of the law of the land because it is followed in subsequent relevant cases which come before the courts. This is called *judicial precedent.* Many of the liberties of the subject (such as the freedoms of assembly, speech, movement and privacy) are rooted in common law.

Conventions

Many matters concerning the operations of government are governed by practices which have become the accepted way of behaving. One example of this concerns ministerial responsibility which governs the relationship between the executive and legislative branches of government.

MINISTERIAL RESPONSIBILITY IN BRITAIN

There are two types of ministerial responsibility, *individual* and *collective.*

Individual Ministerial Responsibility

This concerns the relationship between ministers and the departments they control. As the political head of a department, a minister is expected to be accountable for all actions which it undertakes. If a serious error is committed by that department, the minister may be required to resign. This convention does not apply to ministers who resign (or who are forced to resign) as the result of some form of personal indiscretion or shortcoming (as was the case with Peter Mandelson and Geoffrey Robinson in 1998 which is discussed in Chapter 9) but is solely concerned with the formal role which they occupy within a department.

Collective Ministerial Responsibility

This embraces the relationship of the entire executive branch of government to the legislature. It is assumed that major issues of policy, even if associated with one specific department, have been discussed at cabinet level and thus constitute overall government policy. There are two consequences of this.

1   Ministers are collectively accountable to the House of Commons for all items of government policy. Theirs is a 'one out, all out' relationship. A vote of 'no confidence' in the government requires the resignation of all of its members.

2   While a minister has the right to voice opinions on an issue discussed within the Cabinet, once a decision has been reached it is binding on all of its participants. A minister who is not in agreement with what has been decided should either resign or 'toe the line' and be prepared to publicly defend the outcome which has been reached.

Question

Provide THREE examples of each of the following to serve as your own examples of the sources of the UK's uncodified constitution.

○ Acts of Parliament

○ Common Law.

An advantage of a convention is that it can be disregarded if peculiar circumstances justify this course of action. The Labour Prime Minister Harold Wilson suspended the principle of collective ministerial responsibility during the referendum campaign on Britain's continued membership of the European Economic Community in 1975. This was an example of political expediency overriding normal constitutional practice. It enabled the government to avoid the damaging internal disunity which would have arisen had it been forced to make this decision itself.

The Case for Constitutional Reform in the UK

The lack of a codified constitution is of profound significance. With the exception of European legislation there is no constitutional enactment superior to ordinary statute law passed by Parliament. Other sources of the constitution are ultimately subordinate to this. Accordingly, the constitution is whatever Parliament decrees it to be. This has major implications for the conduct of government. The actions taken by Parliament (and the government which exercises control over it) are constrained only by adherence to popular conceptions as to what is correct behaviour. The restraints which the UK's constitution imposes on the workings of government are thus spiritual rather than legalistic.

Within this general context specific arguments have been put forward in recent years to justify constitutional reform. This is discussed below.

The Operations of the Institutions of Government

The UK has a unitary political structure with power concentrated in national political institutions. The over-centralised nature of the British State and its alleged neglect of issues such as industrial decline and unemployment have often been cited as explanations for the periodic interest in national Parliaments for Scotland and Wales. Such would involve the devolution of power from Whitehall and Westminster and the creation of centres of decision-making away from London.

The workings of the courts have also been criticised. The media frequently highlights what are depicted as judicial shortcomings. The main problem concerns the relative freedom from political accountability which judges enjoy. This grants them a wide degree of autonomy. Although this may be justified (since it prevents governments applying direct pressure onto the judiciary to secure verdicts which it favours) it might enable gender, race or class prejudices to influence judicial decisions. This issue is discussed more fully in Chapter 15.

Executive Domination of the Legislature

A second criticism which has been put forward to justify constitutional reform has been directed at the relations between the branches of government, particularly between the executive and legislature. Politicians of a variety of political persuasions have periodically decried the power of the executive, especially when their own party was in opposition. In 1976 Lord Hailsham referred to an 'elective dictatorship', while during the 1980s the apparent emergence of a 'one-party state' led many Labour politicians to scrutinise the operations of the electoral system which resulted in the Conservative Party continually securing office with the support of a minority of the voting public.

Various reforms have been suggested to remedy this situation. These include devolution, reforming the House of Lords, changing the voting system or limiting the power of Parliament through a written constitution.

The Erosion of Individual Freedoms

A third reason for the emergence of constitutional reform onto the UK's political agenda has been the perception that individual freedoms have been eroded, especially by the actions of the executive. Groups such as Charter 88 have voiced such concerns which can be illustrated by the following examples.

Emergency Legislation and Northern Ireland

In Northern Ireland, legislation such as the Emergency Provisions Act (introduced in 1973 and whose provisions included giving soldiers powers to search people and their property and to detain people) and the introduction in 1971 of internment (that is, detention without trial) and, in 1973, of Crown Court trials without juries (the so-called 'Diplock Courts') have had an adverse effect on civil and political liberties.

In both Northern Ireland and mainland Britain, the Prevention of Terrorism Act (initially introduced in 1974) has also had a detrimental impact on such matters. For example, this legislation enabled the Secretary of State to proscribe political parties (thus making the membership of them a criminal offence), and to deport people suspected of involvement in terrorist affairs from either mainland Britain or Northern Ireland. This legislation also provided the police with additional powers concerning arrest, detention and control of entry of suspected terrorists: these measures initially applied solely to the politics of Northern Ireland but were extended in 1984 to cover international terrorist activity. In 1998 the Labour government announced proposals to extend further the scope of anti-terrorist powers by applying them to any organisation using serious acts of violence to further its ends. Militant animal-rights groups, for example, would be affected by these reforms.

The Criminal Justice (Terrorism and Conspiracy) Act, 1998

Many members of the Labour Party had traditionally been opposed to the Prevention of Terrorism Act because of its adverse impact on civil liberties. However, in 1998 the Labour government felt compelled to introduce anti-terrorist legislation of their own in response to a car bomb attack by the 'Real IRA' in Omagh, Northern Ireland, which killed 28 people. This measure, the 1998 Criminal Justice (Terrorism and Conspiracy) Act, was hastily passed through both Houses of Parliament which were reconvened during the Summer recess for this purpose. It made membership illegal of those loyalist and republican paramilitary organisations which continued to resist the Northern Ireland peace process. These were the Real IRA, the Continuity IRA, the Irish National Liberation Army, and the Loyalist Volunteer Force.

In short, the law was designed to make it easier to convict a suspected terrorist. A senior police officer's opinion that a person was a member of a proscribed organisation would be admissible evidence. Membership would have to be corroborated, although a suspect's refusal to answer questions would be regarded as sufficient in this respect. Ministers defended the changes both to the rule of law and the rules of evidence by insisting that the measure (which was subject to annual review) would be applied sensitively and directed at those whom intelligence had assessed to be terrorists. The Liberal Democrat peer, Lord Avebury, however, suggested that it would be overturned in the European Court.

The second part of the measure was directed at terrorist groups which were based in the UK but whose operations were conducted abroad, especially in Asia and the Middle East. The powers of the UK courts were extended to convict British-based individuals engaged in conspiring to commit terrorist offences anywhere in the world. This aspect of the law was criticised for its sweeping scope, which previously would have asserted the legitimacy of South Africa's apartheid regime and branded Nelson Mandela and members of the African National Congress as terrorists.

The speed with which basic human rights were removed by an Act of Parliament provided an important argument in favour of a codified constitution which could only be amended by a procedure separate from the normal law-making process.

CIVIL RIGHTS AND A CODIFIED CONSTITUTION

Ireland has a codified constitution, but this has not proved to be a totally effective safeguard against the erosion of civil and political rights contained in measures such as the 1939 and 1985 Offences Against the State Acts. In 1998, amendments to British anti-terrorist legislation (which have been discussed above) were enacted in tandem with anti-terrorist legislation passed by the Irish Dail.

Restrictions on Protest and Dissent

Legislation such as the 1986 Public Order Act placed restrictions on the ability of individuals to protest and express dissent. Its provisions gave the police the ability to ban a procession and to impose conditions on demonstrations. Additionally, the 1994

Public Order and Criminal Justice Act introduced new powers under the heading of 'collective trespass or nuisance on land' which could be directed against groups such as pro-environment protesters, anti-hunt saboteurs and participants of 'raves'. This Act further eroded the right to silence which many saw as a cardinal feature of the English criminal justice system. Henceforth the refusal by an accused person to answer questions put by the police might be drawn to the attention of the jury by a trial judge.

Curbs Imposed on Trade Unions

A range of measures passed in the 1980s had a profound effect on trade union organisation and activity by placing restrictions on 'rights' such as striking and picketing, and on the internal regulation of their affairs. Unions were banned from the Government Communication Head Quarters (GCHQ) between 1984 and 1997, implying that they were subversive organisations.

Proposals for Constitutional Reform in Britain

A Bill of Rights

It has been argued that the defence of individual rights would most readily be facilitated by the enactment of a Bill of Rights. This would put citizens' rights on a statutory basis and make it more difficult for the executive branch to restrict them. One way to achieve this would be to incorporate the European Convention of Human Rights into British Law. The implications of the introduction by the Labour government of such a reform in their Human Rights Act are discussed more fully in Chapter 23.

A Codified Constitution

Apart from the fact that codified constitutions are usually produced following a major political upheaval, there are many practical objections voiced against such a reform.

Erosion of the Sovereignty of Parliament

A written constitution would undermine the principle of the sovereignty of Parliament. However, such a development has already effectively occurred following the UK's entry into the European Community.

Civil Liberties May Not be Protected

A codified constitution would not necessarily ensure that civil rights were more effectively protected. Legal discrimination against women persisted for many years in countries such as France despite constitutional provisions seeming to outlaw such practices. The former state of West Germany imposed restrictions on the freedom of speech even though the constitution seemed to prohibit such actions. Conversely, the current British position whereby personal rights are rooted in common law may provide a more effective defence of such freedoms than is the case when they are contained in a constitutional document. Thus a Bill of Rights incorporated into a written constitution might prove an inadequate safeguard of these rights.

Enhancement of the Powers of the Judiciary

A final objection to a written constitution concerns the ability of the judiciary to interpret legislation in relation to this document. Although there may be objections to the power exercised by modern executives, it is open to question as to whether the situation would be improved by subjecting actions of the legislature or executive to socially unrepresentative, unelected and politically unaccountable judges.

Tony Benn.

TONY BENN'S COMMONWEALTH OF BRITAIN BILL

In 1991 the Labour MP Tony Benn introduced the Commonwealth of Britain Bill. This sought to transform Britain into a 'democratic, secular, federal Commonwealth, comprising the Nations of England, Scotland and Wales'.

The key provisions of this Bill included the establishment of a bicameral legislature (the House of Commons and the House of the People) elected for a fixed term of four years. The Prime Minister would be elected by the House of Commons and the government would be accountable to that body. The head of state would be a president elected by both Houses of Parliament, who would preside over a Council of State also chosen by these two Houses. A High Court would be responsible for reviewing any administrative act of the executive. The Monarchy would be abolished and the Church of England disestablished. The Bill proposed that such provisions should be incorporated into a written constitution which would be subject to popular approval in a referendum.

Labour and Liberal Democrat Proposals for Constitutional Reform

In 1996, the leaders of the Labour Party and Liberal Democrats asked two of their senior Parliamentarians, Robin Cook and Robert Maclennan, to discuss the possibility of cooperation between the two Parties concerning constitutional reform. This resulted in the formation towards the end of that year in a Joint Consultative Committee 'to examine the current proposals of the Labour and Liberal Democrat Parties for constitutional reform: to consider whether there might be sufficient common ground to enable the Parties to reach agreement on a legislative programme for constitutional reform; to consider means by which such a programme might best be implemented and to make recommendations'. This body reported in 1997.

A key concern of this report was that the British constitution needed to be changed 'in order to renew democracy and to bring power closer to the people'. The programme which was presented 'represents a transfer of power to make political institutions more responsive to the people. It is a programme which ... will share power with the many, not preserve it in the hands of the few'. A number of specific proposals were put forward to implement these objectives. The main proposals are summarised below.

Bringing Rights Home

It was proposed to incorporate the European Convention of Human Rights into UK law. A new Joint Select Committee of both Houses of Parliament would monitor the operation of the legislation drawn up to implement this proposal and scrutinise pending legislation to ensure the compatibility of future measures with the European Convention. A Human Rights Commissioner or Commission would also be established to provide advice and assistance to those seeking the protection of the rights enshrined in the European Convention and would be able to bring proceedings to secure effective compliance with it.

Freedom of Information

Both parties expressed a commitment to a Freedom of Information Act which would give the public proper confidence in matters of current public concern (such as public health and food safety). It would also give access to information about the workings of government and allow individuals to see information held on them by government agencies. Independent machinery and procedures would be set up to achieve such purposes. Access to personal files would, however, be restricted to provide exemptions in areas such as national security, personal privacy and policy advice given to ministers by civil servants.

Bringing Power Closer to the People

It was argued that the UK is one of the most centralised countries in Europe and that Conservative rejection of devolving power to the nations and regions of Britain had resulted in political disaffection, administrative inefficiency and a strain on the Union. Accordingly, devolution based on the principles of popular consent, the maintenance of the Union, the preservation of local government, the pooling of resources distributed on an agreed basis, and the establishment of proper constitutional provision for the resolution of disputes was proposed.

Scotland

It was pointed out that both the Labour Party and Liberal Democrats in Scotland took part in the Scottish Constitutional Convention which was established in 1989 and which subsequently published a report, *Scotland's Parliament, Scotland's Right*. This recommended a Parliament elected by the Additional Member System of proportional representation (explained in Chapter 4) with legislative competence over matters which were currently the responsibility of the Scottish Office (including health, housing, education, local government and law and order). Both Parties endorsed this report as the basis for legislation to establish a Scottish Parliament.

Wales

Both Parties supported the establishment of a directly elected Assembly (elected by the Additional Member System of proportional representation) providing democratic control over the functions currently discharged by the Welsh Office. It would also ensure that quangos and other unelected bodies performing public functions in the country would be subject to political accountability.

The Regions of England

In order to bring power closer to the people of England, the arrangements whereby government offices for the regions operated throughout England and whereby public policy were discharged by regional quangos lacking proper local democratic control required reform. It was, however, accepted that the sense of regional identity and the demand for regional government was subject to wide variation. A 'stage by stage' approach was proposed whereby indirectly elected regional chambers, based on the existing regional local authorities, would be established. These would allow directly elected regional assemblies to be established when this development had been approved by referendum.

London

It was pointed out that London was the only capital city in Europe without an elected authority. It was asserted that the Conservative government's dogmatic refusal to allow Londoners a say in the running of their own city was a handicap to a world-class capital. Both Parties thus endorsed the establishment of an elected authority for London and Labour further endorsed the proposal for an elected mayor.

Quangos

The power of such bodies was stated to have grown in recent years. They spent £60 billion a year, one-fifth of all public expenditure. The decentralisation proposals for Scotland, Wales, the English regions and for London would 'bring the quango state under the proper level of scrutiny that a modern democracy demands'. Both Parties endorsed the appointment proposals for such bodies outlined in the Nolan report and proposed to extend scrutiny and accountability at local, regional and national levels.

Electoral Systems

In addition to supporting proportional representation for the Scottish Parliament and Welsh Assembly, both Parties agreed that a referendum should be held within the first term of a new Parliament in which there should be a single question offering a straight choice between the first-past-the-post system and one specific proportional alternative. The choice put to the voters would arise from a commission on voting systems appointed early in the new Parliament and asked to report within one year of its establishment. Both Parties agreed that elections to the European Parliament should be by the regional list system of proportional representation. A full discussion of electoral reform is provided in Chapter 4.

Reform of the House of Commons

It was argued that this House no longer held ministers to account and legislation was not given the scrutiny it required. Both Parties thus agreed on a number of reforms which included the programming of parliamentary business to ensure fuller consultation, more effective scrutiny of bills and better use of MP's time, improving the quality of legislation by better prelegislative consultation, and the use of mechanisms such as the special standing committee procedure where evidence was taken before legislation was passed. It was also proposed to alter Prime Minister's Question Time to make it a more genuine and serious means of holding the government to account, to overhaul the process of scrutinising European legislation so that decisions from the EU were more transparent and Parliament's role was more clearly defined, to strengthen the ability of MPs to make the government answerable for its actions, and to enhance the role of Select Committees to ensure the accountability of departments. It was argued that Parliament itself should take the lead in its own reform by setting up a special Select Committee in Modernising the House of Commons early in the new Parliament. The review undertaken by this committee should be open to the views of others by bringing in outside advisers and canvassing the views of MPs, organisations involved in the work of Parliament, and members of the general public.

Reform of the House of Lords

It was stated that there was an 'urgent need for radical reform of the Lords. Its current composition is indefensible, in particular the fact that the majority of its members are entitled to take part in the legislative process on a hereditary basis'. Both Parties thus agreed to remove the rights of hereditary peers to sit and vote in the House of Lords. The role of a cross-bench or non-party element in a reformed House of Lords was accepted as valuable, and it was agreed that such members should remain at their present proportion of around one-fifth of the total membership (following the removal of hereditary peers). An 'open and legitimate' mechanism for appointing such cross-bench peers should be developed. A limited number of existing hereditary peers who had performed an active part in the work of the Lords might become life peers. Existing life peers would not be required to step down but there would be a procedure for voluntary retirement. A guiding principle of reform was that no one political party should seek a majority in the House of Lords. The removal of hereditary peers would leave an imbalance in party representation in the interim stage. Thus following their removal it was suggested that over the course of the next Parliament a reform should be introduced whereby the proportion of peers who took a party whip more accurately reflected the proportion of votes received by each party in the previous General Election. The removal of the hereditary element of the House of Lords was the first stage in its reform. This change would be followed by the establishment of a joint committee of both Houses to bring forward detailed proposals in structure and functions for the later stages of reform. This body should produce recommendations for 'a democratic and representative second chamber'.

The Civil Service

Both parties agreed that a Civil Service Act should be enacted which would give legal force to the existing code of conduct for the civil service. In addition, this code should be tightened up to ensure its political neutrality. This code would also be reviewed in relation to other published authorities to clarify lines of civil service and ministerial accountability and responsibility.

The Implementation of the Labour and Liberal Democrat Proposals

Progress was initially made in the following areas.

❍ *Bringing rights home:* legislation to incorporate the European Convention of Human Rights into British law was included into the government's Human Rights Bill, introduced in 1997. This is discussed more fully in Chapter 24.

❍ *Freedom of information:* a White Paper on this topic was published towards the end of 1997. This is also discussed in Chapter 24.

❍ *Bringing power closer to the people:* referendums on the establishment of a Scottish Parliament and Welsh Assembly were held in 1997. These endorsed the reforms, and elections to these bodies were held in 1999 on the basis of proportional representation. These reforms are discussed in Chapter 16.

❍ *Quangos:* moves which extend the principle of open government to these bodies were announced in 1997. This issue is discussed in Chapter 13.

❍ *Electoral systems:* in 1997 the Prime Minister announced support for the introduction of proportional representation for the 1999 elections to the European Parliament. He also appointed a commission on electoral reform, chaired by Lord Jenkins of Hillhead, to examine alternatives to the first-past-the-post system of electoral reform and recommend an alternative to be passed before the people in a referendum.

❍ *The reform of the House of Commons:* a Select Committee on Modernising the House of Commons was appointed in 1997. Some reforms, including the streamlining of Prime Minister's Question Time, were also introduced.

Further Reading

Rodney Brazier, *Constitutional Reform: Reshaping the British Political System* (Clarendon Press, Oxford, 1991). This examines a number of key areas of British government and assesses the nature and prospects of reform.

A useful contribution to this debate is also found in **Mark Franklin**, 'Whatever Happened to the English Constitution?', *Talking Politics*, Autumn 1988.

Chapter Eleven

The Executive Branch of Government

The aims of this chapter are:

1 To define the term 'executive branch of government', drawing a distinction between the role performed by politicians and that of civil servants.

2 To examine the relationship between the executive and legislative branches of government in a selected number of countries.

3 To analyse the manner in which power is distributed within the executive branch of government, distinguishing between presidential and cabinet government and assessing the relevance of the cabinet system of government in contemporary Britain.

4 To analyse the factors which are relevant to the power wielded by chief executives, drawing particular attention to the British Prime Minister and the American President.

5 To evaluate the strengths and weaknesses of the bureaucracy which serves contemporary chief executives.

6 To distinguish between chief executive and head of state, analysing the arguments for and against the retention of an hereditary monarch as British head of state.

The Role and Composition of the Executive Branch

The key role of the executive branch of government is to direct the affairs of the nation by both formulating and implementing policy decisions. Its work is performed by two distinct sets of people. These are politicians and paid, permanent officials. As the workings of the bureaucracy will be discussed in the following chapter, the discussion here will concentrate on the role performed by politicians within the executive branch of government.

The political control of a state's affairs is under the direction of a group of officials who are referred to as 'the government'.

❍ In the United Kingdom the government consists of the Prime Minister, cabinet and junior ministers.

❍ In the United States of America the government is composed of the President and the cabinet.

In this chapter the term 'executive' is used interchangeably with 'government'.

Relationship Between the Executive and the Legislature

Liberal-democratic political systems possess different political structures. One key distinction concerns the relationship between the executive and legislative branches of government. This underpins the functioning of the executive branch of government and gives rise to two main forms of government (and one variant) whose main characteristics are described below.

❍ *Parliamentary government:* here the personnel of government is drawn from the legislature and is located within that body. The government is collectively accountable to the legislature for its actions and remains in office only while it retains the confidence of that body. Countries which include the UK, Australia and New Zealand have this form of government. Most features of parliamentary government exist in Germany, save that cabinet ministers are not required to be members of the Bundestag.

THE GERMAN CHANCELLOR

The Chancellor is appointed from the largest party in the Bundestag (or the one which is able to construct a majority coalition). The Chancellor possesses considerable power, which includes control over economic policy, defence and foreign affairs, and the appointment of ministers who compose the federal government.

The office of Chancellor was held by Helmut Kohl from 1982 until 1998. He was replaced by Gerhard Schröder, the leader of the Social Democratic Party which emerged as the largest party in the 1998 General Election, and subsequently formed a coalition with the Greens.

❍ *Presidential government:* here the personnel which compose the executive and legislative branches are different. The USA possesses this system of government. The President is elected for a four-year term of office in an election which is separate from those held to elect members to Congress. Neither the President nor other members of the government can be serving members of Congress.

❍ *Hybrid forms of government:* the above classifications do not, however, encompass all forms of government which can be found within liberal democratic political systems. France is an

In 1988 Gerhard Schröder became Chancellor. He took over from Helmut Kohl who held this office for 16 years. The vitality of his coalition government was, however, threatened by the resignation of the Finance Minister, Oskar Lafontaine, in March 1999.

example of a country utilising a hybrid system which includes features associated with both presidential and parliamentary forms of government.

The French System of Government

In France, the traditional division which exists between a parliamentary and presidential system of government has been obscured by the emergence of dual leadership within the

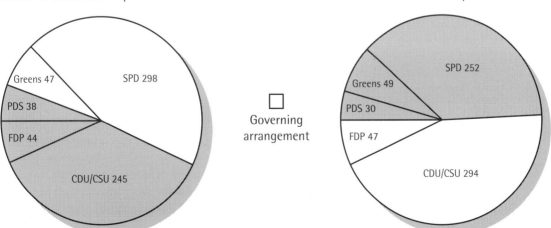

Number of seats **after** Sept 1998 election

Greens 47
SPD 298
PDS 38
FDP 44
CDU/CSU 245

☐ Governing arrangement

Number of seats **before** Sept 1998 **election**

SPD 252
Greens 49
PDS 30
FDP 47
CDU/CSU 294

Key to parties: **SPD**: Social Democrats, **CDU**: Christian Democrats, **FDP**: Free Democrats,
CSU: Christian Social Union, **PDS**: Democratic Socialists

Bundestag seats.

executive branch of government. The 1958 Constitution established the new office of President with powers additional to those normally associated with a head of state. The President was given a very wide range of functions and powers. These included acting as guarantor of national independence and protecting the functioning of public powers and the continuity of the State. Key duties included appointing the Prime Minister, presiding over the cabinet, and acting as commander-in-chief of the armed forces. Special emergency powers can also be exercised by the President. The power and prestige of the Presidency has grown, especially since direct election was introduced in 1962. The 'monarchical drift' of the office was acknowledged by the new president, Jacques Chirac, during the 1995 Presidential Election. The president serves for a period of seven years and the office is seen as France's key political prize.

The division of power between the President and Prime Minister is of central importance to an understanding of the operations of the French system of government. A major role of the President is to appoint (and dismiss) the Prime Minister. A newly appointed prime minister does not have to seek a specific vote of confidence from the National Assembly although he or she is accountable to that body. In making such a choice, however, the President is constrained by the political composition of the National Assembly. It follows, therefore, that the power of the President is greatest when the President's Party controls this body. The Prime Minister is effectively a presidential nominee, which was the case with President Chirac's first appointment to this post, Alain Juppé.

However, if the Party affiliation of the President and the majority in the legislature is different, the President is forced to select a Prime Minister and a government who enjoy the support of the National Assembly. The Prime Minister is more likely to be assertive in such situations since he or she possesses a separate power base and is not totally reliant on presidential support to obtain or remain in office. This may thus reduce the President's power, which occurred during 1986–88 and 1993–95 when a socialist President (Mitterrand) was forced to coexist with a right-wing government dominated by the Gaullists. It subsequently occurred in 1997 when the Gaullist President Chirac was forced to appoint the socialist Lionel Jospin as Prime Minister following the latter's victory in the 1997 elections to the National Assembly.

In such periods of what is termed 'cohabitation', however, a president is far from impotent. Ultimately it is possible to dissolve the legislature. However, this would be politically difficult to justify. The President would be undoing the results of elections to the National Assembly merely because he or she disapproved of the outcome. A newly-elected president, however, might find it easier to justify dissolving the National Assembly if its composition was politically hostile. Thus Lionel Jospin (the unsuccessful Socialist candidate in the 1995 Presidential Election) stated that, should he win, he would dissolve the National Assembly in the hope of securing a Socialist majority in a general election.

Collective Ministerial Responsibility

One feature of parliamentary government is *collective ministerial responsibility*. This convention asserts the supremacy of the legislature by insisting that a government which loses the confidence of that body must resign. Collective responsibility of the executive to the legislature does not apply to presidential forms of government, since its members are not drawn from that branch of government.

The mechanics of collective ministerial responsibility vary.

The UK

In the UK governments may be occasionally defeated in votes on relatively minor aspects of their policies. This would constitute an embarrassment to the government but would not lead to its downfall. However, a vote of 'no confidence' passed by the House of Commons would result in the government's resignation and a general election. This situation last occurred in 1979. James Callaghan's Labour government was defeated by such a vote in the House of Commons. A general election followed which resulted in victory for the Conservative Party led by Margaret Thatcher.

Question

Compare and contrast the main features of the UK's parliamentary form of government with the USA's Presidential political structure. To do this, organise your material under the following headings:

○ **Method of choosing the chief executive**

○ **The composition of the government**

○ **The relationship of the government to the legislature.**

Germany

To oust a government in Germany the Bundestag is required to pass what is known as a 'constructive vote of no confidence'. This entails a vote of no confidence in the Chancellor coupled with the selection of a replacement (who is required to obtain an absolute majority vote in the Bundestag). This process occurred in 1982 when Chancellor Schmidt was replaced by Chancellor Kohl following the decision of the Free Democrats to end their support for the social democrats and form a coalition government with the Christian Democrats.

Relations Within the Executive Branch of Government

The Role of a Chief Executive

Government is led by a *chief executive*. This person appoints other members of the government and usually exercises a pre-eminent position within it, being regarded as the nation's 'leader'. The main functions associated with this office are as follows.

❍ *Initiating proposals for government policy:* these often derive from the Party's election manifesto, although chief executives are also required to respond to unforeseen issues.

❍ *Overseeing policy and the overall conduct of the government:* the exercise of this strategic role may mean that the chief executive intervenes in the specific activities performed by individual government departments. As the result of this involvement the work of government is given a degree of coherence.

❍ *Mobilising support for policies:* this may involve liaison with members of the legislature or rallying public opinion in support of government initiatives.

❍ *Acting in times of crisis:* firm leadership is usually best provided by a single person. Some constitutions provide the chief executive with emergency powers to facilitate decisive action.

❍ *Appointing (and dismissing) public officials:* the ability to 'hire and fire' ensures that the chief executive's policy directives are carried out, and may be used to assert the power of a chief executive in response to criticisms of his or her policies. In the USA, President Truman's dismissal of General MacArthur for insubordination during the Korean War in 1951 dramatically illustrated the use of the dismissal power to counter dissent.

Presidential and Cabinet Systems of Government

There are broadly two models which describe the manner in which political power is allocated within the executive branch of government.

Power May be Concentrated in the Chief Executive

This is the case in the USA where the President is regarded as the main source of power within the executive branch of government. He is separately elected and can thus claim an electoral mandate to initiate recommendations concerning public policy. The American constitution made no reference to the concept of cabinet government. Although the first President, George Washington, commenced the practice (which subsequent Presidents followed) of holding regular meetings with senior members of his administration, cabinet government (in the sense of a group of equals meeting regularly and making collective decisions concerning policy) has never assumed the importance attached to it in other liberal democracies.

Power May be Dispersed Within the Executive Branch

The term 'cabinet government' is used to describe a situation whereby power is held by a group of individuals including the chief executive and other leading members of the government. Major issues of public policy are discussed by all members of the government as a team, presided over by the chief executive. This situation is more likely to be found in parliamentary systems of government. The cabinet is recognised in Germany's Basic Law and is given a number of powers. These include the right to introduce legislation and the power to veto laws which increase expenditure or decrease income. In the UK there is a strong tradition of cabinet government, the contemporary operations of which are discussed below.

Cabinet Government in the UK

The traditional perception of the British cabinet is that it operates as a decision-making body at the very heart of government, exercising general superintendence over policy, providing cohesion to its affairs, and enabling a number of different departmental perspectives to be brought to bear on a common issue. In recent years the nature of cabinet government in the UK has been the subject of debates which have questioned the extent to which the cabinet fulfils its traditional role. The decline of cabinet government has been alleged and the following arguments have been put forward to explain this situation.

Ministerial Preoccupation with Individual Departments

This argument suggests that most members of the cabinet are preoccupied with the task of running their own departments and thus lack the time or the inclination to involve themselves in affairs other than those with which they are directly concerned. Additionally, ministers in charge of departments may become parochial, that is, they seek to advance their department's interests to the detriment of concern for overall national objectives. This tendency is abetted by the system of 'departmental briefs'. These are drawn up by civil servants and are designed to guide their ministers through negotiations in cabinet committees. They are not, however, meant to be shown to the minister's other political colleagues, thus inducing a sense of insularity. In the early months of Tony Blair's Labour government in 1997 there was a tendency for ministers to depart from this practice and share such information around, thus enhancing the informed nature of collective decision-making.

Decisions are Taken in Alternative Forums

The extent of the work of contemporary government and its specialised nature may mean that decisions are made outside of cabinet meetings. These alternative arenas of policy-making include cabinet committees, which operate within the framework of the cabinet system. These are chaired by senior ministers (usually the Prime Minister or Deputy Prime Minister) and enable ministers or civil servants to examine issues in depth, perhaps reporting the conclusions of their deliberations to the full cabinet. There are two types of such committees, permanent and ad hoc. In July 1998 there were 15 cabinet committees, 11 sub-committees and a consultative committee (whose membership included some senior Liberal Democrats).

Alternatively, decisions may be made using more informal structures divorced from the structure of the Cabinet. These include liaisons between ministers and informal groupings. It has been argued that Tony Blair's decision that members of the cabinet should address each other by their first names masked the extent to which the Cabinet was devalued as a policy-making body in his government. The *Guardian* on 29 July 1997 said that 'major policy statements, including plans to charge university students tuition fees and the detailed blueprint for the Welsh and Scottish assemblies have seen little or no discussion in the Cabinet after being thrashed out in cabinet committee and smaller, informal groups'.

Prime Ministerial Government?

The above arguments suggest that the role of the Cabinet has been reduced and that its purpose is merely to rubber-stamp decisions which have been reached elsewhere. In doing so it associates them with its authority, thereby serving as a legitimising rather than a decision-making body. It has thus been concluded that a fundamental shift of power has occurred at the heart of British government and that cabinet government has been replaced by prime-ministerial government. The belief that modern prime ministers dominate the proceedings of their governments is explained by a number of factors.

○ *Party leaders play a prominent role in general election campaigns:* this enhances the status of that person should he or she become Prime Minister.

○ *The power to appoint and dismiss other members of the government:* they are thus dependent on the Prime Minister for their positions. In the UK, the reshuffle undertaken by Tony Blair in July 1998 (which included the dismissal of four Cabinet ministers) emphasised the Prime Minister's ability to construct a government in his or her own image, in which personal loyalty may be the main qualification for office-holding.

○ *The Prime Minister is able to dominate cabinet proceedings:* this situation arises through the ability to control its agenda and sum up its proceedings.

○ *The development of a prime-ministerial office:* the power of this office has increased due to a bureaucracy which gives advice on major issues of policy. This ensures that the Prime Minister possesses much information on the key affairs of state.

It is thus concluded that the UK's government has become prime ministerial or even presidential in nature.

The Continued Vitality of Cabinet Government

The argument that cabinet government has declined in the UK is not universally accepted. The following arguments have been put forward to refute this charge.

The Personal Style of Government

The style or character of individual Prime Ministers has a bearing on the extent to which they wish to exercise initiative or resort to the teamwork of cabinet government to decide major policy issues. Margaret Thatcher and John Major were identified with different approaches to the conduct of government.

The Need to Avoid Overbearing Behaviour

Prime Ministers need to be wary of conduct which is viewed as overbearing by their Cabinet colleagues. Resignations can have a significant bearing on the Prime Minister's hold on office. Sir Geoffrey Howe's resignation from Prime Minister Thatcher's government in November 1990 had a major impact on her authority within the Conservative Parliamentary Party and hence the vitality of her administration.

The Cabinet Retains an Important Role

Although the Cabinet's role has changed, it retains a number of key functions which are set out below.

❍ *A mechanism for the government to be made aware of key political issues:* one benefit which derives from some decisions being taken elsewhere is that this permits the Cabinet's limited time to be devoted to the main issues facing the country. This selection is heavily influenced by the views of the Cabinet Office which traditionally places foreign, defence and economic matters ahead of domestic policies.

❍ *Public image:* the Cabinet provides the semblance of a unified government involved in collective decision-making.

❍ *Arbitration of disputes:* it may act as a final court of appeal to arbitrate disputes between ministers.

Question

Basing your views on the arguments above, do you think that the UK has a prime-ministerial or cabinet system of government?

The Power of Chief Executives

It is often assumed that chief executives occupy a dominant position in the political system from which they are able to successfully advance policy initiatives. This section analyses the constraints on the power wielded by chief executives in the USA and the UK which may prevent them attaining their political objectives.

The American President

The American constitution placed the executive branch in the hands of a president who is directly elected. The President serves a term of four years and may be re-elected on one further occasion. The power exercised by a president to some extent depends on personal choice. Presidents may view themselves as officials who should merely enforce the laws passed by Congress or they may see themselves as dynamic initiators of public policy. These views are further flavoured by popular perceptions concerning the desirability of vigorous action from the chief executive.

THE IMPEACHMENT PROCESS

The American constitution contains a procedure whereby presidents can be removed from office. This is through a process known as *impeachment*, which applies to those office holders who are deemed to be guilty of having committed 'treason, bribery or other high crimes and misdemeanours'.

The present operation of this process is as follows.

1 The Judiciary Committee of the House of Representatives conducts hearings to determine whether impeachment proceedings should go ahead. Witnesses (who could include the President) may be summoned to assess the situation.

2 The judicial committee debates and approves formal changes which are embodied in an article (or articles) of impeachment.

3 Following these proceedings, the House of Representatives votes (by a simple majority) to approve or reject the article(s) of impeachment.

4 If the House approved an article of impeachment, the Senate would then be required to conduct a trial, presided over by the chief justice of the US Supreme Court. A two-thirds majority is needed to convict a president, which has the effect of forcing him to resign.

The belief that American Presidents should be strong and assertive in the conduct of public affairs was bolstered by the need for decisive presidential action to cope with the Depression in the 1930s. But this view has subsequently been revised by the perceived failings of strong Presidents as revealed by the outcome of the Vietnam war (which was associated with presidential initiative) and the belief that strong executive action can lead to abuse of power (as evidenced in the break-in at the Democratic National Committee headquarters at Watergate in 1972 and the subsequent enforced resignation of President Nixon in 1974 who was implicated in this event and subsequent attempts to cover it up). Such factors have tended to make the public suspicious of Presidents who wish to exercise dynamic leadership.

Their ability to initiate actions has further been weakened by the size of the budget deficit which grew enormously during the Reagan–Bush years (1981–93) and served as a constraint on Presidents who might wish to promote policies involving State intervention. However, the anticipation that the 1999 Budget would inaugurate an era of balanced budgets (only the second since 1958) led the Clinton administration to declare that government could henceforth be an affirmative force, a 'force for good', promoting social security and education programmes.

The above considerations have greatly affected the climate within which contemporary presidents operate. But within such a climate, presidents retain a considerable degree of manoeuvre. They possess a range of formal and informal powers and may also exploit their position as the only national unifying force to secure the attainment of their goals. There are a number of factors which affect the ability of a modern American president to achieve policy objectives. These include the federal form of government and the power of the Supreme Court to declare actions initiated by the executive branch to be unconstitutional. In the following section, however, attention is confined to the ability of presidents to manage Congress in order to attain their aims. The topic of executive–legislature relations which constitutes a key point of difference between presidential and parliamentary forms of government.

The President's Control of Congress

In a presidential form of government the President is not a member of Congress and is thus reliant on ways of mobilising that body to secure the attainment of policy goals. There are various factors which influence the President's ability to do this.

The President's Mandate

The mandate which a president obtains in a general election may greatly influence his or her subsequent behaviour. A president may feel it is legitimate to take the initiative in public affairs when the outcome of an election provides a clear statement of public support for a programme put forward during the campaign. When the outcome of an election is less clear (for example, if the president fails to secure a majority of the popular vote) or it appears that the result was determined more by the rejection of one candidate than the popular endorsement of the winner, the president may find it more difficult to promote policy with rigour. Both of these factors played a part in the effectiveness of President Clinton during his first term of office. In the 1992 election Clinton scored only 43.3 per cent of the popular vote in an election which was widely seen as a vote against President Bush. At the same time, the Democratic Party lost nine seats in the House of Representatives.

Clearly Focused Policy Goals

Presidential success in dominating policy making may be most easily realised when the chief executive's policy goals are clearly focused. This suggests the desirability of a limited set of key objectives. This enables both Congress and the public to appreciate the president's fundamental concerns. One problem associated with President Carter (1977–81) was that at the outset of his presidency he put forward too disparate a range of proposals. This presented a confusing statement of presidential objectives. Accordingly, President Reagan (1981–89) presented a programme which included fewer key issues and his subsequent relations with Congress concentrated on achieving them. President Clinton's efforts early in his first term to focus on domestic policy issues was impeded by the emergence of defence and foreign policy issues (including the Bosnian crisis) which demanded attention at the expense of his original objectives.

Congressional Assertiveness

The President (unlike the British Prime Minister) has no direct connection with the legislature, and Congress may not be inclined to follow the presidential lead. As the following examples illustrate, Congress has become more assertive since the 1970s to the detriment of presidents seeking to exercise a dominant role in both domestic and foreign affairs.

Domestic Affairs

Legislation such as the 1974 Budget and Impoundment Control Act introduced innovations designed to enable Congress to compete with the President in the preparation of the budget.

Foreign Affairs

Foreign policy was traditionally controlled by the President, but legislation such as the 1973 War Powers Act and the 1976 National Emergencies Act limited the scope of presidential initiative. Congress's control over appropriations was used to stop aid to the Nicaraguan rebels in 1987. The end of the 'cold war' has further enhanced Congressional involvement in foreign affairs. A major example was the vote of both Houses of Congress in 1995 to overrule the president's policy of an embargo on the sale of arms to Bosnia.

Party Loyalty

Theoretically the party system might secure support for the President in Congress. However the role performed by the

President as a party leader is a relatively neglected one and party loyalty in Congress is much weaker than it is in the UK. Changes to the process by which presidential candidates are nominated and the manner in which presidential election campaigns are financed has been to the detriment of the relationship between a president and established party organisations. Further, parochialism exerts considerable influence over the conduct of members of Congress. They are more likely to follow the President's lead when they feel this will bring them personal political benefits, but they will distance themselves from the administration if they feel that association with the President constitutes an electoral liability.

Thus even when the President's party controls both Houses of Congress, this is no guarantee that all members of that party will support the chief executive on every major policy initiative. Such difficulties beset President Carter who failed to construct good working relationships with his own Party which controlled both Houses of Congress throughout his presidency. In 1997, President Clinton's trade legislation was adversely affected by a revolt of Democrats in the House of Representatives, marshalled by Dick Gephardt, the Democrat leader in that body.

Divided Government

The position of the president is potentially weaker when the opposition party controls either or both houses of Congress. This is a situation which post-war Republican presidents frequently had to endure but which was inflicted on President Clinton following the loss of Democrat majorities in both Houses at the November 1994 Congressional elections (and which he has experienced ever since). In a situation of 'divided government' there is no onus on the Congressional majority to aid the passage of the president's programme and their own leadership might attempt to seize the initiative in policy-making. Thus in the period immediately following the November 1994 elections, the Republican Speaker of the House of Representatives, Newt Gingrich, and the Republican majority leader in the Senate, Robert Dole, exercised a role in policy initiation which seemed to eclipse that exerted by President Clinton.

In such situations presidents may seek to bargain with Congress in order to retain some influence over the legislative process. If Congress puts forward legislative proposals, the President is able to veto them. Although Congress may be able to override this veto, the threat or actuality of using it may trigger off a process of bargaining between the President and Congressional opposition. However, the result may be that neither side will give way to the other and a situation of 'gridlock' arises. The inability of the President and Congress to resolve disagreements on the budget in 1995 led to a shutdown in government in which federal employees were sent home. This arose when conditions attached by Congress for the approval of government expenditure were rejected by the President.

How Presidents Overcome Problems with Congress

Contemporary presidents may seek to overcome the difficulties which have been discussed above in a number of ways.

Coalition Building

In situations of 'unified' and 'divided' government a president is required to seek the support of sufficient members of Congress to ensure the passage of key legislation. This is referred to as 'coalition building' and requires the chief executive to engage in the art of bargaining. This process, however, has been complicated by Congressional reforms initiated after Watergate (especially in connection with the committee system) which have tended to disperse power, thereby making it more difficult for the President to manage Congress by negotiating with a small number of influential politicians.

Contemporary coalition building often involves securing support from politicians of different political allegiances by lobbying, persuading or even coercing them to support the President. It may require coalitions to be constructed on an issue-by-issue basis and has become a key feature of what has been termed the 'no win' presidency. Presidents such as Lyndon Johnson who had wide experience of the operations of Congress were able to conduct this 'wheeling and dealing' successfully especially in connection with his 'Great Society' programme. Others whose political experience was different (such as President Carter who was elected as an 'outsider' to Washington politics) were less successful coalition builders and had difficulty in persuading Congress to implement their programmes.

The Media

Relations with the media may also influence a president's power. A popular president is likely to find it easier to secure support within Congress for the administration's policies and traditionally presidents went to great lengths to ensure that they received favourable treatment by the media. However, in the post-Watergate period the media has become prone to critical analysis which may weaken the President in the eyes of the population. There are ways to counter this, in particular by seeking to ensure that the President's message is not delivered by the media but is heard (or received) directly by the people. This technique was particularly developed by President F. D. Roosevelt whose 'fireside chats' enabled him to address his message directly to the American people. In doing so, he sought to utilise the authority which he derived from his role as head of state (which is discussed below) to further his political objectives.

Executive Orders

Executive orders enable the President to act without having to consult Congress. These orders cover circumstances which range from implementing the provisions of the Constitution, to treaties and statutes. They may also be used to create or modify the organisation or procedures of administrative agencies. The President's power to issue such orders derives from precedents, custom and constitutional interpretation, and particularly from discretionary powers embodied in legislation passed by Congress. The British equivalent of executive orders is the use of the Royal prerogative, but its usage is more restricted.

The above discussion has suggested that in assessing the power of the President it is necessary to depart from an examination of the formal powers of this office and to examine the informal powers which are at the President's disposal. These form a key aspect of what Richard Neustadt described as the power of the president to *persuade*. This may also effect the more controversial use of executive orders whose effectiveness may be dependent on whether they will secure the endorsement of public opinion.

Question

Both the UK and the USA have liberal-democratic political systems, the former with a parliamentary and the latter with a presidential political structure. One key difference concerns the relationship of the executive with the legislative branch of government.

To what extent does the different relationship between the executive and legislative branches of government found in these two different forms of government make it easier for a British prime minister to achieve his or her political goals than is the case for an American president?

THE AMERICAN VICE PRESIDENCY

The American constitution provided for a vice president who would take over on the 'death, resignation or inability' of the President. The circumstances under which this official would assume the office of president was subsequently expanded upon in the twenty-fifth amendment, passed in 1967, covering contingencies which included the temporary or permanent disability of the President. Otherwise the vice president's main function was to act as president of the senate with the power to vote when there was a tie.

In modern election contests voters are asked to endorse a 'ticket' which consists of candidates nominated to fill the offices of president and vice president. Although the vice president is only 'one heartbeat away' from becoming president, it has not traditionally been a highly regarded or sought-after office. When Lyndon Johnson considered Kennedy's invitation to stand as the Democrat nominee for the vice presidency at the 1960 election, he contacted John Garner who had occupied this post under President Roosevelt from 1933–41. Garner reputedly informed Johnson that the office was not worth 'a pitcher of warm spit'. However, some recent presidents have given their vice presidents a more significant role. President Carter (1977–81) made prominent use of Walter Mondale whose role included involvement in the operations of the White House.

Service as vice president is no guarantee of becoming president when the incumbent retires. George Bush in 1988 was the first serving vice president to be elected to the office of chief executive since Martin Van Buren in 1836.

The British Prime Minister

The Prime Minister possesses considerable control over the conduct of British political affairs. However, while there are few formal restraints on this office, the Prime Minister is subject to a range of informal pressures which may greatly limit that person's power. These are discussed below.

Relations Within the Executive Branch of Government

The Prime Minister exercises pre-eminent power in the executive branch of government. There are, however, limitations on the exercise of the key functions of appointment and dismissal.

The Composition of the Cabinet

The Prime Minister may not possess total freedom in the appointment of their leading ministers. Senior politicians within the Party may effectively pick themselves for high government office and it may further be necessary for the Cabinet to reflect key divisions within the Party should these exist. This may affect the power relationship between the Prime Minister and the Cabinet. The problem may be resolved by devaluing the Cabinet as a policy-making body and taking key decisions in alternative forums in which the Prime Minister is dominant. This effectively sidelines those whose views do not coincide with the Prime Minister (as was the course of action adopted towards the Conservative 'wets' during Margaret Thatcher's premiership). The danger with such a course of action, however, is that ministers who feel themselves to be ignored may resign, which could have an adverse effect on the Prime Minister's authority within the Party.

Changing the Composition of Governments

Prime ministers in a number of Western liberal democracies have responded to adverse political developments by *reshuffling* their governments. This involves dismissing ministers who by implication are blamed for the government's unpopularity. The tendency for prime ministers to sacrifice their 'friends' in order to save their own political lives (as a former leader of the Liberal Party, Jeremy Thorpe, once commented in response to Prime Minister Macmillan's 'night of the long knives' government reshuffle in 1963) was demonstrated by John Major in 1993 when he dismissed his Chancellor of the Exchequer, Norman Lamont. It was also evident in France in 1995 when the French Prime Minister, Alain Juppé, dismissed 13 ministers in an attempt to reverse the decline in popularity experienced by his government. This can, however, backfire. Public opinion may view such action as evidence of a government in a terminal state of decline, and sacked ministers may provide an alternative source of leadership within the Party.

Relations With the Legislative Branch of Government

Executive domination of the legislature is a key feature of Britain's parliamentary form of government. However, such dominance is not consistently assured and is dependent on a number of factors.

The Government's Parliamentary Majority

The parliamentary situation may restrict the ability of a prime minister to achieve political objectives. The Prime Minister is the leader of the majority Party in parliament, which means that the chief executive's ability to exercise control over political affairs is potentially greatest when that Party has a sizeable majority in the House of Commons. A government with a small, or no, majority may have to rely on Members drawn from other parties to sustain it in the regular votes which occur. In this circumstance, the Prime Minister may have to agree to demands made by other politicians, on whom the government is forced to rely, or else face the threat of defeat. The latter situation led to the downfall of Romano Prodi's government in Italy in 1997, when the Communist Refoundation (a party which held the balance of power in the lower House of Parliament) refused to support his budget for 1998/99.

The Unity of the Parliamentary Party

A prime minister's power may also be affected by the unity of his or her parliamentary party. Internal divisions may exercise considerable influence on the composition of the government as the Prime Minister may be constrained to ensure that party balance is reflected in its make up. A disunited parliamentary party may make it difficult for the Prime Minister to secure the passage of policies through the House of Commons, especially if the government's overall majority is small. Discontented Members may abstain, vote against their own party or even defect to the opposition. This situation adversely affected the power of John Major in the 1990s. His Parliamentary Party was riven with internal dissension, primarily associated with European policy. In December 1995 the government lost a key vote on fishing policy due to Eurosceptic hostility towards the European Union's common fishing policy. Three of the government's members defected to opposition parties. This situation can increase the government's reliance on other parties to secure the passage of government business.

While a prime minister may threaten to quell revolts by the threat of dissolving parliament and holding a general election, this is a double-edged sword and is rarely a credible sanction since the prior public display of disunity is likely to cost electoral support and make defeat in a general election more likely. Although a government with a large Parliamentary majority can afford occasional backbench rebellions, they are politically embarrassing. Thus the Blair government has sought to impose tight discipline over the Parliamentary Labour Party through the Whips office. This issue is discussed more fully in Chapter 6.

The Government's Popularity

Public opinion may affect the power of the Prime Minister. The extent to which prime ministers pay attention to public opinion varies. The loss of public support in the early period of office may be ignored, especially by a prime minister with a strong nerve who believes that the electorate will ultimately see the wisdom of a course of action which is initially unpopular. Margaret Thatcher, for example, pursued unpopular economic policies after 1979 which had begun to elicit increased public approval before the outbreak of the Falklands war in 1982. However, prime ministers may find it easiest to assert themselves when there is a demonstrable degree of support from the electorate. When the level of this support declines (tested in opinion polls, parliamentary by-elections or local government elections) a prime minister is in a weaker position. There are, however, a number of ways in which prime ministers may seek to reverse a decline of public opinion. In addition to government reshuffles (which are discussed above) prime ministers may utilise the media to court public opinion.

Prime ministers may seek to 'sell' themselves and their policies by making a direct appeal to the general public through the media. Alternatively they may seek to ensure that favourable media presentation is secured by tactics such as utilising the 'lobby' system to cultivate support. The ability to manipulate the media is of crucial importance to a contemporary prime minister. Margaret Thatcher's press secretary, Bernard Ingham, performed a major role between 1979 and 1990 in bolstering the power of the Prime Minister.

Question

○ Analyse the limitations on the power of the British Prime Minister.

○ Discuss how a prime minister might seek to overcome such limitations and thereby enhance his or her power.

The Chief Executive's Bureaucracy

The scope of contemporary government requires those exercising control over it to possess detailed knowledge of complex and technical policy areas. Bureaucracies have thus been developed to serve the chief executive, enabling him or her to exert overall control within the executive branch of government. Such bureaucracies fulfil a number of functions. These include the following.

○ *The provision of advice on policy matters:* this gives the chief executive expertise which may provide leverage in dealings with civil servants employed elsewhere within the executive branch.

○ *Aiding the success of policy initiatives put forward by the chief executive:* this task may involve a number of duties which include coordination and monitoring policies put forward by the chief executive.

○ *Implementation of policy:* one advantage of using the chief executive's bureaucracy to implement policy is that it is not subject to detailed scrutiny by the legislature to which the 'regular' civil service is subject.

EXAMPLES OF BUREAUCRACIES SERVING CHIEF EXECUTIVES

The USA

In 1939, President F. D. Roosevelt established the Executive Office of the President. This contains three bodies – the National Security Council, the Council of Economic Advisors and the Office of Management and Budget. Their work is supplemented by the White House Staff which contains key aides.

Germany

The German Chancellor has a personal department, the *Bundeskanzleramt.* This body, which consists of around 400 members, is chiefly responsible for coordinating, planning and implementing policy and also ensures that the Chancellor's policies are disseminated throughout the Party and to the general public.

France

The French president has a presidential office, the General Secretariat of the Presidency, which includes a number of advisors. There is also the *cabinet du president* which contains personal presidential aides.

The UK

The British Prime Minister has the Prime Minister's Office. This contains a policy unit (sometimes referred to as the 'Number 10 Policy Unit') which in 1998 numbered seven members of staff whose role is to give advice on, monitor and develop policy. The Prime Minister's office gives the Prime Minister detailed knowledge of the affairs of government and enhances his or her ability to initiate policies. It is headed by a chief of staff, and in 1998 employed a total of 152 people. In 1998, the Labour Prime Minister, Tony Blair, sought to enhance his ability to coordinate the work of government by revamping the Cabinet Office, a reform which could have the effect of transforming it into the Prime Minister's private office. This development is discussed in more detail in Chapter 13.

Problems Associated With Chief Executives' Bureaucracies

While personal bureaucracies give chief executives a greater ability to assert control over governments, there are problems associated with the role which these bodies perform.

Size

As the number of staff which are employed within such bodies grows, it becomes increasingly difficult for the chief executive to maintain control over its work. This was a major problem for President Reagan whose personal reputation suffered in the Iran–Contra affair. The President was held responsible for actions concerned with the 'backdoor' sale of weapons to opponents of the Sandinista government in Nicaragua which were undertaken in his name but about which he had little, if any, knowledge.

Insulation

Personalised bureaucracies may insulate the chief executive from outside pressures to such an extent that he or she loses touch with the 'real world'. This may damage the chances of re-election to office.

Relationship With Other Branches of the Executive

The role performed by the chief executive's advisers may eclipse that of departments headed by leading members of the government. President Nixon's national security adviser in his first term, Dr Henry Kissinger, had a national and international profile which surpassed that of the Secretary of State. Leading politicians may resent being effectively sidelined by an entourage of unelected advisers and this friction may have damaging repercussions for the stability of the government. In 1989, the British Chancellor of the Exchequer, Nigel Lawson, resigned because of the influence exerted by Prime Minister Thatcher's adviser on economic affairs, Sir Alan Walters.

Question

○ Why do modern chief executives have personal departments?

○ What dangers do these pose for the smooth conduct of government?

Chief Executives and Heads of State

There is considerable variety within liberal democracies concerning the office of head of state. The UK, Holland, Belgium and the Scandinavian countries have *constitutional monarchs* as heads of state. Their position is derived from birth. In other countries the head of state is subject to some form of election. Such countries are accordingly termed *republics*. This may involve a process of direct election (as is the case in Ireland) or indirect election as occurs in Italy (where the President is elected by a college of 'grand electors' which includes members of both houses of parliament and regional governments) and Germany (where the president is elected every five years by the federal Assembly, a body composed of members of the Bundestag and representatives of the state parliaments.

The Functions of a Head of State

The office of head of state is separate from that of chief executive (although in some countries, such as the USA, it is exercised by the same person, the President). This office possesses a higher degree of authority than that enjoyed by governments since it is viewed as standing above party politics. Heads of State fulfil a number of functions in connection with the government of a country.

Physically Embody the Nation

The head of state performs a number of ceremonial functions such as receiving dignitaries from abroad or presiding over a range of official functions such as state dinners. Additionally, this role may provide a focus for national unity in times of emergency such as war or on occasions of rejoicing such as the VE and VJ celebrations held in Britain in 1995. The role of a monarchy as a symbol of national unity is especially important in Spain and Belgium.

Appoint Chief Executives

In most cases these are formal endorsements of decisions which have already been made. But the participation of the head of state to some extent neutralises the party political dimension of the activity. The involvement of a head of state in selecting a chief executive, for example, suggests that this official serves the whole nation and not merely the political interests which were responsible for securing the office for that person.

Ensure the Smooth Conduct of Political Affairs

A head of state usually possesses the ability to intervene in the conduct of political affairs. This intervention may seek to get a particularly contentious issue further examined. Or the head of state may possess certain reserve powers (such as the ability to dismiss the government or dissolve the legislature) which serve to make the executive branch accountable to a higher authority. These powers are particularly important when there is an impasse in a government whose operations consequently grind to a halt. This happened in 1975 when the Head of State's representative in Australia, the Governor-General, dismissed the Labour Prime Minister Gough Whitlam.

Promotion of Political Reform

An *elected* head of state may seek to translate the authority derived from the position of an apolitical national leader into power and seek to exercise a major role in the political life of a country. The following examples illustrate this process.

Italy

The Italian president Francesco Corsiga (1985–92) was accused of seeking to transform the country's parliamentary system of government into a presidential one which would make wide use of referendums. He was unsuccessful in securing this transition, but a later Italian president, Oscar Luigi Scalfaro, also sought to initiate political actions. In 1997, he utilised his prerogative power of pardon to free six members of the Red Brigade terrorist group from prison. This gesture was intended to induce parliament to declare a general amnesty for those convicted of terrorist offences.

Ireland

Mary Robinson used her tenure as President of Ireland (1990–97) to promote radical politics which served to advance the position of the needy and remedy the perception of women as second-class citizens. She assumed the status as Ireland's first citizen at a time of national transition, and during her period of office a number of social reforms (including the legalisation of divorce and homosexuality) were enacted.

Mary Robinson led Ireland through times of social change.

The British Monarchy

The British Monarch is head of state and also head of the Commonwealth. Criticisms have been directed at this institution in Britain and also within the Commonwealth, most notably in Australia. The Australian Republican Movement was founded in 1991 to seek a republic by the year 2001 (the centenary of federation) so that an Australian citizen would be head of state. In 1993, the then prime minister, Paul Keating, appointed a Republic Advisory Committee to prepare options for public discussion and in 1995 he announced that a referendum would be held on this subject. Keating's defeat in the 1996 General Election initially served to temporarily take this issue off the political agenda as the new Prime Minister, John Howard, did not have republican sympathies. However, in 1997 the process of voting for delegates to a constitutional convention commenced. This body would determine whether there was any consensus for a republic and, if so, how to set one up. Its conclusion would be put to a referendum, which was due to be held in 1999.

Criticisms of the British Monarchy

A number of criticisms have been directed at the Monarchy, most notably that it is not compatible with a liberal-democratic political system.

There are five key problems which can be identified.

Inappropriate Values

The hereditary principle instils society with values which are inappropriate to liberal democracies. It transforms 'citizens' into 'subjects' and in particular suggests that birth rather than merit is a key determinant of a person's status in society.

Undemocratic Government

The royal prerogative enables governments to act in an undemocratic manner by giving the government the ability to perform functions without having to consult Parliament. Declarations of war or the occasional use of troops in strikes are examples of actions undertaken by governments based on the use of the royal prerogative. This is essentially inconsistent with the operations of a liberal-democratic political system in which those who make decisions should be answerable to the people through their elected representatives in Parliament. This criticism has been partially addressed by reforms designed to introduce an element of accountability into the use of some limited aspects of the royal prerogative (such as making the work of the intelligence services accountable to Parliament in the 1994 Intelligence Services Act).

Interference in Political Affairs

The Monarch has the potential to exercise power in the conduct of political affairs and thus 'rule' as well as 'reign'. The Monarch's choice of Prime Minister in Britain is normally confined to the leader of the largest Party after a general election and thus involves rubber-stamping the choice made by the electorate. However, if third parties assume a more dominant role in future years, the Monarch may be required to exercise a more significant political role, as has been the case in Belgium and the Netherlands. This involvement may extend to decisions relating to the dissolution of Parliament or the dismissal of a prime minister.

Cost

The British Monarchy has been compared unfavourably with other European constitutional monarchies, for example that of Spain or the 'bicycling monarchies' found in Scandinavia. A key issue concerns the costs of the Court. In response to such criticisms it was announced in November 1992 that the Queen would pay tax on her personal income and would assume responsibility for the payments made from the Civil List to most members of the Royal Family. But although the Civil List voted by Parliament is a declining source of royal finance, public money is provided from other sources including government departments.

In 1997, the Treasury spent £28 million on the staffing and maintenance of the five Royal Palaces, and the *Guardian* on 17 November 1997 stated that the cost of the Monarchy to the taxpayer would be £42 million in 1998/99. The amount of public money spent on the Monarchy prompted suggestions by the government that such expenditure should in future be scrutinised by the Public Accounts Committee and the National Audit Office. The issue of cost must be considered in conjunction with considerations as to whether the Monarchy provides good value for money. Many actions performed by the Monarch are ceremonial (such as the State Opening of Parliament) or are performed at the behest of others (such as granting Royal Pardons, which are determined by the Home Secretary).

Remoteness

The extent to which the Monarchy understands the needs and expectations of its subjects in the late twentieth century was starkly questioned by events relating to the death of Diana, Princess of Wales, in 1997. The importance attached to protocol ensured that Royal Palaces (initially at Balmoral and latterly at Buckingham Palace) were the only major public buildings in the country not to lower their flags to half-mast as a gesture of respect. Only when the Queen had left Buckingham Palace for the Princess's funeral was it felt possible in accordance with established protocol to substitute the Royal Standard for the Union Flag which then could be flown at half-mast.

Advantages of the British Monarchy

The issues raised above have led to demands for a head of state who is politically accountable for his or her actions. However, supporters of the Monarchy will claim that it possesses a number of advantages. These include the following.

Popular Support

The evidence of some opinion polls suggest that the Monarchy continues to enjoy a relatively high level of public approval. For more than ten years, *Guardian*/ICM polls evidenced 70 per cent popular support for the Royal Family. This slumped to 48 per cent in August 1997, following the death of Diana, Princess of Wales. However, support for the Royal Family slowly recovered. In December 1997, for example, a MORI poll for *The Times* indicated that 55 per cent of respondents felt Britain would be worse off without this institution, 27 per cent felt it would make no difference and 15 per cent believed Britain would be better off without it.

Economic Benefits

Much of the ceremony attached to the Monarchy aids the tourist industry, while royal tours abroad may help exports.

Non-Partisan Nature

Governments are able to receive impartial advice from a seasoned political observer who may serve to depoliticise contentious political decisions should these need to be made.

REFORM OF THE BRITISH MONARCHY

The Monarchy appreciates the need to keep up to date. In 1992 the 'Way Ahead' group of Royal advisors was established. This body meets twice a year to review the state of the Monarchy. It is presided over by the Queen, and is attended by other senior members of the Royal Family.

The need for reform became more pressing following the death of Diana, Princess of Wales, in 1997. Opinion polls revealed popular unease over the Monarchy in the wake of this tragedy. An ICM poll in the *Daily Mail* on 18 October 1997 revealed that 70 per cent of Britons felt the Queen should consider retiring and handing over to a younger successor, rather than delaying the issue of succession until after her death. This poll also indicated that while 46 per cent of the nation felt that Charles should succeed, the high figure of 44 per cent believed he should step aside for his elder son. Concerns that the Monarchy was remote from the public resulted in the appointment of a Royal Director of Communications in early 1998. Suggestions were also put forward by the 'Way Ahead' group in 1998 to facilitate progress towards developing a 'people's monarchy'. These included restricting the future use of the title of 'His or Her Royal Highness' to children of the sovereign and the heir to the throne, and abolishing the procedures of bowing and curtseying to members of the Royal Family.

Question

Basing your views on the arguments presented above (including the section discussing the functions of a head of state), list a series of points for and against the proposition that 'The British Monarchy should be replaced by a head of state who is elected by the people.'

Further Reading

David Mervin, *The President of the United States* (Hemel Hempstead: Prentice Hall/Harvester Wheatsheaf, 1993). This work discusses the impact of key presidents on the development of the office. It also examines the constraints on the President.

The issue of presidential power is the subject of a classic study by **Richard Neustadt**, *Presidential Power* (New York: John Wiley, 1960). Although very dated, it remains relevant: it was said that President Kennedy entered the White House in 1961 with a copy of the book in his back pocket!

The relationship between the executive and legislative branches is discussed in **Michael Foley** and **John Owen**, *Congress and the Presidency* (Manchester: Manchester University Press, 1996).

R.A.W. Rhodes and **Patrick Dunleavy** (editors), *Prime Minister, Cabinet and Core Executive* (Basingstoke: Macmillan, 1995). This book provides a thorough assessment of the workings of the British executive. It extends the analysis beyond a consideration of the roles of and the relationships between the Prime Minister and the Cabinet to an assessment of the operations of the 'core executive' which embraces all mechanisms designed to coordinate the various aspects of the government machine.

The decline in the traditional role of the Cabinet (especially under Margaret Thatcher) is assessed in **Simon James**, *British Cabinet Government* (London: Routledge, 1992).

Chapter Twelve | The Bureaucracy

The aims of this chapter are:

> 1 To discuss what is meant by the term 'bureaucracy' and define its role and working practices.
>
> 2 To define the key characteristics of the British and American civil service.
>
> 3 To analyse the extent to which the British higher civil service acts as a policy maker and how governments may seek to avoid civil service obstruction of their political objectives.
>
> 4 To assess the civil service as a 'ruling elite', devoting particular attention to France.
>
> 5 To evaluate the main trends underlying the reform of the civil service, with particular reference to the UK.

The Role and Development of the Bureaucracy

The executive branch of government is broadly divided into two parts. These consist of those who give it political direction (namely the chief executive and other members of the 'government', whose work is discussed in the previous chapter) and those who perform administrative tasks. The latter work is performed by paid officials or *bureaucrats*, many of whom are categorised as *civil servants*. This means that key matters such as recruitment, pay, promotion, grading, dismissal and conditions of work are subject to common regulations which operate throughout the national government. Such common regulations are enforced centrally by bodies such as the American Office of Personnel Management or the British Civil Service Commission.

Civil servants perform a variety of roles in liberal-democratic states, but there are two which have traditionally been emphasised.

1 *To advise on the content of policy:* this role is carried out by the most senior civil servants, who in the UK are collectively referred to as the *higher civil service*. These include the *permanent secretaries* who are the most senior officials within government departments.

2 *To exercise responsibility for policy implementation:* this is

typically characterised by the impersonal application of established rules and procedures. The term 'red tape' is commonly used to describe the consequences of this method of operation. Policy implementation involves a wide range of activities and includes the delivery of a service to the public (such as the payment of welfare benefits).

DELEGATED LEGISLATION

Civil servants in Britain may perform the task of law-making through their ability to draft what is termed 'delegated legislation'. This arises when an Act of Parliament establishes broad principles whose detailed substance is left to civil servants who draft *statutory instruments*.

There are many advantages to this process. The ability of civil servants to draw up or amend delegated legislation is speedier than would be the case were Parliament required to carry out this process. This means that the law can be speedily updated. Additionally, civil servants may be better equipped than politicians to devise detailed and technical regulations.

Nonetheless, Parliament retains a scrutinising role over delegated legislation. All statutory instruments must be referred to Parliament and some require an affirmative resolution to be passed before they become law. A Select Committee was set up in 1944 to monitor delegated legislation, and in 1973 a joint committee of both Houses of Parliament was established to perform such work.

The Development of the Bureaucracy

The development of the bureaucracy differs from one country to another. Initially jobs in government service were allocated through the patronage system. This meant that people were employed on the basis of personal or family contacts rather than their ability. This system, in which political loyalty was more important than personal competence, tended to promote inefficiency in the operations of the public sector. It was a problem which many countries addressed during the nineteenth century. Below we briefly examine the experience of two countries – the UK and the USA.

Civil Service Reform in the USA

Political patronage influenced the appointment, promotion and dismissal of those employed in American federal public service for much of the nineteenth century. Andrew Jackson played a key role in developing the *spoils system* when he assumed the office of president in 1829. This viewed public office as a legitimate prize with which politicians could reward their supporters. Only towards the end of that century did pressure exerted by bodies such as the National Civil Service Reform League succeed in promoting change. Two key characteristics of the modern American civil service are appointment by merit and political neutrality.

Appointment by Merit

In 1883 the Pendleton Act established the Civil Service Commission (later renamed the Office of Personnel Management). This was a bipartisan (that is, staffed by supporters of both main political parties) board of three members which was charged with setting examinations for appointment into certain civil service jobs. Initially a relatively limited number of posts were affected by this reform, but the number extended during the twentieth century. Today the bulk of civil service posts are covered by 'civil service rules' operated by the Office of Personnel Management. The main criterion for obtaining a job is merit demonstrated in a competitive examination.

Political Neutrality

Under the provisions of the 1939 and 1940 Hatch Acts, civil servants are forbidden to take any active part in political management or political campaigns. However, this situation is offset by the fact that a considerable number of posts in the federal government's civil service remain at the disposal of the President. An incoming President retains the ability to appoint a number of key personnel in the federal government, although the most senior (at deputy-secretary, undersecretary and assistant-secretary levels) are subject to Senate confirmation. These total about 600 posts. The President's appointing power for a further group of senior executive service posts (about 700 in number) is constrained by the 1978 Civil Service Reform Act.

Civil Service Reform in the UK

In the UK the major impetus to the reform of the nineteenth-century civil service was provided by a commission which included Sir Stafford Northcote and Sir Charles Trevelyan. This reported in 1854 and recommended that a distinction be drawn between routine work and that which required intellectual ability. It was suggested that the latter should be carried out by appointees who were chosen on the basis of their performance in an examination of a literary kind, based on subjects studied at the universities. In 1855, three civil service commissioners were appointed to conduct such examinations, which in 1870 were made open to all suitably qualified members of the general public.

This report gave the British civil service certain key characteristics. These are discussed below.

The Generalist Tradition of the Higher Civil Service

This tradition placed the ability to implement decisions more highly than expertise in policy areas. It also facilitated the movement of civil servants between government departments, thus fostering the concept of a *unified* civil service.

Permanence

This viewed employment within the civil service as a career performed by servants of the Crown rather than a temporary position dependent on political patronage. However, 'careerism' led the civil service to become an insular organisation. There was a reluctance to appoint 'outsiders' (perhaps from the world of commerce and business) to senior posts on the grounds that only those who had chosen to make employment within the bureaucracy a permanent career were capable of understanding how the civil service operated. This principle has, however, been marginally affected by the tendency for ministers to appoint a limited number of advisors who are effectively temporary members of the higher civil service. This issue is discussed in more detail below.

Neutrality

This derived from the permanence principle and suggested that a civil servant could serve any government impartially, regardless of its political complexion. One consequence of this is a tendency for the civil service to itself define objectives and judge the policies of incoming governments in accordance with these. This prompted recent prime ministers (particularly Margaret Thatcher) to appoint to senior posts those who were willing to speedily follow government directives.

Anonymity

The doctrine of individual ministerial responsibility (discussed in Chapter 10) suggests that ministers are accountable for the actions undertaken by government departments. They, rather than their officials, take the blame when errors occur. Anonymity further suggests that civil servants should not publicly discuss policy (particularly contentious issues) since, technically, policy-making is the preserve of ministers not civil servants, whose role is merely to implement it.

CONTEMPORARY DEVELOPMENTS IN THE BRITISH CIVIL SERVICE

The issue of neutrality surfaced in 1997 in connection with the work performed by Departmental Directors of Information who worked within the Government Information Service. The role of these officials in presenting government information is set out in a Code of Practice contained in the Whitehall 'Red Book'. This stipulates that officials should not issue material which contains tendentious (that is, biased) material. However, a perception by the new Labour government that such officials should actively promote government policy and effectively act as 'spin doctors' (a term discussed more fully in Chapter 9) led to a number of resignations. By June 1998, 25 heads of information and their deputies had resigned, many of whom were replaced by political appointees.

Jack Cunningham – The 'Enforcer'.

The desire to coordinate the activities of the various ministries in areas which included policy presentation resulted in the establishment in 1997 of the Strategic Communications Unit based in the Cabinet Office and the appointment of Jack Cunningham as the 'enforcer' in 1998. (His role is discussed in more detail in Chapters 9 and 13.) The Strategic Communications Unit initially consisted of senior civil servants and political appointees including the key Labour personnel concerned with the government's portrayal by the media, Peter Mandelson and Alastair Campbell. One difficulty with this reform was that it implied Whitehall in general (and the civil servants operating in this unit in particular) had a legitimate interest in promoting the political interests of the government, particularly by guarding against conflicting statements of government policy being issued from diverse sources.

Question

The above section has discussed the key characteristics of the British civil service which were derived from the Northcote–Trevelyan report. Organising your material under the following headings, consider both the strengths and weaknesses of these characteristics in relationship to the conduct of contemporary British government.

○ **Generalist tradition**

○ **Permanence**

○ **Neutrality**

○ **Anonymity.**

Civil Service Influence over Policy-Making

In theory there is a sharp division between politics and administration, which are the preserve of different sets of officials. This suggests that senior civil servants give advice to ministers but it is the ministers who make decisions. The role of the civil service then becomes that of implementing the minister's decisions. However, the differentiation of roles between civil servants and politicians is not a totally accurate portrayal of what actually happens. Civil servants possess a considerable ability to influence the content of public policy through the advice which they give to ministers and the control which they exert over the processes of policy formulation and implementation.

The accusation that civil servants have usurped the role of ministers and have themselves become policy makers has been voiced in the UK in recent years. This argument is examined in greater detail below.

Ministerial Acquiescence in Civil Service Policy-Making

The accusation that senior civil servants (who are frequently termed *mandarins*) exercise a considerable role in policy-making does not necessarily lead to conflicts between politicians and civil servants. Various factors may induce or even compel civil servants to undertake functions that theoretically ought to be performed by ministers. There are various explanations for ministerial acquiescence in civil service policy-making, which are discussed below.

Permanence

Civil servants are permanent officials with expertise. Ministers hold office temporarily. Ministers may thus be content to let civil servants play a dominant role in the affairs of a department, particularly if they have no personal interest in its work but view it, for example, as a stepping stone to a higher ministerial office.

Knowledge

Ministers may know little or nothing of the work of a department until they are placed in charge of its operations. In theory, therefore, civil servants (with their expertise either of a policy area or of the workings of the administrative machine) are in a powerful position to dominate departmental policy-making, and ministers, aware of this, may defer to their knowledge and experience. The disinclination of some ministers to involve themselves in departmental matters may actually force civil servants to take a dominant role in policy-making whether they wish to do so or not. In such cases the role of ministers becomes that of *legitimating* decisions which are taken on their behalf by the civil service.

A Minister's Workload

The task of heading a government department is onerous. Large quantities of material (such as policy papers, briefing papers and letters) are prepared for ministers by their civil servants and are presented in traditional red boxes. Ministers are required to work at night and at weekends. The time-consuming nature of this work may have been partially ameliorated by the introduction in 1998 of 'virtual red boxes' designed to enable ministers to handle computerised paperwork at home. Additionally, ministers fulfil many diverse roles. In addition to heading a government department, ministers have other functions.

❍ They are Members of Parliament who need to devote time to constituency affairs.

❍ They are leading members of a political party who are expected to perform activities to promote that party.

❍ Those who are senior ministers are also members of the Cabinet and thus need to devote energy to the overall work of government.

'Knowing the Minister's Mind'

The above section has suggested that it is physically impossible for ministers to supervise all aspects of a department's affairs.

Civil servants are thus compelled to use their initiative and resolve unimportant or routine issues on their minister's behalf. Such matters constitute the bulk of a department's work which does not, therefore, come before the minister for consideration. This gives the civil service the ability to make decisions over a very wide range of departmental activities in which the only political guideline might be that of 'knowing the minister's mind' – that is, assessing how the minister would act if he or she were available to deal with the situation personally. The accurate assessment of which issues need to come before the minister and which can be resolved by the department's officials is thus a key task of administration.

Conclusion

These arguments suggest that ministers may acquiesce in a wide range of civil service policy-making. Problems arise only when ministers perceive civil servants to be acting improperly by seeking to control the policy-making process by the manipulation or obstruction of ministers. Attention is now turned to this issue.

Civil Service Usurpation of a Policy-Making Role

The term 'usurpation' in this context refers to a situation in which civil servants seize control of the policy-making machinery without prior authorisation to do so.

CIVIL SERVANT SPEAK

The belief that civil servants conspire to dominate the policy-making process and prevent ministers from attaining their political objectives is frequently mentioned by politicians. Prime Minister Tony Blair drew attention to this situation in his speech to the Labour Party conference in October 1997. He stated that when civil servants referred to a minister's idea as 'ambitious' or 'interesting' they meant that it was 'a stupid idea, dreamt up at the last minute for the manifesto'. If they said a proposal was 'challenging' they meant there 'was not a hope in hell of making it work'. If a policy was labelled a 'brave proposal', it 'means they've got the doctor outside waiting to sign the certificates'.

The spectre of a minister being manipulated by a wily civil servant was vividly brought to life on British television screens in the programmes *Yes Minister* and *Yes Prime Minister*. These implied that civil servants viewed themselves as the policy makers and that their role was to prevent ministers interfering. This gave rise to a perception that the role of the civil service was to inform ministers of all the conceivable objections to any initiatives which they put forward, rather than seeking to implement them.

Such views suggest that civil servants do not only exercise a policy-making role because ministers want them to do so, as has been suggested above: their own inclinations induce them to undertake this role, which may bring them into conflict with ministers. This section examines the tactics which the civil service might use to ensure that their views dominate departmental policy-making.

Manipulation of Options

Many ministers make decisions by selecting from options presented to them by the civil service. This gives the civil service ample opportunity to guide ministers in the direction in which they wish them to go. They may do this, for example, by producing an incomplete list of options designed to direct the minister towards the course of action favoured by the department. Alternatively they may attempt to 'blind a minister with science' that is, making an issue seem so technical that the minister, as a layperson, feels uncomfortable and thus disposed towards accepting the preferred option of the civil service.

Obstruction

Some ministers may wish to have a more prominent role in policy-making. They enter office with clearly defined policy objectives and an appreciation of how these goals should be accomplished, rather than being willing to rely on options presented to them by the civil service. However, this does not guarantee that the civil service will then follow their ministers' leads. They may utilise an array of devices to stop, or slow down, the implementation of the ministers' wishes.

Minister–Civil Servant Relationship: an Assessment

The impression of a civil service which dominates the policy-making process through either acquiescence or usurpation is *not* wholly accurate. There are a number of contrary arguments concerning this issue which are discussed below.

Controversial Plans are Implemented

The civil service has shown itself to be willing to implement controversial proposals, especially in the early period of a

OBSTRUCTION BY THE CIVIL SERVICE

The tactics associated with obstruction include the following.

Delaying the Implementation of Ministerial Directives

This involves the civil service 'sitting it out' in the hope that after a period of time the minister (or even the entire government) will have gone and the instructions of the minister thus become redundant. One way to avoid this problem is for ministers to attach dates to their proposals, which thus requires civil servants to report progress on the implementation of them at regular intervals.

Mobilising Opposition

Many issues involve more than one civil service department. Ministers meeting to take a decision may find themselves vastly outnumbered by civil servants from the affected departments. Inter-departmental committees (which are staffed by senior civil servants, and from which ministers are traditionally excluded) may be used to mobilise opposition to a minister's policy from a number of departments. One way to avoid this is for ministers to sideline their officials and take decisions themselves. On 4 October 1997 the *Independent* reported that the decision by Jack Cunningham (then Minister for Agriculture) and Frank Dobson (Secretary of State for Health) to ask the Prime Minister to set up a judicial inquiry to track down those to blame for the introduction of BSE into cattle and the human food train was taken with no civil servants present.

Manufacturing Political Pressure Against a Minister

This is designed to secure the abandonment of the politician's preferred course of action. They may do this by appealing over the head of the minister to the Prime Minister or the Cabinet, possibly utilising the argument that the minister's intended actions are contrary or damaging to overall government policy. The success of such a tactic is considerably influenced by the minister's standing among his or her political colleagues.

The ability of civil servants to mobilise pressure against ministers was aided by the innovation introduced by the 1997 Labour government. Permanent secretaries were asked to provide reports on the competence and efficiency of junior ministers in their departments. The aim of this exercise was to enable the Prime Minister to make informed judgements concerning the promotion and dismissal of ministers. One unintended consequence of this reform will be to make ministers wary of clashing with their civil servants since they now possess the ability to heavily influence the continuance of their careers in government.

government's life. Unlike the USA, the UK does not have any official period of transition from one chief executive to another which would enable the civil service to draw up plans to implement key political objectives: an incoming prime minister moves into Number 10 Downing Street the morning following an election victory and assumes immediate control for the running of the country.

In recent years, however, the civil service has come to the aid of incoming governments by considering the policies and priorities of opposition parties in advance of an election, which aids their implementation should they secure victory. Harold Wilson's ability to speedily nationalise the iron and steel industry in 1967 (soon after his 1966 election victory) was facilitated by the civil service drawing up plans to do this in advance of the election. Prior to the 1997 General Election, contacts were made between permanent secretaries and leading Labour spokespersons at which issues including the structure of government were discussed. The ability of the civil service to adapt to the policies of a new political master was subsequently demonstrated in 1997 when the Treasury worked at considerable speed to implement Chancellor Gordon Brown's directive concerning the Bank of England and the determination of interest rates.

Ministers and Civil Servants Need Each Other

The relationship between ministers and their civil servants is frequently harmonious. Each 'side' depends on the other. The minister relies on the civil service for advice and the handling of routine business to ensure a manageable workload, but the civil service requires the minister to promote the department's interests. This may involve defending the department when its activities are scrutinised by the Cabinet or within Parliament. It may also involve performing an ambassadorial role to convince the general public that the department fulfils a vital role in civil affairs.

Ministers' Political Control Over the Bureaucracy

In addition to the two arguments referred to above, the ability of civil servants to exercise a dominant role in policy-making may be prevented by ministers taking measures designed to impose political control over the operations of the bureaucracy. These methods include the following actions:

Ministerial Involvement in Appointments and Promotions

The ability to appoint, and in particular to promote, civil servants is one way whereby government might seek to assert control over the bureaucracy. Traditionally, however, these matters have been conducted independently of the government. Candidates for promotion are put forward by a Civil Service Board, composed of senior officials, and it is normal practice for a minister to endorse its recommendation. Political involvement in appointments became a contentious issue in Britain during the period of Conservative governments (1979–97).

During its long period of office, Conservative administrations were responsible for appointing a large number of permanent secretaries and were thus able to subject the civil service to political influences. The 'one of us' test was allegedly applied by the government to the promotion of civil servants to the post of permanent and deputy secretary. This did not mean that such civil servants had to be Conservative Party members, but it suggested they had to be prepared to advance speedily the progress of government initiatives. A major difficulty with such intervention is that the civil service becomes politicised. This means it becomes so closely identified with the policies and working practices associated with a particular political party that its neutrality (which is essential if it is to serve a government of another political persuasion) is questioned.

'EASING OUT'

One further way for ministers to exercise control over the civil service is by 'easing out' those they find it difficult to work with.

A number of differences of opinion surfaced after 1997 in the Treasury between the Labour Chancellor, Gordon Brown, and his permanent secretary, Sir Terence Burns. In 1998, Sir Terence took early retirement and was subsequently awarded a peerage. This enabled a new permanent secretary, Andrew Turnbull, to take his place in the Treasury.

Ministerial Advisors

The operations of the bureaucracy can be politicised by ministers appointing their own advisors (who are paid as temporary civil servants) to offset the activities of civil servants. However, these posts are limited in number and post holders are thus heavily outnumbered by permanent officials. One further problem is that if these advisors are outsiders they may effectively be 'frozen out' of the operations of a department by its permanent officials. In France, this difficulty is solved by ministers appointing existing civil servants to act as their advisors. These are located in the *cabinet ministeriel*. They operate under the minister's direct control and usually revert to their previous posts when their service to the minister has ended.

Advisors and the Blair Government

The use of temporary advisors was increased following Labour's election victory in 1997. The overall number increased from 35 to 50, 18 of whom were employed within the Downing Street policy unit. Some of these were concerned with policy advice whilst others were 'spin doctors' (a term discussed in Chapter 9) mainly involved with media liaison. The influence of these advisors also increased after 1997, and they have been described as a 'third tier' in the policy-making process, standing between ministers and senior civil servants.

The Senior Civil Service as a 'Ruling Elite'

The description of senior civil servants as an 'elite' particularly refers to their social background. In many countries such officials derive from a middle and upper middle class background. The stereotypical British senior civil servant is white, male, middle class, educated at public school and Oxbridge (Oxford or Cambridge Universities) and middle aged. One danger with this is that the elite may inject attitudes and values derived from their social exclusiveness into public policy. These may be out of tune with public opinion. A similar situation exists in France where, despite efforts by socialist administrations to broaden the recruitment base of such officials, a large number derive from socially exclusive backgrounds. There are, however, exceptions: in New Zealand, for example, the main source of recruitment into the civil service is from secondary-school graduates. Preference is given to internal promotions to fill higher-level vacancies.

In Britain, reference is sometimes made to the grip exerted by the *establishment* over the conduct of public affairs. This term refers to a class or group of persons who exert dominance over the State's key institutions (including the government, judiciary and civil service) primarily based upon their social background. In France, elitist control over the affairs of the nation is particularly identified with the senior civil service whose social background, education and training is seen as equipping them to exercise dominant roles throughout all areas of society, including its political life. This situation is discussed below.

Question

Based on your reading of the above section, consider the view that 'it is inevitable that civil servants dominate the British policy-making process.' What dangers do you think may occur as a result of this situation? Can these be avoided?

FRANCE: THE ADMINISTRATORS' STATE?

In France, an elite group of persons trained as administrators occupy key positions not only in the civil service but also in political life and the commercial activities of both the public and private sectors. Specialist training schools function as recruiting agencies for key areas of government activity. The most influential are the *Ecole Nationale d'Administration* and the *Ecole Polytechnique*. Their role is to recruit and train candidates for the higher-level civil service posts. Such training involves education and practical experience. Successful graduates are able to secure posts in the most prestigious areas of government activity. Additionally, however, their background and training enable them to move from the public to the private sector and occupy senior positions there or to occupy key positions in other aspects of public affairs.

The absence of any requirement that civil servants should not participate in political activities increases the likelihood of administrators playing an active part in politics. In the 1990s, the Gaullist president, Jacques Chirac, and his socialist Prime Minister, Lionel Jospin, were both graduates of the Ecole Nationale d'Administration. Although the French administrative elite do not monopolise influential jobs throughout society, the dominant positions held by many from such a background has given rise to accusations that France is an 'administrator's state' in which persons trained as civil servants are dominant in all walks of life. These are the French equivalent of Britain's 'establishment'.

The Reform of the Civil Service in Britain

One compelling reason for reforming the civil service was the need for the administrative machinery to be kept up to date, thus enabling it to face the challenges posed in the second half of the twentieth century. This was especially important for the higher civil service who held the most influential posts. These comprised of the *administrative class* of the civil service which was divided into a number of grades. The reform of the civil service was particularly directed at the workings of these senior ranks. A major series of reforms were proposed by the *Fulton Report* in 1968 which are evaluated below.

The Fulton Report

In 1966 the Labour Prime Minister, Harold Wilson, appointed a committee to examine the 'structure, recruitment and management of the civil service'. It was chaired by Lord Fulton and reported in 1968. Several major criticisms of the civil service were put forward in this report. These are discussed below.

Fulton's Criticisms

○ *Elitism:* the senior ranks of the civil service were dominated by persons from a public school and Oxbridge background who had effectively become a self-perpetuating elite, remote from those it was meant to serve. The expansion of educational opportunities in postwar Britain questioned this elitist dominance.

○ *The cult of the generalist:* the higher civil service was divided into two main groups – administrators and specialists. Although specialists such as scientists were employed, the organisational structure utilised by the service served to marginalise them and ensure that the highest posts were filled by generalist administrators, many of whom lacked knowledge in subjects of contemporary importance which included economics and accountancy.

○ *Inadequate training:* it had been traditionally assumed that 'on the job training' (that is, learning based upon the practical experience derived from performing a job) was adequate for civil servants. As the processes of government and the policy areas embraced by it became more technical, this assumption was challenged.

○ *Deficient management:* two main issues were identified in the Fulton Report – the tendency for senior civil servants to view their key role as being to advise the minister rather than to manage their departments, and the extent to which the Treasury saw its key function being to manage the economy with consequent neglect of its other task of management of the civil service.

○ *Imperfect accountability:* the working practices of the civil service tended to give insufficient responsibility to individual civil servants whose working practices were to constantly refer matters upwards in the hierarchy when decisions were required. This tended to make it difficult to pinpoint responsibility for decisions or to hold civil servants accountable for them.

Fulton's Reforms

To address the problems identified above, the Fulton Committee put forward a series of specific recommendations (158 in total) to equip the civil service to discharge the functions required of it in contemporary government. The main ones were as follows.

Organisational Reform

This entailed the abolition of the separate classes on which the organisation of the civil service was based and the creation of one unified hierarchy (termed a *classless* service) within which posts would be graded. A main intention of this proposal was to enhance the ability of those with specialist knowledge in specific areas of government activity to achieve the highest posts in the civil service, thereby ending the dominance exerted by the generalist administrators at the highest levels. Additionally, it would enhance the corporate identity of the civil service. A further suggestion to secure the implementation of the principle of promotion by merit was to establish an Administrative Trainee system which would provide for accelerated promotion of entrants judged to be the most able.

Enhanced Specialisation

The desire to make the civil service reflect the demands placed upon it by new areas of governmental activity was reflected in a number of recommendations. These included introducing the 'principle of relevance' into civil service entry examinations which would reduce the advantage then possessed by Oxbridge candidates with degrees in subjects such as Classics. It was proposed that careers would be planned around either the economic/finance functions of government or its social service functions and that transfer between these two areas of work would not usually be permissible. This would improve the specialist knowledge and training available to generalist administrators. It was further suggested that increased use be made of late entrants and secondments both from and into the civil service, thus enabling the insular culture and working practices of the civil service to benefit from broader organisational contacts. It was, however, recommended that the careerist nature of the civil service should be retained.

Improved Training

This was designed to enable civil servants to constantly upgrade their skills and knowledge in relationship to the changing demands placed upon them by the work they performed.

Reforms to Civil Service Management

It was proposed that senior civil servants should devote more time to the management of their individual departments and consequently less to advising ministers regarding policy. The shortfall in the advisory function would be taken up by policy experts having greater contact with ministers. It was thus proposed that the overall management of the civil service should be taken out of the hands of the Treasury and allocated to a newly-created Civil Service Department (CSD) with control over all matters of personnel management and staffing.

Improved Accountability

This involved giving clearly defined responsibilities to individual civil servants throughout the civil service machinery, thus enabling them to be held accountable for their actions both within Whitehall and in the broader political environment. This reform would be implemented by creating units of accountable management to which tasks could be allocated, money provided and performance monitored. The Fulton committee further recommended 'hiving off' (that is, transferring the responsibility for) certain areas of activity to semi-independent bodies or agencies.

Implementation of Fulton's Reform Proposals

A number of reforms were implemented in response to the recommendations of the Fulton Committee. This section examines their implementation in the key areas identified above and the subsequent impact which they had on the civil service.

Organisational Reform

Certain changes were made to civil service organisation. An 'open structure' was created for the higher civil service whereby posts of undersecretary level and above (extended to assistant-secretary level in 1985) were open to all civil servants whether they were administrators or specialists. Additionally, moves towards creating a unified grading structure were made. In 1971 the Administration Group was established by merging the Administrative, Executive and Clerical grades which comprised the four Treasury Classes. This group consisted of 10 grades with different entry and examination requirements which closely approximated the former arrangements and thus suggested a change that was primarily a cosmetic one. Generalists continued to dominate the highest ranks of the civil service, one reason being that experts are possibly too insular whereas generalists may have a broader, more rounded view. An Administrative Trainee System was set up in 1971 (remodelled in 1982) for graduate entrants.

Specialisation

Relatively little progress was made with the introduction of 'outsiders' into the civil service or with secondments from the civil service into other organisations. One difficulty with secondments is that those from the civil service who go into commerce, finance or industry may find the conditions or pay there more attractive and this may prompt them not to return to the civil service.

Training

The main innovation was the establishment of a Civil Service College in 1970 (with branches in London and Sunningdale) designed to train around 8,000 civil servants a year. The focus of its work was primarily on managerial functions. One difficulty posed with training is the extent to which it provides courses which are viewed as valuable within the organisation.

Management

The tendency for permanent secretaries to concentrate on advising ministers to the detriment of managing their departments largely remained, perhaps reflecting the desire for most ministers to discuss departmental affairs with their most senior civil servants.

In 1968, all matters relating to the staffing and management of the civil service were transferred out of the Treasury and became the responsibility of the CSD whose permanent secretary was head of the Home Civil Service. This body did not, however, fulfil the expectations of improved civil service management or efficiency. In particular there was a tendency for the CSD's permanent secretary (initially Lord Armstrong and latterly Sir Ian Bancroft) to act as advisor to the Prime Minister to the detriment of managing the civil service. Also, the increased concern attached to the level of public expenditure during the 1970s resulted in the Treasury and CSD having diverse views on civil service staffing and related costs. Accordingly the CSD was abolished in 1981 and its functions were divided between the Management and Personnel Office of the Cabinet Office and the Treasury. In 1987, the Treasury took over this former body and thus effectively restored the pre-Fulton situation of Treasury control over the civil service.

Accountability

The principle of accountable management made little headway. It conflicted with the principle of the anonymity of civil servants and was difficult to make compatible with the convention of individual ministerial responsibility. The Fulton committee was not empowered to examine the constitutional position of the civil service, which was a necessary prerequisite for a reform of this nature.

Question

In what ways do you consider that the civil service which the Fulton Committee examined in 1966 was out of date and in need of reform?

Evaluate the success of any TWO reforms put forward by the committee to modernise the British civil service.

Conclusion

The Fulton report made a significant impact on the development of the British civil service in the late twentieth century. Concern was expressed, however, at the pace of reform and at a perception that the elite administrative class of the civil service was left too free to decide which of Fulton's recommendations would be acted upon and which should be ignored. In particular, therefore, structural or organisational reforms which enhanced career prospects or job opportunities tended to receive attention ahead of other recommendations which seemed to threaten the established culture and working practices of the civil service. This implies, therefore, that only when a government itself takes a key interest in the progress of administrative reform will any radical changes be introduced.

Civil Service Reform in the Late Twentieth Century

The growth in the role of the State in a number of countries after 1945 resulted in large civil services. This was costly. Thus governments wishing to prune public spending were induced to cast a critical eye at the workings of the bureaucracy. Reform of the civil service has been advocated in many countries. In Ireland, the Devlin Report put forward reform proposals in 1969. In the UK, the Fulton Report in 1968 (which has been discussed in detail above) and the Ibbs Report in 1988 influenced significant changes. In the USA this subject was considered by Vice President Gore's *National Performance Review* published in 1993. Governments influenced by 'new right' ideology have been especially interested in civil service reform in recent years. While it would be impossible to chart all the directions which civil service reform has taken in various countries, there are certain developments which have occurred widely. Three of these key common themes are considered below.

Efficiency and Value for Money

The objectives of efficient and effective management have commonly been implemented by drawing upon a number of management techniques utilised in the world of business. In commercial undertakings, profit and loss are the main indicators of organisational efficiency. Such assessments are rarely appropriate to organisations providing public sector services, which require alternative methods to be devised. These are discussed below in relationship to developments in the UK 1979–97.

The Quest for Efficiency and Value for Money in the UK

In the UK the concern for the elimination of waste and promotion of efficiency and value for money resulted in a number of initiatives.

Accountable Management

As has been referred to above, this suggestion was initially made in the Fulton Report in 1968 and was pursued more vigorously following the 1979 General Election when emphasis was placed on ministers' being more fully aware of their departments' operations. This paved the way for devolving managerial and budgetary responsibility to units within departments which could then more easily be held accountable by the minister. In 1982, the objective of accountable management was sought through the *Financial Management Initiative*.

The Financial Management Initiative (FMI)

This innovation derived from earlier attempts (namely PESC and cash limits, which are discussed in Chapter 7) to maintain control over the level of public spending. The Financial Management Initiative required departments to specify *objectives* (that is, what would be achieved through spending a specific sum of money). The attainment of these objectives would then be assessed against *performance indicators*. The FMI further facilitated managerial accountability, since civil servants with managerial roles were given personal responsibility for specific areas of departmental activity. There were, however, difficulties encountered with this initiative. Organisations providing a range of services to the public often found it difficult to precisely define their objectives. This consequently made it difficult to measure the extent to which these had been attained.

Lord Rayner's Efficiency Unit

In 1979, the Efficiency Unit was established (initially under Lord Rayner and subsequently under Sir Robin Ibbs) within the Cabinet Office. It was broader in scope than Policy Analysis and Review (which was introduced in 1970 but abandoned in 1985) and sought to tackle inefficiency and unnecessary bureaucracy. It examined specific policies, activities and functions in order to make savings and enhance effectiveness. Solutions to any problems which were identified would be introduced within a year of the commencement of the scrutiny. A key feature of these investigations was the involvement of all officials associated with the policies or procedures under review in order to generate a commitment to examination and reform.

Management Information System for Ministers (MINIS)

This was introduced into the Department of the Environment by Michael Heseltine in 1980. It sought to remedy the difficulties which ministers (especially those who headed 'giant' departments, which are discussed in the following Chapter) experienced in understanding the operations of the departments they headed. This knowledge was important to the attainment of their objectives.

The process involved each of the 63 units (termed 'directorates') into which the Department of the Environment was divided, providing Heseltine with a document which listed the directorate's objectives and activities, together with statements related to the fulfilment of its objectives and planned future performance. These documents were collected centrally, evaluated and then passed on to each minister. They enabled the ministers to take managerial decisions which, after discussion with the civil servants, were incorporated into an 'action document'. This, coupled with the original MINIS document, constituted the directorate's programme of action for the following year. This exercise would be repeated at regular intervals, thus making for continuous review and monitoring of the department's work. This innovation affected the objectives, activities, organisation and personnel levels of the Department of the Environment in a relatively short space of time. It was, however, unpopular with the civil service. One reason for this was the amount of information this exercise made available to the general public on the work and internal processes of the department. This initiative was personally associated with Heseltine and not widely utilised elsewhere within British government.

The Separation of Policy Planning and Service Delivery

A second direction of civil service reform has been a redefinition of the role and organisation of national bureaucracies. Typically this involved the separation of policy planning from service delivery. There are two main advantages associated with this reform.

1   *Civil servants can engage in long-term planning:* the day-to-day administration of services is placed into the hands of bodies other than government departments. This reform would enhance the capacity of senior civil servants to plan, which might help to overcome their traditional dislike of change and innovation.

2   *Those responsible for implementing services (usually in 'agencies') can exercise a considerable degree of discretion and*

operational freedom: this improves the morale and motivation of the staff employed in such work. Within the confines of policy objectives and a budget set by a government department, those who deliver services are delegated a wide degree of authority as to how they achieve their set goals.

The 'Next Steps' Programme

As has been observed in the above account, the Fulton Report (1968) recommended a number of reforms to improve the overall efficiency of the civil service. These included accountable management, the 'hiving off' of functions and an enhanced degree of attention being paid by senior civil servants to day-to-day departmental management at the expense of their role of advising ministers. These ideas were subsequently developed in a report, *Improving Management in Government: The Next Steps*, which is generally referred to as the *Ibbs Report* and was published in 1988.

This recommended that the national bureaucracy should be divided into a central civil service and peripheral agencies.

❍ *A central civil service:* this would advise ministers and be responsible for strategic planning within a department.

❍ *Agencies:* these would deliver the services within the framework devised by the department's central civil service.

The rationale of this reform was two-part.

❍ *To break up the civil service:* the size and diverse nature of the tasks undertaken by departments (especially 'giant' ones) tended to give rise to departments which were large and unwieldy.

❍ *To secure efficiency:* efficient service delivery was impeded by traditional civil service working practices, which were dominated by obedience to routine. It was thus proposed that those who performed services should be given a wide degree of discretion as to how they secured the results which were allotted to them.

Agencies

The Ibbs report proposed that the executive functions of central government would be performed by *agencies*. These would be 'hived off' from Whitehall and headed by a chief executive. This official would be directly accountable to Parliament and serve as the agency's accounting officer, although he or she would remain under the nominal control of the department's permanent secretary. Agencies would be staffed by civil servants but the concept of a unified civil service was effectively ended. The essence of this latter principle was that civil servants were able to move across departments and work anywhere within the bureaucracy. Such movement is less likely as this form of hiving off promotes the view that workers are agency rather than government employees. The view of the civil service as a career is also eroded by the creation of agencies. This is especially apparent regarding chief executives who are appointed on fixed-term contracts and paid bonuses to meet targets.

Before an agency is set up ministers have to agree that the activity needs to be discharged by government. The alternatives of contracting out or privatisation must first be considered (which are discussed below). The relationship between departments and agencies are defined in a framework agreement. Innovations which were introduced included flexibility in recruitment, the development of pay and grading structures specific to agencies, and the requirement that such bodies produce business plans and performance targets. Agencies now dominate the central machinery of government. Over 60 per cent of all civil servants are employed by such bodies and their total cost to the taxpayer exceeds £10 billion a year.

A number of criticisms have been made of the operation of agencies. These include imperfect accountability and problems arising from the separation of policy and administration.

❍ *Imperfect accountability:* agencies are insufficiently accountable for their actions. The convention of individual ministerial responsibility is harder to enforce when a wide range of operational decisions are made by civil servants who operate at arm's length from ministerial control. This problem is compounded by the ability of ministers to use the existence of agencies to disclaim responsibility when problems arise.

PRISON ESCAPES

The use of agencies may undermine the accountability of government to Parliament.

In October 1995, for example, the then Home Secretary (Michael Howard) denied responsibility for day-to-day operational activities in the prison service. These were stated to be the concern of the Director General of the Prison Service. Issues related to prison security such as high-profile prison escapes were thus declared to be an agency matter for which ministers refused to be held to account.

○ *Problems arising from the divorce of policy and administration:* agencies assume that it is possible to separate these two functions. In reality, however, this may not be the case since they are often fused as opposed to distinct processes.

Privatisation

A third direction which civil service reform frequently takes is for services to be delivered by private sector organisations. This is commonly referred to as privatisation, which in the UK was particularly associated with the transfer of the former nationalised industries into private ownership. Services may be contracted out (in which case the civil service is involved in drawing up contracts, which are subject to *competitive tendering*, and then in monitoring the performance of those to whom contracts are awarded) or they may be divorced from government completely. Such reforms view competition as the main way to make services efficient.

Contracting out was pursued in the USA during the 1980s and the *National Performance Review* (1993) urged that increased use should be made of service provision by non-governmental bodies. During the 1990s, 'market testing' was introduced by the British government. This sought to establish the advantages of government departments contracting out a range of services to the private sector.

A full evaluation first needs to be undertaken to ascertain if it is appropriate for a service to be delivered by the private sector. If a service is contracted out, it is essential that efficient monitoring procedures are put in place by departments to ensure that services are efficiently provided and to safeguard the interests of consumers. Such mechanisms involve cost and also may create tensions by seeking to evaluate the performance of those involved in commercial activities according to civil service standards.

There are, however, a number of problems associated with privatisation. Civil service inertia needs to be overcome. Bureaucracies are often resistant to change, especially when organisations and jobs are threatened. Thus political will to implement reforms is important. The commitment of the Conservative government during the 1980s was thus crucial to bringing about alterations to the British civil service. A further difficulty concerns the involvement of the private sector in administering public policy. It is alleged that the private sector's main concern is profitability. The organisations which administer privatised services are said to be primarily motivated by a desire to make profits rather than to deliver a quality service to the public.

Question

Using additional material selected from books, journals and contemporary newspapers, discuss the strengths and weaknesses of ONE reform introduced into the civil service after 1979 and which has been referred to above.

In the UK, the government's response to such arguments was to place emphasis on *consumerism*. The *Citizens' Charter* (1991) sought to make all providers of public services (including those administered by the private sector) aware of their duties to their clients, and to establish standards of service which consumers had the right to expect. This awareness was reinforced by agencies' being set performance targets which could be monitored to assess efficiency.

Further Reading

Peter Barberis, (editor) *The Whitehall Reader* (Buckinghamshire: Open University Press, 1996). This provides a broad selection of views concerning the operations of the contemporary British administrative machine. There is an informative introductory essay which gives a detailed account of developments affecting the civil service since the Fulton Report.

The same author's *The Elite of the Elite* (Aldershot: Dartmouth, 1996) is specifically concerned with permanent secretaries.

Gavin Drewry and **Tony Butcher**, *The Civil Service Today* (Oxford: Blackwell, 1991, 2nd edition). This book offers an informative account of the development of the civil service. It also examines key issues which include minister–civil-servant relationships.

Chapter Thirteen | The Machinery of Government

The aims of this chapter are:

1 To describe the different forms of machinery of government utilised by liberal democracies.

2 To evaluate the way in which the machinery of government is subject to political control.

3 To analyse the manner in which government departments are organised in the United Kingdom, paying particular attention to rational and political considerations.

4 To analyse the role of quangos and related bodies and to assess the problems which they pose for liberal-democratic government, with particular reference to the UK.

5 To discuss developments affecting the coordination of public policy in Britain.

The Organisation of the Work of Government

The previous two chapters have discussed the way in which responsibility for the work performed by national government is shared between politicians and full-time officials, who are usually civil servants. This chapter focuses on the organisational structures within which the affairs of government are conducted.

THE MACHINERY OF GOVERNMENT

As the following brief examples demonstrate, the machinery of government utilised by liberal democracies does not conform to any standard pattern.

◆ *The United States of America:* the machinery of the federal government comprises the cabinet departments, independent regulatory agencies, government corporations and independent executive agencies.

◆ *Ireland:* the machinery of government consists of departments and State-sponsored bodies. The latter have become increasingly important since 1945 in discharging important areas of central government activity.

◆ *The UK:* the machinery of government consists of government departments (much of whose work, as Chapter 12 argued, is now performed by agencies) and ad hoc bodies termed *quangos.* After 1945 a range of industrial or commercial activities were performed by nationalised industries whose operations were managed by a public corporation, which was a specific type of quango. These, however, were subject to the privatisation policies pursued by Conservative governments between 1979 and 1997.

The machinery of government operates in a political environment. These bodies, and particularly the working practices they adopt, can become a source of intense political debate. In the UK, for example, the operations of the Child Support Agency (a body established by the Conservative government in 1991 to ensure that fathers made significant contributions for the upkeep of children following the breakup of a marriage) received prominent attention in the 1990s. In the USA accusations of overzealous conduct by revenue collectors employed by the Internal Revenue Service became a major issue of public concern which prompted presidential intervention. In 1997, President Clinton introduced a package of 200 measures to make this body more accountable and responsive to taxpayers' complaints. These examples highlight the importance of mechanisms to ensure that political control can be exerted over the machinery of government when the need arises. The following sections examine the way in which such control is exerted in America and Britain.

Political Control of the Machinery of Government in the USA

An assessment of the effectiveness of political control of the bureaucracy needs to appreciate a potential conflict between *accountability* and *managerial freedom.* Although those whose activities are financed by public money need to account for what they do, excessive accountability may stifle initiative and make civil servants operate in a cautious manner. Ideally, therefore, agencies should be accountable for their results but given a degree of discretion as to how these are achieved.

Control of the American Federal Bureaucracy

In the USA the control of the federal bureaucracy involves both the President and Congress. Their involvement is sometimes prompted by a belief that inadequate control results in waste and inefficiency. In 1982, President Reagan appointed a commission chaired by Peter Grace to find ways to reduce government spending and to eliminate bureaucratic waste and mismanagement. This commission reported that the government was the worst run enterprise in the USA.

Control by the President

The President may seek to exert control over the bureaucracy in a number of ways.

❍ *Appointment of key personnel:* normally the president is responsible for appointing agency heads and this power may be used to implement presidential objectives. Additionally, political appointees and advisors may be installed into the federal bureaucracy to advance policy initiatives.

❍ *Commissions* may be appointed to scrutinise the bureaucracy's workings.

❍ *Executive orders* may be issued to agencies.

❍ *Scrutiny of the workings of the federal government:* during the 1980s, for example, President Reagan sought to use the Office of Management and Budget to ensure that agency regulations conformed to administration policy.

There are, however, a number of problems which impede effective presidential control over the federal bureaucracy. These include the following.

❍ *Fragmentation:* the bureaucracy is composed of a variety of departments, agencies, bureaux and commissions which possess varying degrees of autonomy.

❍ *Relationship with Congress:* presidential control may also be hindered by the relationship which such bodies establish with Congress. Congress is required to approve proposals put forward by the President to reorganise government departments. Its opposition prevented President Nixon from amalgamating seven departments into four 'super' departments in 1971 and halted President Reagan's plans to abolish the Departments of Education and Energy during the 1980s.

❍ *'Iron triangles':* the relationships which may be constructed between agencies, congressional committees and clients or interest groups may also prove impenetrable to presidential control. This issue is examined more fully in Chapter 8.

Control by Congress

There are a number of ways whereby Congress may involve itself in the working practices of the federal bureaucracy.

○ *Appointments:* some appointments require the approval (or confirmation) of the Senate. Members of Congress may additionally put forward suggestions concerning the appointment of key personnel within the bureaucracy, even when they have no formal involvement in the process.

○ *Legislation:* this provides Congress with the ability to intervene. Acts routinely contain instructions to administrators which can be amended to ensure that the views of Congress are carried out. Additionally, the exercise of discretion is governed by the 1946 Administrative Procedures Act and the 1990 Negotiated Rule Making Act.

○ *Annual renewal:* some agencies or programmes are subject to annual renewal which is dependent upon an assessment by Congress as to whether their aims are being accomplished.

○ *Oversight:* bodies such as the General Accounting Office and the Office of Technology Assessment help to procure information to aid this function. Control over funds is a key aspect of Congressional oversight which is asserted during the annual appropriations procedure. This may be supplemented by investigations into particular government activities. An example of this was the Congressional hearings into the operations of the Internal Revenue Service in 1997.

Congressional intervention may be prompted for two main reasons.

Efficiency and Effectiveness

Congressional intervention into the operations of the federal civil service may be prompted by a desire to ensure that it performs both effectively and efficiently. This concern was displayed by the requirement in 1978 that all major agencies should appoint inspector generals who were concerned with problems such as fraud and waste, and who were accountable to Congress. The 1993 Government Performance and Results Act compelled agencies to prepare (initially on a pilot basis) annual development plans with measurable objectives to enable performance to be monitored.

Political Considerations

The desire by Congress to exert control over the operations of the federal bureaucracy may, however, be politically motivated. It may seek to ensure that its policy goals are fulfilled by the federal bureaucracy. This is especially important in a situation of 'divided government' when Congress and the President may differ on the objectives which they wish the bureaucracy to achieve.

The Organisation of Government Departments in the UK

In the UK, prime ministers ultimately decide how the work of government will be allocated between government departments. This section seeks to differentiate between rational and political factors which govern decisions of this nature. There are three options available to the chief executive when organising the tasks of government:

○ the establishment of new departments

○ the abolition of existing departments

○ the reallocation of the tasks performed by an existing department to another department or departments.

Rational Factors

The expanded role of the State during the First World War prompted the Prime Minister, David Lloyd George, to appoint a Machinery of Government committee, headed by Lord Haldane, to consider the future organisation of government departments. This committee reported in 1919. Haldane considered two alternative methods of organising departments.

1 *Around a specific category of citizen:* this was termed the 'client principle'. The establishment of a department which catered for all the needs of children, for example, would have been compatible with this principle.

2 *According to a particular service delivered by a department:* this suggested that departments should be organised according to the specific nature of the work they performed. Utilising the example referred to above, the adoption of this principle would thus differentiate the numerous functions which children might need to receive (such as education, health care, welfare benefits) and place the responsibility for them in the hands of separate bodies.

Haldane's report recommended the latter method of organisation which became the dominant rational formula utilised by subsequent Prime Ministers to determine the organisation of government departments. It was not, however, the sole principle relied upon to determine how the work of government should be organised. (The Scottish Office (established in 1885) and the Welsh Office (set up in 1964) provided a geographic basis around which the work of government was organised.)

Problems With the Haldane Principle After 1945

The increase in state functions during and particularly after the Second World War (which is discussed in Chapter 19 of this work) resulted in the creation of a large number of separate government departments. This situation posed a number of political problems.

❍ *It devalued the role of the Cabinet:* in order to restrict the membership of the Cabinet to a size which was compatible with effective discussion, it became necessary for prime ministers to exclude ministers in charge of some departments. This ability of the Cabinet to coordinate the disparate tasks of government was adversely affected when it did not contain representatives from all key areas of government activity.

❍ *It weakened collective ministerial responsibility:* the expectation that all ministers should abide by a decision is more difficult to enforce when some are not involved in the decision-making.

❍ *It led to perceptions of neglect by government:* those concerned either as clients or as practitioners with the services provided by departments not within the Cabinet tended to conclude that the government had a low opinion of the importance of such areas of governmental activity.

❍ *It resulted in too narrow a range of policy options:* the existence of large numbers of government departments organised around a relatively narrow area of public policy could mean that insufficient options were available when considering how to spend taxpayers' money. The Concorde supersonic airliner project was initiated in the 1960s by the Ministry of Civil Aviation. It is debatable if a wider-ranging Transport Department would have begun this programme.

The Emergence of 'Giant' Departments

Various reforms were introduced to remedy the problems identified in the previous section in connection with the operation of the Haldane principle.

The 'Overlord' System

Prime Minister Winston Churchill introduced the Overlord System in 1951. It involved the appointment of three coordinating ministers (Lords Cherwell, Woolton and Leather) to represent at Cabinet level the interests of a number of departments which retained their independent status. In practice, however, it resulted in a blurred system of accountability in which it was difficult to determine whether responsibility for a particular decision should rest with the departmental minister or with the overlord. Thus this system was abandoned in 1953.

Merger of Departments

The 'overlord' system was followed in the 1960s by physically merging departments whose responsibilities were related. The term 'giant department' described these newly-created bodies. This term related both to the broad policy areas which were performed by such departments (in comparison to the responsibilities previously associated with Haldane's 'service provided' principle of organisation) and to the consequential large number of staff which they employed to administer them. The advantage possessed by giant departments was that they enabled a Prime Minister to ensure that all major areas of government activity were represented at Cabinet level. However, the scope and staffing arrangements of these departments later raised doubts as to whether effective managerial or political control could be exerted over them. Innovations seeking to respond to such problems, especially MINIS (Management Information for Ministers), are discussed in Chapter 12.

EXAMPLES OF GIANT DEPARTMENTS

The following giant departments were created before 1970 when a White Paper issued by the newly-elected Conservative government gave a rationale for this method of organisation.

◆ *1964:* the Ministry of Defence was established from the separate 'service' departments responsible for the army, navy and air force.

◆ *1966:* the Ministry of Technology was created by absorbing the Ministry of Aviation, much of the work performed by the Department of Economic Affairs, and some of the functions of the Board of Trade.

◆ *1968:* the Foreign and Commonwealth Office and the Department of Health and Social Security were formed.

The Functional Principle

In 1970, Prime Minister Ted Heath's newly-elected Conservative government produced a White Paper entitled *The Reorganisation of Central Government*. This proposed that the organisation of the machinery of government should be according to what was termed the 'functional principle'. This objective of this proposed reform was summarised by the assertion that 'organisation should be the servant of policy' and implied that the machinery of government should be structured according to specific objectives which ministers wished to achieve. Its main benefit was stated to be that the planning and implementation of a programme would be in one set of hands rather than being shared between a number of departments with the inevitable problems of coordination and communication. In practice, however, the White Paper did not initiate any major departure in the manner in which government departments were organised. The two new organisations which were established following its publication (the Department of the Environment and the Department of Trade and Industry) were essentially giant departments in the mould of those created during the 1960s. Other developments put forward in this White Paper (particularly 'hiving off') are discussed in Chapter 12.

Subsequently changes have been made to departmental organisation with the creation of new departments, the division or abolition of existing departments, and the reallocation of functions between them. But these alterations have not been based on any attempt to recast the structure of government according to any new rational principle or formula.

Political Factors

Although attempts to organise government departments according to a rational formula have been illustrated in the previous section, decisions relating to the establishment, abolition or merger of departments are not solely determined by such rational criteria. Political considerations may influence or provide the predominant explanation for decisions of this nature. These are discussed below.

Evidence of Governmental Action

A Prime Minister's desire to convey evidence of the government's intention to respond to a particular issue or problem may result in the creation of new departments. Thus following his victory at the 1964 General Election, Harold Wilson set up the Ministry of Technology (under the trade union leader, Frank Cousins) to prove to the public that his government was fully attuned to 'the white hot heat of the technological revolution'.

To Indicate a Change in the Direction of Policy

Departmental mergers are often influenced by the desire of a Prime Minister to indicate a change in the direction of government policy or to give added emphasis to the approach favoured by the government's political issues. For example, the desire to emphasise the association of education with vocational training (in line with the philosophy governing the 1991 White Paper, *Education and Training for the Twenty First Century*, and the subsequent development of the General National Vocational Qualification) was one reason why John Major abolished the Department of Employment in 1995 and reallocated its main functions between the re-named Department of Education and Employment and the Department of Trade and Industry. A similar attempt to convey to the public a change of emphasis in the direction of government policy underlaid the creation of the National Heritage Department in 1992.

Internal Political Pressures

The creation or merger of government departments may be fashioned by a Prime Minister's need to ensure that senior party colleagues are provided with administrative responsibilities appropriate to their status in the Party. This was one factor which influenced Harold Wilson to establish the Department of Economic Affairs in 1964, to ensure that George Brown (Labour's deputy leader) had a major area of governmental activity to superintend.

External Political Pressures

The creation, abolition or merger of departments may be forced upon a prime minister by public opinion. Public concern regarding outbreaks of salmonella poisoning led Margaret Thatcher to give serious consideration to establishing a separate Ministry for Consumer Protection which would be divorced from the Ministry of Agriculture, since there appeared to be a possible clash between the interests served by the existing department. However, while external political pressures may promote change, they may also serve to prevent them from occurring. The power of the National Farmers' Union, for example, is one reason why a Ministry of Agriculture, Fisheries and Food exists separately from the Department of Trade and Industry. Farmers feel they will get better treatment from a body whose focus is on their specific concerns.

The Role of Parliament in the Organisation of Government Departments

Unlike the role performed by the American Congress, Parliament plays a much reduced role in decisions related to the machinery of government. It is not involved in decisions related to the establishment, merger or abolition of departments which are exercised by the chief executive. Its role, therefore, is limited to scrutiny of the expenditure and working practices of these bodies. In addition to this scrutiny the Public Accounts Committee and the departmental select committees may conduct investigations into the performance of aspects of their work. One example of this was the hearings of the Home Affairs Select Committee into the work of the Lord Chancellor's Department in 1997.

Question

To provide a comparison with the material on American government presented above, select a British government department and make a brief assessment as to how this body is subject to political control. To do this, arrange your material under the following headings:

○ **Control by the Prime Minister and Cabinet**

○ **Control by Parliament.**

Give TWO examples which explain why there is such control and how it is exerted.

The Role of Quangos in the Machinery of Government

This discussion has primarily been concerned with the work performed by civil servants in government departments. However, bureaucrats working for national governments are employed in organisations other than central departments. In most countries a vast range of alternative mechanisms concerned with the formulation and implementation of public policy exist at both national and sub-national levels. In the UK, the staff employed in this 'alternative machinery' of government may be civil servants but often are not, as is described below.

Definitions

This section considers three similar types of organisation. These are all discussed below.

Quangos (quasi-autonomous non-governmental organisations)

These operate within the public sector and are partly funded by central government. They are, however, subject to little central or local government control and thus exercise considerable freedom in the conduct of their affairs. The National Rivers Authority is an example of a quango.

Qgas (quasi-governmental agencies)

These are typically bodies which operate at the level of national government and are concerned with one issue. They derive some finance from central government and unlike quangos are subject to mechanisms of Parliamentary accountability. The Arts Council is an example of a qga.

Quelgos (quasi-elected local government organisations)

These operate at local government level and usually perform a function across the boundaries of a number of local authorities. Their membership is composed (at least in part) of local people through a process of indirect election. The Police Authorities introduced following the passage of the 1994 Police and Magistrates' Courts Act are examples of quelgos. These consist of persons nominated by the Home Secretary, councillors drawn from the constituent district councils, and magistrates.

There is, however, a tendency (especially in newspapers and by politicians) to lump all of the above organisations under the one heading of 'quango'. The absence of a precise definition makes it impossible to provide a completely accurate estimate of the number of such bodies or their expenditure.

The Work of Quangos and Related Bodies

Although quangos, qgas and quelgos perform a wide range of functions, their work may broadly be grouped under one of three main headings.

1 Executive Bodies

The use of such bodies to implement public policy is justified by a belief that central departments or local authorities (which in the UK are the main alternative mechanisms to carry out public functions) are not appropriate to the task in hand. The construction of new towns following the Second World War was handed over to ad hoc bodies (termed New Town Corporations which were supervised by a Commission for the New Towns) since local government did not have the finances to carry the required redevelopment (especially house building).

EXAMPLES OF QUANGOS

The work of quangos and related bodies is varied. A newspaper report in the *Guardian* on 20 October 1997 listed a small number of them. These included:

◆ the Environment Agency

◆ the Commission for Racial Equality

◆ the Equal Opportunities Commission

◆ the Arts Council

◆ the Charity Commission

◆ the Millennium Commission

◆ the Legal Aid Board

◆ the Further and Higher Education Council

◆ the Funding Agency for Schools

◆ the Football Licensing Authority

◆ the Sports Councils

◆ the Gaming Board

◆ the Expert Advisory Group on AIDS

◆ the Law Commission

◆ the Particle, Physics and Astronomy Research Council

◆ the Welsh Development Agency

◆ the Scottish Enterprise Board

◆ the Meat and Livestock Commission.

In the 1980s, the task of urban regeneration in Merseyside and London Docklands was handed over to two Urban Development Corporations. These were able to focus on a problem which traversed existing local authority boundaries and they were also deemed more likely than local government to enter into partnership with the private sector.

2 Advisory Bodies

The main advantage of advisory bodies is that they provide expert advice to ministers at relatively low cost. Such expertise may not be available within the formal civil service machinery, although there have been occasions when ministers have established advisory machinery to give them advice to rival or challenge that provided from within Whitehall. One example of this was the Centre for Environmental Studies which was established by Richard Crossman when he was Minister for Housing in the Labour government elected in 1964.

3 Regulatory Bodies

The main regulatory bodies are the tribunal systems. These adjudicate in disputes between individuals to avoid their having to be referred to the courts whose procedures and costs may not be appropriate to the matter in hand. Examples include industrial tribunals which play a major role in determining issues of gender and racial discrimination in employment.

Advantages and Disadvantages of Quangos and Related Bodies

Incoming governments often scrutinise the actions of quangos very closely. Critical comments from influential Parliamentarians such as Philip Holland prompted the Thatcher government to task an official enquiry to examine these bodies. This was chaired by Leo Pliatzsky, and it reported in 1980. Similarly, in 1997 the newly-elected Labour administration considered plans to abolish or merge numerous quangos as part of its spending review.

Advantages

The main advantage arising from the use of such machinery is that policy can be implemented by organisations which are purpose-built to perform a specific function. It does not have to accord to the organisation and structure utilised by the civil service. Thus people can be recruited with expertise which would not normally be possessed by civil servants (for example experience in conducting a large-scale business enterprise) and rewarded by a salary which does not have to conform to civil service pay scales. In both the UK and Ireland such bodies have been used to link the public and private sectors.

Disadvantages

There are three major problems affecting quangos and similar bodies.

○ accountability

○ patronage

○ impact on the scope of state activity.

Accountability

Accountability may be secured in two ways:

1 *To the executive branch of government:* this may involve the chairperson (a political appointee) reporting to the minister or may entail the chief executive (a paid official) reporting to the department which is associated with the body (perhaps in the form of an annual report or a corporate plan indicating targets and performance).

2 *To the legislature:* the legislature may scrutinise the operations which such bodies perform. The consideration of annual reports might aid legislative scrutiny of such bodies but select committees (such as the Irish Joint Committee on State Sponsored Bodies, established in 1976, or the UK's system of departmental select committees) possibly possess greater potential for enabling legislatures to effectively examine the activities of these bodies.

The extent to which the above mechanisms ensure that these bodies are adequately accountable for their actions has been questioned. There may be a conscious attempt to avoid detailed accountability equated with the constant 'interference' of politicians. Organisations which pursue commercial or quasi-commercial activities require a certain amount of freedom so that enterprise can flourish. Others which pursue non-economic tasks may also justify a relative degree of insulation from political control on the grounds that the task with which they are concerned should not be subject to the constant to and fro of political debate: thus bodies such as quangos effectively depoliticise the function with which they are concerned. This advantage might apply, for example, to the Commission for Racial Equality which is allowed to proceed with its role of eliminating racial discrimination without being subject to constant political battles. Such problems would be more likely to occur were the work performed by a government department such as the Home Office.

However, accountability remains an important issue as such bodies are concerned with the administration of public policy. Additionally some rely on state funding to finance all or some of their activities. In his publication *Quango, Quango, Quango* (1980), Philip Holland identified in excess of 3,000 quangos whose combined expenditure of £8 billion was then approximately the size of the defence budget. In his first speech in the House of Commons after winning the 1997 General Election, the Prime Minister, Tony Blair, argued that it was necessary to change a situation in which unelected quangos spent more money than elected local government.

THE 1997 LABOUR GOVERNMENT AND QUANGOS

In 1997, David Clark, Chancellor of the Duchy of Lancaster, published a consultation paper, *Opening Up Quangos*, which proposed to enhance the accountability of around 1,000 of such bodies responsible for spending in excess of £18 billion of taxpayers' money. The principle of open government would be extended to their operations thereby ending what the minister described as the 'unaccountable, secret and unresponsive world of the quango state'. This involved the disclosure of information to the public such as policy documents and the minutes of their meetings, and many would be required to hold their meetings in public.

Patronage

In 1978 Philip Holland and Michael Fallon estimated in their study, *The Quango Explosion*, that 17 ministers were then responsible for filling 8,411 paid appointments and 25,000 unpaid ones. There was concern that paid appointments to such bodies offered opportunities for 'jobs for the boys'. The accusation of 'snouts in the gravy train' became a particular source of political debate in the UK during the 1990s when it was alleged that the main criterion for the appointment of managers of such organisations had been their political sympathy to the government which appoints them rather than their ability to perform the job. This led the Nolan Committee to recommend that appointments to quangos should be scrutinised by an independent commissioner for public appointments. The role of this office (whose first holder was Sir Len Peach) was extended by Tony Blair's Labour government to ensure that future appointments were non-partisan and that a much wider number of people (including more women and members of ethnic minorities) were encouraged to apply for such jobs. The reforms which were introduced to achieve this objective included a requirement that every quango should open up an Internet site. This would disclose top appointments, salaries and contact numbers.

Nonetheless, accusations of political bias in appointments to such bodies continued to be made. In December 1997, the Conservative Party spokesman on health, John Maples, called for an inquiry by Sir Len Peach into the 'politicisation' of health service boards which ran NHS Hospital Trusts arising from the removal of nominees appointed by the previous Conservative government and their replacement by Labour councillors. It was alleged that this broke the Nolan Code of Practice on openness and transparency. The validity of such accusations was, however, denied by the Secretary of State for Health, Frank Dobson, who claimed the removal and appointment process was being used to increase the number of women and local representatives on such boards.

Impact on the Scope of State Activity

A particular objection which was directed at quangos and related bodies by the incoming Conservative government in 1979 was the manner in which they served to extend the role of the State in 'back-door fashion'. This in itself was a serious objection to a government which sought to 'roll back the frontiers of the state' but it additionally posed administrative difficulties. The proliferation of bodies such as quangos made it virtually impossible to keep a proper check on their operations, which posed the danger of administrative inefficiencies arising from factors such as duplication of work or the overlapping of functions.

Question

Using books, journals or newspaper articles, carry out your own independent study of a quango/qga/quelgo currently operating in British government.

In conducting this exercise you should seek to ascertain when and why the body was established, the nature of the work it performs and what advantages this body possesses over alternative means of carrying this work out (such as a government department, local authority or the courts).

The Coordination of the Work of Government

A key issue which arises from the work of government being performed by a wide variety of agencies and departments is the manner in which public policy is coordinated. A particular concern is to ensure that a government's political priorities are enforced throughout the machinery of government, and to guard against the possibility of departments' pursuing their own objectives without considering how their activities relate to other aspects of the government's work. This section considers the main initiatives introduced into the centre of British government to secure the coordination of political affairs.

The Coordination of British Government

The coordination of the work of government has traditionally been carried out by two bodies: the Cabinet and the Treasury.

The Cabinet

The role of the Cabinet is discussed in Chapter 11. Its ability to effectively coordinate the affairs of government is handicapped by a number of factors. These include the following.

❍ *Size:* Tony Blair's first Cabinet in 1997 contained 22 members, which was too large for meaningful discussion of all aspects of the work of government.

❍ *Inability to undertake long-term strategic planning:* the Cabinet lacks the capacity to undertake long-term strategic thinking. The Central Policy Review staff sought to remedy this problem in the 1970s, but its influence waned by the end of that decade. Normally, therefore, initiatives concerned with policy were promoted by individual government departments.

❍ *The relative autonomy of government departments:* even if the Cabinet were able to determine priorities, it could do little to enforce them throughout the machinery of government, since individual departments possess a considerable degree of independence of action.

The Treasury

The Treasury is a key government department. Its political head is the Chancellor of the Exchequer, and in 1998 its staff totalled 895 civil servants. It exercised a key strategic function of setting levels of public expenditure and taxation through the budget and spending reviews, and was responsible for a wide range of activities which required it to involve itself in the affairs of other government agencies. These included ensuring that public services were cost effective by restricting their budgets. There were, however, problems with coordination being driven by the Treasury, a major one being that this might enhance the power of the Chancellor of the Exchequer above that of the Prime Minister.

The problems posed by these traditional methods of coordinating public policy resulted in a number of new initiatives by the Labour government elected in 1997.

The Early Reforms of the Blair Government

After 1997, a number of developments took place to enhance the coordination of government policy from the centre.

The Social Exclusion Unit

As the functions of government became broader and more complex, coordination could be achieved by the establishment of a high-level task force at the centre of government to focus on the attainment of a specific objective or set of goals across the boundaries of a number of separate departments. One example of this was the Social Exclusion Unit. This was established in 1997 and staffed by 12 civil servants and outsiders. Its role was to aid the victims of the 'vicious cycle' of linked problems which included unemployment, poor housing and high crime by ensuring that all relevant departments pursued policies designed to improve the social position of the poor and bring them back into mainstream society. The term applied to this form of coordination was 'horizonality'. The Social Exclusion Unit had no budget of its own and was designed to conduct research into the solutions to social exclusion and make recommendations on policy designed to ensure that central and local government and other agencies spent money on these groups more effectively.

The role of a similar body, the Women's Unit, is discussed in Chapter 22.

The Cabinet Office

This is a large organisation at the heart of central government. In 1998, it was composed of 1,875 civil servants, headed by the Cabinet Secretary, Sir Richard Wilson. Its work included acting as the administrative arm of the Cabinet and Cabinet Committees, providing support to the Prime Minister's Office, and coordinating policy across government departments. It also housed the Office of Public Service, which was responsible for all aspects of civil service personnel policy.

The need for a strong central structure to ensure that government policy and its presentation were coherent and coordinated resulted in a number of changes within the centre of government. In early 1998 a Strategic Communications Unit was established to harmonise the presentation of policy across all government departments. The key reform, however, concerned the operations of the Cabinet Office, whose role was examined in a report prepared by Sir Richard Wilson in 1998.

The Wilson report proposed to develop the role of the Cabinet Office in order to secure enhanced strategic direction to the entire work of government. This reform was approved by the Prime Minister, who gave it sanction by promoting Jack Cunningham to head the revamped Cabinet Office in his July 1998 government reshuffle. The role of the Cabinet Office became that of monitoring, advising on and enforcing the delivery of services across the machinery of government. Cunningham was dubbed the 'enforcer'. His role was to oversee the implementation of strategic policy objectives and cross-departmental cohesion.

The centre of British government had traditionally been fragmented, with both the Cabinet Office and the Prime Minister's Office exercising key responsibilities of this nature. These reforms sought to end this division by effectively transforming the Cabinet Office into the Prime Minister's department in all but name and making it responsible, under Cunningham, for driving Tony Blair's agenda in Whitehall.

Technology

The ability of the centre of British government to control the activities of individual departments will be enhanced by technology. By the beginning of the twenty-first century all government departments and agencies would be connected to the 'intranet'. This project was the responsibility of the Cabinet Office, enabling the Prime Minister to communicate throughout the machinery of government. The 'top down' approach which underlay this development will enhance the power of the centre of British government at the expense of departmental autonomy.

Further Reading

Anthony Barker (editor), *Quangos in Britain* (London: Macmillan, 1982). This provides a detailed examination of the characteristics and roles of quangos, and assesses their strengths and weaknesses.

Useful literature on the machinery of government is found in a number of books concerned with public administration. Such includes **John Greenwood** and **David Wilson**, *Public Administration in Britain* (London: Unwin Hyman, 1989).

Also the chapter by **Clive Gray** in **Robert Pyper** and **Lynton Robins** (editors), *Governing the UK in the 1990s* (Basingstoke: Macmillan, 1995).

The coordination of policy is discussed in the context of the 'core executive' in **R. Rhodes** and **Patrick Dunleavy**, *Prime Minister, Cabinet and Core Executive* (Basingstoke: Macmillan, 1995).

Chapter Fourteen | The Legislative Branch of Government

The aims of this chapter are:

> 1 To describe and discuss the functions performed by legislative bodies.
>
> 2 To analyse the manner through which legislative bodies perform their functions.
>
> 3 To assess the advantages and disadvantages of bicameral legislatures.
>
> 4 To analyse developments affecting the power and authority of contemporary legislatures and to evaluate (in conjunction with studying reforms to the operations and working practices of such bodies) whether there has been a decline of legislatures.
>
> 5 To examine specific contemporary issues related to the operations of the British House of Commons and the reform of the House of Lords.

The Function of Legislatures

The legislative (or law-making) functions of government are performed by legislatures. Elected legislatures are usually viewed as the symbol of representative government: as it is not possible for all citizens to directly share in policy-making, they elect persons who perform these duties on their behalf. These representatives meet in the country's legislature. This is thus the institution which links the government and the governed. Each liberal democracy has its own term for the body which performs the legislative function. In the United Kingdom the legislature is referred to as *Parliament*, in the United States of America as *Congress* and in the Irish republic as the *Oireachtas*.

Additionally, legislatures undertake a number of specific tasks which are considered below.

Initiating Constitutional Change

Legislatures play a key role in the process of changing a country's constitution. In countries with a flexible constitution (that is, one which can be altered by the normal law-making process) the legislature is solely responsible for initiating and determining constitutional change. This is the situation in the UK. In countries with rigid constitutions (where amendment involves a separate process from the normal law-making procedure), the role of the legislature in providing for change is reduced, although important as the following examples show.

The USA

Two-thirds of both Houses of Congress (the House of Representatives and the Senate) must separately agree to call a Constitutional Convention to determine change when asked to do so by two-thirds of the States (which last occurred in 1787) or themselves propose a specific amendment to the Constitution which three-quarters of the States (which number 50 plus the District of Columbia) must then approve. A recent example of this process was the Equal Rights Amendment proposed by Congress in 1972, which sought to eliminate discrimination on the basis of sex. This failed to secure the required level of support from State legislatures since only 35 approved it, three short of the number required to meet the ratification deadline.

Ireland

Proposed changes to the constitution are initially put before the Oireachtas (Irish Parliament) and, if approved, are then placed before the country's citizens in a referendum. The number of amendments has been small. In 1972, the third amendment allowed Ireland to join the EEC and the tenth amendment authorised the State to ratify the 1987 Single European Act. In 1995, a proposal to legalise divorce was narrowly approved in a referendum.

Law-making

Legislatures constitute the law-making body within a country's system of government. Thus making the law (or amending or repealing it) is a key function which they perform. A specific, although important, aspect of this role is approving the budget and granting authority for the collection of taxes. A key issue concerns the extent to which legislatures themselves initiate law or respond to proposals put forward by the executive branch of government.

Although there is a tendency for legislatures to respond to the initiatives of the executive branch in both presidential and parliamentary systems of government (thus transforming the legislature into a body which legitimises decisions rather than one which initiates them), this is not invariably the case. The committee system of the German Parliament is particularly influential in securing a policy-making role for this body. Much of the work of the Bundestag is carried out through specialised committees whose areas of activity correspond to the federal ministries. These committees provide a forum in which ministers, civil servants and members of parliament (including those of the opposition parties) jointly engage in the process of policy-making.

Scrutiny of the Executive

Legislatures examine the actions undertaken by the executive branch of government. The term 'executive branch' is discussed more fully in Chapter 11, but for convenience may be referred to here as 'government', which in the UK is composed of the Prime Minister and Cabinet and in the USA the President and the administration which he heads.

Governments are required to justify their actions to the legislature which may thus exert influence over its conduct. This scrutiny may be retrospective (that is, it occurs after an action has taken place and seeks to examine the actions of those responsible for it). In some cases, however, the legislature may be required to give its consent in advance to an operation which the executive branch wishes to undertake. In the USA, for example, Congress has to approve an official declaration of war.

In countries with parliamentary forms of government, such scrutiny is linked to the concept of *ministerial responsibility*. Governments are collectively responsible to the legislature. Perceived deficiencies in the activities undertaken by the government may result in its dismissal by the legislature (usually through the mechanism of a vote of 'no confidence'). Individual ministers may also be individually responsible to this body for the performance of specific aspects of the work of the executive branch. The ability of legislatures to force individual ministers to resign varies. In Germany, for example, the Bundestag formally lacks such a sanction although criticism by the legislature may result in a minister's resignation. In the UK, individual ministerial responsibility is effected by the ancient sanction of debating the reduction of the salary of a minister whose actions are disapproved of, thereby forcing the minister to defend his or her actions. This rarely succeeds, one example being the unsuccessful attempt to censure Douglas Hogg (then Minister of Agriculture in the Conservative government) in 1997 for his handling of the BSE crisis. If such a vote was passed, the Minister would either resign or the opposition would table a 'no confidence' motion in the government as a whole.

Confirmation of Governmental Appointments

Scrutiny may also extend to approving the nomination of individual members of the government put forward by the chief executive. This form of legislative scrutiny operates in some countries with parliamentary forms of government such as Ireland but not in the UK. The scrutiny of nominations for public office by the legislature also is a feature of some presidential systems of government, as is discussed below.

THE AMERICAN SENATE AND POWERS OF CONFIRMATION

The Senate is required to confirm a wide range of presidential appointments. The rationale for this process is to ensure that those nominated for high government office have the relevant credentials. In practice, however, this form of scrutiny might involve delving into a person's private life (to demonstrate personal failings which are allegedly incompatible with office holding) or might be determined on political grounds. In 1997, for example, William Weld abandoned his attempt to get the Senate's Foreign Relations Committee to endorse his nomination as American ambassador to Mexico. This situation arose because the chairman of that committee, Senator Jesse Helms, was a conservative who objected to Weld's liberal views on a wide range of social issues. Although both Helms and Weld were Republicans, their differences made the successful outcome of such hearings unlikely.

Judicial Functions

Legislatures may also perform judicial functions whereby members of all three branches of government may be tried and sentenced for offences connected with the performance of their official duties.

In the USA, for example, Congress has a judicial power, that of *impeachment*. This is a formal charge that a member of the executive or judicial branch of government has committed an offence whilst in office. The accusation of inappropriate conduct is laid before the House of Representatives and if they believe that there is a case to answer, a trial takes place in the Senate. If guilt is determined by this body the official would effectively be dismissed from public office. The fear that this process would be successful was sufficient to persuade President Nixon to resign from office in 1974 over the Watergate revelations. These concerned the break-in at the Democratic Party's National Committee headquarters in 1972 and the subsequent attempts to cover up White House involvement in this event.

The Conduct of Legislators

Legislatures may exercise judicial-type functions in relation to the conduct of their members. The processes used vary. In the USA, for example, each House of Congress has an Ethics Committee to which accusations of wrongdoing are referred. Accusations of sexual harassment, soliciting job offers for his wife, misusing campaign funds, and obstructing a congressional investigation by failing to hand over his diaries to the Ethics Committee resulted in Senator Bob Packwood of Oregon resigning his seat in 1995. Members of the legislative branch of government cannot be impeached, but wrongdoings by legislators may be punished by an alternative process of *censureship*. This rarely involves removal from office but embraces alternative sanctions which adversely affect the status of the condemned legislator.

The actions undertaken in the 1990s to combat 'sleaze' in Britain are discussed in Chapter 2.

Investigatory Functions

Legislative bodies may also perform the function of investigating issues of public importance, in addition to the task of scrutinising the actions of the executive. In the USA, Congress has the right to *subpoena* (that is, to force persons to appear and answer questions on the topic which is subject to investigation).

Supervisory Functions

Legislatures may concern themselves with the manner in which an institution of government or an activity which is reliant on public funds is being run. This function (which in the USA is termed *oversight*) is concerned with monitoring the bureaucracy and its administration of policy. This entails ensuring that an agency is meeting the goals specified for it, that public money is being spent for the purposes for which it was intended, or that an operation is conducted in accordance with any restrictions which were initially placed upon it by the legislature. The American Congress actively performs supervisory functions through committee hearings and the review of agency budgets but these procedures are less prominent in other legislatures such as the UK. An example of this were the hearings held by the Senate Finance Committee in 1997 into the operations of the Internal Revenue Service.

Raising Issues of Local and National Importance

Legislatures debate policy and other issues of public importance. Such debates are published in official journals and are publicised

CONGRESSIONAL INVESTIGATIONS

Prominent examples of Congressional investigations have included the following:

◆ The investigations mounted by the Senate Internal Security Committee into alleged communist infiltration of the American government in the 1950s (in which Senator Joseph McCarthy played an influential role).

◆ The Senate Select Committee on Campaign Practices (which was established in 1973 to investigate the Watergate break-in and which is referred to above).

◆ The Iran–Contra investigations which were conducted by a special 26-member investigating committee which included members of both Houses of Congress in 1987.

◆ The Congressional enquiry in 1995 into the Waco tragedy in which the FBI launched an attack on the Branch Dividian sect in their compound in Waco, Texas in 1993. Seventy-six men, women and children were either shot, gassed, burned alive or crushed by tanks.

◆ Investigations into campaign funding practices conducted by the Senate Governmental Affairs Committee in 1997.

by the media, thus providing a source of information for the general public. This enables the electorate to be politically informed and educated.

These bodies further provide a forum in which representatives can advance the interests of their constituencies and intercede on behalf of any of their constituents, especially those who have encountered problems in their dealings with the executive branch of government. Much work of this nature takes place in private, but it is usually possible to raise such issues publicly, within the legislative chamber. In the UK, times are set aside for MPs to put questions to ministers (either in a face-to-face confrontation which takes place in the chamber of the House of Commons, or in writing). Additionally, the adjournment debate (which takes place at the end of a Parliamentary day and lasts for 30 minutes) is a further mechanism which can be used by an MP to air problems of a local nature.

The Operation of Legislatures

Legislatures conduct their affairs through a number of mechanisms. These are considered below.

Question

Conduct your own analysis of the key functions performed by the House of Commons.

Take a good newspaper which has space devoted to Parliamentary proceedings. Provide examples of the activities which are performed over a period of one week by placing them under the following headings:

○ **Law-making**

○ **Scrutiny of the executive**

○ **Raising issues of national importance**

○ **Raising issues of local importance.**

You may get a more detailed and accurate examination (involving a group of people) of the work of Parliament by analysing its journal, *Hansard*, over a similar period of time or by monitoring Radio 4's *Today in Parliament* programme or cable television's *Parliamentary Channel*.

Debate

Legislatures are first and foremost debating institutions. This means that functions including the consideration of legislation, the articulation of constituency issues or the discussion of matters of national importance are performed orally. Members of the legislature deliver speeches in which they put forward their views and listen to the judgements of their fellow legislators on the same issue. The issue may then be resolved by voting. To facilitate debate, members of legislative bodies may enjoy certain immunities which ordinary members of the general public do not possess. In the UK, for example, Members of the House of Commons enjoy freedom of speech. This is one of a number of *Parliamentary privileges*. This means that in Parliament Members may effectively say what they want (subject to the Speaker's rulings) to facilitate the maximum degree of openness in debate. Speeches made by a Member of Parliament, no matter how defamatory, cannot be subject to an action for slander.

Committees

Much of the work performed by contemporary legislative bodies is delegated to committees. In turn, these bodies may devolve responsibilities to sub-committees. These are useful devices as they enable a legislature to consider a number of matters at the same time and thus cope with the increased volumes of work associated with developments such as the expanded role of the State following the Second World War, or membership of supra-national bodies such as the European Union. They further enable small groups of legislators to investigate the affairs of government in considerable detail and through their reports the entire assembly becomes more knowledgeable of these matters and thus less dependent on the government for information.

There are various types of committees existing in modern legislatures. In the British House of Commons a key division is between *standing committees* (which are used to consider legislation) and *select committees* (which are used for various purposes, including examination of the work performed by key government departments). A similar division exists in the American Congress. In countries whose legislatures consist of more than one chamber, joint committees may be established to enable the two chambers to cooperate for specific purposes. In the UK, for example, the Intelligence and Security Committee (which was established by the 1996 Intelligence Services Act to monitor the work of the Security Services) is composed of members drawn from both Houses of Parliament.

Committees are an especially useful means for considering legislation. In the USA, the examination of legislative proposals is aided by the system of hearings in which the committee or sub-committee considering the proposal invites interested parties to give evidence to ensure that their decisions are based on a diverse range of informed opinion. The committee's decision whether to endorse a measure with a favourable recommendation or to 'kill' it is influenced by this procedure.

The Party System and Committee Membership

The party system may have an important bearing on the effectiveness with which committees operate in modern legislatures. The appointment of members to committees usually involves the party leadership and the fact that committee members are affiliated to a political party may influence the manner in which issues before a committee are viewed by its members. In countries with parliamentary forms of government, such as the UK, the party system may help the executive branch dominate the legislature, since the governing party usually possesses a majority on Parliamentary committees.

In countries with presidential forms of government, such as the USA, committees may exercise a far greater degree of autonomy since the executive branch is not directly involved in appointments. Appointments are allocated by the party apparatus which exists in both Houses, although a member's desire to serve on a particular committee may be taken into account. Membership is not confined to a particular session of Congress: once appointed to a committee a member will usually remain on it for the remainder of his or her career. The chairmanship of such bodies is largely – although now not exclusively – determined by *seniority*. This was a procedure whereby the longest-serving committee member whose party controlled Congress automatically headed the committee.

Questions in Parliament

Questions constitute a further method of transacting business in countries with parliamentary forms of government. These may be oral or written and are addressed to members of the executive branch of government. These can be of use in eliciting information, clarifying an issue, or seeking to secure action by the government. They provide a means whereby the civil service (who prepare the answers to such questions) respond to an agenda set by legislators, as opposed to members of the executive branch. In the German Bundestag questions aid the process of ministerial accountability. The oral questioning of a minister may be followed by a vote which enables members of the legislature to express whether they are satisfied with the answers with which they have been provided.

In the UK questions are rarely of importance to the process of policy-making and may merely serve as a device to embarrass the government and reduce its self-confidence or public standing. Here the *supplementary question* is used as a device to catch members of the executive offguard. A traditional way to do this is to ask a generalised question and to follow this up with a very specific one in the hope that the minister will not have been briefed by the civil service and will thus look foolish. The belief that no major function of government was served by exchanges which took place at Question Time led Prime Minister Tony Blair in 1997 to restrict the period available for questions to the Prime Minister from two sessions a week to one.

Bicameral and Unicameral Legislatures

In most liberal-democratic political systems the legislature is divided into two separate bodies which form separate debating chambers. For example, in the UK, Parliament consists of the House of Commons and the House of Lords. In the USA the legislative branch is divided into the House of Representatives and the Senate. The Irish Parliament consists of the Dail Eireann and the Seanad Eireann. In France, the legislative function of government is shared between the National Assembly and the Senate. In the new Republic of South Africa, the legislature is divided into a 400-member National Assembly and a 90-member Senate. These countries have what is termed a *bicameral legislature*.

The opposite of this is a *unicameral* system in which the legislature consists of only one body. Examples of this are found in New Zealand, Finland and Denmark. In 1970, Sweden also abandoned its bicameral system and replaced it with a unicameral one.

Bicameral legislatures possess a number of advantages which are discussed below.

A Revising Chamber

One main benefit of a bicameral legislature is that one chamber can give the other an opportunity to think again and thus reconsider its position. On occasions when the content of legislation is contentious and the period surrounding its passage through the first of the legislative bodies is charged with emotion for and against the measure, it is useful that a second chamber can coolly and calmly reevaluate what has been done and if necessary invite the first chamber to reassess the situation. The second chamber either rejects the measure or proposes amendments to it. In this case the second chamber performs the function of a *revising chamber*.

Differences in Composition

In bicameral systems, the two chambers of the legislature are often composed differently. This may be an advantage in that it enables issues to be examined from different perspectives. Thus in the UK, the House of Commons is elected by popular vote, whereas the House of Lords consists of persons who are members by birth (hereditary peers), nomination (life peers) or by virtue of holding high office in the Church of England (the lords spiritual) or the judiciary (the law lords).

In many countries with bicameral legislatures, one chamber represents popular opinion as expressed in elections, while the other seeks to ensure the representation of specific interests which are usually either territorial or functional. This situation is illustrated in the following examples.

COMPOSITION OF THE BRITISH HOUSE OF LORDS

The House of Lords descended from the Witengemot, a body summoned by English Kings before the Norman Conquest (of 1066). King William I (1066–87) transformed it into an Assembly of barons from which it has subsequently developed.

In 1992 there were:

777   hereditary peers
382   life peers
 24   bishops
  2   archbishops
 20   law lords

Figures taken from Andrew Adonis, *Parliament Today* (Manchester: Manchester University Press, 1993, 2nd edition).

Territorial Representation

In some countries one chamber of the legislature is concerned with territorial representation – advancing the more localised views of the areas, states or regions into which the country is divided. These are various examples of this.

America

A conflict of interest between the sparsely populated States and those in which large numbers of people resided became apparent while the constitution was being drafted. Thus a compromise position (which was termed the 'Connecticut Compromise') was adopted. This resulted in representation in one chamber being based on population, which would give the populous States a greater voice (the House of Representatives). However each State, regardless of size, was given equal representation in the second chamber (the Senate).

Germany

The Bundestag consists of representatives elected by the voters whereas the Bundesrat provides a forum at national level in which the views of the states (or Länder) can be put forward. Each state sends delegations to this latter body. They are mandated to act in accordance with the instructions given to them by their State government. Each state is allotted three votes in the Bundesrat, with extra votes being given to the more populated ones.

France

The second chamber, the Senate, possesses a strong base in the localities. Its members are elected for a term of nine years by an electoral college which is composed of deputies of the National Assembly and local politicians drawn from the Departments and City Councils. Local influences are further reflected in the National Assembly, many of whose members are local politicians, serving as mayors or regional councillors.

Australia

The Australian Parliament consists of two chambers, the House of Representatives and the Senate. The latter's role is to represent the States and Territories. Each of the six States elect 12 Senators, and the Australian Capital Territory and the Northern Territory each elect two.

South Africa

A key role of the South African Senate is to exercise responsibility for regional affairs. To facilitate this, each provincial legislature, regardless of size, elects ten Senators to this body.

Functional Representation

Second chambers may also put forward concerns other than territorial ones. They may represent the interests of specific groups within a country. This is referred to as *functional representation*. The Irish Seanad is theoretically constituted in part on this basis. Members of this body are not directly elected but are supposed to reflect vocational interests. The majority of its members are thus chosen from lists of candidates representing key vocational groups in Irish society (education and culture, agriculture, industry and commerce, labour and public administration and social services). An electoral college composed of members of local authorities and Parliament then selects 49 Senators from these lists, and the Prime Minister (Taoiseach) appoints a further eleven members. In reality, however, party affiliation is the key for election to this body.

The Problems Posed by Bicameral Legislatures

Resolution of Disagreements in Bicameral Legislature

Bicameral legislatures possess inherent problems which need to be resolved. It is conceivable that disputes between the two bodies will sometimes arise. These situations are usually catered for in a country's constitution or by the adoption of political practices which seek to avoid a situation in which one chamber effectively vetoes the work of the other.

Germany

The Bundesrat is not technically an upper house, but a body to represent the States (Länder). Accordingly, all legislation affecting State responsibilities must be approved by this body. It may additionally suggest amendments to other items of Bundestag legislation, referring disputes to a conciliation committee composed of members of both houses.

Ireland

The resolution of disagreement is catered for by the constitution. This established the Seanad as inferior to the Dail in terms of the functions which it performs. The latter body nominates the Taoiseach and approves the government. The government is responsible only to the Dail and most legislation is introduced into this house. The Seanad's subsidiary role thus minimises its ability to disrupt the process of government.

France

The French constitution provides for the pre-eminence of the National Assembly over the Senate. Only the former body can dismiss a government and it also possesses the ultimate ability to determine legislation, through its ability to override a veto by the Senate by what is termed a 'definitive vote'. However, in the event of disagreements between the two chambers, an attempt will usually be made to seek a compromise. The Senate does, however, possess important powers (including the need to consent to changes in the constitution) and has on occasions asserted itself, especially during periods of socialist government when this Party controlled the National Assembly. This situation is referred to as 'conflictual bicameralism'.

The UK

The two chambers are not coequal in power. The 1911 and 1949 Parliament Acts provided for the dominance of the House of Commons over the House of Lords, which now possesses only a temporary veto over some aspects of the decisions of the House of Commons.

The USA

Both branches of the legislature are equal in status. The institution of direct election for senators in 1913 resulted in both Houses of Congress being popularly elected. Disagreements between the two chambers on legislation are resolved through the mechanism of a *Conference Committee*. If a Bill is passed in different versions by the two Houses, a committee composed of members of each House is appointed to resolve the differences and draw up a single Bill. This is then returned to each House for a vote. Should either house reject this bill, it is returned to the Conference Committee for further deliberation. It is not necessary to resort to this mechanism frequently, but when it is used it may provide a forum in which 'trade offs' between the House of Representatives and the Senate are made.

Lack of Time

One difficulty which may affect the operations of a bicameral legislature is the time available for a second chamber to adequately examine legislation sent to it by the first. A solution to this is the process of 'pre-study' which has been utilised by the Canadian Senate on occasions since 1945. This is a process by which the subject matter of a bill under consideration in the House of Commons can be considered by a Senate committee at the same time. The report of this committee's deliberations is made available to the House of Commons, which may consider the Senate's reactions and if necessary introduce amendments before transmitting the bill for the formal consideration of this body. This process enables the Senate to examine legislation placed before them relatively quickly but also ensures that they are able to make a valid contribution to the law-making process.

Question

Study the proceedings of both Houses of Parliament (for example by using a good daily newspaper which reports Parliamentary proceedings or by examining the official report of Parliament, *Hansard*). Assess whether the work performed by the House of Lords is a valuable aspect of British parliamentary politics.

This analysis will enable you to judge whether the advantages of bicameral legislatures as outlined above are met in practice in the British system of parliamentary government.

The Power of Legislatures

The power possessed by legislatures varies from one country to another and is affected by constitutional or procedural rules. In the UK, for example, scrutiny is aided by the opposition parties being granted a number of occasions during each Parliamentary session when they may initiate debates. This enables them to probe the actions of the executive. These are termed *Supply Days* and since 1985 have comprised 20 days of Parliamentary time. But such facilities do not exist universally in legislatures with a parliamentary forms of government. This section seeks to assess a number of contemporary political developments on the power and authority of legislative bodies.

Development of Traditional Functions

Developments have occurred in a number of countries which have had an adverse effect on the ability of legislatures to perform their traditional functions. Several factors which have affected their role include the following.

○ *Membership of supranational bodies:* this has implications for both the law-making and scrutinising role performed by national legislatures. In the UK, for example, membership of the European Union has resulted in the loss of some of Parliament's traditional legislative functions. It has also added to the volume of governmental activity which this body is expected to monitor.

This issue is discussed more fully in Chapter 18.

○ *Developments affecting 'direct democracy':* the use which many liberal democracies now make of referendums has eroded the law-making role performed by legislatures, particularly when they are bound to legislate in accordance with the wishes expressed by the public. This issue is discussed in more detail in Chapter 2.

○ *The role of the media:* the ability of the legislature to scrutinise the actions of the executive, to air grievances or to educate the public concerning political affairs is often effectively conducted by the media. Investigative journalism, in particular, may secure the accomplishment of these roles. This issue is explored more fully in Chapter 9.

○ *Bypassing the legislature:* the ability of legislatures to scrutinise the actions of the executive is handicapped when political leaders bypass such assemblies. In July 1998, for example, the British Prime Minister, Tony Blair, chose to deliver his 'end of term' report in the garden of Number 10 Downing Street to a quiescent audience of ministers and civil servants, rather than in the House of Commons where he could be questioned by opposition MPs.

All of the above factors have had an adverse effect on the ability of legislatures to perform their traditional functions.

Additionally, the power of such bodies has been affected by the ability in many countries of the executive branch of government to dominate the work of legislatures. The reasons for this are varied and are discussed below.

Domination by the Executive

A major explanation which is offered for changes in the power of legislatures is the tendency for such bodies to be dominated by the executive branch of government. In many countries, the initiation of policy and the control over finance has passed to the executive branch. In the UK, for example, the bulk of public legislation is initiated by the government, which thus sets the Parliamentary agenda. Parliament may subsequently be able to influence the detailed content of such legislation but is not the driving force behind it. Additionally, governments may be able to utilise procedural devices to expedite the progress of their legislation. In the UK, one such device is the *guillotine*. This is a mechanism which limits the time devoted to a debate ensuring that the progress of a government measure is not halted by unnecessary or excessive parliamentary scrutiny. This is a safeguard against the *filibuster* which enables members of the American Senate to halt the progress of legislation by speaking indefinitely. Unlike the American House of Representatives, there is no time limit on debate in the Senate.

This situation of executive dominance of the legislature has occurred in both parliamentary and presidential forms of government. There are three reasons which might account for this development.

1 The Ability to Initiate Action

The ability of the executive branch to act independently of legislatures in certain circumstances has tended to enhance the power of the former, eroding the latter's ability to initiate public policy or scrutinise the activities of government. In the UK, the government may make use of the *royal prerogative* and undertake some actions without having to first obtain Parliamentary approval. In other liberal democracies, chief executives are given emergency powers in certain circumstances or may govern by some form of decree. As has been observed in Chapter 11, the American president may issue executive orders and thus act in some circumstances without the approval of Congress.

2 The Volume of Government Business

A second explanation for executive dominance concerns the volume of postwar State activity, much of which is of a complex and technical nature. This has made it difficult for members of legislatures to keep abreast of the affairs of modern government and has tended to result in ministers and civil servants within the executive branch exercising a dominant position in policy-making because of their expertise and the superior information which they have at their disposal.

3 The Party System

The final explanation for the power of executives over legislatures is the development of the party system. This aligns members of the executive and legislative branches. Members of both branches, when belonging to the same party, have common ideological and policy interests. They have a vested interest in successfully translating these common concerns into law. Such mutual interests are underlaid by party discipline which serves to induce members of the legislature to follow the lead given by their party chiefs within the executive branch of government. In extreme cases where party discipline is strong, disobedience to the wishes of the executive might result in expulsion from the Party, a fate which befell the British Conservative Party's 'Eurorebels' in 1994. The emergence of disciplined political parties thus has the effect of ensuring that legislatures do not act as corporate institutions exercising their functions on behalf of the nation as a whole. Instead they operate under the direction of the executive branch of government.

The French Party System

The party system possesses obvious advantages for the executive branch of government in its dealings with the legislature. It helps to prevent legislative anarchy (in the sense of members seeking to pursue individual interests to the exclusion of all else) and organises the work of such bodies, thus ensuring that specific goals and objectives are achieved. The manner in which party discipline can enhance executive dominance of the legislature is illustrated in France where the situation in which governments were placed at the mercy of constantly shifting coalitions in the National Assembly was replaced during the 1960s by the development of parties which were organised in support of, or opposition to, the government. This situation was termed *le fait majoritaire*. It supplemented other developments contained in the 1958 constitution which were designed to subordinate the legislature to the executive. These included limitations on the ability of the National Assembly to dismiss governments and facilities for governments to secure the passage of legislation lacking majority support in either the National Assembly or the Senate.

LEGITIMISING

This is an important consequence of executive domination of legislatures.

The power of legislatures is potentially devalued if the initiative in proposing legislation is passed to the executive branch of government which then controls the progress of that legislation through the legislature by the workings of the party system. Its main role becomes not that of making law but of confirming decisions that have been reached elsewhere (for example in cabinet meetings or in inter-party discussions).

Nonetheless, when passed by the legislature, the law applies to all citizens, who are required to obey it. Compliance is most effectively achieved by downplaying the political forces which have shaped legislation and associating it with the actions of a body whose authority is widely acknowledged. Law is therefore depicted as the outcome of a process engaged in by the entire legislative body: legislation is viewed as the collective decision of this assembly which is ultimately responsible to the people. Legitimising thus entails enhancing the status of the actions of the government. The power of the latter is augmented with the authority of the legislature, thereby ensuring wide public compliance to the government's measures.

The Authority of Legislatures

A consideration of developments affecting contemporary legislatures should extend beyond an examination of changes affecting the power of these bodies. It is necessary to consider allegations that the aura and prestige of these institutions has suffered in recent years, and that this has had an adverse effect on the authority of these bodies.

The Economic Climate

Public confidence in legislatures may be especially affected by the economic climate. Factors such as recession are likely to have an adverse impact on the way the public view all institutions of government, especially when it appears that they have no instant solutions. Recession is further likely to reduce the capacity of institutions of government to act as innovators: rather than act as dynamic proponents of reform (which may enhance the standing of such bodies in the public eye) executives and legislators are disposed towards inaction and pruning public spending. This is a less adventurous exercise than initiating new programmes.

Performance of a Diverse Range of Functions

Legislatures perform a wide range of functions. However, not all of these are compatible. In particular, prominent attention to the role of promoting local considerations may detract from the legislature's ability to exercise superintendence over national affairs and may give the appearance of a fragmented body with no overall sense of purpose. This may also result in the decline of the aura and prestige of that body and thus its authority.

Localism in Practice

The role which legislators perform in providing a service to their constituents is an important one in many countries. In the UK reference is often made to a Member of Parliament's 'personal vote'. This implies that some candidates secure support from their local electors on the basis of who they are and what they have done (especially in connection with the past services provided to their constituents). Such support is, however, far less important than a candidate's party label.

In other liberal democracies, however, the defence of local interests (which is termed *parochialism*) may be a prominent concern of legislators. This may have an adverse effect on the authority of a legislative body which in extreme situations may be merely viewed as an arena in which local concerns are advocated to the relative exclusion of issues of national importance.

Ireland

Members of the Dail are often prominent participants in the local political affairs of the constituency they represent and view the promotion of local interests and articulation of individual grievances as more important than formulating national legislation. Even Ministers are not immune to these parochial pressures.

The USA

The parochialism of members of Congress detracts from that body's ability or willingness to view matters from an overall national perspective. Although American Congressional elections are fought by candidates who represent the nation's major Parties, the main influence on the outcome of these elections is the personal vote which a candidate can attract. This personal vote may be secured on the basis of that person's campaigning style and how they 'come across' to local voters. However, the key basis of a personal vote is the candidate's previous record when in office. This record can be based on factors which include accessibility to local constituents (especially the provision of help to those with problems), the voicing of support for local interests or causes, and particularly the ability to attract government resources into the constituency which the candidate represents.

It follows, therefore, that incumbent candidates (that is, those who are seeking re-election) are in a far better position to win seats in the House of Representatives or Senate than is a candidate who has no record and is striving to win a seat for the first time. Only factors such as a dilatory record in advancing constituency interests or being involved in some form of scandal are likely to offset the incumbent's advantage. Although sitting candidates do sometimes lose, a key feature of elections to Congress is that incumbents are in a good position to win, and usually do so.

It has been argued that this situation results in Congress having a dual character: it is at one and the same time a body composed of politicians with a keen interest (or even a preoccupation) with local affairs but is also a forum for making national policy. Concern with the former may detract from the latter and reduce Congress's effectiveness in responding to current or future problems.

Adversarial Politics

The operations of the party system have one further consequence which may devalue the authority of legislatures. Party systems often give rise to adversarial politics. The UK and New Zealand are examples of countries whose political affairs are traditionally conducted in this manner. Adversarial politics denotes a situation in which one party is automatically disposed to oppose the views and suggestions of another as a point of principle. If this style of politics influences the operations of the legislature, it means that any sense of common purpose is lacking. The work of the legislature is less concerned with a genuine search for the best solutions to issues and problems but is mainly activated by the furtherance of partisan acrimony and the pursuit of party advantage. Members of the legislature who are supporters of the same party from which the executive is drawn are likely to back that government and deride proposals made by the opposition party (or parties) regardless of the merits of the cases put forward. Similarly, those who are not supporters of the government are likely to make destructive rather than constructive assessments of initiatives put forward by the executive branch. This may affect the way in which members of the public feel towards the legislature. It may be viewed as an institution whose main function seems to be playing party politics rather than advancing national concerns.

The actual extent to which adversarial politics has dominated British politics since 1945 is discussed in Chapter 19.

'CONSTRUCTIVE OPPOSITION'

One development related to the above discussion of adversarial politics was the decision of the Liberal Democrats to embark upon a course of action termed 'constructive opposition' to the Labour government which was elected in 1997.

The main benefit of this approach to the Liberal Democrats was a limited form of involvement in government affairs which included offering five senior Liberal Democrats places on a cabinet sub-committee to consider the issue of constitutional reform. The main problem posed by this stance, however, was that cooperation with the Labour government on this matter made it difficult for the Liberal Democrats to criticise any of its actions even when it involved matters about which they had not been consulted.

Corruption

One of the main explanations for legislatures experiencing reduced authority concerns corruption. If the public perceive that the main purpose of seeking election to such bodies is to further a member's personal interests rather than to serve the nation, citizens are likely to hold both legislatures and legislators in low regard. This issue is discussed more fully in Chapter 2.

The Decline of Legislatures?

It has been argued above that contemporary legislatures face two related sets of problems – changes affecting the powers of such bodies which have impeded their ability to discharge traditional functions and changes in public perceptions of their aura and prestige. This has had an adverse effect on the authority which they are able to command. These arguments can be amalgamated to suggest that there has been a decline in legislatures.

However, although major developments which have contributed to allegations of the decline of such bodies have been charted, legislatures continue to perform vital roles in political affairs. Some of the problems to which attention has been drawn are neither universal nor insuperable. For example, the dominant hold which governments exercise over the law-making process is greater in some countries than in others. In both Germany and Italy, for example, there remains a considerable degree of scope for legislation to be initiated by ordinary (or 'backbench') members of the legislature.

Legislatures and the Party System

The impact of the party system on the role of legislatures is also subject to a wide degree of variation and this has an obvious bearing on the subservience of legislature to the executive. For example, the nature of the party relationship between Congress and the President in America is one factor which explains why Congress has retained an extremely significant role in law-making. Additionally, the dominance which governments possess over the conduct of legislatures through the operations of the party system is not always a constant feature in the political affairs of a country. There are occasions when legislatures may assert themselves to a greater degree, and these situations may arise in both parliamentary and presidential forms of government.

❍ *In a parliamentary system:* when no one party possesses overall majority support in the legislature.

❍ *In a presidential system:* when the executive branch of government is controlled by a different party than that which controls the legislature.

Some examples of this are considered below.

Ireland

During the 1980s, the absence of one party with an overall majority gave the Dail the opportunity to exercise its right to dismiss governments. Two were dismissed and a third was forced to resign and seek a dissolution.

France

When the presidency and National Assembly in France were controlled by different political parties during periods of what is termed *cohabitation* (1986–88, 1993–95 and since 1997), the President was forced to appoint a prime minister who enjoyed the support of the National Assembly. In 1997, President Chirac was accordingly obliged to appoint his defeated opponent in the 1995 Presidential election, the socialist Lionel Jospin. In such situations governments become accountable to the legislature rather than to the President, thus enhancing the power of the former at the expense of the latter.

The USA

The November 1994 American Congressional elections resulted in the Democratic Party losing its majority in both the House of Representatives and the Senate. This enabled Congress to seize the initiative from President Clinton in major policy areas, especially in the area of public expenditure. This is discussed more fully in Chapter 11.

Conclusion

The above examples suggest that the party system is a double-edged sword. Although it sometimes aids executive dominance over the legislature, it may also enable legislatures to assert themselves at the expense of executive power. Their ability to do this may further be enhanced by reforms which are discussed in the following section.

Reforms to the Working Practices of Legislatures

The Role of Select Committees

Legislatures may seek to provide themselves with mechanisms to elicit information on the affairs of government, thus enhancing their ability to effectively scrutinise the actions of the government. Individual legislators may be provided with financial aid to employ staff, or be able to draw upon the services of those with expert knowledge of specific policy areas. British Members of Parliament and members of the Irish Dail are extremely poorly served in this respect while American legislators fare far better, with large personal staffs and the support of expert research services.

Select committees constitute a key reform to facilitate legislative scrutiny of the government. Their deliberations provide a source of information which is separate from that provided by the executive branch. Further, the non-partisan climate within which select committee discussions are held may reduce the domination exerted by the executive branch of government, thereby enhancing the status of the legislature. This has been the case in Ireland, France, the UK, New Zealand and Canada.

❍ *Ireland:* the Fine Gael–Labour coalition (1982–87) established a number of select committees in 1983 but most of them were abandoned by the Fianna Fail government in 1987.

❍ *New Zealand:* major reforms to the system of select committees were introduced into parliament by the incoming Labour government in 1985. These reforms were designed to subject the government to enhanced parliamentary and public scrutiny. One significant innovation was the power of such committees to inquire on their own initiative into any area of government administration, policy or spending.

❍ *Britain:* the Public Accounts Committee was an early example (established in 1861) of a select committee monitoring the work of government. It examines the accounts of government departments and seeks to ensure that money is spent effectively and for the purposes which were intended. Its work is aided by the Comptroller and Auditor General and the National Audit Office. The post-1979 select committee system is discussed in more detail below.

Question

❍ To what extent (and why) do you believe that the power and authority of the House of Commons has declined in recent years?

❍ In conjunction with material contained in the following section, consider ONE measure whereby this decline might be reversed.

The British House of Commons

This section explores a number of issues related to the contemporary operations of the British House of Commons.

Law-Making in the UK

In the UK, there is a difference between public and private legislation. The former constitutes the general law of the land, and the latter is limited in jurisdiction (often being promoted by public bodies such as local authorities to extend their powers). A number of stages are involved in translating a proposal into law.

THE PROCESS OF PUBLIC LEGISLATION

The following outline applies to public legislation. It is assumed that this legislation is first introduced into the House of Commons, which is generally (but not exclusively) the case.

First Reading This is merely the announcement of an intention to introduce legislation on a particular topic. No debate occurs at this stage.

Second Reading This is a debate on the general principles embodied in a legislative proposal (which is termed a *Bill*). If these principles are approved the Bill progresses to the next stage in the legislative process.

Committee Stage	This involves a detailed examination of the contents of the Bill. Amendments can be made provided that they do not destroy the Bill's fundamental principles which have been approved in the second reading.
	This stage usually takes place in a standing committee which involves a relatively small number of MPs, although a committee of the whole House or a select committee may be used instead. A committee of the whole House is used in connection with the most important issues raised by a government's Finance Bill (which has the effect of turning the Budget statement into law).
Report Stage	This is the stage at which the changes to the Bill proposed by the committee are considered by the full House of Commons and either approved or rejected.
Third Reading	This is a consideration of the Bill as amended in its progress through the House of Commons.

If the Bill receives its third reading, it then goes through a similar process in the House of Lords.

If amendments are proposed by the House of Lords, these need to be separately considered by the House of Commons. By convention the House of Lords will normally give way to the sentiments of the Commons if there is a dispute between the two chambers.

When such differences are reconciled, the Bill is passed for *Royal Assent*. This is granted automatically, but is the process by which the Bill becomes an *act*.

It is necessary for a Bill to complete all stages of the above process in both Houses of Parliament in a single Parliamentary Session. If it fails to do this, the Bill must be reintroduced in the following session, commencing at the first reading stage when the process begins all over again.

Private Members' Legislation

Most bills are put forward by the government. However, backbench MPs also have a limited ability to initiate law-making. Members have the ability (under the *ten minute rule* procedure) to propose legislation. They do this by making a brief (ten minute) speech at the commencement of Parliament's proceedings. This is unlikely to produce reform and is mainly used by an MP to express support for an issue.

Additionally, a minimum number of days (consisting of ten Fridays each Parliamentary session) are set aside for backbench MPs to promote legislation. The allocation of this scarce time is determined by ballot. Private Members rely heavily on pressure groups for ideas on subjects requiring legislation and for aid in drafting bills. The time allotted to such legislation is limited, thus giving opponents ample opportunity (especially through their ability to table large numbers of amendments at the Bill's Report State) to ensure that it does not become law before the end of a Parliamentary Session. Controversial proposals are thus unlikely to succeed unless the government steps in and donates some of its own Parliamentary time to ensure the passage of the legislation. This was the case concerning the 1967 Abortion Act. The reluctance of the Blair government to give such extra time to the Bill put forward by Michael Foster to ban the hunting of stags and other animals with dogs in the 1997–98 Parliament ensured that the measure had to be abandoned. This Bill failed despite the overwhelming support of MPs, who at its Second Reading stage voted to approve it by the margin of 411:151.

The 'countryside march', a procession through the streets of London on 1 March 1998 joined by approximately 250,000 people expressing the concerns of rural Britain.

The Select Committee System

In 1979, a new system of select committees was introduced into the House of Commons to monitor the work performed by all the key government departments. Initially 14 of such 'departmental' committees were appointed. There are currently 19 Select Committees which are additional to others set up for specific purposes often of an ad hoc nature. One example of the latter is the Select Committee on the Modernisation of the House of Commons, which was established in 1997.

The role performed by the Select Committees which were established in 1979 has been varied. The main functions which these bodies have carried are as follows.

❍ *Monitoring departments:* the work of Select Committees has included scrutinising the operations of government departments, and seeking to expose shortcomings. In doing this they have used their powers to secure a wide range of additional information on the operations of departments and the quangos which are responsible to them.

❍ *Policy-making:* Select Committees discharge this role either by involving themselves in the initiation of policy or by aiming to persuade departments to change the direction of existing policy.

Strengths of the Select Committees

The system of Select Committees which was established in 1979 sought to alter the balance between the legislative and executive branches of British government. The strengths of these committees are discussed below.

❍ *The scope of their work:* the new Select Committee system covered the major tasks of government as opposed to monitoring the activities of merely one or two departments. This made it difficult to abolish any particular committee (as had happened with the Agriculture Committee in 1969) if its work offended the government, since they all 'stood or fell' together.

❍ *The ability to secure expert advice:* to aid them in their deliberations, such committees were empowered to hire staff with expertise in the area of government with which they were concerned. They also possess the power to call for 'persons and papers', which means they may secure evidence from persons with knowledge of the subject area under discussion, including civil servants.

❍ *Diluting the hold exerted by party politics:* members of such committees may display a sense of corporate loyalty which overrides Party affiliation. This is most apparent in the production of a unanimous report, critical of government policy, as occurred in 1997 when the Health Select Committee unanimously condemned the government's decision to exempt Formula 1 racing from the proposed tobacco sponsorship ban.

○ *Offering an alternative to government office:* members who do not aspire (either by choice or minor party membership) to hold government office may find in select committees an alternative political 'career structure'. This was illustrated in 1997 when the chairmanship of the powerful Social Security Select Committee was given to a Liberal Democrat MP, Archie Kirkwood.

○ *Securing additional functions:* select committees may improve their ability to monitor the activities of the government by adding to their responsibilities. This includes considering evidence on a topic before a Bill is drafted, or holding American-style confirmation hearings. Such were conducted in 1997 by the Treasury Select Committee for appointees to the Bank of England's Monetary Policy Committee whose role was to exercise day-to-day control over interest rates.

Weaknesses of the Select Committees

There are, however, certain problems connected with the operations of the new Select Committee system.

The Civil Service

A civil servant has no right to refuse a summons to appear before a Select Committee, although by convention such a request is made to a department as opposed to a named civil servant. This enables the Minister to determine which civil servant should attend a Select Committee hearing. Problems have arisen concerning the nature of the information which such officials might be expected to reveal. This matter is governed by the *Osmotherly Rules* which were originally drawn up in 1988, and redrafted in 1994. They emphasise that a civil servant giving evidence before a Select Committee does so on behalf of the minister, and acts under his or her directions, thereby upholding the convention of ministerial responsibility to Parliament. These rules urge civil servants to be as helpful as possible in giving evidence to Select Committees, but require them to avoid making contentious comments on government policy, confining their responses to questions of fact and explanation.

The Role and Status of the House of Commons Becomes Devalued

The authoritative work of Parliament may become transferred from the floor of the House of Commons to the Select

Committees. This development poses the danger of fragmenting the ability of Parliament to exercise scrutiny of the overall role and performance of government.

The Workings of the Committees are Not Effectively Integrated Into Parliament's Business

Select Committees were designed to extract information which would then be published for the benefit of all Members of the House of Commons. However, the reports of Select Committees (which are not routinely debated) often make a marginal impact on the activities of Parliament.

Domination of Membership by the Party Whips

Members of Select Committees are appointed by the Committee of Selection, which prior to 1979 had been responsible for appointing members of Standing and Private Bill Committees. Although this reform was designed to reduce the ability of party leaders to dominate the appointments to these committees, it was recognised at the outset that the two front benches would play an influential role in this matter, thus threatening to undermine the ability of committee members to exercise independent thought. This continues to be the case. In 1997, for example, the Labour whips office was accused of improper influence in securing the removal of Diane Abbott from the Treasury Select Committee.

Consensus Politics

One problem faced by Select Committees is that their quest for agreement across party lines may require 'trade offs' between members of different political parties, resulting in the production of a unanimous report which consists of a 'soggy compromise'. The lack of biting edge makes it of little use in the scrutiny of the actions of the executive.

Partisanship

Select Committees may on occasions operate in a party political manner. In 1998, the Liberal Democrat Treasury spokesman, Malcolm Bruce MP, criticised the report of the Labour-dominated Treasury Committee into the Budget as 'superficial, incomplete and unsatisfactory', and accused it of failing to provide for detailed, constructive criticism of the economic policy of the Labour government. Later that year, an investigation by the Public Administration Committee into allegations of the politicisation of the government's press machine resulted in the Conservative and Liberal Democrat members publishing an 'alternative' to the report endorsed by the Labour majority.

Reforms of the Labour Government After 1997

The Modernisation of the House of Commons

To outside observers, many of the rituals of the House of Commons seem at best to be outdated, and at worst border on farce. Unlike the legislatures of many other liberal democracies where voting is performed electronically, British MPs must vote by personally passing through the division lobbies. Cries of 'hear, hear' and the throwing of Order papers into the air are the means of applauding a member's valid contribution to a debate instead of clapping which is not permitted. The requirement that an MP must be 'seated and covered' whilst seeking to make a point of order during a division gives rise to the wearing of top hats and other forms of bizarre headwear, as was evidenced in the acrimonious exchanges which took place during the debates on Michael Foster's bill designed to outlaw the hunting of certain wild mammals with dogs. It was against the background of seemingly outdated practices that the Labour government elected in 1997 appointed a cross-party committee to consider the modernisation of the House of Commons.

SUGGESTED REFORMS

The first report of the committee established to consider the modernisation of the House of Commons was issued in March 1998. The reforms which were suggested are outlined below.

◆ *Suspension:* MPs suspended for bad behaviour should not receive pay.

◆ *Privy councillors:* these senior politicians should not receive precedence over other backbench MPs in being called by the Speaker to make speeches.

◆ *Passage of legislation:* Bills which had first been considered by a Select Committee or a special standing committee might proceed through the House of Commons more slowly over two sessions as opposed to the present one.

The government's initial response to modernisation was delivered in June 1998. It proposed that the House should not sit on Fridays (thus allowing Members to spend more time in their constituencies), and that the committees responsible for examining legislation should meet during September rather than having to wait until mid-October when the House traditionally reconvened.

The Case for Reforming the House of Lords

It has been argued above that most liberal democracies have bicameral legislatures. The problem which affects Britain's bicameral system concerns the composition of the upper house, the House of Lords, whose membership remains dominated by *hereditary peers* (that is, those who owe their position to birth). There are two key problems with the composition of the House of Lords.

1 An Anomaly in a Liberal-Democratic Political Structure

The unelected House of Lords possesses the ability to thwart the will expressed by the House of Commons, whose members *are* elected. In 1998, an amendment to the government's Crime and Disorder Bill which sought to equalise the age of consent to 16 for homosexuals and heterosexuals was passed by the House of Commons with a majority of 207 votes. It was rejected by the House of Lords by the margin of 168 votes. This reform had to be abandoned at that time in order to ensure that the government was able to secure the prompt enactment of a major piece of legislation containing 12 of its 1997 election manifesto pledges.

2 A Bias Towards the Conservative Party

The presence of hereditary peers (the majority of whom are members of the Conservative Party) gives the House of Lords a potential Conservative bias.

COMPOSITION OF THE HOUSE OF LORDS

In 1998, the Party membership of peers was as follows:

490   Conservative

143   Labour

 59   Liberal Democrat

322   Crossbenchers (a term which means a member of no political party).

Hereditary peers were overwhelmingly Conservative. In 1998 the numbers of hereditary peers were:

325   Conservative
 17   Labour
 23   Liberal Democrat

Figures taken from the *Guardian*, 8 January 1998

Between May 1997 and July 1998, the Labour government was defeated in divisions on 28 occasions. However, even if the House of Lords is consistently anti-Labour, it is not unquestionably pro-Conservative. Between 1979 and 1997, Conservative governments suffered a number of defeats on key items of legislation. These included the Local Government (Interim Provisions) Bill (designed to pave the way for the abolition of the Greater London Council and the Metropolitan County Councils) in 1984, and the Police and Magistrates' Courts Bill which was introduced in the House of Lords in 1993. Former Conservative Home Secretaries Viscount Whitelaw and Lord Carr marshalled opposition to the latter measure on the grounds that it gave ministers too much power to direct the police service. They were successful in securing some key amendments to the Bill.

The Progress of Reform of the House of Lords

Reforms to the Powers of the House of Lords

Initial reforming measures were mainly directed at the powers of the House of Lords, seeking to minimise opposition to the existence of this body by reducing its ability to thwart the will of the elected chamber, the House of Commons. Thus in the case of disagreement between the two Houses of Parliament, the one with the elected base will ultimately prevail. This situation is enshrined in the 1949 Parliament Act which gives the House of Lords the power to delay the progress of non-financial legislation which has been passed by the House of Commons for the maximum period of one year, after which (provided the measure is reintroduced in the House of Commons) it will become law. The only exception to this is the retention of the absolute veto of the House of Lords to a proposal to extend the life of Parliament beyond the limit of five years.

The 1949 Parliament Act was applied in 1998 in connection with the Labour government's European Elections Bill. This sought to introduce proportional representation into elections for the European Parliament. The majority of the House of Lords objected to the closed list system proposed in the Bill (whereby candidates would be chosen by the parties rather than the voters) and sent it back to the House of Commons on five occasions. This ensured it failed to become law in the 1997/98 Session of Parliament. However, the decision by the majority of peers to deny this Bill a second reading in the new Session of Parliament, more than a year after the House of Commons had originally approved it, meant that the Bill automatically became law under the terms of the 1949 Act.

Reforms to the Composition of the House of Lords

Reforms to the composition of the House of Lords have been limited in scope, being mainly designed to dilute the hold possessed by hereditary peers but not to abolish them. One reason for this is that any attack on the hereditary principle would inevitably raise the question of the place of the hereditary Monarchy in the British political system. The key reforms to the composition of the House of Lords have been twofold.

❍ *1958:* the 1958 Life Peerages Act made it possible for men (and, for the first time, women) to receive peerages which could not be passed on to their descendants.

❍ *1963:* the 1963 Peerage Act made it possible for hereditary peers to give up their peerage and thus be eligible to stand for election to the House of Commons.

Reforms Introduced After 1997

There were various options for reform available to the incoming Labour government.

Minimal Reform

This would involve abolishing the voting rights of hereditary peers but retaining the remainder of the institution more or less intact. The advantage of this would be that prime ministers could continue to utilise the life peerage system as a key form of political patronage. Tony Benn pointed out in 1997 that the last ten prime ministers had made great use of this power and appointed 900 life peers. One advantage of this is that prime ministers can bring 'outsiders' into their government if these latter people possess expertise which will benefit the conduct of public affairs. In 1997, for example, Tony Blair recruited the chairman of the British Petroleum oil company (who took the title of Lord Simon) to act as Minister for Trade and Competitiveness in Europe. However, the removal of the hereditary peers would considerably enhance the dependency of this body on the Prime Minister, effectively transforming it into what Lord Irvine described in the *Independent* on 24 December 1997 as 'the biggest quango in our nation's history'.

Radical Reform

This would entail replacing the House of Lords in its entirety with a directly elected second chamber. The main problem with this proposal is that it may lead to both Houses of Parliament being equal in power. This poses the possibility of one being able to exercise a veto over the work of the other, resulting in stagnation in government. A secondary consideration is the cost. It is likely that radical reform would require members of the second chamber to be paid a salary: currently they are merely entitled to allowances (which in 1998 amounted to £34.50 a day for subsistence, £78.50 for overnight subsistence when the House sits late into the evening, £33.50 a day for secretarial assistance, and a first class rail fare).

Compromise Reform

This would entail the removal of the hereditary peers. The House of Lords would then be composed of a mixture of nominated (life) peers coupled with a directly elected element.

The Progress of Reform since 1997

As is stated in Chapter 10, reform of the House of Lords was supported by both the Liberal Democrats and the Labour Party before the 1997 General Election. In 1998, a cabinet committee was appointed under the Lord Chancellor, Lord Irvine of Lairg, to consider this issue. The pace of reform was affected by the Prime Minister's desire to achieve consensus. The Conservative Party responded to this situation by appointing their own Constitutional Commission which was designed to outflank the government by producing concrete reform proposals.

The government's intention was to proceed in stages: *stage 1* would involve the abolition of the right of hereditary peers to sit and vote in the House of Lords. The composition of an 'interim' second chamber would be based on the existing life peers (with some additional members designed to redress the Conservative majority). Its powers would be similar to those currently possessed by the House of Lords. In March 1998, the Prime Minister referred to the possibility that newly-appointed members to this body could be chosen by an independent panel, thus undermining the criticism that it would constitute the 'house of patronage', controlled by the Prime Minister's nominees.

Political expediency might mean that reform did not progress beyond stage 1. If it did, *stage 2* (which would be preceded by a Royal Commission) would entail abolishing the interim chamber and replacing it with an institution directly elected in whole or in part. Consideration would also have to be given to the powers appropriate for a body of this nature.

Divisions in the Conservative Party

One problem with reforming the House of Lords was that their opposition to change could slow down the progress of other

Question ?

○ Using newspapers and journals, chart the progress of the reform of the House of Lords embarked upon by the Labour government elected in 1997.

○ What are the strengths and weaknesses of the reforms implemented by this government?

items of Labour policy. In an attempt to avoid this, the Prime Minister and the then Conservative leader in the House of Lords, Lord Cranborne, agreed to a compromise whereby 91 hereditary peers (elected by their own parties in proportion to their current strength) would remain members of the upper chamber until stage 2 reform was implemented. This 'deal' was struck behind the back of the Conservative Party leader, William Hague. When he became aware of it, he sacked Lord Cranborne from his frontbench team, insisting that stage 1 not be concluded until the details of stage 2 had first been determined.

Further Reading

Andrew Adonis, *Parliament Today* (Manchester: Manchester University Press, 1993, 2nd edition). This thoroughly discusses the functions, structure and day-to-day operations of the House of Commons and House of Lords, and analyses contemporary issues which include the impact of the EU on Parliamentary sovereignty.

A useful account of such issues is also provided by **Paul Silk** and **Rhodri Williams**, *How Parliament Works* (Harlow: Longman, 1995, 3rd edition).

Philip Norton (editor), *Legislatures* (Oxford: Oxford University Press, 1990). This book contains a number of valuable essays which contribute towards an understanding of the role and operations of legislatures. Issues such as the relationship between legislatures and executives are thoroughly explored in a comparative context.

Chapter Fifteen | Law Enforcement and the Judiciary

The aims of this chapter are:

1 To provide an appreciation of the manner in which law enforcement is a major political issue in liberal-democratic systems of government.

2 To analyse the mechanisms of control and accountability of the police in liberal-democratic systems of government.

3 To examine the control and accountability of the British policing system.

4 To evaluate the strengths and weaknesses of trial by jury.

5 To analyse the varied activities undertaken by the courts, differentiating between civil, criminal, administrative and constitutional law enforcement, focusing particular attention on the process of judicial review.

6 To evaluate the arguments related to judges being described as law makers, with particular reference to the United Kingdom.

7 To analyse the constraints which prevent judges operating in a totally impartial manner, concentrating on an examination of British judges and the state.

The Politics of the Criminal Justice System

In liberal-democratic systems of government the key roles in the system of law enforcement are performed by police officers and judges. Common to all liberal-democratic systems is the *rule of law*, whose main principles are:

○ *Equality before the law:* all individuals accused of a crime are treated in the same manner – the system of law enforcement is impartial and operates without fear or favour.

○ *An open, visible system of law enforcement:* those accused of wrongdoing are entitled to a free trial which follows established procedures.

The state will intervene against those persons whose actions seriously conflict with a country's criminal code. They will be arrested by the police, tried by a jury (where this system operates) and sentenced by judges. The rule of law emphasises the protection of individual rights from arbitrary interference (that is, official action subject to no control) by officials of the State. The guarantees provided by the rule of law are thus in stark contrast with the operations of a *police state* in which the actions performed by agencies such as the police are not subject to legal restraints, and citizens lack adequate protection in their dealings with such bodies.

The Political Environment of Law Enforcement

It is necessary that the system of law enforcement in liberal-democratic countries should be seen as impartial in order for its actions to be accorded widespread popular consent. This situation is most easily guaranteed when the agencies and personnel engaged in this work are free from political pressures and biases and thus able to apply the law in the same manner to all persons within a country. However, total freedom from political pressures or influences is impossible in any liberal-democratic system of government. This is so for reasons which are discussed below.

Law and Order is a Major Political Issue

A government's record in combating crime and lawlessness may have a significant bearing on its ability to retain power in an election. It was argued, for example, that the Conservative Party's ability to condemn Labour's record as inadequate in this area was a crucial factor in Mrs Thatcher's election victory in 1979.

Alternatively, deficiencies in the response by a government to such issues will be exploited by opposition parties and may cost it public support. The damaging effects to a government arising from failures concerned with crime control and the criminal justice system were displayed in Belgium in 1998. The escape from custody of the serial child killer and convicted paedophile, Marc Dutroux, resulted in a Parliamentary censure motion. The government narrowly won this, but only after ministers secured the resignation of the country's chief of police.

Law and Order and Public Policy

Those who work in the public sector must be subject to adequate mechanisms of political control and accountability. Control and accountability ensures that government policies are enforced, and also that political objectives (such as the need for the agencies involved in such work to maintain law and order and to provide adequate value for money) are accomplished. A

LAW ENFORCEMENT AS A POLITICAL ISSUE IN THE UNITED STATES OF AMERICA

The political importance of crime ensures that the police and courts do not operate in a vacuum. These bodies may be subject to both informal and formal political pressures designed to enhance the government's overall standing. The political dimension of law enforcement is enhanced when key actors in the judicial process are themselves political figures. This is the case in the USA where state law officers are popularly elected. The need for those seeking such office to court public opinion was regarded as one factor behind the decision of a Massachusetts district attorney (Thomas Reilly) to seek a first-degree murder indictment for the British au pair, Louise Woodward, in 1997 following the death of a child who had been in her care. It was believed that the successful prosecution of this charge (as opposed to one of manslaughter) would considerably enhance his prospects for election as Attorney General of the state.

balance, however, has to be struck between the control exerted by politicians over the area of law enforcement and the legitimate desire for a degree of independence by the professionals involved in such work. This is illustrated below using the British system of law enforcement.

The Autonomy of the British System of Law Enforcement

In the UK, Conservative governments between 1979 and 1997 made strenuous efforts to exert control over the operations of the system of law enforcement. There were two aspects to these reforms which are discussed below.

The Erosion of Professional Autonomy

The operational independence of the police and judiciary was reduced by two pieces of legislation. These were the 1994 Police and Magistrates' Courts Act (which is discussed below) and the 1997 Crime (Sentencing) Act. This latter legislation was designed to counteract allegations that judges were often too 'soft' on criminals. It thus proposed to extend the principle of mandatory sentences (which previously existed only for murder) to a range of offences. Judges would be expected to apply these sentences unless there were compelling reasons not to do so.

Value for Money and Quality of Service

The changes introduced into the police service to secure the objective of enhanced value for money are discussed below.

Additionally, the emphasis on consumerism also affected the role of bodies concerned with law enforcement. The philosophy of the 1991 *Citizen's Charter* influenced the adoption of quality-of-service initiatives by police forces, and the operations of the judicial system were directed by the *Court's Charter*, which became operational in 1993.

Question

Give TWO reasons to explain how and why the control exerted by central government over EITHER the police service OR the judicial system increased during the 1990s. What dangers do you see from such developments?

To do this, organise your material under the following headings.

○ **Effectiveness:** the need for central government to be seen as effective in the 'war' against crime and lawlessness.

○ **Value for money:** the requirement for central government to guarantee that public money is spent wisely and efficiently by the agencies of the criminal justice system.

Control and Accountability of the Police

The main role of the police is to ensure that all citizens obey the law. If citizens fail to do so the police can invoke a range of sanctions. These may include *cautioning* or *arresting* a person who is breaking the law. Mechanisms of control and accountability seek to ensure that the police carry out their duties fairly and efficiently.

There are three main models governing the control and accountability (or governance) of policing. These are discussed below.

National Government Control of Police Work

If a police force is controlled by, and accountable to, national government there is a danger that the main role of that organisation will be to promote the political interests of the Party or Parties from which the government is formed. Typically the government will depict its interests as being identical to those of the State. Police operations would be directed by the national government to whom the police are accountable. The police therefore personify the State: they are the 'State in uniform'. Such a situation existed, for example, when South Africa was subject to white minority rule.

The main danger which might arise from such a close identification between the police and national government concerns the style of policing. If the main role of the police is to uphold the interests of the government, policing may be coercive in nature, directed against all those who disagree with the policies pursued by that government. Coercive policing is frequently pursued by paramilitary police bodies who take their orders from a minister in the national government. Their attitude may be that of 'shoot first and ask questions later' since there is no organisation other than the government to hold the police accountable for their actions.

POLICING AND CENTRAL GOVERNMENT

Current examples of national control of police work include France and Ireland.

France

Central government performs a major role in police affairs. There are two main police forces. The *police nationale* is controlled by the Ministry of the Interior while the *gendarmerie nationale* is technically part of the armed forces under the control of the Ministry of Defence. Officers from these bodies are also used as investigating officers to conduct enquiries under the supervision of an investigating judge or a public prosecutor. In this capacity they are termed the *police judiciaire* and are responsible to the judiciary.

Ireland

The *garda siochana* operates on a national scale, controlled by a commissioner who is appointed by and accountable to the Minister of Justice.

Local Control of Policing

In some countries the police are subject to local control secured through State governments, local authorities or the direct election of police chiefs. This is the case in Germany, where policing is primarily a State responsibility. This situation ensures that the police are ultimately accountable to local public opinion for their activities. It results in the existence of a number of police forces within a country and since it is likely that a range of political parties will exercise control over local governments, police work is not identified with the advancement of the interests of one particular political party. In this situation police work is focused on issues felt to be of concern to ordinary members of the general public rather than towards achieving the political priorities of national government. This role is appreciated by the public who support the police in their work. Policing is thus carried out with the *consent* of most members of the population. There are, however, problems associated with local control and accountability of policing, as is illustrated by the following brief discussion of the USA.

Control of American Policing

In the USA policing is primarily a local affair, controlled by units of local government operating at county or municipal levels. The Federal Bureau of Investigation is an agency of the justice department with the responsibility of enforcing federal laws, and additionally the national guard which exists at State level may also perform police-related functions. Local control, however, does not necessarily take the politics out of policing. State or local governments also have political objectives, and the police may be used to further these.

The development of urban policing in the USA, for example, was considerably influenced by local 'machine politics' in which local politicians exerted considerable influence over matters such as the recruitment and promotion of police officers and the tasks which they performed. Lack of efficiency and even corruption stemmed from this situation which persisted for a number of decades in the late nineteenth and early twentieth centuries. Today, the desire of local politicians (especially mayors) to secure re-election might entail a significant level of involvement in police affairs.

Professional Control of Policing

A final option is that police work should be controlled by, and accountable to, those professionals who actually perform the work. Under this model, senior police officers exercise control over whole forces and individual police officers. This system of control and accountability might seem the best guarantee of political impartiality in the exercise of police work as it leaves the professionals free to determine what are the most important functions to discharge.

There are, however, problems with such a system. The police and the public may have different views concerning which matters should receive priority attention and the manner in which these should be addressed. There is the danger that the lack of police accountability to the public may result in the police and public becoming so distanced that their role is seen as illegitimate by citizens. It is also possible that members of the general public will distrust a system in which police officers are subject to internal mechanisms of accountability. Remedies

Question

Based on your reading of the above account, who do you feel should exercise control over police work — central government, local government or the police themselves?

against abuse of power are difficult in a situation in which the police effectively operate as a 'law unto themselves'. The British concept of *constabulary independence* comes closest to the model of professional control.

The British Policing System

The models which have been examined in the above section imply that police accountability is most efficiently secured when control is in the hands of one body. This exercises control over policing, and the police service is accountable to that body for the performance of its work. The system of accountability is, however, considerably complicated when more than one party exercises control over police work. The following discussion of British policing investigates this problem.

The Historical Development of British Policing

When the new system of British policing was developed in the early decades of the nineteenth century it was controlled by, and accountable to, local government. The exception to this was the Metropolitan police (which was controlled by the Home Secretary). Elsewhere, policing was organisationally attached to local government and was supervised by a committee of councillors in urban areas (termed the watch committee) and by the magistrates in rural parts of Britain (who until 1888 exercised the functions of local government in such places).

As the century developed, however, others became involved in police affairs. The decision by central government in 1856 to pay some of the costs of provincial police forces was accompanied by a mechanism to ensure that each force benefiting from these new financial arrangements was conducted in an efficient manner. This was effected by an inspectorate whose responsibilities included visiting each and every force. The role of central government increased when the size of the government grant to police forces was doubled in 1874, and was further strengthened when the 1919 Police Act made a number of issues (such as pay and conditions of work) subject to the central direction of the Home Office.

Additionally, chief constables also sought to carve out for themselves areas of control over police work. These people began to see themselves less as servants of the local authorities which employed them but, instead, as professionals who needed a certain degree of insulation from outside pressures in order to perform their work effectively. Chief constables began to insist that they were accountable to the law but not to local or national politicians.

The 1964 Police Act and the Tripartite System

By the middle of the twentieth century, control over police work was shared between three bodies – local government, national government (the Home Secretary) and chief constables. The 1964 Police Act sought to regularise this situation by stipulating the precise areas of responsibilities attached to each of these parties. Outside of London, the role of local government was to be discharged by a new body, the *police committee* (latterly termed *police authority*). This was normally a committee of a county council, whose boundaries, when remodelled by the 1972 Local Government Act, provided the geographic basis for policing in England and Wales.

The system of accountability introduced by this legislation was a complex affair, based upon a system of checks and balances. Certain aspects of work were controlled by one of these three bodies, but could be referred to another for sanction or rejection. Examples of this system are discussed below.

❍ *Responsibility for the direction and control of a police force:* this responsibility was allocated to the chief constable, but the police authority could demand information concerning the way in which an area was policed.

❍ *The appointment and dismissal of chief constables:* this power was given to a police authority, but the Home Secretary had the ultimate power to accept or reject police authority decisions.

Assessment of the Tripartite System

The tripartite system of police governance proved to be defective in practice. The main problems which emerged after 1964 were as follows.

Control Over Police Work Lacked Precision

Each body was provided with generalised responsibilities, but their actual substance and detailed application was undefined. Such imprecision made it possible for one body to encroach on the work of another, resulting in 'turf wars'. This difficulty was a major explanation for the disputes concerning the accountability of police forces to local communities which occurred in some areas in the early 1980s.

Ineffective Accountability

There were a number of deficiencies in the system of accountability provided for in 1964.

❍ *The absence of effective sanctions:* for example, if the Home Office was unhappy with the performance of a police force it could withhold its certificate of efficiency and the government's financial contribution towards its costs. But the practical impossibility of bankrupting a police force meant that this became a toothless sanction.

❍ *The possibility of avoiding responsibility:* thus, a chief constable who was required by a police authority to produce a report on police activities could appeal to the Home Secretary to override the request. This entanglement of responsibilities meant it was difficult to hold any one body accountable for its actions.

The 1984 Police and Criminal Evidence Act

A particular problem which arose from the system of control and accountability which was introduced in 1964 was the perception that the views of local people regarding policing were not taken into account. Initially, disputes arose between some police committees and their chief constables

---

THE POLICE AND CRIMINAL EVIDENCE ACT

The main reforms introduced by this Act were as follows.

◆ *Safeguards to the use of police powers:* the use of police powers including stop and search became subject to safeguards. These stipulated the circumstances in which such powers should be used and also provided for monitoring of an individual officer's conduct by supervising officers.

◆ *The Police Complaints Authority:* the machinery used for investigating complaints by members of the public against police officers was reformed. The Police Complaints Board (established in 1976) was abolished and replaced by the Police Complaints Authority. Although outside investigation of complaints against the police was not instituted, this new body was given the ability to supervise such police investigations.

◆ *Consultation:* allegations that friction between police and public could be partly attributed to the absence of effective mechanisms to make the police accountable for their actions resulted in the requirement that regular consultative exercises should be conducted.

(especially in Merseyside and Greater Manchester) where it was alleged that chief constables unilaterally implemented policies and paid insufficient attention to the views and requirements of local people. It was argued that police work should be more accountable to police committees and to the general public.

The relevance of such a demand was underlined by the outbreak of public disorder in many of the UK's inner-city areas in the early 1980s (especially in 1981). One popular explanation for these events was the poor relationship between the police and public, especially black youths, who it was alleged experienced racist conduct and abuses of power by the police. The government appointed an enquiry into these disorders, chaired by Lord Scarman. This reported in 1981 and was responsible for initiating a number of reforms to police methods (especially the promotion of community policing), recruitment and training policies. A particular objective of such reforms was to improve the relationship between the police and ethnic minority communities. Other reforms were included in the 1984 Police and Criminal Evidence Act.

The Increased Role of Central Government in Police Affairs

The 1980s witnessed a considerable increase in the control exercised by central government over police affairs. The 1964 Police Act made the Home Secretary responsible for superintendence over the entire police service. The importance of this responsibility was demonstrated in 1983 when a Home Office circular applied the Financial Management Initiative to the police service, thus requiring that its operations be efficient and provide good value for money. This involved a number of developments, which included setting measurable objectives for the service whose attainment could be assessed by performance indicators. These were drawn up by bodies which included the Audit Commission. This body had been established by the 1982 Local Government Finance Act, and its subsequent activities involved scrutinising the working practices of police forces. As has been referred to above, the emphasis of the Citizen's Charter on consumerism also imposed outside constraints on the way in which policing was delivered.

The 1994 Police and Magistrates' Courts Act further enhanced the degree of control exerted by central government over police affairs. Senior officers were placed on fixed-term contracts. Key national objectives and performance indicators were drawn up by the Home Office to ensure that police actions became accountable to central direction. The national government set force budgets and also had the ability to subject them to cash limits. But there was little debate concerning the mechanisms needed to ensure that central government became adequately accountable for the way in which it exercised its control over police work. Critics argued that central government had been given power without adequate responsibility.

A Revitalised Role for Local Government

The Labour government's 1998 Crime and Disorder Act provided local government with a key role in police activities. In conjunction with the chief constable, local authorities were made responsible for formulating and implementing a strategy to reduce crime and disorder in their areas. This responsibility may develop into a situation whereby local government exerts a dominant influence over local crime-and-disorder issues, leaving central government to concentrate on coordinating the police response to serious crime.

Question

'Prime responsibility for policing should be in the hands of chief constables.' List arguments for and against this proposition.

Trial by Jury

Juries are designed to provide a trial by one's peers (which in this sense means 'social equals'). Their key role in a criminal trial is to listen to the evidence which is presented by the defence and prosecution and to determine the guilt or innocence of the defendant based upon an objective consideration of the facts. Trial by jury is not found in all liberal democracies: Japan, for example, does not utilise this system. Additionally, a jury's autonomy in determining the outcome of a trial also varies. In the UK, for example, they follow instructions given to them by the trial judge who further sums up proceedings for them.

Advantages of Trial by Jury

There are a number of advantages to the system of trial by jury.

Participation

Juries facilitate widespread public involvement in the operations of the criminal justice system. This may mean that the application of the law corresponds to what public opinion believes to be just and fair. The ability to enforce 'everyman's concept of justice' is particularly obvious in juries' ability to pronounce a verdict of 'not guilty' in the face of overwhelming evidence to the contrary. This may lead to the law being changed to mirror possible perceptions of fairness. Recent jury trials in the USA have emphasised that this situation is not necessarily an advantage, however. The acquittal in 1992 by a Los Angeles jury of police officers for beating Rodney King reflected the depth of racism in American society which denied justice to a black citizen.

Defence Against the Lack of Judicial Impartiality

The socially elite nature of judges in many liberal democracies may result in a perception of class, race or gender bias in the operations of the criminal justice system. The involvement of juries may lessen this concern. This advantage is, however, offset by two main problems.

❍ *Juries are not socially representative of the population as a whole:* the perception that British jurors were 'predominantly male, middle aged and middle class' has not been totally redressed by reforms introduced in 1974 (which are discussed below). Women and members of ethnic minority communities remain under-represented, and outside of urban areas, black defendants will usually face an all-white jury.

❍ *In some systems judges can overturn verdicts:* this arose in the trial of the British au pair, Louise Woodward, in 1997 in the American State of Massachusetts. The trial judge disagreed with the jury's verdict (guilty of murder in the second degree). He reduced it to that of involuntary manslaughter, giving him the ability to drastically reduce the sentence imposed on her.

Defence of Civil and Political Liberties

Juries safeguard the liberties of the subject which are of paramount importance in a liberal-democratic political system. In 1985, for example, a British jury rejected the assertion by a judge that the interests of the government and the State were identical, and acquitted the civil servant, Clive Ponting, of an offence under the Official Secrets Act.

TRIAL BY JURY IN BRITAIN

Between 1825 and 1974 there were a number of qualifications needed to serve on a jury, the chief of which was a property requirement – the necessity to be a householder. However, the 1974 Juries Act provided that all persons aged 18–65 whose names were included on the electoral register were eligible to serve. This legislation was designed to broaden the social composition of juries, since former qualifications tended to prevent membership drawn from particular key groups in society, especially women. It did not, however, totally resolve the issue of juries being socially unrepresentative. There are a number of reasons which explain the persistence of this problem. These include non-registration for voting (which, although a legal requirement, is higher among young people and members of ethnic minority groups), and the tendency of certain categories of persons to seek exemption when summoned by the jury officer. Professional and self-employed people are least prepared to give up their time or money to serve as jurors and are thus relatively under-represented on such bodies. Initially the universal agreement of all 12 members of the jury was required to reach a verdict but the 1967 Criminal Justice Act permitted majority verdicts of 10:2 to determine the outcome of a trial. One reason for introducing this reform was to make it more difficult for associates of a defendant to intimidate individual jury members.

Decision-Making by British Juries

It is difficult to accurately assess how juries reach decisions in the UK. The *New Statesman* attempted to scrutinise the operations of the jury which deliberated in the trial of the former leader of the Liberal Party, Jeremy Thorpe, for conspiracy to murder in 1979. Following this, the 1981 Contempt of Court Act prevented further journalistic investigation into the workings of juries, although the Labour government elected in 1997 indicated it would permit research into this field. The key problems which have been identified in the operations of juries are discussed below.

Biases and Prejudices May Influence the Decisions of Juries

Factors such as accent, dress, occupation, and level of articulation may affect the behaviour of juries, while gender and racial prejudice may also undermine the fairness of trial by jury. In cases involving sexual violence, defence lawyers will often seek (through aggressive cross-examination) to reveal details of a female victim's sexual history in the belief this will aid their client's cause. Racism may also undermine the ability of juries to listen dispassionately to a case and then pronounce a verdict based upon an objective assessment of the evidence.

Lack of Legal Training

This may result in jurors' being swayed by factors other than the evidence presented in a trial. In addition to prejudices and biases, these may include body language, the performance of lawyers retained by the defence and prosecution, or irrational considerations in which a juror's emotions form the basis of a decision. Additionally, jurors may lose track of the evidence in lengthy trials. Collective memory, however, may help to offset the shortcomings of individual memory.

Reform of the British Jury System

Factors such as the time and cost of jury trials, coupled with the belief that guilty people are sometimes acquitted because of the problems – identified above – with jury decision-making, have prompted suggestions that the system of trial by jury should be reformed. There are a number of directions which such reform could take.

○ *Reducing the types of offence eligible for trial by jury:* this would be accomplished by increasing the number of offences which can only be tried summarily, in a magistrates' court, thus confining trial by jury to the more serious cases. In 1998, a Home Office consultation paper proposed to abolish the right to trial by jury for around 20 per cent of cases currently heard by Crown Courts. This would result in major financial savings.

○ *Enhancing the ability of jurors to make objective judgements:* this could include permitting jurors to take notes during the trial, enabling jurors to question witnesses, and providing jurors with facilities to see video tapes of the trial and thus replay confusing or forgotten issues.

○ *Streamlining the jury system:* this would provide for trial by a reduced number of persons. During the 1939–45 World War, British juries consisted of seven persons, and six are used in many American States. There are, however, problems associated with such an innovation, which include whether this number of jurors is sufficient to provide an adequate social mix or facilitate robust conversation.

Abolition of the jury system

A more radical reform would be to abolish the system of trial by jury. There are a number of alternatives which might replace it.

○ *Trial by judges or people with professional expertise:* such a system is used in a number of European countries in cases such as fraud in which lay jurors may not understand the complex nature of the evidence.

○ *Trial before several judges:* this is the system currently used in the British Court of Appeal.

○ *Trial before one judge:* this system was introduced in Northern Ireland in 1973 for trials involving 'scheduled offences' (that is, crimes associated with politically motivated violence). Such courts are named *Diplock Courts* after the author of this reform, Lord Diplock. A particular problem is a belief that the high level of guilty verdicts in these courts arise from judges having a bias against acquittal. This perception of unfairness will inevitably

Question

Based on your reading of the above section and supplemented by additional material drawn from jury trials reported in the newspapers or journals, do you believe that the advantages of trial by jury outweigh its disadvantages?

result in the end of this innovation if the 1998 peace settlement proves to be permanent.

The Courts

The main role of the courts is to adjudicate in a dispute between two parties. These may be private citizens who are in dispute with each other. Alternatively, the State may be involved in a case which comes before the courts.

TRIAL PROCEDURE

No two liberal-democratic countries have an identical judicial system. Differences especially exist concerning the conduct of trials.

◆ *The adversarial system:* this system is used in the UK and the USA, the essence of which is that two parties seek to prove their case by countering the arguments put forward by their opponents. The trial is presided over by a judge whose main function is to ensure fair play.

◆ *The inquisitorial system:* this system is used in a number of European countries. Here the gathering of evidence is the responsibility of a magistrate or judge and the main function of the trial is to resolve issues uncovered in the earlier investigation. The judge will actively intervene in the trial in order to arrive at the truth. France, for example, utilises this system.

Civil and Criminal Law

The work of the courts is usually divided into civil and criminal matters:

❍ *Civil law:* this is concerned with the resolution of disagreements in which, typically, one party seeks some form of redress (such as damages) from a second party. Slander is an example of a civil action.

❍ *Criminal law:* this involves activities which have broader social implications and which thus require the State to initiate a prosecution with a view to punishing the offender. Murder is an example of a criminal charge.

In many countries civil and criminal matters are heard in different courts. This is not invariably the case, however. In France, civil and criminal matters are heard in the one court, the *ordre judiciaire*, utilising the same judicial personnel. In the UK, a circuit judge may hear both civil and criminal cases and magistrates' courts perform some civil functions.

The Organisation of the Courts in the UK

The civil and criminal courts in the UK are organised in a hierarchical fashion. This is illustrated in the following diagram.

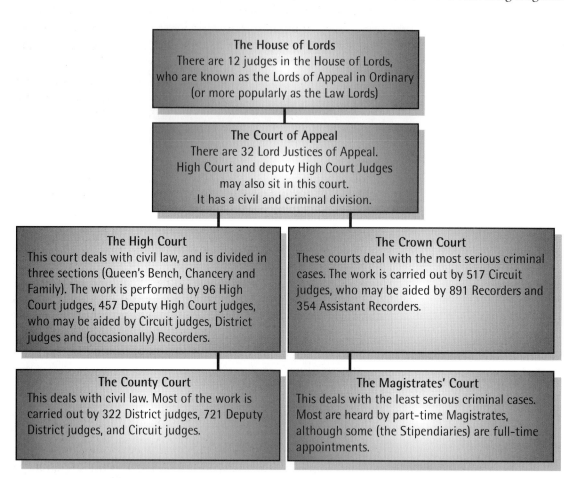

The House of Lords
There are 12 judges in the House of Lords, who are known as the Lords of Appeal in Ordinary (or more popularly as the Law Lords)

The Court of Appeal
There are 32 Lord Justices of Appeal. High Court and deputy High Court Judges may also sit in this court. It has a civil and criminal division.

The High Court
This court deals with civil law, and is divided in three sections (Queen's Bench, Chancery and Family). The work is performed by 96 High Court judges, 457 Deputy High Court judges, who may be aided by Circuit judges, District judges and (occasionally) Recorders.

The Crown Court
These courts deal with the most serious criminal cases. The work is carried out by 517 Circuit judges, who may be aided by 891 Recorders and 354 Assistant Recorders.

The County Court
This deals with civil law. Most of the work is carried out by 322 District judges, 721 Deputy District judges, and Circuit judges.

The Magistrates' Court
This deals with the least serious criminal cases. Most are heard by part-time Magistrates, although some (the Stipendiaries) are full-time appointments.

Minor civil matters may be handled by the small claims procedure which seeks to resolve a dispute without the need to take it to open court. Most civil cases which go to court are heard by county courts, although the High Court of Justice may hear cases in which large sums of money are involved. Appeals against a verdict reached in a county court or the High Court will be heard by the Court of Appeal (Civil Division).

Most criminal cases are tried in magistrates' courts. These courts handle cases in which a verdict can be delivered 'on the spot' and are thus courts of summary (or immediate) jurisdiction. The more serious, carrying heavier sentences, are heard on indictment in crown courts presided over by a judge and making use of a jury. Appeals against the verdicts reached in crown courts are heard by the Court of Appeal (Criminal Division).

The House of Lords is the final court of appeal for both criminal and civil cases. There is no appeal against a decision of the Law Lords, although in December 1998 they agreed to set aside a decision that the former Chilean dictator, General Pinochet, did not have immunity from prosecution and could thus be extradited as requested by the Spanish government. The revelation that one of the judges who was party to this decision, Lord Hoffmann, had links with the human-rights organisation Amnesty International, prompted this unprecedented action, the effect of which was to cause a new hearing in 1999.

Administrative Law

Administrative law is concerned with the relationship between a government and its citizens. In the UK a challenge by a member of the general public to the actions or operations of the executive branch of government may be heard in the courts. The legality of delegated legislation or accusations of abuse of power may be challenged in this manner. Minor issues (such as a dispute arising from a decision taken by a civil servant) may, however, be resolved by a tribunal. Complaints of maladministration (that is an accusation that incorrect procedures were followed to arrive at a decision) may be submitted to the Ombudsman. These issues are discussed more fully in Chapter 23.

THE FRENCH SYSTEM OF ADMINISTRATIVE COURTS

In France, the separate system of administrative courts arose from a belief that the executive branch of government would become subordinate to the judiciary if the ordinary courts were able to review its actions. Administrative courts have exclusive jurisdiction in a wide range of cases covered by public law which involve disagreements between individuals and the State. Such conflicts include allegations of illegal actions undertaken by ministers, civil servants and public bodies.

The French system of administrative courts is headed by the Conseil d'Etat. This is staffed by senior civil servants and is the final court of appeal in disputes between the citizen and the government. Below this is the *cour administrative d'appel*. This court possesses judicial powers alone and hears appeals from the *tribunal administratif*. The latter operates on a regional level and like the *Conseil d'Etat* is an advisory and judicial body.

In other countries, however, a separate court system exists to adjudicate upon such matters. Germany and France have a distinct system of courts concerned with administrative law.

Constitutional Law

In some countries, the courts may be also called upon to adjudicate in disputes arising from the constitution. This work may involve the following activities:

○ *Assessing acts passed by the legislature:* this work seeks to ensure that legislation is in accord with the statement of fundamental law contained in the country's constitution.

○ *Scrutinising actions undertaken by the executive branch:* the executive orders issued by the American President are an example of this activity, which is performed by the Supreme Court.

○ *Determining the constitutionality of actions undertaken by sub-national bodies:* in federal States such work includes scrutiny of the actions of State governments to ensure that they do not exceed their powers as specified in the constitution.

○ *Examining the allocation of responsibilities within and between the institutions of government:* this task is designed to ensure that this division remains as was provided for in the constitution. It is designed to ensure, for example, that the work of one branch or tier of government does not encroach upon the responsibilities allocated elsewhere within the system of government.

If the courts decide that the actions placed before it for examination are in breach of the constitution, these actions may be declared 'unconstitutional'. This has the effect of overturning them, and they are thus rendered 'null and void'.

Judicial Review

The process of scrutinising actions undertaken by the legislature, executive or other tiers of government is termed *judicial review*. The manner whereby this process is performed and the tasks which it involves vary greatly from one country to another.

The USA

Judicial review encompasses the scrutiny of actions undertaken by the legislative and executive branches of government. The process of judicial review is performed by the supreme court which consists of nine judges appointed by the President (subject to the consent of the Senate). Their right to act in this manner was not explicitly written into the Constitution but was asserted in one of its early decisions (that of *Marbury* v. *Madison*) in 1803. The court's intervention occurs when cases are referred to it on appeal either from the highest courts of appeal in the States or from the federal court of appeal. One important consequence of this body's interpretation of the constitution was to establish the civil rights of black Americans during the 1950s and 1960s.

France

The *Conseil Constitutionnel* is responsible for ensuring that decrees and legislation proposed by the government and National Assembly conform to the constitution. This body was instituted in the 1958 constitution. It consists of nine members who are not required to be legally trained judges. Three of these are appointed by the President of France, three by the President of the National Assembly and three by the President of the Senate. They serve for nine years and may not be renominated. Former Presidents of the republic may also serve on this body. Unlike the American supreme court, there are some limitations placed on the jurisdiction of this institution and it further exercises a range of advisory power (including the requirement that it has to be consulted if the President intends to exercise emergency powers). Advice on the constitutionality of bills may also be provided by the *Conseil d'Etat*.

Germany

The Federal Constitutional Court ensures that the constitution is obeyed. This body was established in 1951 and it is staffed by 16 judges. These are nominated by all-party committees and are formally appointed by the Bundesrat and Bundestag. In addition to its ability to declare law unconstitutional it has further involved itself in the process of law-making by suggesting how a law which it has declared to be unconstitutional can be amended in order to comply with the constitution. This court also adjudicates disputes between the federal government and states.

Italy

The task of upholding the constitution is shared between a constitutional court and the President of the Republic. The former's role includes acting as a court of impeachment for the President, Prime Minister and other ministers. The latter's tasks include ensuring that the actions of the executive and legislature conform to the relationship specified in the constitution.

Question

What do you understand by the term 'judicial review'?

Using examples taken from newspapers and journals, illustrate the manner in which this process occurs in the UK.

JUDICIAL REVIEW IN THE UK

Unlike the countries discussed above, the UK lacks a codified constitution. With the exception of commitments associated with its membership of the European Union (the implications of which are discussed in Chapter 18), judicial review in the UK was historically confined to a narrower range of activity. It sought to ensure that the actions undertaken by the executive branch of government were strictly in accordance with the law. Traditionally the courts were unwilling to make wide use of this power, but they did so with increased frequency in the 1990s. Examples of defeats experienced by the Conservative government between 1992 and 1997 are discussed below.

◆ *1995:* the Appeal Court delayed the process of rail privatisation by a decision which hinged on the interpretation of 'minimum standards'.

◆ *1996:* the High Court set aside the Home Secretary's decision to expel the Saudi dissident, Professor Mohammed al-Mas'ari, to Dominica.

◆ *1996:* the High Court (and latterly the Court of Appeal) overturned the Home Secretary's attempt to fix a 15-year minimum term for the child killers of James Bulger.

Decisions of the nature referred to above projected the judiciary forcefully into the political arena but were viewed by the Conservative government as an attack on its ability to govern. Judicial review may also extend to sub-national units of government where a particular desire is to ensure that the activities undertaken by local government do not exceed the powers granted by Parliament. In 1982, for example, the House of Lords overturned the 'cheap fares' policy of the Labour-controlled Greater London Council.

Judicial Interpretation

In theory, the role of judges is to apply the law to the specific issue which comes before them. However, it is often argued that judges go beyond this role and effectively determine the contents of the law. This situation arises as a result of judicial interpretation which may effectively give judges the ability to act as law makers. Judges differ, however, in the principles they apply when interpreting the law. These contrasting views are discussed below.

The Strict Letter of the Law

Some judges rigidly apply the wording of the law to the case which is before them. The judge's 'interpretation' is thus determined according to the strict letter of the law. This tends to promote a conservative approach to judicial interpretation. It suggests that issues which are not contained in a country's law or constitution cannot be inserted into it by judges. Those who subscribe to such a view regard this either as the work of legislators or (when the issue before the court concerns a codified constitution) as a matter which should be responded to by the process of constitutional amendment.

Judicial Activism

Other judges, however, exercise a wider degree of discretion when interpreting the law. This situation may arise for one of the following reasons.

○ *The need to apply the law to changed circumstances:* some judges when faced with a situation which is not strictly covered by existing law or constitutional provision may believe it to be their responsibility to bring the existing law or the constitution up to date. Judicial interpretation may help to ensure that the law reflects changing public sentiments as to what constitutes reasonable conduct.

○ *The need to clarify the law:* a statute or constitutional provision at issue in a case may lack precision or be ambiguous and thus capable of having more than one meaning. The judge will thus be required to give an opinion as to the correct course of action which should be pursued.

In both of these situations judicial interpretation departs from the precise wording of the law or constitution. This is termed judicial activism, which enables a judge to advance beyond the mere administration of the law and, instead, to act in the capacity of a legislator exercising a positive role in policy-making. That is, they advance existing law or create new law through the power which they give themselves to interpret laws and constitutions. Critics of this role argue that judges ought to distinguish between interpreting the law and actually writing it. They assert that judicial interpretation leads judges to perform a role which ought to be carried out by the legislative branch of government or through the process of constitutional amendment.

Judicial activism may be guided by one or other of two principles.

1 Judgement According to the Spirit of the Law

This means that judges reach a verdict based upon what they believe to be compatible with existing law or constitution, rather than with what is precisely contained in them. In reaching their judgement, judges may seek to determine what was in the minds of those who initially drafted the law or constitution and apply this to the case before them.

2 Judgement According to Judges' Views

Some judges may consider it their duty to adjudicate a case according to what they believe *should* be contained in the law or constitution, rather than what actually is there. This is a radical form of judicial activism, implying that judicial judgements of this nature are rooted in the judge's preferences rather than being founded on the law or constitution.

Judicial Activism in the UK

The ability of British judges to act as law makers is influenced by the diverse sources of law.

Interpretation of Statutes

Although the absence of a codified constitution limits the extent of judicial activism in the UK, judges' ability to act as law makers is justified by the need to interpret the law in order to resolve the meaning of words and phrases contained in Acts of Parliament. Michael Zander argued that there were three basic rules governing this form of statutory interpretation.

1 *The 'literal rule'*: here the courts rigorously applied the literal meaning of the words contained in a statute regardless of whether the outcome made sense.

2 *The 'golden rule'*: here the literal meaning of the words in an Act might have been departed from in order to prevent an absurdity. In this case the judge would have looked for alternative meanings conveyed by such words.

3 *The 'mischief rule'*: this encouraged the courts to depart from the precise language of the statute and instead to consider the context within which the act was passed: this may include considering the 'mischief' which arose in common law which the statute was designed to remedy.

Although the literal rule would normally be followed by a judge in determining the outcome of a case, judicial creativity is

Question

Discuss the argument that British judges often act in the role of law makers rather than law enforcers. List TWO benefits and TWO dangers which arise from such a course of action.

facilitated by the application of the golden rule and particularly the mischief rule.

Interpretation of Common Law

Statutes constitute only one source of English law. There is additionally common law which consists of judicial precedent created either by historic custom or the earlier decisions of judges which become binding. Judges are able to exercise creativity in connection with common law which has been said to provide a general warrant for judicial law-making. Judicial creativity arises either because the common law is imprecise or because a judge decides to ignore precedent. Lord Denning was associated with the latter course of action. He held that the prime purpose of the law was to secure justice. Thus in trying a case a judge was entitled to apply his or her own judgement concerning what was the just outcome, regardless of precedent.

The Politics of the Judiciary

The above discussion has argued that the work of judges goes beyond that of merely enforcing the existing law. Their ability to act as law makers highlights the importance of the manner in which they are appointed, and the extent to which they are accountable for their decisions.

Judicial Appointment

This section compares the process of appointing judges in three liberal democracies – the USA, France and the UK. In particular it seeks to discuss the political significance of the appointment process.

Judicial Appointment in the USA

In the USA presidents often seek to promote their political values through the appointments which they make to the federal judicial system, especially to the supreme court. All federal judges and justices of the supreme court are appointed by the President. Enquiries into a candidate's background are initiated on behalf of the chief executive. Following this, however, they are required to be confirmed by the Senate whose Judiciary Committee conducts hearings into a nominee's suitability. Judges of the supreme court serve for life subject to 'good behaviour'. The ability of this body to overrule state and federal legislators and the chief executive influences presidents to appoint judges whose political views closely correspond to their own. For similar reasons, the Senate may pay regard to issues other than professional competence when a nominee comes before them for confirmation.

Some presidents have the opportunity to appoint a large number of federal judges, and others very few. However, when one party has filled the office of president for a number of years, it is likely that the composition of the federal courts will reflect this control. Thus when President Clinton entered office in 1992 he was faced with a conservative supreme court whose personnel had been mainly chosen by previous Republican presidents. They thus had the ability to thwart the President's plans regarding affirmative action and the desegregation of schools, both of which were announced in 1995.

Judicial Appointment in France

The political importance of judicial appointment is especially evident in the *Conseil Constitutionnel*. A specific function of this body is to adjudicate on disputes between the President and Prime Minister, especially concerning legislation. These are most likely to occur in a period of 'cohabitation' when these two officials are drawn from different parties. The appointment of a chairman who is politically sympathetic to one of them may heavily tip the balance of power in his or her favour. In 1995, the then socialist President, François Mitterrand, appointed M. Roland Dumas as president of the *Conseil Constitutionnel*. In 1998, his position was jeopardised by an investigation into an alleged defence contract fraud involving the sale of frigates to Taiwan when he had served as Foreign Minister, 1984–93. If he were forced from office on this issue, the Gaullist President, Jacques Chirac, would be empowered to replace him with a rightwing nominee, thus gaining advantage in the 'cohabitation' struggle with the socialist Prime Minister, Lionel Jospin.

Judicial Appointment in the UK

An important political issue affecting judicial appointment in the UK concerns the social unrepresentiveness of judges. The dominance of white, male, middle-class, public school and Oxbridge-educated persons may serve to undermine the legitimacy of the judicial system to those social groups who feel themselves to be excluded from its composition.

In the UK, judges are appointed by the Lord Chancellor's Department, although selections for the most senior appointments are forwarded to the Prime Minister and are made in the name of the Monarch. A judge will initially be appointed at the bottom end of the judicial hierarchy (that is, as district court judge or as an assistant recorder). In securing appointment it is necessary for the applicant to have the requisite number of years' experience as either a barrister or a solicitor in the court for which appointment is sought. This is laid down in the 1990 Courts and Legal Services Act. Additionally, the Lord Chancellor's Department applies three guiding principles in the procedure for selecting judges.

1   *Appointment on merit:* this means that appointment disregards factors such as ethnic origin, gender, marital status, sexual orientation, political affiliation, religion or disability.

2   *'Soundings':* the Lord Chancellor's Department asks serving members of the judiciary for their views on the candidate's suitability and past performance. This aspect of the appointment process in particular has been criticised for its tendency to promote an 'old boys' network', thereby ensuring a socially unrepresentative and conservative judiciary.

3   *Probation:* a candidate for full-time judicial office must first serve in a part-time capacity (either as an assistant district court judge or an assistant recorder) in order for that person's competence and suitability to be fully established.

Judicial Accountability

In a liberal-democratic political system, members of the legislative and executive branches of government (who in theory are charged with initiating and carrying out legislation) are accountable for their actions. Ultimately they rely on public support to enter or remain in public office. Judges, however, are usually insulated from any direct form of political accountability for their actions, even when these have a fundamental bearing on political affairs. They are usually unelected (although this method of appointment does apply in some American States) and, once appointed, enjoy security of tenure.

○ *The UK:* here senior judges can be removed only by an address on the part of both Houses of Parliament to the Queen.

○ *Ireland:* here judges can be dismissed only for misbehaviour and incapacity, and to do this requires resolutions from both houses of Parliament (the Dail and the Seanad). Additionally, an Irish judge's remuneration cannot be reduced during that official's term of office.

While this situation may aid the judges to operate independently of the government, it may mean they are insufficiently accountable for the actions they undertake whilst in office.

COMPOSITION OF THE JUDICIARY

The soundings system used to appoint members of the judiciary has resulted in the senior judiciary being drawn from markedly similar backgrounds. The *Guardian* on 5 August 1998 reported that:

'there are no women among the law lords, only one among the 35 Appeal Court judges, and seven among the 97 High Court Judges. Ethnic minorities are completely absent from the higher judiciary. There are no black full-time judges at any level, and only four (mainly Asian) ethnic minority circuit judges out of 558.'

Women are underrepresented in the judiciary.

Formal Controls

These include the jury system (which has been discussed above), and the ability to offset decisions made by the courts through a revision to the law or an amendment to the constitution. The ability of politicians to enact legislation governing the conduct and practices of the criminal justice system may help to offset judicial biases. As has been discussed above, in the UK, for example, the 1992–97 Conservative government sought to restrict the autonomy of judges in sentencing policy: the 1997 Crime (Sentencing) Act thus introduced mandatory sentences for certain types of offence, which judges were routinely meant to follow.

Informal Controls

Additionally, judges may be subject to informal pressures. There is the important informal sanction of media publicity with episodes when it is felt that judges have 'got it wrong'.

In particular, judges may be influenced by a consideration of what is acceptable to the public at large and may seek to ensure that their judgements are in accord with the prevailing political consensus. It has been argued that the American supreme court watches the election returns. This is of particular importance when the courts are required to determine a politically emotive issue, and suggests that public and political opinion may play a role in determining judicial decisions. Courts possess authority rather than power. Compliance to their decisions (for example by lower-level courts or by public officials) is thus more likely when these are supported by a degree of political or public approval. But it may not always be a straightforward matter to operate in this fashion. Contentious issues will divide the public and make it impossible for the judiciary to avoid political controversy.

Judges and the State

Judges are depicted as both objective and impartial. For these reasons they are often selected by governments to conduct enquiries into contentious issues of public policy. The extent to which it is accepted, however, that the State, law and hence the work of judges is neutral is much dependent on a person's own political viewpoint. A very broad division of opinion separates what might be labelled 'liberal' and 'Marxist' opinion on this subject.

JUDICIAL NEUTRALITY?

Liberal Analysis

Liberal analysis suggests that the State is neutral. That is, it has no interest in defending and advancing the views held by the majority of its citizens. It follows from this, therefore, that the law also seeks to embody the common perception of right and wrong, and that in enforcing the law judges merely reinforce such popular attitudes.

Marxist Analysis

Marxist analysis asserts that the State is not impartial but, rather, seeks to defend and advance the interests of those who hold economic power within society. The law, therefore, is not neutral but seeks to perpetuate the unequal property relationships which exist within society. Thus judges, when enforcing the law, are not acting in the interests of all citizens but perpetuating the inequalities which underpin it. The Marxist view that the operations of the State and the content of the law exist to serve the interests of the ruling class highlights the problem of securing popular consent for both. They assert this is achieved through the ideological apparatus of the State which proclaims what Marxists regard as the 'myths' of the neutrality of the law and the impartiality of judges.

Judges and the State: a Case Study of the UK

Judges constitute a key aspect of the machinery of government in any political system. They will regard the preservation of that system of government to be of paramount importance. This suggests that those whose actions pose fundamental challenges to the State or the values which underpin it cannot receive impartial treatment by judges. This assertion is allegedly borne out in the definition which judges accord to the term 'public interest', the upholding of which is an essential yardstick governing judicial behaviour.

Griffith, a neo-Marxist, asserted that judges had acquired a 'strikingly homogeneous collection of attitudes, beliefs and principles' as to what the public interest consists of. This was based on their common experiences derived from education, training and pursuit of the profession of barrister. The perception that all judges adhered to the view that the public interest embraced 'the interests of the State (including its moral welfare) . . . the preservation of law and order; and . . . the promotion of certain political views normally associated with the Conservative Party' led him to conclude that it was demonstrable that on every major social issue which has gone before the courts during the last 30 years – concerning industrial relations, political protest, race relations, government secrecy, police powers, moral behaviour – the judges supported the conventional, established and settled interests.

However, the Marxist view has been challenged by what is termed the 'pluralist' position. This disputes the Marxist perception that the actions of judges are characterised by a sense of uniformity of approach. The frequent occurrence of clashes between the Court of Appeal and the House of Lords suggested there was no single conception of public interest, and such a view held that, while most judges are conservative, there were elements of independence and variety to be found amongst them.

Iraqgate

The absence of a consistent direction pursued by judicial decisions can be illustrated by two trials in the 'Iraqgate' affair (involving the sale of arms to Iraq by British companies), a common feature of which was the attempt by the government to utilise Public Immunity Certificates to withhold material from the defence on the grounds that this would prejudice national security. The trial judge had the ability to agree with this suppression of evidence or overturn it.

In the first of these cases, involving the firm Ordtec in 1992, the trial judge agreed with the government's actions. Following plea bargaining, two persons were given suspended sentences, and one was fined in connection with trying to export a shell-fuse assembly line to Iraq. In the second case, involving Matrix-Churchill, the judge overruled the government and the trial quickly collapsed in 1992. Whether the motive for the inconsistency between two very similar trials illustrated the extent of judicial diversity or was designed to advance the myth of judicial impartiality is ultimately dependent on a political interpretation of the nature of the State, the purpose of law and the function performed by the judiciary.

Question

Assess the arguments for and against the view that 'the judiciary constantly uphold the interests of the State.'

Making use of newspapers which report court proceedings, compile a file of cases which either support or disprove this view.

Judges and Government Policy

The defence of *state* interests needs to be differentiated from the defence of *government* interests. It is open to debate as to whether the judiciary display a relatively consistent line in connection with the defence of the State. However, their actions may be less constant when a matter which is referred to them for adjudication has significance for the policy of the government but is not in the interests of the State. It has been observed above that the willingness of the judiciary to act independently of the executive branch of government in the latter circumstances was particularly obvious for much of the 1990s when the courts regularly utilised the process of judicial review to overturn actions undertaken by Conservative governments.

Further Reading

The constitutional position and role performed by judges is discussed in a number of key works which include **John Griffith**, *The Politics of the Judiciary* (London: Fontana Press, 1991, 4th edition).

Robert Stevens, *The Independence of the Judiciary* (Oxford: Clarendon, 1997).

Richard Hodder-Williams, *Judges and Politics in the Contemporary Age* (London: Bowerdean, 1996) provides a comparative discussion based on material from the UK and the USA.

The law-making function of the judiciary is evaluated in works which include **Michael Zander**, *The Law Making Process* (London: Butterworths, 1994, 4th edition).

Dianne Woodhouse, 'Politicians and the Judiciary: A Changing Relationship', *Parliamentary Affairs*, Volume 48, Number 3, July 1995, specifically examines the process of judicial review in the UK.

Chapter Sixteen | Sub-National Government

The aims of this chapter are:

> 1 To define the term 'sub-national government'.
>
> 2 To analyse the key distinctions which exist between federal and unitary political structures and confederations.
>
> 3 To evaluate the strengths and weaknesses of federal political structures.
>
> 4 To assess the role played by regional bodies in states with unitary political structures.
>
> 5 To analyse the pace of constitutional reform affecting Scotland and Wales.

Definition and Forms of Sub-National Governments

A major role performed by government is to provide services for the benefit of the general public. Many of these are provided by national government. However, others are controlled and administered by bodies covering only part of a particular country, and are termed 'sub-national government'. There are a wide variety of these, but this chapter will confine attention to State and regional authorities.

Unitary and Federal Political Structures

Sub-national government is subject to considerable variation. A key distinction concerns the autonomy which such units enjoy.

Unitary Structures

Political power is centralised in the hands of the national government in States with unitary political structures. Countries which include the United Kingdom, Sweden and France possess such arrangements. However, such States often possess a unit of government which is intermediate between national and local government. These are usually regional bodies which provide services for a relatively wide geographic area whose inhabitants share some form of common identity such as language, culture or race. Regional authorities vary according to the autonomy which they possess: some exercise power which is devolved from national government, thus giving them a wide degree of control over such delegated responsibilities, while others merely function as administrative bodies whose role is to provide regional services according to guidelines laid down by national government.

Federal Structures

Federal political structures are characterised by the division of power (or sovereignty) between the national (or federal) government and the constituent states. Examples of this include Germany, Australia and the United States of America. The division of responsibilities is provided for in a single source, usually a written constitution, which allocates specific functions to each sphere of government. Each enjoys autonomy in its own area of jurisdiction, which means that one may not intrude into the operations of the other. There may also be functions which are exercised jointly by both tiers of government.

Confederations

A confederal political structure bears some relationship to a federal structure. The key difference concerns the powers of the national government. In a confederation, the national government has extremely limited powers relative to the responsibilities of State governments, thus making for a weak central authority. A particular feature of a confederation is that the national government has no direct powers over citizens: functions such as taxation and law enforcement are exercised by the constituent governments.

A confederal system of government lacking an effective executive branch existed in America between 1781 and 1788. The southern States of America which seceded in the Civil War also had this form of government between 1861 and 1865. The Commonwealth of Independent States (which was established in 1991 following the collapse of the Soviet Union) is a recent such creation.

Local Government

In states with unitary and federal political structures a range of services are provided by subordinate authorities, termed 'local government'. The scope of their activities and extent of their autonomy is subject to wide variation. In many Western European and Scandinavian countries local government is created by national constitutional enactment, and in the USA is provided for in state constitutions. In countries which include France, Italy, Sweden and Denmark, local government has the ability to perform any function unless expressly forbidden to do so by law. This is termed 'general competence'. In the UK and Ireland, however, local government has no constitutional status. Its existence is derived from legislation and it may only perform those functions which are expressly allocated by law passed by parliament. This situation tends to vastly curtail the autonomy which is exercised by local authorities in these two countries, although in the UK discretionary powers provide such bodies with a significant degree of operational and innovatory freedom.

Local government is considered in more detail in Chapter 17.

Question

Distinguish between unitary and federal political structures.

To do this you should:

- ○ Define a unitary political structure in your own words.

- ○ Outline in your own words the main characteristics of a federal political structure.

- ○ Discuss TWO main differences between these two types of political structure.

Federal Political Structures

The division of power between a national government and constituent units such as states or provinces is the essence of a federal political structure. This section analyses this political arrangement in detail.

Advantages of Federal Political Structures

There are a number of advantages associated with a federal political structure.

Aids the Relationship Between the Government and its Citizens

Federalism was historically viewed as a safeguard against the overbearing power of a strong, central government. In large countries it breaks down the remoteness which would otherwise occur if government were provided by a distant national authority. Government is thus brought closer to the people, who are provided with the means to participate through the process of voting or through their involvement with locally-orientated pressure groups.

Facilitates Diversity in One Country

New right ideology emphasises the benefits which are based upon the diversity with which a federal system of government may be associated. Variations within one country in matters such as taxation or the level of services may prove attractive to citizens or to commercial organisations who are encouraged to move from one part of the country to another to benefit themselves. Diversity may thus encourage competition between States to attract resources such as people and industry.

Maintains National Unity

The autonomy possessed by State governments in States with federal political structures may benefit nations whose existence is threatened by significant internal divisions. Provided that a nation secures recognisable political or economic benefits to all of its citizens, groups with divergent interests may be encouraged to remain within the one State when the power possessed by the national government is limited to allow most functions to be provided by governments controlled by local people. Federalism thus empowers localities to run most aspects of their affairs in accordance with the wishes of the people who reside there. It may thus contribute towards stability in States threatened by separatist tendencies. Belgium granted considerable powers of self-government to its Flemish and Walloon communities within the confines of a federation, in order to prevent the break-up of the State along linguistic lines. For similar reasons a wide degree of autonomy has been granted to the Canadian province of Quebec.

FEDERALISM IN CANADA

Canada consists of a federation of ten provinces and two territories. Strong separatist forces exist in the province of Quebec. This is underlaid by its French language and culture. In an attempt to retain national unity, Canada's federal political system has provided Quebec with considerable powers of self-government, especially in connection with the official use of French. However, this situation has not been to the satisfaction of many Quebeckers who desire separation. This would enable Quebec to negotiate future relations with the remainder of Canada on its own terms. In 1995, a referendum was held on the issue of separation. Quebeckers rejected it by the narrowest of margins. In 1998, the Canadian supreme court ruled that the province could not secede unless the federal government gave its consent, although it ruled that the federal authorities would have a duty to conduct

> negotiations about secession if a majority of Quebeckers supported independence in a fair referendum.
>
> The existing level of self-government contributed to the rejection of separation: the continued unity of the nation may depend on the national government redefining its relations with Quebec through provisions such as decentralisation and power-sharing which would provide an enhanced degree of autonomy within a federal state. The appeal of this course of action was evidenced in the 1998 provincial elections in which the secessionist Parti Québécois lost ground.

Disadvantages of Federal Political Structures

There are, however, problems associated with federal political structures. The main ones are discussed below.

Fragments Government

Government is fragmented in states with federal political structures. Diverse standards of service provision within a single country are not necessarily desirable, and a minority may be given the means to frustrate the will of the majority. The progress of civil rights in the USA has been impeded by the ability of southern State governments to resist or to slow down the implementation of such legislation. Some of these problems may, however, be partially or wholly overcome. In the USA, for example, the existence of intergovernmental bureaucracies, composed of paid officials operating at all levels of government, has served to promote common approaches to problems pursued by all tiers of government.

A Tendency for the Power of National Governments to Become Enhanced

A particular difficulty with federalism concerns the distribution of power between the national and constituent governments. This division is typically provided for in the constitution, and disputes between the two tiers of government are arbitrated by a constitutional court. However, a tendency for the power of national governments to be enhanced at the expense of states has been observed in many federal countries. In the USA, this alteration to the fundamental nature of federalism has partly arisen from the willingness of the supreme court to interpret the constitution in a manner which is favourable towards national governments' playing an increased role in economic and social policies. A particular consequence has been an increased reliance by the States on revenue provided by national government.

Financial aid to State governments may erode the independence of the latter. This became a particular issue in Germany following unification, since the States which comprised the former country of East Germany were heavily dependent on federal financial support. Such money may be given to States largely to use as they please (as occurs in Germany, and was the case with President Nixon's General Revenue Sharing policy in the USA), or it may be attached to stringent conditions which States have to meet (as occurred in America under President Reagan). The States' freedom of action may also be limited by requirements imposed by the national government which are designed to enforce conformity and set minimum standards of service provision. In the USA, pre-emption is an example of the latter. This imposes a legal requirement on States to meet certain minimum standards or to provide stipulated services.

Nonetheless, States continue to play an important role in the economic and social life of a federal country. In the USA, for example, the ability of the States to raise some of their own revenue and their role as implementators of public policy may enhance their image as dynamic institutions, even if they are subject to relatively strong central control.

FEDERALISM IN THE USA

America pioneered federalism. Its subsequent history suggests that the division of power within such a political structure is not fixed but, rather, is fluid and adaptable to changed political and economic circumstances. It has progressed through the following stages.

◆ *Dual federalism:* this emphasised central and State governments' exercising sovereignty in their own spheres of activity. This view was based upon the Tenth Amendment to the Constitution which reserved to the States all powers not specifically delegated to the federal government in the constitution.

◆ *Cooperative federalism:* this emerged after 1933 when States were required to act in a partnership with the national government and implement programmes to alleviate the effects of the Depression, for which they received financial aid. The grant in aid provided by the federal government was the main mechanism to secure such coordinated action.

◆ *Creative and new federalism:* this enhanced the role of local government as a third partner in solving problems of national importance. Creative federalism was associated with President Johnson (1963–69), and new federalism with Presidents Nixon (1969–74) and Ford (1974–77).

Question

List TWO arguments in favour of and TWO arguments against the replacement of the UK's unitary political structure with a federal one.

◆ *'Coercive federalism'*: President Reagan (1981–89) sought State and local compliance to federal policies through methods such as increasing the mandatory duties imposed on them, and granting federal aid to persons rather than localities. Although increased use was made of block grants to increase the discretion of State and local officials, the overall approach of Reagan and his successor, President Bush (1989–93), led to conflict between federal and State governments.

Regional Machinery of Government

States with unitary political structures are often accused of being centralised: power resides in the capital city, and citizens living in areas which are geographically distant from this area may feel neglected by a government which they regard as remote. Some unitary states, therefore, have utilised regional apparatuses to offset the disadvantages which are sometimes perceived in a centralised state. This involves a state being divided into a number of smaller areas within which certain tasks of government can be discharged. The role and composition of regional machinery is variable, and many different forms may be used even in one state. The main varieties of regional machinery are considered below.

Advisory

Regional machinery may be purely advisory. It can be utilised as a consultative mechanism to provide for overall government planning of particular functions, or it might be established by individual government departments to aid the flow of information between that department and citizens living in each region. This may enable central government to adjust the operations of a policy to suit the particular requirements of a region and its inhabitants, or it may be used to provide advice on government policies to people or public authorities residing or operating there. Such machinery typically includes civil servants and possesses no power other than the ability to act as a vehicle for the two-way process of communication between government and the governed.

Coordination

Regional machinery may seek to coordinate the work of government on a sub-national level. This may involve attempts to ensure that government departments, quangos, local authorities, and voluntary agencies all work towards a common objective, and to guard against the possibility that the activities of one agency conflict with the objectives of another. One task of the regional machinery introduced by the Labour government after the 1964 General Election was to secure a coordinated approach to achieve the development of the region and make the best use of its resources. This machinery consisted of regional planning boards and regional economic planning councils. The boards (with the advice of the councils) were responsible for drawing up a regional economic plan and for coordinating the work of various ministries in its execution.

REGIONAL ECONOMIC POLICY IN THE UK

The goal of regional economic growth required a degree of coordination at the centre of government. This was provided for through regional economic policy, which originated in the 1930s to provide aid selectively to those regions experiencing high levels of unemployment. This policy was developed in the postwar period by a 'carrot and stick' approach which was designed to persuade firms to locate in economically depressed regions (by giving them financial inducements), and to deter them from moving to the relatively prosperous South East or Midlands (through the use of disincentives in the form of Industrial Development Certificates and Office Development Permits). Rising unemployment through the 1970s questioned the overall effectiveness of regional policy, and it was drastically curtailed by Conservative governments in the 1980s whose philosophy was to let the operations of the market, not the activities of the State, remedy regional imbalances.

Administrative and Governmental

A region may alternatively provide the geographic unit around which services are administered. There are many varieties of regional machinery discharging administrative or governmental functions.

❍ *Discharging individual services:* in Ireland, for example, health services have been provided by Area Health Boards since 1971.

❍ *Coordinating several governmental functions:* in the UK (before the implementation of legislation enacted in 1998 to establish the Scottish Parliament and Welsh Assembly), the Scottish and Welsh Offices were responsible for a range of services in these two countries which were performed by individual government departments in England. Those who administer services in this fashion may possess some discretion to tailor them to address specific regional needs or requirements.

○ *Providing government:* regional machinery may be given some degree of power. This will often be exercised by representatives elected at regional level who then discharge a range of services over which they possess partial or total control. Scottish local government introduced a regional tier in 1975, and the Labour government's enactment of legislation in 1998 to provide for 8 Regional Development Agencies could pave the way for regional government in the UK. This could occur if these regions are given a guaranteed status in Parliament. This might be achieved either by providing places for regional representation in a reformed House of Lords or by establishing standing committees in the House of Commons. These could comprise MPs for each region, and their role would be to develop provincial policy.

STRUCTURE OF SCOTTISH LOCAL GOVERNMENT

The 1973 Local Government (Scotland) Act (which was implemented in 1975) provided for a regional dimension to the structure of local government. Responsibilities were shared between regional and district councils, save in the most remote areas where island councils carried out the entire range of local government functions.

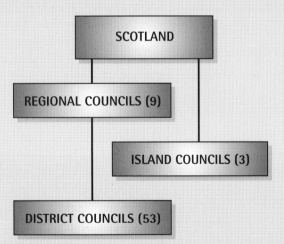

The structure of Scottish local government, 1975–96.

Island Councils were single-tier structures: elsewhere in Scotland a two-tier system of local government operated. Provision was also made in the legislation for the creation of community councils.

Particular criticism was levelled at the regional tier, which was accused of being remote, inefficient, and varying too greatly in terms of area, population and resources. Accordingly (in line with other Conservative reforms to local government in the 1990s) the entire structure contained in the 1973 Act was scrapped by the provisions of the 1994 Local Government (Scotland) Act. It was replaced by 25 unitary (that is, one-tier) local authorities. This new structure was introduced in 1996.

Regional Government in Europe

The following States possess unitary political structures which include a regional dimension.

France

In 1973, 22 regional councils were established for mainland France, and four for its territories overseas. They were initially indirectly elected advisory bodies whose role was primarily concerned with economic planning. Since 1986 they have been directly elected.

Italy

Italy is divided into 20 regions which vary greatly in terms of size. Five of them (Sicily, Sardinia, Trentino-Alto Adige, Friuli-Venezie Giulia and Valle d'Aosta) have a special status and enjoy a greater degree of autonomy. Each region has a popularly elected council, and since the mid–1970s increasing powers have been devolved from central government to the regions.

Spain

Regional government may possess sufficient power to alter the nature of a unitary political structure into one that approximates a federal one. This degree of power may be important in enabling national government and strong regional affiliations to be reconciled. This is the case in Spain and may be illustrated by the example of the regional government of Cataluña (Catalonia) promoting the use of their language (Catalan) in that area.

In 1979, 17 regions (or 'autonomous communities') were set up, each with an assembly (elected by the party list form of proportional representation), and a president (elected by the assembly). The 1978 constitution made Castilian the pre-eminent language in Spain but at the same time also recognised others, leaving regional parliaments with the ability to determine the balance. In 1983, the regional parliament in Catalonia decreed the mandatory use of Catalan in regional government. In 1998, a law was proposed to require that 50 per cent of new films shown in Catalonia should use this language,

Question

Using TWO examples drawn from the area in which you live, indicate the importance of regional machinery in the British political structure.

and that private radio stations operating there should broadcast half of their output in that language.

In March 1996, the Conservative Party led by José Maria Anzar formed a minority government which relied on support in parliament from regional parties from Catalonia, the Basque country and the Canary Islands. This resulted in the speeding up of proposals to transfer powers to regional governments, especially in connection with economic affairs.

The 'Home Rule' Debate in Scotland and Wales

The Contemporary Political Importance of Nationalism

Sovereignty is often associated with nationalism. Postwar history contains numerous examples of national identity being the driving force of movements which seek the establishment of self-governing states. Nationalism creates feelings of patriotism, and inspired independence movements in African countries directed against European colonial powers. In Latin America, it was the main force behind anti-American movements in many countries, including Cuba and Nicaragua. More recently it dominated events in the former country of Yugoslavia in which nationalism was the justification for 'ethnic cleansing'. The desire to establish a self-governing state has considerable influence on the contemporary politics of Canada and Spain. Here national minorities (the Quebeckers, Catalans and Basques) desire self-government.

In the UK the case for Scottish and Welsh home rule has been vocally expressed since the late 1960s. In the following section the progress of this demand is discussed. Before doing so, however, it is important to differentiate between three terms which have arisen in connection with this debate.

❍ *Devolution:* this involves the transfer of power from a superior to an inferior political authority. The dominance of the former is generally exhibited through its ability to reform or take away the power which it has bestowed.

❍ *Federalism:* this necessitates a division of power between central and sub-national governments. The existence of the latter and the general range of powers they possess is usually embodied in a codified constitution.

❍ *Home rule:* this requires the break up of a nation into a number of sovereign states, each exercising total control over their internal and external affairs. This demand is usually based on the existence of a national identity.

Scottish Home Rule

Brief History

Scotland has been part of the United Kingdom since the 1707 Act of Union, although its government was characterised by a number of key differences from England and Wales, most notably in the operations of the criminal justice system. The assertion that Scotland has a distinct national identity is put forward in support of the demand for total control over domestic and internal affairs. This demand is articulated by the Scottish National Party.

Home rule has been traditionally justified by the argument that the Westminster Parliament neglects the special interests and problems faced by the Scots. The Scottish Office, headed by the Scottish Secretary, has had responsibility since 1885 for coordinating a wide range of policy areas in Scotland but such an arrangement lacked any form of accountability to Scots people which had once been provided by a separate Scottish parliament. Sentiments in favour of home rule were reinforced during the 1970s by the discovery and development of oil around the Scottish coast. The fact that some countries within the European Union have a smaller population than Scotland has further strengthened the SNP's demands for an independent Scotland within Europe. This would provide the country with access to world markets, while developments in communications have boosted Scotland's ability to attract investment. Between 1979 and 1997 Scotland's distinct political identity was displayed by the overwhelming support given to the Labour Party during a period when English politics was dominated by the Conservatives. Following the 1997 General Election, none of Scotland's 72 MPs were drawn from this Party.

Welsh Home Rule

Welsh national feeling has traditionally been weaker than Scottish nationalism. England and Wales have a longer history of integrated government: the last Welsh Parliament met in 1404, and the Act of Union between the two countries was passed in 1536. Unlike in Scotland, Welsh nationalism is not fuelled by a desire to re-establish a national Parliament as a symbol of national identity. Welsh nationalism is primarily based on culture and language and was particularly identified with the Welsh Language Movement in the 1970s. These factors have proved to be divisive forces in the postwar period since Wales contains large numbers of English people who have migrated there, and many others (especially in South Wales) are not

Welsh-speaking. The support for Welsh nationalism is thus primarily confined to North and Mid Wales, and in 1997 Plaid Cymru secured the return of 4 of Wales's 32 MPs. In the 1979 referendum vote, Welsh people voted against the proposed arrangements by the margin of 4:1.

The Views of the UK's Main Political Parties

The views of the UK's major political parties towards Scottish nationalism are briefly discussed below.

❍ *The Conservative Party:* this is pledged to defend the constitutional status quo and has displayed the least interest in fundamental constitutional reform. However, it has occasionally supported some measure of adjustment to the Parliamentary committee system which reviews Scottish affairs.

❍ *The Liberal Democrats:* they support a federal system of government which would give the Scots a considerable degree of control over the administration of their domestic affairs, but with issues such as the economy and defence being determined by a federal parliament.

❍ *The Labour Party:* the problem for the Labour Party was that any concession towards home rule might reduce the number of Scottish MPs elected to Westminster. A significant reduction in their numbers would make it more difficult to secure the election of a Labour government. To retain the status quo at Westminster would enable Scottish and Welsh MPs to vote on English affairs but not vice versa, a matter referred to as the 'West Lothian question'.

Scotland and Wales in the 1970s

The main developments which took place in this period were as follows.

❍ *1973:* the Royal Commission on the Constitution reported: it made recommendations for legislative assemblies to be set up in Scotland and Wales, funded by an independent exchequer board. The assemblies would be at liberty to decide how to spend the global sums they were allocated.

❍ *1975:* a White Paper (*Our Changing Democracy – Devolution to Scotland and Wales*) proposed elected assemblies for both countries, financed by a block grant. The actions of these bodies would be subject to veto by the respective Secretaries of State who would further exercise responsibility for a wide range of policy, including economic planning and industrial promotion, and agriculture and fisheries.

○ *1978:* the Scotland and Wales Acts were passed: these stipulated that the devolution proposals would be put to a referendum, and, to be implemented, 40 per cent of the registered electorates in each country would be required to vote 'yes': an abstention was effectively a 'no' vote. The referendums held in 1979 failed to secure this level of support with only 32.9 per cent of Scots voting in favour. The proposals were thus abandoned.

Constitutional Reform in Scotland and Wales

This section analyses the progress of constitutional reform in the 1990s, culminating with two pieces of legislation which established a Scottish Parliament and Welsh Assembly in 1998.

Political Developments Affecting Scotland and Wales 1992–97

The Scottish National Party

The level of support for the Scottish National Party since the 1992 General Election prompted fresh initiatives from the major political Parties. The SNP proposed the establishment of a Scottish Parliament elected by a mixture of the first-past-the-post system and the Additional Member System, with an elected Chancellor as its presiding officer. This body would govern an independent Scotland, and links with England, Wales and Northern Ireland would be retained through an organisation entitled the 'Association of States of the British Isles'.

The Scottish Labour Party and Liberal Democrats

The Scottish Labour Party and Liberal Democrats have cooperated since 1989 in the operations of the Scottish Constitutional Convention which recognised the principle that Scots people had the right to determine the structure of their own government. In 1995, these two Parties announced proposals under the auspices of the Convention which involved a Scottish Parliament elected for a fixed term by a method which was designed to add an element of proportionality to the first-past-the-post system. This parliament would elect a chief minister and possess limited powers to vary the UK rate of income tax. It would be responsible for policies which are currently the responsibility of the Scottish Office.

The Conservative Party

In 1993, the then Conservative government's White Paper, *Scotland in the Union*, suggested amended provision for the consideration of Scottish affairs at Westminster. In 1995, proposals were announced to increase the powers of Scottish MPs in this area of activity. Scottish Bills would normally be referred to the Scottish Grand Committee for their second and third reading stages, and ministers would be required to attend meetings of that committee to explain the government's Scottish policies. A special standing committee, meeting in Scotland, would be established. This would listen to evidence related to Scottish legislation undergoing its committee stage. Enhanced powers for Scottish local authorities were also put forward.

The Labour Government and Scotland and Wales After 1997

The Labour government elected in 1997 pushed ahead with proposals for constitutional reform in these countries. A White Paper was published in July 1997 which offered the people of Scotland and Wales separate referendums on the government's proposals.

❍ *Scotland:* people in Scotland were asked to approve the establishment of a Scottish Parliament, and also to determine whether it should have the ability to raise some of its own finances by varying the standard rate of income tax by 3p (the so-called 'tartan tax').

❍ *Wales:* Welsh people were asked to endorse the proposal to establish a Welsh Assembly: this body would have no ability to raise any of its own expenditure.

A significant feature of the 1997 referendum campaign was the support for a 'yes' vote by the Scottish National Party which had traditionally opposed devolution as an inadequate dilution of its policy of home rule. It wanted 'independence or nothing'. However, in 1997 this Party perceived that a Scottish parliament could subsequently be developed into outright independence. Later, in mid-1998 (when opinion polls suggested that it would be the biggest Party in the new Parliament), the SNP promised an immediate referendum on independence following the 1999 elections.

RESULTS OF THE SEPTEMBER 1997 REFERENDUMS

Scotland: 1,775,975 (74.3 per cent) voted in favour of a Parliament
614,400 (25.7 per cent) voted against this proposal
(A lower figure than the first, 63.5 per cent, voted in favour of the 'tartan tax'.)
60.3 per cent turned out to vote

> Wales: 559,419 (50.3 per cent) voted in favour of an Assembly
> 552,698 (49.7 per cent) voted against this proposal
> 51.3 per cent turned out to vote
>
> The Scottish referendum was held one week earlier than the Welsh one.
>
> Popular support for the government's programme resulted in the publication of two pieces of legislation in December of that year, the contents of which are discussed below.

Scotland

The government's legislation proposed a system of devolution whose main features were as follows.

○ *A Scottish legislature:* a Scottish Parliament of 129 members would be created, serving a fixed term of four years. This body would have power to make laws on all domestic matters including health, education and training, law and home affairs, economic development and transport, local government, the environment, agriculture, fisheries and forestry, and sports and the arts.

○ *Finance:* the Scottish parliament would be financed by the Scottish block grant (which in 1997 was £14.3 billion), supplemented by the 'tartan tax' applied to all who lived in Scotland for more than half of the year. It was estimated that the revenue from the latter in 1998 would be £450 million.

○ *A Scottish executive:* the Monarch would appoint a First Minister for Scotland, and receive that person's resignation. The First Minister would initially be selected by the Members of the Scottish Parliament (MSPs), and the role of the Monarch would be to ratify this choice.

○ *The European Union:* the Scottish Parliament would be able to move at its own pace to legislate on the implementation of European laws. However, Scottish ministers and officials would be only able to participate in the Council of Ministers' meetings as part of the UK delegation.

○ *Reserve powers:* a wide range of matters (including the UK constitution, foreign affairs, fiscal, economic and monetary policy, defence and national security, medical ethics, social security and employment) would be reserved to the Westminster Parliament. Additionally, the Scottish Secretary would have powers to overrule the Scottish Parliament and halt legislation believed to be inappropriate, and to ensure that the UK's international treaties were implemented in Scotland.

❍ *Scottish representation at Westminster:* the legislation repealed the requirement (currently provided for in 1986 legislation) regarding the minimum number of Scottish MPs at Westminster.

Elections to the Scottish Parliament were to take place in 1999. As is discussed in Chapter 4, the Additional Member System would be used for these elections. It was originally intended that this body would sit for the first time in the year 2000. In 1998, however, the Scottish Secretary, Donald Dewar, suggested that this body might meet nearer to the date of the elections.

Wales

The government's proposals for Wales were different in a number of key respects from those for Scotland. It proposed to establish an Assembly of 60 persons, elected by the Additional Member System which is discussed in Chapter 4. Powers currently administered by the Welsh Office would be transferred to this new body, thereby subjecting them to accountability. The Assembly would possess no law-making or independent tax-raising powers, and would remain totally reliant on the block grant (which in 1997 totalled £6.9 billion). This provided for a system which democratised existing administrative arrangements rather than introducing devolution.

Question

Compile your own information on the operations of EITHER the Scottish Parliament OR the Welsh Assembly. In doing so you should consider:

❍ the manner in which the executive and legislative branches of government are constructed

❍ the powers possessed by these new bodies

❍ the nature of the electoral system used to elect members to these bodies

❍ the outcome of the 1999 elections.

Further Reading

A historical account of the progress of devolution in Northern Ireland, Scotland and Wales is provided by **Vernon Bogdanor**, *Devolution* (Oxford: Oxford University Press, 1979).

Also, **Tom Nairn**, *The Break Up of Britain: Crisis and Neo-Nationalism* (London: NLB, 1977).

Federalism in the USA is discussed in general books on American government. Examples include the chapter by **John Kincaid** in **Gillian Peele**, **Christopher Bailey**, **Bruce Cain** and **Guy Peters** (editors), *Developments in American Politics* (Basingstoke: Macmillan, 1994, 2nd edition).

Also **David Walker** in **Philip Davies** and **Fredric Waldstein** (editors), *Political Issues in America Today: The 1990s Revisited* (Manchester: Manchester University Press, 1996).

An interesting account of federalism in some European countries is provided in **Jurg Steiner**, *European Democracies* (Harlow: Longman, 1998, 4th edition), Chapter 5.

Chapter Seventeen | Local Government

The aims of this chapter are:

1 To consider the advantages which local governments bring to the operations of a liberal-democratic political system.

2 To analyse the extent to which the theoretical benefits associated with local government are realised with reference to the operations of British local government.

3 To evaluate the constraints affecting the autonomy of local government.

4 To analyse changes to local government in the United Kingdom introduced between 1979 and 1997.

5 To assess reforms proposed for local government after 1997.

Local Government and Liberal Democracy

Local government has responsibility for the administration of a range of services to people living in a relatively small geographic area. Many of the functions traditionally associated with local government are utilised by large numbers of citizens on a daily basis. These include the provision of housing, social services, environmental services, refuse disposal and planning. Education is frequently provided by local government: in France this service has traditionally been subject to a considerable degree of central control, but changes proposed by the then Minister of Education, Charles Allègre, in the late 1990s sought to devolve control over this service to local level. Below, the advantages which local government brings to the workings of a liberal-democratic political system are considered.

Advantages

Local Accountability

A major benefit of local government is that it is composed of elected officials. In English-speaking liberal democracies these are usually termed 'councillors'. They can be held accountable to the local electorate for the way in which services are provided. In this way the functions discharged by government can be made compatible with the needs and requirements of local people. There are alternative ways to provide services (such as through development corporations which have been used selectively in the UK since 1979), but the elected dimension of local government is the key to its responsiveness to local issues and problems.

Efficiency in Service Provision

Local government is often considered to be the most efficient way to provide public services. Its size enables local issues (which may be peculiar to a particular part of the country) to be addressed. Such issues might be overlooked were all government services administered by larger geographic units such as State or regional authorities. Local government is also flexible in its approach to problems and has the ability to innovate in an attempt to find solutions to them. In the UK a wide variety of equal opportunities policies were pioneered by local authorities during the 1980s. The proposals of the 1997 Labour government to reform the administration of local government was influenced by experiments in local authorities such as Hammersmith and Fulham in London which installed a mayor and small cabinet to speed up decision-making.

Pursuit of Social Objectives

Local government may serve as a vehicle to advance social objectives such as gender or racial equality which may have a low priority on the national political agenda. It may do so through its role as an employer, purchaser or provider of services. Since the passage of the 1976 Race Relations Act, local government has a statutory duty to eliminate racial discrimination and has been at the forefront of developing equal opportunities policies.

The receptiveness of local government to social concerns may help to overcome the problem of marginalisation whereby particular minority groups perceive that the operations of the conventional political system do not cater for their needs. These may be encouraged to become involved in conventional political activity at local level as this presents a realistic possibility that some of their concerns might be addressed. In both the UK and the USA a significant number of councillors derive from ethnic minority backgrounds. This involvement may reduce the likelihood of such minority groups having to resort to more extreme forms of political activity which have a damaging effect on social harmony.

Participation

The existence of local government enhances the ability of citizens to participate in government. In addition to voting in national elections they may also vote in local government elections or put themselves forward for service as elected members of local authorities. Local government thus increases the number of people able to take decisions related to the administration of its affairs.

CONSULTATION AND PARTICIPATION

In addition to voting or standing for office, local people may also be enabled to play a role in the day-to-day affairs of local government. This is achieved through the processes of consultation and participation.

◆ *Consultation:* this involves mechanisms whereby the general public are able to make their views known to those who take decisions. This may be achieved through surveys, exhibitions or advisory bodies. The key feature of consultation is that policy makers are not bound to follow the opinions expressed to them: they agree to listen but are not required to act in accordance with them.

◆ *Participation:* this entails a change in the power relationship between citizens and policy makers. It is thus more radical than consultation since power is shared with the general public and policy making becomes a joint exercise involving governors and the governed. Mechanisms to achieve this in the UK include a local authority's ceding to tenants' associations the control of the running of a council housing estate.

Consultation and participation might be regarded as beneficial to liberal democracies as they permit the views of the public to be considered or acted upon by public officials. However, the lack of information in the hands of the general public might make meaningful discussion impossible and may even result in the public being manipulated into giving their backing to contentious proposals put forward by the policy makers.

Linking Citizens with National Government

In many countries local government is viewed as a training ground for politicians who later occupy high national office. Serving as an elected member of a local authority provides a person with experience in taking political and administrative decisions and representing local constituents. In the UK, former Prime Minister John Major commenced his political career as a councillor in Lambeth, London.

Local government may also further serve as an institutional mechanism which links local people with national government.

This is especially apparent in France where leading politicians sometimes hold elected office in municipal government. Jacques Chirac, for example, who served as Prime Minister between 1986 and 1988, also held the powerful position of Mayor of Paris between 1977 and 1995. This situation provides national politicians with powerful localised bases of support.

Acting as a Pressure Group

An important role performed by local government is its ability to act as a pressure group, putting forward local needs or concerns to other tiers of government and seeking remedies, perhaps through the provision of increased funds to the locality or by changes in central government policy.

The early 1980s witnessed some Labour-controlled local authorities' providing confrontational opposition to Conservative government policies which they believed were harmful to local people. This was particularly evident in Liverpool following the May 1983 local elections which obtained a clear majority for the Labour Party. Confrontation with the Conservative government over spending cuts led many Labour Councillors to propose setting a deficit budget (which was illegal). The strengthened hold of those who endorsed this course of action in the 1984 round of local elections forced the Conservative government to compromise and provide the Council with increased financial aid for housing and the urban programme. The ability of local government to act in this manner is enhanced by its elected base which implies it is acting with the support of local majority opinion.

Barometers of Public Opinion

Although local government elections should be concerned with local issues, their outcome is frequently determined by national considerations. This arises because in many liberal democracies local government elections are contested by the same parties as those which compete for power nationally. This may mean that the outcome of such contests is heavily influenced by voters' opinions on the performance of the parties (especially the record of the government) at national level. Local government elections may thus provide evidence of the political mood of the nation and serve as a means whereby the general public can exert influence over the conduct or composition of the national government. For example, the good performance of the Popular Party and the poor showing of the Socialists in Spain's 1995 municipal elections was one pressure exerted on the socialist Prime Minister, Felipe Gonzalez, to call an early general election in 1996, before the opposition forces could grow any stronger. However, he was narrowly defeated.

Question

Conduct your own study of political participation in a local authority of your choice.

Using a relevant set of election results, assess:

○ the number of wards in which elections took place

○ the total number of candidates contesting these elections, with a breakdown of their Party affiliation

○ the number of seats which changed hands from one Party to another

○ the turnout in each ward: this is expressed in percentage terms by dividing the total number of votes cast in each ward by the total number of voters registered as electors in each ward.

UK Local Government in Practice

The above section has discussed the benefits which local government theoretically brings to the operations of liberal-democratic political systems. This section analyses the extent to which such benefits are realised in practice in the UK.

Local Accountability

One major problem which arises from the almost universal tendency for local elections to be contested by political parties concerns the ability of a Councillor to consistently place local opinion at the forefront of his or her political agenda. In the UK, a Councillor performs a number of roles which are discussed below:

○ *Party representative:* most Councillors are nominated by political parties and owe their election to the Party label and the efforts exerted at election time by local party activists. This means that a Councillor will be expected to follow the Party line on issues which come before the council and may be subject to disciplinary sanctions for failing to do so.

○ *Policy maker:* one task which Councillors perform is to take decisions relating to the services which the Council implements. This duty may be discharged by serving on committees or sub-committees whose work involves specific areas of local authority activity. The specialised knowledge gained from this activity might result in overall policy-making concerns governing a Councillor's actions.

○ *Representative of local ('ward') residents:* Councillors are required to pay attention to the needs and problems of those whom they represent. This task is often discharged by holding regular advice 'surgeries' at which members of the public can seek the aid of an elected member.

These roles are not always compatible. On some occasions, a Councillor may have to give preference to one role at the expense of another. An issue such as the closure of a local school, for example, may result in a Councillor toeing the Party line even though those the Councillor represents are opposed to such a measure. In the sense that political or administrative considerations may outweigh a Councillor's duty to put forward the views of local people, it can be argued that local government is not always as accountable to local residents in practice as it should be in theory.

Efficiency in Service Provision

The ability of local government to effectively cater for the needs of its inhabitants by providing flexible or innovative approaches to problems has been impeded by a number of factors. In particular, the ability of local government to respond to local needs may be impeded by the scale or nature of these problems being beyond its capacity to solve. Its organisational base may be inappropriate, and its revenue-generating capacity inadequate to offer workable solutions to problems such as urban poverty which are manifested at local level, especially in inner-city areas. In such places the demand for services is high but the ability of people to pay for them is low. This tends to drive up the level of local taxes and encourage wealthier people to move away. This situation may result in increased reliance on finance supplied by national government or lead to the delivery of services by purpose-built bodies detached from the organisational structure of local government.

The perception that local government could not efficiently provide a range of services required in postwar Britain resulted in functions being transferred to other bodies. Examples of this include:

○ *New towns:* the 1946 New Towns Act provided for the construction of communal developments. These were built and planned by New Town Corporations which were financed by central government. This approach was based upon the belief that local government lacked the resources to build housing and construct relevant infrastructures on the scale required in postwar Britain.

○ *Development corporations:* two were initially set up in 1981 in London Docklands and Merseyside to secure the economic rejuvenation of these areas, and others were latterly established. They were preferred to local government since the affected areas were not confined to areas contained in one local authority and because it was thought that Labour-controlled authorities would not encourage private sector involvement.

The development corporations established by Conservative governments in the 1980s were wound up in March 1998. However, the Labour government proposed to continue this approach by legislating to establish Regional Development Agencies in 1998. The key function of these bodies is to develop a regional economic strategy which involves cooperating with other bodies such as local authorities and the voluntary sector. These agencies were also given powers and funds to advance economic development and regeneration.

LOCAL GOVERNMENT IN IRELAND

Local government was responsible for a wide range of key services when the Irish state was established following partition in 1921. These included roads, housing, health, income maintenance, fire-fighting, and water and sewerage. Some local authorities also controlled electricity and gas services. Progressively the number of functions was reduced with the removal of electricity, income maintenance, health and electricity services. These changes resulted in the main concerns of local government by the 1980s being reduced to environmental infrastructure and cultural activities.

Pursuit of Social Objectives

The ability of local government to effectively pursue social objectives which may not figure prominently at a national level is facilitated when such bodies are socially representative: in particular, local councillors should consist of a cross-section of the local electorate to ensure that the interests of specific groups of residents are properly catered for. In the UK, this ideal does not exist.

In 1967, a study carried out by Sir John Maud indicated that Councillors were untypical in terms of age, class, gender, property ownership and length of residence in an area. The situation had not greatly changed when a further study (chaired by D. Widdicombe in 1986) revealed that the councillors remained socially unrepresentative. This study indicated that 81 per cent of councillors were male, 32 per cent were employers or managers, and only 5 per cent were semi-skilled or unskilled manual workers. Ethnic minorities are also poorly represented at this level of government: in 1998 only 500 of 23,000 councillors nationally were black.

This means that the pressure on a local authority to pursue social objectives to advance the interests of neglected groups may be less intense and the overall approach ineffective.

Participation

The ability of local government in the UK to aid public involvement in local political affairs is handicapped by two main problems. The first is the level of public interest in the affairs of local government and the second is the traditional tendency of some local authorities to operate in a manner which has discouraged such interest.

Voter Participation in Local Elections

Public interest in UK local election contests is often very low and compares unfavourably with many other European countries. In May 1998, for example, the turnout in Iceland's municipal elections was approximately 82 per cent. Turnout in the UK was extremely low in the May 1998 local elections, when voter apathy was displayed on an almost unprecedented scale. Several reasons might explain this situation and are discussed below.

❍ *The outcome of an election is felt to be unimportant:* voters may feel that the results of the election will have relatively little bearing on the actions of the local authority. Factors which include wards (and sometimes entire local authorities) being strongholds for one particular political Party may be a disincentive to voting either by supporters of the dominant Party (on the grounds that their Party is going to win anyway) or by its opponents (in the belief that voting for their Party would be a waste of time).

❍ *The role of local government fails to command public respect:* this view suggests that many of the concerns of local government seem trivial in comparison to key political issues such as the economy, law and order, or Europe. Accordingly, people do not vote in large numbers. This perception that local government affairs are unimportant has been influenced by reforms both to its role and to its finances, reforms introduced between 1979 and 1997 and discussed below.

❍ *Local influences fail to dominate policy-making:* the views of local people form only one influence which may determine local policies. Services are administered by full-time officers whose professional views or interests may have a decisive effect on the nature of local policies. Other 'non-local' influences which

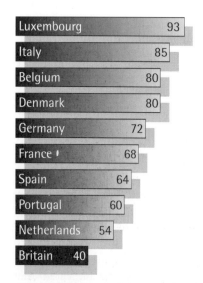

Voter turnout in 1998 local elections in Western Europe, %. Taken from the *Guardian*, 22 April 1998.

shape local decisions include political parties and central government.

❍ *Sleaze:* popular involvement in local government affairs is not encouraged by accusations of corrupt behaviour by public officials. The 'homes for votes' scandal in Westminster City Council led its former leader, Dame Shirley Porter, and her senior colleagues being surcharged £31 million by the District Auditor in 1996. Accusations of sleaze were also levelled against Labour-controlled councils including Doncaster, Coventry, Birmingham and Glasgow in the late 1990s.

Remoteness

Local government has sometimes been depicted as remote from those it serves. Reform provided for in the 1963 London Government Act (which established the Greater London Council and the London Boroughs), and 1972 Local Government Act (which provided for the two-tier system of County and District Councils outside of London) created larger units over which services were provided. The perception of remoteness was compounded by developments concerned with *corporate planning* and *corporate management* which were pursued during the 1970s. These innovations (which are discussed in Chapter 7) were designed to break down the excess departmentalisation of local government activities which would be subject to an enhanced degree of coordination. In practice, however, the corporate approach to local government affairs sometimes tended to centralise power in the hands of a small number of senior councillors and chief officers (especially the authority's chief executive), effectively 'freezing out' the majority of councillors and the general public.

To counteract the accusation of remoteness, a number of reforms took place.

Decentralisation

Decentralisation incorporated a wide range of initiatives pursued after the 1970s, designed to bring service provision physically closer to local people. Such included *area management* which typically involved the provision of advice or the delivery of a service at sub-local authority level. Decentralisation has not been pursued in the UK with the vigour found in other European countries such as France and Spain, although the Liberal Democrat administration in the London Borough of Tower Hamlets did make considerable advances with this approach between 1986 and 1994. This involved the creation of seven neighbourhoods controlled by committees whose political complexion reflected that of the ward councillors. These controlled a wide range of local services, leaving the Borough Council responsible for a reduced number of policy-related functions.

Structural Reform

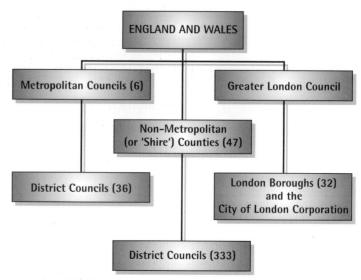

The structure of local government in England and Wales, which was provided for by the 1963 London Government Act and the 1972 Local Government Act.

Secrecy

Local government was sometimes accused of operating in a secretive manner which did not encourage members of the general public to share any interest in its affairs or guarantee that policy decisions reflected the needs of local residents. An early attempt to force local authorities to become more open in their affairs was the 1960 Public Bodies (Admission to Meetings) Act, which compelled local authorities to admit the press and public to meetings of the full council and to all committees provided that these were composed of the entire membership of a local authority. The spirit of this measure was built upon in the 1972 Local Government Act which extended this principle of openness to all local authority committee meetings regardless of whether they consisted of only a proportion of local authority members. It was assumed that a more open local authority would become more sensitive to local opinions and needs.

This measure was, however, deemed to be insufficient to break down the secrecy which governed the operations of some local authorities. Organisations such as the Campaign for the Freedom of Information and the Community Rights project argued for increased information being made available to the public concerning local government affairs. This pressure

LOCAL GOVERNMENT IN ENGLAND AND WALES

The division between metropolitan and shire counties was justified by the different responsibilities possessed by such councils. Education and social services, for example, were the responsibility of Metropolitan *district* councils and shire *county* councils. The 1972 Act also authorised the establishment of Parish (or Community) Councils. These possessed few executive functions, and their main purpose was to represent local opinion to other authorities and public bodies.

The structure of local government was subsequently affected by two further reforms.

◆ *The 1985 Local Government Act:* this abolished the Metropolitan County Councils and the Greater London Council. Their responsibilities were either devolved to the surviving District or Borough Councils or became the responsibility of newly-created joint boards.

◆ *The 1992 Local Government Act:* this reform was directed at the two-tier system of local government in the shire counties. It permitted the establishment of one-tier (or unitary) 'all-purpose' local authorities. By the end of 1998, 46 such authorities had been established.

Although political motives and administrative considerations influenced such reforms (especially the belief that it was more efficient and cost effective for services to be administered by one set of hands), they also served to create units of government which were physically closer to local residents.

resulted in the 1985 Local Government (Access to Information) Act. In addition to stipulating that all meetings of the council, its committees and sub-committees should normally be open to the public, the Act sought to secure the provision of material such as agendas and minutes of meetings, reports and the background papers utilised by officers when writing such official documents. This would enable the public to be more equipped to evaluate local authority decisions and thus facilitate the process of accountability of elected members to those they represented. This would thus place an added pressure on local government to serve more effectively the needs of local people.

Linking Citizens and National Government

Local government remains a training ground for some of those who seek national political office. At the 1997 General Election, for example, newly-elected Members of Parliament included Graham Stringer who had served as leader of Manchester City Council. Additionally, 17 of the 27 Liberal Democrat MPs who were newly-elected in 1997 had prior service as councillors. Local government has also served as a training ground for other aspects of political activity. The extent of 'hung councils' (that is, local authorities where no single Party has overall control) in the 1980s forced political Parties to sink their traditional differences and cooperate. The ability of the Liberal Democrats and Labour Party to achieve this helped to create an environment after the 1997 General Election in which the Liberal Democrats adopted a stance of 'constructive opposition' towards the Labour government.

Acting as a Pressure Group

The elected base of local government legitimises its ability to seek to exert influence on the policies pursued by other private and public sector bodies who may respond positively to suggestions which possess the support of local people. In this sense local government may make a major contribution to the operations of a pluralist society. However, the effectiveness of the tactic of confrontation by local governments in order to perform the role of a pressure group is adversely affected by its constitutional position. Ultimately central government is able to ensure compliance from those local bodies which challenge its actions. This was the case in Liverpool where the stand against the Conservative government mounted by Labour Councillors resulted in defeat in the High Court in 1985, the imposition of a surcharge by the District Auditor, and the subsequent rate-capping of the authority in 1986.

Barometers of Public Opinion

Local elections provide some evidence of the popularity of the main political parties. The degree of popular support for the national government may be more influential in determining the outcome of a local election than the performance of the authority and the personnel in control of it.

Local affairs may, however, remain significant in determining the outcome of local government elections in some areas. In the UK the former Liberal Party and latterly the Liberal Democrats pioneered a strategy referred to as 'community politics'. Although this term has a number of definitions, in practice it usually entails local Party activists placing purely local issues at the forefront of their campaigns, thereby offering the electorate an effective form of representation based on regular communication, including *Focus* newsletters. This approach has

Question

Based on the material you have gathered, and your reading of the above section, discuss THREE factors which you think might explain the relatively low level of voter participation in the local elections you have studied.

succeeded in dramatically increasing Liberal Democrat representation on local authorities.

Central Control Versus Local Autonomy

In most liberal democracies, local government is subject to a considerable degree of control by national or State governments. This may be exercised in a number of ways which are discussed below.

Control by the Executive Branch

The executive branch may impose a range of controls on the operations of local government. These include specific controls over individual services, limits on local government spending or detailed controls over local government borrowing. In Ireland central supervision is also exerted over the personnel employed by local authorities. A further way in which local government can be controlled by higher political authorities is through the prefectoral system which is discussed below.

The Prefectoral System

The prefectoral system involves the imposition of an official appointed by central government to act as its eyes and ears in the localities, and to provide a link between central and local government, effectively fusing the two levels of administration.

THE PREFECTORAL SYSTEM IN FRANCE

In France the prefect (who was termed 'Commissioner of the Republic' between 1983 and 1987) is a civil servant appointed by the Ministry of the Interior and placed in each Department and, after 1972, in each region. The prefect formerly exerted considerable day-to-day powers over the Departments and their constituent local government units (termed 'communes'). The extent of such power over local authority actions was subject to variation but was universally reduced by reforms enacted by the Socialist government in the 1980s. These served to lessen the high degree of central control formerly exercised over French local government. However, prefects continue to wield supervisory powers over local government. The importance of this might be displayed should any of the three cities controlled by the National Front following the 1995 municipal elections seek to implement their 'national preference' policy. If this occurred the prefects could intervene to ensure that the equality and anti-discrimination provisions in French law were upheld.

The system whereby a representative of central government (usually termed a 'prefect' or 'governor') is appointed alongside an elected regional or provincial assembly is relatively common in Europe. Arrangements of this nature exist in Denmark, Sweden, Spain, Greece and Italy. In Italy the prefect is the State's representative in the localities (termed 'provinces'). This official is usually an official of the Ministry of the Interior, but is sometimes a career politician. In theory, the prefect's main role is to coordinate the work of central government Ministries at a local level, although in practice much attention is directed to the maintenance of public order and security.

Judicial Control

In countries in which the powers of local government are rigidly controlled by legislation, judicial control may constitute an important restraint. In the UK, for example, the courts are able to intervene and prevent local authorities from performing functions which they are not legally empowered to perform (and, possibly, to surcharge the councillors who authorised such 'illegal' expenditure). They may also force a council to discharge its mandatory duties if it is ignoring these. The former of these controls is known as *ultra vires*, and the latter is termed *mandamus*.

Reforms to UK Local Government 1979–97

This section evaluates the main changes which were made to local government in the UK between 1979 and 1997. In this period Conservative governments displayed a critical attitude towards local authorities. It was accused of waste, inefficiency, poor management and putting political interests before service to the community. This resulted in increased central control being exerted over local government, and a loss of functions with which it was traditionally associated.

Loss of Functions

Government policy reduced the role performed by local government in responsibilities such as the provision of public housing. At the behest of government policy initiated in the 1980 Housing Act, one million council houses were sold, and much of the work previously carried out by local authorities in this area have been assumed by housing associations. Additionally, services were taken out of the hands of local government and transferred to a range of alternative authorities including joint boards, quangos and central government.

One major innovation was the reduction of local authority control over education. This was affected by two developments contained in the 1988 Education Reform Act. The first was the enhanced degree of control which central government exerted over the content of education through the imposition of a National Curriculum and proposals for universal assessment at the ages of 7, 11, 14 and 16. The centralising tendencies of this measure were subsequently developed in the Labour government's 1998 School Standards and Framework legislation which provided a wide array of powers for the government to intervene if teachers, schools or local education authorities failed to meet performance targets drawn up by Whitehall.

Centralisation was accompanied by a second development which removed power from local education authorities and instead placed it in the hands of head teachers and school governors. They were given control of their school or college budget under the system of Local Management of Schools. Proposals put forward in 1998 by the Labour government to delegate even more of the education budget to heads and governors posed the possibility that the ability of local education authorities to influence education would be still further reduced.

Controls Over Local Government Spending

When the Conservative Party entered government in 1979, local government expenditure was financed in a number of ways.

❍ *The rates:* these were levied by individual local authorities, and an individual's contribution was based upon a notional rent which could be obtained for the property he or she owned. A major problem with the rates was that it was a regressive form of taxation which hit the poor hardest, since it was based on property value and not on an individual's ability to pay. Since 1967, however, rate rebates to lower-income households substantially redressed this deficiency.

❍ *Central government grant:* since 1966 this had been termed the 'rate support grant'. It consisted of a number of elements which were designed to ensure increased aid to areas of need.

❍ *Charges:* these were derived from the users of particular local government services.

The level of local government spending was primarily determined by the local authority itself. Suggestions to curb spending could be made by central government, but local authorities were free to ignore such advice. To remedy this situation, the Conservative government embarked upon a number of reforms, the main features of which are discussed below.

The 1980 Local Government Planning and Land Act

Estimates of what each local authority needed to spend in order to provide services of a national uniform standard were drawn up by civil servants. This was known as *Grant Related Expenditure*. Central government then established a figure which determined what each local authority should raise through the rates (which was effected by setting a national uniform rate). The difference between these two figures was paid by central government in the form of a 'block grant'.

One difficulty with Grant Related Expenditure was that it required cuts in spending for some local authorities which could not be reasonably met within one financial year. Accordingly, 'volume targets' were prepared so that a local authority which overspent in terms of its Grant Related Expenditure figure but which kept within its volume target was deemed to be performing satisfactorily. These Grant Related Expenditure and volume target figures were subsequently amalgamated in the 1982–83 financial year to provide one overall figure prepared by central government to guide the level of spending by individual local authorities. In 1990, Standard Spending Assessments were introduced to determine local spending.

The 1982 Local Government Finance Act

This measure placed holdback penalties on a statutory footing. This meant that a local authority which proposed in its budget to spend above the target figure prepared by central government would lose a proportion of its block grant as a punishment for overspending. This Act also ended the ability of local authorities to levy a supplementary rate if, as a result of holdback penalties, it sought to maintain its initial level of spending by making additional demands on its local inhabitants.

The 1984 Rates Act

Initial Conservative reforms were based on the belief that public opinion would prove to be the ultimate sanction against high-spending local authorities. It was assumed that councils which ignored spending limits and which sought to override the loss of money through the imposition of holdback penalties by levying high rates on local residents would be voted out of office. But this sanction failed to occur, a major explanation being that the system of exemptions and rebates meant that the poorest people contributed little or nothing to local authority expenditure. It was thus irrelevant if their rate bill was £500 or £5,000 as it would be paid for them.

Accordingly, a new sanction was introduced in the form of 'rate capping'. This enabled central government to place a limit on the amount of money which any local authority could raise through the rating system. This power was used selectively, directed against those Councils which in the view of central government had been spending irresponsibly. The sanction of 'capping' was incorporated into subsequent reforms, including the introduction of Standard Spending Assessments in 1990. These calculations formed the basis of central government's contribution towards local expenditure in the rate support grant (alternatively called the Standard Spending Grant), and sought to ensure that the council taxes charged by every local authority would be identical.

The 1988 Local Government Finance Act

The Conservative Party's key reform to local government finance was the introduction of a new method through which they would fund their operations. Rates (which were a tax levied on property) were replaced by a tax on individuals. This was the *community charge*, more infamously known as the 'poll tax'. It was designed to enhance the accountability of local government to its residents by forcing all citizens to contribute towards the costs of local government. In this way it was envisaged that high spending councils would be more readily sanctioned by local electors as everyone would make some contribution towards the cost of local services. This new system was introduced in Scotland in 1989 and in England and Wales in 1990. In 1990 a Uniform Business Rate was introduced to govern the financial contribution made by business concerns towards the costs of the local authorities in which they are situated.

However, the introduction of the poll tax was surrounded with controversy. It was an extremely difficult and expensive tax to collect, problems which were compounded by a campaign encouraging people not to pay. It was argued that the tax was essentially unfair as it made all contribute regardless of their means. Eventually the government was forced to back down. The poll tax was abandoned and the 1992 Local Government Finance Act replaced it with the council tax which became local government's independent source of finance. This was essentially a tax on property, the level of which was determined by its estimated value (which was viewed as reflecting the financial status of its occupants).

Compulsory Competitive Tendering

This reform was based upon a perception that in many cases local councils were better at planning, financing and regulating services than they were at owning, managing and directly providing them. It enabled the concept of market forces to be introduced into the operations of local government which, rather than directly providing services, was given greater flexibility to determine how a particular function should best be achieved. One way to achieve this was to make services subject to compulsory competitive tendering. This entailed the local authorities inviting tenders from interested parties to carry out a particular operation (such as refuse disposal) for a period of years, at the end of which the contract would again be put out to tender. Legislation such as the 1988 Local Government Act thus moved local government in the direction of an *enabling authority* rather than one which directly provided services.

The Role of the Private Sector

In addition to the role of the private sector in administering services previously operated by local government, Conservative administrations also sought to involve the private sector in broader projects which included the rejuvenation of declining urban areas. Although this approach sometimes involved local government working in partnership with financial and business interests, on occasions it resulted in the establishment of bodies such as urban development corporations and task forces which bypassed local government and whose activities were not subject to any form of control or accountability to local people.

Question

Analyse the extent to which Conservative policies pursued between 1979 and 1997 made local government subject to enhanced central control.

Evaluation of Conservative Reforms 1979–97

The Conservative Party adopted a hostile approach towards local government after 1979. This prompted a subsequent leader of the Conservative Party, William Hague, to express his own commitment to effective local government in 1998. This section evaluates the reasons why such reforms were adopted and the consequences of them, especially in connection with enhanced central control.

Rationale For Conservative Reforms

Reforms to local government introduced by Conservative governments after 1979 could be justified by several reasons which are discussed below.

Economic

The controls which were introduced to curtail the level of expenditure by local government were justified by the argument that the national government should exercise control over the level of public spending. The annual expenditure for local government in 1997/98 (the last year of Conservative government) was £48 billion (of which only 23 per cent was raised through council tax).

Efficiency and Value for Money

Conservative intervention was also justified by a perception that local government was profligate (that is, wasteful in terms of expenditure). In addition to the measures outlined above, a further reform was the introduction of the Audit Commission in the 1982 Local Government Finance Act. The role of this body was to investigate the efficiency of local government. In 1995, it commenced the process of publishing local authority performance indicators, one implication of which was that people might be induced to move to the most efficient and cost-effective local authorities.

Structural reform was also justified on efficiency grounds. The Conservative government's case for the 1985 Local Government Act (which abolished the Greater London and Metropolitan County Councils) included arguments that their strategic role was unnecessary and that they were responsible for a high proportion of the alleged overspending in local government.

Political

The attitude of the Conservative Party towards local government after 1979 was flavoured both by the dominant hold which the Labour Party held in many urban areas and also by the manner in which some in the Labour Party viewed local government as a forum to advance the ideology of socialism.

THE URBAN LEFT AND LOCAL SOCIALISM

A number of Marxists viewed local government as the 'local state'. This implied that the scope for pursuing radical policies at this level was constrained by local government's being part of the machinery of the capitalist state – perceived to be the instrument of class domination. However, after 1979 some within the Labour Party believed that local government could be a launch pad to build socialism in the UK from the bottom up. These, termed the 'urban left', thus sought to use local government in this political sense.

Their approach involved the enhanced control of local government over all aspects of local authority work, and promoted the idea that its main purpose was to satisfy the needs of local people, primarily through the provision of services. Its actions should be governed by social concerns rather than by economic considerations. Attempts were also made to formulate a local economic strategy which was geared towards the needs of local workers. Such included funding cooperative ventures and ensuring that the local authority was a 'model employer'. Some attempts were also made to influence the conduct of the private sector with whom the local authority had dealings through contract compliance (which entailed insisting that private companies adhere to standards of behaviour acceptable to socialist opinion in connection with their commercial activities).

The Conservative government was opposed to the ideals which the urban left sought to promote, and to the tactics which were designed to achieve them. The insistence that the police should be subject to a greater measure of local accountability resulted in the chief constables in Greater Manchester and Merseyside relying on Home Office support against their Labour-controlled police authorities. Confrontation occurred when those local authorities, which were adversely affected by the imposition of limits on their spending, sought to resist. To the Conservative Party, such difficulties provided the justification for the reforms which they introduced after 1979.

Assessment of Conservative Reforms

Conservative reforms to local government between 1979 and 1997 resulted in a considerable degree of increased central involvement in local affairs. In 1983 George Jones and John Stewart wrote *The Case for Local Government*. In this work they argued that such centralisation at the expense of local autonomy was not a desirable development for a variety of reasons.

○ *Concentration of power:* these reforms resulted in a dangerous concentration of power at the centre of British government. Responsiveness to local needs became replaced by adherence to national standards.

○ *Remoteness:* the reforms led to a reduction in the visibility and accessibility of government. Decisions were taken by people far away from those who were affected by them. In particular, the role of the civil service was strengthened by such changes: unlike local politicians, civil servants were anonymous and politically unaccountable for their actions.

○ *Standardisation:* there would be an increase in uniformity at the expense of diversity. The latter was viewed as important since it helped to promote constructive social change.

Such views suggested a move away from *local government* towards *local administration*. The former term implies a degree of autonomy, usually guaranteed by the fact that local government raises a proportion of its own revenue by taxing its inhabitants. The latter suggests that local government has no independence of action and exists to provide services whose content was structured at national level. It effectively becomes an agent of central government.

The Labour Party and Local Government After 1997

The Labour government which was elected in 1997 introduced a number of reforms to local government. The main innovations are discussed below.

The Reform of London Government

The abolition of the Greater London Council in 1986 meant that London (almost alone of capital cities in the world) lacked an elected city-wide authority. There were a number of difficulties arising from this situation, in particular in connection with the administration of services. Some (such as the fire brigade) were administered by joint committees of the London Borough Councils, and others (such as strategic land-use planning) were controlled by Whitehall.

The 1997 Labour government put forward proposals to provide Londoners with a system of government which would be able to take a strategic view of the needs of the people and the delivery of services. This would be achieved through the establishment of a city-wide authority and the introduction of an elected mayor.

A City-wide Authority for London

In August 1998 the Local Government Commission published a blueprint for a London Assembly, which would be headed by an elected mayor. Fourteen members of this body would be elected from 14 constituencies (with an average electorate of 350,000) by the first-past-the-post system, and a further 11 members would be chosen in a capital-wide poll conducted by the party list method of proportional representation. The latter provision was designed to ensure that the political composition of the Assembly was related to party voting strengths. It was envisaged that the first elections would take place in Autumn 1999 or May 2000. The annual budget of the London Assembly would be around £3.3 billion, and it would be responsible for a range of services which included education, social services, housing and local planning.

The London Assembly

An Elected Mayor

The concept of an elected chief executive was novel to the British political system. Local government traditionally possessed a collective executive which was selected from the leading members of the largest political Party represented on the local authority. In some areas, however, one person, termed the 'leader of the council', often wielded considerable control over local authority affairs. The Labour government's proposals thus sought to provide London with a civic leader whose status as a directly elected official would be on a par with that possessed by the mayors of New York, Tokyo or Paris. One advantage of such a reform would be that an elected official can seize the initiative and deal with local problems. The ability to do this has been a feature of the 'new-breed mayors' who have been elected to office in a number of American cities in the 1990s. These include Rudy Giuliani in New York and Richard Riordan in Los Angeles. Their success was achieved by focusing on the key issues of crime, schools and jobs, and by attracting companies and entrepreneurs into their localities.

London voters approved the proposal to establish an elected mayor in a referendum held in 1998. The powers of this official would be subject to scrutiny by the London Assembly which would have to be notified of major decisions taken by the mayor, and which possesses the power to amend a budget prepared by this official.

General Reform of Local Government

In 1998, the Deputy Prime Minister, John Prescott, outlined the future direction of local government reform. These proposals included the following.

○ *Streamlining procedures:* this entailed the establishment of an executive (consisting of a mayor) or a cabinet-style of government to manage the affairs of the local authority and to replace the antiquated committee system. The main aim of such a reform was to promote speedier decision-making. To secure this, the government proposed that if an authority was loathe to make such changes it would be compelled to hold a referendum to ask their voters' opinion on the subject.

○ *Ending compulsory competitive tendering:* this would be replaced by a 'best value' system of price and quality testing overseen by the Audit Commission.

○ *Award of 'beacon' status:* councils with a good record of performance would be able to apply for this status, one benefit of which might be greater financial freedom including the ability to set a small additional business rate.

❍ *Ending 'capping':* what the government dubbed as 'crude and universal' capping of local authority budgets by Whitehall would be ended, although it intended to retain powers of intervention.

❍ *Rooting out dishonesty, corruption and sleaze:* new regionally-based independent Standards Boards would be created in an effort to eliminate this problem. This was in addition to internal reforms (under the heading of Project 99) introduced by the Labour Party to vet its candidates in future local election contests. This enquired into a potential candidate's personal, political and financial dealings, and the Conservative Party contemplated a similar scheme.

Question ?

Select any ONE reform to local government introduced by the Labour Party after 1997.

Using sources which include books, newspapers and journals, analyse:

❍ the key features of this reform

❍ the purposes this reform was designed to achieve

❍ the strengths and weaknesses of this reform

❍ your own evaluation as to whether this reform constitutes a strength or weakness to the operations of local government in the UK.

Further Reading

George Jones & **John Stewart**, *The Case for Local Government* (London: George Allen and Unwin, 1983). The fact that these eminent academics wrote this book was indicative of concern regarding the adverse impact of Conservative reforms on the vitality, and even continued existence, of local government.

Tony Byrne, *Local Government in Britain: Everyone's Guide to How it All Works* (Harmondsworth: Penguin Books, 1994, 6th edition). This provides an extremely detailed account of the structure, financing and internal organisation of local government, and also of the political environment within which local government operates.

An interesting set of essays on subjects which include the role and constitutional position of local government, and party politics is provided in **Lawrence Pratchett** and **David Wilson**, *Local Government and Local Democracy* (Basingstoke: Macmillan, 1996).

Richard Batley and **Gerry Stoker** (editors), *Local Government in Europe: Trends and Developments* (Basingstoke: Macmillan, 1991). This book provides an informative account of the operations of local government throughout the European Union.

Chapter Eighteen | The Nation State in the Contemporary World

The aims of this chapter are:

> 1 To define the term 'sovereignty' and distinguish between this and 'the sovereignty of Parliament' in the United Kingdom.
>
> 2 To examine the continued vitality of the sovereignty of the nation state by analysing the extent to which obligations from international and supranational bodies have eroded this principle.
>
> 3 To describe the evolution of the European Union and discuss the main institutions through which it operates.
>
> 4 To analyse the political debate in the UK concerning the European Union.

The Erosion of the Sovereignty of the Nation State

The Meaning of Sovereignty

Sovereignty implies *self-determination*. The term suggests that a state has the ability to control its own activities without interference from outside bodies and countries. In particular, sovereignty suggests that a state has the exclusive right to pass laws which administer that nation's affairs.

As has been argued in Chapter 16, sovereignty is shared within federal states. In countries which include the United States of America, Australia, Canada and Germany, the national government may enact legislation in certain areas of activity, and other matters are subject to regulation by the States or provinces which comprise these countries. The division of power is provided for in a codified constitution, and a constitutional court arbitrates when problems arise as to whether a particular function is within the jurisdiction of national or sub-national governments. In unitary countries such as the UK and France, sovereignty is not divided. The determination of the country's affairs is solely in the hands of central government, which theoretically has the exclusive and unlimited right to regulate the activities of these nations.

The Sovereignty of Parliament

The term 'sovereignty' must be distinguished from the concept of 'the sovereignty of Parliament'. The latter lies at the heart of the UK's system of government. Initially this doctrine was designed to provide for the superiority of Parliament over the Monarchy. It implies the following.

○ *Unlimited powers to make law:* parliament may pass any legislation it wishes. It cannot be challenged by any other body within the State (such as a court or a local authority). As is argued later in this chapter, membership of the European Union has modified this aspect of the term.

○ *Inability to bind a successor:* the concept of the sovereignty of Parliament also suggests that one Parliament cannot bind a successor to a course of action. Any law passed by one Parliament can be subsequently amended or repealed. In theory this includes legislation securing British membership to supranational bodies such as the European Union.

Globalisation

It is doubtful whether any state has ever enjoyed total control over the conduct of its affairs. Although the nineteenth-century nation state perhaps went some way to realising this ideal, such countries were required to pay regard to outside factors when administering their internal or external activities. In the twentieth century, sovereignty is even less of a reality: the ability of any state to function autonomously has been undermined by a wide range of factors which have contributed towards an enhanced degree of international cooperation. The term 'globalisation' is used to refer to the increased interconnectedness of nation states in political, economic and cultural affairs which has undermined the traditional distinction between 'national' and 'international' politics.

Question

Distinguish between the terms 'sovereignty' and 'sovereignty of Parliament'.

To do this you should:

○ state in your own words what you understand by 'sovereignty'

○ discuss in your own words the definition of 'sovereignty of Parliament' and indicate its historical significance

○ indicate the relationships between these two terms by assessing the links and dissimilarities between them.

The following section will discuss a number of aspects concerned with the erosion of national sovereignty.

International Cooperation

The following section will consider the political dimensions of globalisation by considering a wide range of organisations, membership of which places limitations on a nation's ability to be in total control of its own affairs.

Bodies Which Secure Global Cooperation

Factors which include the desire to prevent a third world war, and the enhanced interdependence of nations arising from contemporary developments in matters which include economic policy and environmental issues have resulted in the establishment of a number of bodies designed to secure cooperation between nations across the world. Below, several examples of such organisations are discussed.

The United Nations

This organisation was formally established on 24 October 1945, and its aims were to:

○ maintain international peace and security

○ develop international cooperation in economic, social, cultural and humanitarian problems.

It is administered by the United Nations Secretariat, whose chief figure is the secretary-general, appointed by the General Assembly (which is the parliament of the United Nations). Its main institutions are the Security Council (whose role is to maintain peace and security, which may involve the use of armed force), and the International Court of Justice, based at the Hague in Holland.

AGENCIES OF THE UNITED NATIONS

Much of the work of the United Nations is carried out through specialised agencies which are funded by the member states.

◆ *The World Health Organisation:* this seeks to assist people in all nations to attain the highest possible levels of health.

◆ *The International Labour Organisation:* this aims to improve labour conditions, raise living standards and promote productive employment through international cooperation.

◆ *The International Monetary Fund:* this was established in 1945 to promote international monetary cooperation, establish a multilateral system of payments, and help remedy any serious disequilibrium in a country's balance of payments by enabling it to borrow from the Fund. Since the Latin American debt crisis in 1982, aid has increasingly been given to developing nations.

◆ *The World Trade Organisation:* this came into operation in 1995, replacing the General Agreement on Tariffs and Trade whose key purpose had been to work towards the reduction of trade barriers. The World Trade Organisation is a permanent trade-monitoring body.

◆ *The International Criminal Court:* member States of the United Nations voted at the Rome Conference in 1998 to create an International Criminal Court to try cases against humanity. This implied that human rights were international in scope.

The Commonwealth

The Commonwealth is a free association of sovereign, independent States, and has no charter or constitution. It is based on a desire for cooperation, consultation and assistance by those who choose to be members of it. The 1931 Statute of Westminster (which gave full autonomy to the Dominions of Australia, Canada, New Zealand and South Africa), is commonly regarded as the origin of the Commonwealth, although the 'modern' Commonwealth stemmed from 1949 when India chose to become a republic whilst remaining a member of this organisation. This meant that the British Monarch was transformed from a legal entity into a symbol. The Commonwealth is serviced by a Secretariat, and headed by a secretary-general. Heads of government of Commonwealth countries meet every two years to discuss international affairs.

Bodies to Secure Inter-Regional Cooperation

A number of organisations seek to provide for the cooperation of nations on a scale which falls short of global collaboration but which goes beyond the geographic boundaries of one single region. Typically, this form of cooperation will embrace nations located in different continents or sub-continents. Examples of inter-regional cooperation include the following.

❍ *The Commonwealth of Independent States:* this was formed following the collapse of the former Soviet Union in December 1991. Its membership consists of a number of the Soviet Republics, and its organisation is based upon a Council of Heads of State and a Council of Heads of Government.

❍ *The Organisation of American States:* this was formed in 1948, and comprises countries situated in North, Central and South America and the Caribbean. Its objectives include promoting solidarity among the American States, defending their sovereignty and independence, and speeding up the process of economic integration.

❍ *The Organisation of African Unity:* this was formed in 1963 and comprises countries throughout Africa and the Middle East. Its aims were to further African unity and solidarity, to coordinate political, economic, cultural, health, scientific and defence policies, and to eliminate colonialism in Africa.

Bodies to Secure Intra-Regional Cooperation

A number of organisations have been formed to secure cooperation between nations in a particular section of the world, typically in the same continent. The European Union (which is discussed in greater detail below) is the main example of a European organisation of this nature, but there are others.

❍ *The Council of Europe:* this was established in 1949 to secure a greater measure of unity between the countries of Europe by discussing common interests and problems and discovering new methods and areas of cooperation. Its membership is broader than that of the European Union.

❍ *The Nordic Council:* this was founded in 1953 by Denmark, Iceland, Norway and Sweden, and was joined by Finland in 1956.

❍ *The European Space Agency:* this was initially formed in 1973 to promote space research and the use of technology for peaceful purposes. Its projects included the Ariane rocket.

Military Cooperation

The defence and security policy of individual nations is often affected by international treaties. One example of this is the 1963 Nuclear Test Ban Treaty. Additionally, a number of formal military pacts exist on a global, inter- or intra-regional basis. One of the most important is the North Atlantic Treaty Organisation. This was established in 1949 to oppose the threat from the Soviet Union and its East European satellites. It initially consisted of the USA, Belgium, the UK, Canada, Denmark, France, Iceland, Italy, Luxembourg, the Netherlands, Norway and Portugal. It was a mutual defence treaty whereby signatories agreed that an armed attack against one or more of their number in Europe or North America would be considered as an attack against all members. Its supreme body is the Council of Foreign Ministers of all the member states, and its Secretariat is based in Brussels.

International Cooperation and Sovereignty

Membership of supranational institutions places limitations on the activities of the member countries, whose sovereignty is restricted by the expectation that they will adhere to the policies determined by the central decision-making machinery of those institutions. This voluntary form of cooperation may be supplemented by more active measures designed to influence the actions of members (and sometimes non-members). These methods are discussed below.

❍ *Moral pressure:* the discussion within the Commonwealth in 1995 on whether to impose sanctions against Nigeria was designed to pressurise that country's government to introduce improvements to its civil rights policies and return to a democratic form of government.

❍ *Sanctions:* trade embargoes constitute a sanction which international bodies may use to force a government to change the direction of its politics.

❍ *Force:* international bodies may use military intervention to accomplish their aims. The UN military coalition which liberated Kuwait from Iraqi occupation in 1991 is an example of this. The use of ground troops in Bosnia under the authority of NATO in 1995 sought to ensure the successful implementation of the peace agreement following its endorsement by the Presidents of Croatia, Bosnia and Serbia.

The Emergence of the Global Economy

In addition to the existence of various formal institutions which have undermined national sovereignty by encouraging nations to cooperate, economic factors have also served to erode the significance of national boundaries. These factors (which are discussed below) have given rise to the emergence of a global economy which has been brought about by international trade and the international character of contemporary commerce and finance. The concept of a global economy rejects the view that the economies of nation states can be seen as independent entities, and instead places emphasis on their inter-relationships. This concept emphasises that the success or failure of the economy of one nation, or block of nations, has a major impact throughout the world.

The global nature of financial markets was evident in 1987, when panic selling in New York spread to the Pacific and

Europe and thence back to the USA. Later, the South-East Asian financial crisis of 1997 triggered a slump in world share prices: at one stage in the UK £43 billion was wiped off the value of the London stock market. The problems in South-East Asia put pressure on Japan's economy. In August 1998 the decline in the unit of Japanese currency (the yen) had an adverse effect on stock markets throughout the world.

THE RUSSIAN ECONOMIC COLLAPSE, 1998

The economic aspect of globalisation was dramatically illustrated by the economic and political events which took place in Russia towards the end of 1998. This problem was initiated by the 'collapse' of the currency (the rouble), that is, it lost its value against key world currencies such as the Dollar and Pound.

The government's response was to devalue the currency and postpone debt repayments. These actions, however, provoked economic difficulties which spread far beyond Russia. They resulted in a flight of capital, since Western investors (who stood to lose huge sums of money from unpaid loans in Russia) sold shares worldwide and turned to safer forms of investment (such as government bonds and fixed-interest-rate stocks). This selling had an immediate consequence for the economic policies pursued by individual Latin American and Asian nations, who were forced to consider devaluation of their currencies or large rises in interest rates. The economic difficulties of Latin American countries had a subsequent effect in the USA and Europe, especially in those countries (such as Spain) whose banks had large investments in that part of the world.

The impact of such problems on the UK was to push up the international value of the Pound since this currency was viewed as a good investment. Its high value, however, made life difficult for exporters (whose markets in countries severely affected by recession had effectively dried up), and created pressure to cut interest rates.

International Trade

International trade has placed restraints on the actions of national governments. Membership of regional trading blocs such as the European Union, or wider international arrangements such as the World Trade Organisation limit the ability of member countries to pursue policies such as tariff protection against other participating nations. Broader agreements have also been made to regulate the world's trading system through international actions which include the Group of Seven (G7) summit meetings, consisting of the UK, the USA, Italy, France, Canada, Germany, Japan. Russia is also involved in some aspects of this arrangement. Such initiatives restrict the control which individual nations exert over economic policies. The discretion possessed by individual governments in these matters is further reduced by the need to consider the reaction of financial markets to political decisions taken by individual governments.

Multi-National Companies

The concentration of large-scale economic activity has resulted in the formation of multi-national companies. These have their headquarters in one country but their commercial activities are conducted throughout the world. Incentives for them to do this include access to raw materials and, in the case of firms locating in the Third World, the availability of cheap labour. Such multi-national companies (many of which are American or Japanese-owned) possess considerable influence over the operations of the government of the countries in which they invest, thereby undermining the economic and political independence of such countries. In return for providing jobs and revenue derived from taxing their operations, multi-national companies may demand concessions from governments as the price for their investment in that country. They may seek direct or indirect control over a country's political system to ensure that government policy is compatible with the needs of the company. If these conflict, the government may suffer. In Guatemala, for example, President Jacobo Arbenz's quarrels with the American United Fruit Company resulted in his replacement by an American-backed military government in 1954.

The desire of multi-national companies to dominate nation states was clearly evident in the Multilateral Agreement on Investment, which was drawn up in 1998 by the Organisation for Economic Cooperation and Development (whose inner core constitutes the 'Group of 8' nations referred to above). This proposed a new set of investment rules to enable giant multi-national corporations to buy, sell and move their capital all over the world without being subject to regulation by national governments. This Agreement would enable multi-national companies to sue governments for damages if they passed laws which discriminated against them, thus enabling investors world-wide to compete on equal terms and not be subject to laws passed by particular countries to aid the investment opportunities of their own nationals.

Foreign Aid

Some countries, especially in the developing world, are in receipt of aid. This includes grants, loans or gifts which may be designed to stimulate agricultural and industrial development or be concerned with military purposes. Such aid to Third World countries is provided either by individual governments (termed 'bilateral aid'), or by international bodies such as the World Bank or the International Monetary Fund (termed 'multilateral aid'). Foreign aid may be awarded subject to conditions which the receiving government is forced to adopt. As is argued in the following section, these may include fundamental alterations in domestic policy.

Dependency

The relationship of First and Third World countries has been described as one of dependency. This suggests that the role of Third World countries is to serve the economic interests of the industrially advanced nations, thereby distorting the pattern of economic development which becomes geared to the needs of the First World and its multi-national companies. Dependency is reinforced by loans made available to Third World countries by bodies such as the International Monetary Fund. The interest rates charged and the conditions stipulated by the lending body erode the sovereignty of the receiving country in both political and economic affairs. Aid provided by Western liberal democracies, for example, may require improvements in the receiving country's human rights record.

The interest paid by Third World countries on their foreign debts became a major issue in the 1980s, and was evidenced by the Latin American debt crisis in 1982. A number of debtor countries are effectively bankrupt. This means either that they cannot keep up their repayments, or that in order to do so governments undertake measures which prejudice their own citizens. Expenditure on key services such as health or education may be sacrificed in order to repay debts, or it may be necessary to export agricultural produce, resulting in the population suffering from hunger and starvation.

COMMUNICATIONS

The cultural aspects of globalisation have been enhanced by developments in communications. A good example of a development in communication which physically brings nations together but at the same time erodes the sovereignty of individual governments concerns the media.

Chapter 9 examined technological developments affecting the structure of the mass media. Developments such as satellite, cable television and particularly the Internet have transformed the media into a global mechanism which transmits across national frontiers. These new forms of communication have made it difficult for governments to exercise control over the spread of information to their citizens since it may be transmitted from installations which operate outside their frontiers and which are beyond their supervision. In response to this situation, the European Community produced a discussion document in 1984 entitled *Television Without Frontiers* which sought to establish a common regulatory framework from broadcasting across Europe. In 1989, member nations signed a directive designed to establish a free market for television broadcasting across national frontiers.

Conclusion

The above sections have documented some of the restrictions imposed on the freedom of action possessed by national governments. It would be wrong to assert that nations now have *no* meaningful control over their internal or external affairs. For example, while national economies are subject to broad global considerations and restraints which have narrowed the scope of national economic policy, individual governments possess considerable freedom to implement policies designed to strengthen the supply side of their economies: such measures include improving skills, promoting investment and enlarging the nation's economic capacity.

Individual governments may further pursue political courses of action regardless of the opinions of other countries. The decision by the French government in 1995 to resume its programme of nuclear weapon testing in the Pacific Ocean provoked widespread opposition from individual countries such as Australia and New Zealand, from international pressure groups such as Greenpeace, and from international organisations such as the Commonwealth. Economic pressure in the form of boycotts against French produce, especially wine, was applied. But the French government ignored such pressures and proceeded with this policy.

Sovereignty also remains a term which enters into the rhetoric of political debate and influences political behaviour. In the UK, allegations that sovereignty is threatened by the policies of the European Union remain a potent argument which crosses traditional political divisions. This will be discussed later in this chapter.

Question

'In the modern world it is impossible for any one state to exercise total control over the running of its political affairs.' Discuss TWO reasons which justify this comment.

In your view, does this mean that sovereignty is a 'dead' political concept?

The Institutions of the European Union

The European Union is an important example of a supranational governmental body. Countries which join this organisation forgo control over their own affairs in areas which are encompassed by its treaties. Decision-making in these areas becomes a collective exercise involving representatives of all the member countries. The UK's voice in the European Union, for example, is put forward by its 87 Members of the European Parliament, two commissioners (who are nominated by the UK government), and the one vote it possesses in common with every other member in the Council of Ministers. The following sections briefly discuss the evolution of the European Union and describe how its work is performed.

The Evolution of the European Union

The Second World War provided a key motivating force for movement towards closer cooperation between the countries of Western Europe. There was a desire by leading politicians from both the victorious and defeated nations to establish institutions to avoid a further war in Europe. The first step towards cooperation was the establishment in 1951 of the European Coal and Steel Community. It was envisaged that the sharing of basic raw materials which were essential to the machinery of war would avoid outbreaks of hostilities. This initiative was followed in 1955 by the formation of the European Investment Fund. The body now known as the 'European Union' developed from an organisation which was initially popularly known as the 'Common Market'. The main developments in the progress of the EU are as follows.

The Treaty of Rome (1957)

This treaty established the European Economic Community (EEC) and Euratom (the European Atomic Energy Community). The EEC initially consisted of six countries (France, West Germany, Italy, the Netherlands, Belgium and Luxembourg). The UK, the Irish Republic and Denmark joined in 1973, Greece in 1981, Spain and Portugal in 1986, and Austria, Finland and Sweden in 1995. Discussions concerning the accession of Poland, Hungary, Slovenia, Estonia, Cyprus and the Czech Republic to the EU began in 1998, and these countries are likely to become members in 2002/3.

The Single European Act (1986)

This Act sought to remove obstacles to a frontier-free community by providing the legal framework to achieve a single market by 31 December 1992. This would entail the free movement of goods, services, capital and people between member states.

The Maastricht Treaty (1991)

This treaty was drawn up by the heads of member governments at a meeting of the European Council and sought to provide a legal basis for developments concerned with European political union and economic and monetary union. The Treaty laid down the conditions for member countries joining a single currency. This required a high degree of sustainable economic convergence measured by indicators which covered inflation, budget deficits, exchange rate stability (which would be guaranteed by membership of the Exchange Rate Mechanism), and long-term interest rates. Moves towards common foreign and security policies, and an extension of responsibilities in areas which included justice, home affairs and social policy were also proposed.

The then British Conservative government objected to the 'Social Chapter' designed to protect workers' rights, and had reservations concerning the terms and timing of monetary union. It thus signed the Treaty only when it was agreed to exempt the UK from the Social Chapter and allow Parliament to determine monetary union. It was further satisfied that the inclusion of the Subsidiarity principle in the Treaty would limit the scope of future policy-making by the EEC (although the precise meaning of the term 'Subsidiarity' was subject to diverse interpretation across Europe). Other countries also experienced problems with this Treaty. It was rejected in 1992 by a referendum in Denmark, a result which was reversed after this country succeeded in securing four opt-out provisions.

Following ratification of this treaty in 1993, the term 'European Union' was employed, implying the creation of an organisation which went beyond the original aims of the EEC.

The Treaty of Amsterdam (1997)

This was agreed at a heads of government summit in 1997, and it amended and updated the Treaties of Rome and Maastricht. It sought to strengthen the commitment to fundamental human rights and freedoms, expressed opposition to discrimination, racism and xenophobia, and aimed for greater foreign policy coordination between member states and the development of a common defence policy. It also proposed enhanced police and judicial cooperation. It promised a move towards common decision-making on immigration, asylum and visa policies, although the UK and Ireland were given opt-outs in these areas.

The Brussels Summit (1998)

At a summit of the European heads of government in May 1998, the finance ministers of 11 countries agreed to implement the objectives of the Maastricht Treaty and create a single European currency, the Euro. On 1 January 1999, the currency of these 11 countries was fixed in relation to the Euro, and a new European central bank was established to manage monetary policy. The Euro was used for paper and electronic transactions after January 1999, and would go into general circulation in 2002 when national currencies would be withdrawn. The UK, Denmark and Sweden remained outside the single currency, while Greece announced her intention to join it in 2002. The UK had joined the Exchange Rate Mechanism in 1990. This required her to maintain the value of the Pound against other EU currencies, using interest rates to achieve this, regardless of domestic considerations. The UK left in 1992 in the belief that high interest rates were prolonging recession.

A single European currency placed restrictions on the sovereignty of those nations which joined. The ability of individual governments to use interest rates to control the growth of their economies was ended, and it seemed likely that, as the economies of participating countries converged, there would be intense pressures for equalisation to take place between wage rates, taxes and social security systems.

Political union, possibly leading to the creation of a European state, could be seen as a logical development which stemmed from the creation of a single currency. Although, in the wake of this development, President Chirac of France and Dr Helmut Kohl, then chancellor of Germany, emphasised that the creation of a European central State was not on their political agendas, this issue became a prominent topic in subsequent debates on the future of the EU. At the 1998 Cardiff summit meeting, a proposal was adopted to establish a council of deputy prime ministers to coordinate the work of EU institutions and national governments. This was designed to enhance the degree of political control exerted by individual governments over Brussels. This theme was subsequently taken up by Paddy Ashdown, then leader of the UK's Liberal Democrats. In 1998, he called for a European constitution to guard against the creeping accumulation of powers by the central decision-making machinery of the EU. This would clarify the relationship between the member States, regions and the EU, and would guarantee the maximum amount of decentralisation of power.

The Main Institutions of the European Union

The Commission (based in Brussels)

This body consists of 20 members appointed by the governments of each member State. Each State appoints one commissioner, and the larger select two. Each commissioner serves a four-year term which may be renewable. On appointment commissioners take an oath not to promote national interests. The commissioners appoint a president who has a five-year term of office. The commissioners are allocated specific responsibilities (termed 'portfolios') by the EU president. They are served by a civil service organised into what are termed Directorates General. The Commission performs a number of key tasks connected with the operations of the European Union.

❍ *The initiation of policy:* this task is performed through the preparation of proposals for the consideration of the Council of Ministers.

The European Commission is based in Brussels.

❍ *The implementation of policy:* laws passed by the Council of Ministers are passed to the Commission for implementation. This role often includes enacting delegated or secondary legislation. Much policy is not directly administered through the Commission's civil service but is discharged by the member States.

❍ *Supervisory functions:* this body also serves as a watchdog, and may draw the attention of the Court of Justice when measures are not being implemented.

❍ *Financial:* the Commission is responsible for preparing draft budget proposals. In 1998, it published the Agenda 2000 proposals which were designed to set the framework of the EU budget for the millennium and beyond.

In 1998, the Commission president, Jacques Santer, proposed to reform the Commission by creating a layer of four or five 'super commissioners' (termed vice presidents). This would elevate key EU activities (including foreign policy and financial affairs) and enable one person to make authoritative pronouncements on them.

The Council of Ministers (based in Brussels)

The Council is composed of ministers of the member States. The Council 'proper' consists of each country's foreign minister, although much of its work is discharged by sub-committees and working groups in which other ministers may participate. The Council is the European Union's supreme law-making (legislative) body. European law is delivered in two main forms.

1 *Regulations:* these are immediately and directly embodied into the law of each member country.

2 *Directives:* these require a member country to take action to adopt the principles contained in a directive into national law by a process termed 'transposition'.

Voting in the Council of Ministers is weighted in favour of the larger member states, although this process is rarely used. Decisions are usually either approved unanimously or (if the ministers of one or more member states object) are shelved. Legislation when approved by the Council becomes part of the national law of member States and it is in this sense that membership of the EU results in a loss of sovereignty. This has been to some extent safeguarded by the practice of unanimity, whereby all members of the Council are required to approve a proposal in order for it to be adopted. This effectively gives individual governments the power to veto proposals and thereby preserve national interests. Since the mid-1980s, however, there has been a movement towards taking decisions on the basis of qualified majority votes which would erode the single nation veto. The Single European Act and the Maastricht Treaty extended the areas which could be determined in this manner. One aspect of what is termed the 'fast track' European integration proposals, enunciated by Chancellor Kohl of Germany and President Chirac of France towards the end of 1995, involved expanding still further the number of decisions which can be made in this manner. Such included tax harmonisation which the French prime minister, Lionel Jospin, and German chancellor, Gerhard Schröder, endorsed at their summit meeting in Potsdam in 1998. Progress in achieving this would be greatly aided by abolishing the unanimity rule.

The presidency of the Council changes hands at six-monthly intervals, with each member state taking its turn. The UK's tenure occurred between January and June 1998.

The European Council (no permanent venue)

This is effectively the most senior level of political authority in the EU. It is composed of the heads of government and foreign ministers of the member countries, and the President and one Vice President of the Commission. Its existence was formally recognised in the Single European Act. Its main purpose is to discuss political issues of overall importance to the European Union, and in this capacity, it has performed a prominent role in the area of foreign affairs. It is not, however, a law-making body, and its decisions would have to be ratified by the Council of Ministers to acquire legal status.

The European Parliament (meets in Luxembourg and Strasbourg)

This consists of representatives who (since 1979) are directly elected by the citizens of each member country, the number of representatives being determined by population. MEPs serve for a term of five years. For much of its existence the European Parliament was regarded as an advisory body, a 'talking shop' which considered proposals put forward by the Commission but which exercised little power over decisions. However, the Single European Act and particularly the Maastricht Treaty sought to provide it with a more vigorous role. Its new responsibilities included the right to reject the EU budget and to be consulted on the appointment of Commissioners, and the ability to play a more significant role in the law-making process. During the 1990s, it sought to use such powers to exert control over the actions of the Commission. In 1995, it threatened to pass a vote of censure against the Commission unless the latter took action to halt French nuclear tests in the South Pacific Ocean. This course of action, which required a two-thirds majority to be successful, would have forced the collective resignation of the Commission. In 1998, it rejected the EU budget in protest against accusations of fraud and mismanagement by the Commission, and subsequently (in 1999) proposed the resignation of individual Commissioners in connection with this issue. This culminated in the collective resignation of the Commission in March 1999.

The European Parliament makes wide use of committees and it is these bodies which consider the content of proposed European Union law. A key deficiency in its powers concerns its lack of control over the Council of Ministers.

The European Court of Justice (sits in Luxembourg)

The Court of Justice (which should not be confused with the European Court of Human Rights) is staffed by judges and advocates drawn from member countries. They serve for six years. The main purpose of the Court is to ensure that European Union law is adhered to within member countries. Disputes between member States, between the European Union and member States, between individuals and the European Union, or between the institutions of the European Union are referred to this Court. It has the power to declare unlawful any national law which contravenes European law and also has the power to fine companies who are found to be in breach of such legislation. A number of national courts (including those of France and the UK) have upheld the view that European law has precedence over national law.

THE COURT OF JUSTICE AND NATIONAL LAW

Examples of the power wielded by the European Court of Justice over the domestic law of member countries are shown below.

◆ *Britain:* in 1995 the Court ruled that men in Britain should receive free medical prescriptions at the age of 60, rather than 65, to bring them into a position of equality with women.

◆ *Belgium:* in 1998 the Court ruled that failure to amend the constitution to enable non-Belgium EU citizens to vote in local elections (as was required under the provisions of the Maastricht Treaty) would result in a fine of £125,000 per day.

Committees

The work of the EU is discharged by a number of committees. Key committees are discussed below.

The Committee of Permanent Representatives (COREPER)

This consists of a body of officials (sometimes referred to as 'ambassadors') who act on behalf of the Council of Ministers. Their main role is to examine proposals put before the Council of Ministers to facilitate their future discussion of the issue. These officials are senior civil servants of member States who are temporarily seconded to the European Union.

The Economic and Social Committee

This is a consultative body comprised of representatives from member countries. Its work is diverse. This is reflected in its membership which may include employers, trade unionists, professionals and agricultural interests.

The Committee of the Regions

This body consists of representatives from all member countries and advises on and debates the EU's regional policy.

Impact on the Institutions of National Government

Membership of the European Union has had an impact on the organisation of the machinery of member governments at a number of different levels.

○ *The executive branch of government:* in the UK, for example, a European Secretariat within the Cabinet Office coordinates national policy towards the EU, and government departments (especially those concerned with trade, agriculture and industry) have divisions concerned with the European dimension to their activities. One key function is to ensure that British and European law are harmonised.

○ *Legislatures:* parliaments in member nations have established specialist committees to monitor the activities of the EU. These include Ireland's Joint Committee of the Oireachtas on Secondary Legislation, the British House of Commons Select Committee on European Legislation, and the short-lived (1983–87) German Europa-Kommission composed of members drawn from the Bundestag and the European Parliament.

○ *Judiciaries:* the decisions of national courts may be overruled by the European Court of Justice where these conflict with EU laws. Membership of the EU also implies that national courts can determine the validity of domestic law in relationship to community law. This aspect of judicial review is novel to some countries, including the UK.

○ *Local government:* local authorities have established formal links with Brussels in connection with proposed bids for aid from sources such as the European Regional Development Fund.

❍ *Pressure groups:* the transfer of decision-making to the institutions of the European Union has had significant implications for those who seek to influence the policy-making process. As was observed in Chapter 8, pressure groups are widely engaged in liaison with the Commission and its officials. Lobbying by groups in Brussels is especially apparent in the areas of agriculture, environmental policy and regional and economic policy.

Question

Select any ONE of the following:

❍ the European Commission

❍ the Council of Ministers

❍ the European Parliament

❍ the European Court of Justice.

Compile your own information concerning this EU institution. You should include its membership, the role it performs, the power it wields, and contemporary developments affecting its evolution.

The European Union and British Politics

The Pressure For Greater Cooperation Between European Countries

In the postwar period a number of pressures contributed towards a movement towards greater European cooperation.

❍ *The desire for peace and security:* as has been noted above, the desire to prevent another world war (those of 1914–18 and 1939–45 having been considerably fuelled by the rivalry between Germany and France) was a key factor motivating European politicians to seek closer ties.

❍ *Economic factors:* a number of issues related to economic policy, trade and industrial research and development might be more effectively managed by cooperation between governments. The potential of the European market was massive: in 1995, the combined population of the 15 member countries was in excess of 350 million, and their combined gross domestic product was approximately 30 per cent of global GDP.

❍ *World influence:* the postwar world was dominated by 'superpowers' (the Soviet Union, the USA and the People's Republic of China). A unified Europe was theoretically more likely to be able to influence the course of world events than individual countries acting unilaterally.

British Politics and the Issue of Closer European Cooperation

The pressures which induced politicians in Europe to secure a greater level of cooperation were less pressingly felt in the UK. Although Britain had played a foremost role in the 1914–18 and 1939–45 World Wars, the Country had not been a battleground in the same way as had many countries in Europe. There was a view (shared by politicians such as Winston Churchill) that closer European cooperation was desirable since it would enable quarrels and rivalries between these countries to be solved without the resort to war into which Britain would inevitably be dragged. But this did not mean that Britain would have to play a prominent role (or necessarily be involved at all) in such developments.

The issue of the relationship between the UK and Europe split the main political parties and created some unusual, perhaps bizarre, political alliances: in the 1975 referendum campaign, for example, the case for leaving Europe was voiced by rightwing politicians such as Enoch Powell and leftwingers such as Michael Foot. The subject itself has also undergone subtle transformations, as is shown below:

❍ *Should Britain join?:* the former Liberal Party was the most enthusiastic advocate of Britain joining the EEC in the late 1950s and early 1960s, but this move was opposed by many in both the Conservative and Labour Parties, as well as by European leaders such as the President of France, Charles de Gaulle. Britain's application to join was vetoed in 1963 but accepted in 1972, thus ending this particular debate.

❍ *Should Britain (having joined in 1973) remain a member?:* reservations (especially in the Labour Party) concerning Britain's membership of the EEC resulted in the government of Harold Wilson renegotiating Britain's terms of membership. These terms were put to a referendum in 1975, and support for them determined the outcome of this question.

❍ *What kind of European cooperation?:* we tend to accept Britain's membership of the EEC (now EU) as a fact, but the debate has shifted to a consideration of the nature which European cooperation should assume. The issue of national sovereignty as opposed to a federal Europe is the fundamental underpinning of this issue.

The Political Debate on Closer European Cooperation

The arguments in relationship to the three questions referred to above have split the main parties. This section briefly puts forward the issues which have been raised in connection with Europe since it first entered the British political debate in the late 1950s.

Sovereignty

UK membership of the European Union clearly has an adverse effect on the traditional doctrine of the sovereignty of Parliament. Further, unlike many other forms of international cooperation which are concerned with specific purposes, the European Union possesses something akin to a blank cheque to extend the area of its control.

However, placing the *loss* of sovereignty at the forefront of British political debate is not a totally accurate portrayal of the reality. The key issue concerns the *pooling* of sovereignty. This means that the UK has the ability to play some part in shaping the domestic policies of all member countries over a wide range of policy areas. In this sense, enhanced cooperation between European countries increases the UK's ability to influence legislation on a supra-national basis.

Remoteness, Centralisation and Lack of Accountability

Apart from the European Parliament, the key decision-making institutions of the EU (the Council of Ministers and the European Council) are not subject to any meaningful form of popular accountability. The gives rise to perceptions of faceless bureaucrats in Brussels passing laws about which British voters are not consulted and about which they can do nothing should they object to what has been enacted. In 1998, the British Foreign Secretary, Robin Cook, addressed such concerns by proposing that a second tier to the European Parliament should be formed, from MPs of the member States, which would sift through decisions made by Brussels and block those which meddled with the finer details of national life.

The direct application of EU decisions in the UK has given rise to accusations of British interests being sacrificed to suit the concerns of other member States. Such views have been especially voiced by the British farming and fishing industries. The movement towards the use of qualified majority voting in the Council of Ministers has heightened such concerns since this may result in EU laws being forced on the UK without the agreement of the British government.

Xenophobia

This term denotes a dislike, even hatred, of foreigners, and in political debate is often accompanied by articulating pride in one's own country, race and culture. Such views have frequently entered into the debate on the UK's place in Europe. In 1962, the then Labour Party leader, Hugh Gaitskell, rejected Britain joining the EEC on the grounds that this would wipe away one thousand years of British history. In 1990, a leading minister of the then Conservative government, Nicholas Ridley, resigned following the expression of anti-German sentiments in an interview in the *Spectator* magazine.

Technical Objections

This covers matters such as the size of the UK's contribution to the EEC/EU budget, and led to the then Labour Prime Minister, Harold Wilson, seeking to renegotiate Britain's terms of entry following his victory at the February 1974 General Election. A major concern was that the UK failed to get good value for money, being a net contributor to the EEC budget. Particular criticism was directed at the expenditure on the Common Agricultural Policy which was viewed as subsidising the inefficient farming practices adopted in countries such as France. Reductions in the size of UK financial contributions during the 1980s helped to reduce the weight of this objection. However, it emerged as an issue in 1998 when Germany (backed by Austria, Holland and Sweden) sought to lower its contribution to the EU budget, which at that time totalled around 60 per cent of its net contributions. This development reflected an increasing unease on the part of the EU's richer countries about paying for its poorer members, but its timing was influenced by Helmut Kohl's attempt to secure the re-election in the German General Election of September 1998.

The Atlantic Alliance

This suggests that the UK's interests (especially in terms of defence and foreign policy) are better served by cooperation with the USA. This relationship could be jeopardised should the UK become closely identified with the cause of enhanced European cooperation. Some European countries (most notably France) have traditionally adopted a hostile attitude towards American influence in Europe, and such views might instigate a more integrated European structure of government, especially if one reason for this development was to rival the existing super-powers. A major dispute within the then Conservative government in 1986 concerning the rescue of the Westland helicopter company by a European or American-backed scheme led to the resignation of a key minister (Michael Heseltine, who favoured the European package), illustrating the 'America versus Europe' dilemma for UK politicians.

Support for the value of the American Alliance was not confined to the Conservative Party. In 1998, the Labour Prime Minister, Tony Blair, depicted the UK as a bridge between Europe and the USA. He wished to use this pivotal world role to guard against American isolationism and to convince Europe of the value of American world leadership. His inclination to deal directly with the USA rather than consult with his EU partners was evident in December 1998 when British and American forces bombed Iraq in response to its failure to cooperate with UN weapons inspections.

The Views of the Major Political Parties

This section briefly evaluates the attitudes of Britain's two main parties concerning European cooperation.

The Labour Party

The Labour Party was traditionally divided concerning membership of the EEC. Many social democrats shared the view of the then Liberal Party that entry was a key underpinning of the quest to modernise the UK in the early 1960s. However, many in the Labour Party were sceptical. The EEC was initially viewed as a 'rich man's club', and later (especially in the late 1970s and early 1980s) as a mechanism dominated by free market ideals which would prevent a future Labour government from pursuing socialist objectives. However, during the course of the 1980s, the attitude of the Party altered. This was so for a number of reasons which are outlined below.

❍ *The dominance of the Conservative Party in British politics:* Europe presented the possibility of offsetting the dominant hold which the Conservative Party exerted over British politics between 1979 and 1997. Policies which the Labour Party and its supporters favoured (such as the social chapter) could be promoted through the mechanisms of the EU.

❍ *Hostility towards Europe was associated with the left of the Party:* as is argued in Chapter 3, the dominant hold exerted by the left of the Party receded after the 1983 General Election defeat. The Party's advocacy of British withdrawal was abandoned. Subsequent Labour leaders adopted a more positive attitude towards Europe, although reservations concerning European monetary union were evident after 1997.

The Conservative Party

This Party was identified with support for the UK joining the EEC: the then Conservative Prime Minister, Harold Macmillan, unsuccessfully applied for entry in 1961, and a later Conservative government, headed by Ted Heath, took the UK into the EEC in 1973. There were, however, opponents to Britain's involvement in Europe who became more vocal in opposition to what they perceived as a project to develop an integrated trading bloc into that of a federal Europe. Divisions within the Conservative Party over Europe had an unsettling impact on the fortunes of the Conservative Party in the latter years of Margaret Thatcher's premiership, and had a detrimental effect on the unity of John Major's Conservative governments (1990–97). Opposition to closer ties with Europe became associated with the so-called 'Eurosceptics'.

THE CONSERVATIVE EUROSCEPTICS

Premier Thatcher's Bruges speech in 1988 led to the formation of a faction (the Bruges Group) within the Conservative Party to oppose progress in the direction of a federal Europe. An influential tendency, the Eurosceptics, also existed within that Party during the 1990s.

Eurosceptics were especially opposed to any further moves towards pooling sovereignty and political integration, moves which they viewed as the underpinnings of the Single Market Act and the Maastricht Treaty. They opposed the latter treaty's goal of economic and monetary union, and did not wish to re-enter the Exchange Rate Mechanism. Eurosceptics were unhappy concerning the seemingly ever-expanding policy-making areas embraced by the EU (especially in connection with social policy), and also criticised the European Court of Justice for enhancing federalism. A number voted against the ratification of the Maastricht Treaty in 1993, even though the then Conservative government made this an issue of confidence. Eurosceptic support for the candidacy of John Redwood in the 1995 leadership contest of the Conservative Party was a major explanation for his good showing against the then prime minister, John Major. It demonstrated the potency of the political appeal of sovereignty.

Question

Compare and contrast the current attitudes adopted by any TWO of the UK's political parties towards closer European integration.

Further Reading

There are a number of good books dealing with the European Union. These include **Stephen George**, *Politics and Policy in the European Union* (Oxford: Oxford University Press, 1996, 3rd edition), and **John McCormick**, *The EU: Politics and Policies* (Colorado: Westview Press, 1996). These discuss the history and institutions of the EU, and examine a number of key EU policy areas.

Another good account of the evolution of the EU and its relationship with the outside world is provided by **Paul Taylor**, *The EU in the 1990s* (Oxford: Oxford University Press, 1996).

The theme of globalisation is fully discussed in **Barrie Axford**, *The Global System – Economics, Politics and Culture* (Cambridge: Polity Press, 1995). This analyses the rise and nature of a world society.

Contemporary
Political Issues

PART FOUR

Chapter Nineteen | The Role of the State

The aims of this chapter are:

1 To briefly describe changing views concerning the level of State activity from the late nineteenth century until 1945.

2 To analyse arguments critical of the role performed by the State after 1945.

3 To evaluate the approaches adopted by Conservative governments between 1979 and 1997 to 'roll back the frontiers of the State'.

4 To assess the policies pursued after 1997 by the Labour Party concerning the role of the State.

5 To analyse the arguments related to the existence of a political consensus between 1945 and 1979.

6 To evaluate arguments related to the emergence of a new political consensus in the 1990s.

The Changing Role of the State

The following section provides a very brief account of changing views concerning the desirable scope of State activity.

The Late Nineteenth and Early Twentieth Century

Historically the role of the State was confined to a few key areas which usually included defence and foreign affairs. Its involvement in economic and social affairs came about slowly. The main reforming party in the nineteenth century was the Liberal Party which was wedded to individualism. It was deemed the responsibility of individuals to improve themselves and considered to be their fault if they failed to do so. It rejected an active role for the State, believing that this 'interference' both undermined the reliance of individuals on their own efforts,
and placed unwarranted restrictions on the ability of individuals to utilise their initiative and seek self-advancement. They were willing to accept State intervention if actions by one citizen prevented others from exercising their liberty, but opposed more positive actions by the State which would respond to economic inequality or social injustices.

The traditional Liberal endorsement of individualism was, however, challenged towards the end of the nineteenth century. Investigations by social scientists into the widespread problem of poverty suggested that this was not always the fault of the individual but sometimes arose from circumstances beyond his or her control (such as trade cycles resulting in periodic economic depression, ill health or old age). This gave rise to a distinction between the 'deserving' and 'undeserving' poor, the latter being those whose habits (such as idleness or drunkenness) were held responsible for their poverty. Towards the end of the nineteenth century a number of socialist societies emerged, which led to the creation of the Labour Party in the early twentieth century. This party endorsed collectivism, an approach which was also embraced by some (termed 'New Liberals') in the Liberal Party.

The First World War served to make collectivism more 'fashionable'. Although the conduct of the early years of war were influenced by the traditional Liberal approach of individualism, the need to respond to the unprecedented demands of total warfare resulted in more prominent State intervention. This was particularly evident in the creation of the Ministry of Munitions in 1915, and State direction or supervision of a range of industries (and those employed within them) which were essential to the war effort. Although many of these innovations were abandoned when the war ended in 1918, subsequent suggestions were made by the economist John Maynard Keynes for State involvement to remedy major social problems such as unemployment.

The Second World War and the Role of the State

INCREASED STATE ACTIVITY, 1939–45

The role of the State was greatly expanded in response to the Second World War. This included the following developments.

◆ *State supervision of industry:* this affected industries which included the railways, air passenger transport, the mines, ports and agriculture. However, the degree of government supervision varied.

◆ *Direct state running of industry:* after 1935 the government embarked on the policy of building munitions and armament factories. Some remained under direct government control when they became operational, although others were subject to 'agency arrangements' whereby once built they were placed under the control of firms in the private sector.

◆ *State control over essential goods:* German submarines sunk Allied ships carrying food and supplies. The government was required to acquire foodstuffs and raw materials whose distribution was then controlled through the process of rationing. The influence which the government secured enabled it to impose price controls.

◆ *State control over labour:* agreements were concluded with the unions over matters which included the arbitration of wage disputes and strikes. Additionally, the government acquired powers to regulate conditions of labour and to direct labour where it was most required. In 1941, a manpower budget was drawn up to balance the personnel requirements of industry and the armed forces.

The role of the State increased in a number of key areas between 1939 and 1945. However, unlike the First World War, the 1939–45 conflict resulted in the acceptance that the State should continue to exercise major responsibilities after peace had been secured. This arose in part out of practical necessity (such as with the need to repair bomb damage to around 3.75 million houses, and to reconstruct and invest in key industries such as the railways and mines). Additionally, however, the war generated feelings that members of the working class who had contributed significantly to the war effort on the home and foreign fronts were deserving of improved economic and social conditions in an era of peace. The mixing of the classes which occurred during the war (especially on the home front where children from working class city environments were evacuated to the countryside) provided graphic evidence of the plight of the urban poor. Thus the sacrifices made by the working class during the war created a moral basis on which aid to the poorer members of society could be justified. These considerations gave rise to an expanded role of the State after 1945, in areas which are discussed below.

❍ *State running of industry:* many of the industries taken over at the outbreak of war were not returned to their private owners in 1945 but were nationalised.

❍ *State responsibility to secure full employment:* this responsibility was derived from a White Paper written by Keynes in 1944.

❍ *The welfare state:* Sir William Beveridge's report on Social Insurance and Allied Services in 1942 resulted in the creation of the welfare state, which embraced a 'cradle to grave' range of social provisions including a national health service. The welfare

Sir William Beveridge, whose 1942 report led to the founding of the Welfare State.

state was directed against the five 'giants' of want, disease, squalor, idleness and ignorance.

Although these reforms were enacted by the Labour government which was elected in 1945, the endorsement of collectivism was more broadly supported. Although there were reservations within the Conservative Party about many of the developments pursued by Clement Attlee's Labour governments between 1945 and 1951, the role of the State (although pruned in some areas) was expanded in others by the Conservative governments of 1951–64. Both Parties endorsed a mixed economy, and the area of social policy was greatly developed after 1951.

Question

Briefly assess any ONE of the main factors which contributed to the increased role of the State between 1914 and 1945.

To do this, select from the following headings:

◯ **Political ideology:** here you need to analyse the collectivist nature of ideology endorsed by the major political parties in this period.

◯ **The impact of war:** here you would need to assess the extent to which war promoted a more vigorous role to be played by the State.

◯ **Academic influences:** these would embrace arguments put forward as part of intellectual opinion concerning the level of State activity.

Critique of the Role of the State After 1945

Little challenge was made to the involvement of the State in a wide range of policy areas embracing industry, social welfare and the handling of the economy in the immediate postwar years. The State assumed an ever-greater range of responsibilities in subsequent years. The Labour Party became especially identified with statism (a belief in the ability of the State to solve a wide range of contemporary problems), although the Conservative Party and to some extent the Liberal Party did not have significantly different views on this issue.

Nonetheless, there were criticisms put forward concerning the role of the State in the postwar United Kingdom. These came from three sources.

❍ *The Liberal Party:* in 1953 a body, the non-servile state group, was formed within the Liberal Party to challenge the view of the State as 'an engine of all advance'. However, the attention paid to their critique was limited because of this Party's political weakness during the 1950s. Its membership included a future Liberal leader, Jo Grimond, who subsequently became a prominent opponent of statism.

❍ *Academic opinion:* leading political scientists put forward the 'overload' thesis in the 1970s. This stated that political campaigning revolved around the 'politics of promising' in which the main Parties sought to outbid each other at election times with promises of what they would do if elected to office. However, the resources on which to fund such promises were declining, which suggested the need for the public to be educated to expect less rather than more from the State.

❍ *The Conservative Party:* in the early 1970s the government led by Ted Heath briefly pursued policies which were designed to reduce the role of the State. These were known as 'Selsdon Man' policies, being named after a Surrey Hotel where they were adopted by the then Shadow cabinet. These were rapidly abandoned in 1972 due to the collapse of Rolls-Royce and increasing unemployment. They were replaced by a more interventionist approach.

The most vigorous attempt to reduce the level of State activity was, however, pursued by Conservative governments after 1979. The following section evaluates the developments which took place in this period.

The Conservative Party and the Role of the State, 1979–97

The Conservative government which was elected in 1979 under the leadership of Margaret Thatcher pursued a political approach which has been variously described as 'Thatcherism', 'neo-liberalism', or 'new right' ideology. As has been briefly referred to above, aspects of this approach were not confined to the Conservative Party but were also endorsed by anti-statist Liberals whose main spokesperson was Jo Grimond, the Party leader between 1956 and 1967 (and again briefly in 1976). The following section identifies a number of key arguments put forward by both of these strands of political opinion.

Objections to the Role of the State

The 'new right' of the Conservative Party and anti-statist Liberals voiced a number of concerns regarding the role of the State after 1945. The arguments presented are discussed below.

Dependency

The activity of the State in the area of social welfare was alleged to have given rise to a culture of dependency. Those in difficulties were encouraged to turn to the State for a solution to their problems rather than seeking to solve them using their own initiative or through the help of their family, friends, neighbours or community. Liberals such as Jo Grimond were particularly concerned that individuals in this situation were devalued as persons since they relinquished to the State the ability to exercise control over matters which affected the conduct of their everyday lives. Conservatives tended to emphasise that the reliance on social welfare served as a disincentive to seek work.

Bureaucracy

Bureaucrats administer a service on behalf of others. Their dominance after 1945 arose from the growth of large-scale industrial, commercial and governmental organisations. This 'big is beautiful' mentality was heavily (although not exclusively) influenced by the increased role performed by the State after 1945 which resulted in a large public sector which gave rise to powerful bureaucracies including professional organisations and trade unions. These were the four further problems alleged to arise from this situation:

○ *The dominance of sectional interests:* bureaucracies within the public sector advanced their own interests to the detriment of the overall requirements of the nation. The common good was thus undermined by sectional interests.

❍ *The loss of power of the individual:* individuals were encouraged to band together and advance their interests as part of a 'herd' rather than through the exercise of their own initiative.

❍ *Lack of accountability:* bureaucracies were often unresponsive to the opinions or needs of those in whose interests they operated.

❍ *Undemocratic:* governments found it necessary to incorporate powerful bureaucracies into the decision-making machinery of the State. This gave rise to the corporate State in which control over key aspects of public policy was taken away from Parliament and handed over to meetings between unions, employers and ministers. These were conducted in secret, and the participants could not be held accountable for their actions.

Economic Inefficiency

A key objection to the public sector was that it was inefficient. This problem arose because it was not subject to the discipline of market forces. This meant that productivity was not the exclusive determinant of the existence of jobs (since the State frequently stepped in to subsidise unprofitable concerns in order to fulfil the social obligation of maintaining a high overall level of employment) or of pay in the public sector. This was perceived to be a major cause of inflation which those on the right of the political spectrum viewed as *the* key political problem, particularly because of its effect on investment.

High Public Spending

Conservatives and anti-statist Liberals viewed with alarm the high levels of public spending in the UK in the late 1970s. This was measured in terms of public spending as a percentage of Gross National Product, and its high level arose from factors which included the scope of welfare services, and also from the need on the part of the nationalised industries for capital. Such requirements resulted in borrowing and high levels of taxation. Liberals such as Grimond asserted that this situation made socialism an almost inevitable outcome: the private sector of the economy would collapse under the weight of taxation, resulting in the State taking over the means of production.

Policies to Reduce the Role of the State After 1979

Conservative governments between 1979 and 1997 pursued a range of policies which were designed to reduce the role performed by the State. The main developments are discussed below.

Monetarism

In the mid-1970s the UK and other Western nations experienced a new problem, that of 'stagflation'. The following two economic problems occurred at the same time, triggered by dramatic rises in the cost of oil.

❍ *Stagnation:* which entailed the lack of economic growth and resultant unemployment.

❍ *Inflation:* which involved rapidly rising prices.

These undermined Keynesian economics, since he had held that these problems would not occur together, and justified a search for new economic methods. An alternative to Keynesian economics was 'monetarism', in which the key priority became that of tackling inflation. Monetarists believed that inflation was caused by there being too much money in the economy, which was derived from factors including the availability of credit. This was underpinned by an excessively high level of government spending. The new approach sought to reduce the level of spending by controlling the money supply. It involved linking targets for the growth of the money supply to targets for government borrowing and was implemented by policies which included imposing cash limits on the expenditure of central government departments, and seeking to establish some form of control over the expenditure of local government. By the mid-1980s, however, government economic policy to control inflation shifted from seeking to impose targets on the growth of the money supply to the use of interest rates to maintain a strong exchange rate.

A Free-Market Economy

The adoption of monetarism inevitably resulted in the endorsement of a free market in which matters such as economic growth and the provision of employment opportunities were secured through the 'natural' forces of supply and demand, rather than as the result of government intervention in economic affairs. The latter had given rise to a variety of policies including State ownership, incentives to industry to locate in deprived regions (or disincentives not to establish in prosperous ones), high taxation and incomes policies. The endorsement of the free market also justified an attack on the activities of trade unions since these were blamed for preventing market forces from operating effectively by insisting, for example, on excessive wage rises not supported by productivity.

The Internal Market

An attempt was made to subject services which remained in the public sector to the discipline of market forces. This was achieved through the implementation of an 'internal' market which sought to create a division between a purchaser of services and then provider of them. This was implemented in the National Health Service, for example, whereby health authorities became 'purchasers' of services offered by hospital service 'providers'.

Privatisation

This policy initially sought to reduce the size of the public sector by denationalising many of the industries which were State controlled. Some (such as Ferranti in 1980) were sold by private sale, but in others which included British Telecom (1984), British Gas (1986) and British Airways (1987), the State's holding was sold off in the form of shares offered to the public. This gave the Treasury an immediate influx of huge amounts of money, and was theoretically designed to advance the concept of 'popular capitalism' in which ordinary members of the general public were able to buy shares (and receive regular dividends on them). In practice, however, many shares in such industries were bought up by large commercial or financial concerns.

Privatisation entailed contracting out and deregulation as well as denationalisation and was one aspect of the Conservative government's policies to improve the operations of the supply side of the economy in order that markets could operate with enhanced efficiency. This approach assumed increasing importance in the mid-1980s, and, as Chapter 16 indicates, was forced on local government through initiatives which included compulsory competitive tendering.

Consumerism

This approach was especially identified with Prime Minister John Major who launched the Citizen's Charter in 1991. This applied to a wide range of public services, but stemmed from earlier initiatives which were designed to hold to account those who delivered public services when these had been privatised. Control was effected in a number of such industries by regulation which was designed to ensure that consumers were provided with services of an acceptable quality. This typically took the form of regulators' (such as OFTEL for British Telecom and OFGAS for British Gas) being able to monitor services and suggest improvements. In some cases (as with the rail industry) they were provided with the power to fine companies whose delivery of services was poor. Thus political accountability gave way to consumerism: the public exercised control over privatised public services by their ability to 'shop around' and go elsewhere if the company delivering the service failed to provide a quality service. This, however, is only possible when competition exists between those who provide a particular service. For much of the period of Conservative governments, consumerism was imperfectly realised since state-controlled monopolies were merely transformed into private sector monopolies with no meaningful public accountability.

Enhanced Self-Reliance

The desire to reduce the role of the State resulted in enhanced importance being attached to the family as a key social unit. Policies were also promoted to construct a property-owning democracy. This entailed encouragement of private home ownership at the expense of local authority house provision. The 'right to buy' was introduced in the 1980 Housing Act, compelling local authorities to sell their property to those of their tenants who wished to buy it. Arguments which depicted lone-parent families as the source of all social evils, and the emphasis placed on welfare state 'scroungers' sought to provide popular support for the Conservative governments' endorsement of a self-reliant society. Encouragement for private enterprise to provide services such as health and education was also given.

Enhanced Individual Freedom

The desire to 'set the people free' from the interference of government underlaid the intention to reduce personal taxation so that individuals could spend more of their money as they thought fit. The enhancement of the freedom of the individual was also extended to organisations such as trade unions which were subject to policies designed to democratise their operations, thereby reducing the ability of leaders to take decisions which were unrepresentative of the views of the membership.

Question

Analyse the strengths and weaknesses of any TWO policies introduced by Conservative governments between 1979 and 1997 to reduce the role of the State.

Increased Power of the State

The policies pursued after 1979 were not underlaid by a consistent objective of reducing the role of the State. Some policies increased the role of the State and the power of central government over policies.

Free Market, Strong State

The adoption of monetarist economic policies resulted in increasing unemployment. This led to the creation of disaffected sections of society whose dissent was graphically displayed in actions such as urban disorders and rioting. The State had to respond to such activities, and one aspect of this response was to increase the powers and weaponry available to the police service so that protest and dissent could be effectively quashed. It has thus been argued that the adoption of the free market requires a 'strong state'. This entailed a number of piecemeal changes being made to the operations of the political system to facilitate a more coercive response to those who challenged their social exclusion by extra-parliamentary methods of activity. This issue is discussed more fully in Chapter 23.

Centralisation

A number of Conservative policies increased the role of central government. This approach influenced Conservative views towards local government and was evident in services such as education where the 1998 Education Reform Act reversed the traditional decentralisation of British education through the imposition of the National Curriculum.

The Labour Government and the Role of the State

SOCIAL DEMOCRACY AND THE WIND OF CHANGE

The policies adopted by the Conservative Party in the UK after 1979 and by the Republican Party in the USA after 1980 had a significant influence on social-democratic Parties throughout the world. The abandonment of Keynesianism in favour of monetarism was subsequently adopted by a number of such Parties, a major exception being in Norway. Significant developments affecting the policies pursued by socialist and social-democratic Parties occurred in countries including France and Germany.

◆ *France:* privatisation policies were increased by France's socialist government after 1997. It rejected demands for more public spending and approved a £2.7 billion tax cut for businesses in the 1999 budget.

◆ *Germany:* Gerhardt Schröder, the leader of the Social Democrat Party which secured victory at the General Election in September 1998, put forward a platform which included embracing the market economy, advocating a partnership between business and labour, supporting private investment, and advocating income and corporation tax cuts.

A major problem faced by the Labour Party in the 1990s was that the emphasis placed on individualism had eroded support for collectivism. Conservative governments had produced a more selfish society, one aspect of which was a disinclination to aid its least fortunate members, especially where this implied a higher level of taxation. Accordingly, the Labour Party was forced in the 1997 General Election to disclaim any intention to raise taxes, but benefited both from the unpopularity of the Conservative government and from genuine concern that unregulated individualism had given rise to undesirable developments such as 'sleaze' and enormous salaries paid to 'fat cat' executives in the private sector. Public criticism was particularly directed at those earning large salaries in formerly state-owned enterprises delivering a service to the general public.

This meant that the Labour government elected in 1997 could claim a mandate to pursue initiatives to create a less selfish society, provided that these did not result in higher levels of public spending. The following section assesses how this concern was addressed in the early period of Labour government.

The Implementation of Stakeholding

Stakeholding has been discussed in Chapter 3. The new Labour government vigorously pursued this concept, which was particularly addressed to those who had been thrown aside after 1979 and had become alienated from the rest of society, believing themselves to be unwanted or irrelevant in an economic sense, since they were unable to contribute to the processes of production. The government's objective was thus to create an inclusive, more tolerant, one-nation society based upon the widening of opportunity but not the redistribution of reward. This objective was clearly put forward by Labour's Chancellor, Gordon Brown. His first budget as Chancellor of the Exchequer in 1997 was couched in the language of inclusion. The government's commitment to reducing inequality and social exclusion was emphasised by the establishment in August 1997 of a special unit within the Cabinet Office headed by the Prime Minister.

Setting the Poor to Work

Labour policy was initially directed at those on 'the edge of the labour force'. It was not envisaged that action undertaken by the government alone would solve this problem, and the role of the private sector was crucial. This was compatible with a view of the State as an enabling body operating in partnership with private enterprise to fulfil social objectives. Labour's Chancellor of the Exchequer, Gordon Brown, sought to give such ideas practical content with his call for a national crusade against unemployment and poverty. He put forward measures which included the following.

❍ *'Welfare to Work':* this was a job-creation scheme funded from £5 billion raised from a windfall tax on the privatised utilities.

❍ *A programme designed to make work pay:* this was achieved through a mixture of the minimum wage and a 10 pence starting rate of tax. These were incentives to encourage the take-up of low-paid jobs.

❍ *An overhaul of the tax and benefits system:* such were designed to lift the low-paid workers from poverty.

❍ *Training:* there were increased opportunities for British workers to improve their skills.

The attention devoted to skills training and raising educational standards was a crucial aspect of Labour's commitment to stakeholding. It was accepted that globalisation tended to produce insecurity and social dislocation, and the government thus sought to guard against the consequences of this by making it possible for workers to constantly adjust the skills they possessed. This would enable them to take advantage of the new forms of work which became available as avenues offered through previous occupations closed. Educational improvement and the development of skills were key aspects of the *Investing in Young People* initiative which was announced towards the end of 1997. This required employers to offer the opportunity of paid study leave to young workers below 18 years of age who had left school with few if any qualifications, and whose employment did not provide any training element. This measure was designed to prevent them becoming trapped in 'dead end' jobs.

Labour's early reforms thus sought to enable the unemployed to become stakeholders through their participation as workers in the market economy. This approach was followed in Chancellor Brown's second budget, delivered in March 1998. In this he put forward the twin policies of Child Care Tax Credit and Family Tax Credit.

○ *The Child Care Tax Credit:* this was designed to encourage mothers back into the workforce by making child care affordable for the lower paid.

○ *The Family Tax Credit:* this was introduced in 1999. It would replace the existing State benefit by a tax credit paid through the pay packet, thereby encouraging work.

The entire approach was dependent on sustained economic growth. Accordingly, the 1988 Budget put forward a range of tax and investment measures designed to stimulate enterprise, aid company growth and create jobs. The encouragement of enterprise was particularly directed at the small-business sector.

The Welfare State

Some advocates of a stakeholder society emphasised a strong universal welfare state as the mechanism to reincorporate those who constituted the 'underclass'. However, the incoming government wished to avoid major increases in the level of public spending. Accordingly, the policies which were designed to set the unemployed back to work were also viewed as a reform to the welfare state. These sought to tackle the problems of poverty and unemployment at their roots, by addressing issues such as low skills and low wages rather than merely responding to the consequences of them by adding a few pounds onto welfare benefits. The first principle of Labour's modernisation of the welfare state was thus to take action to open up work opportunities to those previously denied them. The provision of personal skills and employment were seen as the most effective anti-poverty policies in the long term. The desire to move the focus of welfare away from the payment of benefit and towards enabling people to move to work was a key underpinning of the Green Paper on welfare reform, *New Ambitions for our Country: A New Contract for Welfare*, published in March 1998.

INITIAL LABOUR POLICY ON PUBLIC SPENDING AND THE WELFARE STATE

The initial policy direction of the 1997 Labour government was to provide individuals with the resources and opportunities to become self-reliant through the provision of work, education and skills training. The notion that individuals should be responsible for their own welfare was forcibly expressed in the 1998 Green Paper, which made explicit the responsibility of the individual to work, be independent, support family members and save for retirement. This would enable the direct role of the State in such matters to be reduced, thus enabling those unable to make any contribution towards their own welfare to secure enhanced levels of benefits.

There was a need, however, to respond to criticisms made during the 1997 election campaign concerning the alleged Conservative underfunding of public services, especially health and education. Labour accepted that strong public services were essential for the good of the individual and society as a whole, but it did not endorse a high-spending state as the way to achieve this objective. Additionally, the scale of the problem of poverty made a 'tax and spend' solution unworkable. Labour thus needed to provide improved public services in a manner which did not involve a massive commitment to increased levels of public spending. This would serve to alienate middle England taxpayers (if required to pay more tax) and would have an unsettling effect on the City.

Initially, the government kept to the limits on public sector spending drawn up by the previous Conservative administration and sought to fund improvements in other ways. These included the redistribution of existing funds, since reductions in social-welfare benefits derived from putting the employed back to work would mean that public spending could be redistributed to other areas, including the health service and education. This aim could also be achieved by eliminating waste: the Health Secretary, Frank Dobson, estimated that reforms to the NHS proposed in the 1997 White Paper (*The New NHS – Modern and Dependable)* to eliminate red tape could save £1 billion before the year 2002.

Additionally, money was sought both from the private sector, which was encouraged to be more socially responsive, and through allowing the beneficiaries of certain services to make a more significant contribution towards their cost. Thus the government succeeded in 'levering' money from the private sector to contribute towards the school-buildings programme, and the NHS Private Finance Initiative provided funds for hospital building. In 1998, the government announced the establishment of 25 Education Action Zones. These were located in areas of social disadvantage and jointly funded by the Treasury and business (which included Rolls-Royce, Kellogg, British Aerospace and Tate and Lyle). The policy of forcing graduates to repay their higher education tuition fees was an example of the government seeking to finance public services by levying money from the immediate beneficiaries.

An Assessment of Labour's Stakeholder Reforms

Labour's endorsement of stakeholding entailed an acceptance that the equality of means and rewards was not a pre-eminent political aim. Labour now supported the more modest objective of economic, social and political inclusion. However, this goal was seen as insufficiently radical by some members of the Labour Party who believed it diluted the Party's historic commitment to equality through the redistribution of wealth and power, and constituted less of an attempt to bring socialism up to date than a search for a philosophy to replace it.

The stakeholder economy could be identified with the twin aims of the pursuit of social justice and the smooth operation of a market economy, thus appealing both to the unemployed and to the entrepreneur. The government did not feel that these aims were incompatible. They believed that the market economy was egalitarian and that any who took advantage of the opportunities which it offered could themselves become wealth creators. The 'soak the rich' days were thus formally abandoned in favour of an approach which invited the poor to participate in the market economy and themselves become wealthy. A greater measure of equality would thus be secured not from the top down (as had traditionally been the case with the Labour Party) but from the bottom up, through the actions of individuals making the most of themselves through judicious use of the economic freedom which the free market entailed.

However, the needs of the market and the wishes of the individual are not necessarily complementary. Thus, Labour policies associated with the stakeholder economy revealed a carrot and stick approach in which the minimum wage and the prospect of low income tax for the poorly paid were balanced with an attempt to remove dependency on benefits in favour of incentives to return to work. It thus appeared that economic efficiency required some members of the underclass to become participants in the stakeholder economy and conform to the requirements of the market whether they wanted to or not. Schemes to achieve this aim (which included proposals in 1997 to axe the child benefit supplement paid to lone parents) were politically controversial within the Labour Party.

The emphasis of changes which were designed to reform the welfare state around the work ethic were further questioned regarding the quality of work which people would effectively be forced to undertake. The failure to immediately focus on benefit reform (which meant that social security benefits were only raised in line with prices) resulted in those who continued to rely on them (such as the elderly, the long-term sick or disabled) finding their lot deteriorating and their level of poverty increasing. One rationale for Labour's approach was that they first sought to eliminate the stigma of 'scroungers' which had been previously applied to some categories of social-welfare claimants. Their approach would isolate the genuine cases who would eventually secure an enhanced measure of public support for increased benefits being paid to them.

THE 1998 COMPREHENSIVE SPENDING REVIEW

In July 1998, the Chancellor, Gordon Brown, announced plans to increase public expenditure by £56 billion over the following three years. Much of this money would be spent on health and education. Although this seemed to suggest that the Labour Party was reverting to a public spending regime which was previously associated with 'old' Labour, it did not entail a significant departure from the policies associated with Conservative and 'new' Labour governments. Such additional spending was to be financed in part from savings on debt interest repayments (which total around £5 billion a year) and from future sales of private assets (which were expected to raise around £11 billion). This apparent acceptance of privatisation implied that the public sector was viewed to be desirable only in fulfilling tasks which government alone could carry out (such as health). Additionally, money allocated to departments would be subject to a rigorous application of value-for-money tests.

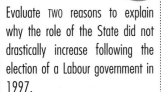

Question

Evaluate TWO reasons to explain why the role of the State did not drastically increase following the election of a Labour government in 1997.

The Postwar Consensus

This term suggests that between 1945 and 1979 there was a broad agreement between the Labour and Conservative Parties on:

○ the style of government

○ the policies which were pursued.

This section assesses the main areas of agreement between the two Parties and seeks to suggest why such consensus emerged. It also evaluates whether or not this term can validly be applied to the conduct of political affairs in this period.

Areas of Agreement

A key source for this topic is that of David Kavanagh and Peter Morris, *Consensus Politics From Attlee to Thatcher*. This details agreements between the two Parties over five broad policy areas. Some (although not all) of these indicated an acceptance of an increased level of state activity between 1945 and 1979.

1 *The mixed economy:* the nationalisation of many industries taken over by the Labour governments of 1945–51 was justified on technical rather than on political grounds. Their management by public corporations distanced them from control by the government. These developments made it easier for the Conservative Party to accept nationalisation, and agreement emerged between the Parties on a mixed economy consisting of public and private sectors.

2 *Full employment:* the economist John Maynard Keynes advocated government involvement in the operations of the economy to achieve full employment. He proposed this should be done through 'demand management' whereby the government would set levels of spending, investment and taxation to achieve the required level of demand to sustain a high level of employment. Labour and Conservative governments alike pursued the approach suggested by Keynes.

3 *The welfare state:* the postwar Labour government acted on the proposals drawn up by Beveridge in 1942 and introduced a national health service and a range of measures designed to aid the poorer members of society. The Conservative Party subsequently endorsed the philosophy of the welfare state, and spending on welfare services increased, especially during the 1960s.

4 *The role of the trade unions:* both parties accepted the principle of free collective bargaining, and both accepted that unions had a legitimate role to play in government, especially in connection with economic policy.

5 *Foreign and defence policy:* the desire of the 1945 Labour government to distance itself from communism ensured it did not embark upon a distinctive socialist foreign policy. Consensus was thus achieved over issues which included acceptance of the USA's key role in defending British and European interests against the perceived Soviet threat, and the development of the UK's independent nuclear deterrent (which was initially embarked upon by a Labour government in 1947).

Assessment of Consensus

An acceptance that consensus existed between the major Parties between 1945 and 1979 implies that politics was largely devoid of content in this period. This is not, however, correct. Political Parties believed that they were different, and the rhetoric (that is, the language) in which politics was conducted frequently displayed intense hostility between the major Parties. This might suggest, therefore, that the extent of agreement between the two major Parties (as is briefly outlined above) has been overstated. Other arguments might be put forward to suggest a greater level of conflict between the parties in this period. These include the following.

○ *Parties had different objectives:* between 1945 and 1979 political parties embarked on similar policies for quite different reasons. It might be argued, for example, that Labour's endorsement of the welfare state could be explained by a commitment to a greater level of social equality whereas the Conservative Party viewed it as a mechanism to maintain social harmony by giving some benefits to those who least benefited from the operations of capitalism.

○ *Differences between the parties did exist:* the nationalisation of the iron and steel industries evidenced a disagreement between the two major Parties, which were also divided on policies such as defence, Europe and immigration. Divisions between the Parties were, however, sometimes masked by the decisions of their leadership. Thus, consensus may be greatest among political elites, but divisions of opinion become more obvious lower down the Party hierarchy.

○ *The role of the civil service:* as is suggested in Chapter 12, the civil service may serve to neuter what it regards as the more extreme policies advocated by parties (especially when in opposition) in order to maintain a middle-of-the-road political approach. This would suggest, therefore, that differences between the Parties did exist and that it was the influence exerted by the civil service over policy-making which engineered consensus.

The Emergence of a New Consensus?

The social-democratic consensus which emerged after 1945 was especially marked by the expanded role of the State in a range of social and economic affairs. The activities undertaken by Conservative governments after 1979 (which have been described above) indicated the abandonment of many key aspects of the postwar consensus, particularly on the role of the State as a solution to a wide range of social problems. However, the above account has also argued that the actions undertaken by the Labour government which was elected in 1997 derived from the policies of previous Conservative governments, being underlaid by a commitment of both parties to a market economy. This posed the question as to whether Conservative governments after 1979 had secured support for a new consensus.

Similarities in the Approaches Adopted by Both Main Parties

The main similarities in the approaches adopted by the Conservative government after 1979 and the Labour government after 1997 are outlined below.

❍ *Opportunity:* both parties sought to widen opportunity rather than redistribute reward.

❍ *A tough rhetoric on law and order:* this was especially the case in connection with juvenile crime.

❍ *Influence of the USA:* however, the Labour government was less Eurosceptic than the Conservative governments and was willing to endorse greater integration, including monetary union.

Differences in the Approaches Adopted by Both Main Parties

The main differences in the actions undertaken by both parties when in government were as follows.

❍ *Social exclusion and inclusion:* the policies pursued by Conservative governments resulted in social exclusion whereby certain sectors of society (the underclass) were 'written off' as unwanted (in an economic sense). The stakeholding approach adopted by the Labour government after 1997 was based on the objective of inclusion.

❍ *The state and empowerment:* the Labour government after 1997 was more willing to advocate State intervention to provide individuals with the skills and education which they needed to succeed in the workplace than were previous Conservative governments.

❍ *Constitutional reform:* a range of policies pursued by the Labour government after 1997 (including devolution and electoral reform) were based on the aim of altering the relationship between the government and its citizens. Conservative governments after 1979 did not embark upon constitutional reform and, instead, adopted policies (such as those pursued towards local government or services such as education) which increased the power of central government.

The Voluntary Sector

One alternative to the State provision of services is for them to be delivered by the voluntary sector, the key components of which are charities and unpaid workers. Such bodies possess a number of characteristics which are discussed below.

❍ *Organisation:* the voluntary sector is composed of organisations, as distinct, for example, from informal groups which may provide care or advice.

❍ *Absence of statutory control:* voluntary sector bodies are not established by statute or under statutory authority and are not directly controlled by statutory authority (although they may have reporting arrangements to mainstream institutions of government such as local authorities).

❍ *Not profit-based:* voluntary sector bodies are not commercial in the sense of seeking to make a profit. Their funding is derived in a variety of ways, which include fees and charges made for the services they provide and grants awarded by central and local government. This included 'urban aid' which was introduced in the 1960s.

The Role of the Voluntary Sector

The voluntary sector provides a wide range of functions.

❍ *Responding to 'statutory failure':* voluntary sector bodies may 'plug gaps' which the statutory sector has left in its provision of services.

❍ *Community mobilisation:* some voluntary sector organisations operate at neighbourhood level and see their role as that of seeking a redistribution of resources in favour of that community. This may involve activities such as lobbying local government.

❍ *Employment:* voluntary sector bodies may provide employment for local people. These include cooperative ventures.

Problems Associated With the Voluntary Sector

The voluntary sector was given a key role when the Labour Prime Minister, Tony Blair, set out his vision of the 'giving age'. In 1998, the Labour government acknowledged the sector's importance when it published a Compact to establish principles guiding the relationship between government departments and agencies within the voluntary and community sector. There are a number of difficulties associated with the voluntary sector.

❍ *Relationship with local government:* some voluntary sector bodies may view their role to be confrontational, which involves conflict with local councillors and council officers.

❍ *Managerial competence:* persons with no experience in handling budgets may encounter problems when seeking to manage the finances of voluntary sector organisations.

○ *Accountability:* voluntary sector bodies may be accountable to their clientele (for example through the local election of a board of management to administer a community-based project), but they are not politically accountable to local or central government. This situation may pose difficulties, for example, in securing the attainment of the latter's objectives or policies.

Further Reading

Dennis Kavanagh and **Peter Morris**, *Consensus Politics From Attlee to Thatcher* (Oxford: Blackwell, 1989). This book provides a detailed analysis of the extent to which consensus did exist between 1945 and 1979.

The issue of consensus after 1979 is fully explored in **Dennis Kavanagh**, *Thatcherism and British Politics – the End of Consensus?* (Oxford: Oxford University Press, 1987).

A detailed account of the policies pursued by Conservative governments after 1979 is provided by **Stephen Savage** and **Lynton Robins** (editors), *Public Policy Under Thatcher* (Basingstoke: Macmillan, 1993).

Chapter Twenty | Politically Motivated Violence

The aims of this chapter are

---

1 To provide an understanding of the terminology associated with politically motivated violence, distinguishing between terrorism and urban and rural guerrilla warfare.

2 To examine the political objectives which those who utilise politically motivated violence seek to advance and the methods by which they use to attain these ends, particularly differentiating between selective and indiscriminate violence.

3 To analyse the manner in which liberal-democratic political systems respond to campaigns of politically motivated violence.

4 To provide an understanding of the emergence of politically motivated violence in Northern Ireland in the mid-1960s.

5 To evaluate the State's response to the 'Troubles' in Northern Ireland, drawing a particular distinction between security policy and political initiatives.

6 To provide an understanding of the contradictory nature of the main political responses to violence in Northern Ireland, placing particular emphasis on the difficulties involved in constructing a political settlement during the 1990s.

Terrorism and Guerrilla Warfare

This section discusses the main terms associated with the study of politically motivated violence.

Definition of Terrorism

Terrorism involves the use of violence for political motives. The British Prevention of Terrorism Act (originally introduced in 1974) defined the term as:

> the use of violence for political ends and includes any use of violence for the purpose of putting the public or any section of it in fear.

However, the emphasis placed on intimidation in this definition could equally be applied to States engaged in conventional (or customary forms of) warfare which may utilise tactics such as saturation or blanket bombing of civilian populations to advance their cause. This suggests that terrorism is a *subjective* term whose usage is primarily determined by one's political perspective: one person's terrorist is another person's freedom fighter.

Guerrilla Movements and Terrorism

Individuals and groups which engage in acts of violence to further their cause often dispute the use of the term 'terrorist' in relation to their activities. They may more readily identify themselves as guerrilla movements engaged in warfare designed to further the cause they advocate. It is difficult to provide a precise distinction between 'terrorism' and 'guerrilla warfare'. Although guerrilla movements are composed of irregular fighters (that is, their members are not drawn from State organisations such as the police or army) and may fight in accordance with the conventions of war, they are unlikely to do so, and their violence is usually characterised by its indiscriminate nature. A further difference between guerrilla movements and terrorism concerns the extent to which violence is utilised in conjunction with other tactics to achieve a political objective. Individuals and organisations may legitimately be described as 'terrorist' when intimidatory violence is pursued to the neglect of other activities and may appear to become almost an end in itself.

Guerrilla warfare may take the form of urban or rural movements.

Strategy and Tactics

Organisations might use violence to advance a cause which is unlikely to make headway through the use of conventional political activity. Such activity may be advanced either from a position of strength (based on a degree of popular support for the cause) or weakness (whereby violence is utilised out of a sense of desperation in the knowledge that other political tactics are unlikely to succeed). Politically motivated violence has been used to achieve a wide range of objectives utilising a variety of methods. The main strategies and tactics are discussed below.

Strategies

Revolutionary Objectives

These are designed to overthrow the State and institute an alternative economic, political or social order. Violence is typically directed against the government, the political arm of the State. In the nineteenth century, revolutionary violence often targeted monarchs in the belief that their deaths would eliminate authoritarian rule and result in an alternative system of

RURAL AND URBAN GUERRILLA WARFARE

Guerrilla warfare operates in two major ways. The distinction is primarily concerned with the tactics adopted by such movements.

Rural Guerrilla Movements

These movements are modelled on the activities of Mao Tse Tung in China. Rural guerrilla warfare was one aspect of the revolutionary struggle which was waged by the communists in that country. It sought to build a revolution through mass participation and support of the peasantry leading to a situation in which the cities would eventually be encircled by the countryside. Rural guerrilla organisations took advantage of a rural terrain to openly exercise freedom of movement. Isolated areas effectively became 'liberated zones' which the communists controlled. The tactics of such movements are particularly directed at those whose operations are deemed essential to the effective functioning of the State. The methods of violence are usually those of 'hit and run', enabling the guerrillas to utilise their mobility to their advantage.

Urban Guerrilla Movements

These organisations adopt alternative tactics. Revolution is viewed as an activity advanced by military tactics performed by a relatively small group of activists. The urban environment makes it difficult for such groups to operate openly, and they have tended to adopt alternative organisational models. Some form of cell structure is frequently utilised, characterised by its secretive nature. This has been employed by many groups active in urban areas, such as the Basque separatist movement (ETA). In the late 1970s, the IRA has adopted this structure in the United Kingdom, involving the use of 'sleepers'. These are activists sent to Britain with no previous police record and who blend in with the local population, awaiting the call to arms.

The cell structure ensures that those called together to carry out a mission have little personal knowledge of each other. This is a defence against information leaks, especially from informants, and prevents those who are captured and subsequently interrogated from being in a position to reveal details concerning the full membership of a group. Cells often practise a high degree of independence which may be at the expense of the centralised coordination of guerrilla activities.

government offering a greater measure of social justice. In the twentieth century, revolutionary socialist groups have utilised violent methods in an attempt to bring about the downfall of capitalism.

In more recent years, revolutionary violence has been guided by religious impulses. In 1979, the fundamentalist Party, Hezb-Allah, came to power in Iran. This placed that country at the forefront of Islamic revolutionary movements whose aim is to secure the world-wide implementation of Islamic law. The main mechanism to achieve this is the Jihad (or Holy War) which may involve acts of violence against secular (that is, non-spiritual) governments and their populations. Activities associated with Islamic fundamentalists include the assassination of President Sadat of Egypt in 1981 and the placing of bombs at an American airforce base in Saudi Arabia in 1996.

Sub-revolutionary Objectives

This refers to reforms which can be secured within a country's existing economic, political or social system. However, if a government is unwilling to enact such reforms, some form of violence may be used in an attempt to force it to do so. There are numerous examples of reforms which have been brought about in the UK by such mechanisms, including the campaign launched by the Welsh Language Society in 1972 against holiday homes in Wales. Groups with sub-revolutionary objectives may often be pitted against forces other than governments. The activities mounted by organisations such as the Animal Liberation Front, for example, are frequently directed against private individuals and companies.

Liberational Objectives

These are motivated by a desire to rid a country of foreign rule. The use of violence to achieve this objective has met with a number of successes across the world, most notably in opposition to colonial rule exercised by European countries in Africa and Asia. Nelson Mandela (the President of South Africa), and Yasser Arafat (President of the Palestinian Authority), were both leaders of organisations (the African National Congress and the Palestine Liberation Organisation respectively) which were associated with politically motivated violence. Success is achieved because nationalism is likely to find support among some sections of the population who view violence as an acceptable means to achieve such a goal. The campaign by republican groups to remove the British presence from Northern Ireland has constituted a key postwar example of the use of violence to achieve what they (but not their unionist neighbours) perceive as liberation. In Spain, the ETA embarked upon violence in 1959 to advance its objective of an independent Basque socialist state.

State-Sponsored Violence

This is violence sanctioned by governments. States use coercion in their everyday activities. It is thus necessary to draw a distinction between force involving the legitimate use of state power to prevent, restrain or punish breaches of the law, and violence which is not based upon constitutional and legal provisions. Although states are frequently on the receiving end of the latter form of violence, they may also conduct such activities themselves against their external or internal opponents. In the former case, state-sponsored violence may substitute for a formal declaration of war by one country against another. States may additionally seek to eliminate internal opposition and dissent through the use of violence conducted by organisations termed 'death squads', which are either directly controlled by the government or which operate at arm's length from the State so that their activities are condoned by, but not directly accountable to, the government.

Tactics

The prime aim of political violence is to cause a state of disorientation. That is, violence undermines the authority and credibility of the government and destroys community life. Individual citizens become uncertain as to whom they can trust and rely upon. A broad range of tactics are associated with politically motivated violence.

Selective Violence

This is directed against those whose activities are deemed to be crucial to the functioning of the State and its institutions. Politicians, police officers, soldiers, informers and members of the judiciary may be targeted in an attempt to reduce the ability of the State to respond to violence and in general terms to disrupt its smooth running. Additionally, such activity tends to encourage those who carry out violence by demonstrating that the State and its key personnel can be overthrown in this manner. Ultimately the level of such violence may undermine a government's desire to retain power.

Indiscriminate Violence

This is directed against the general public in a random fashion. A government which is unable to counter such activities will be accused of failure to perform its key function of safeguarding the lives of its citizens. Some aspects of the campaign of violence conducted by Northern Irish republican organisations on mainland Britain have constituted an attempt to use violence to secure political objectives through fear, by seeking to intimidate the general public who then exert pressure on the government to give in to demands. The ability to do this has been considerably enhanced by developments affecting weaponry. The development of the highly explosive substance semtex, for example, has made it possible to carry out acts of violence against both persons and property on a devastating scale which further serve to provide publicity for a group and the cause with which it is associated.

Violence Directed at Economic Targets

This may involve attacks against property connected with the nation's trading, business or commercial life. The campaign of Northern Irish republican groups on mainland Britain has involved attempts to disrupt the tourist industry and the commercial life of the City of London, and to cause damage and disruption to shopping centres. One example of this was the destruction of Manchester's central shopping centre by an IRA bomb in 1996. The key reasons for such activities are to stretch the government's resources and to place it under pressure from key economic interests who suffer from the destruction of their business and commercial property. One difficulty with violence of this nature is that attacks directed against property may result in the death or injury of people. This affects public support for the group associated with such actions.

Kidnapping, Hi-jacking and Robbery

These tactics may be used to secure various ends which include raising money, securing publicity, discrediting the government or obtaining concessions (such as the release of jailed members of organisations associated with the use of violence). In the early 1990s, the IRA required to raise £5 million–£7 million each year. Declining contributions from the United States of America meant that this money was chiefly derived from the proceeds of robberies, drinking clubs and cross-border smuggling between Northern Ireland and the Irish Republic.

The State's Response to Politically Motivated Violence

A number of methods have been commonly utilised by liberal-democratic governments to respond to campaigns of politically motivated violence. These include the development of new police powers, the imposition of restrictions on political activity, the introduction of reforms to the judicial process (especially in connection with trial procedures and the penalties for involvement in acts of political violence), and the formulation of international cooperation. The response to such campaigns, however, is governed by a number of key considerations.

Underreaction

A government must be seen to be responding decisively to a campaign of politically motivated violence, especially when this uses indiscriminate tactics. This may involve the use of public relations techniques to convince citizens that effective measures are being pursued. In the UK the government's reaction to public outrage occasioned by the Birmingham bombings in 1974 was to pass a piece of legislation calculatedly entitled the *Prevention* of Terrorism Act. A government which acts indecisively may be accused of being 'soft' on terrorism. This may lose it public support and also encourage the further use of violence, since the sanctions are insufficient to discourage it.

Overreaction

Governments must also avoid taking actions which are viewed as being too extreme. The Brazilian urban guerrilla, Carlos Marighella, identified the aim of politically motivated violence as being to force those in power to pursue actions which alienate the general public. He wrote:

> the police networks, house searches, arrests of innocent people and of suspects, closing off streets, make life in the city unbearable.

An ever-increasing spiral of violence would thus occur whereby the degree of force used by the government and its opponents grew in response to each other's activities. This was a main feature of the activities associated with the Marxist Uruguayan urban guerrilla group, the Tupamaros. Their violence, conducted against the background of a declining economy, resulted in the abandonment of liberal democracy and the institution of military government in that country in 1973. The authoritarian nature of military rule makes it easier to justify violence against an established government. Thus governments need to avoid responses to politically motivated violence which might serve to legitimise the actions of its opponents.

Martyrs

Governments need to avoid creating martyrs. These secure support for those who practise politically motivated violence by providing the basis of legend which inspires others to continue the campaign. The death of Bobby Sands through hunger strike in 1981 boosted support for the political objectives of Northern Irish republican groups.

Propaganda

The response by a government to a campaign of political violence must demonstrate an awareness of the effects of its measures on both internal and external political opinion. Violence utilised by the State against its political opponents may result in a propaganda war being lost at home or overseas. British actions undertaken in Northern Ireland have come under the close scrutiny of the governments of the Irish Republic and the USA and have on occasions had an adverse effect on the UK's standing in the international community.

International Cooperation

This may be pursued at various levels. A broad distinction exists between multilateral and bilateral responses. Multilateral action has been taken by a number of countries acting in concert, perhaps within the structure provided by a supranational body such as the European Union. In 1977, the Council of Europe adopted a European Convention for the Suppression of

Question

Select an example of an organisation which uses violence to further its political aim, and conduct your own research on it. This might be, for example, a republican or loyalist paramilitary group which has been associated with the politics of Northern Ireland since the late 1960s, or you could draw material from abroad (such as ETA in Spain).

Write a brief report on the activities of the organisation you have chosen to study, organising your material under the following headings:

○ **Aims:** what are the political aims of this organisation?

○ **Rationale:** why does it utilise violence in an attempt to accomplish these aims?

○ **Methods:** what forms of violence does the group utilise, and how are these designed to further the cause with which it is associated?

○ **Your views:** do you regard this organisation as a political party, a terrorist organisation or a guerrilla movement? Explain your conclusion.

○ **Counter action:** what measures has the State adopted to counter the campaign of politically motivated violence? How successful have these been?

Terrorism which sought to ensure that extradition for certain actions (including kidnapping, hi-jacking and hostage-taking) would not be refused on the grounds that such crimes were considered to be political. Multi-lateral action was also pursued by the Group of Seven (G7) summit meetings. In 1984, the London summit of this body issued a declaration proposing closer coordination between the police, security organisations and other authorities (especially in the exchange of information, intelligence and technical knowledge). Bilateral agreements (that is, arrangements concluded between two governments) exist between a number of countries including the UK and the Irish Republic.

Northern Ireland and Politically Motivated Violence

DEATHS IN NORTHERN IRELAND

The worst manifestations of political violence in the UK since 1945 have occurred in Northern Ireland. Between 1970 and 1993, 3,000 people were killed, 14,000 bombs were planted and 34,000 shootings took place. In that period, the IRA and its splinter groups were responsible for the deaths of about 1,800 people – 635 soldiers, 297 police officers, 800 local civilians and a further 108 civilians living on the British mainland.

The following sections seek to evaluate why these events occurred and the policies which were put forward to solve them. Particular attention is devoted to political initiatives pursued during the 1990s.

Background

Northern Ireland consists of two ethnic groups.

❍ *The unionists:* their allegiance is to the Northern Irish State and the British Crown.

❍ *The nationalists:* they view themselves as Irish and favour a unified Irish State.

Their differences are particularly reflected in religion, resulting in what is termed the *sectarian divide*: unionists are Protestant and nationalists are Catholic. Religion underpins the politics of Northern Ireland: Protestants mainly support the unionist Parties while most Catholics either back the nationalist Social Democratic and Labour Party or the republican organisation, Sinn Fein.

For much of its history, all of Ireland was part of the UK. Nationalists sought its independence from Britain. This culminated in a war being fought between 1919 and 1921, at the end of which self-government was granted to 26 of Ireland's 32 counties. This initially assumed the name of the Irish Free State (now called the Irish Republic). The remaining six counties (which contained the bulk of Ireland's unionist, Protestant population) were given a devolved form of government, whilst remaining part of the UK. This government took the form of a Northern Irish parliament (which met at Stormont), a prime minister, and system of local government. Northern Ireland was primarily run in the interests of the Protestant unionists who initially comprised a clear majority of its population. This State was biased in the treatment accorded to its Catholic population who were discriminated in a number of important ways. These are discussed below.

Political Rights

Catholics were denied equal political rights with their Protestant neighbours. The property qualification for voting contravened the liberal-democratic principle of 'one person, one vote'. By the mid-1960s, areas with Catholic majorities were governed by Protestant local Councils because local government boundaries were arranged to the benefit of the dominant Unionists. This was known as *gerrymandering*.

Provision of Services

Political discrimination led to other injustices, especially in the provision of services provided by government bodies. Education was effectively organised on sectarian lines, and Protestants benefited in housing allocation. Employment opportunities also tended to benefit this community, which had the effect of ensuring that Catholics suffered from relative economic deprivation. The discriminatory nature and practices of the Northern Irish State were overlaid with a perception that the police force (the Royal Ulster Constabulary, which was controlled from Stormont) operated to uphold unionist dominance.

Reforms in the 1960s

Demands to end the discriminatory practices within Northern Ireland arose during the 1960s. These were voiced by the Campaign for Social Justice (established in 1964), and the Northern Ireland Civil Rights Movement (formed in 1967). These demands were especially put forward by the newly emerging Catholic middle class. The issue of civil rights for Catholics was hesitantly met by the leadership of the Unionist Party. The Northern Irish Prime Minister, Capt. Terence O'Neill, introduced a number of reforms during the 1960s which were broadly directed at some of the injustices faced by Catholics. Such included the establishment of a Ministry of Development in 1965.

The Emergence of Violence

Although one aim of the civil rights campaign was to build bridges between the Catholic and Protestant working classes (since the latter also suffered from economic disadvantage), the activities of the civil rights movement led to a violent response by some Protestants who whipped up anti-nationalist, anti-Catholic feeling. However, Catholic appetites had been whetted by the reforms initiated by O'Neill. There thus emerged a gulf between the demands of the Catholics and the ability (or inclination) of the government to satisfy them. Violence seemed an inevitable consequence of such frustrated expectations which were not appeased even when (under pressure from the British government) O'Neill conceded the principle of 'one person, one vote' in local elections in 1969.

The militant Catholic demand for civil rights and the violent Protestant opposition to reform resulted in sectarian disorders. The situation came to a head in Londonderry. On 12 August 1969, the Loyalist Apprentice Boys were permitted to march through the Catholic area of the Bogside. Rioting commenced which the police could not contain. Accordingly, the Home Secretary (James Callaghan) complied with a request from the RUC and ordered British troops onto the streets of Londonderry on 14 August 1969. The use of military aid to the civil power was seen as a temporary measure while peace could be restored. This objective was supported by a number of reforms which included the passage of the 1970 Prevention of Incitement to Hatred Act, the establishment in 1971 of a Housing Executive, the introduction of job-creation schemes coupled with grants to industrialists to move to Northern Ireland, and measures designed to eliminate discrimination in public employment against Catholics.

The Intensified Polarisation of Society

The violence which emerged during the 1960s was often spontaneous, founded on a deep-rooted distrust of one community by the other. Many of the activities which occurred between 1969 and 1972 (such as 'free Derry') were effectively popular 'risings' by the Catholic working class against the

Northern Irish State. The advocacy or resistance to civil rights reforms was not obviously associated with traditional sectarian organisations. But such violence was soon provided with leadership to intensify the historic bitterness felt between Catholics and Protestants.

The Democratic Unionist Party

The emergence of Ian Paisley as a major political force in Northern Ireland provided evidence of the extent to which society was polarising around extreme sectarian positions. In 1970, he was elected to both Stormont and Westminster, and the following year he and Desmond Boal formed the Democratic Unionist Party to provide a voice for militant Protestant views which sought to resist any political concessions to nationalists. The growth of the latter at the expense of the traditional (or 'official') unionists resulted in the growth of a more extreme (and traditional) Catholic movement – the Provisional IRA.

The Provisional IRA

The Irish Republican Army had not performed a prominent role during the civil rights activities of the 1960s and the resultant sectarian violence, although its members had engaged in some actions to defend Catholics who were under attack from Protestant mobs. The main reason for such relative inactivity was an internal dispute which ultimately split this organisation. The key divisions concerned ideology and political tactics, and led to the IRA splitting into 'provisional' and 'official' wings in 1971. The former sought to utilise existing Catholic militancy as the means to secure the political goal of Irish reunification by driving the British from Northern Ireland. The latter called off the armed struggle against Britain, placing political reform in Northern Ireland ahead of nationalist objectives. It took the name of the Workers' Party during the 1970s until its demise in 1992.

The SDLP

The 1970s also witnessed the growth of another new political party, the Social Democratic and Labour Party. This was formed in August 1970 as a radical Left of Centre political party which sought to work for the nationalist objective of the reunification of Ireland by constitutional means (which differentiated it from republicans who sought to achieve this objective by violent methods). It developed into the political vehicle for moderate Catholic opinion. Its initial leader was Gerry Fitt who was replaced by John Hume in 1979.

The Security Forces and Political Violence

Much of the organised violence which occurred in Northern Ireland and on mainland Britain after 1970 was the responsibility of the provisional IRA. The failure of the 1916 Easter Rising convinced republicans that a conventional 'stand-up' fight, army against army, could not deliver their political objectives. Accordingly, republican paramilitary groups now sought to secure their aims by a guerrilla war utilising acts of violence. Those engaged in the conduct of violence were few, the strength of the Provisional IRA being estimated at 500 gunmen in March 1972, rising to 1,500 later that year.

The Initial Role of the Army

A considerable amount of police work after 1969 was initially performed by the military. The army further provided specialist services such as bomb-disposal operations, and the Special Air Services regiment was deployed in 1976 to carry out surveillance and undercover tasks. The responsibilities of the military also included gathering intelligence on terrorists. In Northern Ireland this task was facilitated by the use of computer technology from army headquarters in Lisburn.

A number of problems arose in connection with the use of the military in policing roles. Initially, the difficulty was believed to be one of inadequate powers. This was remedied by the passage of the 1973 Emergency Provisions Act, but a more serious consideration concerned the manner in which soldiers are trained not to operate by consent but to confront those they regard as enemies. The initial control exerted by unionist politicians at Stormont over the army ensured that the enemy was identified for them as the Provisional IRA. These factors heightened the likelihood of military overreaction to events in nationalist communities. In January 1972, a protest against internment (an activity in which the army had performed a prominent role) in Londonderry left 13 persons dead when paratroopers opened fire on a block of flats in the Bogside. This was known as 'Bloody Sunday'. What was depicted as the indiscriminate killing of innocent civilians boosted support for the Provisional IRA, legitimised their targeting of troops and soldiers, and aided the polarisation of society, which an effective anti-terrorist policy should have sought to avoid.

Legal and Judicial Reform

A number of developments took place which are discussed below.

Internment

This was introduced in 1971 and resulted in persons suspected of involvement with politically motivated violence conducted by the Provisional IRA being arrested and detained without trial. Those who were denied civil rights in this fashion were granted the award of a 'special category' status which entitled them to a range of privileges related to visits, the receipt of letters and parcels and the wearing of their own clothes. However, internment failed to remove terrorists from the streets of Northern Ireland. Most senior IRA men evaded capture while the indiscriminate arrest of Catholics led to the detention of persons who were not directly involved in the campaign of violence. This thus alienated moderate Catholic opinion. The weakness of this policy was further highlighted by the escalation of republican violence following its introduction. In 1971 there had been 174 deaths in Northern Ireland. In 1972, the year internment was introduced, this figure rose to 467.

The Diplock Courts

The Emergency Provisions Act was first enacted in 1973. Its main intention was to create conditions such that the response to politically motivated violence could be by due process of law. This process was termed 'criminalisation'. The 1973 measure was based upon the Diplock Report of the same year and created a distinction between crimes loosely associated with terrorism (termed 'scheduled' offences) and other criminal activities. The former were to be tried by a judge sitting without a jury. From the end of 1973 (when the Diplock Courts began functioning), terrorists would be tried by this innovatory procedure. However, the process was viewed as unfair within nationalist communities who perceived that the absence of a jury would result in injustice.

Nationalist opposition took the form of the 'dirty protest' which commenced in 1978, involving prisoners smearing cells with their own excrement. It was followed by waves of hunger strikes. In the second of these (led by Bobby Sands in 1981), 10 people died, thus becoming martyrs for the republican cause. Political support for Sinn Fein dramatically increased. The imprisoned Sands (and on his death his election agent, Owen Carron) was elected to the House of Commons. Sinn Fein's new-found popular appeal influenced it to endorse the twin strategy of military action coupled with conventional political activity ('the armalite and the ballot box') at its 1981 meeting (*Ard Fheis*). In the 1983 General Election Sinn Fein closed the gap on the SDLP, suggesting that government policy had facilitated the intensified polarisation of society which was especially at the expense of the moderate SDLP.

Police Reform

At the outbreak of violence in the 1960s, policing was in the hands of the Royal Ulster Constabulary (which numbered 2,600 officers) and the Ulster Special Constabulary, whose 425 full-time and 8,481 part-time members were under RUC control. This force had been formed following partition in 1921. Its organisation was centralised, covering all six counties. It was paramilitary in style, and lacked popular support from Catholic members of the community. Policing was under the operational control of an Inspector General and was ultimately accountable to the Northern Irish Minister of Home Affairs at Stormont. The use of the army in a policing role provided a breathing space for police reform and reorganisation. The Hunt Committee advised on the changes required to provide efficient law and order enforcement in Northern Ireland. The key initial changes included the establishment of a Northern Ireland Police Authority in 1970 (which sought to distance policing from the control traditionally exercised by the unionist government), and the replacement of the Special Constabulary with the Ulster Defence Regiment, which had the status of a regiment of the British army and was thus independent of Stormont.

Police Primacy

Problems associated with the military performing a policing role made it important to develop a less militarised and more acceptable form of policing, which would be effective in its response to politically motivated violence but which would also operate with the consent of all communities. A number of developments took place to secure both of these objectives after 1969 which are collectively referred to as 'Ulsterisation'. Improvements were made to RUC intelligence gathering, improved mobility was provided by the establishment of the Divisional and Headquarters Mobile Support Units, and the RUC was enlarged. It numbered 7,718 in 1982 (with an additional 4,840 reservists) at an annual cost which exceeded £200 million. By 1994 it comprised 13,183 officers at an annual cost of £600 million.

Police 'professionalism'

Attempts to make policing more broadly acceptable to all communities were especially associated with chief constables Kenneth Newman (who was appointed in 1976) and John

Hermon (who occupied this office 1980–89). Both instilled into the RUC an element of professionalism which entailed a greater evenhandedness on the part of the police, including operations conducted against disorderly loyalists (especially in connection with their opposition to the Anglo–Irish Agreement in 1985, which is discussed below). Efforts were also made to build contacts with Catholic communities by the adoption of numerous community policing initiatives. In 1994 a six-day Community Awareness Session was introduced into the training programme for new recruits to the RUC. Approximately half of Northern Ireland lacks resident police officers, and an eventual aim is to increase their number.

METHODS UTILISED BY THE SECURITY FORCES

The main security policies which have been utilised to respond to politically motivated violence are described below.

Interrogation

This initially played a major part in the campaign of the security forces to combat political violence. It was used to gather intelligence and in particular to extract a confession from an accused person, using methods which verged on intimidation. Initially criticism was directed at 'interrogation in depth' which involved sensory deprivation. The use of such techniques was banned by Ted Heath's Conservative government in the early 1970s, but other forms of physical or mental abuse continued, enhancing the image of the police as a brutal organisation. In 1978 (in a case brought by the Irish Republic) the European Court of Human Rights declared the UK to be guilty of using 'inhuman and degrading' techniques. This led to the Bennett Inquiry into Police Interrogation Practice in Northern Ireland (1979), which proposed a range of reforms including the use of close-circuit television to monitor interviews.

The Supergrass Policy

This was a new tactic developed by the RUC in the fight against politically motivated violence. It involved a person who had taken part in such activities giving evidence against others who had participated in those same crimes. A supergrass would secure immunity from prosecution provided they named others who were involved in political violence. Between November 1981 and November 1983, 7 loyalist and 18 republican supergrasses were responsible for nearly 600 people being arrested and charged with offences connected with paramilitary activities in Northern Ireland. But there were problems with the procedures adopted. A person named by a statement from a supergrass was arrested and held in custody until a trial date was set. This usually took several months, and led to the system being described an 'internment on remand'.

Shoot to Kill

This term has various definitions. These range from accusations that members of the security forces have used their weapons and caused injury to persons which might have been avoided, to allegations that the security forces have embarked upon a deliberate policy of assassination of those they believe to be involved in terrorist offences. There were a number of instances throughout the 'Troubles' when it seemed that deaths had occurred in dubious circumstances. Prominent attention was accorded to the deaths of six people in South Armagh in 1982, who were shot by members of the RUC's southern region Headquarters Mobile Support Unit. Three trials took place in 1984 in connection with these latter incidents. The RUC officers were acquitted, but in each trial there was evidence suggestive of a cover-up by senior officers, allegedly designed to protect informers.

The official investigation into these killings was concerned with the circumstances which had allegedly led the police to fabricate cover-up stories. It was instituted in 1984 and was initially headed by John Stalker, then deputy chief constable of the Greater Manchester Police, and was subsequently taken over by Colin Sampson in 1986. This aspect of 'shoot to kill' implied that civilians had been the victims of the kind of 'death squad' activity normally associated with third-world dictatorships. However, such an accusation was resisted within police circles which subscribed to the notion of 'honest mistakes', suggesting that police officers (who were frequently targeted by terrorists) took a split-second decision to use deadly force, which hindsight suggested was not necessarily appropriate.

The 'Dirty War'

Accusations have been made of security-force involvement with loyalist paramilitary squads. It has been alleged that these squads operated with the collusion of the security forces and, effectively, did their dirty work for them by eliminating republican terrorists or terrifying the Catholic community in general. A particular aim of collusion was alleged to be that of improving the targeting of the loyalist paramilitary organisation, the Ulster Defence Association (UDA), so that active members of the IRA rather than ordinary Catholics would be killed. Republicans believed that the rise in loyalist terrorism in the 1990s was attributed to such cooperation.

Political Solutions to Violence in Northern Ireland

Suggestions regarding a political solution for Northern Ireland range from perceptions that none exist (since the problem is deemed to be insoluble), to the belief that there are too many options available, which has resulted in politicians flitting from one to another rather than attempting to secure progress in a consistent direction over a sustained period of time. In this section, options with relatively little appeal or chance of success (including repartition and independence) are omitted. This discussion seeks to provide a background to the practical attempts to implement a political settlement in the 1990s.

Direct Rule

In 1972, the Northern Irish Parliament at Stormont was *prorogued* (a term which means its meetings were discontinued without the assembly being dismissed) and the administration of the State was taken over by the newly-created Northern Ireland Office. This development served to further deepen sectarian divisions, nationalists viewing it as evidence that Ulster was in a colonial situation, governed and occupied by an alien and illegitimate power. Direct rule was designed to provide a breathing space during which time military and/or political initiatives could be put forward to restore social harmony. However, attempts to re-establish the basis of self-government (most notably through the Northern Ireland Assembly of 1982–86) failed, and direct rule continued until the end of the 1990s.

Integration and the Internal Settlement

A number of unionists came to favour developing direct rule into a permanent political settlement. This was termed 'integration' and become associated with attempts to submerge Northern Irish affairs into mainstream British politics. This approach was especially promoted by the former leader of the Official Unionists, James Molyneaux, who urged that Northern Ireland should be governed like any other part of the UK and be fully integrated into political structures at Westminster. The establishment of a Select Committee on Northern Ireland in 1994 was seen as a key measure to advance integration. The major difficulty with it was that nationalists continued to live under what they regarded as foreign occupation of their country, which served to legitimise republican violence. This political option was sometimes referred to as an 'internal solution' as it sought to eliminate the role which the government of the Irish Republic had begun to play in the affairs of Northern Ireland after the mid–1980s.

Reunification

Ireland was partitioned in 1921. Nationalists seek to end this situation and place the entire country under the control of an Irish government. Northern Irish nationalist Parties (the SDLP and Sinn Fein) both aspire to the establishment of a unitary Irish State, and republican paramilitary groups have fought to secure this objective. The attainment of this solution would require two conditions to be satisfied. First, the British government would have to relinquish its control over Northern Ireland. Secondly, Northern Ireland's Protestants would have to give their consent to it.

It was not inconceivable that the first condition would eventually be met. The possibility of reunification by consent was included in the Conservative government's 1982 White Paper, *A Framework for Devolution*, and also in the 1985 Anglo–Irish Agreement. In the 1993 Downing Street Declaration (which is discussed below) the British government formally declared that it had 'no selfish, strategic or economic interest in Northern Ireland'. But it is difficult to see how the second condition could ever be achieved, at least in the short term. The Northern Irish State was established in the face of Protestant opposition to the principle of Irish home rule. Protestants are unlikely to suddenly be converted to accept rule by Dublin. However, attempts were made (particularly by Garret Fitzgerald's *New Ireland Forum* in 1984) to consider alternative political structures which would make a reunified Ireland more acceptable to Protestant opinion. This could take the form of federal or confederal forms of government, whereby established governmental units would retain a considerable degree of political power. This would facilitate continued unionist control of areas in which they were in the majority.

There is one further difficulty with this historic nationalist aim. The North is currently heavily dependent on subsidies paid from the British Exchequer. Reunification would inevitably lower the standard of living experienced by Northern Ireland's population unless some form of outside financial aid was obtained.

Power Sharing

Power sharing involved the establishment of an executive composed of Northern Irish politicians drawn from the major political parties on both sides of the sectarian divide. Its main objective would be to give Catholics as well as Protestants an attachment to a self-governing Northern Irish State. A discussion paper in October 1972 (*The Future of Northern Ireland*) led to a White Paper in 1973, and the establishment of a newly elected 78-member Assembly in June 1973, the majority of whose members favoured a power-sharing arrangement. The details of this were subsequently discussed at Sunningdale in 1973 between representatives of the British and Irish governments and the new assembly. This resulted in a Northern Irish executive composed of representatives from the SDLP, the Alliance Party and some sections of the Official Unionists. It took office on 1 January 1974 and was accompanied by a proposal to establish a Council of Ireland to coordinate matters of mutual interest in Ireland and Northern Ireland.

Power sharing was, however, a short-lived development. Many Protestants did not agree with the willingness of some of their political leaders to share ministerial offices with politicians representing nationalist opinion. On the other hand, many nationalists were opposed to the continued existence of the Northern Irish State. Protestant opposition to these new arrangements was displayed by the formation of the United Ulster Unionist Council which won 11 of Northern Ireland's 12 seats in the February 1974 General Election, thus depriving the executive of legitimacy. The strike called by the Ulster Workers' Council in May 1974 succeeded in causing the collapse of the executive authority.

Developments in power sharing were, however, accomplished in local government during the 1990s. By 1993, some form of power-sharing arrangement existed in 11 of Northern Ireland's local authorities.

The Constitutional Convention

The Labour government of Harold Wilson subsequently abandoned the attempt to impose power sharing from above and instead tried to persuade local politicians to introduce it from below. This was the aim of the Constitutional Convention which sought to encourage Northern Irish politicians to consider a range of options for the Province's future governance (subject to a Whitehall veto) provided a mechanism for power sharing was included. Elections to this body took place in 1975 but no progress was made as Protestants opposed to power sharing refused to participate. The initiative was abandoned in 1976.

Rolling Devolution

In 1979, Margaret Thatcher's newly-elected Conservative government issued a White Paper expressing support for devolution and power sharing. Little support was secured for this proposal, and in 1982 the Northern Ireland Act abandoned support for power sharing in favour of what was termed 'rolling devolution'. This involved the election of an assembly with scrutinising, deliberative and consultative powers, and provided for partial or substantial devolution of legislative and executive powers from Westminster to Northern Ireland. The extent of devolved power was to be dependent on the ability of parties in Northern Ireland to agree on the process which would 'roll on' at a pace determined by them. Nationalists refused to participate in an innovation which failed to discuss power sharing or possess an Irish dimension (that is, an acceptance that the government of the Irish republic had a valid role to perform in the affairs of Northern Ireland). The assembly was eventually dissolved in 1986.

Joint Authority

This involved the Irish Republic playing a direct role in the political affairs of Northern Ireland. Although it fell short of reunification, it held out the hope that this may be accomplished as a long-term objective. The initial involvement of the government of the Irish Republic in Northern Irish affairs may thus be developed incrementally in a political direction desired by the nationalists.

In 1984, the New Ireland Forum (composed of representatives drawn from Northern Ireland's SDLP, and the Irish Republic's Fianna Fail, Fine Gael and Labour Party) voiced support for joint authority. Although their preferred goal remained that of reunification and the formation of a 32-county unitary State, they proposed a federal arrangement for the 32 counties involving joint authority being exercised by both London and Dublin over Ulster. Margaret Thatcher initially expressed outrage at a proposal which gave insufficient attention to unionist concerns, but a year later she signed the Anglo–Irish Agreement with the then Irish Taoiseach (Prime Minister), Garret FitzGerald. Although this insisted the consent of the majority in Northern Ireland was required to change its constitutional status, it moved hesitantly in the direction of joint authority by establishing an Intergovernmental Conference of British and Irish ministers to consider political development in Northern Ireland, security and legal issues (especially extradition arrangements), and matters related to cross-border economic and social cooperation. It was supported by a joint secretariat.

Although both major unionist Parties became willing to consider cross-border cooperation during the 1990s, they were totally opposed to any form of involvement by the Irish government in Ulster's affairs. Unionist MPs sought to demonstrate the weight of Protestant opinion against the Agreement by resigning their Westminster seats and forcing by-elections to secure a mandate to oppose it. Protestants were further antagonistic to what they perceived as the 'democratic deficit' inherent in the Hillsborough Agreement: in their view the affairs of Northern Ireland would be determined by the governments of London and Dublin without the direct involvement of Northern Irish people. The Anglo–Irish Agreement ensured the Irish Republic would henceforth play an important part in Northern Ireland's politics, and it subsequently became more difficult for the British government to pursue unilateral policies because of the adverse impact such might have on this agreement.

Euro-Federalism

The accession of the UK to the European Community in 1973 provided another potential solution to Northern Irish political affairs. It led to the possibility of enhanced cross-border projects, increased trade, and economic and commercial cooperation between North and South. Initially, however, these consequences did not materialise. Membership of the EC had a differential effect on North and South which tended to emphasise the border more clearly than previously, while the UK and Ireland frequently clashed on issues which included European agricultural and regional policies.

However, subsequent developments in the direction of a single market in 1992 and the possible future pooling of economic and political sovereignty have suggested a political solution based upon the reduced importance of national frontiers and the expectation that internal squabbles would give way to broader issues affecting the interests of Ireland as a whole. The leader of the SDLP, John Hume, believed that the single market would allow the border to ebb substantially from economic life on the island. Other pressures supportive of Eurofederalism have come from outside Northern Ireland. In 1993, the report of the Opsahl Commission emphasised the importance of the regional dimension to the future development of Northern Ireland within Europe. The main difficulty is the assumption that regional loyalties and the acceptance of supranational authority will develop rapidly enough to erode the traditional sectarian concerns around which Northern Irish politics revolves.

Question

○ Describe ONE major initiative pursued by the British Government over 1972–93 to solve the Northern Ireland problem.

○ Why did it fail to achieve this objective?

Political Developments in the 1990s

Between 1969 and 1989, governments of both parties maintained that constitutional and security initiatives had to be advanced in tandem since they were mutually reinforcing and, additionally, needed to be bolstered by economic regeneration and social reform. Such policies were directed at the political centre ground which comprised of constitutional nationalists and liberal unionists, and sought to isolate the republicans, loyalist paramilitaries and the Democratic Unionist Party. However, factors which included the marginal position of Northern Ireland to the British public policy-making process prevented this form of integrated response. Accordingly, the objective of social harmony was not achieved.

By the early 1990s, the need to construct a fresh political initiative had become acute. The level of violence had escalated, in particular due to the enhanced role performed by Protestant paramilitary groups such as the Ulster Defence Association and the Ulster Freedom Fighters. Their violence was designed to ensure that Protestant concerns would not be marginalised by the desire of British government to appease nationalist sentiments and heed the opinions of the Irish and American governments. Their terror was often unleashed against Catholics in an indiscriminate manner: 36 deaths were attributed to the Protestant paramilitaries in 1991, and 44 in 1992. The British government responded by proscribing the Ulster Defence Association in 1992, but this had little positive impact on the level of violence which often assumed a 'tit for tat' character. The commencement by the Provisional IRA of a new campaign of violence on mainland Britain in 1992 was an added inducement in the quest for a political initiative. This section briefly assesses the main political developments which occurred in this period.

The All-Party Talks and Unionist Reaction

The British government initially sought to seize the political initiative by convening all-party talks, which were designed to establish common ground between Northern Ireland's constitutional Parties. The four main Parties sat down around the one conference table in June 1991, but unionists adopted a negative stance towards these discussions, viewing them as an attempt to legitimise a 'sell out' by the British government to the goal of a united Ireland. They thus succeeded in halting any progress by drawn-out procedural wrangles over issues such as the venue and agenda. The talks were reconvened following the 1992 General Election. The unionists' insistence that Dublin relinquish its claims to the territory of Northern Ireland which were contained in articles 2 and 3 of its constitution resulted in the talks breaking down in November 1992 without any agreement being reached.

The Hume–Adams Talks

John Hume had been a driving force in the initiation of all-party talks in 1991 and 1992. In the absence of progress made by these, he recommended discussions with Gerry Adams, President of Sinn Fein, in 1993. Previous discussions had been held in 1988 but the potential for an agreement between the two parties had increased. Sinn Fein was moving to an acceptance that its objectives were unlikely to be realised by either its military campaign or the current nature of its political activity. Adams's attempts to 'plug it into' mainstream British Labour politics had failed under Kinnock, Smith and Blair, and the links which had been constructed were primarily with its leftwing, whose influence had declined. The Party's support was declining in Northern Ireland, and its poor showing in the Irish elections in 1987 emphasised its marginalised political position in the South. The discussions embarked upon by John Hume and Gerry Adams thus sought to end the marginalisation of Sinn Fein and enable it to participate in the conventional political process in Northern Ireland. This would buttress the voice of Northern Irish nationalism, lend weight to their opposition to an internal settlement, and guard against the possibility of this opinion being bypassed or substituted for the views of the Irish government.

THE HUME–ADAMS TALKS

Seven principles underpinned the Hume–Adams discussions.

◆ The Irish people as a whole had the right to national self-determination.

◆ This was a matter for agreement between the people of Ireland.

◆ The consent and allegiance of the unionists was essential to establishing a lasting peace.

◆ The unionists should not have a veto over British policy.

◆ The British government should join the 'persuaders' (which entailed urging unionists to broaden their political horizons).

◆ The London and Dublin governments had the major responsibility to secure political progress.

◆ An internal solution was specifically rejected.

The British Government's Response to Hume–Adams

The British government was initially sceptical of the benefit of such discussions, viewing them as an obstacle to the resumption of their inter-party talks which had broken down in 1992. Additionally, the British government had traditionally supported the principle of self-determination for the people of Northern Ireland, and insisted that the Provisional IRA declare a permanent end to the violence (not a ceasefire which might prove a temporary measure). However, the British government needed to announce a response to these proposals to prevent the Irish government either siding with Hume–Adams in the absence of any other initiatives, or adopting a 'go it alone' approach of their own to a political solution. Thus in his Guildhall speech on 15 November 1993, John Major reasserted that if the IRA ended its campaign of violence, after a 'sufficient interval to ensure the permanence of their intent', Sinn Fein would be invited to participate in inter-party talks. He specifically stated that under these circumstances unionist politicians would possess no veto on Sinn Fein's participation.

The Downing Street Declaration

A joint declaration was signed by the Prime Ministers of the UK and Ireland on 15 December 1993. This stated that the ending of divisions could only come about through the 'agreement and cooperation of the people, North and South, representing both traditions in Ireland'. The British Prime Minister reaffirmed that the British government would 'uphold the democratic wish of the greater number of the people of Northern Ireland' on the issue of whether they preferred to support the Union or a sovereign united Ireland, and reiterated that Britain had no selfish strategic or economic interest in Northern Ireland. The Taoiseach recognised that stability and well-being would not be found under any political system which was refused allegiance, or rejected, by a significant minority of those governed by it. He thus accepted that a united Ireland required the consent of a majority of people living in the North.

The Declaration reflected compromises in the positions of each signatory government. The British government acknowledged (without endorsing) the nationalist aspiration for a united Ireland, and it was accepted that the 1920 Government of Ireland Act, which guaranteed Northern Ireland's position as part of the UK, was negotiable in accordance with the wishes expressed by the majority of its people. In return the British government achieved some concessions. These included a somewhat vague reference to the possible repeal of articles 2 and 3 of the Irish constitution. But key republican demands were absent. There was no statement by the British government of its support for a united Ireland nor any commitment to British withdrawal. The inclusion of a 'unionist veto' in the provisions governing self-determination additionally failed to treat the Irish people as a whole. Sinn Fein was courted by the possibility of being included in the political process, and this Party would also be included in the Irish government's Forum for Peace and Reconciliation.

The 1994 Ceasefire

There had been three ceasefires during the 1970s which failed to yield any concessions to the IRA. By 1994, Adams was willing to settle for reduced demands at the outset in the expectation that the eventual outcome of negotiations entered into after a ceasefire would prove acceptable to republicans. The Downing Street Declaration, accompanied by its clarifications, was considered by a special Sinn Fein Conference in County Donegal on 24 May 1994. It was rejected, the key stumbling block being the retention of the 'unionist veto'. However, by 1994 nationalism was a formidable political force: a 'pan nationalist front' consisting of the SDLP, Sinn Fein and the Irish government had emerged which was strengthened by the USA, whose financial aid would be vital in supporting reconciliation in Northern Ireland. Such considerations induced the IRA to renounce a 'complete cessation of military operations' on midnight 31 August 1994. The Loyalist paramilitaries followed suit on 13 October.

Aftermath of the Ceasefire

Progress towards achieving a lasting peace in Northern Ireland following the ceasefire was impeded by a number of factors which are discussed below.

The Decommissioning Issue

Sinn Fein had urged the ceasefire on the IRA, believing this would result in their immediate participation in all-party talks without preconditions or vetoes on their eventual outcome. The British government, however, was mindful of considering unionist reaction to any gesture towards Sinn Fein and was unwilling to let it participate in discussions until the republican movement indicated this ceasefire entailed a permanent renunciation of violence. Thus the ceasefire failed to yield republicans any immediate, tangible political advantage. On 21 October 1994, John Major told a meeting of the Institute of Directors in Belfast that he was willing to make 'a working assumption' that the ceasefire was permanent. However, the decommissioning of arms held by the IRA then emerged as a new obstacle to the convening of all-party talks. The British government insisted these must be handed over as a precondition of Sinn Fein's participation in discussions. The IRA viewed such an action as equivalent to a surrender, and refused to contemplate it until a permanent political solution had been achieved through all-party talks. In that situation decommissioning could be associated with the broader policy of 'demilitarisation', involving the withdrawal of British troops and the radical reform of policing arrangements. This deadlock continued into 1995.

Failure to advance the peace process placed severe strains on the Anglo–Irish relationship. The divergent stances adopted by the Westminster and Dublin governments eventually resulted in the adoption of a 'twin track' approach. This entailed the establishment of an international body to examine the issue of decommissioning, and at the same time the governments would hold meetings with the Northern Irish political Parties to pave the way for all-party talks. A three-person independent international body was appointed under the chairmanship of former Senator George Mitchell to consider decommissioning, and the British and Irish governments agreed to a target date of February 1996 for the commencement of all-party discussions. Groundwork talks (consisting of bilateral and trilateral meetings) to prepare for these would be initiated by both governments immediately.

The Mitchell Commission

This was charged by the British and Irish governments to identify and advise on a suitable and acceptable method for full and verifiable decommissioning and also to report on whether there was a clear commitment by those in possession of such arms to work to achieve this end. It reported on 24 January 1996, arguing that Britain's insistence on paramilitary arms being handed over before the commencement of all-party talks was impractical. It set out six principles as a 'democratic test' to which parties to the all-party talks would be required to subscribe their 'total and absolute commitment' before they were permitted to participate.

Sinn Fein was potentially placed in a difficult position. Acceptance of these principles entailed agreement that the ceasefire was permanent and that violence would no longer be used to further their political objectives. Alternatively, rejection of them would result in the loss of support in both the USA and Ireland. The British government, however, removed this

THE SIX PRINCIPLES OF THE MITCHELL REPORT

These consisted of:

- the affirmation of an exclusive commitment to democratic means to resolve political issues

- the renunciation for themselves, and opposition to any efforts by others, to use or threaten to use force to influence the course or outcome of the all-party negotiations

- a pledge either to abide by the outcome of such discussions or to utilise purely peaceful means to alter their conclusions

- the total disarming of paramilitary organisations

- the independent verification of the disarmament process: but it was argued that decommissioning could run in tandem with the peace talks rather than having to be initiated before they commenced

- an end to paramilitary 'punishment' killings and beatings.

It was argued that any party which affirmed these principles should be included in all-party talks.

dilemma for them by insisting that there should be a prior election of an all-party forum. The government envisaged unionists would abandon their insistence on decommissioning as a precondition for holding talks with Sinn Fein if the latter could demonstrate it possessed a democratic mandate to enter discussions. However, the insistence on elections made it possible for Sinn Fein to transfer the focus of attention away from the six principles and towards opposition to elections. It was easier to justify this position since all nationalists were hostile to this proposal. The SDLP viewed it as an attempt by the British government to freeze Dublin out of the Northern Irish peace process and to seek a solution through the process of internal politics which would inevitably be dominated by the unionists.

The Framework Document

The Framework Document provided substance to the Downing Street Declaration. It proposed the establishment of an assembly for Northern Ireland whose 90 members would be elected under a system of proportional representation and serve for a fixed term. A range of issues (including those with constitutional implications) would be determined by a weighted rather than a simple majority, thus giving substantial minorities an effective veto. The assembly would discharge executive and legislative responsibilities, the latter being performed by a number of departments. The Framework Document also proposed the establishment of a three-member Panel, elected by proportional representation, to advise the assembly and act as a liaison between the assembly and the Secretary of State, who would remain responsible for matters not transferred to the assembly. New North–South institutions to cater for present and future political, social and economic interactions were further proposed. These would include a new Cross-Border body to exercise a range of consultative, harmonising and executive functions, accountable to the assembly in Northern Ireland and the Irish Dail. It would be composed of departmental heads of both institutions, but all members of the Northern Irish assembly would be obliged to attend its meetings. The continued cooperation of the British and Irish governments was to be facilitated by the establishment of a new Intergovernmental Conference to act as the main forum through which both governments would work together to pursue joint objectives.

The End of the Ceasefire

The ceasefire dramatically ended with the planting of a bomb in Canary Wharf, London, on 9 February 1996. A period of 527 days had elapsed: Sinn Fein had not been involved in all-party talks, and the peace process had run out of momentum. Although minor concessions (such as the withdrawal of daylight army patrols in Northern Irish cities) were secured, no substantial progress was made in securing any republican objectives, and it was perceived to be unlikely that a change of government in Britain would significantly alter government policy. The resumption of violence thus indicated an intention to exert force on the peace process to produce an outcome acceptable to republicans.

Elections to the All-Party Forum

The government responded to the end of the ceasefire by pressing ahead with elections to the all-party forum and committing themselves to a specific date for the commencement of all-party talks. It was hoped that announcing a date when talks would commence would split Sinn Fein and republican militants. Sinn Fein was able to field candidates in the forum elections but their inclusion in talks was dependent on a new ceasefire.

This result provided Sinn Fein with its best ever performance in Northern Ireland. The government responded to this situation

THE FORUM ELECTIONS

The Forum elections were the gateway to all-party talks. They took place on 30 May 1996. In a 64.5 per cent turnout, the share of the vote obtained by the major parties was as follows:

Official Unionists	24.1 per cent
SDLP	21.3 per cent
Democratic Unionists	18.8 per cent
Sinn Fein	15.4 per cent
Alliance party	6.5 per cent

by offering it gestures to secure a new ceasefire which would pave the way for their involvement in the all-party talks. It was agreed that decommissioning could be delayed for three months, during which deliberations, chaired by Senator Mitchell, could discuss the process in detail. No ceasefire occurred, however, the IRA persisting with its view that decommissioning could only be considered as part of an agreed political settlement.

Unionist Politics

By early 1996 the peace process was in jeopardy. Unionist opinion had failed to make positive responses to the changed political circumstances, and refused to enter into dialogue with Dublin or to participate in the Forum for Peace and Reconciliation. A particular feature of unionist politics in the 1990s was the absence of any leader willing to break ranks with their Party (as Brian Faulkner had in 1974 in connection with the power-sharing executive) and advocate a course of political action contrary to established traditions. Most unionists would not contemplate any fundamental adjustment to Northern Ireland's constitutional status as part of the UK and thus sought a political solution which entailed nationalists abandoning their pursuit of Irish unity and the Irish government accepting this by relinquishing its constitutional claim to the six counties. Unionist resolve was strengthened by the emergence of Protestant extremism articulated by Loyalist paramilitary organisations (the Ulster Volunteer Force and the Ulster Freedom Fighters) and their associated political parties (the Progressive Unionist Party and the Ulster Democratic Party). These sought to defend Protestant interests militarily, and viewed reforms to the operations of the Northern Irish state, to make it more acceptable to nationalist opinion, as an acceptable political position.

British Government Policy

The unwillingness of the unionists to enter into talks with Sinn Fein was seemingly endorsed by the British government which produced obstacles (in the form of preconditions to all-party talks). Although a Conservative government was not ideologically disposed towards breaking up the UK, this solution (as the Downing Street Declaration made clear) was not ruled out provided it had majority support in Northern Ireland. But the situation was further complicated by the government's small majority in the 1992–97 Parliament. The unionist position was vigorously supported by the Conservative Party's rightwing, and the government depended on the votes of the unionists to sustain its majority. Although Prime Minister John Major denied that his actions concerning Northern Ireland had been solely motivated to support the unionist position, his reliance on their votes at Westminster made the government susceptible to the charge that it placed its own survival ahead of the peace process. The tough terms which the Prime Minister announced towards the end of November 1996 for Sinn Fein's inclusion in all-party talks (which included a demand for a lasting ceasefire) were seen in this light: John Hume, the leader of the SDLP, stated that 'if he had a clear majority we would have had peace in Ireland quite some time ago.'

The lack of progress in securing movement by Northern Ireland's political parties resulted in the government's pursuing measures designed to win over the 'hearts and minds' of the majority of Northern Irish people and to enable the direction of the peace process to be determined by ordinary people who might lead it in a direction not necessarily associated with the traditional goals of either unionists or nationalists. Such policies included improvements in the areas of security, financial aid, business confidence and tourism, and projected police reform. In adopting this approach, the government sought to build on the sentiments which had been periodically expressed in developments such as integrated schools and peace movements or peace rallies and which were politically articulated by organisations which included the Alliance Party and the Northern Ireland Women's Coalition.

Drumcree, 1996

Events at Drumcree in 1996 effectively terminated the peace process. The intention of the Orange Order to march to Drumcree Parish Church outside Portadown, along a route which took it past a Catholic housing estate, was initially thwarted by the chief constable of the RUC who banned the parade. Large numbers of Orangemen descended on the venue, and a four-day 'standoff' occurred in which they faced large numbers of police and soldiers. The police eventually gave way to prevent serious disorder from occurring, and the chief constable gave permission for the march to go ahead. For unionists, the issue was whether they could exert their traditional rights to march anywhere they chose, symbolically demonstrating their territorial domination of the Northern Irish State. This ban epitomised to unionists the increasingly pronationalist stance which they perceived the government was adopting and which threatened their fundamental culture and traditions. The event further illustrated how the Orange Order could act as a bridge and unite all shades of unionist opinion.

Nationalists supported the cancelling of an event which caused offence to the community where it would be held. The decision to let the march proceed left the peace process in tatters. The decision suggested to all nationalists that the Northern Irish State had not altered since the inception of the peace process and that (as in 1974) a display of Protestant resistance and the threat of disorder would suffice to cause the abandonment of any developments which they disliked. The government sought to avoid future problems of this nature by setting up a review of parades and marches, chaired by Peter North, (whose report in 1997 recommended the establishment of a parades commission to mediate in disputes). But compromise was not on the political agenda in 1996. Old sectarian hatreds were resurrected: the *Independent* on 17 July 1996 quoted RUC sources which estimated that 600 Protestant and Catholic families had been driven out of their homes in the previous week as both sides attempted to 'ethnic cleanse' their areas.

Assessment of the Peace Process, 1992–97

The events which occurred after 1992 evidenced the difficulties of establishing a political settlement based upon the agreement of parties which were historically opposed to each other. The nationalists sought to alter the balance of the traditionally hostile political equation in Ulster by building upon the involvement of Ireland in Northern Irish affairs and by seeking to secure unity of action between republicans and nationalists. This 'pan nationalist front' was supplemented by the USA playing a more vigorous role in Northern Irish affairs. However, nationalists required the peace process to be conducted with speed so that it acquired an unstoppable momentum: unionists would be overcome by the tide of events and take a pragmatic decision to flow with them. The attainment of nationalist objectives also required the British government to act in the role of a persuader to convince unionists that their future should not rest exclusively within the UK.

The government, however, recognised that the ethnic forces which underlaid unionism would not tolerate incorporation into an Irish nation. They regarded this prospect as alien in terms of values, culture and history, and backward looking because of its perceived sectarianism. It accepted that in the long term it might be possible to suggest that unionists should broaden their economic and political horizons but recognised this could not be accomplished overnight. Accordingly the government sought to tone down the aspirations of Irish nationalists and resist the pressures exerted by Dublin and Washington towards Irish unity. This resulted in the periodic tendency of the British government to 'go it alone' and follow a unilateral course of action with regard to Northern Irish political affairs when they perceived attempts were being made to coerce unionists. The insistence on decommissioning and holding elections following the publication of the Mitchell report were announced unilaterally without first consulting Dublin. The approach of the government, however, gave republicans the impression that they had gained nothing from the ceasefire, whilst stiffening the resolve of unionists to resist making concessions.

The republican movement had been divided on the wisdom of a ceasefire, a significant group wishing to utilise the twin-track tactics associated with the ballot box and the armalite (which in the 1990s had become known as TUAS, The Tactical Use of the Armed Struggle). The absence of progress in the peace process cemented over divisions in that movement on the wisdom of a return to violence. A further problem was that Sinn Fein viewed the then Irish Taoiseach, John Bruton, as hostile to republicanism and assumed that a Fianna Fail government would be more sympathetic to their cause. This perception served as an inducement to remain politically isolated and to continue with the campaign of violence. The key objective was to force the Protestant paramilitary organisations to abandon their ceasefire and thus forfeit any benefits the 'fringe' Protestant parties might secure from their involvement in the all-party talks.

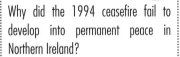

Question

Why did the 1994 ceasefire fail to develop into permanent peace in Northern Ireland?

The 1997 General Election and its Aftermath

An attempt to secure an electoral pact between the SDLP and Sinn Fein for the 1997 General Election proved impossible to achieve, resulting in the forces of nationalism being divided. Nonetheless, Sinn Fein performed well. Gerry Adams regained his former seat of Belfast West from the SDLP and additionally

Martin McGuinness captured Mid Ulster from the Unionists. The SDLP secured the return of three MPs. The combined result obtained by the nationalists and republicans suggested that a new approach was justified from the British government.

There seemed no sign of this initially, however. The Labour government's new Secretary of State, Mo Mowlem, rejected Sinn Fein's involvement in all-party talks. Various moves were initiated in an attempt to get the peace process moving, including the possibility of John Hume contesting the election for the Irish Presidency (a course of action which he did not embark upon). His intention of doing this was to give a clear indication that Northern Irish and Irish politics were inseparably intertwined, thus legitimising the continued involvement of the Irish government in the process. This government, following the 1997 Irish General Election, was led by Bertie Ahern.

Sinn Fein subsequently sought to grasp the political initiative. The IRA ended its attempts to provoke Loyalist paramilitaries into abandoning the ceasefire and itself announced a cessation of violence at a meeting of the Army Convention in October 1997. This provoked a split in the movement and the formation of the 32 County Sovereignty Committee by those who believed the leadership of the IRA and Sinn Fein were engaged in 'selling out' their historic commitment to drive the British out of Northern Ireland. The new strategy was designed to force the unionists to reach an accommodation with nationalism or be branded with the accusation that their intransigence (that is, refusal to compromise) was responsible for the inability to secure a political settlement. The British government subsequently entered into talks with Sinn Fein which 'signed up' to the Mitchell principles, thus ending the impediment to its involvement in all-party talks. The onus was now firmly with unionists to either sit down with Sinn Fein or be held responsible for the continued political stalemate.

The All-Party Talks and the Good Friday Peace Accord

All-party talks commenced in October 1997 against a background of sectarian violence waged by republican paramilitary groups which refused to end violence, and similar Loyalist organisations. The talks were chaired by Senator Mitchell, who set a deadline for agreement between the various parties. This ultimately led to an agreement which was signed on 10 April 1998.

THE GOOD FRIDAY PEACE ACCORD

This provided for a three-strand constitutional settlement, as is outlined in the following diagram.

Strand 1 Internal arrangements of Northern Ireland	Strand 2 North/South Ministerial Council	Strand 3 Council of the Isles
Assembly (run by the executive committee): • Elections for the Assembly took place in June 1998. • Made up of 108 members, 6 from each constituency elected by proportional representation. • Has legislative powers. Its first duty was to set up the North/South ministerial council. • The assembly will be suspended if it does not set up the council within a year. • Decisions are made by a weighted majority system to ensure unionists cannot dominate nationalists.	A forum for ministers from Dublin and Belfast to promote joint-policies.	Representatives from: • Dublin government • Belfast administration • Westminster • Scottish Parliament • Welsh Assembly
Executive Committee: 12 ministers; a first minister, deputy minister plus heads of departments including: • Health • Education • Environment • Economic Development • Agriculture • Finance	Can implement all-Ireland policies – but only with the approval of the Belfast Assembly and Dublin Parliament. Potential areas of responsibility: • Agriculture • Transport • Policing • Relationships with EU	Meet twice a year for discussions but have no administrative or legislative powers

Taken from the *Guardian*, 11 April 1998

This agreement was designed to offer some concessions to all key parties involved in the talks. The establishment of a new devolved structure of government for Northern Ireland (the Assembly) was aimed at unionists (including some of the splinter groups of this Party), while the 'Irish dimension' in the North–South ministerial Council and the Council of the Isles was designed to secure nationalist approval. There were, however, numerous difficulties before a lasting peace could be established in Northern Ireland. The Party leaders had to 'sell' the agreement to their memberships, and the proposals would also be placed before the electorates of both Northern Ireland and the Irish Republic for their endorsement in a referendum (which in the Republic was concerned with amending articles 2 and 3 of the Constitution). Key issues (which included the decommissioning of weapons and the release of paramilitary prisoners) would also ultimately have to be resolved.

The Referendum and the Establishment of the Northern Ireland Assembly

The popular acceptance of the peace accord in Northern Ireland was considerably aided by the roles played by the leader of the Official Unionist Party (David Trimble) and the President of Sinn Fein (Gerry Adams). Many of Trimble's Parliamentary Party opposed (or had sceptical attitudes towards) the agreement, but he succeeded in getting the Ulster Unionist Party ruling council to endorse it in April 1998 by the margin of 540:210. Many republicans were also unhappy about the accord and the decision to abandon the armed struggle, but Adams was able to persuade Sinn Fein to amend its constitution to enable the Party to take up seats it would win in the elections to the new Assembly. (This marked the abandonment of its policy of abstentionism.) Such firm displays of leadership helped to ensure that the population of Northern Ireland gave their support to the Good Friday arrangement in the 22 May referendum by the margin of 71.1 per cent to 28.9 per cent in an 80.9 per cent turnout. The lower turnout in the republic (55.6 per cent) evidenced overwhelming support there to amend the republic's constitutional claims to the North by the margin of 94.4 per cent to 5.6 per cent.

Elections took place to the new Assembly in June 1998. The Ulster Unionists emerged as the largest Party in terms of seats, and David Trimble was elected as the new First Minister. His deputy was the SDLP deputy leader, Seamus Mallon.

ELECTIONS TO THE NORTHERN IRELAND ASSEMBLY, JUNE 1998

The seats obtained by the Parties were as follows:

Ulster Unionists	28
SDLP	24
Democratic Unionists	20
Sinn Fein	18
Alliance	6
UK Unionists	5
Independent Unionists	3
Progressive Unionists	2
Women's Coalition	2

The inability of Ian Paisley's Democratic Unionists and their associates to muster 30 seats was important since this figure would have required votes in the Assembly to be taken on a cross-community voting system as opposed to a simple majority.

Prospects for a Lasting Peace

The fragile nature of the peace process was apparent in events which occurred after the assembly elections. The Orange Order's intention to march at Drumcree in the face of the event being banned, again posed the potential for wrecking the entire process. The lack of progress in decommissioning weapons resulted in Trimble harbouring suspicions towards Sinn Fein that the republican campaign of violence had not been ended, and that the IRA was using different organisational names to mask its involvement in such activities. Two tragedies helped to defuse these initial problems.

Drumcree

The murder of three Catholic children by an arson attack at their home in the vicinity of Drumcree eroded the resolve of the Orange Order to continue with their 'stand off'. Trimble, who had traditionally supported the Orangemen, called on them to disperse from Portadown and declared that 'no road is worth these lives.'

Omagh

In August 1998, a car bomb exploded at Omagh. Twenty-nine people were killed and 220 were injured in the attack which was carried out by the 'Real IRA' (which has political links with the 32 County Sovereignty Committee). Initially this threatened to aggravate tensions between unionists and republicans, with Trimble stating that this massacre would not have occurred had the IRA handed in its weapons. However, the actions of this republican splinter group were immediately condemned by Gerry Adams who stated that he was 'horrified by this action. I condemn it without any equivocation whatsoever.' Sinn Fein had never used such unambiguous language in relation to an act of violence conducted by a republican group, and his words underlined the commitment to the peace process of both Sinn Fein and the IRA. Public revulsion to the Omagh bomb aided Sinn Fein to exert influence over other republican groups (including the Real IRA and the Irish National Liberation Army) to end their campaigns of violence, and on 1 September 1998 Adams effectively declared that the war waged by republican groups was at an end. This facilitated the initiation of discussions into the decommissioning of IRA weapons, but also made it possible for Trimble to have a face-to-face meeting with Adams on 10 September 1998. This was the first time since 1922 that leaders of the Ulster Unionists and Sinn Fein had met for discussions.

In 1998, John Hume and David Trimble were awarded the Nobel Peace Prize for their work in trying to resolve the 'Troubles' in Northern Ireland.

Conclusion

Events which occurred towards the end of 1998 (including the meeting of the Northern Ireland Assembly on 14 September 1998) held out genuine hopes for a lasting peace. There are, however, numerous problems which will have to be overcome. The most significant concerns the development of the political arrangements put forward in the Good Friday agreement. For nationalists and republicans, these are viewed as stepping stones towards their goal of a unified Ireland. For unionists, however, these arrangements are perceived as barriers to prevent this event from ever occurring. Compromise between these two diametrically opposed views of this settlement will prove hard to fashion.

THE INTERNATIONAL PEACE DIVIDEND

Events in Northern Ireland were closely observed by the Basque separatist group, ETA. This was founded in 1958 and used violence to further its cause of independence from Spain. Almost 800 people have been killed in this campaign. Its nationalist objectives were similar to those of the IRA, and the political wings of these organisations (Sinn Fein and Herri Batasuna) maintained close contacts. The Northern Irish peace process influenced ETA to declare a ceasefire in September 1998.

Further Reading

P. Wilkinson, *Terrorism and the Liberal State* (Basingstoke: Macmillan, 1986, 2nd edition). This provides a good account of the nature of terrorism and politically motivated violence, and the response of the liberal-democratic State.

Gerry Adams, *Free Ireland: Towards a Lasting Peace* (Dingle, County Kerry: Brandon Book Publishers, 1995, revised edition).

Steve Bruce, *The Edge of the Union: The Ulster Loyalist Political Vision* (Oxford: Oxford University Press, 1994). These two works provide readers with a good understanding of the complexities of the politics of Northern Ireland.

Sabine Wichert, *Northern Ireland Since 1945* (Harlow: Longman, 1991).

Michael Cunningham, *British Government Policy in Northern Ireland, 1969–1989, its Nature and Execution* (Manchester: Manchester University Press, 1991). Both books offer a comprehensive account of the problems of Northern Ireland and the political solutions put forward in response to them.

A further book, **Caroline Kennedy-Pipe**, *The Origins of the Present Troubles in Northern Ireland* (Harlow: Longman, 1997) gives valuable material on security policy.

Chapter Twenty-one | Racism

The aims of this chapter are:

1	To define the key terms of 'racism', 'racial prejudice' and 'racial discrimination'.
2	To assess explanations of the causes of racism.
3	To examine the extent to which political parties and other political organisations have promoted racism in the postwar United Kingdom.
4	To evaluate the operations of race relations legislation enacted since 1965.
5	To analyse what further steps might be undertaken by the British State to counter racism.

Definition of Racism

Racism is a *social construction*. This means that the views which are based on it, emphasising the superiority of one race of humans over another, are not objective or underpinned by indisputable facts. They are merely the views and value judgements of individuals. Thus, arguments which assert the inferiority of black persons in comparison to whites are grounded not on scientific evidence but on opinions and ideas which lack any rational basis.

The aim of racism is to justify the control which one set of individuals wishes to exert over another. It establishes (and subsequently perpetuates) an unequal relationship between white and black people in which the former exercise power and the latter are subservient. To achieve this aim, it is necessary to assert that the intended victims of racism are subhuman: the rhetoric (that is, language associated with) racism frequently downgrades humans to animals or vermin. The denial by one group of another's humanity creates a climate in which violence, ranging from genocide (that is, the extermination of a racial group) to racial harassment, occurs and in which prejudice and discrimination is encountered. These terms are defined as follows.

○ *Racial prejudice:* this may be defined as blind and irrational hatred based upon the victim being assigned stereotypical characteristics. The assertion of a linkage between crimes such as 'mugging' and black youths is based on racial prejudice.

○ *Discrimination:* this involves the acting out of these negative feelings. Denying employment to a person solely due to the colour of their skin constitutes an example of racial discrimination.

Explanations of Racism

There is no agreement concerning the root causes of racism. This section examines some key arguments which are put forward to explain it.

Racism and the Colonial Heritage

This explanation views history as a crucial underpinning of racism, in particular the colonial context within which black and white races first encountered each other. This 'colonial context' involved white nations conquering and subsequently governing black African countries during the nineteenth century. The right to exert this control was justified by social Darwinism (which justified the dominance of white over black nations on the grounds that some races had evolved to a greater degree than others), and by biological and genetic theories which asserted the innate (that is, inborn) superiority of the white race. The subsequent teaching of history in schools glorifying the Empire further served to reinforce negative images of black people.

Colonisation thus gave rise to perceptions that black people were inferior to whites, and this view was reinforced by the manner in which domination was subsequently exercised. This assumed two key forms:

○ *Economic domination:* this entailed the economies of colonised countries being required to serve the needs of the colonial, or conquering, power. The conquered country's roles were that of supplying raw materials at low prices to the more powerful country, and to act as a market for the goods the latter produced.

○ *Cultural domination:* this is based on allegations that the conquered peoples were backward and would benefit greatly from their association with the nations of Western Europe whose advantages included the Christian religion and education. Those subject to colonisation were thus constrained to abandon their culture (and often their language) and adopt those of the colonial power.

IMMIGRATION AND RACE RELATIONS IN THE UK

The above factors had a profound impact on race relations when people from colonised countries subsequently came to the conquering country as immigrants. For example, black people who came to the UK after 1948 (when the ship *Empire Windrush* brought the first Afro-Caribbean migrants) were subject to sentiments which had been promoted in literature and history and passed on almost unquestioningly from one generation to the next.

The colonial heritage had an additional consequence for those who entered the UK as immigrants. Colonial societies contained numerous tensions. Newly-arrived settlers competed for jobs and land with indigenous (or native) people, while conquered or enslaved people occasionally rose in revolt. British history portrayed such hostilities in terms which were unfavourable to black people, often depicting them as heathen savages who wantonly massacred white people. Such accounts suggested that black people were uncivilised. However, to black people the same events signified the lack of social justice and the heritage of exploitation which they and their descendants had suffered at the hands of greedy white usurpers (that is, those who had seized land without permission).

Immigration resulted in such pre-existing tensions being translated to countries which encouraged postwar immigration, such as the UK.

Psychological Explanations of Racism

The extent to which the prejudice of an individual can be solely attributed to the existence of a racist culture has not, however, been universally accepted. All societies contain people who are racially prejudiced and others who are not. This suggests that the source of prejudice cannot be attributed to the operations of society and the process of socialisation (that is, adaptation of an individual's behaviour so that it becomes compatible with the views held by the majority of members in a particular society). Psychological explanations of racism thus focus on the personality of the individual as the source of this problem. There are various opinions within psychology concerning why an individual may adopt racist tendencies:

○ *An individual's failure to achieve satisfaction:* this may result in frustration leading to aggression. Although this anger should be directed at those responsible for such frustration, it could be targeted at a scapegoat. This theory has been used as an explanation of white racism in the American Deep South.

○ *The authoritarian personality:* research associated with the Frankfurt School of Critical Theory asserted that racism was a consequence of an authoritarian personality. A measurement (the 'F-scale') was devised to indicate willingness to submit to a form of rigid authority coupled with aggression against those who rejected it. Persons who scored highly in this test were deemed likely to be anti-semitic and racist.

Marxist Explanations of Racism

Marxists assert that capitalism is the source of racism. The economic system is based on the exploitation of labour in order to produce profits for those who control the means of production (who are the bourgeoisie). The continuance of this system requires both the guaranteed existence of an abundant supply of labour, and also mechanisms to ensure that class conflict can be resolved before it assumes revolutionary proportions. Thus Marxist analysis would assert the following points.

○ *Immigration:* this was initially designed to secure the abundance of unskilled and semiskilled labour.

○ *Racial prejudice:* this hindered the development of class consciousness. Problems such as low wages or scarcity of employment resulted in the working class fighting itself on racial lines rather than pooling its resources against those who benefited from social injustice. Thus the bourgeoisie are accused of deliberately nurturing racism in order to divide (and thus rule) the proletariat.

○ *Racial discrimination:* this impeded the social mobility of immigrants and their descendants and ensured that they would remain at the bottom of the social ladder, performing menial jobs. These were the original members of Britain's underclass who were deprived of a range of social rights including adequate employment, housing and education opportunities.

The Expression of Racism

Racist views may be promoted in a number of different ways. This section examines the manner in which extra-parliamentary and conventional political activity has contributed to this problem.

Extra-Parliamentary Political Activity

The extreme right has been linked with a number of disorderly activities. This includes football hooliganism, which included the riot which caused the abandonment of the international

MAX WEBER

Marx applied the word 'class' solely to the relationships arising in the labour market: class membership was determined by an individual's relationship to the means of production. Later sociologists inspired by Max Weber used the term more widely, observing a variety of markets and a wide range of class situations which resulted from them. A class was defined as a number of individuals who shared a particular market situation. Conflict arose between classes when one sought to promote its own interests at the expense of others. This analysis has been developed to include racism.

People who came to the UK from new Commonwealth countries entered into an *existing* situation of conflict which was played out in the city. Here competition for space led groups to compete for housing resources. This was one important source of conflict between native whites and black immigrants. Latterly, such competition involved other policy areas including local government resources, welfare benefits and jobs. Immigration did not *cause* social tensions but it served to aggravate existing conflicts. The prior existence of racial prejudice ensured that newly-arrived immigrants became scapegoats for an urban social setting based upon injustices derived from the unequal distribution of material resources (such as wealth). Subsequent public expenditure cuts affecting employment and the social and welfare services intensified the extent of prejudice and discrimination which was directed against those who were blamed for the problems affecting large numbers of the urban working class.

Question

What do you consider to be the main cause of racism in contemporary British society?

To answer this question, use the following headings:

○ **History and the colonial experience**

○ **Psychology**

○ **Marxist analysis.**

Express the explanation each offers for racism in your own words. Which of these views do you consider offers the best explanation for this social problem?

match between England and Ireland at Lansdowne Road, Dublin in February 1995. This was allegedly provoked by Combat 18 and other extremist rightwing groups. After this event Scotland Yard established a special unit to tackle neo-nazi groups. The connection between the extreme right and football hooliganism was highlighted by police seizures of racist and hooligan literature in Operation Harvest in 1996. This was designed to tackle potential disruption to the Euro '96 football competition.

Racial Attacks

Members of ethnic minority communities have frequently been subject to various forms of racially motivated violence ranging from verbal abuse and incivility to physical attacks on themselves and their property. These attacks are inflicted upon individuals or groups purely because of their colour, race, nationality or ethnic and national origins. They challenge the right of ethnic minorities to live in the UK, and inflict deep psychological damage on their victims. In 1994, the Home Affairs Committee declared that racially motivated violence constituted a serious threat to social harmony: 'an assault motivated by racism is more socially-divisive than any other assault, and if allowed to pass unchecked will begin to corrode the fabric of our tolerant society.'

Historically the victims of racial attacks were Jewish people who still experience violence directed at communal property such as cemeteries and synagogues, unprovoked assaults and the receipt of anti-semitic literature. However, many of the contemporary examples of racial violence have been directed against black people. Although racial harassment may be targeted at individuals who become subject to a sustained campaign of intimidation, violence is often directed at individuals who are randomly attacked purely because of the colour of their skin. A number of murders have been committed. These include the murders of Akhtar Ali Baig in 1980, and Fiaz Mirza and Stephen Lawrence in 1993. This violence frequently results in black people being unable, or too scared, to leave their homes in which they exist as virtual prisoners.

RACIAL ATTACKS – A CAUSE FOR CONCERN

In 1994, the House of Commons was informed that the number of incidents of racial violence reported to the police in England and Wales was rising.

◆ 5,900 in 1985

◆ 7,734 in 1992

◆ 9,762 for 1992/1993

◆ 11,878 in the year ending March 1995.

Official figures, however, are believed to provide an inaccurate picture of the problem as racial attacks are frequently not reported. One estimate by Aye Maung and Mirrlees-Black in 1994 based upon a victimisation survey suggested that there were 130,000 racially motivated crimes in 1991 directed against South Asians and Afro-Caribbeans.

The Criminal Justice System and Racially Motivated Violence

One difficulty concerning society's reaction to racially motivated violence has been that ethnic minority communities do not believe that the agencies of the criminal justice system have mounted a sufficiently vigorous response to such problems. Perceived indifference to such violence indicates to those on the receiving end that they are officially regarded as second-class citizens.

The Police and Racial Attacks

Numerous allegations have been made of police indifference to black victims of racial violence. It has been alleged that police responses to such actions traditionally involved a denial that there was any racial motive, a desire to avoid official intervention in favour of treating the incident as a civil dispute between neighbours, the provision of misleading advice, hostility towards victims and delays in responding to requests for help. It has been further alleged that attempts by communities to protect themselves against racial attacks have been met with an unsympathetic police response. For example, in 1994 an Asian, Lakhbir Deol, was charged with murder when he sought to defend himself and his property against a racial attack.

Several explanations might be offered for the stance adopted by the police towards racial attacks.

○ *Inadequate powers:* the problem of racial harassment was not specifically regarded as an offence until the combined impact of the 1997 Protection From Harassment Act, and the 1998 Crime and Disorder Act made it so.

○ *Stereotyping:* some police officers allegedly have a stereotyped view of black people, one consequence of which is the 'black-youth–black-crime linkage'. The acceptance of this stereotyping makes it difficult to view black youths as the victims of crime. In 1998, research suggested that black people were eight times more likely to be stopped and searched by the police than were whites.

○ *Absence of corroborating evidence:* the frequent absence of corroborating evidence (that is, evidence from others to back up the statements made by a victim) hinders the successful detection of those involved in such attacks and their subsequent prosecution.

To respond to such criticisms, ACPO (the Association of Chief Police Officers) published *Racial Attacks – ACPO Guiding Principles* in 1985. The following year a common reporting and monitoring system for racial attacks was established, supervised by the Inspectorate. However, in 1986 the Home Affairs Committee argued that the police had failed to make racial attacks a priority and urged that this should be done. It was recommended that the police should receive special training in handling racial violence. In 1988, the Home Office required all police forces to record details of 'racial incidents'. This approach has been criticised for relating to any incident of an inter-racial nature rather than only to violence perpetrated by white persons on members of ethnic minorities where the aim is to reinforce social inferiority as well as to inflict physical harm.

The Crown Prosecution Service and Racial Violence

Perceptions that the Crown Prosecution Service had a poor record in dealing with racist violence led the Home Affairs Committee in 1989 to recommend the introduction of a comprehensive scheme of monitoring. However, such advice was not immediately acted upon. In 1992, the Code for Crown Prosecutors was amended so that a clear racial motive would be regarded as an aggravating feature when assessing whether a prosecution was required in the public interest. The following year the CPS began monitoring racial incident cases. However, progress in improving the image of the CPS was hampered by allegations presented in the *Observer* on 5 May 1996 that actions taken against its own black employees could be interpreted as discriminatory.

The Courts and Racial Violence

Accusations of inappropriate treatment by the courts have also been made in connection with racially motivated violence giving rise to the perception that a black life is worth less than that of a white. In 1976, the killer of an Asian in Southall was sentenced to four years imprisonment. Kingsley Read (then chair of the National Front) referred to this episode in a speech delivered in Newham, stating 'one down, a million to go'. He referred to immigrants as 'niggers, wogs and coons'. In 1978, he was acquitted of an offence under the Race Relations legislation. The judge advised him to moderate his language in future, and concluded the trial by wishing him well.

Black people may be dealt with unfairly by the courts when they are victims of crime. In 1993, two youths who subjected an Asian teenager to an attack which left him partly blinded in one eye were jailed for only three and a half years. According to the *Independent* on 22 September 1993, the trial judge admitted that 'we are going to kill you, you smelly Paki' constituted racial undertones but did not amount to an 'aggravating feature'. However, the most publicised examples of perceived racial injustice occurred in 1993 with the murder of Stephen Lawrence, and the death of Joy Gardner who collapsed following a struggle with police whilst being served with a deportation order.

In the Stephen Lawrence case the Crown Prosecution Service refused to pursue charges against three youths who were alleged to have been involved in the attack on the grounds of insufficient evidence. The Lawrence family subsequently

Neville Lawrence during a news conference. His son Stephen was a victim of racial violence and the subsequent failure of the criminal-justice system.

initiated a private prosecution which broke down in 1996. In the case of Joy Gardner an Old Bailey Jury cleared two police officers of manslaughter in 1995. A third officer was cleared on the directions of the judge earlier in the trial. The Police Complaints Authority subsequently declined to insist that these three officers should face disciplinary charges.

The newly-elected Labour government instituted an enquiry into the Stephen Lawrence case which took place in 1998, chaired by Sir William Macpherson. During its proceedings the Metropolitan police commissioner, Sir Paul Condon, apologised to the family for the manner in which his force had handled this case. The findings of Sir William Macpherson were published in 1999. He criticised the Metropolitan police for incompetence and institutionalised racism, and recommended a number of reforms which included subjecting the police service to the scrutiny of the Commission for Racial Equality.

RACISM IN GERMANY

Racism in Germany emerged in the late 1980s and has a particular appeal for young East German people of the so-called 'lost generation'. They suffered as the result of the economic crisis following unification, especially in connection with employment prospects. Racism is articulated by methods which include neo-nazi (the term 'neo' meaning 'new') skinhead bands and through direct physical assaults. The Turkish community are a specific target of the xenophobia unleashed by German neo-nazis who seek to establish 'liberated zones' – no-go areas for all deemed to be 'un-German'. This includes foreigners, gays, punks and leftwingers. In 1997, official figures recorded a total of 11,719 crimes with a rightwing extremist background, the highest level since 1945.

The Expression of Racism by the Political Parties

Racism may also constitute the basis of conventional political activity conducted by political parties. This is a growing problem. In 1998, five EU countries (Austria, Italy, France, Belgium and Denmark) had far Right Parties which secured in excess of 5 per cent of the vote in elections. Three of these (the Austrian Freedom Movement, the French National Front, and the Italian National Alliance/Social Movement) enjoyed support on a scale similar to that of the British Liberal Democrats.

The following section illustrates the ability of race to form the basis of a party or bring about the realignment of existing ones.

Neo-Nazis on the march during the 1998 German General Election.

Germany

In addition to racial violence which has been discussed above, conventional political activity in Germany has also given rise to neo-nazi political parties. One of these (the German People's Party or DVU) secured 13 per cent of the vote in elections to the Saxony-Anholt parliament in East Germany in 1998. Its slogans included 'Jobs for Germans' and 'Foreign bandits out', suggesting that unemployment among Germans was significantly aggravated by the number of foreigners working in the country legally and illegally. This vote constituted the highest percentage secured by the far Right in any German State election since the days of Adolf Hitler. Other parties on the far right include the National Democratic Party of Germany (NPD).

France

The French National Front is a Party whose key demand (that of 'national preference') makes it clearly racist. However, towards the end of the 1980s, it appeared that race did not merely constitute the basis for this Party's appeal but, further, presented the possibility for a realignment of Parties on the right.

The National Front polled well in the 1995 municipal elections, and took control of four big towns in Southern France. The Party built upon this success in the elections to the regional councils in March 1998. It obtained 15.3 per cent of the national vote, secured the return of 275 of its candidates and outpolled the traditional right in many areas. This election result meant that it held the balance of power in a number of regions where the combined vote of councillors from the orthodox and extreme Right could outvote the Left. This gave it a crucial role in the election of the Presidents of these bodies, which took place soon after the regional elections. The leader of the National Front, Jean-Marie Le Pen, made an appeal to the traditional parties on the Right, offering his Party's support for their candidates for regional presidents (which would be reciprocated in areas where his Party was strong). This appeal was designed to secure the goal of 'saving' regions from six years of 'socio-communism', and was based upon an acceptance of policies which included the defence of the French national identity.

The offer of support split the Right. The official attitude of the traditional Right (which comprised the Gaullist RPR and the UDF) was to oppose any cooperation with the extreme Right. In the Alpes-Cote d'Azur region, a number of councillors from the traditional Right voted for a socialist nominee as regional president to deny this office to Le Pen. However, some local leaders of these parties (particularly of the UDF) shunned the advice of their leaders and accepted the support of elected Front National candidates to obtain regional Presidencies. The distaste of many moderates towards such arrangements was one explanation for the large gains chalked up by the Left (which embraced 400 seats and control of 11 councils) in the Departement elections which were held soon after the regional contests.

In the wake of the regional elections, major developments took place in 1998 which presented the possibility of a future realignment of the forces of the Right.

❍ *La Droite:* this organisation sought to establish closer links between the traditional Right and the National Front. Leading members of the old Right moved towards embracing racist policies: Edouard Balladur (of the RPR who had served as Prime Minister in 1993–95) called for a special commission to withdraw family and medical benefits from North African and black residents who lacked French citizenship.

❍ *L'Alliance:* in May 1998 a new grouping, L'Alliance, emerged, consisting of a confederation of all groups on the Right of the political spectrum who refused to have any dealings with the National Front. It involved a formal alliance between the Gaullists and other Parties and presented the possibility of the eventual creation of a single 'conservative' Party in France.

Although the National Front would seem to be the main beneficiary of the split in the traditional (or 'orthodox') French right, suggestions of cooperation with the mainstream parties caused disunity within its ranks towards the end of 1998. Additionally, the continued prominent role played by race in France might be reduced by that country's success in winning the World Cup football competition in July 1998. The French team was a multi-ethnic one. A French journalist, Philippe Jérôme, commented that 'the two goals of Zidane (whose parents were Algerian) in the World Cup final did more for the equal rights of citizens than a thousand speeches from the Left denouncing racism and the policies of Jean-Marie Le Pen's National Front.'

Britain

The Conservative Party

At the 1964 General Election a leading Labour politician, Patrick Gordon Walker, lost his seat at Smethwick after an overtly racist campaign mounted by his Conservative opponent, Peter Griffiths. The slogan 'If you want a nigger for your neighbour, vote Labour' was circulated during the contest. Outrage at such overt racism led the Labour Prime Minister, Harold Wilson, to challenge the Conservative leadership to refuse Griffiths the party whip so that he would spend his time in Parliament as a 'Parliamentary leper'. This was not done and, although Griffiths lost the seat to Labour in 1966, he subsequently served as Conservative Member for North Portsmouth from 1979 until his defeat at the 1997 General Election.

The speeches of the Conservative MP Enoch Powell also fuelled racist sentiments. His 1968 'rivers of blood' speech intensified existing racial prejudice by suggesting that the streets of Britain would eventually run red with blood arising from factional fighting. He referred to white Britons being made to feel strangers in their own country by the influx of immigrants which resulted in neighbourhoods being changed beyond recognition.

The Conservative Party has been associated with a range of other actions which have been seen by some people as racist. The 1948 British Nationality Act had permitted all citizens of the British Commonwealth to enter the country to settle and seek work with their families. Limits on immigration were first introduced by a Conservative government in 1961. The 1971 Immigration Act (which required those coming to the UK to prove a close connection with the country) particularly pandered to such feelings by suggesting that black people were a problem for society and a threat to British culture and traditions. The introduction of a tiered system of citizenship in the 1981 Nationality Act, further restrictions on immigration contained in the 1988 Immigration Act, and attempts to impose limitations on asylum seekers in the 1993 Asylum and Immigration Act have further reinforced the negative view of immigrants as the source of social problems whose entry should only be permitted in an ever-narrowing range of circumstances.

The Labour Party

Many Working Men's Clubs operated a colour bar in the 1960s and 1970s, and the abandonment of Labour's outright opposition to all forms of immigration control was perceived as pandering to racist sentiments. The mid-1960s witnessed the 'dutch auction of illiberalism' in which the main Parties sought to outbid each other with 'tough stands' on immigration against the background of the economic recession of the late 1950s and early 1960s. Allegations of racist conduct by members of the Labour Party again surfaced following its election victory in 1997 when allegations were made that the image of 'new' Labour was that of an almost exclusively white organisation, containing few black MPs. The Commission for Racial Equality indicated it had received a number of complaints from black and Asian councillors regarding their deselection by local parties. Two of these, Raghib Ahsan and Muhammad Afzal, were advised by lawyers that they had a case under the Race Relations legislation.

The Liberal Democrats

The activities of some Liberal Democrat councillors in the London Borough of Tower Hamlets were also tainted with racism. An internal Party enquiry conducted by Lord Lester in 1994 into alleged racist election leaflets recommended the expulsion of three local Party members.

The National Front

The National Front was formed in 1967 following the fusion of a number of groups on the rightwing of the political spectrum. The Party contested its first by-election in 1968 at Acton, and in 1973 gained 16 per cent of the poll at West Bromwich. It secured several good results in local government elections after the second 1974 General Election but declined towards the end of that decade. For several years in the 1970s, however, the National Front posed a significant threat to the urban support of the main political Parties although it never succeeded in getting any of its candidates elected to local or national political office. Its chief political impact was to force the issue of race onto the political agenda.

The main plank of the National Front's programme was to end immigration and initiate a programme of repatriation. The Party blamed most of the problems faced by contemporary urban society (such as poor housing conditions, crime, employment prospects, and the strains placed on the welfare state) on those who came to the UK from the new Commonwealth countries. Additionally the Party placed itself at the forefront of a defence of Britain's national identity by decrying attempts by governments of both Parties to achieve assimilation, the consequences of which included mixed marriages. After the 1966 General Election, however, factors which included a toughening Conservative stance on immigration, led to the National Front's adopting a new political stance.

The Party embraced a populist appeal in which it depicted itself as the standard bearer for the views of 'ordinary' members of the general public which were ignored by the major political Parties. These were said to be dominated by 'unrepresentative liberals', and resulted in allegedly unpopular policies such as immigration, the abolition of capital punishment and abortion being forced on the country. Additionally, the National Front moved into new policy areas by opposing the Common Market and the power of multi-national corporations. These were allegedly driven by considerations which were prejudicial to the interests of the working class or those engaged in small business enterprises.

The National Front also sought to benefit from the economic and political climate of the early 1970s. The extent of industrial unrest and the indecisive results of the two 1974 General Elections legitimised the attempt by the National Front to present itself as a movement which could mobilise the support of all classes and political Parties and provide firm and effective leadership in order to 'save the nation'.

By the end of the 1970s, however, the appeal of the National Front was waning. Several factors contributed to this situation in addition to the mobilisation of organised support against the Party by the Anti Nazi League. Some of its appeal, particularly in the 1974 General Elections, had been in the nature of a protest vote. The National Front failed to make any substantial impact on the degree of class loyalty which underpinned support for both main political Parties. The election of Margaret Thatcher as Conservative leader in 1975 resulted in a more pronounced emphasis on issues such as law and order, and a less liberal attitude towards immigration, which thus lessened the unique appeal of the National Front. Internal divisions, often based on personality rather than policy, also had a detrimental effect on the vitality of the Party: in 1975 a former chairman, Kingsley Read, left and formed the National Party which secured some limited local successes especially in Blackburn. In 1995, this Party was renamed the National Democrats.

The British National Party

The British National party was formed in 1982 following a split within the National Front. Its policies are racist and anti-semitic. The *Guardian* on 12 February 1994 estimated that the membership of the BNP was 2,000. At the 1994 local elections it called for the repeal of all race relations laws, and made a facetious demand for the legalisation of children's golliwogs. The Party won a local authority by-election in Tower Hamlets in 1993, and the following year saved its deposit in a Parliamentary by-election at Dagenham. It is alleged to have close links with the organisation Combat 18 which was formed in 1992 (although a similar organisation, Column 88, existed in the 1960s). Combat 18 presents a particular threat to social harmony through its association with acts of violence against racial minorities. These seek to spark 'tit for tat' violence resulting in intensified residential segregation (or ethnic cleansing). It was initially formed to guard BNP meetings, but the relationship between the organisations has become less overt in the 1990s. The BNP proscribed Combat 18 in 1994 in order to sustain its image as a political party rather than a street gang.

Organised Opposition to Racism in Britain

Racism has been countered by a number of organisations which have engaged in activities including demonstrations and various forms of direct action. Following the Second World War, Group 43 mounted militant opposition to the Union Movement, which had replaced the former British Union of Fascists.

The National Front was opposed by organisations which included the Anti Nazi League, established in 1977 by the Socialist Workers' Party. The League's tactics included protest marches, public meetings and rock concerts. Its strength waned with the virtual demise of the National Front, but it was reformed in 1992 to respond to the emergence of the British National Party. In 1991, a new organisation, the Anti-Racist

Question

With reference to events in any ONE European country, to what extent and in what ways can it be said that racism has been a significant political issue since 1960?

Alliance, was formed mainly by black political activists who had been working in the Labour Party. Opposition of a more violent kind has also been mounted by the Anti-Fascist Alliance which was formed in 1985 to confront the BNP both ideologically and physically. One of its 'successes' was to prevent hundreds of skinheads attending a gig by the neo-nazi group Skrewdriver in 1992. Confrontational opposition to the extreme Right has also been waged by anarchist groups such as Class War.

Reforms to Combat Racism

The need to combat racism in society may be justified on moral grounds but is necessary also because of racism's overall effect on social harmony. Racism breeds a climate of violence against members of ethnic minority communities and may, in turn, encourage such groups to reject white-dominated society, thus undermining progress towards a multi-ethnic society. Groups which include the Nation of Islam (whose leading figure is David Farrakhan) advocate separatism whereby black people control their own lives and destinies without interference from whites.

This section seeks to assess the initiatives which have been developed to counter racism within British society.

Race Relations Legislation

In countries such as the USA minority communities are far more sizeable, which means that political Parties have to cater for their needs in order to secure electoral success. In 1998, for example, the Hispanic community in the USA (that is, those of Latin American descent) numbered some 30 million (11 per cent of the population), and in some States (including California and Texas), Hispanics comprised 25 per cent of the population. Although this community does not vote as a cohesive block, its overall size is a guarantee against political marginalisation. A further 13 per cent of the American population at this time was black, and 5 per cent were Asian. On the other hand, the ability of Britain's ethnic minority communities to place the issue of discrimination firmly onto the political agenda has been impeded by their small size.

There have been three measures concerned with race relations since 1965.

Total Population (in 000s)	56,206.1
White	53,062.3
Black Groups	929.6
South Asian Groups	1,548.8
Other Groups	665.3

THE SIZE OF THE UK'S ETHNIC MINORITY POPULATION (1991 CENSUS)

The figures in the table opposite indicate that ethnic minority communities in total comprise 3,143,700 persons, or 5.6 per cent of the total population of Great Britain.

Figures taken from Office for National Statistics (Peter Radcliffe editor), *Ethnicity in the 1991 Census* (London: HMSO, 1996).

The 1965 Race Relations Act

This measure constituted the first official attempt to deal with racial discrimination. It owed much to the operations of the pressure group CARD (Campaign Against Racial Discrimination). Its main provisions embraced the following points.

○ *'Places of public resort':* it became illegal to discriminate on grounds of colour, race, ethnic or national origins in places which included restaurants and theatres.

○ *Housing:* it outlawed racial discrimination in the transfer of tenancies.

○ *Incitement to racial hatred:* this became a new criminal offence.

○ *Establishment of enforcement machinery:* a Race Relations Board and Conciliation Committees were established to enforce the legislation. These investigated complaints and sought to ensure that acts of discrimination would not be repeated. The consent of the Attorney General was required to initiate a prosecution if this intervention failed.

The 1965 legislation was, however, limited in scope, and the majority of cases which were referred to the Race Relations Board were outside its remit. The National Commission for Commonwealth Immigrants and local Voluntary Liaison Committees were additionally established to help immigrants overcome problems of social adjustment, to alert local communities to the realities of racial inequality and to offer opportunities to ethnic minorities to become more involved and integrated in the wider community.

The 1968 Race Relations Legislation

Following the passage of the 1965 Act, the organisation Political and Economic Planning investigated the extent of racial discrimination in the UK. The findings contained in its 1967 report formed the basis of the 1968 Race Relations Act which sought a more vigorous response to racial discrimination.

❍ *Extension of the provisions of the 1965 Act*: discrimination was defined as a situation where 'a person on racial grounds treats another less favourably than he treats or would treat other persons on racial grounds', and covered a range of activities relating to employment, housing, the provision of goods, facilities and services to the general public, and the publication of discriminatory advertisements.

❍ *The Community Relations Commission*: this was designed to coordinate the work of local voluntary community relations organisations, and to promote harmonious community relations.

The 1976 Race Relations Act

Between 1972 and 1975 the organisation Political and Economic Planning conducted research into the disadvantage experienced by racial minorities, and the sources of this problem. It was estimated that the weak enforcement powers of the Race Relations Board (which was unable to summon witnesses, issue orders or initiate an investigation unless an individual complained) had hindered the alleviation of discrimination. In spite of previous measures, black unskilled workers had a one in two chance of being discriminated against when applying for a job. The Race Relations Act of 1976 thus sought further reforms.

❍ *Further extension of the scope of the legislation*: the new legislation was extended to cover new areas of public life including education and training. Complaints concerning discrimination in employment are now made to industrial tribunals, and the other matters are dealt with through County Courts.

❍ *Indirect discrimination*: the Act covered indirect as well as direct discrimination. The former constituted conditions or requirements which had a discriminatory effect, and which could not be justified without reference to race, colour, nationality or ethnic or national origin of the person affected.

❍ *The Commission for Racial Equality*: this replaced the Race Relations Board and the Community Relations Commission.

Effectiveness of the Commission for Racial Equality

The effectiveness of the work of the CRE may be assessed by the following information:

❍ *Assistance and advice*: the CRE can offer advice and assistance to individuals with complaints of racial discrimination. In 1995, the Commission for Racial Equality received 1,682 applications from individual complainants, and provided advice and assistance to 1,305 applicants.

FUNCTIONS OF THE COMMISSION FOR RACIAL EQUALITY

The 1976 Race Relations Act gave this newly-established body four main functions:

1   to work towards the elimination of racial discrimination

2   to promote equality of opportunity and good relations between members of different ethnic groups

3   to review the workings of the Race Relations Act

4   to make proposals for changes to the government.

It was also empowered to conduct formal investigations into any subject of its choice, and may be required by the Secretary of State to carry out a particular enquiry. The Commission could compel persons to give evidence or provide documents in such circumstances. Such formal investigations may give rise to a non-discrimination notice being issued, requiring the discriminating person or organisation to cease unlawful discrimination. The impact of such a notice is monitored, and if discrimination continues, the CRE may apply for an injunction through the courts, ordering the person or organisation to desist. Breach of such an injunction constitutes contempt of court.

An example of the use of this procedure arose in 1996, when the CRE threatened the Ministry of Defence with a non-discrimination order unless it took immediate steps to increase the number of soldiers from ethnic minority communities in the Household Cavalry.

○ *Redress:* complainants may secure financial redress if the discrimination is proven. In 1995, industrial tribunal awards in cases supported by the Commission amounted to £209,292, an average of £5,105 per case. Additionally, 94 cases assisted by the CRE were settled on terms, with industrial tribunal settlements amounting to £617,942. Nineteen non-employment cases were settled on terms totalling £28,000.

Further Steps to Secure Racial Equality

Although, as has been indicated above, some individuals have made successful use of race relations legislation and secured personal redress of their grievances, race relations legislation has failed to eradicate the overall problems of racial prejudice and discrimination within British society.

Race relations legislation has made only a limited impact on

THE EFFECTIVENESS OF RACE RELATIONS LEGISLATION

Some individual complaints of racial discrimination may be satisfactorily remedied by existing race relations legislation.

In 1998, four young Asian women were awarded £48,000 by an industrial tribunal, whose report described their employers as 'unbelievable, evasive, contradictory and out to smear'. Two of these women further won a constructive dismissal case against the firm. The women were ordered not to speak Urdu at work, barred from observing religious holidays, and were subject to racial taunts by senior staff.

In 1998, an industrial tribunal found that a senior black employee of Hackney Borough Council had been subjected to 'four years of living hell' by a colleague who had 'a fixed mental impression that Africans, particularly West Africans, have a propensity to commit fraud'. He was awarded damages totalling £380,000.

The amount which might be paid has been increased following the removal of the upper limit for awards by the 1994 Race Relations (Remedies) Act. However, it is not easy to win a case since the onus of proving the allegation is on the complainant. Further, access to the courts is available only to individuals. This means that the 'class actions' which are a feature of American anti-discrimination legislation (and the large fines which have sometimes been awarded) are absent in the UK.

redressing racial inequality in Britain. One explanation for this was the unfavourable political climate between 1979 and 1997. Many Conservatives contended that emphasising racial discrimination eroded individual responsibility for a person's social situation, and enabled the blame for problems ranging from educational under-achievement to delinquency to be foisted on 'the system' rather than be located within the individual.

An ICM poll published in the *Guardian* on 20 March 1995 stated that an overwhelming majority of people in the UK believed that there was widespread racial prejudice in the country: 79 per cent of white respondents believed that there was prejudice towards black people. A European-wide survey published in 1997 suggested that one in three Britons was a self-confessed racist. This figure was higher than in Portugal, Sweden and Luxembourg (where below one in five admitted to this sentiment) but lower than that in France, Belgium and Austria.

The Office for National Statistics concluded in 1996 that ethnic minorities had generally fared worse than the white population on grounds of unemployment, pay, housing or as victims of crime. The educational system has been accused of racial bias. A report by OFSTED (the body which inspects schools) in 1996 asserted that the rate of expulsion of Afro-Caribbean pupils was six times higher than for white children, which was likely to result in the emergence of an alienated, underqualified group. The exclusion of black pupils from schools arose from, and served to support, a perception that these children posed a problem for the school and were educationally subnormal.

Such problems justify further measures being taken. The cause of racial equality might be aided by the following measures:

○ reforms to the legislation

○ the promotion of measures to provide for positive discrimination

○ pursuing the goal of integration to achieve a multi-ethnic society.

Reforms to the Race Relations Legislation

In 1998, the Commission for Racial Equality put forward a number of proposals to reform the Race Relations Legislation in order to eradicate discrimination from society. It proposed the following.

○ *The scope of the Act should extend to discrimination by all public bodies:* this would provide protection in areas which included policing, and the treatment of prisoners.

○ *All new legislation should have to comply with the Race Relations Act:* ministers would be required to confirm that new legislation which they brought forward either did not conflict with the legislation or would be required to justify those cases where a discrepancy was necessary.

○ *The definition of indirect discrimination:* a reform to amend the definition of indirect discrimination would reflect the EU Burden of Proof Directive, which called for a new definition in the Sex Discrimination legislation. Compensation would be available for indirect discrimination without having to prove intent, thus focusing on the consequence rather than the motive of those practising this form of discrimination.

○ *Protection should extend to voluntary workers:* these workers should have the same protection as employees, and the organisations for which they worked should be liable for discriminatory acts and racial harassment by third parties.

○ *Ethnic monitoring should become compulsory for all employers with over 250 workers:* this was deemed to be an essential tool to measure the progress towards racial equality, and could be used to aid an individual complainant.

❍ *'Class actions':* it was proposed that where a number of persons were affected, courts and tribunals should be able to consider a group complaint rather than requiring each individual to make a separate submission.

Positive Discrimination

The approach embodied in British race relations is that of equal opportunities. This seeks to ensure that ethnic minorities are treated in the same manner as white people and that colour of skin is not an obstacle in securing employment, housing or other social necessities. The approach is, however, an essentially passive process which does little to tackle the underlying reasons for discriminatory practices.

An alternative approach is that of positive discrimination. This accepts that ethnic minorities have historically been denied equal treatment in white-dominated societies and seeks to remedy this through the more radical approach of pursuing a range of measures which are designed to redress the imbalance by discriminating in favour of disadvantaged groups. This approach has been adopted in the USA, for example, where it is usually referred to as 'affirmative action'. A diverse range of initiatives is required to guarantee equal employment opportunities. These are directed at areas which include recruitment, training and the setting of goals and targets. The latter may include the use of *quotas* which seek to ensure enhanced employment opportunities for ethnic minority communities. This approach may also be extended to other areas, including access to higher education.

Integration and a Multi-Ethnic Society

The Race Relations Acts discussed above have been mainly directed at the symptoms of racial injustice (that is, prejudice and discrimination) and not its root cause. In 1974, Parekh argued that the forces of economic and political power and cultural domination which caused racism had to be addressed. This involved immigrants organising themselves into a powerful force in the country's economic and political life, and recreating their black identity through the recomposition of their historical heritage. This approach would result in minority groups being placed in a position which commanded respect from the host society rather than having to rely on its benevolence, and also having pride in their own culture and heritage rather than having to seek social acceptance by adopting the traditions and behaviour of those who had previously colonised them.

Parekh's approach was compatible with attaining a multi-ethnic society through the strategy of *integration*. It is based on power sharing whereby minority groups are able to exert a degree of autonomy within a host society. This presents an alternative approach to *assimilation* whereby minority groups are encouraged to abandon their heritage, culture and separate identity and merge themselves with the dominant society. British race relations legislation has been primarily geared towards aiding the process of assimilation by removing impediments which prevent the attainment of this latter goal. A more radical approach towards eliminating racial discrimination would be to abandon any attempt to assimilate minority groups and encourage them to stand on their own feet both economically and politically. This approach is designed to generate respect from the white community which, in turn, would aid the removal of discriminatory practices based on the underlying perception of black inferiority.

Question

Discuss the main functions of the Commission for Racial Equality and the way in which these duties are carried out.

Using examples of your own, discuss evidence which suggests that legislation enacted since 1965 has failed to eliminate racial discrimination in the UK. What reasons would you put forward to explain such lack of success?

MUSLIM SCHOOLS

The move to establish separate Muslim schools is an important aspect of integration. The UK had a longstanding tradition of Roman Catholic, Anglican, and Jewish schools, but Muslim institutions (which numbered around 60 towards the end of the 1990s) received no form of State funding and thus had to be operated privately, charging those who used them. In January 1998, the Secretary of State for Education, David Blunkett, approved applications from two Muslim schools to secure grant-maintained status.

Banning Racist Political Parties

The quest for racial equality may be aided by banning racist political parties. This section analyses the arguments for and against this course of action.

Arguments for Banning Racist Political Parties

A number of arguments can be presented in favour of banning (or proscribing) political parties whose policies serve to promote racism.

○ *The activities of racist parties create a climate in which racial violence is likely to occur:* the number of violent incidents rose sharply in south-east London after the BNP moved its headquarters into that area in 1989. Banning organisations which use or encourage violence to further their political ends would be compatible with the test applied by the Prevention of Terrorism Act towards Northern Irish terrorist groups.

○ *Banning would constitute a positive political statement:* this action would demonstrate a commitment by both the executive and legislature to a multi-racial society in which the articulation of racism is deemed an unacceptable form of social and political behaviour.

○ *Financial considerations:* banning might also save police resources which have often been expended on demonstrations and processions involving racist parties and their opponents. Some of these (such as Red Lion Square in 1974 and Southall in 1979) have been particularly violent events at which demonstrators have died.

Arguments Against Banning Racist Political Parties

However, there are problems associated with such a course of action.

○ *Freedom of speech:* this is a key feature of a liberal-democratic political system. Banning political organisations raises the issue as to who should possess the right to decide what is politically acceptable and what should be prohibited.

○ *Monitoring becomes more difficult:* banning a party is unlikely to result in its disappearance. Instead this action may drive it underground whereby it continues to operate in a secretive, covert fashion. This poses problems for the police, who need to monitor its activities.

○ *Violence may be intensified:* banning may result in an organisation's pursuing more extreme tactics to further its political objectives, since it is no longer constrained by the need to court political support in a conventional manner. The aggrieved group will also have a grudge against the State which instituted the ban, and may further direct violence against its key personnel (including politicians, judges and police officers).

○ *Martyrdom:* there is also a danger that a party which is banned may secure popular sympathy by being viewed as an 'underdog', denied the liberal-democratic right of freedom of speech. The extent to which this is likely to occur depends on whether the public discern any dignity in the cause espoused by the Party.

○ *Selective banning is discriminatory:* as has been shown at the start of this chapter, all political Parties have, on occasions, shown themselves willing to pander to racism. It might thus be deemed unfair to select some organisations for such extreme treatment whilst ignoring others.

Question

Based on the above arguments, would you advocate banning a party whose policies are overtly and unambiguously racist?

○ *Banning is unnecessary:* banning racist parties may also be resisted on the grounds that it is possible to utilise existing legislation to deal effectively with the activities of their members.

Legislation Concerning Racial Attacks

A further reform to secure racial equality is for the law to be amended to ensure that racial harassment and violence become seen as serious issues. Such legislation is found in a number of American states, and a number of attempts have been made to introduce similar measures in the UK. In 1994, a report of the Home Affairs Select Committee suggested that a charge of violent assault in which there was evidence that the attack had been motivated by colour, race, nationality or ethnic or national origins could result in an additional and consecutive sentence of up to five years' imprisonment for the racial element of that offence.

Arguments in Favour of New Legislation

The main arguments in favour of the introduction of new legislation to deal with racial violence is the inadequate protection historically afforded to those who fall victim to it. A new offence of racially motivated violence would secure the following advantages:

○ *Encourage public bodies to address this issue:* a specific offence of racial violence would inform the police, courts and the general public of the commitment by the government and Parliament to eradicate this social problem. It would also be possible to monitor the precise extent of such activity.

○ *Provide a more effective recourse for the victims of such violence:* issues such as harassment and violence are often civil offences which invite personal remedies to major social problems. Existing criminal law has often been subject to unfavourable interpretation by judges, which, coupled with the lenient sentences, has not deterred racial misconduct.

Opposition to New Legislation

There is, however, opposition to such a reform. The main arguments against establishing a new law on racially motivated violence are discussed below.

Focuses on Motive

An offence of racial violence would entail concentrating on the motive for a criminal action. Not only is this unusual in British law (which traditionally focuses on the offence itself) but it might also prove difficult to establish motive in a court of law.

Adequate Remedies Exist

It can be argued that there exists sufficient criminal and civil law to deal with both violence in general and racial harassment in particular. The offence of incitement to racial hatred contained in the 1986 Public Order Act is of particular importance. This made it an offence to use threatening, insulting or abusive words or behaviour with the intention of stirring up racial hatred, or when it could be proved that such actions were likely to stir up racial hatred whether intended or not. The law also covered the publication and broadcast of socially inflammatory material through media such as films, video and sound recordings. The consent of the Attorney General remained a requirement for a prosecution to be initiated. The offence related to disorderly conduct in section 5 of the 1986 Act might also be utilised in relation to threatening, abusive or insulting behaviour of a racial nature. The 1994 Criminal Justice and Public Order Act latterly introduced the new offence of intentional harassment to deal with persistent problems of this nature.

Judicial interpretation may also render new legislation to deal with racially motivated violence unnecessary. In 1994 Lord Chief Justice Taylor (in *R. v. Ribbans, Duggan and Ridley*) ruled that although the law did not have any specific offence of racial violence, a proven racial motive in any crime of violence could lead the judge to exercise discretion and give an increased sentence.

New Legislation May Have Unintended Consequences

One problem is that the offence of racial violence might be utilised in a manner not anticipated by its proposers. A main dilemma would be to decide whether this offence was designed to deal only with incidents in which the victim was a member of a minority group (in which case it might result in accusations of preferential treatment being accorded to minorities), or whether the offence could be applied to any crime of an inter-racial nature, which was the proposal of the Select Committee in 1994.

Enforcement of New Legislation

It has been argued above that traditionally the criminal justice system has not always treated racially motivated violence with the seriousness the issue would seem to deserve. Any new offence would only prove effective if the agencies within the criminal justice system regarded racial violence as a serious issue.

There are some signs that such changes are occurring. The 1991 Criminal Justice Act required the Home Secretary to publish information annually as a safeguard against discrimination on grounds including race and gender. This required agencies within the criminal justice and penal systems to collect data on minority groups as victims, offenders and workers.

Question

The Labour government's 1998 Crime and Disorder Act contained provisions concerned with racially aggravated offences.

Based on your reading of the above section, analyse the strengths and weaknesses of introducing new law to deal with this issue.

THE RESPONSE OF THE POLICE AND COURTS TO RACIAL VIOLENCE

In 1993, the newly-installed Metropolitan Commissioner of Police, Paul Condon, indicated that his force had to be 'totally intolerant' of racially motivated attacks and of those who used racial hatred for political ends. Problems including the low clear-up rate for such incidents prompted the Home Affairs Committee to assert in 1994 that, while progress had been made by the police in this area of work, it was necessary for the Home Office to re-emphasise that tackling racial incidents should be regarded as a priority task. Subsequent initiatives have included the cooperation between the Campaign for Racial Equality and Association of Chief Police Officers in 1996 to develop management standards for police forces around the country concerning responses to racial harassment.

The attitude of the courts in dealing with cases related to racial violence is not consistently biased. There has been a greater willingness to initiate prosecutions for offences such as publishing racially inciting material, and the conviction rate in prosecutions concerned with racism began to rise during the 1990s. There are also examples of those found guilty of racial attacks being given severe sentences. In 1993, for example, two men (one 22 and the other 19 years of age) were jailed for life for the racist killing of an Asian minicab driver, Fiaz Mirza. The judge recommended that one of these men should serve a minimum sentence of 22 years in prison.

Further Reading

Bhikku Parekh, *Colour, Culture and Consciousness: Immigrant Intellectuals in Britain* (London: Allen and Unwin, 1974). Although dated, this collection of essays written by non–white intellectuals regarding their life in England and the problems they encountered provides an informative account of racism.

Richard Skellington, '*Race' in Britain Today* (London: Sage Publications, 1996, 3rd edition). This offers a thorough and readable account of the experiences of black people in a number of policy areas, and assesses the effectiveness of policies designed to respond to racism.

Chapter Twenty-Two | Male and Female Inequality

The aims of this chapter are:

> 1 To examine the nature of male and female inequality, differentiating between explanations based on biology and social processes.
>
> 2 To evaluate the main aspects of the social processes which create gender discrimination within society.
>
> 3 To analyse the effectiveness of reforms to combat gender discrimination in contemporary societies.
>
> 4 To evaluate the development of the role of women in politics.
>
> 5 To evaluate contemporary political reforms which seek to combat gender discrimination.

The Roots of Male–Female Inequality

This chapter is concerned with the existence of an unequal power relationship between the two sexes. This gives rise to discrimination whereby one is accorded a different and inferior status in society. There are two broad explanations which can be put forward to explain female inequality.

○ *Biology:* this suggests that inequality is based upon chromosome or hormonal differences between the sexes. It is thus rooted in nature.

○ *Social processes:* this asserts that inequality is not 'natural' but, instead, is an artificial creation which is based upon social or cultural processes. It is derived from 'common sense' assertions concerning the obvious physical differences between the sexes which are then developed by social institutions and culture to provide for (and subsequently reproduce) the dominance of one sex and the inferiority of the other. It is thus rooted in society and its institutions.

These two explanations give rise to different perceptions of the nature of male and female inequality. Biology is concerned with *sexual inequality* whereas social processes relate to *gender inequality*. In the remainder of this chapter the term 'gender' will be used in relation to male–female inequality. Although there is some evidence from studies conducted with young children which suggest that differences between the sexes are innate (that is, we are born with such attitudes) and are perceived at early ages, the notion of gender suggests that the operations of society have a crucial bearing on the power relationship between the sexes. The term 'male chauvinism' is used to describe the irrational nature of assertions of female inequality.

PATRIARCHY

In a number of Western societies, the unequal power relationship between the sexes is to the advantage of the male. Males are viewed as superior. This view is the basis of what is termed a *patriarchal* society. This term literally means 'rule of the father' but is more generally used to describe male superiority over women. There is considerable debate within feminism as to whether patriarchal values develop independently of other social forces or whether they are the product of the class relationship within society. The latter view, held by some Marxists, suggests that changes in society's class relationship will free women from oppression.

Question

Account for the inequality of the sexes in contemporary society. To do this, consider how these differences can be accounted for in terms of:

○ biology

○ social construction.

Which of these two explanations do you find the most convincing?

The Social Construction of Gender Inequality

This section examines some of the main social processes through which gender inequality is created and enforced.

The Division of Labour

In industrialised societies, males and females were allocated different spheres of responsibility. These are based upon perceptions of differences in matters such as the capabilities and temperaments of males and females. Thus the male was perceived as a 'breadwinner' whose role was to provide for the welfare of his children and reliant female partner. This provided the male with a socially dominant position over the female whose role was that of performing domestic duties in connection with the running of a home and the care of children. This basic division of labour had a number of important consequences for women.

○ *Social conformity:* those who failed to conform to the social expectations placed upon them of being a wife and mother were traditionally looked down upon.

○ *Differential work:* women who left the home to work were expected to undertake employment which either was compatible with their social role (such as nurses) or by its nature, was not threatening to the male (particularly in the sense of not competing with his 'breadwinning' role).

Recent Changes in the Composition of the Labour Force

Industrialised societies have been subject to two important changes in the 1970s and 1980s.

1 *Deindustrialisation:* this term denotes economic changes which arose from the decline of the manufacturing industry and the growth of the service sector of the economy.

2 *Deskilling:* this arose in part from the extended use of technology in productive processes, leading to a situation in which employers required fewer skills from their workforce.

Both of these changes were to the benefit of the numbers of women in paid employment, which dramatically increased after 1970. However, the nature of the pay and conditions of women workers and the power which they exercised within the organisations which employed them remained anchored on their socially constructed position of social inferiority. Many of the women who entered the workforce were thus employed in poorly-paid, part-time work.

Stereotyping and the Media

The media played an important role in enforcing the division of labour within society. Women's magazines in particular were responsible for promoting the view that females existed to serve males whose social responsibilities justified this inequality.

Reforms to Redress Female Inequality

The discrimination experienced by women in the UK was formerly institutionalised, as is shown by the following examples.

Question

Using some examples of your own (drawn from advertisements or women's magazines, for example), illustrate the manner in which the media is responsible for seeking to ensure that men and women perform different, and unequal, roles within contemporary British society.

The Operations of the Criminal Justice System

In many countries the operations of the criminal justice system enforced the dominance of the male over the female. In the United Kingdom, examples of this include the following.

❍ *Women as second-class citizens:* judicial interpretation of the common law led to women being barred from entry to a wide range of professions and public offices. This was because they were defined as 'women' and not 'persons', and thus not entitled to the benefits and privileges contained in legislation referring to 'persons'. It was not until 1929 that the Privy Council ruled that women were indeed 'persons', thus ending such discrimination.

❍ *Masculinity:* violence by men towards women was (and is) often excused on the basis of the socially acceptable habit of masculinity: this is an implicit defence in rape cases where factors such as the dress or habits of a woman will be cited in mitigation for the male acting out his 'natural' biological urges.

❍ *Women were seen as the property of men:* the view that in a domestic setting women were inferior to men was used as an implicit excuse for the State not to interfere in matters such as domestic violence. Only in the 1990s (in cases concerning Emma Humphreys and Sara Thornton) did judges begin to rule that domestic violence was a factor when provocation was put forward as a defence by women who had killed aggressive partners.

There are a number of prominent women QCs, one of whom is Cherie Booth, wife of the present Prime Minister, Tony Blair.

Education

Women were unable to graduate from English universities until the early 1920s, although Cambridge University retained this form of discrimination until 1948. This meant that women who had taken the same courses and sat the same examinations as their male counterparts were unable to become full members of the University, and had to be satisfied with a certificate which gave them the 'title of a degree'. In 1998, some 900 women attended a special ceremony at Cambridge University to rectify this injustice.

During the 1970s, two pieces of legislation were enacted which sought to address the issue of male–female inequality. These are discussed below.

The 1970 Equal Pay Act

This measure (which was subsequently amended in 1984) stated that an individual woman could not be treated less favourably than a man in the same employment in respect of pay and other terms of her contract of employment in cases where she performed:

○ the same work as him

○ work which was broadly similar

○ work which had been given an equal value to a man's job under job evaluation, or work which was of equal value to that of a man where no job-evaluation scheme existed. The Act also provided that job-evaluation schemes could be challenged if they discriminated by sex between the jobs of men and women.

The Act was a 'two-way' measure in that it also catered for discrimination against men in these three circumstances. It also provided for the removal of discrimination from collective agreements, employers' pay structures and statutory wage orders.

The 1975 Sex Discrimination Act

This measure (which was amended in 1986) set up the Equal Opportunities Commission. It was given three general duties:

○ to work towards the elimination of discrimination

○ to promote equality of opportunity between men and women

○ to keep under review the working of the Equal Pay Act and the Sex Discrimination Act and, when required by the Secretary of State, or when otherwise necessary, to draw up and submit to the Secretary of State proposals for amending them.

It was additionally given one specific duty which derived from the first two of the general duties listed above:

○ to keep under review those provisions contained in legislation dealing with health and safety at work which required different treatment for men and women, including, for example, hours of work.

Scope of the Legislation

The 1975 Act sought to eliminate discrimination against women in the following areas.

○ *Employment:* there is no overlap between an individual's rights under the 1970 and 1975 measures, although for enforcement purposes it is not necessary for a complainant to determine which is relevant to her case: an industrial tribunal will decide a case under the most relevant Act when all the facts have been determined.

○ *Education.*

○ *The provision of goods, facilities and services, and premises.*

○ *Miscellaneous matters:* these include discriminatory advertisements, or instructions and pressure being exerted by one person on another to discriminate.

The 1975 Act outlawed both direct and indirect discrimination.

○ *Direct discrimination:* this is a situation where a person treats a women on the grounds of her sex less favourably than a man is, or would be, treated.

○ *Indirect discrimination:* this consists of treatment which could be described as equal in a formal sense, but which served to discriminate against a woman. It applied, for example, to formal employment qualifications which could not be justified by the nature of the work involved and which served to limit or disqualify female applicants.

Enforcement Procedures

An individual who considers that they have been the victim of conduct which the Act makes unlawful has the right to institute proceedings in a county court (or sheriffs court in Scotland) or an industrial tribunal. The latter deals with all complaints related to discrimination in employment while courts are concerned with other areas covered by the Act.

Industrial Tribunals

There are three possible courses of action available when a tribunal finds in favour of a complainant.

○ *An order declaring the rights of the parties.*

○ *An order requiring the respondent (ie the person whose conduct is discriminatory) to pay compensation to the complainant:* initially the maximum award which a tribunal could make was £5,200, but this ceiling has since been abolished.

○ *A recommendation that the respondent take a particular course of action:* the intention of this course of action is to obviate (that is, counteract) or reduce the adverse effect on the complainant. Usually, such action has to be implemented within a specified period of time. Failure to comply with a recommendation may be penalised by an increase in the level of compensation awarded.

The Courts

County or sheriff courts which adjudicate when there are allegations of discrimination not concerned with employment have three courses of action open to them if they find in favour of the complainant.

○ *An order declaring the rights of the parties.*

○ *An injunction or order:* this requires a person or body to perform, or not to commit, or to cease committing, acts specified in the injunction or order.

○ *Damages:* the amount awarded is based on damages for expenses or other losses sustained by the claimant which are capable of being precisely calculated (such as loss of earnings), and also for damages or losses for matters such as hurt or injured feelings which are incapable of such clear-cut assessment.

Additionally, a county or sheriff court has the power to modify a discriminatory term in a contract.

DISCERNING ANTI-DISCRIMINATORY LEGISLATION (OR PRACTICE)

The Sex Discrimination Act may provide adequate remedies for individual complaints. For example: in 1997, an industrial tribunal in Croydon awarded record non-pregnancy-related sex-discrimination damages to an employee of Southwark Borough Council, London, for a catalogue of problems which culminated in a 'sham redundancy' under the guise of departmental restructuring. She was awarded £78,000 for loss of earnings, £98,000 for four years' loss of pay, £43,000 for loss of pension, an investment sum of £2,500 and £12,500 for being made 'seriously depressed' by her treatment.

The Council had failed to comply with a tribunal order to hand over papers relevant to the case, thereby barring itself from being able to defend either the claim or the damages award.

The Strategic Role of the EOC

The right of the individual to legal protection is reinforced by certain strategic functions of the Equal Opportunities Commission. These are outlined below.

○ *Formal investigations:* in order to carry out its duties the EOC may conduct formal investigations into any matter. Where an investigation uncovers conduct which contravenes the 1970 or 1975 Acts, the EOC may issue a non-discrimination notice.

○ *Instigation of legal proceedings:* the EOC may commence legal proceedings in respect of persistent discrimination, and has the sole right to initiate such actions in connection with discriminatory practices and advertisements, or instructions and pressure to discriminate.

○ *Provision of assistance to individuals:* the EOC has powers to aid individual complainants where special considerations justify this assistance. These are when the complaint covers a matter of principle, where the complex nature of the matter makes it inappropriate for an individual to proceed unaided, or where some other special consideration applies. 'Aid' includes giving advice, seeking a settlement and arranging for legal advice or representation.

The Effectiveness of the 1975 Legislation

The 1975 Act was based on the philosophy of equal opportunities between the sexes in the areas of activity which it covered. There were, however, some aspects of the legislation which permitted certain forms of *positive action* to aid women who in the past have been discriminated against to 'catch up'. Such measures included, for example, employers providing special training facilities whereby women could aspire to areas of work in the organisation in which they were traditionally not employed. Equal opportunities remain, however, and it is unlawful under the Act to bias recruitment or selection procedures to achieve a balance between the sexes.

Reforms to the 1975 Legislation

Legislation initially introduced in the 1970s has failed to totally eradicate discrimination against women in Britain. Limited improvements have been made, and the proportion of women occupying senior positions in the private and public sectors has increased. However, there are further steps which need to be made. By 1998, the pay gap between men and women stood at around 20 per cent, and towards the end of that year the government's Office for National Statistics reported that the differential had widened for the first time in 10 years. Similarly, the success rate of claims brought under the Equal Pay Act is low: only 1 case in 10 succeeds. Equal-pay cases may take years to be heard by a tribunal, and the outcome only affects the individual who brought the case, even if this was typical of the working practices in a particular organisation. Such weaknesses have led the Equal Opportunities Commission in 1998 to call for a new equality 'super law'. The main provisions are outlined below.

❍ *Outlaw of sexual harassment:* individual tribunal cases have effectively 'invented' a law of sexual harassment, which would become part of the general law of the land through this reform.

SEXUAL HARASSMENT

Sexual harassment is a serious manifestation of discrimination against women. In 1997, two reports revealed widespread discrimination by male commanders against female troops at an American army training base in Maryland. This included sexual harassment and abuse of female soldiers. In the same year, an internal American army survey suggested that sexual coercion of female trainees by their superiors was widespread, and sexual harassment was rampant. In Italy, allegations that female students were subject to sexual harassment by their male professors at the University of Bari in the late 1990s resulted in the formation of a national forum on the exploitation of academic power for sexual purposes. This concluded that cultural rather than legislative changes were required to address this problem.

❍ *Imposition of a duty on all public bodies to promote equal opportunities:* this would include, for example, the selection of judges where it has been argued that the use of the 'old boys network' is a key reason for the overwhelmingly male composition of the senior members of the judicial branch of government.

❍ *Imposition of responsibilities on a wider range of organisations to eliminate sex discrimination:* this duty would extend to public bodies and private employers, who would implement measures including workforce monitoring by gender, and the review of pay structures to ensure equal pay for men and women. Firms seeking public sector contracts would have to demonstrate compliance with such requirements.

❍ *Tightening up on clubs which restrict female membership:* this reform was designed to outlaw practices which included banning women through provisions such as 'men only' bars. Women would either have to be offered full membership rights or be excluded entirely.

❍ *Streamlining and enhancing the effectiveness of equal opportunities legislation:* this would be provided through reforms which included 'class actions' whereby employees could bring cases of discrimination as a group rather than individually. This would mean that the outcome would apply to all those affected.

Further suggestions for reform would provide the EOC with enhanced powers to police equal opportunities legislation.

These would be modelled on the powers of Northern Ireland's Fair Employment Commission, and would include enabling the Commission to take enforcement proceedings before industrial tribunals.

European Law

The ability to have children and return to work is a fundamental issue concerning women's rights. There is, however, no uniformity within the EU member States on this matter. This means that women's entitlement on issues such as maternity leave and child-care facilities varies from one EU country to another. In Holland, for example, child-care facilities were traditionally limited, which meant that few women with children under 18 were able to work full-time. In Finland, however, women are entitled to paid parental leave followed by guaranteed daycare provision for children. If the State could not find such child-care provision, a woman would be entitled to compensation.

Rulings of the European Court of Justice may be concerned with female inequality. In 1995, this court ruled that the use of quotas for female employment as a way to redress the imbalance of the sexes in the workplace was illegal. However, in 1997 the court went some way towards endorsing the principle of affirmative action when it rejected a complaint made by a German teacher. He had lost a promotion in 1994 because the State of North Rhine-Westphalia operated a policy whereby women should be preferred for a job vacancy if they were of equal ability, qualification and suitability compared to a male applicant. The court argued that the procedure of deliberately favouring female job applicants in the public sector, when both male and female candidates were equally qualified, did not infringe sexual-equality or equal opportunity legislation.

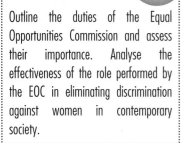

Question

Outline the duties of the Equal Opportunities Commission and assess their importance. Analyse the effectiveness of the role performed by the EOC in eliminating discrimination against women in contemporary society.

Women in Politics

Female enfranchisement (that is, the right of women to vote) was often belatedly granted: in Switzerland, for example, women could not vote in federal elections until 1971. The historic tendency for politics to be dominated by males has meant that women remain significantly under-represented at all levels of government. This has historically been the case in Italy, although in 1998 the new Prime Minister, Massimo D'Alema, appointed women to head six of the country's ministries. Elsewhere, however, women do not play a prominent role in political affairs. In Germany, for example, only one of the 16 States (Schleswig-Holstein) was headed by a woman in 1998. The United States of America has never had a woman president in its

200-year history, and only one woman (Geraldine Ferraro) has ever stood in a presidential election (when the Democrats nominated her as their vice-presidential candidate in 1984). In France, the relatively low number of women in the national legislature prompted the Senate to pass a motion calling for a constitutional amendment to boost sexual equality in parliament in March 1999. Below, the involvement of women in politics in the Irish Republic and in the UK is assessed. This involvement is important not merely because it places women's issues (which include domestic violence, child-care rights, parental leave, and forced marriages) onto the political agenda, but because women in high-profile political positions serve as a source of encouragement and inspiration to all women who aspire to social equality and the ending of discrimination.

Women in Politics in Ireland

The election of Mary Robinson as President of Ireland in 1990 (the first woman to be elected to this office) exerted a significant impact on the role of women in virtually every sphere of Irish life. The process of female emancipation in what had traditionally been a male-dominated society was underpinned by a number of social factors (which included rapid economic growth, an above-average educational system, and a comparatively classless society) but required a symbolic action to 'kick-start' it. This was provided by Mary Robinson's election and her subsequent pledge in 1990 of a new deal for women of every age group, class and creed. She played a significant role in challenging the inequalities experienced by Irish women. Her replacement as President in October 1997 was Mary McAleese, who was elected in a contest dominated by women candidates.

Women in the Irish Republic have subsequently occupied other significant political positions. Mary Harney became the first woman leader of a mainstream political Party, the Progressive Democrats, and occupied the position of Tanaiste (Deputy Prime Minister) in the government formed by Bertie Ahern in 1997. In 1998, the Irish cabinet included two women with senior ministerial posts and a junior minister.

Northern Ireland

The involvement of women in Northern Irish politics also underwent significant change in the latter decades of the twentieth century. Women's concerns were traditionally marginalised by the nature of sectarian politics. However, the peace movement and latterly the Northern Ireland Women's Coalition projected social issues such as child care, health and education onto the political agenda, and forced the traditional

Parties to view such concerns seriously. Fifteen per cent of the candidates who stood in the 1998 Northern Ireland Assembly elections were women. The prominent role played by the Northern Ireland Secretary of State, Mo Mowlam, after 1997 served to promote the role of women in Northern Irish politics.

Women in Politics in the UK

The Social Composition of the British House of Commons

At the 1992 General Election, 651 Members of Parliament were elected. Of these, only 60 (9 per cent) were women. An all-party campaign, the Three Hundred Group, was established to seek the election of 300 women to the House of Commons as one of its objectives. Some parties, such as the Labour Party and Liberal Democrats, have responded to this issue by introducing reforms which were designed to increase the number of women candidates for public office. However, progress in this direction was blunted in 1996 when an industrial tribunal (in the Jepson case) ruled that single-sex candidacy lists were illegal.

The joint proposals of the Scottish Labour Party and Liberal Democrats for a Scottish Parliament included the aim of equal representation of men and women in such an assembly. Latterly, the organisation Scotland Forward advocated gender equality in the new Scottish Parliament. This was a cross-party group supported by the Labour Party, the Scottish National Party, the Scottish Liberal Democrats and the Scottish TUC. However, the Labour government did not proceed with proposals to amend the sex-discrimination legislation to permit bias in favour of women candidates which was at the centre of the Jepson case. It was perceived that the use of proportional representation for these elections in 1999 would help to increase the representation of women in Scottish politics.

The Involvement of Women in Government

The Labour Party, when in opposition during the 1980s, made pledges designed to combat female inequality. These included a promise by the then leader, Neil Kinnock, to introduce a minister for women's rights. Such reforms sought both to remedy a social injustice but also to advance the political fortunes of the Labour Party, whose defeat in the 1987 General Election was partly attributed to its lack of appeal to women voters. Labour's 1997 election manifesto promised a women's minister of cabinet rank, and the increased representation of women in Parliament after the 1997 General Election (many of whom were Labour MPs) prompted the Labour government to advance the role of women throughout the machinery of government.

WOMEN MEMBERS OF THE BRITISH HOUSE OF COMMONS

1997 General Election

Total number of Labour MPs	418
Number of women Labour MPs	101
Total number of Conservative MPs	165
Number of women Conservative MPs	13
Total number of Liberal Democrat MPs	46
Number of women Liberal Democrat MPs	3

The total number of women MPs elected in 1997 was 120 out of a total of 659 (18.2 per cent). In addition to MPs elected for the main political parties, this figure included two SNP women MPs and the Speaker, Mrs Betty Boothroyd. The Equal Opportunities Commission pointed out that this was the smallest group of women in any European parliament apart from France and Greece.

Question

○ Present TWO arguments which can be used to support the call for more women Parliamentary candidates.

○ What factors serve to prevent women from becoming candidates for Parliamentary elections?

The Personnel of Central Government

Tony Blair's Labour government initially contained five women cabinet members and 20 other women members. After the 1998 reshuffle, the number of women cabinet members remained at five, and the number of other women members slightly increased to 22. The number of middle-ranking jobs was significant since it provided women with political experience which would eventually aid them to secure higher-level ministerial appointments.

The media insultingly branded the new women MPs as 'Tony's Babes'.

The Machinery of Central Government

Following the 1997 election, the government established a Women's Unit. This was composed of some 35 civil servants, housed within the Department of Social Security. A cabinet sub-committee on women was also set up. The role of these bodies was to 'feminise' policy-making by ensuring that all government departments placed the concerns of women high on their political agendas. One consequence of this new-found concern was a strategy paper in 1998 which set out proposals to tackle issues which ranged from domestic violence to sexual harassment in the workplace. This evidenced the interdepartmental nature of the government's initiatives, which required action from a range of departments including the Home Office, the Lord Chancellor's office, Health and the Department of Environment, Transport and the Regions.

There were, however, two difficulties with the approach adopted.

1   *Influence of the Women's Unit:* the location of the Unit within the DSS failed to provide it with the political 'clout' to ensure that other departments paid sufficient interest to women's concerns. Accordingly, in October 1998 the Unit was rehoused within the Cabinet Office, alongside the Social Exclusion Unit (which is discussed in Chapter 13). This was designed to enhance the profile of the Women's Unit.

2   *A minister for women:* no separate Minister for Women was appointed although members of the government (initially Harriet Harman and Joan Ruddock and, following the July 1998 reshuffle, Baroness Jay, Tessa Jowell and Helen Liddell) were allocated responsibilities which they combined with their other ministerial duties. This arrangement meant that women's issues were not the exclusive concern of one politician. The fight against female inequality thus lacked a figurehead.

Quangos

In 1998, the Chancellor of the Duchy of Lancaster, David Clark, announced the government's intention to make governmental bodies more accountable and representative of society by increasing the number of women appointed to quangos. The ultimate aim was to secure parity between men and women serving on such bodies by the early years of the twenty-first century. In 1998, there were 26,000 men and 12,200 women appointed to such bodies. Less than one position in five were held by women in quangos associated with the Ministry of Defence, the Home Office and Ministry of

Agriculture. To attract the extra number of women required, the minister instructed officials to look out for people with non-conventional career patterns to fill such posts, and to scrap unnecessary requirements which would discourage applications.

Further Reading

Valeria Bryson, *Feminist Political Theory: An Introduction* (Basingstoke: Macmillan, 1992). This work discusses the origins of feminist ideas and analyses recent feminist theories. It provides a good account of the diverse nature of feminist perspectives on a wide range of issues.

Diane Richardson and **Victoria Robinson** (editors), *Introducing Women's Studies* (Basingstoke: Macmillan, 1993). This book examines a wide range of areas encompassed by women's studies, including 'race', feminist theory, sexuality, health and education. The main issues and debates within each of the subject areas are fully evaluated.

Chapter Twenty-Three | The Citizen and the State in the UK

The aims of this chapter are:

---

1 To provide an understanding of the involvement of the State in regulating political activities whose impact might be deemed subversive.

2 To discuss the main agencies whose role is to defend the State against subversion.

3 To analyse the extent to which agencies defending the State against subversion are subject to adequate mechanisms of control and accountability.

4 To evaluate the extent to which open government operates in the United Kingdom, by analysing the operations of legislation governing official secrecy and data protection, and evaluating proposals for wider access to official information.

5 To examine the manner in which citizens in liberal-democratic political systems can be protected against arbitrary actions undertaken by government, and to analyse the effectiveness of available remedies such as the Ombudsman.

'Political Policing' in the UK

The term 'political policing' implies that the State has a justifiable interest not merely in seeking to eliminate crime against persons and their property but also in countering thoughts and ideas whose impact may be described as *subversive*. A principal difficulty with this term is its imprecise definition which gives rise to the possibility of unwarranted intrusions by the government and agencies of the State into political affairs.

The Definition of Subversion

Subversion is a term used to justify attempts to prevent the spread of ideas and thoughts which may ultimately result in public disorder and even revolution. However, the term 'subversion' has no objective or even constant definition. This gives rise to the accusation that the definition may be adjusted in order to justify State intervention against any group whose actions are disapproved of by a particular government.

The main difficulty with defining subversion in this broad and vague fashion is that it may be used to justify State regulation of a wide range of extra-parliamentary political activities including industrial disputes, protest and direct action. These aim to bring about some form of change to society. The State thereby undermines the liberal-democratic tradition by declaring as illegitimate political and industrial activities which had previously been thought to have distinguished a liberal democracy from an authoritarian or fascist society. The following example illustrates how actions undertaken in the name of the State may be directed against groups which organise such activities or those who participate in them.

Question

Consider the arguments for and against State intervention in the regulation of political ideas and activity. In considering this topic, you should address the following issues:

❍ the way in which political ideas can be viewed as offensive by some groups of people

❍ the fact that political activities might result in some members of the public being harmed emotionally or physically

❍ how the concerns of the State might suffer as the result of political ideas and activities

❍ who should draw the line between 'acceptable' and 'unacceptable' political ideas and activities, if a line should be drawn at all.

Defending the State Against Subversion

The role of the police in countering subversive thoughts and actions is limited, and is primarily carried out by the Special Branch. This is responsible for a wide range of surveillance work (the essence of which is close monitoring and observation), particularly of foreign communities living in the UK. This body played a major role in the enforcement of the Prevention of Terrorism legislation. The other main agencies concerned with this work are discussed below, although additional bodies including the Defence Intelligence Staff (housed within the Ministry of Defence) and the Secret Intelligence Service, MI6 (which is part of the Foreign Office), may also be involved. Commercial bodies operating in the private sector may undertake this work, their main advantage being that they can be disowned by State agencies if their operations become public knowledge.

The Security Service

The Security Service (usually referred to as MI5) was established in the early years of the twentieth century. Its initial concern was to foil the spying activities conducted by foreign powers within Britain. It is controlled by a Director General appointed by the Prime Minister and is accountable to the Home Secretary. Initially MI5 had no legal status, and neither its role nor its duties were defined by statute. However, it was placed on a statutory footing by the 1989 Security Service Act. This Act defined its main roles.

❍ *To protect national security:* in particular 'against threats from espionage, terrorism and sabotage, from the activities of agents of foreign powers and from actions intended to overthrow or undermine parliamentary democracy by political, industrial or violent means'.

❍ *To safeguard the economic well-being of the UK:* this involved countering threats posed by the actions and interests of persons operating outside of the British Isles.

This wide range of functions is mainly carried out by gathering information. The *Guardian* on 21 May 1992 stated that this agency had computerised records on approximately 1,000,000 persons. Traditionally recruitment into MI5 was not subject to civil service rules and procedures, and reliance was placed on factors such as the 'old boy network'. However, the conviction in 1985 of an MI5 agent, Michael Bettaney, for trying to pass information to the Soviet KGB led to reforms in recruitment and personnel management. Subsequently, in 1995, the open recruitment of graduates was introduced.

Special Branch and MI5

Special Branch and MI5 have traditionally enjoyed a close working relationship. This was especially apparent in the procedures adopted to implement the *positive vetting* of state employees and contractors. This procedure was introduced in 1952, being designed to ensure that members of the Communist Party or those with communist sympathies were not employed in connection with secret State work. Currently, one million jobs are subject to some form of security vetting. Cooperation between the two agencies is also required as MI5 officers lack the power of arrest. Although some areas of activity overlap, Special Branch tends to concentrate on short-term activities whereas MI5 handles longer-term surveillance.

Government Communications Headquarters (GCHQ)

This organisation became politically prominent when Prime Minister Margaret Thatcher removed the right of its employees to join trade unions in 1983. However, its origins stem from the First World War when Signals Intelligence (SIGINT) was set up to break enemy ciphers: the designation GCHQ was adopted during the Second World War. During these hostilities its work extended beyond code breaking to the interception of enemy signals and sending and receiving British secret wartime communications. Following the end of this war, GCHQ became part of a multi-national pact to enable the 'free world' to intercept and monitor radio, radar, telex, teletype microwave transmissions, telephone calls and satellite communications made within and between communist countries. Such interception was carried out using spy satellites and listening posts throughout the world.

GCHQ and Domestic Politics

Although the role of GCHQ is theoretically confined to the interception of international communications between foreign governments, international companies or private individuals, the increased use by companies such as British Telecom of microwave radio transmissions to relay telephone conversations across the country has led to assertions that the equipment operated by GCHQ could be applied to internal matters. This accusation was made concerning joint operations conducted by GCHQ and the American organisation, the National Security Agency, in connection with attempts by foreign governments, particularly the USSR, to donate money to the National Union of Miners during the 1984–85 miners' dispute. The threat of sequestration (confiscation of the union's assets) made it imperative to obtain funds to keep the union afloat. However, the British government was able, through international surveillance of the NUM bank accounts and union officials, to keep abreast of attempts by foreign governments to send aid. The belief that the NUM strike threatened to destabilise the government prompted it to utilise GCHQ to monitor a British target.

The Control and Accountability of Agencies Countering Subversion

The control and accountability of agencies defending the State against subversion requires a balance to be struck between two factors.

○ *Operational freedom:* bodies responsible for defending the State against subversion require some degree of autonomy in order to carry out their duties.

○ *The preservation of liberal-democratic political values:* this emphasises the need for State security to be compatible with the political and civil rights normally associated with liberal-democratic political systems. This objective is achieved through ensuring that bodies such as Special Branch, MI5 and GCHQ are accountable for their activities.

Operational Independence and the Problems it Poses

The 1952 Maxwell Fyfe directive, which governed the operations of MI5 until the passage of the 1989 Security Service Act, emphasised that it should be kept free from any political bias or influence and that nothing should be done 'that might lend colour to any suggestion that it is concerned with the interests of any particular section of the community, or with any other matter than the defence of the realm as a whole'. Any breach of the spirit of this directive might result in agencies' being accused of advancing the interests, not of the State, but of the government. An accusation of this nature was made in connection with the activities of MI5 and CND in the 1980s. MI5 was accused of liaising with a unit within the Ministry of Defence (DS 19) which sent information to Conservative candidates in the 1983 General Election on the political affiliations of members of the CND leadership.

Problems of Ineffective Accountability

The main difficulty posed by the requirement of operational independence is that bodies such as MI5 may assert the requirement for autonomy: that is, they insist on the need to be independent organisations which are not subject to the accountability normally associated with public bodies in liberal-democratic political systems. A number of problems derive from this situation.

Liberal Democracy is Devalued

Agencies which are insufficiently accountable for their actions may effectively determine their own roles and the manner in which they perform them. They regard themselves as 'guardians of the State' and may seek to assert their dominance above elected politicians or governments in the belief that these are pursuing subversive activities. A television programme, *Secret History*, shown on 15 August 1996 asserted that the Wilson administration of 1974–76 suffered from operations carried out by MI5 operatives to discredit ministers. The targets of the campaign included Judith Hart and Tony Benn. Such actions thus suggest that agencies may erode the liberal-democratic process by undermining the credibility of those whom the public have elected to represent and govern them.

The Use of 'Dirty Tricks'

The manner in which MI5 discharges its responsibilities may also pose problems. Some aspects of its work are allegedly carried out by the use of 'dirty tricks' which may include tactics designed to undermine, smear or hound those individuals or groups which MI5 believes to be harmful to the State.

MI5 AND ALLEGED 'DIRTY TRICKS'

There are several recent allegations of 'dirty tricks'.

◆ *The miners' dispute:* the chief executive of the National Union of Miners during the coal dispute of 1984–85, Roger Windsor, was alleged to have been an MI5 undercover agent. His activities included making false allegations of corruption against the NUM president, Arthur Scargill, which were designed to destabilise and sabotage the union.

◆ *'Clockwork orange':* this was a secret MI5 operation initially designed to undermine the morale of the IRA and extreme loyalist groups in Northern Ireland but later extended to leading politicians in Northern Ireland and Britain. Colin Wallace (who was associated with covert work of this nature but subsequently distanced himself from it), was allegedly framed by MI5 for manslaughter in 1980 to silence him. In 1996 the Appeal Court quashed this conviction.

Question

Evaluate the arguments for and against MI5 autonomy (that is, being largely free of control and accountability to any other outside body).

Inadequate Funding

Practical problems may arise from the lack of effective mechanisms of accountability. The funding arrangements of these agencies were not historically disclosed. Although there is now a greater degree of openness concerning expenditure (the budget for MI5, MI6 and GCHQ for 1996/1997 being £751 million), practical difficulties have arisen in the past because of secrecy in this matter. MI5 faced perpetual problems due to its lack of adequate financing which resulted in the agency seeking funds from the Americans for the development of technological innovations.

Mechanisms of Accountability

Mechanisms to provide for the control and accountability of agencies involved with defending the State from subversion were traditionally viewed as being inadequate. The role of the media as the 'fourth estate' provided a theoretical check on the ability of the State and its agencies to conduct themselves in an overbearing manner. Investigative journalism may be used to subject the activities and methods utilised by State security agencies to public scrutiny. However, the ability of the press and television media to expose the workings of such bodies was restricted by two mechanisms.

○ *The 'D' notice system:* this provided the government with the ability to persuade the media not to publish material which they deemed to be sensitive.

○ *The Official Secrets legislation:* the 1911 Official Secrets Act imposed the sanction of a fine or imprisonment on journalists or former government employees who sought to publish accounts of the activities of the security services. The cases in the Australian courts between 1986 and 1988 concerning Peter Wright's account of the work of MI5 in his book, *Spycatcher*, demonstrated the extent to which the Conservative government was willing to go to prevent public knowledge of such matters.

Reforms Introduced Since the 1980s

The belief that bodies concerned with the political aspects of policing were insufficiently accountable for their actions became the subject of public debate during the 1980s (particularly in connection with the alleged extent of telephone tapping) and prompted the government to introduce a number of reforms which are discussed below.

Telephone Tapping

The 1980s witnessed a considerable volume of interest in the operations of the security services in general and the practice of telephone tapping in particular. Two related problems emerged in this debate – the impact of technology on telephone tapping and a belief that the extent of the practice was more widespread than the government was willing to admit.

THE EXTENT OF TELEPHONE TAPPING

Governments were traditionally loathe to admit the extent to which telephone tapping was practised. There was a gap in official information between the publication of the Birkett Report in 1957 and a 1980 White Paper. The latter revealed that the number of warrants authorising telephone taps had risen from 129 in 1958 to 467 in 1979. However, the relatively small size of this figure was the subject of debate. It was unclear whether the figure quoted in the 1980 White Paper was the annual total of all *current* warrants or whether it comprised the annual total of *new* warrants issued in each year. It was further admitted in Parliamentary debate that the document made no reference to Northern Ireland (where different criteria applied), it omitted the work of the Defence Intelligence Staff and MI6, and did not refer to GCHQ whose operations were governed by informal guidelines issued by ministers. Such criticism resulted in the government appointing Lord Diplock to examine the interception of communications by the police, post office and MI5. His first report in 1981 expressed general satisfaction that the procedures outlined in the 1980 White Paper were being adhered to. In 1997, the Home Secretary signed warrants for 1,391 telephone taps.

The Interception of Communications Act, 1985

Perceptions that the general public was not adequately protected against the misuse of powers related to telephone tapping by the security services resulted in the 1984 Telecommunications Act, providing redress through the courts for illegal tapping. This procedure was almost immediately amended by the 1985 Interception of Communications Act. This legislation covered the following issues.

○ *Placed warrants on a statutory basis:* interception of communications would usually require a Secretary of State to issue a warrant. This would normally last for two months but could be cancelled at any time and was renewable. These could be issued in the interests of national security, to prevent or detect a serious crime or to safeguard the economic well-being of the UK.

○ *Safeguards:* the Act established a tribunal to investigate claims of interception by members of the public. It possessed the power to quash warrants, to direct the destruction of intercepted material, and to direct the Secretary of State to pay compensation. The office of commissioner was also set up to investigate alleged violations which were not the subject of an individual complaint, to issue reports to the Prime Minister, and publish an annual report to Parliament.

The 1989 Security Service Act

The main provisions of the Act were that it:

○ *Placed MI5 on a statutory basis:* the 1994 Intelligence Services Act subsequently placed MI6 and GCHQ on a similar legal footing.

○ *Gave legislative sanction to the issue of property warrants:* these permitted the 'entry or interference with property' by MI5 personnel. Such warrants to 'bug and burgle' were issued for a period of six months and could be renewed.

❍ *Introduced a complaints procedure:* a Security Services Tribunal consisting of three legally trained persons would investigate complaints against MI5. A Security Services Commissioner, appointed by the Prime Minister from candidates who had held high judicial office, would keep under review the issue of property warrants by the Secretary of State. The Commissioner makes an annual report which is normally laid (in whole or in part) before Parliament.

Legislative Accountability

In 1993, the Home Affairs committee argued that MI5 should be more closely monitored because of the new role it had been allocated in connection with Irish terrorism. It was pointed out that its annual budget was secret and that the official figure of £185 million a year was almost certainly an underestimate. Such arguments ultimately resulted in the 1994 Intelligence Services Act which established the Intelligence and Security Committee. Its role was to examine the expenditure, administration and policy of MI5, MI6 and GCHQ. It consists of nine cross-party MPs and Peers appointed by the Prime Minister.

The Effectiveness of Reforms Introduced Since 1980

Reforms introduced since 1980 were designed to respond to criticisms made of the role, and particularly the methods, utilised by the security services. They have been subsequently complemented by further developments which include the decision in 1991 to name the Director General, and the publication in 1993 of a booklet (*MI5, The Security Service*) which gave information on the activities which it performed. The existence of bodies such as MI5, MI6 and GCHQ is now publicly acknowledged, and information concerning their work is made available on the terms under which they are willing to provide it.

However, reforms introduced since 1980 have not significantly altered the climate of secrecy within which such bodies operate. For example, the extent to which telephone tapping takes place remains the subject of debate. On 14 June 1991 the *Guardian* alleged that 35,000 telephone lines were tapped each year. The difference between this figure and the number of warrants issued annually suggested that a single warrant authorised the tapping of a large number of telephone lines. The adequacy of safeguards to protect members of the public from the abuse of power by the security services has been disputed. Key weaknesses are discussed below.

❍ *Insufficient independent scrutiny of warrants:* warrants to intercept communications and to permit MI5 to break into a person's

In 1991, as part of a policy of greater openness, Stella Rimington was revealed as the head of MI5.

home or vehicle and plant bugs are issued by the Home Secretary, acting on the advice of the civil service rather than the judiciary.

○ *Tribunals lack effectiveness:* the tribunals established by the 1985 and 1989 legislation are merely required to satisfy themselves that correct procedures have been followed, and they lack the power to investigate unlawful interceptions. They do not have to produce evidence to convince a complainant that its findings are justified or to give reasons for its decisions. By 1998 not one single complaint had been upheld by either of these tribunals.

○ *Legislative control remains weak:* the Parliamentary committee established by the 1994 Intelligence Services Act lacks the power to summon 'persons and papers'. Further, its ability to increase public awareness of the role of these bodies is hampered by its members being subject to the duty of silence imposed by the Official Secrets Act. This committee issues an annual report to the Prime Minister who decides what aspects of it may be disclosed to Parliament.

○ *Globalisation:* a further problem is that interception is increasingly carried out on an international basis. The American 'Echelon' communications intelligence system provides for global access to international communications using satellites, taps and monitoring stations placed in key locations.

To redress some of these problems, particularly that of ineffective Parliamentary control, the government announced in 1998 that MI5, MI6 and GCHQ might be subject to regular Parliamentary debates. It was also considering the possibility of replacing the Intelligence and Security committee with a new House of Commons Committee with the power to summon witnesses.

The New Role of MI5

The end of the cold war resulted in MI5 acquiring new responsibilities. In 1992, it was assigned the lead role in countering terrorism on mainland Britain. Around half of MI5's resources were devoted to this function, which provided the main reason for the agency's continued existence. The IRA ceasefires have required the development of further functions. Accordingly, the 1996 Security Services Act allocated MI5 the responsibility for dealing with 'serious crime' in addition to its existing functions. This theoretically gave MI5 a broad area of activity since serious crime is defined as an offence which carries a sentence of three years or more on first conviction, or any offence involving conduct by a large number of persons in pursuit of a common purpose. This posed the problem of demarcation disputes (or 'turf wars') arising between the police and MI5, although the relatively small size of the latter (which has approximately 2,000 staff) made it unlikely that it would seek to take over mainstream policing roles. In 1998 it was revealed that only 2 per cent of MI5's annual budget of around £140 million was spent aiding the police and customs service to combat serious crime.

THE 1996 SECURITY SERVICES ACT

The role to combat serious crime, contained in the 1996 Security Services Act, was contentious. It was criticised by civil libertarians and the police.

◆ *Civil libertarians:* these expressed fears that the term 'serious crime' was broad, and that the Act provided no definition of the categories of persons liable to surveillance, failed to place limits on the activities which were subject to such scrutiny, and gave no definition of the conditions under which information gathered would be retained. Concern was also expressed on the involvement of MI5 with ordinary crime because of its lack of accountability.

◆ *The police service:* senior police officers were concerned MI5 would assume the lead role in matters such as drugs and organised crime. This fear initially arose as only MI5 had legal powers to enter a person's premises and plant a bugging device to effect surveillance. This deficiency was remedied in the 1997 Police Act, which provided the police with powers to 'bug and burgle', using methods such as hidden cameras and listening devices to prevent or detect serious crime.

Question

To what extent have reforms enacted since 1979 succeeded in making MI5 more accountable to outside bodies? How adequate do you consider these reforms to have been?

The Defence of Human Rights

Until the late 1990s, British citizens who felt that their civil rights and liberties had been prejudiced by the actions of the State were forced to take their case to the European Court of Human Rights at Strasbourg. This process was both costly and lengthy: in 1997 it was estimated that the average cost of a case heard by the European Court of Human Rights was £30,000 and the average time taken for judgement to be pronounced by this body was five years. In 1997, the Labour government published a Human Rights Bill which contained proposals to remedy this situation.

The main proposals of this Bill which were enacted in the 1998 Human Rights Act were as follows.

❍ *The European Convention of Human Rights would be incorporated into British law:* this meant that matters which included the right to liberty and security, the right to a fair and public hearing, respect for family and private life, and freedom of thought and expression would become part of UK law and could thus be heard in British courts. The main aim of this reform was to increase the defences available to a citizen against abuse of power by the agencies of the State.

❍ *Contravention of these rights would constitute an offence:* the High Court would be empowered to grant damages to plaintiffs whose complaints were upheld. The new law would make it illegal for public authorities (including the government, courts, and private bodies discharging public functions) to act in contravention of these designated human rights.

❍ *Potential improved defence of individual privacy:* public authorities must act positively to defend the rights included in the legislation. This could mean that expectations would be placed upon the courts to promote the enhanced defence of the privacy of the individual on the grounds that under the new law their role includes that of ensuring that public authorities offer effective remedies against actions which are incompatible with the European Convention on Human Rights.

❍ *Monitoring of human rights:* the Bill did not propose to establish a Human Rights Commission, although the White Paper expressed an open mind on such a reform which would place the oversight of all matters affecting human rights (including the work currently performed by the Commission for Racial Equality and the Equal Opportunities Commission) under one roof. In the interim period, the work of monitoring would be performed by a committee of MPs.

Reaction to the Government's Proposals

Initial reaction to the White Paper and the Human Rights Bill was favourable. Andrew Puddephatt of Charter 88 declared in the *Guardian* on 25 October 1997 that 'for the first time in our history people will be able to challenge abuses of their rights through the British courts. This Bill tips the balance of power from politicians to the people.' There were, however, criticisms voiced concerning the likely impact of such a measure. In addition to concerns voiced by the media concerning privacy (which have been discussed in Chapter 9), a key problem centred on the restricted power of the Convention over other aspects of British law.

The European Convention and the Sovereignty of Parliament

In some countries (such as Canada), human rights legislation empowers judges to strike down any legislation which conflicts with such basic principles. This would *not* be the case in the UK (save in the case of law passed by the Scottish Parliament and Welsh Assembly). Under the human rights legislation, judges would be empowered to declare a law passed by Parliament 'incompatible with the convention', thus upholding the concept of the sovereignty of parliament. Although it was assumed that declarations of this nature by the courts would induce the government and parliament to speedily introduce corrective measures to bring such legislation into line with the Convention of Human Rights, there was nothing to prevent either of these bodies from ignoring the rulings. This might induce an aggrieved person to refer the matter to Strasbourg, thus suggesting that the Act has failed to substantially improve the present situation regarding the defence of human rights.

Question ?

Assess the likely changes to civil and political liberties in Britain which are likely to occur following the passage of the Human Rights Act, 1998.

Open Government

Open government in a liberal democracy can be justified for two important reasons.

1   *Access to personal information:* this covers the right of individuals to see files containing information recorded about them by public bodies. A citizen can determine the accuracy of such information and if necessary secure its amendment before it can cause him or her personal harm or damage.

2   *Knowledge of the affairs of government:* in a liberal democracy, members of the general public need to be able to evaluate the performance of a government in order to give (or deny) it political support. This requires the availability of information through which the activities of government can be judged.

However, the secrecy which often surrounds the workings of government may make it difficult for the public to secure such information. This section analyses two issues – official secrecy and access to information.

Official Secrecy

In countries such as the UK and Ireland, the media has been hampered in its ability to discuss political issues. Here official secrecy has been used to prevent the disclosure of 'official' information. In the UK, the 1911 Official Secrets Act made any disclosure of official information a criminal offence. This was amended in 1989 when a new Official Secrets Act was enacted.

This revised section 2 of the 1911 measure and regulated the disclosure of information regarding the security services in the following ways:

○ *A person who was (or had been) a member of the security or intelligence services:* such persons were prohibited without lawful authority to disclose any information, document or other article related to security or intelligence which was (or had been) in that person's possession by virtue of being a member of such services. A minister was empowered to apply this provision of the Act to any other person.

○ *Crown servants and government contractors:* these were forbidden to make 'damaging disclosures' concerning the security or intelligence services, defence and international relations. It also became an offence for Crown servants and government contractors to make disclosures concerning crime and special investigation powers.

○ *Absence of 'public interest' defence:* the Act contained no public interest defence which might be used by civil servants or investigative journalists who publicised government activities in areas covered by the legislation. In some areas, however (such as defence), it was necessary for the State to demonstrate that the disclosure resulted in 'harm' or 'jeopardy' to State interests.

Whistle Blowing

The 1911 and 1989 Official Secrets Acts posed dilemmas for some civil servants who believed that politicians sometimes confused State interests with their own political considerations and sought to use the former grounds to suppress information which might have damaging political consequences. This gave rise to the phenomenon of 'whistle blowing'. This involved a civil servant deliberately leaking information to bodies such as the media when he or she believed that the public's right to know was of greater importance than the concern of a government to keep such material secret. A danger posed by whistle blowing is that it erodes the trust between ministers and civil servants. It might result in the politicisation of the bureaucracy whereby politicians appoint persons to its upper ranks whose trust and loyalty can be relied upon.

Freedom of Information

Freedom-of-information legislation typically compels public bodies or officials to make available a wide range of material relevant to political affairs, provided that this does not threaten national security or constitute an unwarranted intrusion into an individual's privacy. In the USA the 1966 and 1974 Freedom of

EXAMPLES OF WHISTLE BLOWING

Examples of whistle blowing include the following cases.

The Tomlinson Case

Richard Tomlinson was a former MI6 officer who had operated in Moscow and Bosnia and sought to publish a book related to his work. He was charged with damaging national security following an analysis of his book synopsis which he passed to an Australian publisher, Transworld, in 1997. Although he rejected the possibility that material in the book would damage Britain's national security, he acknowledged that the synopsis contained secret information and thus admitted a charge under the Official Secrets legislation of unlawfully passing information to a third party. In 1997, he was jailed for 12 months for seeking to sell his story to the Australian publisher.

The Shayler Case

In 1998, David Shayler, who had formerly worked for MI5, made allegations that MI6 had been involved in a failed attempt to assassinate the Libyan leader, Colonel Gadafy, in 1996. A bomb had been planted under his motorcade, but the wrong car had been blown up, resulting in the deaths of several bystanders. Shayler was arrested in Paris, pending extradition to the UK to face charges under the Official Secrets legislation. The lengths to which the Labour government was willing to go to prevent any further disclosures of these allegations to the British public was displayed when its lawyers served the BBC with an injunction to prevent it from televising an edition of the highly-respected *Panorama* programme which intended to deal with the Shayler allegations. This affair subsequently prompted the Committee on Intelligence and Security to recommend that an independent investigator be appointed to look into allegations of malpractice by the security services. In November 1998 an appeals court in Paris ordered Shayler's release. The judge, Elisabeth Ponroy, declared his whistle-blowing was political in nature and thus he could not be extradited to face trial.

Information Acts provided citizens and interest groups with the right to inspect most federal records. Although access to some information may be denied, an appeal to the courts may secure the production of the desired information. New Zealand also has an Official Information Act which permits public access to a wide range of information. Similar legislation exists in Germany and is a considerable aid to investigative journalism.

Freedom of Information in the UK

In the 1960s, retrospective examination of official information enabled the public to consult certain government documents after a period of 30 years had elapsed. However, certain documents were exempt from these provisions.

Criticisms were made regarding the release of information held in the files of government departments. Release under the 30-years rule can be blocked (by the Lord Chancellor signing a statutory instrument) for two reasons.

1   *National security:* this prevents release where the interests of the State could be endangered.

2   *Personal sensitivity:* this stops release on the grounds that it might cause substantial distress (or endangerment from a third party) to the persons affected by disclosure, or to their descendants.

The Labour Government and Freedom of Information

A Code on Access to Government Information has existed since 1994 although relatively little use has been made of it. In 1996, only 2,000 requests were made by the public for information. In 1997, a White Paper on Freedom of Information was published. The aim of this document was to implement an EU data-protection directive giving the public the right to inspect files held on them. The scope of the legislation which it proposed was extremely broad, going beyond central government and extending to the whole of the public sector (including local government, quangos, the nationalised industries, public service broadcasters, the courts' administrative functions, the privatised utilities and the work of private bodies performing contracted-out services). The White Paper proposed to require these bodies to open their files to the public on demand within 20 working days.

PROBLEMS POSED BY FREEDOM-OF-INFORMATION LEGISLATION

The opposition of government ministers succeeded in removing a Freedom of Information Bill from the government's legislative programme for the 1998/1999 Parliament. It was likely that a newer, and weaker, version would be placed before Parliament in the following session, 1999/2000.

There were two main problems affecting the progress of the proposals contained in the 1997 White Paper.

Opposition Within the Executive Branch of Government

This measure encountered considerable opposition from within the machinery of government, including from cabinet ministers and senior civil servants. Civil servants who were used to a culture of 'anti-openness' were opposed to the White Paper on grounds which included costs and the power which the ombudsman would possess in relation to disclosure. In response to such criticisms, the Lord Chancellor proposed a national appeals tribunal which would arbitrate between the Ombudsman and Whitehall when they clashed over the release of documents.

The Culture of Government

The enhanced ability of the public to scrutinise documents if and when Freedom of Information legislation is passed cannot be taken for granted. Its effective operation requires the active cooperation of both ministers and civil servants. Without this, it is possible to evade the spirit of these measures.

A further difficulty concerns technology. Documents requested by an individual or the media which may be embarrassing to the government of the day can be more easily altered when they are stored on computer unless procedures such as 'time stamping' are utilised.

Data Protection Legislation

The 1984 Data Protection Act sought to protect individuals from the misuse of information held on them in the computer files of a range of public and commercial bodies. It specified a number of principles which those who stored such information were required to follow. These included requirements that data should be used only for specific, lawful purposes, and should be disclosed to others only for these specified purposes. It also gave individuals the right of access to information held in order to check that it was accurate. Holders and users of computerised information were required to register the database and its use with the Data Protection Registrar who was able to investigate complaints and, if necessary, issue enforcement notices. However, some users (such as the police service) were exempt from key provisions of this legislation and others (such as MI5) were entirely outside its scope, although this latter organisation registered its intelligence computer system in 1995. Additionally, the Act did not apply to information not stored on computers.

In 1998, the government enacted a Data Protection Act. This stemmed from a European Commission directive, and was designed to provide public access to personal information held on them in computer files and other databases by private companies and government agencies in order to prevent the use of data which would cause 'substantial damage or distress'. The Data Protection Commissioner was empowered to issue enforcement notices against organisations which broke the law. Individuals would further have the right to be compensated for an organisation's breach of data-protection principles. However, the scope of the Act was restricted in a number of ways.

○ *The media:* the fear that this Act might result in a backdoor privacy law resulted in exemptions regarding access by the public to information held on them by the media: this issue is discussed more fully in Chapter 9 of this work.

○ *Widespread exemptions were given to government agencies:* the ability of the public to inspect files was limited by considerations of national security and the prevention or detection of crime. Access was also denied to data relating to an individual's physical or mental health and the assessment or collection of tax.

○ *Limited role for the Data Protection Commissioner:* this official was not allowed to make unannounced spot checks on holders of databases.

○ *No reference to certain activities of data-collection bodies:* the Act failed to tackle the dangers arising from technology, especially the 'data matching' of personal information collected by a number of different bodies on one individual. Such practices were given legal sanction in the 1977 Social Security Administration (Fraud) Act, and the 1998 Crime and Disorder Act. A particular danger is that information collected for one purpose may be used for a different reason.

○ *Incentives to evasion:* such cases were subject to lengthy appeal procedures, and the maximum fine would be £5,000.

Question

What do you understand by the term 'open government', and to what extent did the actions undertaken by the Labour government after 1997 extend this concept?

Defence Against Government Errors

A liberal-democratic political system requires mechanisms to prevent the government acting in an overbearing manner towards its citizens and to ensure that adequate redress can be secured when a citizen suffers from mistakes committed by government.

The Ombudsman

This official (who is officially termed 'the Parliamentary Commissioner for Administration') was initially appointed in 1967 to deal with complaints by members of the general public concerning the operation of the machinery of central government. An investigation by the Ombudsman was viewed as a supplement to measures which MPs could initiate to redress the grievances of their constituents (such as tabling a question in Parliament to a minister or introducing an adjournment debate). For this reason, the reference of a complaint to the Ombudsman had to come from a MP and could not be received directly from a citizen.

Benefits of the Ombudsman

The Ombudsman brought a number of benefits to the investigation of a complaint.

❍ *Detailed examination:* the Ombudsman and his staff were able to devote their full-time attention to complaints from the public, which only form one aspect of the job of an MP.

❍ *Strong powers:* the Ombudsman was empowered to call for the relevant files from the department at the centre of the complaint. The 1994 Code of Practice on Access to Government Information, did, however, exclude certain requests.

Weaknesses of the Ombudsman

There were, however, a number of weaknesses affecting the work of the Ombudsman.

❍ *Scope of the terms of reference:* the Ombudsman is only able to investigate accusations of *maladministration*. This is concerned with how a decision made by ministers or civil servants has been reached. The Ombudsman is not, however, able to investigate the wisdom of a particular decision and is confined to considering whether the correct procedures have been followed in arriving at it.

❍ *Powers to enforce a remedy:* if the Ombudsman finds in favour of the complainant, a remedy will be put forward in an official report. However, the Ombudsman has no power to force a government department to provide this remedy. Should a department refuse to follow the Ombudsman's advice, a report will be presented to Parliament and a select committee will further consider the matter. This link with Parliament does usually ensure compliance.

Extension of the Ombudsman System

The Ombudsman system has been extended in a number of areas. In 1969 a Complaints Commissioner was established in Northern Ireland, who was able to take complaints directly from the general public. An Ombudsman was established for the Scottish National Health Service in 1972 and for the remainder of the country in 1973. Local government Commissioners were appointed in 1974. A particular weakness of this system for investigating complaints of maladministration against local authorities is that the Ombudsman is not 'plugged into' any Parliamentary Committee. This means that local authorities have a wider discretion as to whether they choose to implement the advice which has been given, and many fail to do so. In 1994, the post of Prison Ombudsman (to whom prisoners could complain) was established.

Administrative Tribunals

Tribunals provide a mechanism whereby the rights of the citizen can be safeguarded against actions undertaken by central or local government. These are typically concerned with adjudicating on the correctness of a decision reached by officials operating in these areas. Tribunals are viewed as a more effective manner for handling intricate personal cases than the civil courts because of the cost and delay which aggrieved members of the public would be likely to experience. Members of tribunals are appointed by the minister concerned with its area of activity. Examples of tribunals include the following.

◯ *The supplementary benefits tribunal:* this is concerned with appeals from persons who believe that the Benefits Agency has made an incorrect decision concerning their entitlement to supplementary benefit.

◯ *Valuation tribunals:* these are concerned with hearing appeals from members of the general public relating to the banding of property for the payment of Council Tax.

Question

Select a tribunal for your own private study. In doing this, gather your material under the following headings:

◯ **Responsibilities:** the area of activity which is the concern of the tribunal.

◯ **Composition:** the make-up of the tribunal, and how it is appointed.

◯ **Methods:** the procedure adopted by the tribunal for determining cases which are brought before it.

◯ **Assessment:** your own view as to whether a tribunal rather than a county court is the most appropriate way for dealing with such matters.

Further Reading

Mary Seneviratne, *Ombudsmen in the Public Sector* (Buckinghamshire: Open University Press, 1994). This provides a thorough account of the work of the ombudsmen concerned with central and local government and the national health service.

The activities of bodies such as MI5 are covered in a number of highly readable accounts. Such includes **Seumas Milne**, *The Enemy Within: The Secret War Against the Miners* (London: Pan Books, 1994), which deals with the campaign mounted by MI5 during the miners' dispute.

David Leigh, *The Wilson Plot: The Intelligence Services and the Discrediting of the Prime Minister, 1945–1976* (London: Heinemann, 1988) is concerned with activities conducted by state security agencies against Harold Wilson.

Subject Index